Online Trader's Dictionary

The Most Up-to-Date and Authoritative Compendium of Financial Terms

By
R. J. Shook

CAREER
PRESS
Franklin Lakes, NJ

ONLINE TRADER'S DICTIONARY
Cover design by Cheryl Cohan Finbow
Printed in the U.S.A. by Book-mart Press

To order this title, please call toll-free 1-800-CAREER-1 (NJ and Canada: 201-848-0310) to order using VISA or MasterCard, or for further information on books from Career Press.

HG4515.95
S48
2002

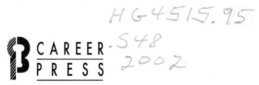

CAREER
PRESS

The Career Press, Inc., 3 Tice Road, PO Box 687
Franklin Lakes, NJ 07417
www.careerpress.com

Library of Congress Cataloging-in-Publication Data

Shook, R. J. (Robert James)
    Online trader's dictionary : the most up-to-date and authoritative compendium
    of financial terms / by R. J. Shook.
        p. cm.
    ISBN 1-56414-567-0 (pbk.)
        1. Electronic trading of securities—Dictionaries. 2. Investments—
        Dictionaries. I. Title.

HG4515.95 .S48 2001
332.63'2'03—dc21   2001042528

Dedication

To Elinore…for her warmth and wisdom.

Acknowledgments

Literally hundreds of traders, bankers, brokers, analysts, money managers, information-systems individuals, Internet leaders, computer specialists, real estate and insurance professionals, and others contributed to the creation of this book. These individuals took time from their busy schedules to speak with me and share their knowledge. Without these obliging contributions—many of the terms in this book don't appear in any other glossary—this book would have been impossible to produce. I am thankful to each and every one of these individuals. I am grateful to my wife, Elisabeth, for endless support and for enduring many late nights as I poured away at my computer. I would also like to thank Erik Niermeyer, Jim Claus and Brad Zucker for their invaluable advice; Robert Liberman and Michael Kleynshag for helping to create www.wallstreetdictionary.com. Thanks to my literary agent, Jeff Herman, who is clearly one of the best in the business.

I am grateful for the talent and expertise at Career Press, namely Stacey Farkas, Editorial Director; Nicole DeFelice, editor; Mike Lewis, Acquisitions Editor; Kirsten Beucler, Marketing Director; and Ron Fry, Publisher.

Preface

When it comes to investing—or every day life—nothing has changed the rules as much as technology. The Internet in particular is breaking through all barriers, helping to make globalization a reality, and offering information and news without regard to geographical boundaries. In business, technology's phenomenal impact is re-writing the rules for even the stodgiest of industries, formerly accustomed to decade's old processes and customs. At home, individuals now wonder how they ever got along with access to the Web, e-mail, and their personal digital assistant.

As a consequence, *The Online Trader's Dictionary* has been written to provide the most complete collection of financial and technology-related terms ever available. Nearly 7,000 terms are included, each term explained with easy-to-understand definitions and complete cross referencing, making this dictionary an essential addition to any investor's or astute businessperson's library. Its contents range from the most basic terms to little-known words and phrases used by the professionals on Wall Street or Silicon Valley.

For anyone interested in investing, business, the Internet, or technology in general, the *Online Trader's Dictionary* is the perfect resource that can be used every day. Included are current buzzwords and new terminology.

The *Online Trader's Dictionary* is also a helpful guide for understanding terminology involving real estate, banking, personal finance, and various other financial matters. Also included are hundreds of phrases and acronyms. This dictionary is perfect for the experienced—or inexperienced—businessperson, banker, trader, and stockbroker, and anyone involved with investing, real estate, and insurance. For anyone interested in investing, business, computers, the Internet, or technology in general, the *Online Trader's Dictionary* is the perfect resource that can be used every day. In this new age, being well-informed is not an option any longer, it has become a necessity.

A

ABC AGREEMENT. A contract explaining a brokerage firm's rights when it purchases a New York Stock Exchange (NYSE) membership for one of its employees. After the purchase, the individual can retain membership and buy another seat for someone else the firm designates, sell the seat and give the proceeds to the firm, or transfer the seat to another of the firm's employees. Only individual brokers may own seats on the NYSE. The individual may work primarily for one major brokerage firm, but a firm may not have a seat titled in its own name. *See Also: contract, exchange, firm, name, New York Stock Exchange, NYSE, proceeds, rights, seat, stock, stock exchange, transfer*

ABOVE PAR. A stock or bond whose market price is higher than its face value. *See Also: bond, face value, market, market price, stock*

ABOVE THE MARKET. A sell order identified as being higher in price than the market's current price for that security. *See Also: current, order, security, sell order*

ABS. Asset Backed Security. *See Also: asset*

ABSOLUTE ADVANTAGE. The power of one producer to make or sell a product below the price of any other producer, sometimes through national subsidies. *See Also: producer*

ABSOLUTE PRIORITY RULE. During bankruptcy or a corporate reorganization, the superseding of the owner's right to equity by creditors' rights and their financial claims. *See Also: bankruptcy, equity, reorganization, right, rights*

ABSORPTION POINT. The point at which the market no longer can accept securities without making price concessions. *See Also: market, point, securities*

ABSTINENCE THEORY. The purchaser of goods or services may receive a rebate if these goods or services are not utilized as such or as quickly as specified in the contract. For example, the owner of a leased automobile that is driven only 12,000 miles per year on a contract allowing 15,000 miles per year may be entitled to a refund. If goods or services are not used right away, some of their cost should be reimbursed through interest or other payments. *See Also: contract, interest, rebate, right*

ACCELERATED AMORTIZATION. Writing off a cost before it normally would be written off, which then reduces taxes. Also, moving up the payment date on a debt by special agreement. *See Also: accelerated depreciation, depreciation, payment date*

ACCELERATED COST RECOVERY SYSTEM (ACRS). This method allows for quicker depreciation of assets than was permitted before 1980. ACRS allows costs to be recovered before an economically useful life span asset's estimated is due. Conversely, in straight-line depreciation, equal charges are made each year throughout the asset's estimated useful life. *See Also: depreciation, straight-line depreciation*

ACCELERATED DEPRECIATION. The writing off of the costs of fixed assets faster than through straight-line depreciation. The higher cost of maintenance and repair during the later years of an asset's useful life are offset by the tax advantages of the early years, thus providing a more steady stream of earnings from the asset. A company's cash flow is aided by the tax benefits of this practice. Accelerated depreciation promotes capital spending and modernization. *See Also: asset, capital, cash, cash flow, depreciation, earnings, maintenance, offset, steady, straight-line depreciation*

ACCELERATION CLAUSE. A provision that the unpaid balance of a mortgage or other contract will become due if the debtor fails to meet interest, principal, or sinking fund payments, if the debtor becomes insolvent, or fails to pay taxes on mortgaged property. *See Also: balance, contract, fails, fund, interest, mortgage, pay, principal, sinking fund*

ACCELERATION THEORY. A change in the consumption rate will cause even greater changes in the amount of purchases and production levels. This action is considered to be the impetus for one form of inflation. *See Also: change, consumption, inflation*

ACCEPTANCE. Agreement to buy or sell a particular security by a specific date for a specific price. *See Also: security*

ACCEPTANCE CREDIT. Substituting the credit of a bank for that of an individual or a firm. *See Also: acceptance, bank, banker's acceptance, credit, firm*

ACCEPTANCE HOUSE. An agency that lends money using bills of exchange as security, or offers its name to endorse a bill drawn on someone else. *See Also: endorse, exchange, name, security*

ACCEPTANCE LIABILITY. A bank's liability when it accepts a negotiable instrument drawn on the bank by one of its customers. *See Also: bank, instrument, liability, negotiable, negotiable instrument*

ACCEPTANCE SUPRA PROTEST. A company or individual other than the debtor who agrees to pay off a debt. *See Also: pay*

ACCOMMODATION ENDORSEMENT. One person endorses a note so a bank will lend money to another person with a poor or inadequate credit history. *See Also: bank, credit, note*

ACCOMMODATION PAPER. A note or other obligation guaranteed by someone other than the beneficiary. *See Also: credit, letter of credit, note, obligation*

ACCOUNT. Any bookkeeping record of a client's transactions, including credit or debit balances, either in cash or securities. Also, an investment syndicate's books that indicate contractual relationships, securities currently or previously owned, and the financial balance between a syndicate participant and the syndicate. *See Also: balance, cash, credit, debit, investment, participant, securities, syndicate*

ACCOUNT BALANCE. The difference between debits and credits in an account. If the debits are higher than credits, the account has a negative balance. *See Also: account, balance*

ACCOUNT DAY. The day stock or commodity exchanges must be settled between exchange members. *See Also: commodity, exchange, exchanges, stock*

ACCOUNT EXECUTIVE. An employee of a broker-dealer who is registered with the National Association of Securities Dealers or one of the exchanges. Account executives are allowed to solicit buy and sell orders for securities, and may handle client accounts. *See Also: account, broker, broker-dealer, client, customer's man, exchanges, handle, registered representative, securities*

ACCOUNT STATEMENT. A periodic report giving the status of a client's transactions, debits, and credits.

ACCOUNTANT'S OPINION. A statement signed by an independent public accountant describing an audit of a company's financial records. The opinion can be unqualified or qualified, the latter warranting investigation. *See Also: audit, statement*

ACCOUNTING CYCLE. Accounting activities that occur during a specific period of time. The period starts and ends with the account balance, all its credits, debits, and any other transactions recorded during the cycle. *See Also: account, account balance, balance, cycle, time*

ACCOUNTING PERIOD. A time span for keeping taxpayers' records. Most businesses operate on the calendar year. A fiscal year is established if the accounting period does not end in December. *See Also: calendar, fiscal year, time*

ACCOUNTING PROCESSES. The classification of accounting procedures and controls through which changes in financial status and condition are recorded.

ACCOUNTING RATE OF RETURN. Any income during a specific period of time divided by the amount of money invested during that period. *See Also: time*

ACCOUNTS RECEIVABLE. Uncollected money owed, for goods or services.

ACCOUNTS RECEIVABLE FINANCING. Short-term financing in which accounts receivable are used as collateral for advances. *See Also: accounts receivable, collateral, factoring*

ACCOUNTS RECEIVABLE TURNOVER. The ratio of total credit sales divided by the accounts receivable for any given accounting period. Divide the total credit sales by the accounts receivable; the answer will indicate the number of times the receivables portfolio has been collected during the accounting period. Business efficiency and profitability is increased by cutting this ratio. *See Also: accounting period, accounts receivable, credit, credit sales, portfolio, profitability, ratio, receivables*

ACCREDITED INVESTOR. An individual with sufficient assets and/or income who is permitted, according to the Securities Act of 1933, to be excluded from the 35 investors in a private limited partnership. To be accredited, the investor must have a net worth of at least $1 million, an annual income of at least $200,000, or must put at least $150,000 into the deal, which cannot account for more than 20 percent of his or her net worth. Private limited partnerships use accredited investors to raise more money than would be possible with 35 less-affluent people. *See Also: account, limited partnership, net, net worth, partnership, private limited partnership, put, securities, Securities Act of 1933, worth*

ACCRETION. The carrying value of a bond bought at an original discount adjusted upwards over time approaching the bond's face value. The Internal Revenue Service clearly and precisely defines its provisions for this upward adjustment. *See Also: bond, carrying value, discount, face value, internal revenue, service, time*

ACCRETION ACCOUNT. A record of the increase between the price of a bond purchased at discount and the bond's face value. *See Also: bond, discount, face value*

ACCRUAL BASIS. An accounting system which revenues are recorded when they are earned, and expenditures are recorded when they result in liabilities for benefits received. This differs from cash accounting, under which an entry is made only when cash is paid or received. *See Also: cash*

ACCRUAL BONDS. Also known as Z-Bonds, an Accrual Bond is a CMO tranche that is sold at a deep discount to its par value. Accrual Bonds accrete interest at a stated coupon rate that is added to the outstanding principal balance instead of being paid to the investor. This accretion can continue until the bond becomes current; subsequent bonds have been retired and the accrual bond becomes a sequential pay bond. At this time, the accrual bond begins making principal payments. *See Also: accretion, balance, bond, CMO, coupon, coupon rate, discount, interest, outstanding, par, par value, pay, principal, principal balance, sequential pay bond, time, tranche*

ACCRUED INCOME. Income which is earned, but not received.

ACCRUED INTEREST. The amount of interest accumulated between interest payments. Accrued interest on bonds must be added to their purchase price. *See Also: interest, purchase price*

ACCRUED LIABILITIES. Liabilities which arise from expenses incurred, but not yet paid.

ACCUMULATED DISTRIBUTION. Money put into a trust to be distributed later. The money is taxed when it is put into the trust, but not when the trust funds are distributed. *See Also: put, trust*

ACCUMULATED DIVIDEND. Dividend owed to stockholders of cumulative preferred stock. *See Also: cumulative preferred stock, preferred stock, stock*

ACCUMULATED EARNINGS TAX. A tax that corporations must pay if they accrue earnings without distributing their dividends to stockholders. Some companies would rather pay this tax than distribute dividends, because the dividends would place the individual stockholders into higher tax brackets. *See Also: earnings, pay*

ACCUMULATED SURPLUS. A company's excess profits that are not held or reinvested.

ACCUMULATION. Absorbing an excess supply of stock, thereby increasing the demand for it. Accumulation generally occurs after a stock's price drops and stabilizes, thus increasing demand. Accumulating shares of a security over a stretch of time avoids attracting attention. The term is also used to describe a base pattern on a chart where long term holders buy under-valued securities with the intention of capital appreciation. *See Also: appreciation, base, capital, capital appreciation, chart, demand, securities, security, stock, supply, term, time*

ACCUMULATION AREA. Price range in which investors buy stock. *See Also: range, stock*

ACCUMULATION PLAN. A method where an investor regularly can buy mutual fund shares in varying amounts, with dividend income and capital gains distributions reinvested in additional shares. *See Also: capital, dividend, fund, mutual fund*

ACID TEST RATIO. Cash and cash equivalents divided by current liabilities. *See Also: asset, cash, cash equivalents, current, current liabilities, current ratio, quick asset ratio, ratio*

ACQUIRED SURPLUS. Working capital received when a company is purchased. *See Also: capital*

ACQUISITION. Controlling interest over an asset, usually referring to one company buying out another. *See Also: asset, interest*

ACQUISITION COST. The sales charge a client must pay to invest in a specific mutual fund, or the costs of acquiring property. *See Also: client, closing costs, fund, mutual fund, pay, sales charge*

ACQUISITION DATE. The day someone commits to buying an asset. *See Also: asset*

ACROSS THE BOARD. Widespread, overall action.

ACRS. Accelerated Cost Recovery System. *See Also: recovery*

ACTING IN CONCERT. Two or more people working together to buy up stock or take over a company. When five percent of the outstanding shares of a stock are acquired, a report must be filed with the Securities and Exchange

Commission stating the acquirer's intentions. *See Also: commission, exchange, outstanding, securities, stock, take*

ACTIVE ASSETS. Physical assets used for a corporation's daily operations. *See Also: operations*

ACTIVE BOND CROWD. New York Stock Exchange bond department members responsible for the heaviest amount of bond trading. *See Also: bond, exchange, stock, stock exchange*

ACTIVE BOX. The place where collateral for securing a broker's loan or a customer's margin position is held, or where securities are held for safekeeping either for a dealer or a dealer's customer. *See Also: collateral, dealer, margin, position, safekeeping, securities*

ACTIVE MANAGEMENT. Ongoing portfolio management that seeks to achieve maximum results. In making investment decisions, active managers rely on timely information such as research, market opinions, and their own assessment and experience. *See Also: assessment, investment, market, on, portfolio*

ACTIVE SERVER PAGES. Also known as ASP, a programming environment developed by Microsoft that is run on a server. ASP provides the easy combination of HTML, scripting, and components to create powerful Internet applications. *See Also: ASP, combination, HTML, Internet, on, run, server*

ACTIVE TRANCHE. A tranche in a CMO transaction that is currently receiving principal payments. *See Also: CMO, principal, tranche, transaction*

ACTIVEX. A Microsoft technology that suggests Active Web pages. ActiveX, a standard for programming blocks known as objects, facilitates the viewing of animated graphics effects, Microsoft Word documents, and more. *See Also: technology, Web*

ACTIVITY. The trading volume of a stock, or a group of stocks, on a particular exchange. *See Also: exchange, stock, trading volume, volume*

ACTUAL. A physical commodity, as opposed to a futures contract, that is present and ready for delivery or storage, sold on a cash market. Delivery is rarely taken; rather, the customer pays a fee to store the commodity. *See Also: cash, cash market, commodity, contract, delivery, futures, futures contract, market, physical commodity*

ACTUAL CASH VALUE. The theoretical value of a contract when it is redeemed, as opposed to its market value. *See Also: contract, market, market value, theoretical value*

ACTUALLY OUTSTANDING. Stocks and bonds that a corporation has issued, but not reacquired. *See Also: corporation*

ACTUARY. An insurance company mathematician who calculates premiums, dividends, and annuity rates, among other figures, using risk factors from experience tables, which are based on the company's history of claims and other data. *See Also: annuity, insurance, risk*

AD HOC. A specific action taken to solve a specific problem.

AD REFERENDUM. A signed contract with provisions and issues not yet resolved. *See Also: contract*

AD VALOREM TAX. Tax based on a property's assessed value.

AD VIEWS. The number of times an advertiser's advertisement is actually loaded to visitors.

ADD-ON INTEREST. A procedure which a certain percentage of the principal is used to calculate the interest cost. The interest cost is then added to the principal to determine the amount the borrower must repay. *See Also: interest, principal*

ADDRESS. Two types of Internet-related addresses: e-mail and a Web page address. *See Also: e-mail, Web, Web page*

ADJUSTABLE RATE CONVERTIBLE NOTE. A debt security that is issued at a higher price than its potential matured value. This note, however, can be traded for shares of common stock that are worth the original price of the note. *See Also: common stock, debt security, matured, note, security, stock, worth*

ADJUSTABLE RATE MORTGAGE. A mortgage agreement that establishes interest rate adjustments made at regular intervals. The adjustments are based on an index that cannot be controlled by the lending institution, such as the interest rate on U.S. Treasury bills, the cost of funds rate, or the average national mortgage rate. Because the borrower takes some of the risk of rising interest rates, he or she receives a lower initial rate than he or she would get on a fixed-rate mortgage. *See Also: average, cost of funds, funds rate, index, interest, interest rate, intervals, mortgage, risk*

ADJUSTABLE RATE MORTGAGE FUND. A mutual fund that primarily buys adjustable rate mortgage securities (ARMs). These mutual funds are subject to the volatility of rising and falling interest rates, which affects the interest rate adjustments of the underlying ARMs. *See Also: adjustable rate mortgage, fund, interest, interest rate, mortgage, mutual fund, securities, volatility*

ADJUSTABLE RATE PREFERRED STOCK. Publicly traded stock collateralized by mortgage backed securities. *See Also: mortgage, securities, stock*

ADJUSTED BASIS. Base price used to calculate capital gains or losses when a stock or bond is sold. The price is adjusted to compensate for stock splits and transactions costs that have occurred since the stock's original purchase. *See Also: bond, capital, stock*

ADJUSTED DEBT BALANCE. Formula used to determine the position of a margin account, calculated by netting the balance owed to the broker with any unused portion of the margin account and any paper profits on short accounts. *See Also: account, balance, broker, margin, margin account, paper, position*

ADJUSTED EXERCISE PRICE. The process the Options Clearing Corporation uses to adjust an option contract because of stock splits or stock dividends. Adjusting is done to maintain the original amount of the contract as much as possible. *See Also: contract, corporation, option, option contract, stock*

ADJUSTED GROSS INCOME. Income figure an individual or couple uses to compute federal income tax. To reach the adjusted gross income, a person subtracts business expenses that weren't reimbursed and other deductions from his or her gross income. *See Also: gross*

ADJUSTMENT BOND. Bondholders exchange a bond for a new security in a company facing bankruptcy. The new security would pay interest or dividends as long as the corporation meets certain financial goals. *See Also: bankruptcy, bond, corporation, exchange, interest, pay, security*

ADJUSTMENT PREFERRED SECURITIES. Following any restructuring these preferred securities would have a priority claim over a company's assets. *See Also: priority, securities*

ADJUSTMENT RATE PREFERRED STOCK. A senior issue of corporate stock usually purchased by another corporation because of tax advantages (85 percent of preferred stock dividends are tax-exempt to another corporation). The dividend, normally paid quarterly, is pegged to a short-term index, such as the three-month Treasury Bill rate, or a Commercial Paper Composite. *See Also: commercial paper, composite, corporation, dividend, index, issue, paper, preferred stock, quarterly, stock, Treasury bill*

ADMISSION BY INVESTMENT. By investing cash in a partnership and increasing that firm's assets, an individual can become a part owner. *See Also: cash, partnership*

ADMITTED TO DEALINGS. Securities approved by the Securities and Exchange Commission for listing and trading on a stock exchange. *See Also: commission, exchange, listing, securities, stock, stock exchange*

ADRS. American Depository Receipts. *See Also: depository*

ADSL. Asymmetric Digital Subscriber Line. *See Also: digital, subscriber*

ADVANCE COMMITMENT. Agreement by an individual buyer to purchase a bond issue on a specific future date. *See Also: bond, issue*

ADVANCE REFUNDING. The exchanging of fixed-income securities before they are due for another issue. This allows the issuer to issue the new bonds at lower rates. *See Also: issue, securities*

ADVANCE-DECLINE. Ratio of stocks that have gone up versus those that have dropped in a specific time period. If stocks advance, analysts consider the market "bullish." If stocks drop, the market is considered "bearish." *See Also: drop, market, time*

ADVANCING MARKET. Widespread increase in market prices, with indications that the market will remain on the upswing. *See Also: market*

AD VIEWS. The number of times an advertiser's advertisement is actually loaded to visitors.

ADVISER. One that advises, such as a person that offers professional advice or firm that is responsible for mutual fund investment decisions. Advisers typically collect fees based on total assets. *See Also: firm, fund, investment, mutual fund, on, professional*

ADVISORY FUNDS. Money a client deposits in his or her bank, which the institution then invests at its own discretion. *See Also: bank, client*

ADVISORY SERVICE. An agency investors use to obtain market information and investment advice. *See Also: investment, market*

AFFIDAVIT. A sworn, notarized statement concerning a financial, legal, or other transaction. *See Also: legal, statement, transaction*

AFFIDAVIT OF DOMICILE. Document provided by the executor of an estate verifying the decedent's place of residence at the time of death. The affidavit is necessary before any securities can be transferred from the estate, because the securities have to be checked for possible liens in the decedent's home state. *See Also: affidavit, estate, home, securities, time*

AFFILIATE. Relationship between at least two companies when one owns less than a majority of the other's voting stock, or when both are subsidiaries of a third company. *See Also: stock, voting stock*

AFFILIATE PROGRAMS. An online business relationship whereby a Website can offer the goods or services of a third-party Website. The third-party will maintain the goods or services, typically including customer service and shipping, in exchange for referral fees. *See Also: exchange, offer, online, service, Web, Website, will*

AFFILIATED PERSON. Person in a position to directly influence a corporation's actions, such as the director, or someone who owns more than 10 percent of the stock. Anyone who can directly influence one of these people, such as a family member or close friend, is also considered an affiliated person. *See Also: close, director, position, stock*

AFFINITY CARD. A debit or credit card that is tied to a particular consumer interest, such as lifestyles or clubs. Affinity cards typically contribute a portion of the user's transaction cost to an interest related to the card, such as a charitable organization. *See Also: credit, debit, interest, transaction*

AFFINITY GROUP. Individuals with a common interest. On the Web, affinity groups may gather for such events as a newsgroup or online chat. *See Also: interest, newsgroup, on, online, Web*

AFTER HOURS BEST ASK. The lowest price at which a security is being offered in the after hours market. *See Also: market, security*

AFTER HOURS BEST BID. The highest price at which a buyer is prepared to pay in the after hours market. *See Also: market, pay*

AFTER HOURS HIGH. The highest price in which a security traded during the current day's after hours trading session. *See Also: current, security, session*

AFTER HOURS LAST SALE. The last price in which a security traded during the current day's after hours trading session. *See Also: current, security, session*

AFTER HOURS LOW. The lowest price in which a security traded during the current day's after hours trading session. *See Also: current, security, session*

AFTER HOURS PERCENT CHANGE. The percent increase or decrease between the last sale of the regular day's trading session and the last sale of the current day's after hours trading session. *See Also: current, last sale, sale, session*

AFTER HOURS VOLUME. The total number of shares in which a security traded during the current day's after hours trading session. *See Also: current, security, session*

AFTER TAX. Corporate or individual profits or losses after state and federal taxes are considered.

AFTER TAX REAL RATE OF RETURN. Comparison of the after tax total return of a taxable investment with the total return of a tax-exempt investment after the amounts are adjusted for inflation. *See Also: after tax, inflation, investment, return, total return*

AFTER-ACQUIRED CLAUSE. A provision in a mortgage whereby a second mortgageable property can be used as additional security on an existing loan. *See Also: mortgage, security*

AFTER-ACQUIRED PROPERTY. Asset or real property purchased after a corporation has executed a mortgage, or after a person has drawn up his or her will. Such asset or property is not subject to the prior mortgage or will. *See Also: asset, corporation, mortgage*

AFTER-HOURS TRADING. Also referred to as post-market trading, trading that occurs after the close of the regular trading session. After-hours trading can refer to inter-company trading, trading via an ECN, or on an international exchange. *See Also: close, ECN, exchange, on, post-market trading, session*

AFTER-MARKET. Market created after a company goes public with its stock. *See Also: stock*

AGAINST THE BOX. Sale of borrowed shares of stock in which an investor's position is long. Sellers may sell "against the box" in order to avoid ownership, disclosure, or to benefit from tax considerations. *See Also: disclosure, order, position, stock*

AGE OF MAJORITY. Age at which a person can legally sign a contract; typically 18 or 21 in most states.

AGENT BANK. A bank that acts as a mediator between customer and broker. *See Also: bank, broker*

AGENTS. Intelligent software used by buyers or sellers in an e-marketplace that can perform various functions, such as monitoring prices and conditions. Agents can also be used to automatically execute transactions. *See Also: e-marketplace*

AGGRAVATED PARTY. One who files a complaint or requests arbitration, claiming to be the victim of an exchange member's unfair practices. *See Also: arbitration, exchange*

AGGREGATE EXERCISE POLICY. Number of shares in a put or call contract, multiplied by the exercise price. *See Also: call contract, contract, exercise, exercise price, put*

AGGREGATE INDEBTEDNESS. Total amount of money or shares a broker or dealer owes to customers. *See Also: broker, dealer*

AGGREGATE SUPPLY. Total amount of goods and services supplied to the market at different price levels during a specific time period; also called total output. The amount corresponds with the number of goods and services demanded by different income levels during the same time period. *See Also: market, time*

AGGREGATION. An e-commerce model in which the buying power of consumers and businesses are aggregated to achieve the best possible prices from suppliers. In general, the higher the volume, the lower the price an item is expected. Aggregation may also refer to a Web-based service of amassing predetermined information on behalf of a business or a consumer. *See Also: buying power, e-commerce, on, service, volume*

AGGREGATOR. A business-to-business company that brings together multiple buyers (or sellers) in a centralized e-marketplace in order to collectively obtain the best prices. *See Also: e-marketplace, order*

AGGRESSIVE GROWTH. Stressing riskiness and profit potential over quality and security. This approach is a philosophy that may be applied to the direction of an individual company or an investment outlook. *See Also: investment, profit, security*

AGGRESSIVE GROWTH FUND. A mutual fund with a rapid capital appreciation objective. Typical investments may include small growth companies and highly volatile stocks. Investment techniques may involve aggressive strategies such as leveraging, options and short selling. *See Also: appreciation, capital, capital appreciation, fund, investment, mutual fund, volatile*

AGGRESSIVE PROTFOLIO. Collection of securities purchased for short-term profit potential rather than defensive quality and income. *See Also: profit, securities*

AGING SCHEDULE. Schedule of monthly receivables shown by maturity and classified as current or delinquent. This classification of accounts helps a company analyze the quality of its receivables investments. *See Also: current, maturity, receivables*

AGNOSTIC TECHNOLOGY. Software applications that can accommodate most systems, particularly useful when connecting two businesses with conflicting standards. *See Also: standards*

AGREEMENT AMONG UNDERWRITERS. A contract among members of an investment banking syndicate which covers many points: appointing the syndicate manager, agent, and additional managers if necessary; defining members' liability; agreeing to pay each member's share on a settlement date; authorizing the manager to distribute units to a selling group; and defining the life of the syndicate. *See Also: agent, banking syndicate, contract, investment, manager, pay, share, syndicate, syndicate manager*

AGRIBUSINESS. Any large-scale farming or agricultural enterprise. As of late, giant corporations are replacing individual family farms.

AI. Artificial Intelligence.

AIR BALL LENDING. The portion of a loan that is based on expectations of business growth, not backed by hard assets, such as equipment. *See Also: on*

AIR POCKET STOCK. When stock prices take a dramatic nose dive and shareholders rush to sell. This action is compared to a plunging aircraft that has hit an air pocket. *See Also: hit, stock, take*

ALIAS. An alternate name, usually easy to remember, that can refer to a network resource, a group of people or an individual. For example, an easy-to-use alias e-mail address, such as webmaster@xyz.com can be used instead of an individual's real address. *See Also: address, e-mail, e-mail address, name, resource*

ALIEN CORPORATION. A company, originally incorporated under the laws of another country, that now operates in the U.S. or another country outside its home nation. *See Also: corporation, foreign corporation, home*

ALIENATION. Transferring interest or property to someone else. *See Also: interest*

ALIENATION CLAUSE. Provision in a contract whereby a note must be paid in full when the mortgage title is transferred. *See Also: contract, full, mortgage, note*

ALL OR ANY PART. Brokers may execute any part of an order in a discretionary account within a client's price limit. *See Also: account, discretionary account, limit, order, price limit*

ALL OR NONE OFFERING. A new security offered publicly with a requirement that the entire issue must be sold by a certain date or all offers will be canceled. *See Also: issue, security*

ALL OR NONE ORDER. A request to buy or sell a security in which all of the security must be involved in the transaction, or all of it will be canceled. For example, an investor may place an order with a broker to purchase 1,000 shares of XYZ stock at $50 per share. If only 500 shares are available at that price, the order will not be completed. *See Also: broker, order, security, share, stock, transaction*

ALLIED MEMBER. Partner or stockholder in a New York Stock Exchange firm who is not a member of the exchange. Since a firm doesn't need more than one partner or stockholder as a member, even a board chairman may be only an allied member, who cannot do business on the trading floor. *See Also: exchange, firm, floor, New York Stock Exchange, stock, stock exchange, stockholder, trading floor*

ALLOCATION. Exchange members issue stock option exercise notices by a random drawing to ensure fair trading through random selection. *See Also: exercise, issue, option, stock, stock option*

ALLOWABLE DEPRECIATION. An amount that could have been deducted as depreciation but instead is added to the value of the asset. *See Also: asset, depreciation*

ALLOWANCE. Money reserved to make up for bad debts or depreciation. *See Also: depreciation*

ALPHA. The premium an investment portfolio earns above a certain benchmark (such as the Standard and Poors's 500). A positive alpha indicates the investor earned a premium over that index. *See Also: benchmark, index, investment, investment portfolio, portfolio, premium*

ALTERNATE ACCOUNT. An account held by at least two people, with any of those named allowed to draw from the account. *See Also: account*

ALTERNATE DEPOSITORS. Two or more people who collectively hold a joint account. *See Also: account, hold, joint account*

ALTERNATIVE MINIMUM TAX. Requires taxpayers with substantial taxable incomes to pay a minimum tax, even if their income normally would not be taxable. *See Also: pay*

ALTERNATIVE MORTGAGE INSTRUMENTS. Various mortgage choices a person may pick to avoid taking out a fixed-rate mortgage. *See Also: adjustable rate mortgage, annuity, graduated payment mortgage, mortgage, reverse annuity mortgage, variable rate mortgage*

ALTERNATIVE ORDER. A buy or sell order that allows several alternatives to be used to fill the order. When part of the order is executed, the unused alternatives will be canceled. For example, an investor may be willing to purchase 20,000 shares of stock at $26 1/2, but he or she may only post an initial bid of 5,000 shares at $26 1/4. The broker may be given some discretion in this matter. *See Also: broker, fill, order, post, sell order, stock*

AMALGAMATION. The union of two or more companies when such a union financially benefits all businesses involved.

AMBAC. American Municipal Bond Assurance Corporation. *See Also: bond, corporation, municipal bond*

AMERICAN BOARD OF TRADE. Provides spot and deferred markets, and offers investors stock market information. *See Also: market, spot, stock, stock market*

AMERICAN DEPOSITORY RECEIPTS (ADRS). Certificates issued by a U.S. bank and traded in this country as domestic shares. The certificates represent the number of foreign securities the U.S. bank holds in that security's country of origin. ADRs make trading foreign securities in the U.S. easier by eliminating currency exchange, legal obstacles, foreign ownership transfers, and the need to trade on a foreign exchange. *See Also: ADRs, bank, currency, easier, exchange, foreign exchange, foreign securities, legal, securities*

AMERICAN MUNICIPAL BOND ASSURANCE CORPORATION (AMBAC). A private holding company that insures the payment of principal and interest on new municipal bonds. AMBAC-insured bonds carry the highest bond rating. *See Also: and interest, bond, bond rating, carry, interest, principal*

AMERICAN OPTION. Any option an investor can exercise before its maturity. *See Also: exercise, maturity, option*

AMERICAN PARITY. U.S. funds equal to the foreign price of securities abroad. *See Also: securities*

AMERICAN STOCK EXCHANGE (AMEX). The second-largest stock exchange in the United States. Otherwise known as Amex, the exchange is the exchange is located at 86 Trinity Place in Downtown Manhattan. The Amex tends to specialize in securities of slightly smaller capitalization. *See also: AMEX, capitalization, exchange, securities, stock, stock exchange*

AMERICAN STOCK EXCHANGE MARKET VALUE INDEX. The average value of all common shares, rights, and warrants listed on the American Stock Exchange. *See Also: average, exchange, rights, stock, stock exchange*

AMERICUS TRUST. A five-year investment trust fund in which American Telephone & Telegraph stockholders deposit their shares. *See Also: fund, investment, investment trust, trust*

AMEX. American Stock Exchange. *See Also: exchange, stock, stock exchange*

AMEX OPTIONS SWITCHING SYSTEM. A computer that transmits incoming orders for options to the proper trading posts. The computer also notifies the exchange member who made the order if the option has been executed. *See Also: exchange, option, order*

AMICUS CURIAE. Usually referring to a "friend-of-the-court," it is a brief filed by a company or other party interested in the outcome of a specific court case, without being an actual litigant. The brief states reasons why the court should decide on one litigant's behalf, and why a ruling that went the other way could be detrimental to the overall business climate. *See Also: actual, an actual*

AMORTIZATION. Method of accounting where the cost of an asset is spread over its useful life. This can be applied to such items as patents, copyrights, and goodwill. *See Also: asset, goodwill, spread*

AMORTIZATION OF PREMIUM. Any premium paid for a bond above its par value or call price is amortized over the life of the bond. *See Also: bond, call price, par, par value, premium*

AMORTIZED LOSSES. Losses may occur when interest-bearing instruments are sold before maturity when interest rates are fluctuating. *See Also: interest, maturity*

AMORTIZED MORTGAGE LOAN. A loan that must be repaid within a specific period through regular payments that reduce the loan's principal and cover interest as it falls due. *See Also: interest, principal*

AMOUNT AT INTEREST. The amount of principal deposited to earn interest. *See Also: interest, principal*

AN ACTUAL. A security that underlies an option or the security that satisfies a contract when it is delivered. *See Also: contract, option, security*

ANALOG. Data that is represented in an electrical signal or wave in which its physical quantities continuously vary. This contrasts to digital, in which data is represented as binary digits. The difference can be explained as analog representing the fluid hands moving on a clock, whereas a digital representation would consist of information describing each movement. *See Also: binary, digital, movement, on, signal*

ANALYST. An investment firm professional who makes estimates on the investment value of companies, industries, and the economy as a whole. *See Also: firm, investment, investment value, professional*

AND INTEREST. The buyer of an outstanding bond must pay the seller any interest that has built up between the last interest payment and the settlement date. *See Also: bond, interest, outstanding, pay, settlement date*

ANGEL FUNDING. A type of very early-stage venture funding usually provided by individual investors. This funding typically requires less paperwork and due diligence than traditional venture capitalists, with friendlier terms. *See Also: due diligence, funding*

ANNOUNCEMENT DATE. The specific day a company announces that its stocks will be paying dividends. The company will also announce the amount of the dividends on this date.

ANNUAL EARNINGS. All income, minus expenses, received in a year (that is, annual profits). *See Also: minus*

ANNUAL FINANCIAL STATEMENT. A document that gives a company's financial status, stating profits and losses, for the year. The document is released on the last day of the company's fiscal year. *See Also: fiscal year*

ANNUAL MEETING. A yearly meeting in which stockholders elect a board of directors and vote on other company concerns. *See Also: board of directors, elect*

ANNUAL REPORT. A comprehensive financial statement corporations issue yearly to shareholders. The report defines the company's financial condition, announces new products or services, explains past performances, and projects future prospects. Mutual funds send their shareholders annual reports, which are detailed with performance numbers, current investment strategy and portfolio holdings. Copies can usually be obtained upon request. *See Also: issue, statement*

ANNUAL RETURN. Based upon dividends, reinvestment of dividends, capital gains or losses, this is the percentage of change that an investment has achieved over a 12-month period. *See Also: appreciation, interest, investment, unrealized appreciation*

ANNUAL YIELD. The amount of money an investment earns in interest or dividends each year. *See Also: interest, investment*

ANNUALIZED LINKED-MEDIAN RETURN. Annualization of the compounded yearly median returns. Companies that do not have calendar year ending dates have comparison returns. *See Also: calendar, comparison returns*

ANNUALIZED PERCENT. Translating a partial year's figures into an annual rate.

ANNUITANT. One who receives an annuity. *See Also: annuity*

ANNUITY. Periodic payments made over a specified period of time, usually in equal amounts, such as interest payments on bonds. *See Also: interest, time*

ANNUITY BOND. A security with no date of maturity that pays interest for an indefinite length of time. *See Also: date of maturity, interest, maturity, security, time*

ANNUITY METHOD OF DEPRECIATION. Derived by subtracting the salvage value from a capital asset's original cost, and the straight-line portion of the difference is charged to each period. *See Also: capital, original cost, salvage value*

ANNUITY PLAN. A retirement fund where a person receives income after paying into the fund for a specific number of years. *See Also: fund*

ANNUITY UNIT. Accumulation units converted to units upon which annuity payments can be made. *See Also: accumulation, annuity*

ANNUNCIATOR BOARDS. A paging device on the stock exchange wall used to direct a floor broker to the firm's booth for orders and executions. Electronic paging boards are used now in the stock exchanges. *See Also: broker, exchange, exchanges, floor, floor broker, stock, stock exchange*

ANTECEDENTS. The determination of whether a corporation has had the same owner for a long time, or if the firm has frequent ownership changes. *See Also: corporation, firm, time*

ANTICIPATED HOLDING PERIOD. The length of time a limited partnership expects to remain in operation before business is terminated. *See Also: limited partnership, partnership, time*

ANTICIPATION. An account payment made before it is due. *See Also: account*

ANTICIPATION NOTE. A short-term municipal debt instrument issued to secure funds backed by current revenues. *See Also: current, debt instrument, instrument*

ANTITRUST. A court action restricting companies that try to monopolize a particular industry or trade. *See Also: industry*

ANY-QUANTITY RATE. A transport charge for any amount of a commodity. *See Also: commodity*

AOB. Any Other Business. AOB is used as a concluding agenda item during a business meeting, usually time permitting. *See Also: time*

API. Application Programming Interface.

APPLIANCE. Also called a network PC denotes a low-cost PC or related device designed for Internet access and other specialized business uses, but without the full capabilities of today's personal computer and software. *See Also: full, Internet, network PC, personal computer*

APPLICATION OF FUNDS STATEMENT. A report taken from balance sheets during two different periods which then provides an overview of changes that occurred during the periods. *See Also: balance*

APPLICATION PROGRAMMING INTERFACE. API is an interface between the operating system and application programs that programmers use to interact with other applications. The API contains hidden functions inside programs that dictates how the operating system and application programs communicate.

APPLICATION SERVICE PROVIDER. An ASP is an online outsourcer or hosting service that licenses, maintains, and rents third-party software systems, via remote access such as the Internet, to businesses or individuals. For a monthly or yearly subscription fee, ASPs typically provide the servers, network access, and applications. *See Also: ASP, hosting, Internet, online, remote, remote access, service, subscription*

APPLICATIONS SOFTWARE. Software, or a computer program, that is designed for the end user, such as word processing, data bases, spreadsheets, Web browsers. Software is generalized as being either systems software or applications software. *See Also: end user, processing, systems software, Web*

APPLIED PROCEEDS SWAP. When one block of bonds is sold to buy another block of bonds.

APPRAISAL. Evaluation of an asset to determine its value. *See Also: asset*

APPRAISAL RIGHTS OF MINORITY STOCKHOLDERS. A statutory right of dissenting stockholders when a company is consolidated or merged with another firm. *See Also: firm, right*

APPRAISAL SURPLUS. The difference between an asset's appraised value over its book value. *See Also: book, book value*

APPRECIATION. The increase in value of an asset over time. *See Also: asset, time*

APPRECIATION POTENTIAL. The expected increase in market value. *See Also: market, market value*

APPROPRIATE SURPLUS. A portion of a company's surplus that the board of directors has set aside for a particular purpose, and should not be considered a liability. *See Also: board of directors, liability*

APPROPRIATION. An amount of money set aside for a specific purpose.

APPROVED DEPOSITORY. A bank or trust company approved by the exchange where the members of that exchange deposit cash and securities. *See Also: bank, cash, exchange, securities, trust, trust company*

APPROVED LIST. A list of approved investments that a fiduciary may buy for a client. *See Also: client, fiduciary*

ARBITRAGE. The buying and selling of stocks, foreign exchanges, precious metals, bonds, or other commodities from one market to a separate but related market. An arbitrage opportunity arises when two companies plan to merge or when one security is convertible into another. *See Also: exchanges, market, security*

ARBITRAGE BONDS. Municipal bonds issued with the intention of refunding higher rate bonds in advance of their call date. In order to gain an interest rate advantage, the proceeds from the new issue will be invested in treasuries until the call date of the issue being refunded. *See Also: call date, gain, interest, interest rate, issue, new issue, order, proceeds, refunding, treasuries*

ARBITRATION. An industry-operated, binding method of eliminating or reducing conflicts between stock exchange members or between members and nonmembers. Arbitration is sought after all involved parties cannot resolve a conflict on their own. They then agree to adhere to whatever decision the arbitration panel may reach. *See Also: exchange, stock, stock exchange*

ARCADE. Trading rooms where floor traders congregate to trade on computer screens. Considered a "cousin" of the trading pits, arcades have financial backing from exchange leadership but are not sponsored by any exchange. Arcades offer certain advantages, such as fewer clerical errors or out trading. *See Also: exchange, floor, offer, on, out trading*

ARCHITECTURE. The reference to the overall design of a computing system, software or networks, including the hardware, software, and protocols within a computing system, plus other designs if referring to a network, such as access methods. *See Also: plus*

ARCHIVE. A collection, or back up, of files stored on a computer network. *See Also: back up, on, up*

ARIEL. The Automated Real-time Investments Exchange is a computer network that handles transactions involving large blocks of stock. *See Also: exchange, stock*

ARITHMETIC INVESTING. A method of investing that reduces the investor's risk by estimating rates of return during a specific period. *See Also: return, risk*

ARM. Adjustable Rate Mortgage.

ARM'S LENGTH SYSTEM. A method of calculating corporate state income taxes where only profits earned in a particular state are taxed by that state. Earnings from elsewhere are not taxed by that state, but may be taxable elsewhere unless they were earned by a parent company abroad. *See Also: earnings*

ARM'S LENGTH TRANSACTION. A contract which the parties involved act independent of each other. *See Also: contract*

ARMS INDEX. See trading index. *See Also: index, up, volume*

AROUND. The number of points on either side of par. For example, when quoting a premium or discount, a "three-three around" would be three points on either side of par. *See Also: discount, par, premium*

ARPANET. Formed by the U.S. Department of Defense during the Cold War, ARPANET is a forerunner to the Internet. The network was designed to be a military command and control center that could withstand nuclear attack. It was created so that authority was distributed over geographically dispersed computers. *See Also: Internet, U*

ARPS. Adjustable Rate Preferred Stock. *See Also: preferred stock, stock*

ARREARAGE. Cumulative unpaid dividends of preferred shares. *See Also: preferred stock, stock*

ARREARS. Any past-due amount.

ARTICLES OF ASSOCIATION. Similar to a corporate certificate, this document is usually associated with nonstock companies, such as charities. *See Also: certificate*

ARTICLES OF INCORPORATION. A document that establishes a corporation and, after certification, becomes the corporation's charter. *See Also: charter, corporation*

ARTIFICIAL INTELLIGENCE. Also referred to as AI, the ability to use computers to perform activities that normally require intelligence, such as game playing, reasoning, learning, responding to human language, and reacting to external stimuli.

AS PRINCIPAL. A brokerage firm which is buying or selling securities for or from its own account. In such cases, commissions are not charged. *See Also: account, firm, securities*

ASCENDING TOPS. A chart that shows that each peak is higher than the previous peak. *See Also: chart, descending tops, peak*

ASCII. Acronym for American Standard Code for Information Interchange is an English-language code that assigns a number to each character, both upper and lower case as well as punctuation. ASCII text does not include special formatting.

ASIAN DEVELOPMENT BANK. An international bank with its headquarters in the Philippines that promotes both social and economic growth in Asia by making loans to underdeveloped countries. *See Also: bank*

ASIAN FUNDS. A mutual fund that invests primarily in the stocks of Asian-based companies. *See Also: fund, mutual fund*

ASK. The lowest price at which a security is being offered to sell. For open-end mutual funds, this is the net asset value. *See Also: offer*

ASKED PRICE. The lowest price at which a security is being offered to sell. For open-end funds, the asked price is the funds current net asset value per share plus its sales charge. *See Also: dealer, security*

ASP. Application Service Provider or Active Server Pages. *See Also: server, service*

ASPIRIN COUNT THEORY. A lighthearted market indicator that says the market will fall a year after aspirin production increases, and will rise a year later if aspirin production goes down. *See Also: fall, market*

ASSAY. Examination of a metal's content, composition, and purity. *See Also: composition*

ASSAY OFFICE BAR. A bar of nearly pure gold or silver from the U.S. Mint that has been tested by an assay office. *See Also: assay*

ASSEMBLAGE. Bringing together two or more people to form an aggregate, or the cost of bringing two or more items into a single ownership.

ASSENTED SECURITIES. Owners of a corporate security agree to change the security's status because of corporate restructuring, bankruptcy, or some other change. *See Also: bankruptcy, change, security*

ASSESSABLE STOCK. A company that goes through a reorganization is subject to an assessment of its stock. *See Also: assessment, reorganization, stock*

ASSESSED VALUATION. The amount of money a government attaches to an asset and upon which it bases taxes. *See Also: asset*

ASSESSMENT. Any charge made against a taxable asset. *See Also: asset*

ASSESSMENT BOND. A municipal bond issued to pay for improvements to government-owned property, such as streets or sewers. *See Also: bond, municipal bond, pay*

ASSESSMENT RATIO. The difference between the assessed property value and the fair market value. *See Also: fair market value, market, market value*

ASSESSMENT ROLL. A list of all legal information with a description of each piece of property and its assessed value. *See Also: legal*

ASSESSOR. A government official responsible for evaluating the value of a piece of property.

ASSET. Everything owned by a corporation or an individual-from buildings and equipment to intangible assets such as patents and reputation. Also, a mutual fund's cash and investment holdings, such as stocks, warrants, options, bonds, CDs, etc. *See Also: corporation*

ASSET ALLOCATION DECISION. Investments are made with a proper mix of assets to achieve certain goals, such as risk level, income, and appreciation potential. *See Also: appreciation, appreciation potential, level, risk*

ASSET ALLOCATION FUND. A mutual fund that seeks to allocate investments in a variety of asset classes. Asset classes may include foreign and domestic securities, real estate, precious metals, etc. Depending on the mutual fund, allocations may be variable as market conditions change, or fixed. *See Also: asset, change, estate, fund, market, mutual fund, on, real estate, securities*

ASSET AND LIABILITY STATEMENT. A balance sheet. *See Also: balance, balance sheet*

ASSET BACKED SECURITY. Also known as ABS, bonds that are securitized by receivables-such as credit cards, second mortgages, automobile loans, equipment leases, airline ticket receivables, boat and recreational-vehicle loans, unsecured personal loans, automobile and truck dealer inventories, and mobile homes. These securities typically are structured to offer high credit ratings. *See Also: credit, dealer, high credit, offer, receivables, securities*

ASSET COVERAGE. The ratio of assets to obligations. The indicator measures a corporation's ability to meet debt service payments. *See Also: debt service, ratio, service*

ASSET DEPRECIATION RANGE SYSTEM. The Internal Revenue Service's guideline in defining and allowing depreciable lives for specific depreciable assets. *See Also: internal revenue*

ASSET FINANCING. The conversion of assets into cash in exchange for security interest in the assets. *See Also: accounts receivable, accounts receivable financing, cash, conversion, exchange, interest, security*

ASSET LIABILITY MANAGEMENT. Matching items on opposite sides of the balance sheet. A corporation that wishes to acquire an asset must decide whether to pay cash, thereby reducing an asset, or take out a loan, thereby increasing a liability. *See Also: asset, balance, balance sheet, cash, corporation, liability, pay, take*

ASSET MANAGEMENT ACCOUNT. A bank or other financial institution that combines regular banking services, such as checking and savings accounts, with brokerage house services. *See Also: bank, brokerage house, house*

ASSET PLAY. An attractive security with a current price that does not reflect the worth of the firm's assets. *See Also: current, security, worth*

ASSIGNMENT. Transfer of ownership from one party to another.

ASSIGNMENT OF LEASES. Securities that sometimes are assumed in association with commercial property mortgages.

ASSIGNMENT OF MORTGAGE. A document that transfers a loan obligation from one owner to another. *See Also: obligation*

ASSIMILATION. The public distribution of a security's new shares by syndicate members and issued underwriters. *See Also: issue, syndicate*

ASSOCIATE MEMBER. A person with limited membership rights at the American Stock Exchange. *See Also: exchange, rights, stock, stock exchange*

ASSOCIATE SPECIALIST. An exchange member who assists a market specialist. *See Also: exchange, market, specialist*

ASSOCIATED PERSON. Anyone connected with a broker-dealer, including (but not limited to) directors, officers, and branch managers. *See Also: broker-dealer*

ASSOCIATION OF INTERNATIONAL BOND DEALERS. An organization based in Switzerland made up of banks and brokers involved in international debt securities. *See Also: securities*

ASSUMABLE MORTGAGE. The buyer takes over the previous owner's mortgage, which usually provides the buyer with a lower interest rate than he or she could have received by taking out a new mortgage. *See Also: interest, interest rate, mortgage*

ASSUMED LIABILITY. One person takes over loan payments or other obligations from someone else.

ASSUMPTION OF DEBT. One person takes over another person's debts.

ASYMMETRIC DIGITAL SUBSCRIBER LINE (ADSL). A digital technology that facilitates the transmission of data over copper phone lines, typically at rates faster than regular dial-up or ISDN lines.

AT A DISCOUNT. A security that sells for a price that is below its par value. *See Also: par, par value, security*

AT A PREMIUM. A security that sells for a price that is above its par value. *See Also: par, par value, security*

AT BEST. A customer order to buy a security at the best rate possible. *See Also: order, security*

AT MARKET. A customer order to buy or sell securities immediately at the best price available. *See Also: order, securities*

AT OR BETTER. A customer order to buy a security at or below a specified price, or to sell a security at or above a specified price. *See Also: order, security*

AT PAR. A security that sells at its par value. *See Also: par, par value, security*

AT RISK. The possibility of a loss. Investors in limited partnership can receive tax deductions if their investments are not guaranteed a rate of return. *See Also: limited partnership, partnership, rate of return, return*

AT SIGHT. A securities payment that is due immediately upon presentation or demand. *See Also: demand, securities*

AT THE BANK'S RISK. The bank, and not the customer, assumes most of the risk of losing money in this type of an investment. In return, the customer relinquishes some of the profit potential. *See Also: bank, investment, profit, return, risk*

AT THE CLOSE. A customer order that is to be completed at the best price possible when the market closes for the day. *See Also: market, order*

AT THE MONEY. A put or call option with an exercise price equal to the underlying security's current market value. *See Also: call option, current, current market value, exercise, exercise price, market, market value, option, put*

AT THE OPENING. A customer order that is to be completed at the best price possible when the trading for the security opens. The order is canceled if not executed immediately. *See Also: order, security*

AT YOUR RISK. The bank customer, and not the bank, assumes most of the risk of losing money in this type of an investment. *See Also: bank, investment, risk*

ATTORNEY-IN-FACT. Written permission to represent another person outside of court, such as a broker with the authority to transfer securities. Also known as "power of attorney." *See Also: broker, securities, transfer*

AUCTION. The buying and selling of real and personal property through a bidding process. Auction types include: Dutch, English, Japanese, Vickrey, and Yankee. Auctions can be forward or reverse, or sealed or unsealed. *See Also: forward, personal property*

AUCTION MARKET. Trading securities through an exchange with buyers and sellers competing against one another to get the best prices. The New York Stock Exchange is a prime example. *See Also: exchange, New York Stock Exchange, prime, securities, stock, stock exchange*

AUDIT. An evaluation of a company's financial records to verify that stated assets and liabilities match the actual assets and liabilities. *See Also: actual, evaluation*

AUDIT TRAIL. The printed and tangible records of a company's financial transactions.

AUSTRIAN SCHOOL OF ECONOMICS. A school of thought that follows a line of human action, skeptical of government intervention in economic affairs. People who hold to this philosophy emphasize the actions of individuals in economics. *See Also: hold, intervention*

AUTEX SYSTEM. A computer network that relates which brokers want to buy or sell large blocks of stock. *See Also: stock*

AUTHENTICATED COPY. A security certified by an appropriate official. *See Also: security*

AUTHENTICATION. A security measure, typically using digital certificates, for checking a business' or individual's identity. *See Also: digital, security*

AUTHORITY BOND. Municipal bond issued by a governmental body for a public services project such as building a new hospital wing or installing new roads. The bonds are repaid from revenues generated by the project. *See Also: bond*

AUTHORIZED STOCK. The maximum amount of stock that corporations may issue. The fixed amount is stated in the company's certificate of incorporation. *See Also: certificate, certificate of incorporation, issue, stock*

AUTOMATED BOND SYSTEM. A New York Stock Exchange computer network that lists all orders for nonconvertible bonds. *See Also: exchange, New York Stock Exchange, stock, stock exchange*

AUTOMATED CLEARINGHOUSE. A firm set up with computers and used by member financial institutions to combine, sort, and distribute payment orders. *See Also: firm*

AUTOMATED CUSTOMER ACCOUNT TRANSFER SERVICE. Members of the National Securities Clearing Corporation can transfer customer accounts through this computer service. *See Also: corporation, National Securities Clearing Corporation, securities, service, transfer*

AUTOMATED PRICING AND REPORTING SYSTEM. The New York Stock Exchange computer network used to process and assign prices to certain odd-lot orders. *See Also: exchange, New York Stock Exchange, stock, stock exchange*

AUTOMATIC INVESTMENT PLAN. A program, such as a payroll deduction plan, that enables the periodic transfer of funds to a specified account that is invested in a predetermined mutual fund. *See Also: account, deduction, payroll deduction plan, transfer*

AUTOMATIC ORDER EXECUTION SYSTEM. An American Stock Exchange system in which market and limit orders for active option series (up to 10 contracts at a single price) are instantly executed. *See Also: exchange, limit, market, option, option series, stock, stock exchange*

AUTOMATIC PROXY BIDDER. An online application that automatically submits bids in a Web-based auction. The criteria is established by the bidder.

AUTOMATIC REINVESTMENT. A system that enables investors to buy new shares with income dividends or other money earned from a particular stock. A mutual fund investor can authorize the automatic purchase of additional fund shares, using dividends and capital gains distributions. Even though no distributions are received directly by the investor, taxes must be paid. *See Also: income dividends, market, stock, stock market*

AUTOMATIC TRANSFER SERVICE ACCOUNT. A savings account with funds that can be transferred immediately by computer to cover checks written against a checking account. *See Also: account, savings account*

AUTOMATIC WITHDRAWAL. A system that entitles mutual fund shareholders to receive regular payments, every month or quarter. Shares are liquidated if the payments cannot be realized by dividends, income and/or realized capital gains on the fund's securities. *See Also: dividend, fund, mutual fund*

AUTOMOBILE LOAN SECURITIES. An Asset-Backed Security backed by automobile loans. These automobile loans are securitized via a pass-through or pay-through structure. Depending on the structure, principal and interest payments are directed to holders of the bonds, typically on a monthly basis. *See Also: and interest, basis, interest, principal, security*

AUTONOMOUS INVESTMENT. A new investment created by unrelated interest rate changes or changes in the national income level. *See Also: interest, interest rate, investment, level, national income*

AUTOREGRESSIVE. Using historical data to predict future data.

AVAIL. The balance after discounts and expenses are deducted. *See Also: balance*

AVAILABLE ASSET. An asset that is not mortgaged or pledged that can be readily sold. *See Also: asset*

AVATARS. Computerized graphical representations of people used on the Web. Avatars respond to the commands of the user, representing the user during discussions and other interactions with other avatars. Avatars can be used commercially to represent salespeople or customer service representatives. *See Also: on, service, Web*

AVERAGE. The buying or selling of securities in order to obtain a better overall price. *See Also: order, securities*

AVERAGE ANNUAL TOTAL RETURN. A measurement of performance, commonly used for mutual funds, that annualizes the percentage of change that an investment has achieved over a given time horizon. This performance is based upon dividends, reinvestment of dividends, and capital gains or losses. *See Also: capital, change, investment, on, reinvestment, time*

AVERAGE DOWN. Buying shares at a lower price in order to reduce a stock's average price. *See Also: average, order*

AVERAGE EQUITY. A trading account's average daily balance. It is used to ensure that margin requirements are met. *See Also: average, balance, margin*

AVERAGE LIFE. The average length of time it is expected to take to retire outstanding debt through amortizing payments, or through serial maturity or sinking funds. Also, a bond portfolio's weighted average maturity. *See Also: average, maturity, outstanding, retire, take, time*

AVERAGE UP. Buying additional shares of a stock at a price higher than the original cost in order to lower the stock's average cost basis. The stock is perceived as a good investment, even at higher prices. *See Also: average, basis, cost basis, investment, order, original cost, stock*

AVERAGES. A single value given to a specific set of market information, used to reflect the market's current strengths or weaknesses. The most widely followed is the Dow Jones Industrial Average. *See Also: average, current, Dow Jones Industrial Average, industrial, market*

AVERAGING. *See Also: dollar cost averaging*

AWARD. A borrower accepts a competitive bid for a security by notifying the high bidder. *See Also: competitive bid, security*

AWAY FROM ME. A market-maker's quote meaning that the best bid or offer price is someone else's. *See Also: offer*

AWAY FROM THE BLUE. A dealer offers municipal securities that he or she has not advertised in the Blue List Book. *See Also: blue list book, book, dealer, securities*

AWAY FROM THE MARKET. A limit-order bid is lower, or the offer price is higher than the stock's current market price. *See Also: current, market, market price, offer*

AX TO GRIND. Securities traders solicit business without telling the salespeople whether they want to buy or sell, which gives them an idea of the market's interest before they commit to a deal. *See Also: interest*

B

B2B. Business to Business.

B2B CONSORTIUM. A group or coalition of buyers or sellers that pool their resources online toward a business objective. Collaboration could include, for example, channel procurement through a marketplace. *See Also: channel, coalition, online, pool, procurement*

B2B2C. Business to Business, Business to Consumer

B2C. Business to Consumer.

B2D. Business to Distributor. *See Also: distributor*

B2E. Business to Employee.

BABY BOND. A convertible or straight-debt bond with a face value of less than $1,000. Baby bonds bring the market within reach of small investors, but they also cost more to administrate, distribute, and process, and they are not part of the active market that guarantees liquidity. For this reason, they are almost extinct. *See Also: bond, face value, liquidity, market*

BACK DATING. Putting a date on a check or other document that is earlier than the actual date drawn. Also, an investor who holds mutual funds and has signed a letter of intent to benefit from a declining percentage sales charge for additional purchases. *See Also: actual, check, letter of intent*

BACK DOOR. A nickname for the U.S. Department of Treasury.

BACK DOOR FINANCING. A government agency borrows money from the U.S. Treasury rather than waiting for Congress to appropriate more funds.

BACK DOOR LISTING. One company that has not qualified for listing on the stock exchange buys another company that is listed, thereby enabling it to qualify for listing. *See Also: exchange, listing, stock, stock exchange*

BACK END LOAD. Investment products that do not have initial sales charges sometimes have a redemption fee. Such charges often are lowered over time. For example, five percent in the first year, four percent in the second year, etc. *See Also: redemption, time*

BACK END RIGHTS. Rights that protect a shareholder's financial interests. This tactic is used by management when a corporation is threatened with a takeover. Stockholders are able to exchange rights and shares for cash, preferred stock, or debt securities in case those attempting the takeover get a percentage of the outstanding stock but do not complete the takeover at a value equal to management's offer. *See Also: cash, corporation, exchange, offer, outstanding, outstanding stock, preferred stock, rights, securities, stock, takeover*

BACK OFFICE. The operational department of a bank or brokerage house. The department is not directly involved in selling or trading, but is responsible for accounting, compliance with government regulations, and interbranch communications. *See Also: bank, brokerage house, house*

BACK UP. The reversal of a stock market trend. *See Also: market, market trend, reversal, stock, stock market, trend*

BACK-END SYSTEMS. Programs or processes that handle order processing, inventory control, and receivables management for buyers and sellers and are not directly accessed by a user. Back-end systems are typically accessed through a front-end system, such as a Web page. *See Also: handle, inventory, order, processing, receivables, Web, Web page*

BACKBONE. The Internet's high speed data links that serve as major network connections.

BACKING AWAY. A market maker in a security fails to honor a firm bid for the minimum quantity. Backing away is considered unethical under the National Association of Securities Dealers guidelines. *See Also: fails, firm, firm bid, maker, market, market maker, securities, security*

BACKSPREAD. An investment strategy that involves the purchase of one option and the sale of two others with either higher or lower strike prices. *See Also: investment, investment strategy, option, sale*

BACKUP LINE. A commercial paper issuer would take out this credit line to cover maturity notes in case new notes could not be found to replace them after they reached maturity. The credit line always should have the same value as the outstanding commercial paper. *See Also: commercial paper, credit, maturity, outstanding, paper, take*

BACKUP SYSTEM. A settlement system established by the Options Clearing Corporation to ensure that its members honor their obligations of exercised options contracts. *See Also: corporation*

BACKWARDIZATION. This occurs in commodities and foreign-exchange trading when deliveries made sooner have a higher price than those made later.

BAD DEBT. An account or loan balance that a company is unable to collect, and subsequently writes off. *See Also: account, balance*

BAD DEBT EXPENSE. The amount of money a company spends on accounts it has been unable to collect.

BAD DELIVERY. A securities certificate that is delivered in less than acceptable form as a result of damage or improper signature. *See Also: certificate, securities*

BAD FAITH. An intentionally misleading or deceptive practice.

BAG. The unit of trading used in silver coin investing. One bag holds coins with face values that total: 1,000 silver dollars, 2,000 half dollars, 4,000 quarters, or 10,000 dimes. *See Also: unit*

BAIL OUT. Selling securities arbitrarily while in a panic without first considering the potential loss. The term also applies to a financially strong company coming to the rescue of a weaker company. *See Also: panic, securities, term*

BAIT AND SWITCH. Advertising an item at a low price, but pressuring a potential buyer to purchase a higher-priced substitute. A common practice is to tell the customer the lower-priced item is no longer available, and the more expensive item would be more beneficial to the customer anyway. Such tactics are illegal, and companies using them have been prosecuted. *See Also: low*

BALANCE. Subtraction of debits from credits in a given account. *See Also: account*

BALANCE OF PAYMENTS. Method that all of a nation's international financial transactions are recorded with double-entry bookkeeping. The system precludes surpluses and deficits by maintaining a balance of payments in a current account (which covers imports and exports), a capital account (which covers investment movements), and a gold account (which covers movement in the gold market). Surpluses and deficits show up in the different accounts. *See Also: account, balance, capital, capital account, current, current account, investment, movement*

BALANCE OF TRADE. The difference between the value of a country's imports and exports. It is considered a favorable trade balance when exports exceed imports. *See Also: balance, favorable trade balance*

BALANCE SHEET. Financial accounting of a company's assets, liabilities, equity, and net worth as of a specific date. *See Also: equity, net, net worth, worth*

BALANCE SHEET EQUATION. Derived by adding liabilities to a stockholder's equity, equaling a company's total assets. *See Also: equity, stockholder's equity*

BALANCED BUDGET. When expected revenues equal expected expenses for a specific time period. *See Also: time*

BALANCED MUTUAL FUND. A fund that buys both growth and income securities, through investments in stocks and bonds, in an effort to obtain the attractive returns while reducing risk through diversification. *See Also: fund, risk, securities*

BALANCED TARGET MATURITY FUNDS. A mutual fund that guarantees a targeted investment return at maturity. The guaranteed return is usually achieved through the purchase of zero coupon U.S. Treasury securities, while the remainder is typically invested for long-term growth, such as stocks. *See Also: coupon, fund, investment, maturity, mutual fund, return, securities, U*

BALLOON. The final payment on a loan or mortgage that is much larger than previous payments, sometimes because interest rates increased during the life of the loan. *See Also: interest, mortgage*

BALLOONING. Manipulating stock prices so they increase far beyond the stocks' real values. *See Also: stock*

BANDWIDTH. Usually expressed in bits per second (BPS), bandwidth is the amount of data that can be sent through a particular network connection. Also used loosely to denote any type of capacity. *See Also: bits per second*

BANK. A financial business, chartered by the state or federal government. Banks borrow money at one rate from individuals and organizations that have excess cash. They then lend the money at higher rates to entities that are in need of cash. In recent years, service charges have joined interest rate spreads as a major source of bank revenue. *See Also: cash, interest, interest rate, service*

BANK ACCOMMODATION. A bank loans a customer money on the customer's own note, or on a note someone else owes to the customer. Such loans allow the customer to avoid transaction costs. *See Also: bank, note, transaction*

BANK CHECK. A check a bank draws upon itself. A bank check is considered beneficial, especially in the securities industry, because payment is assured. *See Also: bank, check, industry, securities*

BANK FOR COOPERATIVES. A government-sponsored corporation that loans money to agricultural cooperative associations. The Farm Credit Administration supervises the bank. *See Also: bank, cooperative, corporation, credit, Farm Credit Administration*

BANK GUARANTEE LETTER. A document issued by a bank and approved by the New York Stock Exchange verifying that a customer has sufficient funds to cover the writing of a put option or enough shares to take care of a call option. *See Also: bank, call option, exchange, New York Stock Exchange, option, put, put option, stock, stock exchange, take*

BANK HOLDING COMPANY. A corporation which controls several companies and whose principle business is commercial banking. A corporation may form a holding company to establish subsidiaries not governed by state banking laws. *See Also: corporation, holding company*

BANK INSURANCE FUND (BIF). Formerly the Federal Deposit Insurance Corporation, this fund insures commercial and savings bank deposits up to $100,000. These monies cannot be commingled with the Savings Association Insurance Fund. *See Also: bank, corporation, fund, insurance, savings bank*

BANK LINE. A lending establishment's implied commitment to loan a client up to a specific amount of money during a given time period. This is not a contractual commitment. *See Also: actual, client, time*

BANK QUALITY. Any bond with a top investment grade rating of AAA, AA, A, or BBB, with AAA being the highest quality rating. Bonds with these ratings are suitable for purchase by institutions such as bank trust departments. Also known as investment grade. *See Also: bank, bond, investment, investment grade, quality rating, top, trust*

BANK RUN. Depositors begin to doubt the solvency of their bank, and they start withdrawing their money. Because most of a bank's assets are not kept on hand in cash, such runs can cause serious damage to a financial institution. *See Also: bank, cash, solvency*

BANK SECURITIES. Capital debentures, preferred stock, or common stock issued by a commercial bank. *See Also: bank, commercial bank, common stock, preferred stock, stock*

BANK TERM LOAN. A loan issued instead of a long-term bond in times of high interest rates, which expires no sooner than one year. *See Also: bond, interest*

BANK TRUST DEPARTMENT. An area of a bank responsible for settling estates, administering trusts, acting as trustees for corporate bonds, and administering pension and profit-sharing plans. *See Also: bank, pension*

BANK WIRE. A computer system that transmits information about credit transfers, loan participants, securities transactions, credit histories, and other material that may require a prompt response from one participating bank to another. *See Also: bank, credit, securities*

BANK-ELIGIBLE ISSUES. Commercial banks can buy U.S. Treasury-issued obligations (usually due within 10 years).

BANK-GUARANTEED BOND FUNDS. A major bank stands behind a portfolio of bonds against default because the bank has agreed to buy the portfolio's underlying securities at agreed upon prices with only six days' notice. *See Also: bank, default, portfolio, securities*

BANKED COST. A dealer who previously charged less than regulations permitted can add those undercharges to current margins to make up for the loss of commissions. *See Also: current, dealer, margins*

BANKER'S ACCEPTANCE. Banks issue this short-term financial instrument to finance international trade. A banker's acceptance produces a high rate of return for the investor, with little risk involved. *See Also: acceptance, financial instrument, instrument, issue, rate of return, return, risk*

BANKER'S SHARES. Stocks issued to an investment banker that have features allowing the banker to control the firm. For example, the stocks may have voting features, while other shares do not, giving the banker an advantage over other stockholders. *See Also: firm, investment, investment banker*

BANKING AND SECURITIES INDUSTRY COMMITTEE. An organization responsible for establishing securities guidelines and certificate handling procedures. *See Also: certificate, securities*

BANKING SYNDICATE. A group of banks that have banded together to underwrite and sell specific issues of securities. *See Also: securities*

BANKNOTE. A bank-issued promissory note that can be used as cash. It is payable on demand and is considered legal tender. *See Also: cash, demand, legal, note, promissory note, tender*

BANKRUPTCY. An individual's or organization's inability to pay debts. Whether the insolvent debtor petitions for such action or the debtor's creditors make the petition, the objective is the same: an equitable distribution of assets to eliminate as many of the debts as possible. *See Also: pay*

BANNER ADVERTISEMENT. A common form of advertising on the Web consisting of a graphic image, oftentimes animated, which provide a hyperlink to more information, usually on the advertiser's Web site. *See Also: hyperlink, on, Web , Web site*

BAR CHART. A market chart that illustrates stocks' highs, lows, closing information, and other index and volume changes that occurred during a specific time period. *See Also: chart, highs, index, market, time, volume*

BARBELL STRATEGY. A bond portfolio strategy whereby holdings are primarily concentrated in bonds with short-term and long-term maturities. *See Also: bond, portfolio*

BARGAIN. A security that represents good relative value when the underlying company's assets and earning power are considered. *See Also: earning power, relative value, security*

BARNEY AGREEMENT. A handshake agreement whose name is derived from the theme song from children's television show "Barney," titled "I love you, you love me." *See Also: name*

BAROMETER. A compilation of market information that simulates overall market trends. *See Also: market*

BAROMETER STOCK. A widely followed issue that is used as a yardstick to predict future market conditions. *See Also: issue, market*

BARREL OF OIL. A barrel is the standard measure of crude oil volume in international trading. It is equal to 42 American gallons of oil at 60 degrees Fahrenheit. *See Also: volume*

BARREN MONEY. Any money that does not earn interest or bring the holder any other additional profit. *See Also: interest, profit*

BARRON'S CONFIDENCE INDEX. Comparison between yields on high-grade bonds and low-grade bonds. As this spread drops, the index reflects investors' building confidence in the economy. *See Also: high-grade bonds, index, spread*

BARTER. A sale whereby goods and services are traded without the use of traditional currency. Bartering can take the form of direct bartering, in which goods are directly exchanged for other goods. Bartering can also take the form of exchanging goods and services for barter credits, which can be used at a later time for other goods or services. *See Also: currency, legal*

BASE. A stock pattern that indicates a long-term, tight price range that usually follows a market decline. *See Also: market, price range, range, stock*

BASE PERIOD. A specific period used for measuring economic data. The data is compared to information from previous periods.

BASE-YEAR ANALYSIS. A company's financial statements for several years are compared to a common base year to analyze the company's performance. *See Also: base*

BASEBUILDING. A long-term, lateral price trend which sometimes is considered necessary after a long decline in the stock market before prices can start going up again. *See Also: market, stock, stock market, trend*

BASEMARKET VALUE. The average price of a group of securities over a specific period. *See Also: average, securities*

BASIC BALANCE. The current balance of payments added to the company's expected long-term capital movements. *See Also: balance, balance of payments, capital, current*

BASIC YIELD. The annual rate of return on a no-risk investment. *See Also: investment, rate of return, return*

BASIS. The original cost plus transaction costs and adjustments for splits, in the case of equity. The Internal Revenue Service requires that this figure be used to calculate capital gains and losses. For commodities, it is the difference between the price of the future and the price of the deliverable cash instrument. *See Also: capital, cash, equity, instrument, internal revenue, original cost, plus, service, transaction*

BASIS BOOK. A reference manual published by the Financial Publishing Company of Boston that contains important securities information, such as coupon interest rates and the time remaining until maturity of many bond issues. This book enables investors to calculate the dollar prices and yields of various securities. *See Also: bond, book, coupon, interest, maturity, securities, time*

BASIS GRADE. An exchange establishes quality standards for a commodity before it is considered acceptable for delivery on a futures contract. *See Also: commodity, contract, delivery, exchange, futures, futures contract, standards*

BASIS POINT. One one-hundredth of one percent. For example, an addition of 40 basis points to a yield of 7.50 percent would increase the yield to 7.90 percent. Basis points normally are used when quoting yields on bonds or notes. *See Also: basis, yield*

BASIS PRICE. A price stated in terms of annual rate of return or yield-to-maturity. *See Also: rate of return, return*

BASIS QUOTE. The difference between the cash price and the futures price of a commodity. *See Also: cash, cash price, commodity, futures*

BASIS RISK. The risk that a hedge does not move as expected relative to the change in market price of the hedged security or loan. *See Also: change, hedge, market, market price, risk, security*

BASIS TRADING. Large investors establish underlying stock and index futures positions. If index futures look cheap, these investors buy futures and sell their stock. When stocks look cheap, the opposite takes place. *See Also: cheap, futures, index, index futures, stock*

BASIS VALUE. A security's value as an investment, and a bond's value at maturity. *See Also: investment, maturity*

BASKET TRADING. Buying or selling a group of assets at one time in an effort to duplicate the performance of a specific market index or average, instead of trying to outperform the market. *See Also: average, fund, index, index fund, market, market index, time*

BAUD. The number of bits per second in which a modem transmits. *See Also: bits per second, modem*

BCC. Short for Blind Carbon Copy, BCC is a copy of an e-mail message to an individual, but is not listed in the address field of the message to whom the message is being sent. *See Also: address, e-mail*

BD FORM. A document that contains the names of principals, capital compliance, and financial information about a broker-dealer firm. All broker-dealers are required to file this form with the Securities and Exchange Commission. *See Also: broker-dealer, capital, commission, exchange, firm, principals, securities*

BEAR. A person who expects the stock market to fall or the economy to slow down. *See Also: fall, market, stock, stock market*

BEAR ACCOUNT. A short account in which a person has sold stock or a futures contract with the expectation of buying it back later at a cheaper price if the stock market falls. *See Also: account, contract, futures, futures contract, market, stock, stock market*

BEAR CAMPAIGN. The selling of securities short in an effort to force prices downwards, then buying the securities back at a profit. *See Also: profit, securities*

BEAR CLIQUE. A group that sells a specific stock short in an effort to drive the price down. Forming such a group is illegal. *See Also: drive, stock*

BEAR COVERING. The act of repurchasing borrowed securities that had previously been sold short. *See Also: securities*

BEAR HUG. A takeover offer. Corporate officers are caught in a bear hug when a takeover offer is good enough to entice some shareholders, but not attractive enough to make everybody happy. No matter which way they decide, they will be in trouble with at least some of the stockholders. *See Also: bear, offer, takeover*

BEAR MARKET. A long-term decline in security prices. *See Also: security*

BEAR PANIC. A wave of bearish liquidation may create a selling climate. Afterwards, bargain hunters may enter the market, driving prices up and panicking bears, particularly those who sold short. *See Also: bargain, liquidation, market*

BEAR RAID. A group of investors manipulate the price of a stock by selling large quantities of it short. The sale of so many shares causes the price to drop dramatically. The investors then buy the stock back, pocketing the difference. Such collusion is illegal. *See Also: drop, sale, stock*

BEAR SPREAD. When an investor simultaneously buys one type of option and sells another type on the same security. The spread becomes profitable when the price of the underlying security declines. *See Also: option, security, spread, underlying security*

BEAR SQUEEZE. Institutions sometimes know bears have sold securities short before prices go up, resulting in a bear panic. High bid prices force the bears to cover their shorts and take losses. *See Also: bear, bear panic, panic, securities, shorts, take*

BEAR STRADDLE. The writing of an uncovered call and a covered put are invested in the same underlying stock with identical striking prices and expiration dates. The writer profits if the underlying security does not vary much in price over the life of the straddle. *See Also: expiration, put, security, stock, straddle, uncovered, underlying security*

BEAR TRAP. A stock price that drops, after which many people sell, but then surges back up again. *See Also: back up, stock*

BEARDING. A large order for securities is split into several smaller orders that will be executed by several brokers. Bearding keeps the intentions of the large investor private so he or she will not drive up the price of the securities before the purchase is complete. *See Also: drive, order, securities, split*

BEARER. Any person who holds a negotiable instrument. *See Also: instrument, negotiable, negotiable instrument*

BEARER BOND. A bond issued and payable to anyone with physical possession, as opposed to a bond issued and registered in the owner's name. *See Also: bond, name*

BEARER FORM. A security the issuing company hasn't registered on its books that is payable to whomever holds it. *See Also: security*

BEATING THE GUN. Accepting orders for a new stock before the security's registration becomes effective. The Securities and Exchange Commission prohibits such a practice. *See Also: commission, exchange, registration, securities, stock*

BED AND BREAKFAST TRANSACTION. A British term for selling a security at a profit at the close of the trading day, then buying it back in the morning after the price has dropped. *See Also: at the close, close, profit, security, term, trading day*

BEDBUG LETTER. A letter the Securities and Exchange Commission sends to a company after the company files a preliminary registration statement for permission to sell stocks. The term came about from the Securities and Exchange Commission's desire to get the bugs out of the registration statement before the company can begin to issue securities. *See Also: commission, exchange, issue, registration, registration statement, securities, statement, term*

BELL. A ringing or buzzing that signals the opening and closing of major stock exchanges each day. *See Also: exchanges, stock*

BELLS AND WHISTLES. Special features, such as subscription warrants that a company may add to a security in order to attract potential investors' attention. *See Also: order, security, subscription*

BELLWETHER. A specific stock, such as Xerox or IBM, that serves as a general indicator of the direction of the overall market. *See Also: benchmark, market, stock*

BELLY UP. Describes a company facing bankruptcy. *See Also: bankruptcy*

BELOW PAR. Selling for a price that is less than the security's face value. *See Also: face value*

BELOW THE LINE. Unusual revenue or expenses that don't normally appear on a company's balance sheet that require a separate classification. *See Also: balance, balance sheet*

BELOW THE MARKET. A bid that is lower than the highest bid for a specific security. *See Also: security*

BENCHMARK. Used for comparison purposes, benchmark, or bellwether, indexes offer standards by which investors can measure, monitor, price or evaluate a security. For example, the Treasury market is the benchmark for bonds such as mortgage backed securities, corporate bonds, international bonds, etc. The S&P 500 is a commonly used benchmark for the equity market. *See Also: bellwether, market, securities, standards*

BENEFICIAL INTEREST. Held by someone who owns something of value, such as stock in a company or placement in a trust. *See Also: placement, stock, trust*

BENEFICIAL OWNER. A person who benefits from owning a security, even if the security's title is in the name of a bank or broker. The classic example is stock held in "street name" by a broker for a client. *See Also: bank, broker, client, name, security, stock*

BERNE UNION. An organization represented by members from 26 countries, that works toward the acceptance of "sound principles of export credit and investment insurance." *See Also: acceptance, credit, insurance, investment*

BEST EFFORTS. Used by underwriters in selling an entire new security issue by a certain date. Instead of buying and reselling the issue, the underwriter leaves the risk with the issuer. *See Also: issue, risk, security*

BEST OF BREED. A no-compromise approach to selecting a software application that is considered a complete application suite with a deep functional focus, supporting users' demand for the best possible application functionality. Best of breed applications usually operate in tandem with other complimentary applications. *See Also: demand, supporting*

BEST'S RATING. Service measuring the quality of insurance companies. *See Also: insurance*

BETA. A measure of risk. The higher the beta, the higher the risk. Beta represents the average percentage change in the price of a stock compared to the percentage change of the market index. A beta value of 1.0 means the stock changes at the same rate as the underlying index. A beta of 2 means the stock will likely move—up or down—at twice the rate as the index. *See Also: average, change, index, market, market index, risk, stock*

BETA SOFTWARE. An application that is in a testing phase for reliability and usability suitable for an end-user environment, but not yet ready for a broad release. *See Also: testing*

BEY. Bond Equivalent Yield. *See Also: bond, yield*

BIAS HUB. A business to business marketplace that favors one party in a transaction, either the buyer, the seller, or even a particular participant. *See Also: business to business, participant, transaction*

BID AHEAD. Orders equal in price are processed on a first-come, first-served basis. *See Also: basis*

BID AND ASKED. The highest price an investor will pay for a security (bid), or the lowest price someone will sell a security (asked). *See Also: pay, security*

BID IN COMPETITION. An investor with a block of securities to sell approaches several dealers, then sells the securities to the one dealer with the highest bid. The dealer may inventory the stock in an effort to attract future business from the investor. *See Also: dealer, inventory, securities, stock*

BID PRICE. The highest buy price at which a security is being offered. For open-end mutual funds, this is the net asset value. *See Also: pay, security*

BID WANTED. An investor, through a broker, announces that he or she wants to sell a security and is ready to accept bids. *See Also: broker, security*

BID WILL IMPROVE. A trader will tell a seller, who requests a market picture, that he or she will pay more than the bid represents, but the seller must first offer a counter-proposal. Often the buyer and seller will split the bid-ask spread. *See Also: bid-ask spread, market, offer, pay, picture, split, spread, trader*

BID-ASK SPREAD. The difference between the best buying price and the best selling price for any given security. *See Also: security*

BIDDING UP. The bid price for a security moves higher and higher as demand for the security increases. *See Also: bid price, demand, security*

BIF. Bank Insurance Fund. *See Also: bank, fund, insurance*

BIG BOARD. The nickname for the New York Stock Exchange, the oldest and largest stock exchange in the United States. Historically, the companies listed on the Big Board are bigger and more established than those listed on the American Stock Exchange. *See Also: exchange, New York Stock Exchange, stock, stock exchange*

BIG FIVE. The five largest accounting/consulting firms in the United States. Listed alphabetically, they are: Andersen, Deloitte & Touche, Ernst & Young, KPMG Consulting, and PricewaterhouseCoopers.

BIG MAC. A nickname for New York City's Municipal Assistance Corporation. *See Also: corporation*

BIG UGLIES. A description for unglamorous companies in industries like mining, steel and oil.

BIGGER FOOL THEORY. Investors buy a security because they believe they can sell it at a later date to someone less knowledgeable. *See Also: security*

BILATERAL CLEARING. All payments from countries with a scarce foreign exchange make payments through a central bank instead of through foreign trade banks. This is done in an effort to economize, with the requirement that the countries maintain a balanced mutual trade every year. Examples of countries with scarce foreign exchange include Guyana and Bulgaria, which produce few products with any demand on the foreign market. Each country has its own currency, but no other nations want the currency because there's nothing in Bulgaria or Guyana they want to buy with it. *See Also: bank, central bank, currency, demand, exchange, foreign exchange, market*

BILL DISCOUNTED. Interest is deducted from the face amount at the time of purchase and the face amount is paid at maturity. The classic example is the U.S. Treasury bill. *See Also: face amount, maturity, time, Treasury bill*

BILL OF EXCHANGE. A short-term debt, the collateral for which is either a commodity or another product in the midst of transit. *See Also: collateral, commodity, short-term debt*

BILL OF MATERIALS FUNCTION. The capability of presenting predefined records of items routinely needed by buyers for a specific purpose. This enhances a seller's ability to reduce the planning process and encourage sales.

BILL PRESENTMENT. The collection of a bill or invoice by a customer. Third-party services, or bill presenters, seek to assemble bills and invoices for consumers, thereby competing with financial services companies for facilitating the transaction. *See Also: transaction*

BILL STRIP. The U.S. Treasury Department auctions Treasury bills of different maturities at the same average price. *See Also: average*

BILLING CYCLE. The period, usually monthly, between customer billings.

BINARY. A numeric system consisting of two unique digits, with 2 as its base, and using 0s and 1s for its notation. The binary system is widely used in computing because two voltage levels on an electronic device can be easily represented as two switches. Each digital switch is called a bit. *See Also: base, bit, digital, on*

BINDER. A written document describing a contract's terms and conditions and serving as a temporary contract until the final agreement can be submitted. Binders are most commonly used in the insurance industry. *See Also: contract, industry, insurance*

BIOMETRICS. A validation methodology that relies on personal traits, such as retina scans and finger prints, to control access in instead of, or in conjunction with, password or identification verifications. *See Also: on*

BIT. The smallest unit of measurement for computer data, expressed as a 1 ("on") or 0 ("off"). *See Also: unit*

BITS PER SECOND. BPS is a measure of how fast a device, such as a modem, communicates. Usually expressed in thousands of bits per second (KBPS) or millions of bits per second (MBPS). *See Also: modem*

BITSY. A nickname for Brokers Transaction Services Incorporated. *See Also: transaction*

BLACKHATS. Highly skilled hackers who break into computer systems with malicious intent. A blackhat will break into a system to destroy files or steal data. Once they compromise a system, the more sophisticated blackhats will implement techniques such as trojans and backdoors. Unlike a blackhat, a whitehat will break into a system without malicious intentions and expose the weakness to the site operators. *See Also: home, Internet, up, whitehats*

BLACK BOX. A computerized portfolio selection model that incorporates any number of economic and company variables. Proponents of such models claim that the value lies in the fact that they are completely objective. *See Also: portfolio*

BLACK FRIDAY. A quick, dramatic drop in the market. The first Black Friday was September 24, 1869. A group of investors tried to corner the gold market, which prompted such a panic in the business community that a depression ensued. *See Also: depression, drop, gold market, market, panic*

BLACK KNIGHT. A person or company that makes a takeover offer that would be hostile to the existing management of the target company. *See Also: offer, takeover, target*

BLACK MARKET. Any illegal securities trading. *See Also: securities*

BLACK MARKET BOND. Dealers who are not part of the investment syndicate trade in a bond registered with the Securities and Exchange Commission between the bond's effective date and the date the account members lift the pricing restrictions. Such bonds can seriously damage the investment syndicate's efforts to distribute the bonds itself. *See Also: account, bond, commission, effective date, exchange, investment, lift, securities, syndicate*

BLACK SCHOLES OPTION PRICING MODEL. Fischer Black and Myron Scholes developed a model to estimate the fair market value of option contracts. The model uses, among other data, interest rate levels and the price volatility of the underlying security to gauge the contracts. *See Also: fair market value, interest, interest rate, market, market value, option, security, underlying security, volatility*

BLACK TUESDAY. Tuesday, October 29, 1929, the day the stock market crashed marking the onset of the Great Depression. *See Also: depression, Great Depression, market, marking, stock, stock market*

BLANK CHECK PREFERRED STOCK. When stockholders allow the company's management to issue preferred stock that includes voting rights to approved parties in an effort to avoid hostile bids. *See Also: issue, preferred stock, rights, stock, voting rights*

BLANK ENDORSEMENT. A person or firm signs a financial instrument to make it negotiable without restriction. *See Also: financial instrument, firm, instrument, negotiable*

BLANK STOCK. A company doesn't set the terms of a stock in the articles of incorporation, but establishes them later when the stocks are issued. *See Also: articles of incorporation, stock*

BLANKET CERTIFICATION FORM. Foreign brokers and dealers provide this document when they buy newly issued securities. The document says the foreign broker or dealer understands and will obey the regulations of the National Association of Securities Dealers. *See Also: broker, dealer, NASD, securities*

BLANKET FIDELITY BOND. The brokerage insurance that protects firms from incidents of fraudulent trading, forgery, and loss of securities. Dealers are required to maintain this coverage by the Securities and Exchange Commission's regulations. *See Also: exchange, forgery, insurance, securities*

BLANKET MORTGAGE. A single debt, or mortgage, that covers all of a company's property. *See Also: mortgage, single debt*

BLANKET RECOMMENDATION. Investors are advised by their broker that they should buy or sell specific securities despite their portfolio size or their investment goals. *See Also: broker, investment, portfolio, securities, size*

BLENDED CREDIT. Credit issued with more than one funding source. *See Also: funding*

BLIND AD. An advertisement that does not name the advertiser, such as job listings that do not name prospective employers. Such ads solicit written replies and eliminate phone calls and personal visits. *See Also: job, name*

BLIND BROKERING. One person acts as an intermediary between a borrower and lender; sometimes one of the parties remains anonymous. *See Also: intermediary*

BLIND ENTRY. An incomplete bookkeeping entry with only account credits and debits listed without any further financial information. *See Also: account*

BLIND POOL. Money from several people is collected, put into a fund and invested for their profit. The investors receive periodic reports on their money, but they cannot manage the money themselves. *See Also: fund, profit, put*

BLIND TRUST. A trust fund established to protect a person from any conflict of interest charges. The person's finances are handled by a designated fiduciary. *See Also: conflict of interest, fiduciary, fund, interest, interest charges, trust*

BLOATWARE. Software programs that require excessive amounts of memory, or disk space and RAM, in proportion to the task it performs.

BLOCK AUTOMATION SYSTEM. A communications computer at the New York Stock Exchange used when institutional investors trade large blocks of securities. The computer allows investors to identify buyers and sellers quickly. *See Also: exchange, New York Stock Exchange, securities, stock, stock exchange*

BLOCK HOUSE. A brokerage firm that specializes in trading blocks of stocks. *See Also: firm*

BLOCK OF STOCK. A trading unit of stock consisting of 10,000 shares or more. *See Also: stock, trading unit, unit*

BLOCK ORDER. An order to buy or sell $1 million or more worth of bonds or 10,000 or more shares. *See Also: order, worth*

BLOCK POSITIONER. A dealer who takes a position in the securities market so his or her client can profit from increased market prices. A block positioner, who must be registered with the Securities and Exchange Commission as well as with the New York Stock Exchange, takes the market position while representing a client who wants to sell a block of stock. A block positioner's clients are usually large, well-capitalized firms. *See Also: block of stock, client, commission, dealer, exchange, market, New York Stock Exchange, position, profit, securities, stock, stock exchange*

BLOCKED. A trader is told that his or her blocks cannot be crossed at the trader's price either because the spread is too tight or because another dealer is offering a deal as good or better. *See Also: dealer, offering, or better, spread, trader*

BLOOD BATH. Occurs when the stock market plummets and investors lose tremendous amounts of money-at least on paper. *See Also: market, paper, stock, stock market*

BLOTTER. A written manuscript of broker or dealer activity for any given day including purchases, sales, and other transactions. *See Also: activity, broker, dealer*

BLOW-OFF TOP. A rapid price increase in a security, followed by a rapid drop in price. This is in technical analysis to help determine market trends. *See Also: drop, market, security, technical analysis*

BLOWING OFF. The peaking of stock prices after a lengthy advance and heavy trading or a buying climax. *See Also: buying climax, climax, heavy, stock*

BLOWOUT. Occurs when all shares of a new securities offering are quickly sold, which brings the corporation higher stock prices, but limits the number of shares a buyer may be able to purchase. *See Also: corporation, offering, securities, stock*

BLUE CHIP. Nationally known common stock with a lengthy history of profit, growth, and quality management. IBM and Du Pont are both examples of blue chip stocks. *See Also: common stock, profit, stock*

BLUE LIST BOOK. A financial list published daily that reports which bonds are for sale, their prices, and their yields. The list includes bonds for sale by more than 700 dealers. *See Also: sale*

BLUE SKY LAW. Securities must be registered according to the laws of each particular state before they can be sold in that state. Those stocks which do not follow a particular state's registration laws become restricted. The nickname came from a judge who once said a certain stock had as much value as a patch of blue sky. *See Also: registration, stock*

BLUETOOTH. An industry-supported wireless personal area networking (WPAN) standard, named after the 10th Century Viking king who united Denmark, is a low-cost radio technology. Bluetooth, a low-power, short-range communications standard, is designed to eliminate the need for cabling in a wide range of products, including cellular phones, computers, personal digital assistants (PDA), printers, digital cameras, audio equipment, headphones, and more. *See Also: digital, range, technology*

BO DEREK. Description for a perfect investment or trade. The name comes from the actress who played a "perfect woman" in the 1979 movie "10." *See Also: investment, name*

BOARD BROKER. A Chicago Board Options Exchange member who acts as an agent for other brokers and who performs the duties of a principal when trading for his or her own account. *See Also: account, agent, exchange, principal*

BOARD OF ARBITRATION. A committee of three to five people who decide the outcome of disputes between stock exchange members as well as nonmember brokerage firms. An arbitration board may also be used to work out disagreements between clients and brokers. Those involved in the dispute first must agree to settle their fight with the board. The board's decision is binding. *See Also: arbitration, committee, exchange, settle, stock, stock exchange*

BOARD OF DIRECTORS. A committee elected by the company's stockholders at their annual meeting. The board's duties include appointing corporate officers, issuing shares of stock, and declaring dividends. *See Also: annual meeting, committee, stock*

BOARD OF GOVERNORS OF THE FEDERAL RESERVE SYSTEM. A committee of seven people who set banking regulation policy for the country. The committee members are heads of the regional federal reserve banks. *See Also: committee, reserve*

BOARD ROOM. Brokerage houses have a room where customers can watch the consolidated tape of stock transactions. To some extent, the "tape" has been replaced by individual quotation machines provided for the customer's use. *See Also: consolidated tape, quotation, stock, tape*

BOBTAIL POOL. A group of investors involved in a speculative venture who have a common goal, but who act independently of each other. *See Also: speculative*

BOGEY. Used for comparison purposes, bogey is the benchmark standard by which a money manager or portfolio manager is compared. *See Also: benchmark, manager, portfolio, portfolio manager*

BOILER ROOM. A room jammed with telephones where salespeople call long lists of prospective investors and try to sell them speculative or fraudulent securities. *See Also: securities, speculative*

BOLLINGER BANDS. Bands, or lines, drawn on a chart below and above the moving average. These lines vary in distance from the moving average of a security's price based on the security's volatility. *See Also: average, chart, moving average, volatility*

BOND. A long-term debt security issued by a corporation or government, with a stated interest rate and fixed due dates when interest and principal must be paid. Specific features are written into each bond's indenture, including whether the interest and principal will be paid to the person in whose name the security is registered, or if it will be payable to anyone presenting it, in which case it is considered a bearer bond. *See Also: bearer, bearer bond, corporation, debt security, indenture, interest, interest rate, long-term debt, name, principal, security*

BOND ANTICIPATION NOTE. A government-issued, short-term debt instrument that will be paid off by the proceeds from another bond sale soon to be issued. *See Also: bond, debt instrument, instrument, proceeds, sale, short-term debt*

BOND BUYER'S INDEX. Published in The Bond Buyer, this index contains gauges to judge the yields from municipal bonds and to help predict future trends. *See Also: bond, index, the bond buyer*

BOND DISCOUNT. The negative difference between a bond's market or purchase price and its par value. *See Also: market, par, par value, purchase price*

BOND DIVIDEND. A stockholder who is owed a dividend receives payment in the form of a bond instead of cash or additional shares of stock. *See Also: bond, cash, dividend, stock, stockholder*

BOND EQUIVALENT YIELD (BEY). Yield for mortgage-backed securities that reflects assumed semiannual payments of cash flows, rather than monthly cash flow payments. This conversion allows for an easier comparison of mortgage-backed securities to other securities, such as corporate and government bonds. *See Also: cash, cash flow, conversion, easier, securities*

BOND FUND. A mutual fund that primarily invests in fixed-income instruments. Bond fund investors typically seek income over growth. Bond funds can generate either taxable or tax-free income. *See Also: fund*

BOND HOLDER. Anyone who owns a bond, whether it is in registered or bearer form. *See Also: bearer, bearer form, bond*

BOND HOUSE. A firm that deals in securities, but concentrates its business on bonds. *See Also: firm, securities*

BOND INVESTORS GUARANTY INSURANCE COMPANY. Insures the timely payment of interest and principal to municipal securities investors. Municipalities pay for this coverage but it often results in lower interest costs. *See Also: interest, pay, principal, securities*

BOND POWER. A certificate that accompanies a bond when it is transferred from one owner to another. The certificate appoints an attorney-in-fact, the seller's broker, who will complete the ownership transfer in the corporation's records. *See Also: attorney-in-fact, bond, broker, certificate, transfer*

BOND PREMIUM. The positive difference between a bond's market or purchase price and its par value. *See Also: market, par, par value, purchase price*

BOND QUOTATION. While corporate bonds carry face values in dollar amounts, they are quoted in points based on the dollar amounts. One point represents $10, with minimum variations of one-eighth of a point. U.S. Treasury Bonds are quoted in 32nds of a point. *See Also: carry, point*

BOND RATING. A rank of quality, ranging from AAA to D (default) given to a bond based on its investment value. The rating is based on such things as the issuer's reputation and its record in paying interest. *See Also: bond, interest, investment, investment value*

BOND RATIO. Divide the total number of bonds outstanding by the same number plus the company's equity. This ratio determines a company's level of leverage. A number higher than 33 percent is considered a high measure of leverage, but this guideline varies with each industry. *See Also: equity, industry, level, leverage, outstanding, plus, ratio*

BOND SWAP. Selling one bond issue and buying another at the same time in order to create some advantage for the investor. Some benefits of swapping may include tax-deductible losses, increased yields, and an improved quality portfolio. *See Also: bond, issue, order, portfolio, time*

BOND WASHING. Some British bonds trade ex-interest instead of on an accrued interest basis; so to avoid paying taxes, an investor would sell the bond to a nontaxable holder before the ex-date, after which the investor buys the bond back at its original price plus interest. By doing this, the interest has become a capital consideration instead of being taxable. *See Also: accrued interest, bond, capital, consideration, interest, plus*

BONUS FUTURES. If executives believe their companies' year-end bonuses will be low, they can hedge their bets by selling futures to a colleague. The buyer guarantees the seller a certain percentage of the seller's annual salary, and if the bonus is more than that percentage, the buyer gets the difference. If the bonus is less, the buyer must make up the difference. *See Also: futures, hedge, low*

BOOK. A written record either of anticipated interest for a proposed underwriting, or the activities of underwriting account members. *See Also: account, interest, underwriting*

BOOK CREDIT. Financial commitments that are not backed by any securities, but show up in ledger accounts. *See Also: ledger, securities*

BOOK ENTRY SECURITIES. Stocks held in "street name," that are recorded in a customer's account, but are not accompanied by a certificate. This trend is leading toward a certificateless society. *See Also: account, certificate, name, trend*

BOOK ENTRY TRANSFER. Eliminating the need for physical certificates, this is a computerized method of making a transfer. *See Also: transfer*

BOOK VALUE. Also known as the net asset value, book value is the original cost of an asset minus any depreciation taken for accounting purposes. The book value of a company is the depreciated value of a company's assets, including cash, accounts receivable and inventories, less its liabilities. *See Also: asset, book, depreciation, minus, net, net asset value, original cost*

BOOK VALUE PER SHARE. Subtract all liabilities and the par value of stock from total assets and divide by the number of outstanding shares of common stock. This figure represents the break-up value per share if a company were liquidated. *See Also: break-up value, common stock, outstanding, par, par value, share, stock*

BOOKKEEPING EQUATION. An one-line balance sheet summary, expressed as assets minus liabilities equaling a shareholder's equity. *See Also: balance, balance sheet, equity, minus*

BOOKMARK. A feature that is standard on most Web browsers that allows users to easily save and catalog links to frequently used Web addresses for future visits. *See Also: on, Web*

BOOKSHARES. A procedure of recording stock shares in investment companies. This process eliminates the need for mutual fund share certificates and records fractional share holdings. *See Also: fund, investment, mutual fund, share, stock*

BOOM. A fast and strong upswing in the economy proceeded by an increase in the stock market. *See Also: market, stock, stock market*

BOOMERNOMICS. An investing strategy that relates to the trends of Baby Boomers.

BOOT. Nickname for branch operations and orientation training, which new brokerage firm employees must go through before they can work in the firm's operations departments. *See Also: firm, operations*

BOOTSTRAP ACQUISITION. A friendly corporate takeover. In a bootstrap acquisition, the target company gives some of its assets to dissident stockholders in exchange for their shares. The acquiree then sells 100 percent of the shares to the acquirer. In the process, the new owner gets 100 percent of the company at a lower price because the purchased company, in essence, helped to finance its own takeover. *See Also: acquisition, exchange, takeover, target*

BORROWED RESERVES. A bank borrows money at the Fed funds rate from another member bank to maintain the reserve ratio mandated by the Federal Reserve Bank. *See Also: bank, Federal Reserve Bank, funds rate, member bank, ratio, reserve, reserve bank*

BORROWED STOCK. A broker borrows shares of a security to complete a client's short sale. *See Also: broker, sale, security, short sale*

BORROWING POWER OF SECURITIES. The amount of money an investor can borrow from his or her broker to buy securities based on the value of assets in their account. The brokerage firm lists each customer's borrowing power on his or her monthly statement. *See Also: account, broker, firm, monthly statement, securities, statement*

BORROWING SHORT, LENDING LONG. A bank makes long-term loans using cash it owes to depositors in the short term. Since long-term rates are generally higher than short-term rates, banks earn revenue from the spread. *See Also: bank, cash, short term, spread, term*

BOSTON INTEREST. Interest based on a 30-day month, no matter how many days a particular month has in actuality. For example, interest in February would be the same as in June and in December, even though the actual numbers of days in the three months vary. *See Also: actual, interest*

BOSTON STOCK EXCHANGE. Located at One Boston Place, this regional stock exchange handles securities not only from the New England area, but from the exchange listings in New York City as well. *See Also: City, exchange, regional stock exchange, securities, stock, stock exchange*

BOT. A bot, short for robot, refers to an automated program designed to collect data, such as a shopping bot that searches for particular products at e-retailers across the Web. *See Also: Web*

BOTTOM. The price level at which a security is not expected to drop below before it starts to go up again. *See Also: drop, level, security, to go*

BOTTOM FISHER. An investor who concentrates his or her efforts on looking for securities that have bottomed out, or those expected to bottom out soon, such as the stocks of companies facing bankruptcy. The investor can buy the stocks at a reasonable rate and expect them not to drop any lower before they start increasing in value. *See Also: bankruptcy, bottom, bottom out, drop, securities*

BOTTOM OUT. The point at which a stock price has dropped so far that demand exceeds supply and the price begins to rise again. *See Also: demand, point, stock, supply*

BOTTOM-UP APPROACH TO INVESTING. An investment strategy that initially concentrates on individual stocks with attractive investment potential, then considers industry trends, followed by broader macro trends, such as the state of the economy. *See Also: put*

BOUGHT DEAL. A commitment to buy the entire issue of a security from the issuing company. *See Also: issue, security*

BOUNCE. A temporary and rapid recovery in a security or index after a steep decline. *See Also: index, recovery, security*

BOUTIQUE. A small brokerage firm that specializes in a limited number of securities with a select number of customers. *See Also: firm, securities*

BPS. Bits Per Second.

BRACKET. The manner in which investment bankers in an underwriting are classified in relation to financial responsibility-the higher the bracket, the higher the financial responsibility and the higher the bank's name appears in the "tombstone" ad. *See Also: investment, name, underwriting*

BRACKET CREEP. As a person's income rises because of inflation, he or she inches into a higher tax bracket. The Tax Reform Act of 1986 lowered the number of tax brackets and thus limited the effect of bracket creep. *See Also: bracket, inflation, tax bracket*

BRAND. An organization's distinctive identifier, such as its name, trademark or symbol, used to establish a certain level of trust or quality among its customers or potential users. A brand may apply to a product, services, or the organization itself. *See Also: level, name, symbol, trademark, trust*

BRAND LOYALTY. The tendency of a consumer to repeatedly purchase the same named product or service. *See Also: service, tendency*

BRAND NAME. The name or identifier used by an organization to distinguish itself or its product and/or service from its competitors. *See Also: name, service*

BRASSAGE. A government orders bullion to be minted into coins. *See Also: bullion*

BREADTH OF THE MARKET. The number of stocks involved in a market move compared to the total number listed. If two-thirds of all stocks rose in price on a given day, investors say the breadth was good for an advancing day. *See Also: market*

BREAK. An abrupt, unexpected reversal in market prices. *See Also: market, reversal*

BREAK-UP VALUE. The separate worth of a company's various components as if they all existed independent of the company. This is equal to the company's book value. *See Also: book, book value, worth*

BREAKAWAY GAP. Price movements with highs and lows that do not overlap the previous day's movement and begin a new trend. For example, a positive trend may be forthcoming if today's low price is higher than yesterday's high price. *See Also: highs, low, movement, trend*

BREAKING THE SYNDICATE. Dissolving the investment organization that was formed to underwrite an issue of securities by eliminating the agreement among underwriters. The members then can sell their holdings without restriction. *See Also: agreement among underwriters, investment, issue, securities*

BREAKOUT. The price of a security increases above its previous high point, or falls below its previous low point. In a breakout, the security is expected to continue in the same direction for some time. *See Also: low, point, security, time*

BREAKPOINT. In buying certain mutual funds, increments in the level of dollars invested will allow the commission percentage to be reduced. *See Also: commission, level*

BREAKPOINT SALES. Occurs when a broker sells mutual funds in dollar amounts slightly below that needed to reduce the commission percentage. Such a practice is considered unethical. *See Also: broker, commission*

BRICKS AND MORTAR. A traditional off-line company with a focus on non-Internet channels as the outlet for the majority of its products and services. *See Also: on*

BRIDGE LOAN. A borrower arranges short-term financing while awaiting the approval of a long-term loan.

BRING OUT. One or more underwriters offers a new security issue for sale publicly. *See Also: issue, sale, security*

BROAD MARKET. When securities trading is unusually heavy. *See Also: heavy, securities*

BROAD TAPE. Wire service stock reports that provide a wider range of information than the ticker tape, which merely shows prices and sizes of trades. *See Also: range, service, stock, tape, ticker tape*

BROKEN CONVERTIBLE. A convertible bond with a yield that has risen to the level of yields from similar nonconvertible securities. *See Also: bond, level, securities, yield*

BROKEN LOT. Fewer than 100 shares of a specific stock. This is also referred to as an odd lot. *See Also: lot, odd lot, stock*

BROKEN PERIOD. A foreign exchange arrangement with a future settlement date and without a standard maturity period. *See Also: exchange, foreign exchange, maturity, settlement date*

BROKER. The intermediary between a buyer and a seller of securities. The broker, who usually charges a commission, must be registered with the exchange in which he or she trades. *See Also: commission, exchange, intermediary, securities*

BROKER-DEALER. A firm that not only handles transactions for customers, but also buys securities for its own account and then sells those securities to customers for a profit. *See Also: account, firm, profit, securities*

BROKER LOAN RATE. The interest rate brokers pay when they borrow money to pay for their customers' positions in the securities market. *See Also: interest, interest rate, market, pay, securities*

BROKER'S FREE CREDIT BALANCE. The New York Stock Exchange provides a monthly report of the amount of money each firm has sitting idle in its brokerage account. *See Also: account, brokerage account, exchange, firm, New York Stock Exchange, stock, stock exchange*

BROKER'S MARKET. Describes heavy trading by brokers in their own accounts, but holds little interest by individual investors. *See Also: heavy, interest*

BROKER'S TICKET. A record of a broker's executed buy and sell orders, including all information pertinent to the orders such as names, dates, and prices.

BROKER'S TRANSACTION SERVICES INCORPORATED. Sells trade processing and reporting services to brokers. *See Also: processing*

BROKERAGE ACCOUNT. A broker will keep records of all transactions in which his or her clients ever have been involved. The customer will receive statements disclosing monthly transactions, current positions, and cash balances. *See Also: broker, cash, current*

BROKERAGE HOUSE. A firm that buys and sells securities for customers. *See Also: firm, securities*

BROWSER. A software program that allows users to access Web pages on the World Wide Web. *See Also: on, Web , World Wide Web*

BROWSER PLUG-IN. Software that can extend features and functionality to a Web browser. *See Also: Web, Web browser*

BSP. Business Service Provider. *See Also: service*

BTW. An abbreviation for By The Way that is commonly used in online communications, such as newsgroups and e-mails. *See Also: online*

BUBBLE. A speculative venture that has little chance of making a profit. When this fact becomes evident, the bubble bursts and prices fall. *See Also: fall, profit, speculative*

BUBBLE COMPANY. A company that never planned to do any legitimate business, created to defraud potential investors.

BUCKET SHOP. A brokerage house will confirm a customer's order at a specific price without executing the order on an exchange in hopes of obtaining a better price. The firm would then pocket the difference between the two prices. Such practices are prohibited by the Securities and Exchange Commission. *See Also: brokerage house, commission, exchange, firm, house, order, securities*

BUCKETING. A broker who executes a customer's order in his or her own account rather than on the open market because the broker believes he or she will profit from a balancing transaction later. The Securities and Exchange Commission prohibits bucketing. *See Also: account, broker, commission, exchange, market, open, open market, order, profit, securities, transaction*

BUCKING THE TREND. Doing the opposite of the rest of the market. For example, buying long when the market is going down, or selling short when the market is on an upswing. *See Also: market, selling short*

BUDGET. The amount of money needed to complete a project, or the amount of money needed to operate an organization during a one-year period.

BUG. A logic or syntax error in a computer program's code that makes it falter or fail. Bugs can also be found in the designs of a computer system or hardware. Bugs are more likely to be found among end users during beta programs. *See Also: beta*

BUILDING AND LOAN ASSOCIATION. A firm that saves and lends money and specializes in financing construction projects. Deposits are often represented by shares in the name of the depositor. These institutions are somewhat antiquated, and have largely been replaced by savings and loan associations. *See Also: firm, name*

BULGE. A short, quick price rise in an entire market or an individual stock. *See Also: market, stock*

BULGE BRACKET. The firms in an underwriting syndicate with the largest participation. *See Also: syndicate, underwriting, underwriting syndicate*

BULK SEGREGATION. Securities owned by individuals, but not registered in their names and kept separate from securities owned by the broker-dealer. *See Also: broker-dealer, securities*

BULL. Someone who expects the securities price, or economy in general, to improve. *See Also: securities*

BULL MARKET. A long-term rise in security prices. *See Also: security*

BULL POOL. Investors organize with the purpose of manipulating stock prices upwards. Members are not permitted to make any individual transactions. Bull pools are illegal. *See Also: bull, stock*

BULL SPREAD. A strategy using option contracts that increase in value with the price of the underlying security. An investor buys a call option while simultaneously selling a put option. The option sold will have a higher exercise price than the one purchased. *See Also: call option, exercise, exercise price, option, put, put option, security, underlying security*

BULL STRADDLE WRITING. An uncovered put option and a covered call option are written on the same underlying option. *See Also: call option, option, put, put option, uncovered*

BULLDOG SECURITIES. Foreign securities traded in England with face values and interest payments quoted in pounds sterling. *See Also: and interest, interest, securities*

BULLET. Borrowed money or a borrowed security that must be repaid in one lump sum at the end of its term, instead of having smaller payments that are due regularly. *See Also: security, term*

BULLET BOND. An interest-bearing bond that returns all principal on the date the bond matures. *See Also: bond, principal*

BULLETPROOF. Any contract, agreement, or other document that contains absolutely no loopholes. *See Also: contract*

BULLION. A refined precious metal, such as gold or silver, that has been melted and shaped into bars, rounds, or another form.

BULLION COIN. A coin with a value close to its bullion content, as opposed to a rare coin with a value higher than its gold content because of its rarity, or collector interest. *See Also: bullion, close, interest*

BUNCHING. Putting together many small orders to be executed at the same time, instead of spending time on them individually. *See Also: time*

BUOYANT. Securities that are rising in price.

BURN RATE. The pace, usually expressed in months, at which a new company spends its venture capital to finance overhead before generating positive cash flow from operations. *See Also: capital, cash, cash flow, operations, overhead*

BURNOUT. When an investor begins to take taxable profits from his or her investment after all available tax shelters have been exhausted. *See Also: investment, take*

BUS. An electronic path or channel that serves as an internal connection among functional areas, such as between a processor and memory. The bus can also serve as an external connection between the CPU and external memory and peripheral devices. *See Also: bus, channel, CPU*

BUSINESS CONDUCT COMMITTEE. Determines the facts and enters a judgment in complaints of improper trade practices. Committees are established in all of the 13 districts of the National Association of Securities Dealers, organized under the association's rules and regulations. *See Also: securities*

BUSINESS CYCLE. The time period from the top of a Gross National Product rise to the bottom of a fall and back to the base line. *See Also: base, bottom, fall, gross, time, top*

BUSINESS DAY. Any day the brokerage community and stock exchanges are open for trading. There are several days during the year where banks are closed but stock trading continues. *See Also: exchanges, open, stock*

BUSINESS INTELLIGENCE. Analyzing data, via data mining, data warehousing, and other related technologies, to explore relationships and trends. The objective is to gain insights to improve business processes and decision making. These insights can be vital to enterprise-wide strategic planning initiatives. *See Also: data mining, gain*

BUSINESS SEGMENT REPORTING. A company divides its income, sales, assets, and other data into separate accounting categories according to the subsidiary or division where they originate so management can compare and analyze strengths and weaknesses from the different branches. *See Also: subsidiary*

BUSINESS SERVICE PROVIDER. A BSP is a company that rents business applications, or third-party software applications, to their customers via the Internet. In contrast to ASPs, BSPs may offer back-office solutions, such as payroll and bookkeeping. *See Also: Internet, offer*

BUSINESS SOLVENCY. When a business has more assets than liabilities.

BUSINESS TO BUSINESS. Also referred to as B2B and B to B, business conducted between two companies, rather than between a company and individuals, usually in either a vertical market or a horizontal market. Business to business networks can facilitate any combination of transactions, information sharing, and communications. They can create value by reducing costs associated with searching or by electronically streamlining processes. *See Also: combination, market, vertical market*

BUSINESS TO BUSINESS TO CONSUMER. Also referred to as B2B2C and B to B to C, a combination of business to business and business to consumer models. For example, a company can facilitate a sell to a consumer for another company. This can exist in various online business models, such as affiliate programs and syndicated programs. *See Also: affiliate, affiliate programs, business to consumer, combination, online*

BUSINESS TO CONSUMER. Also referred to as B2C and B to C, business conducted between companies and individual consumers, rather than between companies. Business to consumer Web sites can facilitate any combination of transaction, information sharing and communications. *See Also: combination, sites, transaction, Web*

BUSINESS TO DISTRIBUTOR. Also referred to as B2D and B to D, communications and transactions conducted between businesses and their distributors.

BUSINESS TO EMPLOYEE. Also referred to as B2E and B to E, Business using the Internet to enhance communications to employees, usually via a company intranet. B2E can also refer to businesses selling goods or services to their employees. *See Also: Internet, intranet*

BUSINESS TO GOVERNMENT. Also referred to as B2G and B to G, business conducted between companies and individual consumers, rather than between companies. Business to consumer Web sites can facilitate any combination of transaction, information sharing and communications. *See Also: combination, sites, transaction, Web*

BUST-UP PROXY PROPOSAL. One group of company stockholders asks the other shareholders to approve the company's liquidation or sale in an attempt to get rid of the existing management. *See Also: liquidation, sale*

BUSTED CONVERTIBLE. One stock that could once have been exchanged for another-conversion is no longer appealing because the underlying equity's price has fallen too low. *See Also: low, stock*

BUTTERFLY SPREAD. Selling two calls and buying two calls with several different expiration dates and exercise prices. The investor will profit from premium income if the market value of the underlying security does not move dramatically by the expiration dates. *See Also: exercise, expiration, market, market value, premium, premium income, profit, security, underlying security*

BUY A PUT. An investor pays extra for the right to sell 100 shares of a specific stock at a preset price within a given time frame. If market conditions are such that proceeding with the sale at the preset price would cause the investor to lose money (if the current market price is higher than the original put price), he or she is under no obligation to sell. *See Also: current, frame, market, market price, obligation, put, right, sale, stock, time*

BUY AND HOLD. The accumulation of a security for long-term appreciation and/or income rather than short-term profits. *See Also: accumulation, appreciation, security*

BUY AND WRITE. An investor buys securities then sells or writes covered call options on the same securities so that he or she can profit from the stock dividends and the call option premiums. The investor sacrifices some appreciation potential in return for the premium. *See Also: appreciation, appreciation potential, call option, option, premium, profit, return, securities, stock*

BUY AT BEST. In the purchase of a large block of over-the-counter securities, the dealer-broker is instructed to buy at the best price available. All of the securities, however, need not be purchased at the same price. *See Also: securities*

BUY IN. A selling broker fails to deliver on time, so the buying broker must obtain the securities from someone else. *See Also: broker, fails, securities, time*

BUY MINUS. An order to buy stock at a price lower than the current market value. Normally, an investor will try to make such a deal when the stock's price is dropping. *See Also: current, current market value, market, market value, order, stock*

BUY ON BID. An investor buys a listed stock from an odd-lot trader who is selling at bid price instead of waiting to buy from the odd-lot trader after a round-lot sale. *See Also: bid price, sale, stock, trader*

BUY ON THE OFFER. When an investor buys an odd-lot stock at the lowest asking price, plus the odd-lot differential, so that he or she does not have to wait for a round-lot sale to determine the odd-lot price. *See Also: differential, plus, sale, stock*

BUY ORDER. A client orders his or her broker to buy a specific amount of stock at a particular price. *See Also: broker, client, stock*

BUY SIDE APPLICATIONS. E-commerce procurement applications that provide solutions for the purchase of both core and non-core items. *See Also: procurement*

BUY SIGNAL. A chart indicator that, because of market movements, shows a buyer that it's a good time to purchase stock or other securities. *See Also: chart, market, securities, stock, time*

BUY STOP ORDER. When a client orders his or her broker to buy a security that increases in value after it has hit a certain price, then to buy at the best price available. *See Also: broker, client, hit, security*

BUY THE BOOK. A client orders his or her broker to buy all the shares of a specific security that are available at the offer price. *See Also: broker, client, offer, security*

BUY TICKET. An investment department document that tells the order department to buy a specific security. The ticket states the date, time, size, and price of the security purchased. *See Also: investment, order, order department, security, size, time*

BUY-IN PROCEDURE. If a broker or dealer does not deliver a promised security to a purchaser, the purchaser can notify the agent. Within two days he or she can buy the security on the open market and charge the delinquent agent with any losses incurred. *See Also: agent, broker, dealer, market, open, open market, security*

BUYBACK. A customer purchases the same type of stock he or she just sold short in an effort to satisfy a contract or to cover a short position in the market. In the corporate sense, a company may utilize excess cash to repurchase shares of their own stock. *See Also: cash, contract, market, position, repurchase, short position, stock*

BUYER DRIVEN AUCTIONS. Also known as a reverse auction, buyers indicate what they are interested in purchasing and sellers compete for the lowest price to sell goods or services.

BUYER'S MONOPOLY. A market with one buyer and several sellers. *See Also: market*

BUYERS' MARKET. Supply exceeds demand, so prices are attractive. *See Also: demand*

BUYING BASIS. The difference between a cash commodity's price and a future that was sold to hedge that price. *See Also: cash, hedge*

BUYING CLIMAX. A quick surge in the price of a security or the overall market, which prompts investors to purchase more. In a short time, there is no one they can sell the higher priced stock to. This climax creates a vacuum and a sudden drop in the stock's price. *See Also: climax, drop, market, security, stock, time*

BUYING HEDGE. A long position in the futures market which equals the cash commodity that eventually is needed. *See Also: cash, cash commodity, commodity, futures, futures market, long position, market, position*

BUYING ON A SHOESTRING. Purchasing securities on the minimum margin. *See Also: margin, securities*

BUYING ON BALANCE. When a broker's buy orders exceed the sell orders.

BUYING ON MARGIN. An investor can buy securities by borrowing money from his or her broker. The amount a customer can borrow is dependent upon the securities and cash in his or her account. *See Also: account, broker, cash, securities*

BUYING ON SCALE. A broker is instructed to buy certain securities at specific intervals while the security's price is dropping. By buying on scale, the investor's price per share drops with each consecutive purchase. *See Also: broker, intervals, scale, securities, share*

BUYING OUTRIGHT. Buying a security by paying 100 percent cash; the opposite of buying on margin. *See Also: buying on margin, margin, on margin, security*

BUYING POWER. The amount of money a person has available to spend on securities. This hinges on the level of assets the person has in his or her brokerage account and how much is on margin. *See Also: account, brokerage account, level, margin, on margin, securities*

BUYING RANGE. If market prices are dropping, an advisor determines the point at which he or she believes prices may start to increase again. Based on that information, the advisor recommends when an investor should start buying stock. *See Also: market, point, stock*

BUYING SIGNAL. A series of prices on a stock chart that does not fall into a normal pattern and, therefore, is used to gauge an attractive price level for purchase. *See Also: chart, fall, level, stock*

BUYING THE INTERMARKET SPREAD. An investor hedges his or her position in the market by buying and selling two different securities at the same time. An example of this might be the purchase of a bond and the short sale of a utility stock. *See Also: bond, market, position, sale, securities, short sale, stock, time, utility*

BUYOUT. Buying a percentage of stock large enough for the purchaser to own the biggest share of a corporation. This permits him or her to take control of a company's management and assets. *See Also: corporation, share, stock, take*

BYLAWS. Self-imposed rules by which an organization or company must abide. Bylaws include such regulations as to how directors are to be named and how stock shares are to be transferred. *See Also: stock*

BYPASS TRUST. A contract with which parents transfer their assets to their children while reducing the amount of money the children will have to pay in estate taxes. Once initiated, the terms of the trust cannot be changed, but the parents can receive income from the trust during their lifetimes and, in some cases, use some of the principal. *See Also: contract, estate, pay, principal, transfer, trust*

BYTE. A group of eight bit, enough to represent a character. *See Also: bit*

C

C++. An extension of the C language, C++ is used to develop programs using the Microsoft operating systems platform and other related programs. *See Also: platform*

C-COMMERCE. Short for Collaborative Commerce, an online trading community among multiple enterprises and trading partners that facilitates activities such as transactions and operating efficiencies. *See Also: collaborative commerce, commerce, online*

CABINET BID. A deal that is not made on the exchange floor and that closes an out-of-the-money option contract for one cent. *See Also: contract, exchange, exchange floor, floor, option, option contract*

CABLE. The spot exchange rate between the dollar and pound sterling. *See Also: exchange, exchange rate, pound, spot, spot exchange rate*

CACHE. Temporary storage of a file on a hard disk. This acts as a timesaver since a file, such as a Web page, is already downloaded onto the hard disk rather than requesting the file from the original server. *See Also: on, server, Web, Web page*

CACHING. Storing or buffering Web page data at temporary locations on a network to speed downloading time and reduce traffic on a server. *See Also: on, server, time, Web, Web page*

CALCULATED RISK. The estimated probability that a business venture will succeed, based on any unknowns associated with the investment. *See Also: investment*

CALENDAR. A list of securities that are offered publicly for sale. Separate calendars are issued for new stock issues, corporate bonds, and municipal bonds. *See Also: sale, securities, stock*

CALENDAR SPREADING. Buying and selling options within the same class (all puts or all calls) but with different expiration dates. *See Also: class, expiration*

CALL AWAY. The exercise of an option contract forces the option writer to relinquish the stock. The security is said to be "called away." *See Also: contract, exercise, option, option contract, option writer, security, stock*

CALL CONTRACT. A call option equivalent to 100 shares. *See Also: call option, option*

CALL DATE. A bond issuer specifies a date that the bond can be redeemed before maturity. *See Also: bond, maturity*

CALL FEATURE. A clause in a senior security that permits the issuing company to buy the security back at a predetermined price, as long as the purchase is made before the security matures. *See Also: security*

CALL LOAN. A loan with the provision that the lender can demand payment in full at any time. Also, a broker deposits collateral with a bank and is loaned money. The broker then loans the money to customers to finance margin activities. *See Also: bank, broker, collateral, demand, full, margin, time*

CALL LOAN RATE. The rate banks charge brokers on call loans; this rate forms the basis for minimum margin interest charges. *See Also: basis, interest, interest charges, margin*

CALL MONEY. Money that banks have lent to brokers that must be paid upon demand. *See Also: demand*

CALL MONEY MARKET. Used by brokers and dealers with call funds secured by stock exchange collateral and government securities to cover a customer's margin accounts as well as the broker's and dealer's own securities inventory. *See Also: collateral, exchange, inventory, margin, securities, stock, stock exchange*

CALL OPTION. The right to purchase 100 shares of a specific stock at a specific price within a given time, in exchange for a premium. The buyer will profit if the stock's market value rises above the sum of the striking price and the amount paid for the call at the time of expiration. Options are traded on several exchanges. The premium can provide extra income for the seller (writer) of the option. *See Also: exchange, exchanges, expiration, market, market value, option, premium, profit, right, stock, striking price, time*

CALL OPTION BUY-SELL RATIO. Divide call option buying by call option selling. If the ratio is higher during a drop in the market, the ratio is considered bearish. If the ratio is lower when the market is moving up, the ratio is considered bullish. This evaluation is based upon the opinion that option buyers are not successful in the long run. *See Also: call option, drop, evaluation, market, option, ratio, run*

CALL PRICE. The price at which a corporation or other obligor is permitted to redeem a bond or preferred stock which contains a call provision or call feature. *See Also: bond, call feature, call provision, corporation, preferred stock, redeem, stock*

CALL PRIVILEGE. A bond issuer can repay the bond at any time before its maturity. Differs from a call feature, which has more limitations. *See Also: bond, call feature, maturity, time*

CALL PROTECTION BONDS. Prevents the issuing corporation from redeeming the bond for a certain number of years. Investors who bought bonds with high yields are protected in case interest rates drop, after which the corporation probably would want to refinance the bond. If the bond is redeemed, investors usually receive a premium over the face value of the bond. *See Also: bond, corporation, drop, face value, interest, premium*

CALL PROVISION. Defines the circumstances under which the issuer can redeem a bond before its maturity. *See Also: bond, call feature, maturity, redeem*

CALL PURCHASE. A person selling commodities holds some pricing options that can be exercised later, as long as the pricing options fall within a specific range of the existing price. The purchase hedges against a swift price rise. *See Also: fall, range, SWIFT*

CALL RISK. The bondholder's risk that the bond may be redeemed, or called, prior to maturity. Bond issuers will call bonds after interest rates drop, in order to refinance the bond at lower rates, leaving the investor with a lower interest-rate environment with which to invest. *See Also: bond, drop, interest, maturity, order, risk*

CALL SALE. An investor agrees to sell a security with the buyer setting the price at a later date. A call sale is the opposite of a call purchase. *See Also: call purchase, sale, security*

CALL SPREAD. A position formed when an investor buys one call and sells one call on the same security, the options having different expiration dates and different exercises. The investor believes that the underlying security will make a quick, but limited move. The proceeds from the sale help to offset the cost of the purchase, but upside potential is limited. *See Also: expiration, offset, position, proceeds, sale, security, underlying security, upside, upside potential*

CALLABLE BOND. A bond in which the issuer has the right to redeem prior to maturity by paying a preset price. *See Also: bond, maturity, redeem, right*

CALLABLE CAPITAL. Capital investors have made commitments to contribute to a company. Under prescribed conditions, corporate directors can demand that this capital be paid. *See Also: capital, demand*

CALLABLE PREFERRED STOCK. Any preferred stock a corporation can redeem for payment at a preset price. *See Also: corporation, preferred stock, redeem, stock*

CALLABLE SWAP AGREEMENT. A provision that allows the investor of the fixed-rate leg of the swap transaction to terminate the swap between the call date and maturity with no penalty. *See Also: call date, leg, maturity, swap, transaction*

CAMBISM. Selling foreign currencies.

CAMBISTRY. The study of foreign currencies.

CANADIAN INSTITUTE OF CHARTERED ACCOUNTANTS. An organization of Canadian public accountants that reports changes in corporate accounting practices ordered by the Canadian government. To be admitted into the organization, an accountant must be a college graduate and must pass a battery of tests. *See Also: pass*

CAP. The highest interest rate a securities issuer will pay on a bond issue, or the highest price at which a securities underwriter will sell a new stock. Also, an upper limit to the interest rate payable on a variable rate bond or mortgage. *See Also: bond, interest, interest rate, issue, limit, mortgage, pay, securities, stock*

CAP ORDER. A large buy or sell order giving the exchange specialist permission to use his or her own discretion in executing the deal. While this practice is formally prohibited by the exchanges, it still is used in some instances for expediency. *See Also: exchange, exchanges, order, sell order, specialist*

CAPITAL. A company's net assets, including all retained earnings. *See Also: earnings, net, net assets, retained earnings*

CAPITAL ACCOUNT. A business owner's account that indicates his or her equity. *See Also: account, equity*

CAPITAL APPRECIATION. The increase in an asset's market value, measured from the time of purchase to the time of sale. *See Also: market, market value, sale, time*

CAPITAL APPRECIATION AND PROTECTION INSURANCE. A variable life insurance policy that allows the owner to change investment premiums between investments, including mutual funds or zero-coupon bonds. Profits from the investments remain in a tax shelter as long as they are not distributed. *See Also: change, insurance, investment, life insurance, variable life insurance*

CAPITAL APPRECIATION BOND. See Zero Coupon Bond. *See Also: bond, municipal bond*

CAPITAL APPRECIATION FUNDS. Mutual funds that invest primarily in growth oriented common stocks. Fund managers, in order to enhance the capital appreciation of the fund, may employ aggressive investment techniques, such as leverage and high portfolio turnover. *See Also: appreciation, capital, capital appreciation, fund, investment, leverage, order, portfolio, turnover*

CAPITAL ASSET. All fixed assets, such as property, buildings and equipment, that are used in the normal course of doing business.

CAPITAL ASSET PRICING MODEL. The relationship between a company's expected risk and anticipated return. According to the model, an asset's or stock's return equals risk-free return plus risk premium. The higher the risk, the higher the premium. *See Also: plus, premium, return, risk, risk premium*

CAPITAL BUDGET. A program used to finance long-term projects, such as advertising, plant expansion, and research and development. *See Also: plant, research and development*

CAPITAL CHARGES. Capital needed to satisfy interest and to amortize money invested in a company. *See Also: interest*

CAPITAL CONSUMPTION. A company's investments earmarked for production.

CAPITAL CONSUMPTION ALLOWANCE. The amount of depreciation that economists subtract from the gross national product-usually about 11 percent. After depreciation is subtracted, the new figure is called the net national product. Economists, however, continue to quote the GNP because NNP figures are not always available or reliable. *See Also: depreciation, GNP, gross, net, NNP*

CAPITAL EXPENDITURE. The amount of money a company spends to buy capital assets or to upgrade their existing capital assets. *See Also: capital, upgrade*

CAPITAL FLIGHT. An investor moves large sums of money from one nation to another in an effort to seek a safe haven. For example, in order to preserve capital, an investor will move money out of countries suffering from political or economic turmoil. *See Also: capital, order*

CAPITAL FORMATION. A company weighs the cost of expanding its capital base through equity or debt offerings, short-term loans, or internal financing. *See Also: base, capital, equity, internal financing*

CAPITAL GAIN. In capital assets, the difference between the sale price and the cost less depreciation. In financial assets, the difference between the sale price and the purchase price adjusted for splits and transaction costs. *See Also: capital, depreciation, purchase price, sale, transaction*

CAPITAL GAINS DISTRIBUTION. Paying investment company stockholders out of long-term capital gains that came from selling portfolio securities. Investment companies are not taxed on such gains if they are passed on to shareholders. *See Also: capital, investment, investment company, long-term capital gains, portfolio, securities*

CAPITAL GAINS TAX. Tax on an asset that has been held for a certain period (usually six months or one year) and then sold for a profit. When the capital gains receive favorable tax treatment, it is advantageous to hold the asset for at least the minimum period. *See Also: asset, capital, hold, profit*

CAPITAL GOODS. Assets, such as production lines for manufacturing or heavy equipment used by a construction company, that are used to support business operations. Capital goods are typically high cost, infrequent purchases that eventually minimize total long-term costs. *See Also: capital*

CAPITAL GROWTH. An investment objective that seeks growth, or appreciation, in value. *See Also: appreciation, investment, investment objective*

CAPITAL INTENSIVE. The cost of capital assets exceeds the cost of labor in the manufacturing of a product. *See Also: capital, cost of capital*

CAPITAL ISSUES. Permanent and fixed securities, such as common and preferred stock. *See Also: preferred stock, securities, stock*

CAPITAL LEASE. A lease in which the lessee gets all of the economic benefits, as well as the risks, of the property. A company is required to show such a lease on its balance sheet as an asset and a liability. *See Also: asset, balance, balance sheet, lessee, liability*

CAPITAL MARKETS. A market in which capital funds, such as equity and debt, are traded. *See Also: capital, equity, market*

CAPITAL REQUIREMENTS. The amount of money needed to finance business operations for the foreseeable future. *See Also: operations*

CAPITAL RISK. The possibility that a person may not be able to recover all of his or her original investment when the investment is liquidated. This is in direct contrast to insured investments, such as certificates of deposit, wherein principal is guaranteed. *See Also: investment, principal*

CAPITAL STOCK. The source of a corporation's equity capital, indicating stocks that represent ownership. Capital stock usually refers to common, not preferred stock. *See Also: capital, equity, equity capital, preferred stock, stock*

CAPITAL STRUCTURE. The structure or condition of a company's long-term debts, preferred stock, and net worth, used as a basis for comparing a company's debt-to-equity ratio. *See Also: basis, debt-to-equity ratio, net, net worth, preferred stock, ratio, stock, worth*

CAPITAL SURPLUS. The amount by which a security's balance sheet value exceeds its par value. *See Also: balance, balance sheet, par, par value*

CAPITAL TURNOVER. A company's annual sales divided by the average shareholder's net worth. This figure indicates whether the company can continue to grow and expand without further investments. *See Also: average, net, net worth, worth*

CAPITALISM. An economic system based on the theory that profit provides motivation to achieve. In a capitalistic society, property is privately owned and profits from a company remain with that company's owners, instead of reverting to the government for control and distribution. *See Also: profit*

CAPITALIZATION. Permanent funds, such as stocks and bonds, used to finance a business venture.

CAPITALIZATION RATE. An interest rate economists use to convert a group of future payments into one present value. An internal discount rate. *See Also: discount, discount rate, interest, interest rate, present value*

CAPITALIZATION RATIOS. The percentage of bonds and other long-term debts, preferred and common stock, retained income, capital surplus, and capital stock premiums, that are capitalized. *See Also: capital, capital stock, capital surplus, common stock, stock*

CAPITALIZE. To categorize a specific cost as a long-term investment instead of charging it to current operations. *See Also: current, investment, long-term investment, operations*

CAPITULATION. A reference to a sharp decline in a security or an index, marked by extremely high volume. Capitulation is viewed by some as panic selling. *See Also: index, panic, security, volume*

CAPPING. A person or group of people try to keep an underlying security's market price below the exercise price of a particular stock option contract because of a personal interest in the security. This practice normally takes place near an expiration date. Depending on how capping is done, the practice often is illegal. *See Also: contract, exercise, exercise price, expiration, expiration date, interest, market, market price, option, option contract, security, stock, stock option*

CAPTIVE. A company owns production capabilities which the company uses solely instead of selling them publicly. For example, a television manufacturer may own a lumber mill so it can use the mill's products to build cabinets for its products. *See Also: mill*

CAPTIVE FINANCE FIRM. A subsidiary formed to finance customer purchases from the subsidiary's parent corporation. For example, an automobile manufacturer may establish an acceptance corporation which makes car loans to people who want to buy cars from the main company. *See Also: acceptance, corporation, parent corporation, subsidiary*

CARAT. A unit of measure of the weight of precious gems, equal to 200 milligrams. *See Also: unit*

CARRY. The act of holding stocks for a customer.

CARRY INCOME OR LOSS. The difference between interest income and the financing cost of an investment portfolio purchased on margin. *See Also: interest, investment, investment portfolio, margin, on margin, portfolio*

CARRYING BROKER. A broker or dealer who holds a customer's investment account. *See Also: account, broker, dealer, investment*

CARRYING CHARGE. The interest incurred for financing a securities position calculated by subtracting the cost of funds borrowed to finance those securities, from the interest earned on the securities held. For commodities, the charge includes carrying the actual commodity, interest, storage, and insurance costs. *See Also: actual, commodity, cost of funds, insurance, interest, position, securities*

CARRYING MARKET. When distant positions hold a premium over nearby positions, with the premium high enough to pay for carrying charges. *See Also: hold, pay, premium*

CARRYING VALUE. A fixed asset's value after deducting its accumulated depreciation reserve from the original depreciable cost. *See Also: depreciation, reserve*

CARRYOVER. United States tax laws allow an individual who had a net capital loss of more than the maximum annual deduction of $3,000 to carry over the remainder to ensuing tax years until the amount is offset against either capital gains or income. *See Also: capital, carry, deduction, net, net capital, offset*

CARTEL. A group organized to manipulate prices by regulating the production and marketing of a specific product, such as silver. The organization of petroleum exporting countries (OPEC) is the world's most famous cartel. Cartels are illegal in the United States. *See Also: Organization of Petroleum Exporting Countries, OPEC*

CARTER BONDS. A medium-term debt instrument denominated in a foreign currency that the United States issued during President Carter's administration in an effort to solve foreign currency imbalances. *See Also: currency, debt instrument, foreign currency, instrument, president*

CARVE-OUT. The partial spin-off of a parent company's business. This usually involves selling a stake, typically 20% or less, in an IPO or rights offering. *See Also: IPO, offering, rights, rights offering*

CASH. Any negotiable currency in spendable form. *See Also: currency, negotiable*

CASH ACCOUNT. A brokerage firm account in which all transactions are completed in cash. *See Also: account, cash, firm*

CASH BASIS. Money is credited to a person's account only as it is received. An alternative is a method in which money is credited to an account when it is accrued. *See Also: account*

CASH BASIS ACCOUNTING. An accounting technique in which the basis for recording transactions is the receipt and payment of cash. It is the date on which cash changes hands, not the date on which goods and services are rendered. *See Also: basis, cash*

CASH BOARD. The part of a commodity exchange's chalkboard designated for the listing of cash commodity contract sales. *See Also: cash, cash commodity, commodity, contract, listing*

CASH BUDGET. The amount of cash a company expects to receive and disburse over a given period of not more than one year. *See Also: cash*

CASH BUYING. Buying securities and commodities that are to be delivered immediately. *See Also: securities*

CASH COMMODITY. The reciprocal of a futures commodity accepted on delivery after a transaction contract is completed at a future date. *See Also: commodity, contract, delivery, futures, transaction*

CASH CONVERSION CYCLE. The time between when cash for raw materials is paid and when finished goods are sold. The shorter the cycle, the more money a company can generate, and the less money it has to borrow. *See Also: cash, cycle, time*

CASH COW. A business that generates a high level of cash flow. *See Also: cash, cash flow, level*

CASH DELIVERY. Securities are traded and delivered in the same day.

CASH DIVIDEND. A cash distribution from earnings or accumulated profits to company stockholders. *See Also: cash, earnings*

CASH EARNINGS. The amount of cash taken in, minus cash paid out, excluding noncash expenses. *See Also: cash, minus, noncash*

CASH EQUIVALENTS. Investments with a high level of liquidity. *See Also: level, liquidity*

CASH FLOW. A company adds the annual depreciation charge for fixed assets to its earnings after interest, taxes, and preferred dividends. *See Also: depreciation, earnings, interest*

CASH FLOW BOND. A fully amortizing debt instrument with a fixed coupon rate and a fixed payment schedule, having an average life equal to or less than its securing collateral. *See Also: average, average life, collateral, coupon, coupon rate, debt instrument, instrument*

CASH FORWARD SALE. A commodity is sold with the actual delivery taking place at a later date. *See Also: actual, commodity, delivery*

CASH ITEMS. A company's bank deposits, government bonds, among other items that are listed on its financial statement as cash equivalents. *See Also: bank, cash, cash equivalents, statement*

CASH MANAGEMENT ACCOUNT. A joint venture of banks and brokerage houses whereby wealthy clients can use a credit card to draw from their investment balances. *See Also: credit, investment, joint venture*

CASH MANAGEMENT BILL. A short-term money market instrument the U.S. Treasury issues to pay for its short-term financial obligations. *See Also: instrument, market, money market, money market instrument, pay*

CASH MARKET. The ownership of a security or commodity is transferred and payment is made in cash when the security or commodity is delivered. *See Also: cash, commodity, security*

CASH POSITION. The percentage of a company's total net assets that is available in cash. *See Also: cash, net, net assets*

CASH PRICE. The amount it would cost to buy a quantity of a commodity to be delivered immediately. *See Also: commodity*

CASH RATIO. Comparing a company's cash and marketable securities to its current liabilities. The ratio is a gauge of the company's liquidity. *See Also: cash, current, current liabilities, liquidity, marketable securities, ratio, securities*

CASH RESERVES. Investment funds being held in short-term assets while awaiting more permanent investment opportunities. *See Also: investment*

CASH SUBSTITUTE. A liquid investment with a dollar value that remains relatively constant. The investment is held in place of cash. *See Also: cash, investment, liquid*

CASH SURRENDER VALUE. The amount an insurer will return upon cancellation of the policy to a policyholder. The cash surrender value of life insurance (CSVLI) can be used as collateral against loans. *See Also: cash, collateral, insurance, life insurance, return*

CASH TRADE. A security transaction in which settlement with payment and delivery on the security occur on the same day as the trade date. *See Also: delivery, security, trade date, transaction*

CASH VALUE LIFE INSURANCE. A type of life insurance in which part of the premium is used to provide death benefits and the remainder to earn interest, this being a protection plan and a savings plan. *See Also: insurance, interest, life insurance, premium*

CASH WITH FISCAL AGENT. The amount of money a person has deposited with a commercial bank or other fiscal agent that will be used to pay for matured bonds and interest. *See Also: agent, and interest, bank, commercial bank, fiscal agent, interest, matured, pay*

CASHBOOK. An accounting record with both cash receipts and cash disbursements. The cashbook's balance should correspond with the cash balance on the general ledger. *See Also: balance, cash, general ledger, ledger*

CASINO SOCIETY. Investors who put their money into undervalued corporate assets, volatile futures contracts, or other speculative ventures in an effort to make fast money. *See Also: futures, put, speculative, undervalued, volatile*

CASUALTY INSURANCE. Insurance that protects a business or homeowner against loss, damage, and related liability. *See Also: liability*

CATALOG AGGREGATORS. Businesses that collect and provide simple sorting and organization of catalogs from multiple vendors. This enables an easy comparison of products and services.

CATALYST. An event that precipitates the movement on a security or index. *See Also: index, movement, on, security*

CATCHER. A trading ring employee who is responsible for recording transactions. *See Also: ring, trading ring*

CATS. Certificate of Accrual on Treasury Securities. *See Also: certificate, securities*

CATS AND DOGS. Speculative stocks with brief histories of sales, earnings, and dividend payment. *See Also: dividend, earnings*

CAVEAT EMPTOR. "Let the buyer beware."

CAVEAT VENDITOR. "Let the seller beware."

CBE. Corporate Bond Equivalent. *See Also: bond, corporate bond*

CBOE. Chicago Board Options Exchange. *See Also: exchange*

CBOT. Chicago Board of Trade.

CC. Short for carbon copy, CC is a copy of an e-mail message to an individual, and is listed in the address field of the message to whom the message is being sent. *See Also: address, e-mail*

CD. Certificate of Deposit. *See Also: certificate*

CD-ROM. Short for Compact Disk Read-Only Memory, a computer storage medium for digital data. *See Also: digital*

CDMA. Code Division Multiple Access is a wireless telephone transmission technology that spreads digitized data across the entire bandwidth in which it has access. Each transmission is assigned a unique sequence code, with multiple calls overlaid over each other. *See Also: technology*

CDPD. Cellular Digital Packet Data is an open specification that supports the Internet's protocol to enable wireless access to the Internet and other public packet-switched networks. *See Also: digital, Internet, open, packet, protocol*

CDSC. Contingent Deferred Sales Charge

CEASE AND DESIST ORDER. Used by the Securities and Exchange Commission to stop people it believes are violating federal trading laws. *See Also: commission, exchange, securities, stop*

CEDEL. A Luxembourg firm that banks and broker-dealers use as a clearing house for Eurobond transactions. *See Also: clearing house, Eurobond, firm, house*

CEILING PRICES. Maximum prices under a system of price controls.

CELLER-KEFAUVER ANTIMERGER ACT. A law that restricts anticompetitive mergers resulting from the acquisition of assets. *See Also: acquisition*

CENTRAL ASSETS ACCOUNT. An account that provides both banking and investment services for the person whose account is carried. *See Also: account, investment*

CENTRAL BANK. A bank established for the government and through which the government issues currency, administers monetary policy (including open market operations), holds deposits representing the reserves of other banks, and engages in transactions to facilitate the conduct of business and protect the public interest. The central bank in the U.S. is a function of the Federal Reserve System. *See Also: bank, currency, Federal Reserve System, interest, market, monetary policy, open, open market, reserve*

CENTRAL CERTIFICATE SERVICE. A service that delivers securities to each other through a bookkeeping computer in order to reduce the physical movement of stock certificates. *See Also: movement, order, securities, service, stock*

CENTRAL PROCESSING UNIT. A CPU is a complex silicon chip that is referred to as the brains of the computer, the CPU processes, or executes, requests from applications. Used more loosely, the CPU can refer to the entire computer.

CENTRAL REGISTRATION DEPOSITORY. A computer system for filing the registrations of representatives, broker-dealer principals, and agents. *See Also: agents, broker-dealer, principals*

CERTIFICATE. A document verifying security ownership. A certificate includes such information as the issuer's name and the terms under which the security was issued. *See Also: name, security*

CERTIFICATE FOR AUTOMOBILE RECEIVABLES. A short-term debt security backed by automobile loans. It originates when lenders package the loans and sell to the public, providing the lenders with more funds for use in additional lending. Cars are relatively safe investments, and the interest rates are usually higher than the interest rates of U.S. Treasury securities. *See Also: debt security, interest, securities, security, short-term debt*

CERTIFICATE OF ACCOUNTS. A certified public accountant's written evaluation of a company's financial records after he or she has audited the accounts. *See Also: evaluation*

CERTIFICATE OF ACCRUAL ON TREASURY SECURITIES (CATS). A U.S. Treasury bond that is sold at a deep discount from its face value. Although it pays no interest, it is redeemable for full face value when it matures. *See Also: bond, discount, face value, full, interest, Treasury bond*

CERTIFICATE OF BENEFICIAL INTEREST. Designates non-voting securities with underlying assets of one corporation as debt securities of another corporation. *See Also: corporation, securities*

CERTIFICATE OF CLAIM. A contingent promise of the Federal Housing Administration to reimburse an insured mortgagee for certain costs incurred during a foreclosure of an insured mortgage. The proceeds from the sale of the property however, must be sufficient to cover those expenses. *See Also: foreclosure, mortgage, proceeds, sale*

CERTIFICATE OF DEBT. A document that shows a borrower still owes a balance on a loan or other debt obligation. *See Also: balance, obligation*

CERTIFICATE OF DEPOSIT (CD). A debt instrument issued by a bank that will pay interest periodically or at maturity (set by competitive forces in the marketplace), and principal when it reaches maturity. Maturities range from a few weeks to several years. *See Also: bank, debt instrument, instrument, interest, maturity, pay, principal, range*

CERTIFICATE OF DEPOSIT ROLLOVER. A person who buys a certificate of deposit on margin can deduct interest on the loan while moving income from the certificate to the next year to defer taxes. *See Also: certificate, interest, margin, on margin*

CERTIFICATE OF INCORPORATION. The charter granted to a corporation's petitioners with which the corporation can legally transact business in the state issuing the certificate. *See Also: certificate, charter, corporation*

CERTIFICATE OF INDEBTEDNESS (CI). A defunct debt security issued by the U.S. Treasury that had a fixed coupon rate and matured within 90 days to a year. The Treasury replaced CIs with Treasury bills that mature in 180 days to a year. *See Also: coupon, coupon rate, debt security, matured, security*

CERTIFICATE OF PARTICIPATION. Investment companies issue such certificates in place of shares of a security to indicate how much interest a customer holds in a particular company. *See Also: interest, issue, security*

CERTIFICATE OF TITLE. A title company provides a person selling property with verification that the seller does own the property.

CERTIFICATED SECURITIES. The number of shares of a particular commodity that are certified and ready to be delivered on a futures contract. *See Also: commodity, contract, futures, futures contract*

CERTIFICATELESS MUNICIPAL. One certificate is issued for an entire series of municipal bonds instead of each bond having its own certificate of ownership. *See Also: bond, certificate*

CERTIFICATELESS TRADING. Trading securities that do not have certificates of ownership issued to the holder. The holder can prove ownership by requesting a nonnegotiable certificate issued in the name of the broker who originally executed the transaction. *See Also: broker, certificate, name, nonnegotiable, securities, transaction*

CERTIFIED CHECK. A personal check that the issuing bank pledges to make good upon presentation. A certified check is not the same as a bank check, which the bank draws on itself. *See Also: bank, bank check, check*

CERTIFIED FINANCIAL PLANNER (CFP). A person who has passed examinations for a certification in coordinating a customer's banking, estate, insurance, investment, and tax affairs. Some planners only charge fees, while others may collect a smaller fee along with a commission on products sold. *See Also: commission, estate, insurance, investment*

CERTIFIED PUBLIC ACCOUNTANT (CPA). An accountant who has passed exams and achieved a designated amount of experience. A CPA is licensed by his or her state of residence and can prepare corporate and personal tax returns, as well as usual accounting and auditing work.

CFP. Certified Financial Planner.

CFTC. Commodities Futures Trading Commission. *See Also: commission, futures*

CGI. Common Gateway Interface is an application that enables a user to request information to a Web server to another application program, and to receive back the requested data. *See Also: gateway, server, Web*

CHAIRMAN OF THE BOARD. The member of a company's board of directors who presides over board meetings. The chairman is the highest-ranking officer in a corporation. *See Also: board of directors, corporation, officer*

CHAMBER OF COMMERCE. A group of business executives that promotes the activities and interests of its members, often by promoting the group's home city. It tries to draw new businesses to town or to attract tourism-both of which ultimately increase the city's tax base. *See Also: base, City, home, tax base*

CHANCELLOR OF THE EXCHEQUER. The United Kingdom's version of the United States Secretary of the Treasury. The chancellor is responsible for his or her government's receipts and payments.

CHANGE. The difference in price between the current price and the previous day's closing price. *See Also: closing price, current*

CHANGES IN STOCKHOLDERS' EQUITY. A section in a company's annual report that shows the stockholders' equity, which is the difference between their assets and their liabilities. *See Also: annual report, equity*

CHANNEL. A middleperson between the creator of a product and the buyers. A retail store or a salesperson is an example of a channel. Also, a reference to a special interest area on a Web site, such as a chat room or Internet relay chat (IRC). *See Also: chat, chat room, interest, Internet, Internet Relay Chat, on, Web, Web site*

CHANNEL CONFLICT. The bypassing, or disintermediation, of a distribution channel, in which a manufacturer, wholesaler, or producer will sell directly to consumers. *See Also: disintermediation, producer, wholesaler, will*

CHANNEL ENABLERS. Rather than creating a new channel, channel enablers use existing distribution channels, maintaining existing relationships.

CHARITABLE LEAD TRUST. Assets are contributed to a trust, with the trust making fixed payments at a predetermined percentage that is at least five percent of the initial fair market value of the trust assets. Annuity payments are made to one or more beneficiaries that are named by the donor at the time the trust is established. Payments can be made to the beneficiaries for a specified term of up to twenty years. Income earned by the trust that exceeds the annuity amount is added to the trust's principal. If the trust's earnings are insufficient to meet the fixed payment, principal will be used to make up the difference. At the end of the term, the qualified charitable organization the donor selected receives the property in the trust and any appreciation. *See Also: fund, trust*

CHARITABLE REMAINDER. If a business venture ends or fails, any remaining interest in the venture goes to a charitable organization. *See Also: fails, interest*

CHARITABLE REMAINDER ANNUITY TRUST. Assets are contributed to a trust, with the trust making fixed payments at a predetermined percentage that is at least five percent of the initial fair market value of the trust assets. Annuity payments are made to one or more beneficiaries that are named by the donor at the time the trust is established. Payments can be made to the beneficiaries for a specified term of up to twenty years. Income earned by the trust that exceeds the annuity amount is added to the trust's principal. If the trust's earnings are insufficient to meet the fixed payment, principal will be used to make up the difference. At the end of the term, the qualified charitable organization the donor selected receives the property in the trust and any appreciation. *See Also: fair market value, fund, market, market value, trust*

CHARITABLE TRUST. A trust fund established to benefit an entire community without a specific, individual beneficiary. For example, a person can establish a trust to benefit a city's arts community, with proceeds from the bust fund going to help build a new art museum. *See Also: fund, proceeds, trust*

CHART. A pictorial display of data. Charts show the historical values of variables frequently used to spot trends that may be used to provide insights in projecting future values. *See Also: spot*

CHART OF ACCOUNTS. A list that shows the names of accounts and the order in which they appear on a company's ledger. *See Also: ledger, order*

CHARTER. A document endorsed and approved by a branch of state government in a company's home state that gives the company legal status as a corporation. *See Also: corporation, home, legal*

CHARTERED FINANCIAL ANALYST. A person certified by the Institute of Chartered Financial Analysts as being proficient in accounting, evaluating financial data, and managing investment portfolios. *See Also: investment*

CHARTERED FINANCIAL CONSULTANT. A person certified by the American College of Bryn Mawr as being proficient in investments, real estate ventures, and tax shelters. *See Also: estate, real estate*

CHARTERED INVESTMENT COUNSEL. A person certified by the Investment Counsel Association of America as being proficient in accounting, economics, portfolio management, and taxation. *See Also: investment, portfolio*

CHARTIST. A technical analyst who maps out stock, bond, and commodity patterns, looks for recurring patterns, and then recommends which securities should be purchased. *See Also: analyst, bond, commodity, securities, stock*

CHARTIST'S LIABILITY. The risk of buying or selling short a security when the transaction is based solely on a chartist's recommendation. *See Also: risk, security, selling short, transaction*

CHAT. Individuals on the Internet communicating, usually in real-time, by typing in messages. Chatting can occur on different levels: one-on-one, a one-to-many (e.g., an interview), or many-to-many. *See Also: Internet, on*

CHAT ROOM. A site on a network, typically as part of a Web site or part of an online service, where on-line, real-time conversations occur among a number of computer users. Chat rooms are usually organized by topic or special interests, such as online investors or cooking. *See Also: on, online, service, topic, Web, Web site*

CHATTEL. Personal property, or property that is not real estate. For example, land is real estate, but a house built on that land is chattel. *See Also: estate, house, real estate*

CHEAP. Used to describe a stock price as low compared to its present value. "Underpriced" is used when a stock price is low compared to its potential future value. *See Also: low, present value, stock*

CHEAP STOCK. Corporate shares of stock that are distributed while the company is still in its speculative stage. *See Also: speculative, stock*

CHECK. A bill of exchange, or draft on a bank drawn against deposited funds to pay a specified amount of money. It is considered cash and is negotiable when endorsed. *See Also: bank, bill of exchange, cash, draft, exchange, negotiable, pay*

CHECK KITING. A person writes a check without having enough money in his or her account to cover it, but he or she expects to be able to deposit the money before the check reaches the bank. *See Also: account, bank, check*

CHECKING THE MARKET. Surveying market-makers to find out what the best bid is for a specific security. *See Also: security*

CHERRY PICKING. Choosing the best stock while ignoring stock that is less valuable. *See Also: stock*

CHICAGO BOARD OF TRADE (CBOT). The largest exchange in the United States for trading futures contracts. The Chicago Board Options Exchange is a subsidiary of the Chicago Board of Trade. *See Also: exchange, futures, subsidiary*

CHICAGO BOARD OPTIONS EXCHANGE (CBOE). The largest market in the United States for trading put and call options. *See Also: market, put*

CHICAGO MERCANTILE EXCHANGE. The second largest commodities exchange in the United States. *See Also: exchange*

CHIEF EXECUTIVE OFFICER. A corporate officer responsible for a company's activities. *See Also: officer*

CHIEF FINANCIAL OFFICER. A corporate officer responsible for signing checks, keeping the books, and planning the finances of the company. *See Also: officer*

CHIEF OPERATING OFFICER. A corporate officer responsible for a company's day-to-day management. *See Also: officer*

CHINESE MARKET. Investors are willing to pay more than the lowest offer for a stock, or sell for less than the highest bid, but only if a large number of the securities are included in the deal. *See Also: offer, pay, securities, stock*

CHINESE WALL. An intangible barrier between the trading side of a broker-dealer firm and its finance and research side. This division prevents broker-dealers from taking advantage of the finance department's inside information. *See Also: broker-dealer, firm, inside information*

CHIPS. See Clearing House Interbank Payments System. *See Also: clearing house, house*

CHOP STOCKS. Easily manipulated penny stocks.

CHUMMING. A person artificially inflates the stock market's volume to attract more orders in one competitive security issue. *See Also: issue, security, stock, volume*

CHURNING. Excessive trading in a customer's account in an effort to increase the broker's commissions. The customer will usually be worse off or in no better condition. Although difficult to prove, churning is illegal under the Securities and Exchange Commission's rules. Also, the continual cycle of acquiring new customers and losing others. *See Also: account, exchange, securities*

CI. Certificate of Indebtedness. *See Also: certificate*

CINCINNATI STOCK EXCHANGE (CSE). The first fully automated stock exchange in the United States. Exchange members trade securities through a computer network, not on a trading floor. *See Also: exchange, floor, securities, stock, stock exchange, trading floor*

CINDY CRAWFORD. Description for a perfect investment or trade. The term comes from the name of a fashion model. *See Also: investment, name, term*

CIRCLE. An indication of how much interest will be expressed in a new security while the security is still in the registration process. Company representatives make lists of potential buyers, then circle the names of those who express an interest. *See Also: indication, interest, registration, security*

CIRCUMFIDUCIATION. Money, which was invested in certificates of deposit, is transferred to another investment. *See Also: investment*

CITIZEN BONDS. A certificateless municipal bond that may be registered on any of the stock exchanges. *See Also: bond, certificateless municipal, exchanges, municipal bond, stock*

CITY. London's counterpart to Wall Street in the United States. Most of England's financial services organizations are concentrated in The City, which is on London's East Side. *See Also: Street, Wall Street*

CLAIM ACCOUNT. A bank account in which a commodity can be deposited. *See Also: account, bank, commodity*

CLASS. Categorization of securities with similar features. For example, puts are one class and calls are another. Also, bonds are one class of security, and stocks are another. Classes are also used to designate tranches, or slices of a pool of collateral. *See Also: collateral, pool, securities, security*

CLASS ONE RAILROAD. A United States railroad that has annual revenues of more than $10 million. Only Class One-designated railroads can use debt securities to borrow money without guarantees from a commercial bank or a parent company. *See Also: bank, class, commercial bank, securities*

CLASS PRICE. Two different groups of people are charged two different prices for the same commodity, with the group less knowledgeable about the market charged a higher price. *See Also: commodity, market*

CLASS SYSTEM. The stagger system of electing board directors in which only part of the board comes up for re-election in any one year.

CLASSES OF SHARES. Mutual funds may categorize a single portfolio into several classes, distinguished by the type of sales charge levied. Class A shares typically levy a front-end sales load, Class B shares levy a back-end sales load and Class C shares have ongoing sales charges, usually classified as annual 12B-1 charges. *See Also: 12B-1 fee, class, load, portfolio, sales charge, sales load*

CLASSIFIED STOCK. Equity securities are separated into groups such as Class A or Class B. The difference between the two will be determined by the provisions of the charter and bylaws. Differences can distinguish privileges in voting power, dividends, and liquidation procedures. *See Also: bylaws, charter, class, liquidation, securities*

CLAYTON ANTITRUST ACT. Federal statute passed in 1914 as an amendment to the Sherman Antitrust Act, prohibiting business monopolies and trade restraints in domestic industries. *See Also: antitrust*

CLEAN. If a block positioner can match buy orders and sell orders without taking the security into his or her inventory, thus taking a risk, the transaction is said to be "clean" (or "natural"). Also, a clean balance sheet is one free of debt. *See Also: balance, balance sheet, block positioner, inventory, risk, security, transaction*

CLEAN ON THE PRINT. A block trade which can be executed on the floor without a broker-dealer firm acting as principal in the deal. *See Also: as principal, broker-dealer, firm, floor, principal*

CLEAN OPINION. An auditing opinion stating that the auditor found a company's financial records to be accurate and reflective of the company's actual state. *See Also: actual*

CLEAR. Verifying the details of a security's trade before its settlement.

CLEARED. When the purchaser of a security pays for and receives the security. *See Also: security*

CLEARING AGREEMENT. A document in which one broker-dealer agrees to execute and settle another broker-dealer's transaction for a fee. *See Also: broker-dealer, settle, transaction*

CLEARING HOUSE. A place where deals between member firms are executed and settled.

CLEARING HOUSE FUNDS. Funds designated by a check that must clear a local or regional bank before the payee can receive credit. *See Also: bank, check, clear, credit, local, regional bank*

CLEARING HOUSE INTERBANK PAYMENTS SYSTEM (CHIPS). The New York Clearing House's computerized system through which most international transactions are cleared. These transactions are ultimately settled through Fed Wire. *See Also: cleared, fed wire*

CLEARING MEMBER. An exchange member who is granted membership in a clearing house. *See Also: clearing house, exchange, house*

CLEARING THE MARKET. Changing the price of a securities transaction to the satisfaction of the buyer and seller. *See Also: securities, transaction*

CLICK. The action of selecting an item on a Web page, usually with the mouse or a verbal command. *See Also: mouse, on, Web, Web page*

CLICK THROUGH. The action of a visitor to a Web site clicking a banner advertisement. *See Also: Web, Web site*

CLICK THROUGH RATE. The percentage of times visitors click through a particular banner advertisement based on the number of times the banner was actually viewed. *See Also: click through, on*

CLICKS AND MORTAR. A traditional off-line company that leverages its infrastructure (e.g., handling returns, salespeople, etc.) to an Internet-related activity. Both channels can serve as the outlet for the majority of its products and services. *See Also: activity, infrastructure, infrastructure*

CLIENT. 1) A customer. 2) A reference to a computer that is connected to a host or server computer. 3) Client also refers to software that facilitates the connection between a computer and a server. *See Also: server*

CLIENT SERVICE REPRESENTATIVE. A salaried person who acts as a registered representative in discount brokerage firms or handles walk-in clients and one-time transactions in larger firms. *See Also: discount, registered representative*

CLIFFORD TRUST. A trust fund established between two or more living people, with assets pledged for at least 10 years. Income from the assets is given to one party until the trust ends, at which time the assets revert to the grantor. The IRS considers this income as a gift to the recipient. *See Also: fund, grantor, IRS, time, trust*

CLIMAX. A time of heavy trading after a long rise or drop in market prices. The climax signals both the top or bottom, so prices usually change directions following it. *See Also: bottom, change, drop, heavy, market, time, top*

CLIQUE. Several investors band together to form a group and agree to match orders and to sell short or wash sales in an effort to manipulate the price of a security. This act is now illegal. *See Also: security*

CLOCKED. Used to describe a major adverse movement in an investment or market. *See Also: investment, market, movement*

CLONE FUND. A fund that is created to mirror an existing fund, with the same investment objective but typically with different managers and different securities. This may be accomplished, for example, when a fund has been closed to new investors due to its large size. *See Also: closed to new investors, fund, investment, investment objective, securities, size*

CLONE MONEY-MARKET FUND. A type of money market fund that is readily created, but must put up a specific percentage of its assets as a reserve. *See Also: fund, market, money market, money market fund, put, reserve*

CLOSE. The final 30 seconds of trading on the stock exchange floor, designated by a bell that rings continuously for the 30 seconds. *See Also: bell, exchange, exchange floor, floor, stock, stock exchange*

CLOSE A POSITION. Eliminating an investment from a portfolio, usually by selling if a long position exists or by buying in the case of a short security position. *See Also: investment, long position, portfolio, position, security*

CLOSE MONEY. When the price differences among successive stock transactions are fractional or when the spread between the bid and ask on the last trade is barely any different. *See Also: ask, spread, stock*

CLOSE PRICES. A fractional difference between bid and ask prices. *See Also: ask*

CLOSE THE BOOKS. When a company's board of directors declares dividends after temporarily closing the company's stock transfer books. *See Also: board of directors, stock, transfer*

CLOSE TO THE MONEY. A put or call contract with a striking price that is close to the current market value of the underlying security. *See Also: call contract, close, contract, current, current market value, market, market value, put, security, striking price, underlying security*

CLOSED ACCOUNT. A brokerage account that the customer or broker has terminated. Although the brokerage house by law retains transaction records, all securities and money involved are sent to the customer. *See Also: account, broker, brokerage account, brokerage house, house, securities, transaction*

CLOSED END FUNDS. An investment company with a fixed number of shares outstanding. The shares of a closed-end fund usually trade on a secondary market and can sell at a premium or discount to its net asset value. Open-end funds can usually be redeemed at its net asset value, and additional shares can be issued. *See Also: asset, at a premium, discount, fund, investment, investment company, market, net, net asset value, outstanding, premium, secondary market, shares outstanding*

CLOSED END INVESTMENT COMPANY. A company that keeps re-investing shareholders' money in securities instead of issuing new shares or redeeming existing ones. *See Also: securities*

CLOSED END MANAGEMENT COMPANY. A management investment company that issues a specific number of shares which the holder usually cannot redeem at his or her option. The shares normally are redeemed through secondary market deals. *See Also: investment, investment company, market, option, redeem, secondary market*

CLOSED END MORTGAGE BOND. A bond issue that prohibits the property that secures it from being used as collateral on any future bond issues. *See Also: bond, collateral, issue*

CLOSED OUT. An investor who cannot meet his or her margin call or who cannot cover a short sale must liquidate his or her position. *See Also: margin, margin call, position, sale, short sale*

CLOSED TO NEW INVESTORS. A fund may declare itself closed to new investors if it is no longer accepting new investments. This may occur, for example, if a fund has attracted more money than the manager feels can be put to work. *See Also: declare, fund, manager, put, put to*

CLOSED TRADE. A transaction closed when a security that was paid for earlier is sold. *See Also: security, transaction*

CLOSELY HELD. Used to describe a company owned by a few stockholders. Closely held companies are tightly governed by law; the maximum number of shareholders and the transfer of shares are restricted. *See Also: transfer*

CLOSING COSTS. The amount of money needed to transfer property from one person to another. Closing costs take care of title searches, attorney fees, insurance costs, and filing charges. *See Also: insurance, take, transfer*

CLOSING OF TRANSFER BOOKS. A company's board of directors sets a date after which stock ownership cannot be transferred for a specific time period. During that time, dividends will be paid and meetings will be held. A company closes the transfer books in an effort to avoid confusion. *See Also: board of directors, stock, time, transfer*

CLOSING PRICE. A security's last transaction price for the day. *See Also: transaction*

CLOSING PURCHASE TRANSACTIONS. An option writer will purchase a same series, creating a net zero position, thus closing the position. *See Also: net, option, option writer, position*

CLOSING QUOTE. The final bid or offer on a security before the exchange closes for the day. *See Also: exchange, offer, security*

CLOSING RANGE. The range of a commodity's high and low prices in one trading day, indicating the amount of money it would cost to buy or sell the commodity. *See Also: commodity, low, range, trading day*

CLOSING SALE TRANSACTIONS. Options deals in which contract holders liquidate their positions and end their obligations to buy or sell shares of the underlying securities. *See Also: contract, securities*

CLOSING TRANSACTION. One securities deal that cancels another securities deal, both of which carry the same terms. *See Also: carry, securities*

CLUB FINANCING. A group of banks that are approximately the same size band together to underwrite a security. Each bank subscribes to equal amounts of the issue. *See Also: bank, issue, security, size*

CMO. Collateralized Mortgage Obligation. *See Also: mortgage, obligation*

COALITION. Groups of buyers or sellers that agree to collaborate towards a business objective, such as channel procurement through a single market-place. Typically, coalitions operate and control a marketplace though some may claim to be neutral so that other participants may join. *See Also: neutral, procurement*

COATTAIL INVESTING. An investment strategy that simulates the investments of well-known investors. *See Also: investment, investment strategy*

COCKROACH THEORY. The belief that bad market-related news tends to be released in groups.

COD TRANSACTION. A broker buys a security for a client's account and delivers it to the client's agent who then pays for the purchase. Also known as "delivery against cost" and "delivery versus payment." *See Also: account, agent, broker, security*

CODE DIVISION MULTIPLE ACCESS. *See Also: CDMA*

CODE OF ARBITRATION. The National Association of Securities Dealers has established this set of rules and regulations to govern submitting and arbitrating disagreements among exchange members or between members and nonmembers. *See Also: exchange, securities*

CODE OF PROCEDURE. The National Association of Securities Dealers has established this set of rules and regulations to govern the submission and settlement of complaints that arise concerning possible violations of fair-practice laws. *See Also: securities, submission*

COEFFICIENT OF DETERMINATION. A gauge that determines the amount of market-imposed risk on a specific security. *See Also: risk, security*

COINCIDENT ECONOMIC INDICATORS. An economic gauge that follows an industry sector or the economy in general. *See Also: industry, sector*

COINSURANCE. The sharing of an insurance risk. This is typical when a claim may be of a substantial size that one company may not want to underwrite the entire risk. *See Also: insurance, risk, size*

COLD CALL. A broker or agent of a broker calls a potential investor for the first time in an effort either to sell a security or to set up a meeting in which a security will be discussed. *See Also: agent, broker, security, time*

COLD CANVASSING. Making up a list of potential investors without any prior knowledge of the customers or whether they have ever purchased securities. An example of cold canvassing is pulling names from a telephone book. *See Also: book, securities*

COLD IN HAND. A person with no money to invest.

COLLABORATIVE COMMERCE. *See Also: c-commerce*

COLLABORATIVE FILTERING. A software application that sifts through users' profiles to compare one particular user. The information is used to make recommendations based on others' purchasing habits or other preferences. *See Also: on*

COLLABORATIVE PLANNING, FORECASTING AND REPLENISHMENT. A software application that enables companies to share production and planning information. This technology can, for example, be beneficial to a retailer and supplier when estimating upcoming supply and demand, and to use that information to synchronize the retailer's merchandise plan with the supplier's sales plan. *See Also: demand, share, supply, technology*

COLLAPSE. Either the sudden drop in a stock's price or the failure of a business venture. *See Also: drop, failure*

COLLAR. The lowest interest rate a bond purchaser can accept or the lowest price the issuer can accept from the underwriters. *See Also: bond, interest, interest rate*

COLLAR PRICING. A company agrees on a specific price range in which a stock will be priced instead of establishing an exact cost per share. *See Also: price range, range, share, stock*

COLLARED FLOATERS. Bonds that pay interest periodically at its reset date according to a formula. The interest rate paid cannot fall below a floor or rise above a predetermined cap. *See Also: cap, fall, floor, interest, interest rate, pay*

COLLATERAL. An asset such as an automobile or a piece of property that a person uses to take out a loan, promising to give the asset to the lender if loan payments cannot be met. Collateral also refers to the collection of recievables, such as mortgages, which are used to back the interest and/or principal of a security. *See Also: asset, interest, principal, security, take*

COLLATERAL BOND. A bond that is used to secure a loan. *See Also: bond*

COLLATERAL INTEREST. For asset-backed securities, the collateral interest is an additional tranche, which represents overcollateralization. *See Also: collateral, interest, securities, tranche*

COLLATERAL SURETY. Commercial papers such as a stock or a bond, that is used to secure a loan. *See Also: bond, stock*

COLLATERAL TRUST BOND. A bond secured by securities owned by the issuing company. A trustee holds the securities for the bond holder. *See Also: bond, bond holder, securities, trustee*

COLLATERAL TRUST NOTES. Bonds (usually issued by holding companies, investment trusts, or railroads) that are secured by other stocks or bonds. *See Also: investment*

COLLATERALIZED MORTGAGE OBLIGATION (CMO). A security that pools together mortgages and separates them into multiclass, or multitranche bonds of varying maturities, coupon rates, prepayment risk and performance characteristics. This system greatly reduces uncertainties associated with the prepayment risks inherent in mortgage securities. *See Also: coupon, mortgage, prepayment, risk, securities, security*

COLLECTIBLE. An item that has an additional value because of its beauty, rarity, or historical representation. Rare coins, antiques, and old baseball cards are all considered collectibles.

COLLECTION RATIO. Derived by dividing a company's accounts receivable total by its average daily sales to come up with the number of days it takes to turn a dollar entered under accounts receivable into a dollar entered under cash. *See Also: accounts receivable, average, cash, to come, turn*

COLLECTIVE BARGAINING. Union members, representing workers at a particular company, negotiate with company management to arrive at fair and equitable salaries, safe working conditions, and acceptable fringe benefits for member employees.

COLLECTIVE INVESTMENT FUND. An investment trust with pension and profit-sharing funds commingled following Internal Revenue Service approval. *See Also: internal revenue, investment, investment trust, pension, service, trust*

COLLECTIVE OWNERSHIP. Several individuals or companies own an asset, with no one entity owning any specific portion of the asset. *See Also: asset*

COLOR. The specifications, such as market conditions, investor preferences, and yield spreads, for a particular security. *See Also: market, security, yield*

COMBINATION. The position of a group of options other than a straddle, which is made up of puts and calls. *See Also: position, straddle*

COMBINATION BOND. A government-issued debt instrument fully backed by the issuer and by revenues from the project for which it paid, such as toll from a toll road or entrance fees from a city museum. *See Also: City, debt instrument, instrument*

COMBINED FINANCIAL STATEMENT. A financial statement that adds the assets and liabilities of at least two affiliated companies, but does not necessarily reflect investment strength or credit responsibility. *See Also: credit, investment, statement*

COMEX. A commodity exchange in New York City formed by the merger of four past exchanges. This exchange trades futures in sugar, coffee, petroleum, metals, and financial instruments. *See Also: City, commodity, exchange, exchanges, futures, merger*

COMFORT LETTER. A document the issuer or seller of a security provides his or her underwriter or agent with in which the issuer or seller promises to repay any expenses incurred because of litigation, tender offers, or omissions in the registration. *See Also: agent, litigation, registration, security, tender*

COMING TO ME. An over-the-counter trader who gives price quotes that are not his or her own. While the prices do represent another dealer's market, it does not necessarily reflect the over-the-counter trader's final offer. *See Also: market, offer, trader*

COMMERCE. The congressional basis for trade, communication, transportation, among other interactions, between independent states and nations. *See Also: basis*

COMMERCE SERVER. A server, or a host computer on a network, that facilitates online transactions. The server is typically capable of handling online transactions and related activities, including database and inventory management, order taking, billing, security and customer service. *See Also: inventory, on, online, order, security, server, service*

COMMERCIAL BANK. A banking corporation which accepts deposits and makes loans to businesses, regardless of its other services. *See Also: corporation*

COMMERCIAL BAR. A brick of a precious metal that is used for nonmonetary purposes. For example, a brick of silver that will be melted down to make jewelry is a commercial bar, while a brick of silver that will be used to make dimes is not.

COMMERCIAL BORROWER. A person who borrows money for a business venture.

COMMERCIAL CREDIT. Credit extended to businesses for the production of goods and services. This is distinguished from personal, investment, agriculture, and bank credit. *See Also: bank, credit, extended, investment*

COMMERCIAL DISCOUNTS. Discounts given to encourage prompt payments.

COMMERCIAL EXCHANGE OF PHILADELPHIA. A commodities exchange that deals in feeds, flour, and grains. *See Also: exchange*

COMMERCIAL HEDGER. A company that tries to stabilize the price of a commodity by taking a position in the commodities markets because it must use the commodity in producing its own goods. For example, ABC Paint Company may take a position in petroleum futures because they want to lock in prices for materials. *See Also: commodity, futures, position, take, take a position*

COMMERCIAL LETTER OF CREDIT. A document that lends its credit to a customer to permit him or her to finance a business transaction. This allows the customer to draw drafts on the bank under the agreed upon terms. *See Also: bank, credit, transaction*

COMMERCIAL LOAN. Short-term financing to act as a company's working capital. *See Also: capital, working capital*

COMMERCIAL MORTGAGE. A loan that has real estate as collateral and is used for a business venture. *See Also: collateral, estate, real estate*

COMMERCIAL PAPER. An unsecured short-term debt instrument issued by a company with only its credit rating backing the security. These securities have maturities ranging from 2 to 270 days. *See Also: credit, credit rating, debt instrument, instrument, security, short-term debt*

COMMERCIAL PAPER HOUSE. A dealer who buys a commercial paper at one price, then tries to sell it at another. *See Also: commercial paper, dealer, paper*

COMMERCIAL STOCKS. Stocks owned by the U.S. Department of Agriculture, representing grain at major grain centers. *See Also: grain*

COMMERCIAL WELLS. Drilling sites that produce enough oil and gas to be workable as a corporate venture. *See Also: sites*

COMMINGLING. Mixing an investor's securities with those owned by a company in the company's proprietary accounts. *See Also: securities*

COMMISSION. Fees charged by a firm for executing trades. *See Also: firm*

COMMISSION BROKER. An agent, usually a floor broker who executes the public's trades for a commission. *See Also: agent, broker, commission, floor, floor broker*

COMMITMENT FEE. A person planning to issue securities gives money to investors to motivate them to buy the securities when they are issued. By paying a commitment fee, the issuer is assured the funds will be available later for the investors to buy the shares. *See Also: issue, securities*

COMMITTEE. A group of exchange employees responsible for admissions and the conduct of members. *See Also: exchange*

COMMITTEE FOR AN INCOMPETENT. A person appointed to handle the financial affairs for someone else who has been deemed physically or mentally unable to handle his or her own money. *See Also: handle*

COMMODITIES EXCHANGE CENTER. An organization used by New York's four commodities exchanges for clearing transactions and checking quotations. *See Also: exchanges*

COMMODITIES FUTURES CONTRACT. A document in which an investor agrees to buy or sell a specific quantity of a commodity at a future date. *See Also: commodity*

COMMODITIES FUTURES STRADDLE. A transaction in which an investor buys a commodity to be delivered in one month, then sells a contract for the same commodity for delivery in another month in an effort to profit from any price differences. *See Also: commodity, contract, delivery, profit, transaction*

COMMODITIES FUTURES TRADING COMMISSION (CFTC). A panel established to regulate commodities exchanges and futures trading. The CFTC, which covers all commodities traded in contract markets, handles fair trading practices, ethical conduct, and commodities information disclosure. *See Also: contract, disclosure, exchanges, futures*

COMMODITY. An agricultural product, mineral, or other tangible asset that investors trade on a cash or futures basis. *See Also: asset, basis, cash, futures, tangible asset*

COMMODITY EXCHANGE INCORPORATED. A New York commodity exchange that trades in coffee, financial instruments, futures, petroleum, precious metals, and sugar. *See Also: commodity, exchange, futures*

COMMODITY FUTURE. A contract to buy or sell a specific commodity at a specified price at a certain future date. *See Also: commodity, contract*

COMMODITY FUTURES TRADING COMMISSION. A committee that regulates commodity exchange trading. *See Also: committee, commodity, exchange*

COMMODITY PAPER. A loan with a commodity as its collateral. *See Also: collateral, commodity*

COMMODITY POOL OPERATOR. A person who pools funds to be used as trade in commodities futures contracts to benefit the people who put money into the pool. *See Also: futures, pool, put*

COMMODITY STANDARD. A monetary system in which commodities are exchanged for a standing currency base, such as gold or silver. *See Also: base, currency*

COMMODITY TAX STRADDLE. An individual profits from a commodity investment, then looks for a capital loss with which to offset the profit in the current tax year. *See Also: capital, commodity, current, investment, offset, profit*

COMMODITY TRADING ADVISOR. A futures expert who advises investors on how and when to buy and sell futures contracts. *See Also: futures*

COMMODITY-BACKED BOND. A debt instrument that is closely connected to an underlying commodity, such as gold or silver. It pays interest dividends based on the commodity's current price, providing the investor with a hedge against inflation. *See Also: commodity, current, debt instrument, hedge, inflation, instrument, interest*

COMMON LAW. Any legal precedent that has been set by a history of court decisions as opposed to a precedent set by a specific ruling. *See Also: legal*

COMMON MESSAGE SWITCH. A computer that connects members with the New York and American stock exchanges over which order instructions are transmitted. *See Also: exchanges, order, stock*

COMMON STOCK. A unit of ownership in a public company for which the holder can vote on matters and receive dividends from the company's growth, but he or she is the last to receive assets if the company liquidates. Preferred stock, on the other hand, has a set dividend rate. *See Also: dividend, preferred stock, stock, unit*

COMMON STOCK EQUIVALENTS. Securities that can be converted into common stock of the same company. *See Also: common stock, stock*

COMMON STOCK FUND. A mutual fund with a portfolio consisting of only common stock. *See Also: common stock, fund, mutual fund, portfolio, stock*

COMMON STOCK INDEX. The average current price of a stock versus its average price at an earlier date. *See Also: average, current, stock*

COMMON STOCK RATIO. The percentage of a company's permanent capital that comes from common stock, paid-in surplus, and retained earnings. When added together, the bond ratio, preferred stock ratio, and common stock ratio equal 100 percent. *See Also: bond, bond ratio, capital, common stock, earnings, paid-in surplus, permanent capital, preferred stock, preferred stock ratio, ratio, retained earnings, stock*

COMMON TRUST FUND. A fund held by a bank or trust company in which the money is collectively invested and profits are reinvested. *See Also: bank, fund, trust, trust company*

COMMUNISM. A political system in which the government controls production and distribution of goods and services.

COMMUNITY PROPERTY. Property and assets acquired during a marriage that are owned equally by each spouse. To dispose of the assets, both spouses must consent. If the couple were to break up, the assets would be divided 50-50. *See Also: break*

COMPANION BONDS. A coupon-paying CMO tranche that absorbs the repayment variability of collateral principal cash flows, enabling scheduled tranches with higher cash flow priorities, such as PAC bonds, to maintain their predicted sinking funds. *See Also: cash, cash flow, CMO, collateral, principal, tranche, variability*

COMPARABLES. *See Also: comps.*

COMPARATIVE. STATEMENTS Financial documents that cover different time periods (but similar in content), used to compare a company's financial situation and to predict where the company is heading. *See Also: time*

COMPARISON RETURNS. Comparing the return of a taxable investment versus a non-taxable investment. *See Also: investment, return*

COMPENSATING BALANCE. The amount of money a bank requires a depositor to have in an account before the bank will have credit available for the depositor. *See Also: account, bank, credit*

COMPETITIVE BID. The awarding of an underwriting contract to the highest bidder based on the best price and terms. *See Also: contract, underwriting*

COMPETITIVE INTELLIGENCE. The sensitive and confidential information learned by one company about a competitor. Competitive intelligence information includes market research, and marketing and strategy plans. *See Also: market, market research*

COMPETITIVE TRADER. An exchange member who trades stock for an account in which he or she holds some interest. *See Also: account, exchange, interest, stock*

COMPLETE AUDIT. A thorough study of a firm's accounts, internal controls and subsidiary records, making sure the firm is obeying the law, keeping accurate financial records, and using appropriate accounting practices. *See Also: firm, subsidiary*

COMPLETION PROGRAM. A limited partnership that takes over an oil-drilling operation when a well has enough oil to support a commercial venture. Completion programs allow limited partnerships to profit from the oil industry without spending money for exploratory drilling. *See Also: industry, limited partnership, partnership, profit, support*

COMPLIANCE DEPARTMENT. A broker-dealer department responsible for ensuring that all members adhere to Securities and Exchange Commission regulations. *See Also: broker-dealer, commission, exchange, securities*

COMPLIANCE REGISTERED OPTIONS PRINCIPAL (CROP). The person who audits a brokerage firm and must determine if the firm is trading options in accordance with federal and state law and with the rules and regulations of the Securities and Exchange Commission and the self-regulatory organization. *See Also: commission, exchange, firm, securities, self-regulatory organization*

COMPONENT OPERATING FIRM. A company owned or controlled by a holding company system that functions as a unit of that system. *See Also: holding company, unit*

COMPOSITE. An average that measures results using information from several different sources. For example, the Dow Jones Composite uses industrial, transportation, and utility averages. *See Also: average, averages, industrial, utility*

COMPOSITE COMMODITY STANDARD. A system in which a monetary unit is defined in terms of a specific number of commodities instead of gold or silver, which normally serve as the currency base. *See Also: base, currency, unit*

COMPOSITE LIMIT ORDER BOOK. A proposed central computer that would show all buy and sell orders of securities, and ultimately could eliminate the need for exchanges because brokers could execute orders directly through the computer. *See Also: exchanges, securities*

COMPOSITION. Creditors agree to accept partial payments from a person or business that cannot pay off debts. By doing this, the troubled business can avoid bankruptcy, and the creditors are assured some payment. If the business were to go through bankruptcy, some of the creditors might not receive any payments, or the payments might be lower. *See Also: bankruptcy, pay, to go*

COMPOUND ARBITRAGE. When arbitrage is achieved using at least four different markets. *See Also: arbitrage*

COMPOUND GROWTH RATE. A number indicating how much a company will grow; profits are taken for each of the last five years and compounded every year. Analysts use this method to determine whether a company is a worthwhile investment. *See Also: investment*

COMPOUND INTEREST. Interest that is computed on the original amount plus all accumulated interest. *See Also: interest, plus*

COMPOUND INTEREST BONDS. Municipal bonds that are issued at a much lower price than their face value, and which pay no periodic interest. These bonds can be redeemed at par when they mature. *See Also: at par, face value, interest, par, pay*

COMPOUND INTEREST METHOD OF DEPRECIATION. A system which the salvage value of a capital asset when it will be discarded is subtracted from the asset's original cost. The difference is spread into equal installments for the duration of the asset's life. During each installment, the depreciation amount is reduced by the amount of interest it would earn. *See Also: asset, capital, capital asset, depreciation, duration, interest, original cost, salvage value, spread*

COMPOUNDING. Interest earned on interest that was previously earned and reinvested. If an investor invests $10,000 in a security that pays an annual fixed interest rate of 10%, the investor will earn $1,000 in interest by the end of the first year. If that interest is reinvested in that security, at the end of the second year the investor will have $12,100 due to the additional interest that is received from the 10% interest rate that is applied to the original principal and the interest received. *See Also: fixed interest rate, interest, interest rate, on, principal, security, will*

COMPS. Short for comparables, describes same-store sales, which helps determine how well a company's revenue is performing. *See Also: comparables*

COMPTROLLER OF THE CURRENCY. A U.S. official who charters, examines, liquidates, and supervises the nation's banks.

COMPUTER ASSISTED EXECUTION SYSTEM. A communication network, sponsored by the National Association of Securities Dealers, that connects broker-dealers to over-the-counter market makers. Through this system, broker-dealers can order the execution of certain transactions. *See Also: execution, market, order, securities*

COMPUTER GRAPHICS. Pictures or images in a digital format. *See Also: digital*

COMPUTER INFORMATION SERVICES. A network through which broker-dealers and commodity futures merchants buy processing, reporting, and surveillance services. *See Also: commodity, futures, processing*

COMPUTER VIRUS. A software program that infects a computer by embedding itself in a computer system or application. The virus becomes active when the attacked program is executed. Viruses behave in different ways, and can be relatively harmless pranks, destroy computer files, wipe out a hard drive, or disable a computer. *See Also: drive*

COMPUTERIZED MARKET TIMING SYSTEM. A computer network that compiles information about buys and sells, then evaluates trends so the user can decide when and if to invest in particular funds.

CONCESSION. The amount paid per share or per bond to members of a selling group in a corporate underwriting. *See Also: bond, selling group, share, underwriting*

CONDENSED STATEMENT. A financial document in which minor details are grouped together into one section, making it easier for the public to study. *See Also: easier*

CONDITIONAL SALES AGREEMENT. The issuer of an equipment trust certificate pledges a minimum amount of equity, but does not acquire title to the equipment until the entire debt is retired. *See Also: certificate, equipment trust certificate, equity, trust*

CONDOR SPREAD. A vertical bull and bear spread on either put or call options and without any duplicate strike prices. *See Also: bear, bear spread, bull, put, spread*

CONDUIT THEORY. An investment organization passes along interest, dividends, and capital gains to investors so that they, rather than the company, will have to pay the federal and state taxes. *See Also: capital, interest, investment, pay*

CONDUIT-TYPE CUSTOMER. The customer of a broker-dealer who does not reveal his or her customers' identities. Financial institutions often are conduit-type customers. *See Also: broker-dealer*

CONFIRMATION. Indicates that at least two indexes verify a market trend or turning point. *See Also: market, market trend, point, trend*

CONFIRMATION SLIP. Verification that a broker sends to a client, acknowledging a transaction. *See Also: broker, client, transaction*

CONFLICT OF INTEREST. A person who is supposed to be objective in a specific transaction places his or her personal interests above that of the customer by taking a beneficial interest in the outcome of the transaction. For example, a city council member who owns stock in a company would have a conflict of interest if the council voted to give the company a zoning variance. *See Also: beneficial interest, City, interest, stock, transaction, variance*

CONFORMED COPY. A document copy that contains all of the legal features of the original, such as a notary seal and a signature. *See Also: legal*

CONGLOMERATE. The merging or combination of unrelated companies. *See Also: combination*

CONGLOMERATE MERGER. The joining of two companies involved in unrelated businesses.

CONSENSUS FORECAST. The average of all financial analysts' earnings forecasts for a company. *See Also: average, earnings*

CONSENSUS RATING. The average recommendation of all analysts for a single company's shares. *See Also: average*

CONSENT TO SERVICE. A document that authorizes an individual to act as an attorney on behalf of another individual in accepting legal processes. *See Also: legal*

CONSERVATION EASEMENT. A charitable donation of property in which the building rights are given up in a deed to a nonprofit charitable organization, such as a land trust, while providing the donor with income-tax, property-tax and estate-tax savings. Conservation easements prevent all development except that specifically allowed by the easement; property owners are required to show that an easement provides a public benefit, such as preserving a wildlife habitat. *See Also: rights, trust*

CONSERVATIVE PORTFOLIO. A group of investments chosen because they are safe, with the investor not entering any risky ventures.

CONSERVATOR. A person appointed by a court to handle the financial interests of another person who has been deemed incompetent because of age or some physical or mental inadequacy. *See Also: handle*

CONSIDERATION. Cash or securities with which a person buys title to an issuer's equity or debt securities. *See Also: equity, securities*

CONSOL. British bonds issued during the Napoleonic wars which paid a fixed coupon rate and never matured. *See Also: coupon, coupon rate, matured*

CONSOLIDATED BALANCE SHEET. A financial statement that shows a parent company's total assets and liabilities without breaking the numbers down to show the assets and liabilities of the company's subsidiaries. *See Also: statement*

CONSOLIDATED MORTGAGE BOND. A debt instrument that has only one coupon rate of interest. This type of bond is issued in an effort to obtain money to refund previously issued mortgage bonds with different interest rates and maturity dates. *See Also: bond, coupon, coupon rate, debt instrument, instrument, interest, maturity, mortgage*

CONSOLIDATED QUOTATION SYSTEM. Gathers current bid and asked prices of listed securities from all of the different exchanges, then distributes the figures to subscribers. *See Also: bid and asked, current, exchanges, listed securities, securities*

CONSOLIDATED SINKING FUND. A sinking fund designed to serve at least two bond issues. *See Also: bond, fund, sinking fund*

CONSOLIDATED STATEMENT OF FINANCIAL POSITION. A document in which a company's current financial status is reported. *See Also: current*

CONSOLIDATED TAPE. A network that continuously reports on all securities transactions on every exchange. *See Also: exchange, securities*

CONSOLIDATED TAX RETURN. The combined tax returns of all of a company's affiliates and subsidiaries.

CONSOLIDATION. Two or more companies combine to form one new company.

CONSOLIDATION LOAN. A loan that combines a person's or business' debts into one debt so that only one payment needs to be made. A consolidation loan usually is taken out to reduce interest rates: the person or business would be paying interest on only one loan, instead of on five or six. *See Also: consolidation, interest*

CONSOLIDATOR. The process by which a company grows by acquiring other companies. Consolidators are also known as Roll-ups.

CONSORTIUM. Groups of buyers or sellers that work collaboratively toward a common business objective, such as channel procurement through a single e-marketplace. Some consortiums may operate and control an e-marketplace, while others may claim to be neutral so that other participants may join. *See Also: e-marketplace, neutral, procurement*

CONSTANT DOLLAR PLAN. A method in which an individual invests a fixed amount of money in a security at set intervals. More shares will be purchased when the price is lower and less when the price is higher. *See Also: intervals, security*

CONSTANT DOLLARS. A hypothetical unit of purchasing power, measured as the number of dollars in a company's base year. Dollars of other years are adjusted against the constant dollars to determine the company's actual purchasing power. *See Also: actual, base, purchasing power, unit*

CONSTANT FACTOR. The total amount of principal and interest a person or business must pay to retire a debt. *See Also: and interest, interest, pay, principal, retire*

CONSTANT PREPAYMENT RATE (CPR). A prepayment measure that expresses the rate at which a specified percentage of the remaining mortgages in a pool will prepay per year. It is expressed as a percentage of the mortgage balance outstanding at the beginning of a period. CPR includes only prepayments, not contractual principal payments. *See Also: actual, balance, mortgage, outstanding, pool, prepayment, principal*

CONSTANT RATIO PLAN. A system in which a specific dollar ratio is maintained in two different types of investments. For example, if an investor had $100,000 and wanted a 50-50 ratio maintained in stocks and bonds, $50,000 would be invested in each. If the investment rose to $150,000, adjustments would be made so that $75,000 would be invested in stocks and $75,000 would be invested in bonds. *See Also: investment, ratio*

CONSTRUCTION AND DEVELOPMENT REIT. A real estate trust fund from which developers can borrow to build a commercial or residential development. *See Also: estate, fund, real estate, trust*

CONSTRUCTION LOAN. A short-term loan used to pay for building a real estate project, with loan funds disbursed to the borrower as needed and repaid after the project is completed. While the interest rate on construction loans usually is higher than the prime rate, the effective yield also tends to be high, and the lender can maintain a secure interest in the property. *See Also: estate, interest, interest rate, pay, prime, prime rate, real estate, yield*

CONSTRUCTIVE RECEIPT. The actual date a taxpayer receives income, as defined by the Internal Revenue Service. Constructive receipt is the actual date the income is available, even if the taxpayer doesn't actually exercise his or her right to take possession of the money. For example, if an investor receives an interest check on December 30, he or she must report it as income for that year, even if the check isn't cashed until after January 1. *See Also: actual, check, exercise, interest, internal revenue, right, service, take*

CONSUMER CREDIT PROTECTION ACT OF 1968. Also known as the Truth in Lending Act, this law requires lenders to tell borrowers the annual percentage rates, the total cost of the loan including interest, and all loan terms. *See Also: interest, total cost, Truth in Lending Act*

CONSUMER DEBENTURE. An investment note that the issuing financial institution markets directly to the public in an effort to raise money to make loans. *See Also: investment, note*

CONSUMER PRICE INDEX (CPI). The primary gauge of inflation in the United States, the CPI is calculated by establishing the price of a fixed basket of goods and services, which are selected because of their direct impact on average citizens. Included in the basket are such things as food, gasoline, housing, and medical care. Increases in the costs of such items indicate a rise in the inflation rate. *See Also: average, inflation, inflation rate*

CONSUMER-TO-BUSINESS. Also referred to as C2B and CtoB, a reversal of the traditional business that is conducted with consumers, where the consumers dictate the price they're willing to pay, with the business determining whether or not to accept. *See Also: pay, reversal*

CONSUMPTION. Using a product until it has no further value.

CONTANGO. When commodities futures prices rise as maturities lengthen, thus creating negative spreads as contracts go further out. These increases usually reflect costs involved in handling the goods. *See Also: futures*

CONTENT PROVIDER. A business to business or business to consumer Web site whose primary business is derived from the delivery of structured, specific content to its subscribers, members or visitors. *See Also: delivery, Web, Web site*

CONTINGENT DEFERRED SALES CHARGE. The Contingent deferred sales charge (CDSC) is a type of back-end load sales charge that is levied when shares are redeemed within a specific period. Typically, the CDSC fee is reduced over a period of predetermined years that the fund is held. *See Also: fund, load, sales charge*

CONTINGENT IMMUNIZATION. An active bond management system that involves a minimum compound annual return and in which strategies are applied to the portfolio as long as its value is more than that needed to achieve the minimum return. *See Also: bond, portfolio, return*

CONTINGENT LIABILITIES. A bank's responsibility to honor letters of credit or other obligations, and the responsibility of a customer, whose account will be charged if he or she opens a line of credit. *See Also: account, credit, line of credit*

CONTINGENT ORDER. An order to buy one security and sell another only if the deal can be made at a stipulated price difference. *See Also: order, security*

CONTINUED BOND. A bond that never matures and continues to pay dividends indefinitely. *See Also: bond, pay*

CONTINUOUS MARKET. A security that is frequently sold, has a narrow spread, experiences minimal price changes, can be promptly executed, and is liquid. *See Also: liquid, security, spread*

CONTINUOUS NET SETTLEMENT. A settlement where the National Securities Clearing Corporation becomes the intermediary between two brokers involved in a securities transaction, creating a securities balance account. Depending on whether the firm was buying or selling, the account is adjusted up or down each day. Most securities deals are settled in this manner. *See Also: account, balance, corporation, firm, intermediary, National Securities Clearing Corporation, securities, transaction*

CONTRA BROKER. The broker handling the other side of a trade. When buying, the seller is the contra broker. *See Also: broker*

CONTRACT. An agreement between two or more individuals for which certain rights and acts are exchanged and bound by law. *See Also: rights*

CONTRACT BROKER. One stock exchange member who trades for other exchange members. *See Also: exchange, stock, stock exchange*

CONTRACT GRADES. A commodity that can be traded on a futures contract, with superior grades that carry a premium, and lower grades that sell at a discount. *See Also: at a discount, carry, commodity, contract, discount, futures, futures contract, premium*

CONTRACT SHEET. The Securities Industry Automation Corporation prepares this daily sheet from information provided to it by brokers. The sheet covers transaction information, including problems or disagreements over any pending settlement. *See Also: corporation, industry, securities, securities industry automation corporation, transaction*

CONTRACTS IN FOREIGN CURRENCY. A document in which investors agree to buy and sell a specific amount of one country's currency for another country's currency at an agreed upon rate. *See Also: currency*

CONTRACTUAL PLAN. A plan in which mutual funds are used to buy additional fund shares, with the investor agreeing to buy a specific dollar amount and paying on an installment basis. *See Also: basis, fund*

CONTRARIAN. An investor who does the opposite of other investors. This kind of investor believes, for example, that if others say the market is going up, they are only saying so because they are fully invested which means the market actually is at its peak and will begin to decline. When others say the market is going down, the contrarian believes they are saying this only because they have sold out, therefore the market actually will go up. *See Also: fully invested, market, peak*

CONTROL STOCK. Securities owned by those who have a controlling interest. *See Also: controlling interest, interest*

CONTROLLED ADJUSTABLE RATE PREFERRED STOCK. A preferred stock with a dividend that changes according to the varying Treasury security rate. The issuer maintains an asset base to make sure the company can pay changing dividends, thus making it "controlled." *See Also: asset, base, dividend, pay, preferred stock, security, stock*

CONTROLLED COMMODITIES. The trading of commodities futures is federally regulated in order to prevent fraud and manipulation in the market. *See Also: futures, manipulation, market, order*

CONTROLLED CORPORATION. One company controlled by another company, with the controlling company owning at least 51 percent of the other company's stock. *See Also: stock*

CONTROLLED FOREIGN CORPORATION. A foreign company that has five or fewer U.S. citizens with voting shares.

CONTROLLER OR COMPTROLLER. The division of a brokerage house responsible for preparing financial statements, complying with the SEC, and supervising internal audits. *See Also: brokerage house, house, SEC*

CONTROLLING INTEREST. When a person, family, or group owns more of a company's voting shares of stock than anyone else. Controlling interest is either more than 50 percent, or can be less than 50 percent if no other investor holds a higher amount of shares. For example, if Janet Jeffries owns 30 percent of the voting stock, but the remaining 70 percent is divided among 10 other people, with no one person holding more than 29 percent, Janet Jeffries still has controlling interest because no one else has enough shares of stock to out-vote her. *See Also: interest, stock, voting stock*

CONVENIENCE SHELF. A registration statement for a security that will be offered publicly for sale. While this particular registration does not require information concerning the price or the underwriter, it does stipulate the maximum number of shares that can be sold. *See Also: registration, registration statement, sale, security, statement*

CONVENTIONAL LOAN. A mortgage loan secured by real estate instead of by a government agency, and with a fixed interest rate and fixed loan payments for the life of the loan. *See Also: estate, fixed interest rate, interest, interest rate, mortgage, real estate*

CONVENTIONAL MORTGAGE. A residential mortgage loan with a fixed interest rate and term, having regular monthly payments due usually for 20 or 30 years, and secured by the property itself. A conventional mortgage is not insured or guaranteed by the Federal Housing Administration or the Veterans Administration. *See Also: fixed interest rate, interest, interest rate, mortgage, term*

CONVENTIONAL OPTION. A put or call option that was negotiated outside of a listed option market. *See Also: call option, listed option, market, option, put*

CONVENTIONAL PASS THROUGH. A security issued by a financial institution that represents a part of a mortgage pool. The government does not guarantee interest or principal. *See Also: guarantee, interest, mortgage, mortgage pool, pool, principal, security*

CONVERGENCE. The price of a futures contract moves toward the price of its underlying cash commodity as the contract nears expiration. Because of its time value, the contract price is higher at the beginning, but then goes down. *See Also: cash, cash commodity, commodity, contract, expiration, futures, futures contract, time, time value*

CONVERSION. The exchange of one type of security for another. *See Also: exchange, security*

CONVERSION CHARGE. Some mutual funds require the investor to pay a fee if he or she switches from one fund to another within the same class. *See Also: class, fund, pay*

CONVERSION PARITY. The dollar values of a convertible security and the security into which it can be converted are the same. *See Also: convertible security, security*

CONVERSION POINT. When the amount of money it takes to convert a stock or bond is equal to the security's current market price plus any accrued interest. *See Also: accrued interest, bond, current, interest, market, market price, plus, stock*

CONVERSION PREMIUM. The difference of a convertible security's market value above the price of its underlying stock. *See Also: market, market value, stock*

CONVERSION PRICE. An underlying security's value after it has been converted into common stock at the conversion ratio. *See Also: common stock, conversion, conversion ratio, ratio, stock*

CONVERSION RATE. The dollar amount of a bond's par value that can be exchanged for one share of common stock. *See Also: common stock, par, par value, share, stock*

CONVERSION RATIO. The number of company shares a convertible security can be converted into. For example, if one share of a security can be converted into 50 shares of Trumbell stock, then the conversion ratio is 50:1. *See Also: conversion, convertible security, ratio, security, share, stock*

CONVERSION VALUE. The value of the number of shares into which a convertible security can be exchanged. The conversion rate multiplied by the current market value equals the conversion value. *See Also: conversion, conversion rate, convertible security, current, current market value, market, market value, security*

CONVERTIBLE CURRENCY. Money that can be exchanged easily for a precious metal or another currency. *See Also: currency*

CONVERTIBLE DEBENTURES. A security that carries a fixed interest rate and has a specific maturity date, can be traded for stock at any time, but also provides the issuer with the right to call it in or redeem it for cash or common stock at any time. *See Also: cash, common stock, fixed interest rate, interest, interest rate, maturity, redeem, right, security, stock, time*

CONVERTIBLE HEDGE. When an investor sells short his or her shares of a company's common stock, while creating a long position with convertible bonds from the same company. *See Also: common stock, long position, position, stock*

CONVERTIBLE MORTGAGE. A mortgage, usually on commercial properties, in which pension funds receive interest, appreciation is based on any rent increases, and the fund carries an option that allows for conversion into equity ownership. *See Also: appreciation, conversion, equity, fund, interest, mortgage, option, pension*

CONVERTIBLE SECURITIES FUNDS. A mutual fund that primarily buys convertible securities. *See Also: convertible security, fund, mutual fund, securities*

CONVERTIBLE SECURITY. Corporate securities, typically preferred shares or bonds, that can be exchanged for the same company's common stock if demanded by the security holder. *See Also: common stock, securities, stock, stockholder*

CONVEXITY. Given a change in interest rates, convexity is the rate at which duration changes and helps to explain the variance between the duration estimated price and actual price of a bond. *See Also: actual, bond, change, duration, interest, variance*

CONVEYANCE. A property deed which is transferred from one person to another.

COOKED BOOKS. Falsified financial records used to entice investors to buy more shares of stock by making the records look like the company will be making outstanding profits when, in reality, it will not. *See Also: outstanding, stock*

COOKIE. A small text file stored on a computer by a Web site that the user has visited. The Web site's server, depending on how it's configured, may request the text message each time a page is requested by the browser. The main purpose of a cookie is to identify users during future visits. The server can use the cookie to identify a user for many purposes, such as customized Web pages and marketing data (tracking users' usage patterns and preferences). Cookies can also eliminate the need to input a name and password for access privileges. *See Also: name, on, server, time, Web, Web site*

COOLING OFF PERIOD. A period of time, usually 20 days, that must elapse between the filing of a registration statement with the SEC and the offering of securities to the public. *See Also: offering, registration, registration statement, SEC, securities, statement, time*

COOPERATIVE. An organization owned by its members, who pool their resources to achieve a common goal. For example, in a food cooperative, a group of people get together so they can buy large quantities of food at discount prices. *See Also: discount, pool*

COOPERATIVE BUILDING. A building which is run by tenants who own stock in a corporation that owns the building. Instead of paying rent, the tenants pay a proportionate fixed rate to cover the building's maintenance and operating costs. *See Also: corporation, fixed rate, maintenance, operating costs, pay, run, stock*

CO-OPETITION. A strategy that combines cooperation and competition. It is based on the premise that business competitors can benefit when they work together. Coopetition is based on the theory that the sum of what is gained by all participants is bigger than the collective sum of the value of each participant prior to joining. *See Also: on, participant*

COORIGINATOR. The customers of several surety companies get together to invest in a specific security. Each customer is a cooriginator. *See Also: security, surety*

COP. See Certificate of Participation. *See Also: certificate*

CORNERING THE MARKET. Holding enough shares of a security to be able to manipulate the price. *See Also: security*

CORPORATE AGENT. A trust company that acts as a corporation's or government's agent in a variety of investment transactions. *See Also: agent, investment, trust, trust company*

CORPORATE BOND. A corporation-issued, long-term debt instrument. *See Also: debt instrument, instrument, long-term debt*

CORPORATE BOND EQUIVALENT (CBE). See bond equivalent yield. *See Also: bond, yield*

CORPORATE BOND FUNDS. A mutual fund that primarily buys corporate bonds. The primary objective of these funds is usually income over growth. *See Also: fund, mutual fund*

CORPORATE BOND UNIT TRUSTS. A trust unit similar to that of the Government National Mortgage Association, but that has no principal or monthly return. *See Also: mortgage, principal, return, trust, unit*

CORPORATE EQUIVALENT YIELD. A yield from a corporate bond selling at par must equal the yield from a government security selling at a discount. *See Also: at a discount, at par, bond, corporate bond, discount, par, security, yield*

CORPORATE FINANCING COMMITTEE. A panel that works with the National Association of Securities Dealers' Board of Governors in reviewing documents that underwriters file with the Securities and Exchange Commission to make sure the underwriters' markups are fair. *See Also: commission, exchange, securities*

CORPORATE INCOME FUND. A fixed-unit investment trust containing fixed-income securities and paying net investment income each month. *See Also: investment, investment income, investment trust, net, net investment income, securities, trust*

CORPORATE INDENTURE. A document in which a bank, protecting the interest of the lender, agrees to act as an intermediary between a company issuing bonds and the investors buying the bonds. *See Also: bank, interest, intermediary*

CORPORATE REACQUISITION. A company tries to buy back its own securities through a tender offer. *See Also: offer, securities, tender, tender offer*

CORPORATE SHELL. A company that has no fixed assets other than its cash, name, and stock exchange listing. *See Also: cash, exchange, listing, name, stock, stock exchange*

CORPORATE TAX EQUIVALENT. The rate of return a par bond must carry to have the same after-tax yield to maturity as a given bond. *See Also: bond, carry, maturity, par, par bond, rate of return, return, yield, yield to maturity*

CORPORATION. An association owned by its shareholders and considered to be a legal entity. Chartered by a U.S. state or the federal government, this "legal person" may own property, incur debts, and may sue or be sued. The owners have limited liability. *See Also: legal, liability, limited liability*

CORPUS. The principal amount of a debt security, or the underlying assets in a trust agreement. *See Also: debt security, principal, principal amount, security, trust*

CORRECTION. The reversal, usually short-term, of a security's price. Reversals are common in any long-term price trend. *See Also: reversal, trend*

CORRECTIVE PHASE. A period of time in which the price of a security, a market sector or an index falls after increasing in price. The fall is considered steep, but less than a crash. *See Also: crash, fall, index, market, sector, security, time*

CORRELATION COEFFICIENT. A statistical measure of how two market movements are related. *See Also: market*

CORRESPONDENCY SYSTEM. The manner in which independent loan correspondents establish and administer mortgage loans for investors. *See Also: mortgage*

COST ACCOUNTING. This process that gives a company's management the figures needed to evaluate production costs.

COST BASIS. The original cost of an assetless depreciation. *See Also: depreciation, original cost*

COST FACTORS. A consumer credit supplier's business expenses upon which his or her fees are based. *See Also: credit*

COST LEDGER. A subsidiary's financial statement with each job, operation, process, and other expenses given a separate, detailed listing so they ultimately can be verified and reconciled with the parent company's general accounting books. *See Also: job, listing, statement*

COST OF CAPITAL. The amount of money a company could make if it invested in another venture with an equal risk. *See Also: risk*

COST OF FUNDS. A percentage of the average amount of saved or borrowed money that is paid or accrued on its interest or dividends. *See Also: average, interest*

COST OF GOODS SOLD. The amount of money spent during a specific accounting period on labor, material, and production. *See Also: accounting period*

COST PER CLICK. Also referred to as CPC. On the Web, short for the cost of one user clicking on a media advertisement, such as a banner, and proceeding to the page designated by the hyperlink. The CPC is higher for click throughs that are better targeted to specific audiences. *See Also: hyperlink, on, Web*

COST PER THOUSAND. Cost per thousand, or CPM, is short for the cost of media advertising for a thousand impressions. The CPM is higher for impressions that are better targeted to specific audiences.

COST PURCHASE ACCOUNTING. A system allowing a company that owns less than one-fifth of another company's stock to include the stock's dividends in its own income. *See Also: stock*

COST RECORDS. Documents that verify the amount of money a company spent to produce goods or to provide services, including vouchers and invoices.

COST-BENEFIT ANALYSIS. Determining whether the benefits of a specific decision will outweigh its costs. For example, a company will use the cost-benefit analysis to determine whether buying a copying machine will cost more money than it will save in labor.

COST-OF-LIVING ADJUSTMENT. Based on the Consumer Price Index, a company adjusts the salaries of its employees to compensate for changes in the amount of money it takes to live at a certain level. For example, if a company did not make cost-of-living adjustments, an employee making

$15,000 in 1975 would not be able to live in the same style in 1990 if he or she still was making $15,000. Because it costs more to live each year, the employee, in essence, would be making less. *See Also: index, level, price index*

COST-PLUS CONTRACT. A document in which a product's selling price is based on its production costs, which is added to a fixed fee. Such contracts are common on new products that have no pricing history. For example, if a company designed a machine that could translate a dog's barks into human words, the company would use a cost-plus contract because it has no other way of determining how much to charge for such a new machine. On the other hand, if the company designed a new flea collar, the price probably would be based on what other flea collars have sold for in the past. *See Also: collar, contract*

COST-PUSH INFLATION. When the costs of labor and materials go up, the prices of the goods also go up.

COSTS THEORY OF CAPITALIZATION. A system in which a company's capitalization is determined by the amount of out-of-the-pocket money that was invested in its fixed assets and by the amount of money it takes to run the company. *See Also: capitalization, run*

COSURETY. A surety company of a group executing a bond. *See Also: bond, surety*

COUGARS. Certificates on government receipts which show interest in principal or in coupon payments to be made later on particular U.S. Treasury bond issues. *See Also: bond, coupon, interest, principal, Treasury bond*

COUNCIL OF ECONOMIC ADVISORS. A panel of economists, selected by the President of the United States, that advises him on economic policies and helps him draw up a budget. *See Also: budget, president*

COUNTER-CYCLICAL SECURITIES. Corporation-issued securities in which earnings are always going in the opposite direction of the general economy. *See Also: earnings, securities*

COUNTERMAND. Canceling an order or command before the order or command has been executed. *See Also: order*

COUNTERSPECULATION. In an effort to counteract investor influence on prices, the government (in a controlled economy) determines what prices would prevail if the buyers and sellers imposed no restrictions. The government guarantees the estimated amount, then reaches the price by buying sales.

COUNTRY CODE. A two-letter code listed at the end of a top-level domain that has been assigned to countries (or geographic areas that aren't countries, such as Antarctica). For the United Kingdom, for example, the country code is listed as .uk.

COUPON. A certificate that accompanies a bond and carries the amount and the date interest is due. The certificate is torn off and presented when the investor wants an interest payment. *See Also: bond, certificate, interest*

COUPON BOND. A debt instrument with a detachable coupon. Anyone who has physical possession of the coupon can present it to an agent for payment of any interest due. *See Also: agent, coupon, debt instrument, instrument, interest*

COUPON RATE. A bond's annual rate of interest, expressed as a percentage of the bond's face value. *See Also: face value, interest*

COUPON ROLLOVER DATE. The day a new interest rate on a floating-rate security will be established. *See Also: interest, interest rate, security*

COUPON YIELD. Divide a bond's yearly interest rate by its face value, which equals the coupon rate. *See Also: coupon, coupon rate, face value, interest, interest rate*

COVARIANCE. The relationship between two variables multiplied by the standard deviation of each. *See Also: standard deviation*

COVER BID. The second highest bid in a competitive distribution.

COVERAGE RATIO. The ratio between debt instrument payments and income before taxes, indicating whether or not a company will be able to cover its debt service. *See Also: debt instrument, debt service, instrument, ratio, service*

COVERED ARBITRAGE. An investor uses forward cover-a contract for future delivery-to eliminate the exchange risks involved in an arbitrage between different currencies. *See Also: arbitrage, contract, exchange, forward*

COVERED FORWARD SALE. The owner of a commodity sells the commodity for delivery and payment at a later time. *See Also: commodity, delivery, time*

COVERED INTEREST PARITY. A forward exchange rate differential will equal the difference between foreign and domestic currency interest rates, which will bring the differential to near zero. *See Also: currency, differential, exchange, exchange rate, forward, interest*

COVERED MARGIN. The interest rate margin between two different currency instruments after considering the cost of the forward cover. *See Also: currency, forward, forward cover, interest, interest rate, margin*

COVERED OPTION. When a person who is selling an option owns either the underlying security or another option with the same terms, the sold option is considered a covered option. *See Also: option, security, underlying security*

COVERED WRITER. An investor who owns a stock sells options against that stock so he or she can collect premium income. If a person writes a call option and the stock price drops, the investor can hold on to the stock. If the price goes up, the investor probably will have to give it up to the person buying the option. *See Also: call option, hold, option, premium, premium income, stock*

CPA. Certified Public Accountant.

CPC. Cost Per Click.

CPFR. Collaborative Planning, Forecasting and Replenishment. *See Also: forecasting*

CPI. Consumer Price Index. *See Also: index, price index*

CPI-W FUTURES CONTRACT. A commodity futures contract that is based on the government's monthly urban wage and salary index. *See Also: commodity, contract, futures, futures contract, index*

CPM. Cost Per Thousand.

CPR. Constant Prepayment Rate. *See Also: prepayment*

CPU. Central Processing Unit. *See Also: processing, unit*

CRACKER. A person who, without authorization, intentionally breaches computer security to break into a computer system. A crackers intent may be malicious, to prove the vulnerability of a system, or simply for the challenge. *See Also: break, security*

CRASH. A dramatic drop in the securities market and in the economy in general. Also, the sudden failure or breakdown of computer hardware, a software application, or operating system. *See Also: drop, market, securities*

CREDIT. Any money lent through loans and bonds or money owed for the payment of goods and services.

CREDIT AGREEMENT. A contract between a broker-dealer and client when the client uses credit to purchase securities. The contract stipulates terms of the credit and the amount of margin to be maintained, as well as how interest will be charged. *See Also: broker-dealer, client, contract, credit, interest, margin, securities*

CREDIT ANALYST. A person who studies and interprets an individual's or a company's financial history to see if the individual or company is creditworthy. Analysts also look at the issuer of a corporate or municipal bond to decide the bond's credit ratio. *See Also: bond, credit, municipal bond, ratio*

CREDIT CARD SECURITY. An asset-backed security that is backed by credit card receivables. These credit card receivables are typically unsecured revolving lines of credit. Credit card payments are variable and paid monthly. When securitizing these bonds, ownership of the credit card receivables are typically sold and transferred to a bankruptcy remote subsidiary. *See Also: bankruptcy, credit, receivables, remote, security, subsidiary*

CREDIT DEPARTMENT. An area within broker-dealer firms where margin accounts are maintained and supervised, and where the financial history of a client seeking credit is investigated. *See Also: broker-dealer, client, credit, margin*

CREDIT RATING. The financial history of an individual or a company, indicating whether the person or business can repay debts. The credit rating is based on the number of outstanding debts and whether debts have been repaid in a timely manner in the past. *See Also: credit, outstanding*

CREDIT RISK. The risk that an obligation will not be completed with the result being a loss. *See Also: obligation, risk*

CREDIT SALES. A sale which time is given for a buyer to make payment. *See Also: sale, time*

CREDIT SPREAD. When the value of the long option on a security is less than that of the short option on the same security, the investor gets credit in his or her brokerage account. *See Also: account, brokerage account, credit, option, security*

CREDIT UNION SHARES. Shares that represent ownership by the members of a credit union. Under the Uniform Securities Act, these shares are not considered securities. *See Also: credit, securities*

CREDITOR. Anyone to whom money is owed.

CREDITOR'S COMMITTEE. A panel that represents creditors of a company facing bankruptcy. The panel also will represent creditors of a smaller company that is having financial problems in an effort to resolve problems and avoid bankruptcy. *See Also: bankruptcy*

CREEPING TENDER OFFER. One person, or a group working together, buys a large percentage of a newly issued stock in an effort to get control of the company without first issuing a proxy statement. *See Also: issued stock, proxy, proxy statement, statement, stock*

CRITICAL MASS. The point at which enough buyers and sellers participate in a market so goods or services change hands efficiently. Also, the time when a market achieves liquidity and gains momentum. *See Also: change, liquidity, market, momentum, point, time*

CRM. Customer Relationship Management.

CROP. The principal in an options transaction who must make sure the firm is abiding with options regulations. *See Also: firm, principal, registered options principal, transaction*

CROP YEAR. In the commodities market, the time between one agricultural harvest and the next. The crop year is different for each crop. *See Also: crop, market, time*

CROSS-CHANNEL MARKETING. A company's use of one of its sales channel to promote sales to another channel.

CROSS HEDGE. An investor owns one security, then buys or sells a different security that has similar market reaction in an effort to keep from losing money. *See Also: market, reaction, security*

CROSS ORDER. One client asks a broker to buy a security, and another client asks the same broker to sell the same security. Such orders cannot be directly paired, and must be executed through the stock exchange. *See Also: broker, client, exchange, security, stock, stock exchange*

CROSS PURCHASE. When a broker improperly executes a cross order directly without going through the stock exchange. *See Also: broker, cross order, exchange, order, stock, stock exchange*

CROSS SHAREHOLDING. Two or more companies hold shares of stock in each other. *See Also: hold, stock*

CROSSED MARKET. When one broker's bid is higher than another's lowest offer. While crossed markets sometimes occur, the National Association of Securities Dealers Automated Quotations prohibits brokers from intentionally crossing the market. *See Also: market, offer, securities*

CROWD. Group of exchange members gathering around the same post to seek executions that are not readily available. *See Also: around, exchange, post*

CROWDING OUT. When the government borrows heavily at the same time that businesses and individuals want to borrow, the government, in effect, closes out the ability of the latter two groups to borrow. The government, which can afford to pay any interest rate, crowds out individuals and businesses who cannot pay the higher rates, thus slowing down economic activity. *See Also: activity, interest, interest rate, pay, time*

CROWN JEWEL. A company's most valuable asset, with the term used primarily in attracting or dissuading takeover attempts. *See Also: asset, takeover, term*

CROWN JEWEL DEFENSE. A company's management agrees to sell the company's most valuable asset to another party in an effort to avoid a hostile takeover by a third party. By selling off its most valuable asset, the company becomes less attractive to the party threatening the takeover. *See Also: asset, takeover*

CRUMMY TRUST. A trust fund with a beneficiary who can continually accept valuable assets from anyone and, in turn, give that person an annual exclusion of up to $10,000 from federal gift taxes. *See Also: exclusion, fund, trust, turn*

CRUNCH. Financial pressures or actions which produce a financial crisis lead to poor economic conditions in a specific market or in the economy in general. *See Also: market*

CRUSH MARGIN. The amount of money a processor earns from selling the derivatives of a product, minus the cost of the product. For example, if a processor made oil and soybean meal, the crush margin would equal the gross amount the processor made after subtracting the amount he or she paid for the soybeans. *See Also: gross, margin, minus*

CRUSH SPREAD. A futures trader believes discrepancies exist between related products, such as soybeans and their derivatives, and therefore takes a spread position in the market in an effort to profit from the differences. *See Also: futures, market, position, profit, spread, spread position, trader*

CRWNS. Currency-related warrants to buy some U.S. Treasury securities that expire in one or two years. *See Also: securities*

CRYPTOLOGY. The scientific study of coding and decoding data.

CSE. Cincinnati Stock Exchange. *See Also: exchange, stock, stock exchange*

CSVLI. Cash Surrender Value. *See Also: cash*

CUFF QUOTE. Without checking the current market conditions, a person takes an educated guess at what he or she believes the bid and ask prices will be on a securities issue. *See Also: ask, current, issue, market, securities*

CULPEPPER SWITCH. A computer based in Culpepper, Virginia, that transfers federal funds and U.S. Treasury securities between the U.S. Federal Reserve System and member banks. *See Also: federal funds, Federal Reserve System, reserve, securities*

CUM DIVIDEND. An investor buying a stock cum dividend receives the dividend that was declared but not yet paid. *See Also: dividend, stock*

CUM RIGHTS. An investor buying a stock with cum rights receives the rights that were declared but not yet paid. *See Also: rights, stock*

CUMULATIVE DIVIDEND. A dividend from cumulative preferred stock that has not yet been paid. *See Also: cumulative preferred stock, dividend, preferred stock, stock*

CUMULATIVE PREFERRED STOCK. A preferred stock issue on which all dividends that have not been paid will accumulate for the shareholders and will be paid before holders of common stock receive their dividends. *See Also: common stock, issue, preferred stock, stock*

CUMULATIVE RATE OF RETURN. A rate of return that has been compounded for more than one year. *See Also: rate of return, return*

CUMULATIVE VOTING. Stockholders can have as many votes for each share they own as there are directors to be elected. For example, if there are three directors to be appointed, each stockholder is allowed three votes per share of stock. *See Also: share, stock, stockholder*

CURB EXCHANGE. The original name of the American Stock Exchange, so named because securities were traded on the street. *See Also: exchange, name, securities, stock, stock exchange, Street*

CURRENCY. Any form of money that is in public circulation.

CURRENCY DEVALUATION. The dollar's exchange rate drops because of market or government action. With devaluation, Americans can buy less from other nations with the same dollar. *See Also: devaluation, exchange, exchange rate, market*

CURRENCY FUTURES. Futures contracts on major currencies (the British pound, the German mark, and the U.S. dollar, among others) that are held by companies doing worldwide business in an effort to reduce their risks by hedging the value of their home country's currency. *See Also: currency, hedging, home, pound*

CURRENCY IN CIRCULATION. Paper money and coins that are exchanged widely and daily, as opposed to money in circulation (this also includes checking account deposits, among others). *See Also: account*

CURRENT. In budget and accounting practices, this designates the operations of the present fiscal period. *See Also: budget, operations*

CURRENT ACCOUNT. A bank account from which the depositor can withdraw funds at any time. *See Also: account, bank, time*

CURRENT ASSETS. All of a company's assets that probably will be converted into cash within the company's fiscal year. For example, accounts receivable are considered current assets. *See Also: accounts receivable, cash, current, fiscal year*

CURRENT COUPON BOND. A debt instrument that has a coupon interest rate that is near its yield to maturity. Such bonds have a competitive cash flow and interest rates that are less likely to change. *See Also: and interest, cash, cash flow, change, coupon, debt instrument, instrument, interest, interest rate, maturity, yield, yield to maturity*

CURRENT COUPON MBS. The coupon of the mortgage-backed security that is trading closest to par. *See Also: coupon, generic securities, par, securities, security*

CURRENT FACE. The monthly remaining principal, or outstanding loan balance, of a mortgage-backed security. This is computed by multiplying the original face by the factor of the current principal balance. *See Also: balance, current, factor, original face, outstanding, principal, principal balance, security*

CURRENT LIABILITIES. All of a company's debts that are payable within the company's fiscal year. For example, a mortgage payment is considered a current liability. *See Also: current, fiscal year, liability, mortgage*

CURRENT MARKET VALUE. The value of a security based on its closing price of the previous day. *See Also: closing price, security*

CURRENT MATURITY. The amount of time left before a bond matures. *See Also: bond, time*

CURRENT PRODUCTION RATE. The maximum interest rate that may be placed on current Government National Mortgage Association mortgage-backed securities. These securities will normally pay half of a percentage point below the current rate to cover clerical expenses. *See Also: current, interest, interest rate, mortgage, pay, point, securities*

CURRENT RATIO. A company's current assets divided by its current liabilities, which provides a measure of liquidity. *See Also: current, current assets, current liabilities, liquidity*

CURRENT SINKER. In an operative bond with a sinking fund obligation, the company must retire part of the outstanding bond issue by exercising a call or through an open market purchase. *See Also: bond, fund, issue, market, obligation, open, open market, outstanding, retire, sinking fund*

CURRENT VALUE ACCOUNTING. An accounting system in which a person's assets are measured according to current prices instead of the prices the person paid when buying the assets. *See Also: current*

CURRENT YIELD. A security's dividend divided by its current market value. *See Also: current, current market value, dividend, market, market value*

CURTSY. The legal interest a man has in any property in his deceased wife's estate. *See Also: estate, interest, legal*

CUSHION BOND. A callable bond with a market price that is artificially suppressed because of its call price, which helps the bond remain stable during a time of intense interest rate changes. *See Also: bond, call price, callable bond, interest, interest rate, market, market price, time*

CUSIP NUMBER. A number assigned by the Committee of Uniform Security Identification Procedure that appears on the face of all securities documents. Each security is given its own number in order for it to be easily identified. *See Also: committee, order, securities, security*

CUSP. Mortgage-Backed Securities that are on the verge of being called due to early prepayments of the underlying loans held by mortgagors. *See Also: securities*

CUSTODIAL ACCOUNT. An account that an adult creates for a minor child. Since the social security number used on the account is that of the minor, all returns are listed on the child's income tax documents. Minors can only make transactions with the custodian's consent. These may only be cash accounts, not margin. *See Also: account, cash, margin, security*

CUSTODIAN. An agent such as a broker or a bank that stores a customer's investments. *See Also: agent, bank, broker*

CUSTOM POOLS. Also known as multiple-issuer pools, these mortgage-backed pools have one issuer, but different interest rates. All interest rates vary within one percentage point. *See Also: interest, point*

CUSTOMER RELATIONSHIP MANAGEMENT. Also referred to as CRM, the services, tools and strategies to support customer relationships, increase customer satisfaction and to minimize potential problems. CRM software achieves this by collecting and analyzing data to customize service, detect patterns that suggest better ways to serve customers. Two ways to determine customers' preferences include transparency, in which the customers' needs are learned without the customers' involvement, and collaboratively, which includes direct communications with the customers. *See Also: service, support*

CUSTOMER SUPPORT. The range of services provided by businesses to assist the use of its products by its customers. Support may come in the forms of telephone, in-person or in-store visits, Web content, and e-mail. *See Also: e-mail, range, support, Web*

CUSTOMER'S FREE CREDIT BALANCE. The amount of money an investor has in his or her brokerage account that is available for use. *See Also: account, brokerage account*

CUSTOMER'S MAN. Synonymous with "Registered Representative" and "Account Executive," but rarely used as more women enter the industry. *See Also: account, industry*

CUSTOMER'S NET DEBIT BALANCE. The New York Stock Exchange provides credit to its member firms so the firms can, in turn, finance their own customers' securities purchases. *See Also: credit, exchange, New York Stock Exchange, securities, stock, stock exchange, turn*

CUTOFF POINT. The least amount of return permitted in an investment. *See Also: investment, return*

CUTTING A LOSS. An individual takes his or her money out of an investment that is losing money and accepts the loss instead of leaving the money in and losing even more. *See Also: investment*

CUTTING A MELON. Profits, either from securities or employee bonuses, are distributed by either cash or stock dividends. *See Also: cash, securities, stock*

CYBERFRAUD. Using the Internet to deprive of a right, money, or property by fraud. *See Also: Internet, right*

CYBERSPACE. A reference to a digital world constructed by computer networks, in particular the Internet. Cyberspace was first used by author William Gibson in his novel "Neuromancer." *See Also: digital, Internet*

CYBERSQUATTING. Registering a trademarked, branded or otherwise generally recognized Internet domain name for the purpose of reselling it at a profit. *See Also: domain name, Internet, name, profit*

CYCLE. A constant pattern of reversals.

CYCLICAL STOCK. Securities such as those in automobile manufacturing plants and real estate ventures that rise quickly when the economy is on the upswing and fall when the economy drops. Noncyclical stocks include those in companies that produce items people need no matter what the economy is doing, such as food and drugs. *See Also: estate, fall, real estate*

D

DAILY ADJUSTABLE TAX EXEMPT SECURITIES. A municipal industrial development revenue bond with interest calculated daily and distributed monthly. It also provides that the holder can redeem the bond at any time for its face value plus any accrued interest. *See Also: accrued interest, bond, face value, industrial, interest, plus, redeem, revenue bond, time, with interest*

DAILY BOND BUYER. A daily newspaper directed toward the municipal bond industry, with additional news included for fixed-income investors. *See Also: bond, industry, municipal bond*

DAILY TRADING LIMIT. The maximum rise or decline permitted by many commodity and option markets in one trading session. *See Also: commodity, option, session*

DATA MINING. Analyzing data via sophisticated data mining software to help companies learn more about their customers by exploring relationships and trends among customers with common interests.

DATE OF MATURITY. The designated day an obligation must be paid. *See Also: obligation*

DATE OF RECORD. The last day a new purchaser will be entitled to a dividend. If an investor buys stock before the date of record, he or she will be entitled to receive a dividend from the stock. *See Also: dividend, stock*

DATE OF TRADE. The day a buy or sell order is executed. *See Also: order, sell order*

DATED DATE. The effective date of a new bond issue, after which accrued interest is calculated. For example, if the dated date is December 2, and the issue is settled on December 14, the buyer pays the issuer 12 days of accrued interest, but will get the money back when he or she receives the first interest payment. *See Also: accrued interest, bond, effective date, interest, issue*

DATED EARNED SURPLUS. The amount of a company's retained earnings that have accumulated since the company reorganized. This date must be included when the company reports its retained earnings. *See Also: earnings, retained earnings*

DATING. A financial institution extends a company's line of credit further than the institution's usual terms. Financial institutions commonly will do this with companies that have seasonal businesses so the companies can continue operating during the lean months. *See Also: credit, line of credit*

DAWN RAIDS. A British company quickly buys a large block of another company's stock at a premium price. *See Also: at a premium, premium, stock*

DAY LOANS. Money that banks or other financial institutions lend to brokers, which brokers need to use as working capital for that particular day. *See Also: capital, working capital*

DAY ORDER. A buy or sell order that expires when the exchange closes for the day. Usually, all buy and sell orders are day orders unless otherwise specified. *See Also: exchange, order, sell order*

DAY TRADE. The purchase and sale of a stock in the same day. *See Also: daylight trading, sale, stock*

DAY-TO-DAY REPO. An open-ended repurchase agreement that expires after one day. If it is not canceled, it is renewed automatically at an adjusted interest rate. *See Also: interest, interest rate, repurchase, repurchase agreement*

DAYLIGHT TRADING. Buying a security and then selling it the same day. *See Also: day trade, security*

DE FACTO CORPORATION. A company formed in good faith that in some way failed after there was an act of corporate power.

DEAD CAT BOUNCE. Also referred to as bounce, a temporary and moderate recovery in a security or index after a steep decline. *See Also: bounce, index, recovery, security*

DEAD MARKET. A market with little trading and little interest or activity. *See Also: activity, interest, market*

DEALER. A person who buys and sells securities for his or her own account and at his or her own risk. A company also can be a dealer. *See Also: account, risk, securities*

DEALER ACTIVITIES. Usually refers to a bank that takes on the responsibilities of a dealer by trading and underwriting securities. *See Also: bank, dealer, securities, underwriting*

DEALER BANK. A bank that continuously deals in government and agency securities. *See Also: bank, securities*

DEALER FINANCING. A bank or other financial institution that loans a market maker money so that the market maker can carry an inventory of stocks and bonds. *See Also: bank, carry, inventory, maker, market, market maker*

DEALER LOAN. A bank loans a market maker money to finance its trading position. *See Also: bank, maker, market, market maker, position*

DEALER MARKET. A market in which all securities are traded between principals for their own accounts, not for the accounts of clients. *See Also: market, principals, securities*

DEALER PAPER. Commercial paper an issuer sells to a broker-dealer, who then marks it up and sells it to institutional investors. *See Also: broker-dealer, paper*

DEALER'S TURN. A broker-dealer's profit when he or she buys a security at bid and sells at the offer price. *See Also: offer, profit, security*

DEALING FOR NEW TIME. In England, a security is bought or sold in the last two days of an account trading period for the next period. *See Also: account, security*

DEALING WITHIN THE ACCOUNT. In England, either a buy and a sell, or a short securities sale and an agreement to buy the securities back within the same accounting period. *See Also: accounting period, sale, securities*

DEATH SENTENCE. All utilities companies must be registered with the Securities and Exchange Commission, and no utility company can have more than three levels (i.e., the parent company, a subsidiary, and a sub-subsidiary). Any other affiliate or holding company must be dissolved. *See Also: affiliate, commission, exchange, holding company, securities, subsidiary, utility*

DEATH STOCK. Stock of a company facing bankruptcy or liquidation. *See Also: bankruptcy, liquidation*

DEBENTURE. A long-term corporate debt instrument issued without any collateral. *See Also: collateral, debt instrument, instrument, long-term corporate debt*

DEBENTURE BOND. A long-term debt instrument that has no collateral other than the issuing company's general credit. *See Also: collateral, credit, debt instrument, instrument, long-term debt*

DEBENTURE STOCK. A security that has fixed payments at designated intervals. As with a preferred stock, a debenture stock's liquidity is in its equity, not in its debt like a normal debenture. *See Also: debenture, equity, intervals, liquidity, preferred stock, security, stock*

DEBIT. A bank account entry subtracting a specific amount of money; the opposite of a credit. *See Also: account, bank, credit*

DEBIT DISCOUNT. When the proceeds of a loan are lower than the note's face value. *See Also: face value, proceeds*

DEBIT SPREAD. When an option sold is cheaper than an option bought, thus creating a debit in the investor's brokerage account. *See Also: account, brokerage account, debit, option*

DEBT FINANCING. Notes or bonds that are issued so a company can meet its financial obligations.

DEBT INSTRUMENT. Any certificate that represents a loan. *See Also: certificate*

DEBT LIMIT. The maximum amount of money the government can legally owe.

DEBT MONETIZING. The Federal Reserve System issues new fiat money (U.S. currency) to pay off government debt. *See Also: Federal Reserve System, fiat money, pay, reserve*

DEBT RATIO. A company's total debt divided by its assets.

DEBT RETIREMENT. A financial obligation that has been repaid in full. *See Also: full, obligation*

DEBT SECURITY. Any security that represents a loan. *See Also: security*

DEBT SERVICE The annual principal and interest payment on a debt, as required by the debt issuer. *See Also: and interest, interest, principal*

DEBT SERVICE FUND. A fund that pays for an account held to receive interest and principal on general obligation debts. *See Also: account, fund, interest, obligation, principal*

DEBT SERVICE REQUIREMENT. The amount of money needed to pay interest on a debt, the serial maturities of a serial bond, and money paid to a debt service fund. *See Also: bond, debt service, debt service fund, fund, interest, pay, service*

DEBT-EQUITY RATIO. Divide a company's long-term debt by stockholders' equity to determine the level of risk involved in the company's financial structure. *See Also: equity, financial structure, level, long-term debt, risk*

DEBT-EQUITY SWAP. One securities issuer exchanges a new issue from another company for an outstanding bond from that same company. By lowering the company's mount of long-term debt, such a swap often can increase the company's earnings. *See Also: bond, earnings, exchanges, issue, long-term debt, new issue, outstanding, securities, swap*

DEBT-TO-EQUITY RATIO. A gauge that measures the amount of leverage a company's financial structure has, usually achieved by dividing the par value of the company's preferred stock by its common stock equity, and adding that quotient to the company's long-term debt. *See Also: common stock, equity, financial structure, leverage, long-term debt, par, par value, preferred stock, stock*

DECAPITALIZE. Withdrawing an investment from a company. *See Also: investment*

DECAY. The gradual loss of premium over time in an options or futures contract. Also a client disclaiming connection with responsibility for a trade. *See Also: client, contract, futures, futures contract, premium, time*

DECLARATION DATE. The day a company announces it will pay dividends, when it will pay them, and how much they will be. *See Also: pay*

DECLARE. An authorization by a company's board of directors to pay a dividend on a particular day. *See Also: board of directors, dividend, dividend on, pay*

DEDICATED BOND PORTFOLIO. An investment portfolio, such as a retirement fund, aimed at making future payments with the most cash flow possible from the bonds contained in the portfolio. *See Also: cash, cash flow, fund, investment, investment portfolio, portfolio*

DEDICATED LINE. A telecommunications line that provides a direct, permanent connection to the Internet. Examples of dedicated lines include: Internet access through a cable line, T1 line or DSL connection. *See Also: cable, DSL, Internet, T1 line*

DEDUCTION. An IRS-allowed subtraction of an expense from one's adjusted gross income in determining a person's taxable income. These expenses may include charitable contributions, state and local taxes and interest paid. *See Also: adjusted gross income, and interest, expense, gross, interest, local, taxable income*

DEEP BID. A significant, away-from-the-market bid.

DEEP DISCOUNT BOND. A debt instrument issued at par and currently selling for less than 80 percent of its par value. *See Also: at par, debt instrument, instrument, par, par value*

DEEP WEB. *See Also: invisible Web, Web*

DEFALCATION. When a fiduciary or representative misappropriates funds. *See Also: fiduciary*

DEFAULT. When a debtor fails to either pay interest or repay the principal of a loan. *See Also: fails, interest, pay, principal*

DEFEASANCE. A government or corporation erases a debt from the balance sheet by floating a second bond to retire the first. *See Also: balance, balance sheet, bond, corporation, retire*

DEFEASED BOND-EQUITY SWAP. A bond guarantor swaps its common stock for the same amount of U.S. Treasury securities, which are put in escrow until maturity or until their earliest call date, when they are used to retire the first debt. The dealer who arranged the swap pays for the U.S. Treasury securities by selling the common stock. *See Also: bond, call date, common stock, dealer, escrow, maturity, put, retire, securities, stock, swap*

DEFENSIVE INDUSTRY. A company that does not suffer financially when the economy is poor, such as a utilities company, and therefore does better than the general market during a recession. *See Also: market, recession*

DEFENSIVE INVESTING. Putting money into securities that are safe and stable, even though the profits may not be as great, to avoid risking a loss. *See Also: securities*

DEFENSIVE PORTFOLIO. A group of investments that won't go up or down drastically, with emphasis placed on the safety of the investments. *See Also: safety*

DEFENSIVE STOCKS. Stocks that tend to be more stable in times of recession or economic uncertainty in regard to terms of dividends, earnings, and market performance. *See Also: earnings, market, recession*

DEFERRAL OF TAXES. A company or person can put off paying certain taxes until a later year. *See Also: put*

DEFERRED ACCOUNT. Any account, such as an Individual Retirement Account, on which taxes can be paid in a later year. *See Also: account, individual retirement account*

DEFERRED ANNUITY. An annuity that will not make payments until a specified future date. *See Also: annuity*

DEFERRED ASSET. An asset that cannot be converted easily into cash. *See Also: asset, cash*

DEFERRED CHARGES. Expenditures on an asset carried forward over a period of time. These are usually monies a company spends to improve the long-term outlook of its business. *See Also: asset, forward, time*

DEFERRED GROUP ANNUITY CONTRACT. A single premium deferred annuity bought for each person covered in an insured pension plan. The amount of the annuity is equal to the amount the person has accrued in benefits for each year. *See Also: annuity, deferred annuity, pension, pension plan, premium*

DEFERRED INTEREST BOND. A bond such as a zero-coupon bond that does not pay interest until a later date. *See Also: bond, interest, pay*

DEFERRED PAYMENT ANNUITY. An annuity agreement in which the annuitant deposits premiums in a lump sum or in installments at a later date. *See Also: annuitant, annuity*

DEFERRED PAYMENT NOTE. A debt security with a fixed rate that requires a 25 percent initial payment, with the final payment due several months later. *See Also: debt security, fixed rate, security*

DEFERRED PROFIT-SHARING PLAN. A company-sponsored retirement plan, with the company donating either 20 percent of the employee's wages or $3,500, whichever is greater, thus reducing taxable income for the year. *See Also: taxable income*

DEFERRED SPECIAL ASSESSMENTS. An amount of money that has been assessed against a company or an individual, but has not yet come due.

DEFERRED STOCK. A security with a dividend that will not be paid until after a specific date or until after a designated event has occurred. *See Also: dividend, security*

DEFICIENCY LETTER. A letter the Securities and Exchange Commission provides a security issuer during registration of a security. The letter advises the issuer that the registration is inadequate, and changes in the registration must be made before the SEC can approve the security. *See Also: commission, exchange, registration, SEC, securities, security*

DEFICIT. A company's liabilities and debts exceed its income and assets, or a company's spending exceeds its budget. *See Also: budget*

DEFICIT FINANCING. The government borrows money to issue bonds in order to compensate for a revenue shortfall. This procedure strengthens the general economy temporarily, but ultimately becomes a drain because it pushes up interest rates. *See Also: interest, issue, order*

DEFICIT NET WORTH. Liabilities exceed assets and capital stock. *See Also: capital, capital stock, stock*

DEFICIT SPENDING. The government spends more money than it takes in. This deficit must be financed through borrowing. *See Also: deficit*

DEFINED BENEFIT PLAN. A pension plan stipulating the exact amount of money the beneficiary will receive. *See Also: pension, pension plan*

DEFINED CONTRIBUTION PLAN. A pension plan stipulating the exact amount of money the participant must contribute. *See Also: participant, pension, pension plan*

DEFINITIVE SECURITY. A permanent security issued to replace a temporary certificate, which may have been offered on a new issue. *See Also: certificate, issue, new issue, security*

DEFLATION. A drop in general price levels, usually caused by increased demand for money that isn't offset by an increased money supply, or a drop in the money supply that isn't offset by a drop in the demand for money. *See Also: demand, demand for money, drop, in the money, money supply, offset, supply*

DEFLATOR. Used to adjust the difference between one value and the same value as it is affected by inflation. *See Also: inflation*

DEFLECTION OF TAX LIABILITY. One person's tax burden is shifted to someone else.

DEGREE OF COMBINED LEVERAGE. Combining a company's operating leverage and financial leverage creates a gauge of the company's earnings per share variability. *See Also: earnings, leverage, share, variability*

DEGREE OF FINANCIAL LEVERAGE. A company's fixed financing costs create a gauge of the company's earnings per share variability. *See Also: earnings, share, variability*

DEGREE OF OPERATING LEVERAGE. A company's fixed operating costs create a gauge of the company's earnings before interest and taxes. *See Also: earnings, interest, operating costs*

DEL CREDERE AGENCY. An agency that tries to guarantee a client that a buyer will pay off his or her debt. *See Also: client, guarantee, pay*

DELAY. The amount of time elapsed from the first day of the month that the security was purchased to the first payment date that interest and principal is paid. *See Also: interest, payment date, principal, security, time*

DELAYED DELIVERY. A securities contract is settled after a regular delivery of the security, which usually is after five business days. *See Also: contract, delivery, securities, security*

DELAYED DELIVERY CONTRACT. A contract for an agreed-upon future date of the purchase or sale of a security. The specific security is not included in the contract. This also may be known as a TBA (to be announced), because the seller has not identified certain terms of the contract as of the trade date. *See Also: contract, sale, security, TBA, trade date*

DELAYED ITEMS. Transactions that occurred in a previous year.

DELAYED OPENING. The opening of trading for a security is delayed temporarily, usually when there are a lot of buy and sell orders for it and the market specialist wants to maintain an orderly market. *See Also: lot, market, security, specialist*

DELINQUENCY. Failure to meet a financial obligation. *See Also: obligation*

DELIST. A company's fights to list its securities on the exchange is withdrawn, usually because the firm has stopped meeting the minimum requirements. After delisting, the security still can be traded over the counter. *See Also: exchange, firm, over the counter, securities, security*

DELIVERABLE BILLS. Treasury bills that meet the requirements on the exchange on which it is traded. *See Also: exchange*

DELIVERY. An options exercise or a futures contract is fulfilled by handing over the stock certificates or the commodity. *See Also: commodity, contract, exercise, futures, futures contract, stock*

DELIVERY AGAINST COST. *See Also: COD transaction, transaction*

DELIVERY DATE. The specific day a futures contract will be delivered. *See Also: contract, futures, futures contract*

DELIVERY NOTICE. The seller confirms that he or she will deliver a stock or commodity on a specific day at a specific place. *See Also: commodity, stock*

DELIVERY POINT. Where a commodity that is covered by a futures contract can be delivered to fill the contract. *See Also: commodity, contract, fill, futures, futures contract*

DELIVERY PRICE. The price settled on for a commodities contract. *See Also: contract*

DELIVERY VERSUS PAYMENT. Payment for a security must be made when the security is delivered. Usually, the payment is made to a bank, which in turn pays for the stock certificates. *See Also: bank, security, stock, turn*

DELTA. The change in an option premium for each single point of change in the underlying security's price. For example, a delta of 0.5 means a stock's premium goes up by half of a point for each point the underlying stock goes up. *See Also: change, option, option premium, point, premium, stock*

DEMAND. The amount of interest in a security or commodity. *See Also: commodity, interest, security*

DEMAND AND SUPPLY CURVES. A graph of the highest buying and lowest selling prices on a specific security at a particular time and place. *See Also: security, time*

DEMAND DEPOSIT. A customer's deposited assets that are available to be drawn upon by a check or a draft. For example, if a customer deposited an amount of money in his or her checking account, that amount would constitute a demand deposit. *See Also: account, check, demand, draft*

DEMAND FOR MONEY. The portion of a person's wealth that he or she holds in money, as opposed to investing it.

DEMAND LINE OF CREDIT. A bank customer can borrow a predetermined amount of money from the bank each day. *See Also: bank*

DEMAND LOAN. A loan that has no maturity date and must be repaid immediately upon the lender's demand. *See Also: demand, maturity*

DEMAND MORTGAGE. A mortgage that must be repaid in full upon the lender's demand. *See Also: demand, full, mortgage*

DEMAND NOTE. A loan that is due immediately upon demand. *See Also: demand*

DEMAND PRICE. The most amount of money a buyer will pay for a specific security or commodity. *See Also: commodity, pay, security*

DEMAND-PULL INFLATION. When demand is greater than supply, inflation results. Increased demand causes prices to go up, which causes wages to go up, and thereby causes the costs for goods and services to go up as well. *See Also: demand, inflation, supply, to go*

DEMOGRAPHIC TRENDS. A gauge that measures how population trends will affect specific industries.

DEMONETIZATION. A currency or currency base that is taken out of circulation. *See Also: base, currency*

DEMONSTRATION. A sudden and unexpected change in a security's activities. *See Also: change*

DENIAL OF SERVICE ATTACK. Also referred to as DOS attack, the deprival of Internet resources or services by a user, who would ordinarily be able to gain access. This is oftentimes a malicious attack, though it can be accidental. Though a DOS attack is a security breach to a computer system, it usually does not result in theft. *See Also: gain, Internet, security*

DENOMINATION. The number of shares appearing on the face of a security, or the principal amount appearing on the face of a bond. *See Also: bond, principal, principal amount, security*

DEPLETION. A figuratively stated amount of money that a company sets aside from its annual earnings to replace a natural asset-such as lumber from a forest or oil from a well-that is being used up and cannot be replaced. Because the asset cannot be replaced, the company usually gets a tax break on the amount. *See Also: annual earnings, asset, break, earnings*

DEPLETION ALLOWANCE. The Internal Revenue Service allows companies to take a tax deduction for wasted assets. *See Also: deduction, internal revenue, service, take*

DEPLOYMENT. Money from a fund is distributed into asset categories. *See Also: asset, fund*

DEPOSIT ACCOUNT. A bank account with withdrawal restrictions that normally provides a higher rate of interest than regular accounts. *See Also: account, bank, interest*

DEPOSIT ADMINISTRATION CONTRACT. An insurance company's unallocated account which is held for active participants in a pension plan. The participants receive annuities after they retire. *See Also: account, insurance, pension, pension plan, retire*

DEPOSITORY. A bank that accepts deposits of securities and government funds. *See Also: bank, securities*

DEPOSITORY INSTITUTIONS DEREGULATION COMMITTEE. An ad-hoc panel that creates government-insured, interest-bearing deposit accounts at financial institutions to compete with mutual funds.

DEPOSITORY PREFERRED STOCK. A preferred stock with a high par value that is deposited with a bank, which then issues more shares of a preferred stock with a lower par value. The lower-valued stock is entitled to a portion of the deposited security's interest. *See Also: bank, interest, par, par value, preferred stock, stock*

DEPOSITORY TRUST COMPANY. A firm through which members can use a computer to arrange for securities to be delivered to other members without physical delivery of the certificates. A member of the Federal Reserve System and owned mostly by the New York Stock Exchange, the Depository Trust Company uses computerized debit and credit entries. *See Also: credit, debit, delivery, depository, exchange, Federal Reserve System, firm, New York Stock Exchange, reserve, securities, stock, stock exchange, trust, trust company*

DEPRECIATED COST. A fixed asset's original cost minus all accumulated depreciation. *See Also: depreciation, minus, original cost*

DEPRECIATED CURRENCY. The exchange value of a currency drops, and the currency no longer can be accepted at face value. *See Also: currency, exchange, face value*

DEPRECIATION. An amount of money that represents a tangible asset's drop in value over time. The amount is subtracted from the asset's purchase price to give its residual value. For example, an automobile depreciates each year the more it is used. The more miles that are racked up, the more wear and tear the car goes through, the greater the depreciation becomes. *See Also: drop, purchase price, residual value, time*

DEPRECIATION FUND. Money or securities set aside and designated to replace depreciating fixed assets. *See Also: securities*

DEPRESSED PRICE. A security's price is lower than it should be when considering the issuing company's financial condition.

DEPRESSION. A long-term decline in living conditions.

DEPTH. The amount of general interest investors show in the market, representing the number of issues traded compared to the number of issues listed. Logically, the more issues traded, the greater the market depth. Depth also describes the market's ability to absorb a large buy or sell order without a dramatic change in the security's price. *See Also: change, interest, market, order, sell order*

DEREGULATION. Stopping or cutting down government control over a particular industry in an effort to free the market and promote competition. *See Also: industry, market*

DERIVATIVE MEDIUM TERM NOTE (DMTN). A structured security whose value is linked to the value of another financial instrument, such as interest rate indices, foreign-exchange rates, financial indices, or equities. *See Also: financial instrument, instrument, interest, interest rate, security*

DERIVATIVE SUIT. A stockholder sues the issuing corporation, charging that the officers did not protect the best interest of the corporation. In essence, the stockholder is suing the corporation on behalf of the corporation. *See Also: corporation, interest, stockholder*

DERIVED DEMAND. The need for a good or service as a result of the demand for another good or service. *See Also: demand, service*

DESCENDING TOPS. A bearish chart pattern in which each new high price for a security is lower than the security's last high price. *See Also: chart, new high, security*

DESIGNATED CONCESSION. A syndication order for a number of securities that designates nonmembers of the account who will receive the concession for the securities' sale. *See Also: account, concession, order, sale, securities*

DESIGNATED NET. Someone who is not a member of the Municipal Securities rule making board gives an order, to be executed at the public offering price. The order, given to a municipal security syndicate, directs that the concession be credited to the accounts of at least three syndicate members. Municipal investors often use designated net to reward account members who have come up with valuable ideas. *See Also: account, concession, net, offering, offering price, order, public offering, public offering price, securities, security, syndicate*

DESIGNATED OPTIONS EXAMINING AUTHORITY. A panel responsible for overseeing individual broker-dealers.

DESIGNATED ORDER. Orders given to a municipal syndicate, designating one or more members of the syndicate to receive credit for the sale. These types of orders are generally from large institutions. *See Also: credit, sale, syndicate*

DESIGNATED ORDER TURNAROUND. A computer New York Stock Exchange members use to route market orders from one to 499 shares directly to a market specialist, who represents the orders. If the specialist cannot find a contra broker, he or she executes the order against the book. If the specialist can make the deal immediately, he or she does not charge the member a fee. *See Also: book, broker, contra broker, exchange, market, New York Stock Exchange, order, specialist, stock, stock exchange*

DESTINATION CLAUSE. A contract that allows an oil monopoly to designate what nations will get its oil, which in turn keeps the oil out of the spot market. *See Also: contract, market, monopoly, spot, spot market, turn*

DETAILED AUDIT. When all of a company's internal control systems, financial ledgers, and subsidiary records are examined extensively and completely for accuracy. *See Also: internal control, subsidiary*

DETERMINATION DATE. The last day in a month that a person can deposit money in a savings account and still earn interest from the first day of the month. *See Also: account, interest, savings account*

DETROIT STOCK EXCHANGE. This exchange is used primarily for trading unlisted securities. *See Also: exchange, securities*

DEUTSCHE MARK. German currency, commonly referred to as a mark. *See Also: currency*

DEVALUATION. A drop in one country's currency when it is exchanged for another country's currency. For example, if the U.S. dollar was worth 1,200 Italian lire yesterday and devalues 1,100 today, a person with lire could buy more American goods today than he or she could have bought yesterday. *See Also: currency, drop, worth*

DEVELOPMENTAL DRILLING PROGRAM. Drilling for oil and gas in an area that previously has produced oil and gas. While the program usually provides a stable income, it normally does not yield enormous profits. *See Also: yield*

DIAGONAL SPREAD. An investor takes long and short positions in the same class of options with different strike prices and different expiration dates. *See Also: class, expiration*

DIAMOND INVESTMENT TRUST. A trust fund that invests in diamonds, but where the investors do not have physical possession of the stones. *See Also: fund, trust*

DIARY. A listing of maturity dates for financial instruments. *See Also: listing, maturity*

DIFFERENTIAL. A fee paid to a dealer, usually 1/8 of a point, for completing an odd-lot transaction. Or, when the dealer increases his or her quoted fee to a customer because the customer is buying or selling a small amount of securities. *See Also: dealer, point, securities, transaction*

DIFFERENTIAL DUTY. Different duties two blocks of the same commodity may be subject to depending on their place of origin, the type of labor involved in their production, or some other factor. *See Also: commodity, factor*

DIGESTED SECURITIES. Securities owned by an investor who plans to hold onto them for a long time. *See Also: hold, time*

DIGITAL. An electronic representation of words, numbers, sound, or graphics. This digital data is represented as the binary digits 0 and 1, and can be understood by computers. Before digital technology, electronic transmission was limited to analog systems, which is represented by an electrical signal or wave, which changes in amplitude and frequency. *See Also: signal, technology*

DIGITAL CASH. *See Also: e-cash.*

DIGITAL CERTIFICATE. Online identification using encryption that authenticates an individual or business. *See Also: encryption*

DIGITAL SIGNATURE. An electronic representation of a signature, in the form of a graphical impression of a handwritten signature or one based on encryption, which electronically verifies the identification of the sender. *See Also: encryption, on*

DIGITAL SUBSCRIBER LINE. *See Also: DSL*

DIGITAL SUBSCRIBER LOOP. *See Also: DSL*

DIGITAL WALLET. Encryption software that stores the information required to conduct an e-commerce transaction. This information includes credit card numbers, and shipping and billing information. The information may be stored in a third-party's database as part of a service, or in the user's computer system. *See Also: credit, e-commerce, service, transaction*

DIGITS DELETED. A designation on the exchange tape that appears when the tape has been delayed, displaying only the variations instead of the variations and the digits. *See Also: exchange, tape*

DILUTION. When a company issues additional shares of stock even though its income has not increased, the company's equity ratio, earnings per share, and book value per share will drop. *See Also: book, book value, book value per share, drop, earnings, equity, ratio, share, stock*

DIME. Equal to 10 basis points, or 0.1 percent, on a debt security's yield. *See Also: basis, yield*

DINGO. Nickname for Australia's discounted investment in negotiated government obligations. These are government-issued securities that do not carry coupons and are sold at a discount. *See Also: at a discount, carry, discount, investment, securities*

DIP. A slight drop in securities prices in an upward trend, usually marking a good time to buy. *See Also: drop, marking, securities, time, trend*

DIRECT EARNINGS. Earnings of a parent company without the upstream dividends of its subsidiaries.

DIRECT FINANCING. Raising money without using an underwriter.

DIRECT INVESTMENT. Equity is invested in property, securities, and service companies. *See Also: securities, service*

DIRECT PAPER. A commercial paper a company sells directly to the public without going through a broker-dealer. *See Also: broker-dealer, commercial paper, paper*

DIRECT PARTICIPATION PROGRAM. A partnership agreement that calls for tax consequences to flow through to participants. *See Also: partnership*

DIRECT PLACEMENT. An issuer sells a new security directly to institutional clients without using a broker. *See Also: broker, security*

DIRECT PROCUREMENT. The purchasing of raw materials and parts necessary for the manufacturing of finished goods.

DIRECT REDUCTION MORTGAGE. A mortgage that is liquidated in equal payments throughout the life of the loan. As regular payments reduce the amount of principal, the interest rate drops accordingly. *See Also: interest, interest rate, mortgage, principal*

DIRECTED COLLATERAL REMICS. A CMO bond backed by two or more subsets of collateral with cash flows directed to specific groups or classes within a REMIC. *See Also: bond, cash, CMO, collateral, REMIC*

DIRECTED TRUST. A fund, such as a pension plan, that allows the owner to tell the trustee how to invest the money. *See Also: fund, pension, pension plan, trustee*

DIRECTOR. A person who serves on a company's board.

DIRTY. A British stock that is cum divided and is near the date when interest will be paid. *See Also: interest, stock*

DISBURSEMENT. Funds paid in the discharge of an expense or debt. *See Also: expense*

DISBURSING AGENT. A person responsible for paying interest or dividends to stockholders. *See Also: interest*

DISC. The Domestic International Sales Corporation enables American companies to compete with subsidized foreign companies by providing tax advantages to foreign exporters of American goods. *See Also: corporation, Domestic International Sales Corporation*

DISCHARGE OF BANKRUPTCY. An order that ends a bankruptcy procedure and removes the debtor from all financial responsibilities. *See Also: bankruptcy, order*

DISCLOSURE. A company must report all of its management practices, its financial situation, and its legal involvement, when it could influence an investment decision. *See Also: investment, legal*

DISCONTINUOUS MARKET. Securities that are not listed from a separate market. *See Also: market*

DISCOUNT. The difference between a security's redemption value and its current market price. *See Also: current, market, market price, redemption, redemption value*

DISCOUNT BOND. A bond that once sold near par, but that now sells for less. *See Also: bond, par*

DISCOUNT BROKER. A broker who charges a lower fee because he or she executes transactions but provides clients no other services, such as investment advice. *See Also: broker, investment*

DISCOUNT ON SECURITIES. The difference in amounts when a security is traded for less than its par value. *See Also: par, par value, security*

DISCOUNT RATE. The interest rate member banks pay the Federal Reserve when they use securities as collateral. Banks use the rate to determine the lowest interest rate they will charge loan customers. For example, if the bank is paying the Federal Reserve nine percent interest, it will not loan a customer funds with an interest rate below nine percent. *See Also: bank, collateral, interest, interest rate, pay, reserve, securities*

DISCOUNT WINDOW. A place provided by the Federal Reserve where member banks borrow against collateral at the discount rate. *See Also: collateral, discount, discount rate, reserve*

DISCOUNT YIELD. A yield obtained by dividing a security's discount by its face value, multiplying that number by the approximate number of days in the year (360), divided by the number of days left to maturity. The figure provides the interest on a security's face value instead of on the amount of money invested. *See Also: discount, face value, interest, maturity, yield*

DISCOUNTED CASH FLOW. The value of expected cash receipts and expenses on one specific day. A discount rate is based either on the marginal cost of capital to future cash flow, or on the current value of future cash flow to the original cost of the investment. *See Also: capital, cash, cash flow, cost of capital, current, discount, discount rate, investment, marginal cost, original cost*

DISCOUNTED VALUE. The current value of future obligations, as determined by a specific interest rate. *See Also: current, interest, interest rate*

DISCOUNTING THE NEWS. When the price of a stock or the level of one of the markets moves up or down, in anticipation of good or bad news. *See Also: anticipation, level, stock*

DISCRETIONARY ACCOUNT. A brokerage account that allows an employee of an exchange-member firm to make investment decisions on the client's behalf, such as buying and selling, choosing securities, when to buy or sell, and at what price to buy or sell. *See Also: account, brokerage account, firm, investment, securities*

DISCRETIONARY INCOME. The money a person has available after paying all of his or her bills.

DISCRETIONARY ORDER. An employee of an exchange-member firm agrees to a buy or sell order because he or she has only a limited power of attorney over a client's account. *See Also: account, firm, order, power of attorney, sell order*

DISCRETIONARY POOL. One group of people authorizes another group of people to buy and sell securities on the first group's behalf. *See Also: securities*

DISCRETIONARY TRUST. A trust fund or mutual fund that can be invested in any way and is not limited to a particular security. *See Also: fund, mutual fund, security, trust*

DISHONORED. A financial instrument that is rejected after it is offered for payment. *See Also: financial instrument, instrument*

DISINFLATION. When price inflation drops without going below zero. *See Also: inflation, price inflation*

DISINTERMEDIATION. An investor who deposited money with a portfolio intermediary withdraws the money and directly invests it in securities. Also, the displacement of a middleman, or intermediary, in the process of a producer or manufacturer selling directly to a consumer. *See Also: intermediary, portfolio, securities*

DISINVESTMENT. Capital goods are eliminated or capital assets are not maintained or replaced, thus reducing the capital investment. *See Also: capital, investment*

DISPOSABLE INCOME. All money a person has left after paying taxes. Disposable income includes money used to pay bills as well as discretionary income. *See Also: discretionary income, pay*

DISPROPORTIONATE IN QUANTITY. When more than 100 shares, or bonds, with face values totaling more than $5,000 are sold to anyone representing or associated with an underwriter, or to officers of financial institutions.

DISSOLUTION. When a company disbands after its charter expires, either voluntarily or through a government order. *See Also: charter, order*

DIST. Appears on exchange tapes to represent an exchange distribution. *See Also: exchange, exchange distribution*

DISTRESS SELLING. Selling a security out of necessity. *See Also: security*

DISTRIBUTING SYNDICATE. A group of brokers or banks that unite to distribute a large block of securities. *See Also: securities*

DISTRIBUTION AREA. A security has not changed in price much in a long time. The distribution area is this narrow price range. *See Also: price range, range, security, time*

DISTRIBUTION DATE. The day a company pays its stockholders interest or dividends. *See Also: interest*

DISTRIBUTION OF RISK. An investment is spread out over several areas instead of being concentrated on one specific security, which could prove financially disastrous if that one security bottomed out. *See Also: investment, security, spread*

DISTRIBUTION STOCK. After a shelf registration, the issuer's affiliates publicly sell the stock. *See Also: registration, shelf registration, stock*

DISTRIBUTOR. Wholesaler or middleman of securities to the retailers. *See Also: securities*

DISTRICT BUSINESS CONDUCT COMMITTEE. A panel, appointed by district members of the National Association of Securities Dealers (NASD), that hears complaints of unfair trade practices lodged against either an NASD member or someone associated with an NASD member. *See Also: NASD, National Association of Securities Dealers, securities*

DITHERING. The simulation of a display of colors that are not in the color palette of an image. *See Also: color*

DIVERGENCE. When market trends go in a different direction than market indicators predicted, usually signaling the onset of a trend change. *See Also: change, indicators, market, trend*

DIVERSIFICATION. An investor reduces his or her financial risk by spreading his or her investment over a large number of securities, instead of risking it all in one area. *See Also: investment, risk, securities, spreading*

DIVERSIFIED. When 75 percent or more of a management investment company's assets are in four different types of cash or securities, no more than five percent of its total assets can be invested in one issuer's security, and the company holds no more than 10 percent of any issuer's voting shares. *See Also: cash, investment, securities, security*

DIVERSIFIED COMMON STOCK FUND. An investment firm that holds a diversified stock portfolio, with the portfolio value following the market's general trends. *See Also: diversified, firm, investment, portfolio, stock*

DIVERSIFIED HOLDING COMPANY. A company that controls several other companies, but that does not participate in their management or day-to-day operations. *See Also: operations*

DIVEST. To sell or get rid of an investment. *See Also: investment*

DIVESTITUTE. One company that was holding a large block of stock in another company distributes the stock. *See Also: block of stock, stock*

DIVIDED ACCOUNT. Each member of an underwriting syndicate is responsible for his or her allocation only, and not the allocation of any other member. *See Also: account, allocation, eastern account, syndicate, underwriting, underwriting syndicate*

DIVIDEND. The amount of money or securities distributed out of net profits to the company's shareholders. *See Also: net, securities*

DIVIDEND APPROPRIATIONS. The amount of a company's retained income that will be paid in dividends for outstanding preferred or common stock. *See Also: common stock, outstanding, stock*

DIVIDEND CAPTURE. A tactic where a company buys stock shares right before the dividend is paid, holds it for a while, and then sells it without losing any money. The company profits greatly because it pays only a minimal amount of taxes on dividend income. *See Also: dividend, right, stock*

DIVIDEND CLAIM. A person buying stock asks the registered holder for the amount of the dividend because the trade was made before the ex-dividend. The actual transfer was not completed until after the record date. *See Also: actual, dividend, ex-dividend, record date, registered holder, stock, transfer*

DIVIDEND DEPARTMENT. The area in a broker-dealer's firm where employees accept and pay clients those dividends from securities for which the firm is responsible. *See Also: firm, pay, securities*

DIVIDEND DISBURSING AGENT. A financial institution that pays clients interest and dividends on certain securities. *See Also: interest, securities*

DIVIDEND EXCLUSION. The dollar amount of nontaxable dividends.

DIVIDEND ON. A person buys stock with the understanding that he or she will receive the next dividend payment. *See Also: dividend, stock*

DIVIDEND ORDER. A document asking the issuing corporation to send dividend checks to a specific address. *See Also: address, corporation, dividend*

DIVIDEND PAYOUT RATIO. A ratio calculated by dividing the amount of a company's earnings that is available for common stock by the annual common stock dividend. The quotient provides a gauge for comparing different companies. For example, a company with a low ratio probably is considered a growth company. *See Also: common stock, dividend, earnings, low, ratio, stock, stock dividend*

DIVIDEND PRICE RATIO. The difference between the current dividend rate and the stock's market price. *See Also: current, dividend, market, market price*

DIVIDEND RECORD. A newsletter published by Standard & Poors listing dividend payments and the dividend policies of securities issuers. *See Also: dividend, listing, securities, Standard & Poors*

DIVIDEND REINVESTMENT PLAN. Instead of receiving cash dividends, investors can put the money into buying more shares of the security. *See Also: cash, put, security*

DIVIDEND REQUIREMENT. The amount of money a company needs to earn annually in order to pay dividends on preferred stock. *See Also: order, pay, preferred stock, stock*

DIVIDEND ROLLOVER PLAN. A plan in which stocks are bought shortly before the announcement that dividends will be paid, then sold shortly thereafter. By doing this, the investor can make a small profit and collect the dividend. *See Also: dividend, profit*

DIVIDEND WARRANT. A document ordering a corporation to pay dividends to stockholders. *See Also: corporation, pay*

DIVIDEND YIELD. Derived by dividing a stock's market price per share into its dividend per share. *See Also: dividend, market, market price, share*

DIVIDENDS PAYABLE. The exact dollar amount of a dividend. *See Also: dividend*

DIVIDENDS PER SHARE. The amount of money an investor receives in dividends for each share of stock he or she owns. *See Also: share, stock*

DK (DON'T KNOW). Refers to a dealer who receives a confirmation but does not recognize the trade. The receiver replies by sending a DK notice. *See Also: confirmation, dealer, receiver*

DMTN. Derivative Medium Term Note. *See Also: note, term*

DNE. An acronym for "discretion not exercised." DNE appears on order tickets after a client has given a broker a discretionary order, but ultimately made the deal without the broker. *See Also: broker, client, discretionary order, order*

DOCUMENTED DISCOUNT NOTES. A Federal Reserve Discount Bank member bank qualifies this commercial paper as collateral as long as it is accompanied by a different commercial bank's letter of credit or an unrelated private insurance company guarantee. *See Also: bank, collateral, commercial paper, credit, discount, guarantee, insurance, letter of credit, member bank, paper, reserve*

DOG AND PONY SHOW. A broker-dealer firm puts on a seminar to introduce a company's new product or service in an effort to attract the interest of its representatives. *See Also: broker-dealer, firm, interest, service*

DOLLAR BONDS. A long-term municipal debt instrument quoted in dollars instead of its yield to maturity; or foreign bonds denominated in U.S. dollars. *See Also: debt instrument, instrument, yield*

DOLLAR CONTROL. A company guides its inventory based on the amount of money it has, instead of on the number of tangible assets it has. *See Also: inventory*

DOLLAR COST AVERAGING. *See Also: constant dollar plan.*

DOLLAR CREDIT. A bank issues this document so that a customer can draw drafts in dollars. *See Also: bank*

DOLLAR DRAIN. The amount that a foreign country's U.S. imports exceed its U.S. exports. Because the country pays more for the American goods it takes in than it receives for its own goods, the country's dollar supply dwindles. *See Also: supply*

DOLLAR PREMIUM. British investors must pay this additional fee when they buy dollars to invest outside of the country. *See Also: pay*

DOLLAR PRICE. A bond's cost is expressed as a percentage of its face value. For example, a bond with a face value of $1,000 is quoted at 95.5. The bond's dollar price would be 95.5 percent of the face value, or $955. *See Also: bond, face value*

DOLLAR ROLL. A transaction in which an investor of a mortgage-backed security agrees to sell the security to another investor, while agreeing to buy back a similar mortgage-backed security for a specified price on a specified date. The investor who sells the security gives up the cash flows during the roll period, but instead has use of the proceeds. Dollar Rolls are typically used to cover short positions, take advantage of an arbitrage situation, or obtain attractive financing rates for other investments. *See Also: arbitrage, cash, proceeds, security, take, transaction*

DOLLAR SHORTAGE. Occurs when a foreign country that imports American goods runs out of dollars, and must borrow money from the U.S. before it can import anything else from the U.S.

DOLLAR STABILIZATION. An attempt by the government to stop fluctuations in the U.S. dollar's foreign exchange rate. *See Also: exchange, exchange rate, foreign exchange, foreign exchange rate, stop*

DOLLAR STOCKS. British description of U.S. securities. *See Also: securities*

DOLLAR VALUE OF A BASIS POINT (DVBP). The change in the value of a security for a one basis point shift in yield. *See Also: basis, basis point, change, point, security, yield*

DOLLAR WEIGHTED RATE OF RETURN. A gauge of an investment fund's growth rate, measuring the cash flow's weight on the fund's assets during a specific time period. *See Also: cash, investment, time*

DOLLAR-DENOMINATED FOREIGN CURRENCY OPTION. An option that allows the purchase of a foreign currency at an exercise price denominated in U.S. dollars. *See Also: currency, exercise, exercise price, foreign currency, option*

DOMAIN EXPERTISE. Experience within a particular industry or field. *See Also: industry*

DOMAIN NAME. The address that identifies an Internet site, consisting of two parts; the name, followed by the highest subdomain, whether a country code (such as .fr for France) or a commercial code (such as .com). The DNS translates the IP address is into the domain name. *See Also: address, country code, Internet, ip, ip address, name*

DOMAIN NAME SYSTEM. A process that translates an IP address into a domain name. For example, a numeric address like 111.111.111.1 can become abc.com. *See Also: address, domain name, IP, IP address, name*

DOMESTIC CORPORATION. An American company, or a company operating in the same country in which it was created.

DOMESTIC INTERNATIONAL SALES CORPORATION. *See Also: DISC.*

DON'T FIGHT THE TAPE. Some analysts say it is not wise to trade securities against the general market trend. *See Also: market, market trend, securities, trend*

DONATED CAPITAL STOCK. Stockholders donate capital stock shares back to the issuing company. *See Also: capital, capital stock, stock*

DONATED SURPLUS. A stockholder's equity account is credited when the stockholder donates stocks back to the issuing company. *See Also: account, equity, stockholder, stockholder's equity*

DONOGHUE'S MONEY FUND AVERAGE. A weekly listing, published in many newspapers, of seven- and 30-day money market fund yields, along with money fund portfolio maturities, with short maturities indicating that interest rates will go up. *See Also: fund, interest, listing, market, money market, money market fund, portfolio*

DORMANT ACCOUNT. A brokerage account that has not had any activity for a long time. *See Also: account, activity, brokerage account, time*

DORMANT PARTNER. A person who is a partner in a business and who financially benefits from profits and suffers from losses but who is not publicly associated with the business.

DOS ATTACK. Denial of Service Attack. *See Also: service*

DOUBLE AUCTION MARKET. Buyers and sellers constantly vary their prices in an attempt to make the market. When the investor making the highest offer and the seller with the lowest asking price agree on a price, a transaction is made. *See Also: market, offer, transaction*

DOUBLE BOTTOM. Occurs when a stock drops to the same low price twice. Analysts use the double bottom to determine if a stock will continue a decline. Usually, they will predict further decline if the stock drops to that level a third time. *See Also: bottom, level, low, stock, time*

DOUBLE DECLINING BALANCE METHOD. A method of calculating accelerated depreciation with the IRS permitting twice the rate of annual depreciation as the straight-line method. *See Also: accelerated depreciation, depreciation, IRS*

DOUBLE DIGIT INFLATION. Inflation reaching 10 percent or more.

DOUBLE DIPPING. A company issues industrial revenue bonds so it can build a project in the same city that issued the bonds. The company raises the finances at lower rates, then uses accelerated depreciation to get the money back. *See Also: accelerated depreciation, City, depreciation, industrial*

DOUBLE ENDORSEMENT. A note or other negotiable instrument with two signers. If one fails to meet the obligation, the other will become responsible. Both signers are equally responsible for the instrument. *See Also: fails, instrument, negotiable, negotiable instrument, note, obligation*

DOUBLE ENTRY. When one financial account entry shows an increase, another entry must show either an increase or decrease so that all of the debits equal all of the credits. *See Also: account*

DOUBLE EXEMPTION BOND. A bond, usually municipal, with the holder and issuer in the same state, that is free from federal and state taxes. *See Also: bond*

DOUBLE TAXATION. The government taxes dividends of shareholders after it already has taxed a corporation's profits.

DOUBLE TOP. When a stock hits the same peak high price twice. Analysts use the double top to determine if a stock will continue to go up. Usually, they will predict further increases if the stock reaches that peak a third time. *See Also: peak, stock, time, to go, top*

DOUBLE WITCHING HOUR. The time from 3 to 4 p.m. on the third Friday of eight months of the year institutional traders have their last chance to close out June stock-index options and futures positions before the options expire. *See Also: close, futures, time*

DOUBLE-BARRELED. The interest and principal of a municipal revenue bond guaranteed by a municipality, which will make payments out of its tax revenues if necessary. For example, if the school board issues a bond to build a children's museum, but the museum ultimately does not bring in enough money to pay the principal and interest, the city will use its tax revenues to make up any differences. *See Also: and interest, bond, City, interest, municipal revenue bond, pay, principal, revenue bond*

DOW JONES AVERAGE. A composite of the price movement of 65 stocks, including 30 industrials, 20 transportation, and 15 utilities. *See Also: composite, movement*

DOW JONES BOND AVERAGE. An index of six bond groups that represent the general bond market's strength. *See Also: bond, index*

DOW JONES COMMODITY FUTURES INDEX. An index of 12 commodities that represent the strength of the commodities market. The index is based on such data as average prices, trading volume, among other factors. *See Also: average, index, market, trading volume, volume*

DOW JONES INDUSTRIAL AVERAGE. A composite of the price movement of 30 actively traded industrial stocks which purports to reflect the overall stock market movement. *See Also: composite, industrial, industrial stocks, market, movement, stock, stock market*

DOW JONES MUNICIPAL INDEX. The average weekly market value of discounted municipal bonds. *See Also: average, market, market value*

DOW JONES TRANSPORTATION AVERAGE. An index of 20 transportation companies that measures the transportation market's strength. *See Also: index*

DOW THEORY. The theory that no market trend will last longer than a year unless such a trend is indicated by the movements of the industrial, transportation, and utility averages. *See Also: averages, industrial, market, market trend, trend, utility*

DOWN GAP. When the lowest price in a given market day is higher than the highest price of the next day, an open space appears on the stock chart. *See Also: chart, market, open, stock*

DOWN MARKET. A trend of declining market prices. *See Also: market, trend*

DOWN REVERSAL. A sudden drop in prices after prices had been moving up. *See Also: drop*

DOWN ROUND. A venture capital round of financing that is priced at a lower valuation than the previous round. *See Also: capital, valuation, venture capital*

DOWN TREND. A dropping security price that looks like it will continue to go down. *See Also: security, to go*

DOWN UNDER BONDS. A Eurobond from Australia or New Zealand that is not registered in the U.S. American investors can buy "down under" bonds only after they have been traded in Europe for a long time. *See Also: Eurobond, time*

DOWN-AND-OUT OPTION. A block of 10 or more call options with the same exercise price and expiration date, stipulating that if the underlying security's price drops a specific amount, the contract is canceled. *See Also: contract, exercise, exercise price, expiration, expiration date*

DOWNDRAFT. A stock market decline. *See Also: market, stock, stock market*

DOWNLOAD. To copy or receive a file from one computer to another over the Internet. *See Also: Internet*

DOWNSIDE PROTECTION. The range a security's price must drop before an investor starts to lose money. *See Also: drop, range*

DOWNSIDE RISK. A prediction of a security's lowest value probably in the future.

DOWNSIDE TREND. A continuing long-term drop in a security's price. *See Also: drop*

DOWNSTAIRS MERGER. A merger between a parent company with one of its subsidiaries. *See Also: merger*

DOWNSTREAM. A corporation's financial activity, such as a loan, that flows from a parent company to its subsidiary. *See Also: activity, subsidiary*

DOWNSTREAM BORROWING. A company borrowing money using the credit standing of one of its subsidiaries. *See Also: credit*

DOWNTICK. An exchange-listed security that is sold for less than the last regular-way transaction involving the same security. *See Also: security, transaction*

DOWNTURN. A financial cycle that begins to go down. For example, when a bullish market becomes bearish, the market is experiencing a downturn. *See Also: cycle, market, to go*

DOWPAC. An over-the-counter Dow Jones option contract that allows the holder to buy or sell a block of eight stocks. Most of these stocks are the blue-chip stocks Dow uses to calculate its industrial averages. *See Also: averages, contract, industrial, option, option contract*

DRAFT. An instrument used to transfer money from one person's account to another's, with the debit appearing only after the instrument is presented for payment. *See Also: account, debit, instrument, transfer*

DRAG ALONG RIGHTS. The right given to a majority shareholder to influence, or drag, minority shareholders to participate in the sale of a company. All shareholders, minority or majority, are given the same terms and conditions. *See Also: majority shareholder, right, sale, shareholder*

DRAINING RESERVES. The Federal Reserve System cuts down the amount of available money banks can loan out by decreasing the money supply. This is usually done through raising reserve requirements, increasing the interest rates at which banks borrow money from the government, and selling bonds at attractive rates. *See Also: Federal Reserve System, interest, money supply, reserve, supply*

DRAWBACK. The syndicate manager has taken back some of the issues the underwriter was selling to his or her customers so that the manager can sell the shares to institutional accounts. *See Also: manager, syndicate, syndicate manager*

DRAWN SECURITIES. A security ready to be redeemed. *See Also: security*

DREW'S ODD-LOT THEORY. A theory that advises investors to sell if odd-lotters were buying, and to buy if odd-lotters were selling, because odd-lotters' actions are indicators of general market trends. *See Also: indicators, market*

DRIED UP. A buying or selling order is removed from the market. *See Also: market, order*

DRIVE. Manipulation of the market by sellers by forcing prices down, which is illegal. *See Also: market*

DROP. In a Dollar Roll transaction, the drop is the difference between the initial selling price and the predetermined repurchase price. *See Also: dollar roll, repurchase, transaction*

DROP LOCK. A feature on a floating-rate note that allows the holder to convert the note into a fixed-rate note if overall interest rates drop to a predetermined level. *See Also: drop, interest, level, note*

DROP LOCK SECURITY. A feature on a floating rate security that allows the holder to exchange the security for a fixed-rate security if the popular interbank loan rate drops to a predetermined level. *See Also: exchange, level, security*

DRT. An abbreviation, meaning "disregard tape" that appears on orders when the buyer or seller wants the floor broker to use his or her own discretion in determining when to execute the transaction and how much the price should be. *See Also: broker, floor, floor broker, transaction*

DSL. Short for Digital Subscriber Line or Digital Subscriber Loop, a technology that enables the two-way transmission of data over phone lines at very high speeds. *See Also: digital, digital subscriber line, digital subscriber loop, subscriber, technology*

DU-OP SECURITY. A dual option security in which the holder can have his or her choice of an issue of common stock or an issue of preferred stock. *See Also: common stock, issue, option, preferred stock, security, stock*

DUAL BANKING. American banks are chartered either by the state or the federal government, creating differences in regulations and services provided to customers.

DUAL CURRENCY YEN BONDS. A Japanese security with interest paid in yen and the principal paid in a different currency. *See Also: currency, interest, principal, security, with interest, yen*

DUAL EXCHANGE MARKET. Occurs when the same people operate two exchange markets, using one for specific types of underlying transactions, and the other for dealing in the foreign exchange market. *See Also: exchange, foreign exchange, market*

DUAL MUTUAL FUNDS. A fund with portfolios invested in capital growth issues and income investments. *See Also: capital, capital growth, fund*

DUAL PURPOSE FUND. A closed-end mutual fund with one type of share that gives holders all dividends and interest income, and a second type that gives holders the benefits of capital gains earned when the securities are sold. *See Also: and interest, capital, fund, interest, mutual fund, securities, share*

DUAL SAVINGS PLAN. Two different authorities can post savings deposits and account withdrawals. *See Also: account, post*

DUAL SERIES ZERO-COUPON DEBENTURE. In an effort to attract two different markets, a company issues a short-term, zero-coupon note, as well as a long-term, fixed-coupon bond at the same time. *See Also: bond, note, time*

DUAL TRADING. An investor trades the same security on two different exchanges at the same time. *See Also: exchanges, security, time*

DUAL-PURPOSE INVESTMENT COMPANY. A closed-end investment firm that issues income and capital shares, with the owners receiving all of the interest, dividends, and profits. *See Also: capital, firm, interest, investment*

DUALLY LISTED. A security listed on more than one stock exchange. *See Also: exchange, security, stock, stock exchange*

DUE ANNUITY. A clause that requires annuity payments to begin being paid immediately. *See Also: annuity*

DUE BILL. A broker selling a security attaches this document, which gives the buyer title of ownership to the security when it is delivered. *See Also: broker, security*

DUE DILIGENCE. Representatives of an underwriting syndicate who make sure that all available information on a new issue is released. *See Also: issue, new issue, syndicate, underwriting, underwriting syndicate*

DUE ON SALE CLAUSE. A mortgage clause stating that if the property is sold, the entire balance of the loan must be paid immediately, eliminating the possibility of a mortgage assumption. *See Also: balance, mortgage*

DUFF AND PHELPS. A Chicago firm that numerically rates banks, finance companies, and industrial and utility securities. *See Also: firm, industrial, securities, utility*

DULL. When prices of securities do not change much and trading is relatively inactive. *See Also: change, securities*

DUMB TERMINAL. A device with no built-in processing capabilities that consists of a display monitor and a keyboard that facilitates the transmission of data to and from a network server or mainframe computer. *See Also: mainframe, processing, server*

DUMMY. A person who acts on behalf of someone else in a business situation. The dummy controls the other person's votes, but has no personal financial interest or ownership. *See Also: interest*

DUMMY INCORPORATORS. A group of people who act as incorporators at a company's inception, then resign and transfer their interest to the real owners. *See Also: interest, transfer*

DUMMY STOCKHOLDER. A person who holds stock in his or her name when the stock actually belongs to someone else. By doing this, the actual owner's name is kept confidential. *See Also: actual, name, stock*

DUMP. To sell a security at a reduced price just to get rid of it. *See Also: security*

DUMPING. Selling a large number of stocks with little concern about their market price. *See Also: market, market price*

DUN & BRADSTREET. A firm that deals in collection services and credit reporting, used primarily by brokers and dealers. *See Also: credit, firm*

DUN'S NUMBER. The Dun's Market Identifier, or the Data Universal Numbering System, is included in a list of companies. The list contains identification numbers, farm names, addresses, numbers of employees, corporate affiliations, etc. *See Also: market*

DURABLE POWER OF ATTORNEY. One person acts on behalf of another if the other becomes mentally or physically disabled.

DURATION. The average time to receipt of all the cash flows of a bond weighted by the present value of each of the cash flows. The duration value of the bond gives bond investors an indication of how interest rate changes will affect the bond's price. It is the percentage by which the bond's price will move, given a 100 basis point change in yield. *See Also: average, basis, basis point, bond, cash, change, indication, interest, interest rate, point, present value, time, yield*

DUTCH AUCTION. An auction format in which the seller offers property at successively lower prices until a point is reached where all the property is sold to the highest bidders at the lowest price. The Dutch auction process draws its name from traditional flower auctions in Holland. It has long been used for other types of financial transactions such as stock buybacks and IPOs. *See Also: auction, IPO, security*

DUTCH AUCTION RATE TRANSFERABLE SECURITIES. An adjustable rate, preferred, nonconvertible stock with a dividend rate that is reset every 49 years through competitive bidding. *See Also: dividend, stock*

DUTY. A tax on imported or exported goods.

DVBP. Dollar Value of a Basis Point. *See Also: basis, basis point, point*

DWARFS. Fannie Mae mortgage-backed securities collateralized by 15-year mortgages. *See Also: securities*

DYNAMIC COMMERCE. Business transactions with prices not set, but adjusted according to a set of rules, such as in an auction format.

DYNAMIC HTML. Also referred to as DHTML, the production of Web content that changes dynamically in the browser window, created by combining HTML with interactive languages, such as JavaScript. *See Also: HTML, JavaScript, Web, window*

DYNAMITER. A broker who uses the telephone to try to sell unregistered or outright fraudulent stocks and bonds. *See Also: broker*

E

E. Appears in newspaper stock listings to designate that an item has been either declared or paid within the last year. Also, a commonly-used prefix that refers to "electronic." *See Also: stock*

E-BUSINESS. Short for electronic business, this refers to any online business related activity, including transactions, information sharing, and communications. *See Also: activity, online*

E-CASH. Money that is downloaded into an online bank account or onto a computer chip, whether a computer or a smart card. E-cash is primarily targeted at small transactions, typically under $10 and can be even less than a penny. The money can then be used online, by transferring it from an online bank account or the computer. E-cash can also be used in the offline world by transmitting it from a computer or handheld PDA, or a smart card. *See Also: account, bank, offline, online, PDA*

E-CHECK. Electronic check. *See Also: check*

E-COMMERCE. Short for electronic commerce, this refers to the buying and selling of goods and services over the Internet. *See Also: commerce, Internet*

E-FRASTRUCTURE. An underlying foundation, such as equipment and support services, of an Internet-based organization or system. E-frastructure components can include servers and software applications. *See Also: foundation, support*

E-LEARNING. Internet-based training or education, using electronic forums such as video-conferencing, e-mail, and online chat. *See Also: e-mail, online*

E-MAIL. Short for Electronic Mail, e-mail is a way of sending electronic messages or other data via local or global networks, such as the Internet. *See Also: electronic mail, Internet, local*

E-MAIL ADDRESS. The electronic mail address is a string of characters used to specify the source or destination of an electronic message. On the Internet, addresses follow an established protocol, beginning with an identifier, @, then the hosting server (e.g., name@domain name). *See Also: address, electronic mail, hosting, Internet, name, on, protocol, server*

E-MARKETPLACE. *See Also: e-markets*

E-MARKETS. Electronic marketplaces where buyers and sellers assemble to do conduct business.

E-RETAILING. Electronic retailing refers to Internet-based consumer-oriented retail stores that facilitate online transactions. *See Also: online*

E-TICKET. Electronic ticket.

E-TRADE. Electronic trading.

E-WALLET. *See Also: digital, digital wallet*

EACH WAY. Commissions earned by a broker on the buy and the sell of a trade. *See Also: broker*

EAGLE. A restricted and tightly-controlled computer system at the New York Stock Exchange containing corporate information. *See Also: exchange, New York Stock Exchange, stock, stock exchange*

EARLY EXERCISE. A person holding an options contract exercises the contract before it expires. *See Also: contract, options contract*

EARLY MOVER ADVANTAGE. The competitive edge of an individual or company establishing itself as an early player in a market. *See Also: market*

EARLY OWNERSHIP MORTGAGE. Contains the provision that the first six years of payments are sufficient to pay off the loan in 30 years, and after the six years, the loan payments will increase, but the interest rate will stay the same. With this type of mortgage, the loan will be paid off in less than 30 years. *See Also: interest, interest rate, mortgage, pay*

EARLY WITHDRAWAL PENALTY. If a person holding a fixed-term investment withdraws his or her money before the investment matures, the person is charged this fee. *See Also: investment*

EARN-OUT. Future payments that must be made after someone buys a business if that business's profits exceed a predetermined limit. The buyer pays the seller if such rights are specified in the contract. *See Also: contract, limit, rights*

EARNED GROWTH RATE. The yearly compounded internal rate that reinvesting earnings causes a company's per share equity to grow. *See Also: earnings, equity, share*

EARNED INCOME. Any income from wages or taxable gifts.

EARNED SURPLUS. The amount of money a company keeps in its business after dividends are paid.

EARNEST MONEY. To seal a deal, one person signing a contract gives the other signer this money, which is forfeited if the person who gave the money fails to honor the contract. *See Also: contract, fails*

EARNING ASSETS. The loans and investments that comprise most of a bank's profits.

EARNING POWER. The amount of money an asset or security is expected to earn and the current value of those earnings. *See Also: asset, current, earnings, security*

EARNINGS. A company's profits after paying all expenses, but before paying dividends.

EARNINGS BEFORE TAXES. The amount of money a company has after it pays dividends but before it pays taxes.

EARNINGS PER SHARE (EPS). A company's net profit minus its preferred stock obligations, with the difference divided by the number of outstanding shares of common stock. *See Also: common stock, minus, net, net profit, outstanding, preferred stock, profit, stock*

EARNINGS PRICE RATIO. The relationship between a security's earnings per share and its current price. This earnings yield compares the benefits of and differences between bonds, money markets, and stocks. *See Also: current, earnings, earnings yield, share, yield*

EARNINGS REPORT. A document that provides an accounting of a company's income, expenses, profits, and losses.

EARNINGS STATEMENT. A written review of a company's earnings, such as an income statement. *See Also: earnings, income statement, statement*

EARNINGS SURPRISE. A company's earnings report that differs positively or negatively from the consensus forecast. *See Also: consensus forecast, earnings, earnings report*

EARNINGS YIELD. A security's earnings divided by its market price. *See Also: earnings, market, market price*

EASIER. Dropping bid prices.

EASTERN ACCOUNT. Also known as a divided account, this is an underwriting system, usually with municipal bonds, wherein an entire syndicate assumes responsibility for the success of the distribution of that amount. For example, if one firm has 20 percent participation but sells more, that firm will be responsible for 20 percent of any remaining securities. *See Also: account, divided account, firm, securities, syndicate, underwriting*

EASY MONEY. An expanded money supply, which creates an economy in which money is readily available for loans. *See Also: money supply, supply*

EBIT. Designates a company's earnings before it pays any interest or taxes. *See Also: earnings, interest*

ECN. Electronic Communications Network.

ECONOMETRICS. The relationship among such economic forces as government policies, labor, interest rates, and capital expressed in mathematical terms derived from a computer. Through these terms, economic changes can be tested. For example, an econometric theory may study the relationship between the government's policy on agriculture and food prices at the supermarket. *See Also: capital, interest*

ECONOMIC GROWTH RATE. The annual percentage change in the Gross National Product. If the growth rate drops during two consecutive quarters, the country is in a recession. If the growth rate increases during two consecutive quarters, the country's economy is expanding. *See Also: change, gross, recession*

ECONOMIC INDICATORS. Gauges of the nation's economic strength, such as wages and prices, with emphasis on whether that strength will grow or dwindle in the future.

ECONOMIC LIFE. When a fixed asset can be depreciated against a company's current earnings; the life of the asset's usefulness. *See Also: asset, current, fixed asset*

ECONOMIC RECOVERY TAX ACT OF 1981. Among other things, this legislation provided an across-the-board tax cut to U.S. citizens, indexed tax brackets to interest rates, lowered the marriage penalty tax, reduced estate and gift taxes, and lowered the rates of exercising stock options. *See Also: estate, interest, stock*

EDGAR. The Electronic Data Gathering, Analysis, and Retrieval is a Securities and Exchange Commission computer that allows registered securities issuers to file reports with the SEC by computer instead of having to file physical documents. *See Also: commission, exchange, SEC, securities*

EDUCATION IRA. An IRA for the education of parents' children that allows up to $500 a year contributions for each child under age 18. The money grows tax-deferred, and withdrawals are tax-free once the child enters college. *See Also: IRA, up*

EFFECTIVE ANNUAL YIELD. The amount of money an investment makes as expressed in its equivalent simple interest rate. *See Also: interest, interest rate, investment, simple interest*

EFFECTIVE DATE. The day a newly registered security can be offered for sale, which normally is 20 days after the registration statement is filed. *See Also: registered security, registration, registration statement, sale, security, statement*

EFFECTIVE DEBT. The total amount of money a company owes.

EFFECTIVE DURATION. A measure used to quantify a bond, which contains embedded options, such as call features, put feature, or sinking fund features. This is calculated by determining the difference in price of a bond given a small change in interest rates, with the percentage change in price representing the bond's effective duration. *See Also: bond, change, duration, fund, interest, put, sinking fund*

EFFECTIVE EXCHANGE RATE. A spot exchange rate the public has either paid or received, including taxes, subsidies or banking commissions paid on the transaction, with all rates falling within the allowed margin near par. *See Also: exchange, exchange rate, margin, par, spot, spot exchange rate, transaction*

EFFECTIVE GROSS REVENUE. A company's total income minus any collection losses, contingencies, and vacancies, but before the company deducts any amount for operating expenses. *See Also: minus*

EFFECTIVE LIFE. The amount of time left on an unexecuted order, or the expected duration of a self-amortizing security. *See Also: duration, order, security, time*

EFFECTIVE MARGIN (EM). For a given interest rate or prepayment scenario, the effective margin is the net earned yield spread, or margin, that is in excess of financing costs. *See Also: interest, interest rate, margin, net, prepayment, spread, yield, yield spread*

EFFECTIVE NET WORTH. A company's net worth added to its subordinated debt, which is money owed after other, more important, financial obligations are met. *See Also: net, net worth, subordinated, worth*

EFFECTIVE PAR. A preferred stock's par value that corresponds to a specific dividend rate. *See Also: dividend, par, par value*

EFFECTIVE RATE. The yield on a debt security based on the coupon rate, price, time between interest payments, and the amount of time to maturity. This rate determines the overall yield. *See Also: coupon, coupon rate, debt security, interest, maturity, security, time, yield*

EFFECTIVE SALE. The amount of a round-lot sale, which usually is 100 shares of stock, determines the price of the next odd-lot transaction, with 1/8 of a point tacked on as the odd-lot differential. For example, if a round-lot transaction involved stock selling at 42, the next odd-lot purchase would be at 42 1/8. *See Also: differential, point, sale, stock, transaction*

EFFICIENT MARKET HYPOTHESIS. A theory that in a free market, with competition for profits, all knowledge and expectations are accurately reflected in market prices. *See Also: free market, market*

EIGHTY-FIVE PERCENT EXCLUSION. When one company receives cash dividends from another company, 85 percent of the total is excluded as taxable income in some cases. *See Also: cash, taxable income*

EITHER WAY MARKET. When a bid on a security is identical to an offer price. *See Also: offer, security*

EITHER/OR ORDER. An investor advises his or her broker to have one of two orders executed. When one is executed, the other alternative is automatically canceled. *See Also: broker*

ELASTICITY OF DEMAND AND SUPPLY. The demand for luxury items or for nonessentials is elastic because it can jump dramatically or drop if prices go up or down. Necessities such as drugs, food, and electricity are not elastic because people need to buy the products and services regardless of their costs. Elasticity of supply refers to the increase in supply as production and prices go up. *See Also: demand, drop, supply*

ELBOW. A sharp shift in a yield curve slope on a graph that resembles an elbow. *See Also: yield, yield curve*

ELECT. A round-lot transaction that causes a round- or odd-lot stop order to become a market order. For example, if an odd-lot request is in for 60 shares of ABC Paper Co. with a stop order at 42, and the previous round-lot trade of

ABC went for 41 7/8, the broker can make the odd-lot deal without passing the stop limit. The stop order is elected and becomes a buy order. *See Also: broker, buy order, limit, market, market order, order, paper, stop, stop order, transaction*

ELECTRONIC ACCESS MEMBER. For a fee, the New York Stock Exchange gives some people the right to use electronic communications to buy and sell securities on the trading floor, even though they are not exchange members. *See Also: exchange, floor, New York Stock Exchange, right, securities, stock, stock exchange, trading floor*

ELECTRONIC BILL PRESENTMENT AND PAYMENT. Also referred to as EBPP, the online capability of presenting bills to users and the capability of users paying each bill, using an electronic check. *See Also: check, electronic check, online*

ELECTRONIC CASH. *See Also: e-cash.*

ELECTRONIC CHECK. An electronic means by which cash can be transferred via the Internet from a users checking account to pay bills. *See Also: account, cash, Internet, pay*

ELECTRONIC COMMUNICATIONS NETWORK. Also referred to as ECN, an automated exchange that eliminates third parties by matching orders between market makers and investors in exchange for a fee. *See Also: ECN, exchange, market, matching*

ELECTRONIC DATA INTERCHANGE. Also referred to as EDI, The movement of data between firms electronically, in a structured data format. EDI is considered the older version of electronic commerce between companies, as its costs make it feasible for large companies and their trading partners. Also, EDI is more cumbersome and costly than Internet based commerce, which is using XML (extensible markup language). Many e-marketplaces facilitate EDI to XML transaction to enable small and large companies to easily and inexpensively communicate. *See Also: commerce, Internet, movement, transaction, XML*

ELECTRONIC MAIL. *See Also: e-mail*

ELECTRONIC TICKETING. Also referred to as e-ticket, a ticket that is obtained through computer entry, and functions like a paper ticket. E-tickets are popular for movies, airlines, and concerts. Once an e-ticket is purchased, a hard copy can be obtained upon arrival, pending proper identification. *See Also: e-ticket, paper*

ELECTRONIC TRADING. The process by which investors use a computer, PDA, cellular phone, or other device to directly enter investing orders and receive reports and statements through an electronic connection. This type of electronic trade, or e-trade, may be facilitated via the Internet or over a dedicated telephone line. *See Also: e-trade, Internet, PDA*

ELECTRONIC WALLET. Software that enables a user to conduct online transactions, while managing payments and receipts, and storing digital certificates.

ELEEMOSYNARY INSTITUTION. A philanthropic, nonprofit, tax-exempt charity.

ELEPHANTS. Large investors or traders who make very large-volume trades. With large-volume transactions, these institutional-type investors are able to influence market prices for securities. *See Also: market, securities*

ELIGIBLE INVESTMENT. An investment that earns money and that Federal Reserve System banks can rediscount. *See Also: Federal Reserve System, investment, rediscount, reserve*

ELIGIBLE LIST. A list of securities that banks and other financial institutions can buy. *See Also: securities*

ELIGIBLE PAPER. Commercial paper, notes, and other financial issues that Federal Reserve System banks can submit to the Federal Reserve System for discounting. *See Also: Federal Reserve System, paper, reserve*

ELIGIBLE STOCK. A security in which charities and financial institutions can invest. *See Also: security*

ELIGIBLE STOCKS. Odd-lot stocks on which the odd-lot differential also is applied to the next round-lot sale. *See Also: differential, sale*

ELLIOT WAVE THEORY. Created by Ralph Elliott in 1938, this system predicts future trends and pinpoints the next probable broad market movement by counting and measuring price changes in the Dow Jones Industrial Average. *See Also: average, broad market, Dow Jones Industrial Average, industrial, market, movement*

ELVES. A gauge of 10 market indicators that test economic conditions, investors' psychology, and the stock market's current momentum. *See Also: current, indicators, market, momentum, stock, test*

EM. Effective Margin. *See Also: margin*

EMBARGO. One government bans the exportation of specific goods, an approach usually taken during war time or to protest another country's social or foreign policies. *See Also: time*

EMBEZZLEMENT. The theft or misappropriation of a customer's or company's assets, checks, or securities. *See Also: securities*

EMERGENCY HOME FINANCE ACT OF 1970. Legislation that created the Federal Home Loan Mortgage Corporation to build interest in developing a secondary mortgage market. The corporation puts together and sells mortgages guaranteed by the Federal Housing Administration and the Veterans Administration with investors buying the packages as pass-through securities. *See Also: corporation, home, interest, market, mortgage, mortgage corporation, secondary mortgage market, securities*

EMINENT DOMAIN. The government can take possession of an individual's assets for the general public welfare after it has paid the individual a fair price. For example, the government can force a person off his or her land if the government decides to put a highway through that particular property. *See Also: fair price, put, take*

EMPLOYEE RETIREMENT INCOME SECURITY ACT (ERISA). A law established in 1974 which governs the operations of most private pension and benefits plans to protect the interests of the participants. *See Also: operations, pension*

EMPLOYEE SPENDING ACCOUNT. Employees designate up to 50 percent of the money they earn in profit-sharing to reimburse themselves for benefit expenses or for medical insurance. *See Also: insurance*

EMPLOYEE STOCK OPTION. Also referred to as ESO, stock options granted to a company's employees offering the right but not obligation to purchase a predetermined number of shares in the company at a given price. The price, or exercise price, is usually the market price of the stock at the time the options are granted. *See Also: ESO, exercise, exercise price, market, market price, obligation, offering, right, stock, time*

EMPLOYEE STOCK OWNERSHIP PLAN. Also known as ESOP, a company plan that allows employees to buy shares of the company's stock through a contribution system. This plan gives employees of the company the right to buy shares in the company, usually at or below the market price. These stock options are usually restricted as to when they can be exercised and sold. These plans are intended to motivate employees, often providing tax benefits to the company. *See Also: ESOP, stock*

EMPLOYEE STOCK REPURCHASE AGREEMENT. A company's employees can buy shares of the company's stock, but the company retains the right to buy the shares back. *See Also: right, stock*

ENCRYPTION. The process of using cryptology to protect data from unauthorized access. This translates data into a secret code, which is only available to an authorized party. *See Also: cryptology*

ENCUMBERED. An asset owned by one person, but subject to another's claim. For example, if one took out a mortgage to buy a house, the house would be encumbered because even though the property is owned, the bank holds an interest in it until the mortgage is paid. *See Also: asset, bank, house, interest, mortgage*

END TO END. Also referred to as E2E and EtoE, typically used to describe professional services firms, E2E refers to the full spectrum of services offered within a project or industry. *See Also: industry, professional*

END TO END APPLICATIONS. E-Commerce applications that cover the spectrum of needs for a user, such as delivery and management of goods and services between buyer and supplier. *See Also: delivery*

END USER. The person for whom a product, such as hardware or software, is designed.

ENDIGUER. French for hedging an investment. *See Also: hedging, investment*

ENDORSE. The act of placing a name on a certificate to legally transfer ownership. *See Also: certificate, name, transfer*

ENDORSED BOND. A bond issued by one company, but guaranteed by another. *See Also: bond*

ENDORSEMENT FEE. An options broker pays a New York Stock Exchange member firm to guarantee a customer's performance in an over-the-counter option. *See Also: broker, exchange, firm, guarantee, member firm, New York Stock Exchange, option, over-the-counter option, stock, stock exchange*

ENERGY ISSUES. Securities issued by a company involved in energy research, production, or a related field.

ENERGY TRENDS. An analysis of how and where future energy sources will be tapped and how it will affect industry. *See Also: industry*

ENFORCED LIQUIDATION. When the holder of a security fails to keep enough equity in his or her margin account. *See Also: account, equity, fails, margin, margin account, security*

ENGLISH AUCTION. An auction in which bidding commences at the lowest acceptable price, then bidders successively bid the highest price they are willing to pay for an item. Bidding activity halts when the auction duration is complete, and the item is sold to the highest bidder at their bid price. English auctions allow the seller to specify a reserve price. This price, which may be the price where the bidding commences or higher, is the lowest price the item will be sold. *See Also: activity, bid price, duration, pay, reserve, reserve price, will*

ENTERPRISE RELATIONSHIP MANAGEMENT. Also referred to as ERM, Complex applications that integrate the information systems of front-office departments, including customer service, sales and marketing. *See Also: service*

ENTERPRISE RESOURCE PLANNING. Also referred to as ERP, complex applications, supported by multi-module application software, that manage inventory and integrate business processes. This software is typically used by large companies across multiple divisions and organizational boundaries. *See Also: ERP, inventory*

ENTREPRENEUR. A business owner, and the person who takes the greatest amount of risk in the business venture. *See Also: risk*

EPS. See Earnings Per Share. *See Also: earnings, share*

EPUNTS. In Europe, a payment guarantee that is expressed in terms of gold, with its value based in gold. Each unit weighs about 0.9 gram of gold. If someone owns a bond that is expressed in epunts, the holder can ask that it be paid in any one of 17 different currencies. Epunts, which stands for the defunct "European Payments Union," were originally created to ease the difficulties in exchanging foreign currencies. *See Also: ask, bond, gram, guarantee, unit*

EQUAL COVERAGE. If a company issues bonds for a second time, this clause provides that the second issue will carry the same protection as the company's first issue. *See Also: carry, issue, time*

EQUAL CREDIT OPPORTUNITY ACT. Legislation that outlaws discrimination on the basis of gender, religion, or race in the granting of credit. The lender also cannot discriminate if the person is receiving public assistance. Enforced by the Federal Trade Commission, this act became law in the mid-1970s. *See Also: basis, commission, credit, Federal Trade Commission*

EQUALIZING DIVIDEND. When changes occur in a dividend's normal dividend dates, this is paid to correct any irregularities. *See Also: dividend*

EQUALIZING SALE. A short sale executed at either a lower price than the previous sale, or the same price as a previous sale, which was lower than the sale before. *See Also: sale, short sale*

EQUILIBRIUM PRICE. When the supply of a particular good or service equals its demand, this is the item's cost. *See Also: demand, service, supply*

EQUIPMENT LEASING PARTNERSHIP. A limited partnership formed to buy computers, machinery, and other equipment and, in turn, lease the equipment to other companies. While these partnerships profit from the lease payments, they also receive the tax advantages of the equipment's depreciation. *See Also: depreciation, limited partnership, partnership, profit, turn*

EQUIPMENT OBLIGATIONS. Any bond or note that is secured solely by the lien on a specific piece of equipment or machinery. *See Also: bond, note*

EQUIPMENT TRUST CERTIFICATE. A debt certificate that a company issues when it needs to buy mechanical equipment, with the equipment serving as the debt's collateral. *See Also: certificate, collateral*

EQUITY. A company's value after its liabilities have been discharged.

EQUITY CAPITAL. Money a company earns by selling shares of its stock. Equity capital reflects ownership, while a bond represents a debt. *See Also: bond, capital, equity, stock*

EQUITY EARNINGS. A portion of a subsidiary's surplus earnings that exceed dividend payments and that the parent company does not report. *See Also: dividend, earnings*

EQUITY EQUIVALENT LOANS. A loan with property as collateral that provides the lender with the associated option of buying a percentage of the property. *See Also: collateral, option*

EQUITY FINANCING. A company issues equity shares of stock usually at a time when the stock is trading at a high price. *See Also: equity, stock, time*

EQUITY INCOME. A company's loan interest subtracted from its operating income. *See Also: interest, operating income*

EQUITY INCOME FUND. A fund that holds stocks and bonds, with both earning high dividends and interest. *See Also: and interest, fund, interest*

EQUITY INVESTMENT. Any investment that does not carry a guarantee that the investor definitely will earn a specific amount of money. *See Also: carry, guarantee, investment*

EQUITY KICKER. An offering of debt securities that can be converted into the common stock of the company. Because of this feature, a company will pay less interest. *See Also: common stock, interest, offering, pay, securities, stock*

EQUITY MORTGAGE. A loan in which the lender reduces interest rates in exchange for part of the profits the owner earns when he or she sells the property. The percentage the lender receives equals the percentage by which the lender reduces the interest rate. *See Also: exchange, interest, interest rate*

EQUITY NET WORTH. The amount of interest a company's stockholders own based on capital, retained earnings, and surplus. *See Also: capital, earnings, interest, retained earnings*

EQUITY NOTES. Debt instruments that automatically convert to shares of common stock after a predetermined time. The common stock is issued by the same company as the debt instrument. *See Also: common stock, debt instrument, instrument, stock, time*

EQUITY PURCHASE ACCOUNTING. A company that has at least 20 percent of another company's stock can include a percentage of that company's income into its own net income. The percentage the company can include must equal the percentage it owns. For example, if the ABC Company owns 23 percent of XYZ Company's stock, ABC can include 23 percent of XYZ's income in its own net reported income. *See Also: net, net income, stock*

EQUITY REIT. A real estate investment trust that buys and leases property using equity provided by stockholders. Investors profit from rental income and appreciation. *See Also: appreciation, equity, estate, investment, investment trust, profit, real estate, trust*

EQUITY RISK PREMIUM. The difference between the rate of return on risk-free assets and risky common stocks. *See Also: rate of return, return*

EQUITY SECURITY. Any stock that represents ownership in the issuing company, including common stock, preferred stock, and warrants. *See Also: common stock, preferred stock, stock*

EQUITY TURNOVER. Used to figure common equity's rate of return, this is the relationship between sales and the holder of common stock's equity. *See Also: equity, rate of return, return*

EQUITY-TYPE SECURITY. A security that is not common or preferred, but can be converted or exercised for either. *See Also: security*

EQUIVALENT BOND YIELD. Comparison of discount yields and the yields on bonds that pay interest. For example, if a 90-day Treasury bill is sold for $970, the yield to $1000 is 12.54 percent, based on 365 days. *See Also: discount, interest, pay, Treasury bill, yield*

EQUIVALENT TAXABLE YIELD. The amount of money an investor must earn from a taxable investment to get the same amount of money he or she would have earned on a tax-free investment. *See Also: investment*

ERISA. Employee Retirement Income Security Act. *See Also: security*

ERP. Enterprise Resource Planning. *See Also: resource*

ERR. A designation in the futures market that indicates quotations have been erratic. *See Also: futures, futures market, market*

ERRORS AND OMISSIONS EXCEPTED. "E & OE" appears on customers' statements and relieves broker-dealers from responsibility if the statements contain mistakes.

ESCALATOR CLAUSE. A contract stipulation that cost increases will be passed on, whether the contract is for wages, in which case an employee would receive a raise if his or her employer's profits went up, or for a rent agreement, in which case the tenant would have to pay a higher rent if the property owner's costs went up. *See Also: contract, pay, tenant*

ESCHEAT. The ownership of property reverts to the state if the property is abandoned, but in most cases the owner can claim the property later.

ESCROW. Money or assets involved in a contract are placed with a third party to make sure both sides fulfill their parts of the contract. *See Also: contract*

ESCROW AGREEMENT. Two people or two firms agree to place a specific amount of money with a third person or firm, with the money to be delivered only after all terms of the agreement are satisfied. *See Also: firm*

ESCROW ANALYSIS. A mortgagee reviews escrow accounts to make sure monthly deposits are enough to pay for insurance, taxes, and other expenses. *See Also: escrow, insurance, pay*

ESCROW RECEIPT. Occurs when a depository guarantees it will deliver the securities involved in an option contract as soon as the contract is exercised. *See Also: contract, depository, option, option contract, securities*

ESCROW RECEIPT DEPOSITORY PROGRAM. The Options Clearing Corporation administers this book-entry program, which allows a custodian bank to easily deposit, move, or withdraw escrow receipts that are held as collateral on different series of the same class of option. The program cuts down on the issuing and reissuing of escrow receipts. *See Also: bank, class, collateral, corporation, custodian, escrow, option*

ESO. Employee Stock Option. *See Also: stock*

ESOP. Also known as employee stock ownership plan, a company plan that allows employees to buy shares of the company's stock through a contribution system. This plan gives employees of the company the right to buy shares in the company, usually at or below the market price. These stock options are usually restricted as to when they can be exercised and sold. These plans are intended to motivate employees, often providing tax benefits to the company. *See Also: below the market, employee stock ownership plan, market, market price, right, stock*

ESTATE. All the possessions one owns at the time of death. *See Also: time*

ESTATE TAX. An excise tax imposed by a state or federal government to be paid before assets are transferred to heirs. *See Also: excise tax*

ESTIMATED BALANCE SHEET. An estimate of what a company's assets and liabilities will be at the end of the company's next fiscal year. *See Also: fiscal year*

ESTIMATED TAX. The amount of money a financial officer believes his or her company will have to pay in taxes after all tax credits are subtracted. *See Also: officer, pay*

ETA. An index model that weighs the importance of seven financial variables for more than 1,600 industrial companies, then adds together the weighted values to develop a zeta score index. *See Also: index, industrial, score*

ETF. See Exchange Traded Funds *See Also: exchange*

ETHERNET. A standard for LAN connections, ethernet defines the hardware and communications which sends its communications through radio frequency signals carried by a coaxial cable or fiber. *See Also: cable, LAN*

EURO CLEAR. An organization in Brussels that provides transaction clearing services for member banks dealing in Eurobonds and Yankee bonds. *See Also: transaction*

EUROBILL OF EXCHANGE. A bill of exchange expressed in terms of a foreign currency and payable outside of its country of origin. *See Also: bill of exchange, currency, exchange, foreign currency*

EUROBOND. A company issues a bond through the international market, with interest and principal payments due in the currency in which the bond was issued. *See Also: bond, currency, interest, market, principal, with interest*

EUROCREDIT SECTOR. A part of the European sector in which banks continuously roll over shorter-term loans with rates that fluctuate according to the cost of funds so the banks can act as long-term lenders. *See Also: cost of funds, sector*

EUROCURRENCY. Currency deposited in a foreign bank with one of the parties not necessarily being European. For example, U.S. dollars deposited in Germany and Japanese yen deposited in Canada would both be considered Eurocurrency. *See Also: bank, yen*

EURODOLLAR BONDS. American or European bonds that pay interest and principal in dollars. *See Also: interest, pay, principal*

EURODOLLAR CERTIFICATE OF DEPOSIT. A certificate of deposit that is purchased in dollars and then deposited in a bank outside of the United States. *See Also: bank, certificate*

EURODOLLAR SECURITY. A U.S. or foreign security denominated in U.S. dollars, with the dollars deposited in European banks. *See Also: security*

EURODOLLARS. U.S. dollars deposited in banks outside of the United States, with the foreign banks usually paying higher interest rates. *See Also: interest*

EUROLINE. A foreign bank offers a line of credit to an American, with the credit terms available in the foreign country's own currency. *See Also: bank, credit, currency, line of credit*

EUROPEAN COMPOSITE UNIT. A private account unit with a specific amount of currency from each European community, with the amount of currency based on the significance of the country. *See Also: account, currency, unit*

EUROPEAN CURRENCY UNIT. A weighted package of Common Market nations' currency, with the packages adjusted regularly to represent the different countries' trade balances. *See Also: currency, market*

EUROPEAN DEPOSITORY RECEIPT. A document issued in place of stock shares that represents ownership of the shares and makes it easier to deal in foreign securities because the actual stock certificates do not have to be physically transferred. *See Also: actual, easier, foreign securities, securities, stock*

EUROPEAN ECONOMIC COMMUNITY. Belgium, France, Italy, Luxembourg, the Netherlands, and West Germany entered this alliance called the Common Market in 1957, to create an environment of cooperation in trade. Duties were standardized and barriers were torn down. Since then, Great Britain, Denmark, Greece, and Ireland have joined, as have several dependencies in Africa and the Caribbean. *See Also: market*

EUROPEAN OPTION. A put or call contract that must be exercised within five days of the expiration date. *See Also: call contract, contract, expiration, expiration date, put*

EUROPEAN TERMS. The amount of foreign currency needed to buy one American dollar. For example, if it takes 2.5 Swiss francs to buy one American dollar, the franc would be worth 40 cents, and it would be called "2.5 in European terms." *See Also: currency, foreign currency, worth*

EVALUATION. The process used to determine an investment portfolio's value, with exchange-listed stocks valued at their closing price the previous day, and over-the-counter stocks at their bid price. *See Also: bid price, closing price, investment*

EVALUATOR. An independent party without a beneficial interest that assigns a resale value to an asset which has a limit market. *See Also: asset, beneficial interest, interest, limit, market*

EVEN KEEL. Occurs when the Federal Reserve System's monetary policy is consistent. *See Also: monetary policy, reserve*

EVEN LOTS. Stocks sold in blocks of 100 shares or in multiples of 100 shares.

EVEN SPREAD. A spread position where an investor's premium on his or her long position equals the premium that he or she has to pay on a short position. *See Also: long position, pay, position, premium, short position, spread, spread position*

EVEN-BASIS SWAP. An investor sells one fixed-income security from his or her portfolio and buys another without the portfolio's yield changing at all. The average maturity or face values in the portfolio, however, may change. *See Also: average, change, maturity, portfolio, security, yield*

EVEN-PAR SWAP. Occurs when a block of bonds is sold and another is bought at the same time with the same nominal principal, regardless of any net cash difference. *See Also: cash, net, nominal, principal, time*

EVENING UP. A person profits from an investment, with the profit equaling-thus offsetting a previous loss. *See Also: investment, profit*

EVERGREEN LOAN. A loan to a country to pay for any sovereign lending loss that might be caused by continuous rollovers or by the government's own reluctance to enter bankruptcy. *See Also: bankruptcy, pay*

EVERGREEN PROSPECTUS. A securities issue that is registered with the Securities and Exchange Commission and offered continuously, such as a share in an open-end investment company. *See Also: commission, exchange, investment, investment company, issue, securities, share*

EX-ALL. A security is sold without any rights, dividends, warrants, or other privileges. *See Also: rights, security*

EX-ANTE SAVING. A planned savings that may be either more or less than the planned investment. *See Also: investment*

EX-CLEARING HOUSE. When two contra brokers complete a transaction without using a clearing house. *See Also: clearing house, house, transaction*

EX-COUPON. A stock sold without a coupon. *See Also: coupon, stock*

EX-DIVIDEND. The date when a stock is adjusted for its dividend. The buyer of a stock will not receive a dividend that has been declared on the ex-dividend date, but the seller will. The trade will be ex-dividend because the settlement date will be after the record date, which determines which holder is entitled to the dividend. *See Also: dividend, ex-dividend date, record date, settlement date, stock*

EX-DIVIDEND DATE. The specific day a security begins to be traded without paying a current dividend. Only the person who owned the stock before this day is entitled to the current dividend. *See Also: current, dividend, security, stock*

EX-PIT TRANSACTION. A commodities deal traded off the floor of the exchange or away from a normal dealing area. *See Also: exchange, floor*

EX-RIGHTS. Securities that previously were traded with specific rights, but the rights have been removed. *See Also: rights*

EX-STOCK DIVIDENDS. The time between when the payment of a dividend is announced and the day the actual payment is made. If an investor buys a stock during this period, he or she is not entitled to the forthcoming dividend. *See Also: actual, dividend, stock, time*

EX-WARRANTS. Securities that previously were traded with warrants, which give the holder the right to buy more shares at a certain price, but the warrants have been removed. *See Also: right*

EXACT INTEREST. Financial institutions pay interest based on 365 days per year, instead of the usual 360 days, when calculating the daily interest accrued on large deposits. *See Also: interest, interest accrued, pay*

EXCEPT FOR OPINION. An accountant's designation that an audit could not be completed in a specific area of a public company because the information available was not sufficient for the auditor to form an opinion. *See Also: audit*

EXCESS EQUITY. An account's cash value exceeds the amount needed for buying securities on margin. *See Also: cash, margin, on margin, securities*

EXCESS INTEREST. The amount by which the interest credited exceeds a dividend's lowest acceptable interest rate. *See Also: interest, interest rate*

EXCESS MARGIN. Equity in a margin account that exceeds the lender's requirement. The excess amount can be invested or withdrawn. *See Also: account, margin, margin account*

EXCESS MARGIN ACCOUNT SECURITIES. A client's securities that exceed the value of that needed to pay the debit balance in his or her margin account. If the securities are worth more than 140 percent of the debit, the debit balance must be segregated in case the broker becomes insolvent. *See Also: account, balance, broker, debit, margin, margin account, pay, securities, worth*

EXCESS PROFITS TAX. Because of a certain historical base, the government can determine that a company's profits are too great and tax the amount that exceeds a certain limit. *See Also: base, limit*

EXCESS RESERVES. Federal Reserve System bank deposits that exceed the Federal Reserve Board's minimum requirements. *See Also: bank, reserve*

EXCESS RETURN. A security's return minus the return from a no-risk security during the same time period. *See Also: minus, return, security, time*

EXCHANGE. The physical location where securities bought and sold. Also, e-marketplaces where buyers and sellers negotiate prices for goods or services.

EXCHANGE ACQUISITION. An order to buy a large block of stocks combined with several orders to sell the same security put together on the exchange floor. *See Also: exchange, exchange floor, floor, order, put, security*

EXCHANGE CONTROL. A government prohibition of importing or exporting financial instruments, including bank deposits and notes. *See Also: bank*

EXCHANGE DISTRIBUTION. An order to sell a large block of securities combined with several orders to buy the same stock put together on the exchange floor. *See Also: exchange, exchange floor, floor, order, put, securities, stock*

EXCHANGE FLOOR. The physical area of an exchange where securities are bought and sold. *See Also: exchange, put, securities, stock, stock exchange*

EXCHANGE FOR FUTURES. A person buying a cash commodity transfers the cash commodity of a long futures position to the seller, with any difference between the futures contract and the spot paid out in cash. *See Also: cash, cash commodity, commodity, contract, futures, futures contract, position, spot*

EXCHANGE FOR PHYSICAL PROGRAM. A method of trading index futures and their component stocks in which a computer shows deviations between the futures and the stocks in a spread. The trader then tries to buy the index future and sell the stocks short, or vice versa. After the deviations disappear, and the spread returns to normal, the trader closes out the positions for a profit. *See Also: futures, index, index futures, profit, spread, trader, trading index*

EXCHANGE OF SPOT FOR FUTURES. Occurs when two investors swap a specific amount of a cash commodity for the same quantity of futures. *See Also: cash, cash commodity, commodity, futures, swap*

EXCHANGE PRIVILEGE. A stockholder can convert his or her mutual fund into another fund in the same family at no additional charge. *See Also: fund, mutual fund, stockholder*

EXCHANGE RATE. How much of one currency is worth another. For example, if 1,000 Italian lira is worth one U.S. dollar, that would be the exchange rate. *See Also: currency, exchange, worth*

EXCHANGE SEAT. Stock exchange membership, with a limited number of seats available. *See Also: exchange*

EXCHANGE SUPERVISORY ANALYST EXAMINATION. Employees of stock exchange-member firms who are responsible for reviewing research reports which will be issued to the public, must pass this test, which determines an employee's knowledge of financial analysis and exchange research standards. *See Also: exchange, pass, standards, stock, test*

EXCHANGE TRADED FUNDS. A portfolio of stocks that trades as a single security, like a common stock. Exchange Trade Funds (ETFs) typically track a specific index, such as the S&P 500, or a particular industry, such as technology. *See Also: common stock, index, industry, portfolio, security, stock, technology*

EXCHANGE-TRADED OPTION. An option that is listed on one of the exchanges. *See Also: exchanges, option*

EXCHANGE-TYPE COMPANY. Now illegal, management companies formerly allowed their clients to trade in the securities they owned for diversified mutual fund shares without paying capital gains taxes. *See Also: capital, diversified, fund, mutual fund, securities*

EXCHANGES. Any type of financial instrument given to a clearing house for collection. *See Also: clearing house, financial instrument, house, instrument*

EXCISE TAX. A tax placed on the manufacture of a commodity. *See Also: commodity*

EXCLUSION. Any item that isn't covered in a contract, or a specific item that is listed as not being covered by the contract. For example, some expenses for which a person does not have to pay taxes are considered exclusions. *See Also: contract, pay*

EXECUTABLE FILE. A reference to a program file which is executable. Executable files in usually have extensions of .exe or .com in DOS and Windows. Executable files can have any name in UNIX and Macintosh environments. *See Also: name, UNIX, Windows*

EXECUTION. Completing a buy or sell order, or a securities transaction. *See Also: order, securities, sell order, transaction*

EXEMPT SECURITIES. Securities such as government and municipal bonds that do not have to be registered or that do not have to comply with some securities laws, such as those governing margin, dealer registration, and reporting requirements. *See Also: dealer, margin, registration, securities*

EXEMPTION. The government allows a taxpayer to deduct a certain amount from his or her total annual earnings for each family member, as long as the taxpayer can prove he or she paid at least half of that family member's support. The government also allows specific deductions for those with some physical impairments. *See Also: annual earnings, earnings, support*

EXERCISE. The investor holding a put or call option decides to proceed with the transaction. *See Also: call option, option, put, transaction*

EXERCISE ASSIGNMENT. Notifying the person who wrote an options contract that the option is being exercised. *See Also: contract, option, options contract*

EXERCISE CUT-OFF TIME. The time frame in which the holder of an options contract must exercise the option. If the holder does not exercise it, the contract is canceled. *See Also: contract, exercise, frame, option, options contract, time*

EXERCISE LIMIT. Options exchanges prohibit investors and groups of investors working together from exercising more than 2,000 options in each class within five days. *See Also: class, exchanges*

EXERCISE NOTICE. A broker advises the Options Clearing Corporation that a long-option contract must be exercised, after which the OCC assigns another broker to fulfill the contract. *See Also: broker, contract, corporation, OCC*

EXERCISE PRICE. The price for which a call holder can buy, or a put holder can sell, the underlying security. *See Also: put, security, underlying security*

EXERCISE RATIO. The number of common stock shares an investor is allowed to exchange for each warrant he or she owns. *See Also: common stock, exchange, stock, warrant*

EXERCISE VALUE. On a call option, the amount of money which an underlying security exceeds the exercise price. On a put option, it is the amount of money the exercise price exceeds the underlying security. *See Also: call option, exercise, exercise price, option, put, put option, security, underlying security*

EXHAUSTION GAP. A gap that reverses a market trend. *See Also: gap, market, market trend, trend*

EXIT. The time period in which an investor can convert his or her holdings into cash or stock to be liquidated over a designated period of time. *See Also: cash, stock, time*

EXIT FEE. A bank fee designed to discourage investors from transferring their accounts to another trustee. *See Also: bank, trustee*

EXIT STRATEGY. The plan by which an investor seeks to close out an investment. Known as a liquidity event when referring to a venture capitalist, business owner or angel investor that may be seeking an IPO or acquisition as an exit strategy. *See Also: acquisition, close, exit, investment, IPO, liquidity, liquidity event, venture capitalist*

EXLEGAL. A municipal security that is not accompanied by a bond counsel's legal opinion, the buyer must be advised of this fact before purchase. *See Also: bond, legal, security*

EXPECTED YIELD. The amount of money an investor expects to earn from a specific security divided by the total investment, usually expressed in a ratio or percentage. *See Also: investment, ratio, security*

EXPENDABLE FUND. A fund designed to hold cash or assets to be used for administrative actions or other predetermined purposes. *See Also: cash, fund, hold*

EXPENDITURE. A payment or the promise to make a future payment.

EXPENSE. The amount of money it costs to make money.

EXPENSE RATIO. Mutual fund expenses are compared to the average net asset value of outstanding shares. The ratio normally is expressed as a number of cents for $100 of investment. For example, if the expense ratio is 58 cents, the investor is paying 58 cents per $100 to pay for the expenses incurred in operating the fund. *See Also: asset, average, expense, fund, investment, net, net asset value, outstanding, pay, ratio*

EXPIRATION. The last day an option can be exercised. *See Also: option*

EXPIRATION CYCLE. One of three times in which options can be traded. One cycle includes January, April, July, and October, the second includes February, May, August, and November, and the third covers March, June, September, and December. *See Also: cycle*

EXPIRATION DATE. Equity options normally become void at 11:59 p.m. Eastern Standard Time on the Saturday following the third Friday of the contract. *See Also: contract, time, void*

EXPIRATION MONTH. The specific month an option contract expires, after which its terms cannot be exercised. *See Also: contract, option, option contract*

EXPLORATORY DRILLING PROGRAM. A limited partnership engaged in a risky venture to find oil or gas at a sight that previously has not been drilled. *See Also: limited partnership, partnership*

EXPONENTIAL MARKET. A market in which one party can be both a buyer and a seller. The market benefits as more participants join as liquidity is enhanced. Exponential markets are more prevalent when the items sold are considered easy to buy and sell, such as commodities. *See Also: liquidity, market*

EXPORT-IMPORT BANK OF THE UNITED STATES. Established in 1934 and commonly referred to as the Eximbank, this is an independent federal agency that borrows money from the U.S. Treasury to finance U.S. exports and imports.

EXPOST. Variables that have had an effect on securities in the past, but no longer carry any importance other than providing a historical perspective. *See Also: carry, securities*

EXPOSURE .The highest line of credit a broker-dealer will extend to a customer between the trade and settlement dates of a securities transaction. *See Also: broker-dealer, credit, line of credit, securities, transaction*

EXTENDED. A rise or fall in a security's price that continues a trend. *See Also: fall, trend*

EXTENDIBLE DEBT SECURITY. A debt security in which the holder can redeem the note at face value at maturity or hold it for a specified time, after which the interest rate will be adjusted. *See Also: debt security, face value, hold, interest, interest rate, maturity, note, redeem, security, time*

EXTENSIBLE STYLESHEET LANGUAGE. Also referred to as XLS, a standard that enables businesses to reformat XML documents into internal standards. *See Also: standards, XLS, XML*

EXTENSION SWAP. An investor buys one debt security and sells another, with the new security giving the investor more time before maturity. *See Also: debt security, maturity, security, time*

EXTERNAL FUNDS. Any infusion of capital into a company which does not come from the company's own sources. Bank loans and the proceeds of a bond sale are both considered external funds. *See Also: bank, bond, capital, proceeds, sale*

EXTERNALIZATION. A broker buys and sells securities for clients by sending the orders to the exchange floor for execution. This is the most common practice in securities trading. *See Also: broker, exchange, exchange floor, execution, floor, securities*

EXTRA DIVIDEND. When a special dividend that is not included in the annual dividend amount is paid to investors with no guarantee that they ever will receive such a bonus again. *See Also: dividend, guarantee*

EXTRA-MARKET COVARIANCE. Prices of related securities move together, but not in line with the rest of the market. *See Also: market, securities*

EXTRANET. Connecting two or more intranets. This allows two or more companies to collaborate, whether sharing resources, communicating, or transacting business.

EXTRAORDINARY ITEM. Either income or an expense that probably will not recur. *See Also: expense*

F

FACE AMOUNT. The principal amount of money involved in a financial agreement or designated on a financial instrument. *See Also: financial instrument, instrument, principal, principal amount*

FACE VALUE. The amount of money for which a coin, note, or other financial instrument can be redeemed in cash, or the amount of money for which a financial instrument can be redeemed for cash at maturity. *See Also: cash, financial instrument, instrument, maturity, note*

FACE-AMOUNT CERTIFICATE COMPANY. An investment firm that issues fixed-rate debt securities, but no other types. The owner of a face-amount certificate makes periodic payments to the issuer, who agrees to pay the owner either the certificate's face value at maturity or the certificate's surrender value if it is presented before it matures. *See Also: certificate, face value, firm, investment, maturity, pay, securities*

FACILITATING AGENCY. Any company, such as a stock exchange or a brokerage house, that helps people or other companies obtain ownership of goods, services, securities, etc. *See Also: brokerage house, exchange, house, securities, stock, stock exchange*

FACILITATING ORDER. An order for a broker-dealer's proprietary account that is crossed with a customer's order. *See Also: account, order, proprietary account*

FACSIMILE SIGNATURE. A mechanically reproduced and stamped signature on a financial instrument. *See Also: financial instrument, instrument*

FACTOR. The ratio of the current balance of a mortgage pool to the original balance of the pool, with the initial factor being one and the last one being zero. *See Also: balance, current, mortgage, mortgage pool, pool, ratio*

FACTORING. An investor borrows against securities he or she owns to finance another position in the securities market. *See Also: market, position, securities*

FADED. Prices that were quoted earlier have been either adjusted down or withdrawn altogether.

FAIL FLOAT. The cash balance left after a securities transaction falls through because the security was not delivered by the settlement date. *See Also: balance, cash, securities, security, settlement date, transaction*

FAIL POSITION. A broker-dealer cannot deliver securities to the buyer because the broker-dealer's client has not delivered the securities to him or her. *See Also: broker-dealer, client, securities*

FAIL TO DELIVER. An overdue agreement in which the seller has not delivered the security to the buyer. *See Also: security*

FAIL TO RECEIVE. An overdue agreement in which the buyer has not paid for a security because the seller has not delivered the security. *See Also: security*

FAILS. A broker is unable to complete a transaction by the agreed upon settlement date. *See Also: broker, settlement date, transaction*

FAILURE. When a person or company cannot meet financial obligations.

FAIR CERTIFICATE. An affordable, federally insured savings certificate, not subject to federal income tax, that pays significant returns. *See Also: certificate*

FAIR CREDIT REPORTING ACT. A law that gives people the right to view their credit bureau credit reports, challenge any items they believe to be inaccurate, and submit a letter of explanation for any negative marks. *See Also: credit, right*

FAIR MARKET VALUE. The amount at which the buyer and seller, both with all available information, decide to complete a transaction, with neither having any leverage over the other, and with neither exerting any unfair influence upon the other. *See Also: leverage, transaction*

FAIR PRICE. A regulation that requires a bidder to make the same offer for all shares of the same security he or she purchases during a specific time. *See Also: offer, security, time*

FAIR RATE OF RETURN. The maximum amount the federal government allows a public utilities company to earn as profit, with the amount based on how much the company must pay in dividends and interest, in maintaining equipment and covering overhead expenses. *See Also: and interest, interest, overhead, pay, profit, public utilities*

FAIR RETURN. The amount of profit a person can expect from an investment after considering the amount of money that was invested and the risks that are involved. *See Also: investment, profit*

FAIR TRADE ACTS. Acts which allow manufacturers to set minimum retail prices for their products in an effort to diminish competitive price slashing.

FAIR VALUE. A company's board of directors must determine a fair price, one that is reflective of worth, for any securities or assets that do not have market quotations readily available. *See Also: board of directors, fair price, market, securities, worth*

FAIRY GODFATHER. A prospective supporter or investor in a particular company.

FALL. The seller does not deliver the securities to the buyer by the specified delivery date. *See Also: delivery, delivery date, securities*

FALL OUT OF BED. A market that suddenly drops lower than at any other recent time. *See Also: market, time*

FALLEN ANGEL. A well-known company's security with a value that dropped suddenly after a negative development or news report. *See Also: security*

FALLING KNIFE. Hoping for a quick recovery, the act of buying a security that is falling in price, only to see the price continue to plunge. *See Also: plunge, recovery, security*

FAMILY OF FUNDS. A group of mutual funds that are directed by the same investment manager, but have different objectives. *See Also: investment, investment manager, manager*

FANNIE MAE. Federal National Mortgage Association. *See Also: mortgage*

FAQs. Short for Frequently Asked Questions, a collection of common questions and answers on a Web page for a particular subject area. *See Also: frequently asked questions, on, Web, Web page*

FAQS. Firm Access Query System. *See Also: firm*

FAR OPTION. The stock spread position that expires last. *See Also: position, spread, spread position, stock*

FARM CREDIT ADMINISTRATION. A division of the U.S. Department of Agriculture with the responsibility of aiding farmers during difficult times by offering credit or financial assistance. *See Also: credit, offering*

FARMER'S HOME ADMINISTRATION. A unit of the Department of Agriculture. The FHA loans money for community centers, farms, and homes in rural areas. *See Also: FHA, unit*

FASB-8. The statement of Financial Accounting Standards No. 8 governs how companies account for and report foreign currency transactions. *See Also: account, currency, foreign currency, standards, statement*

FASCISM. An economic system in which the government controls private industry as the producer and distributor of goods and services. *See Also: distributor, industry, producer*

FAST MARKET. A situation in a financial market that is marked by heavy trading and high volatility. *See Also: heavy, market, volatility*

FAT BUTTERFLY. A term used to describe a healthy net market maker, with each wing growing outward to reflect an increasing number of buyers on one side and sellers on the other. The body, or the intermediary, fattens as it grows with the abundance of activity. *See Also: activity, intermediary, maker, market, market maker, net, net market, net market maker, on, term*

FATE. The question of whether a bill of exchange has been accepted, paid, or has some other current status. *See Also: bill of exchange, current, exchange*

FAVORABLE TRADE BALANCE. When a country exports more than it imports.

FAVORITE FIFTY. The fifty largest equity holdings of all institutional investors. *See Also: equity*

FDIC. Formerly the Federal Deposit Insurance Corporation. *See Also: bank, bank insurance fund (BIF), corporation, fund, insurance*

FED WIRE. A computer system that connects the Federal Reserve System with its banks and with some dealers in government securities. Banks can use the computer to transfer the ownership of some securities. *See Also: Federal Reserve System, reserve, securities, transfer*

FEDERAL AGENCY SECURITY. A federally issued debt instrument that has a higher safety rating because it is government sponsored. *See Also: debt instrument, instrument, safety*

FEDERAL CREDIT AGENCIES. Any government unit that loans money to financial institutions, companies, or segments of the country's populace. *See Also: unit*

FEDERAL CREDIT UNION. A cooperative in which people can deposit money for savings, take out loans at low interest rates, and request other types of financial assistance. *See Also: cooperative, interest, low, take*

FEDERAL DEBT LIMIT. The total face amount that the United States can legally issue in outstanding obligations, or can guarantee in principal and interest. *See Also: and interest, face amount, guarantee, interest, issue, outstanding, principal*

FEDERAL DEFICIT. The amount by which a country's spending exceeds its revenue. The U.S. Government normally floats long- and short-term loans to cover the deficit, which reached historic proportions in the 1980s. Economists blame high interest rates and inflation for the mountainous deficit. *See Also: deficit, inflation, interest*

FEDERAL DEPOSIT INSURANCE CORPORATION (FDIC). See Bank Insurance Fund. *See Also: bank, bank insurance fund (BIF), fund, insurance*

FEDERAL FARM CREDIT BANKS. Consolidation of the Federal Intermediate Credit Bank, Banks for Cooperatives, and Federal Land Banks, which joined to reduce financing costs. They provide credit services to farmers. *See Also: bank, credit, Federal Intermediate Credit Bank, Intermediate Credit Bank*

FEDERAL FARM CREDIT SYSTEM. Provides short-term, discounted notes in increments of $50,000 to agriculture and agribusiness enterprises through 12 regional districts, each of which has a Bank for Cooperatives, a Federal Intermediate Credit Bank, and a Federal Land Bank. *See Also: agribusiness, bank, Bank for Cooperatives, credit, Federal Intermediate Credit Bank, Federal Land Bank, Intermediate Credit Bank*

FEDERAL FINANCING BANK. A government-owned bank created to reduce costs of federal agencies with government-guaranteed obligations. *See Also: bank*

FEDERAL FUNDS. The amount of money that exceeds the Federal Reserve System's requirement for daily trading by member banks. These funds can be lent out overnight to other member banks. *See Also: reserve*

FEDERAL FUNDS RATE. The interest rate charged when one Federal Reserve bank borrows money from another Federal Reserve bank. Because reserve accounts bear no interest, banks are motivated to lend reserves beyond those required, plus any excess. Banks needing reserves borrow the reserves. *See Also: bank, bear, Federal Reserve Bank, interest, interest rate, plus, reserve, reserve bank*

FEDERAL HOME LOAN BANK. A corporation, sponsored by the U.S. government that issues bonds with the proceeds providing mortgages to the home building industry. The bank was established to promote home financing during the Great Depression. *See Also: bank, corporation, depression, Great Depression, home, industry, proceeds*

FEDERAL HOME LOAN BANK CONSOLIDATED DISCOUNT NOTES. A short-term issue with no fixed offering schedule, sold in $100,000 denominations with maturities of 30 to 270 days, and sold without government guarantees. *See Also: issue, offering*

FEDERAL HOME LOAN MORTGAGE CORPORATION (FHLMC). Commonly referred to as Freddie Mac, this federally-chartered stockholder-owned corporation, created by Congress in 1970, purchases residential mortgages in the secondary market from savings and loans, banks and mortgage banks. Freddie Mac then securitizes these mortgages and guarantees the timely payment of interest and the ultimate payment of principal on these pass-through mortgage-backed securities, then resells them in the capital markets. *See Also: capital, capital markets, corporation, Freddie Mac, interest, market, mortgage, principal, secondary market, securities*

FEDERAL HOUSING ADMINISTRATION (FHA). A corporate instrument of the U.S. Government, created in 1934 under the National Housing Act to insure residential mortgages. *See Also: instrument, National Housing Act*

FEDERAL HOUSING INSURED LOANS. Private financial institutions that are insured by the U.S. Department of Housing and Urban Development insure mortgages to promote residential home-buying. *See Also: Housing and Urban Development*

FEDERAL INTERMEDIATE CREDIT BANK. A unit of the U.S. government that issues bonds, with the proceeds directed toward farming and other agricultural interests. *See Also: proceeds, unit*

FEDERAL INTERVENTION HOUR. Usually right before noon, the Federal Reserve System enters the market to conduct its own business. *See Also: Federal Reserve System, market, reserve, right*

FEDERAL LAND BANK. A corporation, sponsored by the U.S. government, that issues bonds, with the proceeds providing mortgages for farming interests. *See Also: corporation, proceeds*

FEDERAL LOAN BANKS. Twelve district banks that issue equitable long-term mortgages to farmers so the farmers can own their own farms. *See Also: issue*

FEDERAL NATIONAL MORTGAGE ASSOCIATION (FNMA). Commonly referred to as Fannie Mae, the FNMA is a government-sponsored corporation that buys and sells Farmers Home Administration mortgages, Veterans Administration mortgages, and some nongovernmentally-backed mortgages. *See Also: corporation, Fannie Mae, FNMA, home*

FEDERAL OPEN MARKET COMMITTEE. A panel that makes short-term decisions in an effort to meet long-term Federal Reserve System objectives. The committee either sells securities to cut down on the money supply, or buys government securities to increase the money supply. The panel is made up of the Board of Governors and the presidents of six *See Also: committee, Federal Reserve System, money supply, on the money, reserve, securities, supply Federal Reserve Bank.*

FEDERAL RESERVE AGENT. A federal reserve bank's board chairman who maintains the collateral for all of the federal reserve notes held in his or her bank. *See Also: bank, collateral, reserve*

FEDERAL RESERVE BANK. One of the 12 banks that make up the Federal Reserve System. These banks monitor commercial and savings banks in their regional district to make sure they abide by Federal Reserve rules and regulations. In addition, they provide emergency loans to the institutions. The 12 banks are in Atlanta, Boston, Chicago, Cleveland, Dallas, Kansas City, Minneapolis, New York, Philadelphia, Richmond, St. Louis, and San Francisco. *See Also: City, Federal Reserve System, reserve*

FEDERAL RESERVE BANK RESERVE REQUIREMENT. The amount of uninvested money a Federal Reserve bank must have in reserve, expressed as a percentage of the bank's demand deposits. *See Also: bank, demand, Federal Reserve Bank, reserve, reserve bank*

FEDERAL RESERVE BOARD. The presidentially-elected Federal Reserve System's Board of Governors; it administers the system's regulations and supervises its 12 banks. It also sets margin and bank requirements, as well as the system's discount rates. *See Also: bank, discount, margin, reserve*

FEDERAL RESERVE CHECK COLLECTION SYSTEM. The process by which a bank that accepts an out-of-town check sends the check to the Federal Reserve System, which in turn sends the check to its bank of origin and credits the bank on which the check was drawn. *See Also: bank, check, Federal Reserve System, reserve, turn*

FEDERAL RESERVE CREDIT. All of the Federal Reserve System's credit based on the amount that member banks have supplied to their reserves, mostly earning assets. *See Also: credit, earning assets, reserve*

FEDERAL RESERVE CURRENCY. The Federal Reserve Bank issues this paper money for general circulation to be used as legal tender. *See Also: bank, Federal Reserve Bank, legal, paper, paper money, reserve, reserve bank, tender*

FEDERAL RESERVE NOTE. The most prevalent form of paper currency, ranging in denominations from $1 to $10,000 in the United States. *See Also: currency, paper*

FEDERAL RESERVE REQUIREMENTS. The amount of money that Federal Reserve member banks must have deposited with a Federal Reserve Bank so the member bank can back up any outstanding loans. *See Also: back up, bank, Federal Reserve Bank, member bank, outstanding, reserve, reserve bank*

FEDERAL RESERVE SYSTEM. An organization of 12 banks, with the group serving as a central bank that is overseen by a Board of Governors. The United States is divided into 12 districts, with one Federal Reserve Bank in each. *See Also: bank, central bank, Federal Reserve Bank, reserve, reserve bank*

FEDERAL SAVINGS AND LOAN ASSOCIATION. A federally chartered organization that collects individual savings accounts and uses the money to make residential mortgage loans. These savings and loans are owned either by stockholders or depositors, and are members of the Federal Home Loan Bank System. *See Also: bank, Federal Home Loan Bank, home, mortgage*

FEDERAL SAVINGS AND LOAN INSURANCE CORPORATION (FSLIC). *See Also: fund, insurance, SAIF, Savings Association Insurance Fund.*

FEDERAL TRADE COMMISSION. A government agency that promotes fair competition and works to eliminate monopolies and unfair practices that lead to restraint of trade.

FEDERATION INTERNATIONALE DES BOURSES DE VALEURS. A Paris-based international stock exchange federation, to which the New York Stock Exchange belongs, that allows international investing. *See Also: exchange, New York Stock Exchange, stock, stock exchange*

FEE OWNERSHIP. Occurs when the same person owns both the royalty and working interest in a mineral ownership. *See Also: interest, royalty, working interest*

FEEDING THE DUCKS. An investor sells his or her stock as the stock's price is going up. *See Also: stock*

FEEMAIL. The fees attorneys charge to settle shareholders' suits that try to stop the company's management from ransoming those shares of stock that are held by corporate raiders. *See Also: settle, stock, stop*

FEES AND ROYALTIES FROM DIRECT INVESTMENTS. Represents income that U.S. companies receive from their foreign affiliates, in which the U.S. companies are directly invested, which pays for such things as licensing costs, patent royalties, and management expenses. *See Also: patent*

FENCE SITTER. An investor who can't decide whether to invest in a particular venture.

FEVERISH MARKET. When market prices fluctuate so erratically that no common direction can be detected easily. *See Also: market*

FHA. Federal Housing Administration.

FIAT MONEY. Currency that cannot be converted into gold or silver but is designated as legal tender. The currency has no tangible backing other than a government's good faith. All U.S. currency is fiat money. *See Also: currency, legal, tender*

FIBER OPTICS. The use of light waves to transfer voice or data over glass or plastic fibers. Fiber optics are considered to provide a higher quality transmission and provide more bandwidth than traditional copper telephone lines. *See Also: transfer*

FICTITIOUS ORDER. A person orders a broker to buy or sell a security, but never intends to honor the contract. The buy or sell order is tried only to manipulate prices, making it look like there is a lot of activity in the market. *See Also: activity, broker, contract, lot, market, order, security, sell order*

FIDELITY BOND. Insures employees, officers, and partners of broker-dealer firms against misplaced money or misplaced securities, forged checks, forged securities, and fraudulent trading. *See Also: broker-dealer, securities*

FIDUCIARY. A person or firm entrusted with another person's or another firm's assets. *See Also: firm*

FIDUCIARY ACCOUNT. An account which a bank uses to hold assets for a client. *See Also: account, bank, client, hold*

FIDUCIARY LOAN. A loan that is made without collateral. *See Also: collateral*

FIELD GOAL. Nickname for the U.S. Fidelity & Guaranty Corporation, whose stock symbol is FG. *See Also: corporation, stock, symbol*

FIFO. *See Also: first in, first out*

FILE TRANSFER PROTOCOL. Also referred to as FTP, a protocol within the TCP/IP protocol suite used on the Internet that makes it possible to transfer files from one computer (or host) on the Internet to another. *See Also: FTP, Internet, on, protocol, TCP/IP, transfer*

FILL. An order to execute a buy or sell order for securities. *See Also: order, securities, sell order*

FILL OR KILL ORDER. A broker is ordered to trade an order entirely as soon as it reaches the trading post. If it is not executed immediately, it is canceled automatically. *See Also: broker, order, post, trading post*

FINAL DIVIDEND. In Great Britain, the last payment given to investors in a specific year. Because final dividends are required, they do not necessarily reflect other dividends paid earlier in the year.

FINANCE AND CONTROL. The gauge of a company's financial activities, including future plans, goals, and intended directions.

FINANCE BILL. A domestic bank draws this draft on a foreign bank against securities held in the foreign bank. *See Also: bank, draft, securities*

FINANCE COMPANY. Any financial institution that is not a bank, yet loans money to companies and individuals. *See Also: bank*

FINANCE PAPER. The credit that some companies issue to their own customers. For example, General Motors issues credit to its clients through the General Motors Acceptance Corporation. *See Also: acceptance, corporation, credit, issue*

FINANCIAL ACCOUNTING STANDARDS BOARD. A panel of certified public accountants that reviews and offers opinions on bookkeeping practices, with most companies following the board's recommendations when putting together their financial statements and reports.

FINANCIAL AND OPERATIONS PRINCIPAL. The person who is responsible for keeping financial records and approving financial reports. The individual must be tested and certified under the regulations of the National Association of Securities Dealers and the Municipal Securities Rulemaking Board. *See Also: Municipal Securities Rulemaking Board, securities*

FINANCIAL FLEXIBILITY. The degree to which a company can effectively change the amount and timing of its future cash flow in a need to take care of unexpected costs or opportunities. *See Also: cash, cash flow, change, take, timing*

FINANCIAL FUTURES. An agreement to trade a financial instrument, such as a Treasury bill at a specific price and on a specific future date. *See Also: financial instrument, instrument, Treasury bill*

FINANCIAL GUARANTY. A bond-insurer guarantees the bond will pay a fixed amount of money. *See Also: bond, pay*

FINANCIAL GUARANTY INSURANCE COMPANY. A group of banks and brokerage firms that guarantees municipal securities and unit investment trusts. *See Also: investment, securities, unit*

FINANCIAL INSTRUMENT. Any financial document that has a monetary value or verifies a financial transaction. *See Also: transaction*

FINANCIAL INTERMEDIARY. A financial institution that smoothes the flow of funds, such as redistributing savings, between units where income exceeds consumption and units where consumption exceeds income. Normally, individuals are seen as having income that exceeds consumption, and businesses and the government are seen as having consumption that exceeds income. *See Also: consumption, flow of funds*

FINANCIAL PYRAMID. A structure representing a pyramid that investors aim for in setting up a risk structure. For example, an investor may want the bulk of the portfolio in safe liquid instruments with a small percentage in high-risk investing. *See Also: liquid, portfolio, risk*

FINANCIAL RATIOS. Relationships between various items appearing on balance sheets, income statements, and other items, to measure and evaluate a company's condition and effectiveness. *See Also: balance, on balance*

FINANCIAL STRUCTURE. A company's long- and short-term financing.

FINANCIAL SUPERMARKET. A large retail company or organization that offers a wide range of financial services, such as stocks, bonds, real estate, and insurance. *See Also: estate, insurance, range, real estate*

FINDER'S FEE. A service fee given to a person who refers business to someone else. *See Also: service, service fee*

FINENESS. The degree to which a piece of gold or silver is pure. For example, some bars of silver bullion have a fineness of .999, which means that 99.9 percent of the bar is pure silver. *See Also: bullion*

FINITE LIFE REAL ESTATE INVESTMENT TRUST. An investment trust with real estate as the underlying asset. The assets must be liquidated at a future date, with the profits distributed to the beneficiaries. *See Also: asset, estate, investment, investment trust, real estate, trust*

FIRE SALE. A reference to a security or financial markets in general considered to be extremely undervalued. *See Also: security, undervalued*

FIREWALL. Designed to keep out unwanted visitors and to protect confidential information, a firewall is a security barrier, or gatekeeper, that regulates incoming and outgoing electronic traffic. Firewalls consist of computer hardware and software that are placed between the Internet and intranet. *See Also: Internet, intranet, security*

FIREWORKS. A security's price shoots up quickly.

FIRM. The acceptance of an obligation. *See Also: acceptance, obligation*

FIRM ACCESS QUERY SYSTEM (FAQS). A computer network that the National Association of Securities Dealers offers to its customers to review pending securities registrations as well as the results of qualification tests. *See Also: securities*

FIRM BID. A bid that pledges a specific amount of money for a definite number of securities, with the bid binding on acceptance. *See Also: acceptance, securities*

FIRM COMMITMENT. In a securities offering, the underwriter will assume the risk of selling the entire offering. *See Also: offering, risk, securities*

FIRM MAINTENANCE EXCESS. The minimum equity required of a margined security's long market value, usually about 30 percent at most firms. *See Also: equity, long market value, market, market value*

FIRM MARKET. A nonnegotiable asking or selling price. *See Also: nonnegotiable*

FIRM ORDER An investor tells his or her broker to buy or sell a specific quantity of securities at a specific limit price. *See Also: broker, limit, limit price, securities*

FIRM PRICE. A broker tells a client that a specific cost for a security is nonnegotiable and will be good only for a limited time. *See Also: broker, client, security, time*

FIRM QUOTE. The amount offered for a security that the market maker is willing to accept for a round-lot order. *See Also: maker, market, market maker, order, security*

FIRMING OF THE MARKET. When, after a downturn, the prices of securities stabilize. *See Also: downturn, securities*

FIRST BOARD. An established date that futures will be delivered. *See Also: futures*

FIRST CALL DATE. The first day a bond issuer can redeem all or part of an issue. *See Also: bond, issue, redeem*

FIRST COUPON. Used if the first interest payment on a newly-issued bond will be anything other than six months from the issue date. Subsequent interest payments, however, will be made every six months. *See Also: bond, interest, issue*

FIRST IN, FIRST OUT (FIFO). For accounting and lax purposes, inventory and assets are presumed to be sold in the same order in which they were purchased. Therefore, inventory costs begin with the oldest asset, and move forward toward the most recent purchase. *See Also: asset, forward, inventory, order*

FIRST MORTGAGE BOND. A long-term debt instrument with the first mortgage on the issuer's property serving as the bond's collateral. *See Also: collateral, debt instrument, instrument, long-term debt, mortgage*

FIRST-MOVER ADVANTAGE. The competitive edge of an individual or company establishing itself as the first, or early, player in a market. *See Also: market*

FIRST NOTICE DAY. The first day a person is able to notify a short-position seller that a delivery will be made through a commodities clearing house. *See Also: clearing house, delivery, house*

FIRST PAYDOWN DATE. Given a particular prepayment assumption, the date on which a CMO tranche begins to receive principal payments. *See Also: CMO, prepayment, principal, tranche*

FIRST PREFERRED STOCK. A stock that holds the primary claim on dividends and assets, with priority over common stock and other preferred stocks. *See Also: common stock, priority, stock*

FIRST SINKING FUND DATE. The earliest day a bond issuer can begin making sinking fund payments. *See Also: bond, fund, sinking fund*

FIRST-YEAR REPUBLICAN JINX THEORY. A theory that the market will drop in the first year of any Republican president's incumbency. *See Also: drop, market*

FIRSTS. Any asset's highest quality issue. *See Also: issue*

FISCAL AGENCY SERVICES. Federal Reserve banks, acting on behalf of the federal government, maintain accounts for the U.S. Department of Treasury, cash checks drawn on the Treasury, sell and redeem securities, and perform a variety of other functions for the government. *See Also: cash, redeem, reserve, securities*

FISCAL AGENT. A bank or trust company that acts, under a corporate trust agreement with a corporation, in the capacity of general treasurer. The agent will perform duties like making dividend payments, paying rents, redeeming bonds and coupons at maturity, and handling taxes relating to the issuance of bonds. *See Also: agent, bank, corporation, dividend, maturity, treasurer, trust, trust company*

FISCAL POLICY. Congress' manner of managing taxes and public spending.

FISCAL YEAR. A company's bookkeeping year, which can begin at any time during the actual year. *See Also: actual, time*

FISH. When one dealer tries to identify the buyer or seller working with another broker-dealer who is trying to trade a large block of securities. *See Also: broker-dealer, dealer, securities*

FITCH INVESTORS SERVICES. A firm that rates corporate bonds so investors can judge the investment risks. *See Also: firm, investment*

FITCH SHEETS. Fitch Investors Services provides a list of consecutive trade prices for specific securities. *See Also: securities*

FIVE HUNDRED DOLLAR RULE. A broker-dealer doesn't have to liquidate part of a client's account that has a cash deficiency if that cash deficiency is less than $500. *See Also: account, broker-dealer, cash*

FIVE PERCENT RULE. Set by the National Association of Securities Dealers, this is an ethical standard for markups, markdowns, and dealer commissions on securities transactions. *See Also: dealer, securities*

FIXATION. Establishment of a commodity's current or future price. *See Also: current*

FIXED ANNUITY. An insurance product in which the recipient regularly deposits money, which later will be paid back out to the recipient or the recipient's beneficiary as income. Such annuities protect the person's principal, allow the annuitant to defer taxes on the interest, and exclude the income from any probate proceedings. *See Also: annuitant, insurance, interest, principal*

FIXED ASSET. Any asset a company expects to use in its current operations for at least a year. *See Also: asset, current, operations*

FIXED CAPITAL. The capital that securities investors invest in fixed assets, as opposed to current assets, such as land, buildings, machinery, etc. *See Also: capital, current, current assets, securities*

FIXED CATALOG PRICE. A stated, non-negotiated price with the quantity being the only negotiable parameters. *See Also: negotiable*

FIXED CHARGE COVERAGE. Compares a company's income before paying interest and taxes with the amount the company spends on its yearly interest on funded debts. The result provides a gauge of the bond's safety. *See Also: interest, safety*

FIXED COST. A company's expense that does not change with business volume, such as salaries, interest, and rent. *See Also: change, expense, interest, volume*

FIXED EXCHANGE RATE. A narrow range in which the exchange of two countries' currencies must fall when trading on the open market. *See Also: exchange, fall, market, open, open market, range*

FIXED INTEREST RATE. An interest rate on a debt instrument that remains the same until the debt is retired. *See Also: debt instrument, instrument, interest, interest rate*

FIXED LIABILITIES. A debt obligation that will mature in a year or more. *See Also: obligation*

FIXED OBLIGATION. A debt that was fixed at the time of settlement, remaining fixed during the obligation's life. *See Also: time*

FIXED PRICE. An amount the underwriting syndicate establishes as the public price of a new securities issue. The amount will not change unless the syndicate is dissolved. *See Also: change, issue, securities, syndicate, underwriting, underwriting syndicate*

FIXED RATE. A loan interest rate that does not fluctuate with changing market conditions. Because borrowers are protected from fluctuations, these rates are normally higher than variable interest rates. *See Also: interest, interest rate, market*

FIXED RATE MORTGAGE. A mortgage loan featuring monthly payments that remain constant throughout the term of the mortgage. *See Also: mortgage, term*

FIXED RETURN DIVIDEND. A dividend that does not change during the life of an investment, such as that on a preferred stock. *See Also: change, dividend, investment, preferred stock, stock*

FIXED TRUST. A trust with a portfolio that is made up of specific types and numbers of a security. *See Also: portfolio, security, trust*

FIXED-BALANCE BONUS ACCOUNT. A savings account that pays higher interest rates as long as the holder maintains a minimum balance for a specific time period. *See Also: account, balance, interest, savings account, time*

FIXED-DOLLAR SECURITY. A nonnegotiable debt instrument that the holder can redeem for the amount established in a fixed-price schedule. *See Also: debt instrument, instrument, nonnegotiable, redeem*

FIXED-INCOME INVESTMENT. An investment that pays a predetermined regular rate of return until it matures, such as a coupon bond that pays a fixed rate of interest. *See Also: bond, coupon, coupon bond, fixed rate, interest, investment, rate of return, return*

FIXED-INCOME MARKET. A debt-bearing instrument such as a money market, a corporate bond, or a financial future. *See Also: bond, corporate bond, instrument, market, money market*

FIXED-INCOME SECURITY OPTIONS PERMIT. An American Stock Exchange license that allows the holder to trade interest rate options for his or her own account. *See Also: account, exchange, interest, interest rate, stock, stock exchange*

FIXING THE PRICE. Arbitrarily establishing a price on something in advance rather than via the free market. *See Also: free market, market*

FIXTURE. Any permanent structure or item attached to a piece of property that if removed from the property would cause permanent damage, such as electrical wiring or plumbing.

FLAME. On a newsgroup or mailing list, a flame is an angry comment or message that is often aimed at a particular user in retaliation for a netiquette violation. *See Also: netiquette, newsgroup*

FLASH REPORTING. When transaction reporting at a stock exchange falls six minutes behind the market activity, the prices of 15 stocks are given every five minutes with "FLASH" preceding the prices. *See Also: activity, exchange, market, stock, stock exchange, transaction*

FLAT. Used to describe a bond that is traded without any interest, such as a bond in default or one which is tied directly into the earnings at a company. *See Also: bond, default, earnings, interest*

FLAT SCALE. When the short-term and long-term yields of a municipal bond are about the same. *See Also: bond, municipal bond*

FLAT TAX. A tax that is applied at the same rate to all income levels instead of higher income levels paying higher rates.

FLEXIBLE BUDGET. A report outlining a company's expected revenues and expenses, with costs varying according to sales and output levels.

FLEXIBLE EXCHANGE RATE. Where foreign exchange rates change because of supply and demand, not because any government is trying to manipulate the rate. *See Also: change, demand, exchange, foreign exchange, supply*

FLEXIBLE LOAN INSURANCE PLAN. A mortgage in which part of the buyer's down payment is put into a savings account, with the lender drawing on the account over a period of time to supplement the buyer's low monthly payments. *See Also: account, low, mortgage, put, savings account, time*

FLEXIBLE MANAGER. An investment manager with the ability to change the investments in a client's portfolio, both in the cash amount involved and in the types of securities held. *See Also: cash, change, investment, investment manager, manager, portfolio, securities*

FLEXIBLE REPURCHASE AGREEMENT. A long-term contract, with securities as collateral, between a lender and borrower in which the borrower is required to buy the collateral back in the future. During the life of the loan, the principal and interest are adjusted according to current market conditions. *See Also: and interest, collateral, contract, current, interest, market, principal, securities*

FLEXIBLE-PAYMENT MORTGAGE. A loan in which the first five years of payments are slightly lower because they cover only interest. After five years, the payments must be fully amortizing. *See Also: interest*

FLIER. A person who normally doesn't invest, or who invests conservatively, puts money into a highly speculative investment. *See Also: investment, speculative*

FLIGHT OF CAPITAL. Capital, or liquid assets that were convened from capital, that moves in such a way as to cut losses or to increase profits. *See Also: capital, liquid, liquid assets*

FLIGHT OF THE DOLLAR. An investor uses the dollar exchange to buy foreign securities and thereby avoid the effects of inflation or some other financial force. *See Also: exchange, foreign securities, inflation, securities*

FLIGHT TO QUALITY. An investor who is trying to protect his or her portfolio in an unsettled market immediately moves his or her money to a safe investment. *See Also: investment, market, portfolio*

FLIP MORTGAGE. A loan in which payments are graduated.

FLIP-OVER PROVISION. With this contractual stipulation, a company's preferred stock shares can be converted either into the company's common stock or into common shares of any corporation that takes the company over. With this stipulation, takeovers are less attractive because the percentage of new ownership can be drastically cut, with many shares remaining with the original holders of preferred stock. *See Also: actual, common stock, corporation, preferred stock, stock*

FLIPPER. A trader in the market who is in and out of stocks usually in a matter of days. *See Also: market, trader*

FLOAT. The number of shares of a corporation that have been issued and are available for trading by the public. *See Also: corporation*

FLOATER. A note with a variable interest rate that is tied to another interest rate. *See Also: interest, interest rate, note*

FLOATING AN ISSUE. Distributing a new securities issue. *See Also: issue, securities*

FLOATING CHARGE. A business loan, with assets instead of a particular piece of collateral as security, in which the lender is paid first from the assets after a receiving order is made against the firm. *See Also: collateral, firm, order, security*

FLOATING CURRENCY. A currency with its value based on market forces instead of on the variety of exchange rates, but that can be affected by official government intervention. *See Also: currency, exchange, intervention, market*

FLOATING DEBT. A continuously renewing debt.

FLOATING EXCHANGE RATE. An exchange rate that fluctuates and is not dependent on government activities. *See Also: exchange, exchange rate*

FLOATING INTEREST RATE. An interest rate that changes according to market conditions, Treasury bills, and the prime rate. *See Also: interest, interest rate, market, prime, prime rate*

FLOATING RATE CMO (FRCMO). A CMO bond whose coupon adjusts periodically at a spread above a specified index, such as LIBOR. Considered a bearish investment, floating rate securities earn higher interest payments as interest rates rise and the underlying mortgage collateral prepays slower. *See Also: bond, CMO, collateral, coupon, floating rate securities, index, interest, investment, LIBOR, mortgage, securities, spread, underlying mortgage*

FLOATING RATE NOTE. A bond with its interest rate adjusted according to the interest rates of other financial instruments. *See Also: bond, interest, interest rate*

FLOATING RATE PREFERRED STOCK. A preferred stock with a dividend that is adjusted according to another rate, such as a Treasury bill rate. *See Also: dividend, preferred stock, stock, Treasury bill*

FLOATING RATE SECURITIES. A debt instrument whose coupon adjusts periodically at a spread above a specified index, such as LIBOR. Considered a bearish investment, floating rate securities earn higher interest payments as interest rates rise. *See Also: coupon, debt instrument, index, instrument, interest, investment, LIBOR, securities, spread*

FLOATING SECURITIES. An investor buys a security in his or her broker's name and sells it immediately to make a quick profit. *See Also: name, profit, security*

FLOATING SUPPLY. The number of shares of a security that normally is available for trade. *See Also: security*

FLOOR. The physical area of an exchange where securities are traded. *See Also: exchange, securities*

FLOOR BROKER. A person who executes security or commodity orders, as an agent on the floor of an exchange. *See Also: agent, commodity, exchange, floor, security*

FLOOR OFFICIAL. An exchange employee who settles auction disputes. *See Also: auction, exchange*

FLOOR PARTNER. The officer of an exchange member firm who is responsible for securities transactions on the exchange floor. *See Also: exchange, exchange floor, firm, floor, member firm, officer, securities*

FLOOR REPORT. After an order has been successfully executed on the exchange floor, the price, number of shares, and the name of the security are confirmed. *See Also: exchange, exchange floor, floor, name, order, security*

FLOOR TICKET. Entered by an investor's broker, this contains all the information necessary to complete a buy or sell order. *See Also: broker, order, sell order*

FLOOR TRADER. An exchange member who trades only for his or her own account, or for accounts in which he or she holds a modicum of financial interest. *See Also: account, exchange, interest*

FLOPPY DISK. A reusable, portable magnetic disk on which data and programs can be stored. Also known as a floppy or diskette, these flexible plastic devices were once the primary method of data and software distribution.

FLOTATION COST. The expense involved in issuing a new security. Normally, the flotation costs are higher for stocks than for bonds because distribution is wider and common stocks are generally more volatile. *See Also: expense, security, volatile*

FLOW OF FUNDS. A statement of how municipal revenue from a bond resolution will be spent and how priorities will be set as to what will be funded first, second, third, etc. *See Also: bond, resolution, statement*

FLOWER BOND. A Treasury bond that can be redeemed at par value when the owner dies, in order for proceeds to be used to pay any inheritance taxes. *See Also: at par, bond, order, par, par value, pay, proceeds, Treasury bond*

FLUCTUATION. Changes in a security's market price between transactions, with the movements caused by such factors as supply and demand. *See Also: demand, market, market price, supply*

FLUCTUATION HARNESSING. Dollar cost averaging in which an unchanging dollar amount is regularly invested. *See Also: averaging*

FLUCTUATION LIMIT. Commodities exchanges limit the height and depth of daily price changes. If the price of a commodity reaches the limit, it cannot be traded any more during that day. *See Also: commodity, depth, exchanges, limit*

FLUID SAVINGS. Money that has not been invested.

FLURRY. A security's trading volume suddenly takes a sharp but temporary jump, usually because of a newspaper or magazine report. *See Also: trading volume, volume*

FMAN. An acronym, showing that some classes of listed options expire quarterly in February, May, August, and November. *See Also: quarterly*

FNMA. Federal National Mortgage Association. *See Also: mortgage*

FOCUS REPORT. Broker-dealers must submit Financial and Operational Combined Uniform Single reports to self-regulatory organizations monthly and quarterly. The statements must include the firm's earnings, capital, trade information, etc. *See Also: capital, earnings, quarterly*

FOOTSIE. Nickname for the Financial Times Stock Exchange Index, which includes the 100 largest publicly owned stocks listed on the London Stock Exchange. Footsie is Great Britain's answer to the Dow Jones indexes in the U.S. *See Also: exchange, index, London Stock Exchange, stock, stock exchange*

FOR A TURN. An investor commits to a particular stock for a small, fast profit. *See Also: profit, stock*

FORBES 500. A list published in Forbes magazine of the 500 largest U.S. companies based on sales, assets, and profits, among other requirements.

FORCED CONVERSION. Because the underlying shares of a convertible security are above market value, the convertible security is selling above its call price. The security's issuer calls the security at its call price so the holder must convert to common shares, sell it, or take the loss by accepting the lower call price. *See Also: call price, convertible security, market, market value, security, take*

FORECASTING. Projections in the market or economy by implementation of existing data. *See Also: market*

FORECLOSURE. The lender takes the home and property from a mortgagee who has failed to make timely payments. *See Also: home*

FOREIGN BUY-SELL RATIO. The total foreign purchase of American securities divided by the total foreign sales of American securities provides a gauge of how foreign investors perceive the American securities market. *See Also: market, securities*

FOREIGN CORPORATION. A company created in another country and incorporated under that country's laws. A foreign corporation also can refer to a company formed under the laws of another state. For example, a foreign corporation in Ohio could be a company incorporated in New York. *See Also: corporation*

FOREIGN CROWD. Members of the New York Stock Exchange who trade foreign bonds. *See Also: exchange, New York Stock Exchange, stock, stock exchange*

FOREIGN CURRENCY. Paper money and coins issued by another country. For example, in Germany, the U.S. dollar is a foreign currency. *See Also: currency*

FOREIGN CURRENCY OPTION. An option that allows one to purchase or sell a foreign currency at an exercise price denominated in another foreign currency. *See Also: currency, exercise, exercise price, foreign currency, option*

FOREIGN CURRENCY OPTIONS PARTICIPANT. A person certified by the Philadelphia Stock Exchange who can do business in particular foreign currency options. *See Also: currency, exchange, foreign currency, Philadelphia Stock Exchange, stock, stock exchange*

FOREIGN DIRECT INVESTMENT. A foreign citizen buys most of an American company's stock. *See Also: stock*

FOREIGN EXCHANGE. The handling of foreign trades, including the physical movement of currencies from one country to another to complete a transaction. *See Also: movement, transaction*

FOREIGN EXCHANGE RATE. The amount of money one country's currency is worth compared to another's. For example, the number of francs it takes to buy one U.S. dollar would be the franc's foreign exchange rate. *See Also: currency, exchange, exchange rate, foreign exchange, worth*

FOREIGN INVESTMENT COMPANY. A company created and headquartered outside of the United States, but with Americans or American residents holding the majority of stock, and with securities comprising most of the company's assets. *See Also: securities, stock*

FOREIGN INVESTORS TAX ACT. A 30 percent tax limit for foreign citizens who invest in U.S. securities. The legislation was designed to increase the number of foreign investors of U.S. securities, which could help lower America's international account deficit. *See Also: account, deficit, limit, securities, tax limit*

FOREIGN PERSONAL HOLDING COMPANY. A company created and headquartered outside of the United States, which has less than six Americans or American residents owning more than 50 percent of the stock, with most of the company's income coming from investments. *See Also: stock*

FOREIGN SECURITIES. A security issued by a company incorporated outside of the United States which does most of its business outside of the United States. *See Also: security*

FORGERY. The act of altering any document or signature with the intent to defraud or prejudice an individual. This is a statutory crime.

FORM 10-K. An annual report, released publicly, that all companies with registered securities must issue. The report must include such information as sales, revenue, and operating income. *See Also: annual report, issue, operating income, securities*

FORM 10Q. *See Also: quartlerly report*

FORM 3. An officer, director, or investor who has at least 10 percent of a company's equity must file this report, which states security ownership, with the Securities and Exchange Commission. *See Also: commission, director, equity, exchange, officer, securities, security*

FORM 4. An officer, director, or investor who has at least 10 percent of a company's equity must file this report, which states changes in security ownership, with the Securities and Exchange Commission. *See Also: commission, director, equity, exchange, officer, securities, security*

FORM 8-K. A company files this report with the Securities and Exchange Commission within a month after an event occurred which changed the company's financial situation. *See Also: commission, exchange, securities*

FORM S-1. Before publicly selling a securities offering, a company files this form with the Securities and Exchange Commission. In this form, the company provides detailed information about itself, its securities, and the manner in which the securities will be sold. *See Also: commission, exchange, offering, securities*

FORM S-2. Before publicly selling a securities offering, a company that has been reporting to the Securities and Exchange Commission for three years files this form with the SEC. Less detailed than Form S-l, Form S-2 provides the company's latest financial statements. *See Also: commission, exchange, offering, SEC, securities*

FORM S-3. Before selling personally owned stock, a company official must file this form with the Securities and Exchange Commission. *See Also: commission, exchange, securities, stock*

FORMULA PLANS. Any predetermined system of investing, such as dollar cost averaging or constant ratio investing, that outlines a program based on investing a specific amount of money or investing during a specific time period. Through formula investing, a person can eliminate the risks involved by making financial decisions based on emotion. *See Also: averaging, dollar cost averaging, ratio, time*

FORTUNE 500. A list published by Fortune magazine that names the 500 largest U.S. industrial corporations ranked by sales. *See Also: industrial*

FORWARD. A financial instrument an investor sells for future delivery. This act is in direct violation of federal securities laws. *See Also: delivery, financial instrument, instrument, securities*

FORWARD AUCTION. An auction process in which one seller offers items for sale, and multiple buyers place bids. *See Also: sale*

FORWARD BUYING. An investor purchases commodities at the current market price for future delivery. An investor would forward buy if he or she expected the commodity's price to go up. *See Also: current, delivery, forward, market, market price, to go*

FORWARD CONTRACT. An agreement in which an asset's price is determined now, but the asset will be delivered in the future. *See Also: asset*

FORWARD COVER. A forward foreign exchange agreement that protects the buyer or seller of foreign currency from unexpected changes in the exchange rates. *See Also: currency, exchange, foreign currency, foreign exchange, forward*

FORWARD EXCHANGE TRANSACTION. Buying or selling foreign currencies with the price fixed at a current price, but with delivery to be made later. *See Also: current, delivery*

FORWARD INTEREST RATE. The most common interest rate for a specific forward futures contract. *See Also: contract, forward, futures, futures contract, interest, interest rate*

FORWARD MARGIN. The difference between a currency's cost today and its cost at a specific future date.

FORWARD MARKET. When all transactions are made at the current market price with delivery to be made later. *See Also: current, delivery, market, market price*

FORWARD PRICE. The amount of money an asset costs when it will be delivered and paid for in the future. *See Also: asset*

FORWARD PURCHASE UNDERWRITING. A company raises money by issuing stock at a price higher than the prevailing rate with the understanding that the company will not collect the money until later. *See Also: stock*

FORWARD RATE. The dollar amount a commodity, currency, or bond will cost on future delivery. *See Also: bond, commodity, currency, delivery*

FORWARD SELLING. An investor selling a commodity at the current market price, with the commodity eventually to be delivered later. An investor would forward sell if he or she expected the commodity's price to drop. *See Also: commodity, current, drop, forward, market, market price*

FORWARD TRADING. *See Also: front running*

FORWARD-FORWARD. An investor enters into a contract to be effective on a future date, with the instrument-often a certificate of deposit-maturing on an even further future date. *See Also: certificate, contract*

FOUNDATION. A private, nonprofit, tax-free organization that collects and distributes money for charities.

FOUNDERS' SHARES. Capital stock, usually with special restrictions, issued to the people who created a company. *See Also: stock*

FOUR C GRADING SCALE. The four determinations of a diamond's value: carat weight, clarity, color, and cut. *See Also: carat, color*

FOURTH MARKET. When two large institutions execute a securities deal without using a broker. *See Also: broker, securities*

FRACTION. Less than one share of a stock. Holders normally do not receive dividends. *See Also: share, stock*

FRACTIONAL DISCRETION ORDER. A broker has the right to buy or sell for a client using the broker's own discretion, up to a certain order or price limit. *See Also: broker, client, limit, order, price limit, right*

FRACTIONAL RESERVE BANKING. A system in which the money a bank must pay depositors on demand is invested or lent to other clients. Therefore, the bank could not pay 100 percent of the money it owed if 100 percent of its customers tried to withdraw all their money. *See Also: bank, demand, pay*

FRACTIONAL SHARES. Factors including stock splits, investment plans, and stock dividends create a security share that actually is less than one whole share. *See Also: investment, security, share, stock*

FRAGMENTATION. An inefficient market condition in which there is no dominant group of buyers or sellers. *See Also: market*

FRAME. 1) An HTML tag that allows an independent browser window to be contained within a primary browser window. 2) A boundary that surrounds a computer generated graphic image. 3) A variable-length packet of data containing the header and trailer information required to be transmitted in frame relay technology. 4) A single picture in a film or video that represents a single sequence of motion. 5) A single refresh, or scan, of the computer display screen. *See Also: frame relay, HTML, packet, picture, screen, tag, technology, window*

FRAME RELAY. A dedicated connection on a digital network that provides high-speed data transmission. Frame relay is typically used on a wide area network (WAN) and in private networks with leased lines, such as T1s. *See Also: digital, frame, on, wide area network*

FRANCHISE. A manufacturer or franchiser gives a dealer the right to sell his or her products in a specific area. *See Also: dealer, right*

FRANCHISE TAX. A state tax that state-chartered corporations must pay to do business under their corporate names. *See Also: pay*

FREDDIE MAC. A commonly-used nickname for the Federal Home Loan Mortgage Corporation. *See Also: corporation, home, mortgage, mortgage corporation*

FREE CREDIT BALANCE. The amount of money an investor has in his or her brokerage account that can be withdrawn. *See Also: account, brokerage account*

FREE CROWD. The group that most actively trades bonds on the New York Stock Exchange. *See Also: exchange, New York Stock Exchange, stock, stock exchange*

FREE MARKET. A system of voluntary transactions, with deals made according to unregulated supply and demand. *See Also: demand, supply*

FREE PRICING MODEL. The business model provides for revenues from sources other than charging customers for content or other services. The most commonly used revenue stream in this model is from advertising.

FREE RIDE. After a person makes a buy order, the stock price goes up and he or she sells the stock before actually paying for the buy order. This illegal practice allows a person to profit without actually risking any money. *See Also: buy order, order, profit, stock*

FREE RIGHT OF EXCHANGE. An investor can change his or her security from bearer to registered, or from registered to bearer, without having to pay a fee. *See Also: bearer, change, pay, security*

FREE SUPPLY. When the total number of stocks in the commodities industry is less than that owned by the government. *See Also: industry*

FREE SURPLUS. The part of retained earnings that can be used to pay common stock dividends. *See Also: common stock, earnings, pay, retained earnings, stock*

FREE WHEELING. After breaking a resistance area on the chart, a security's price increases even further. *See Also: chart*

FREED UP. Underwriting syndicate members no longer have to sell securities at the previously agreed upon price. *See Also: securities, syndicate*

FREEWARE. Software available on the Internet that is free to download, and can be redistributed for free. *See Also: download, Internet, on*

FREQUENTLY ASKED QUESTIONS. *See Also: FAQ's*

FRIEDMAN THEORY. Economist Milton Friedman theorized that a country's monetary controls directly affect the country's economic condition, with the economy moving in direct proportion to an expanding or decreasing money supply. *See Also: money supply, supply*

FRIVOLITY THEORY. Hypothesizes that future market trends can be predicted by looking at the amount of money Americans spend on eating and drinking. If the amount is above 36 percent or below 33 percent of a household's income, the market will drop. The theory is that if the percentage does not fall within 33 and 36, Americans are too frivolous or not frivolous enough. *See Also: drop, fall, market*

FRONT RUNNING. An unethical practice in which a market maker trades an equity in advance of clients, based on knowledge he or she has that will predictably move the equity's price. Also referred to as forward trading. *See Also: equity, forward, forward trading, maker, market, market maker, on, will*

FRONT-END LOAD. A sales charge of up to eight percent that investors must pay when buying shares of a mutual fund. *See Also: fund, mutual fund, pay, sales charge*

FRONT-ENDING ORDER. A broker-dealer agrees to buy part of a block order as long as he or she is allowed to act as the agent for executing the rest of the block. *See Also: agent, block order, broker-dealer, order*

FRONTIER MARKETS. Considered the outer reaches of the emerging-markets universe, these markets are considered the least developed of developing markets. This includes places such as sub-Saharan Africa, South Asia, Eastern Europe and the Caribbean. In these markets, stocks may rise and fall in ways that make little sense to an outsider, as local investors respond to a host of complications that can include political uprisings, droughts, floods, and other natural and man-made disasters. *See Also: fall, local, outsider*

FROZEN ACCOUNT. Any account in which no transactions can be made, usually because the bank or carrier of the account has accused the holder of some rules violation, or because of account discrepancies. *See Also: account, bank*

FROZEN ASSET. An asset that cannot legally be liquidated during a specific time period. *See Also: asset, time*

FTP. File Transfer Protocol. *See Also: protocol, transfer*

FULFILLMENT. The process of receiving a consumer's or business's order from a supplier and completing such tasks as order and shipping management, packaging, returns and shipping tracking. *See Also: order*

FULL. A bond that is trading with accrued interest. *See Also: accrued interest, bond, interest*

FULL COUPON BOND. A debt instrument with a coupon rate higher than the market's current interest rate. *See Also: coupon, coupon rate, current, debt instrument, instrument, interest, interest rate*

FULL DISCLOSURE. All pertinent facts about a security and the issuing company must be revealed when the security is offered for sale as required by the Securities and Exchange Acts of 1933 and 1934, and by the major stock exchanges. *See Also: exchange, exchanges, sale, securities, security, stock*

FULL FAITH AND CREDIT. The promise to pay a debt secured only by credit history, not by collateral. *See Also: collateral, credit, pay*

FULL FAITH AND CREDIT BOND. A financial instrument secured only by the issuers' credit history, not by collateral. *See Also: collateral, credit, financial instrument, instrument*

FULL STOCK. Any equity stock that has a par value of $100. *See Also: equity, par, par value, stock*

FULL TRADING AUTHORIZATION. A person other than the investor is permitted to trade on the investor's account. *See Also: account*

FULL-BODIED MONEY. A commodity currency such as gold that is worth its face value. *See Also: commodity, currency, face value, worth*

FULL-SERVICE BROKER. A broker who provides varied services to clients, such as offering advice, tax shelters, and partnerships. *See Also: broker, offering*

FULL-SERVICE FUND. A mutual fund in which the investor's dividends are automatically reinvested in the fund. *See Also: fund, mutual fund*

FULLY DILUTED EARNINGS PER SHARE. A company's earnings figured as if all of the company's convertible securities had been changed into shares of common stock. *See Also: common stock, earnings, securities, stock*

FULLY DISTRIBUTED. When a public securities offering has been completely sold to investors, either private or institutional, but not with large quantities sold to dealers or traders. *See Also: offering, securities*

FULLY INVESTED. All of an investor's available money already is invested, so he or she cannot seek additional investments until liquidating some of his or her existing holdings.

FULLY MANAGED FUND. A mutual fund that puts money in several types of investments, such as common stocks, preferred stocks, and bonds. *See Also: fund, mutual fund*

FULLY MODIFIED PASS-THROUGH SECURITIES. A debt instrument with fractional claims on a multimortgage portfolio, with the issuer distributing guaranteed principal and interest to the holder. If the payments were not guaranteed, the securities would not be fully modified. *See Also: and interest, debt instrument, instrument, interest, portfolio, principal, securities*

FULLY PAID SECURITIES. Securities an investor has paid for, or legal issues for which a company has received cash, goods, or services equal to its par value. *See Also: cash, legal, par, par value*

FULLY REGISTERED BOND. A bond's holders are registered with the issuing company. Any interest or maturity redemptions are automatically mailed to the holders. *See Also: interest, maturity*

FULLY TAX-EXEMPT SECURITY. A municipal debt with interest payments that are not taxable. *See Also: interest, with interest*

FULLY VALUED. The point at which a stock has reached a price that accurately reflects its underlying company's actual earning power. If the price goes above this price, it is overvalued, and if it drops below this price, it is undervalued. *See Also: actual, earning power, overvalued, point, stock, undervalued*

FUND. An asset or sum of money that is set aside and designated for one specific purpose. *See Also: asset*

FUND BALANCE. The amount that assets exceed liabilities and reserves.

FUND GROUP. A collection of funds that share similar purposes, classes, or characteristics. *See Also: share*

FUNDAMENTAL ANALYSIS. An analysis method which considers a company's financial statements, balance sheets, and management commentary to project future price movements of their securities. Historical records of sales, earnings products, assets, and other measures also assist fundamental analysts when seeking future trends. Fundamental analysts will also consider reports from company customers and suppliers, and other general reports about the company. Technical analysis in not considered an aspect of the fundamentals. *See Also: earnings*

FUNDAMENTAL PRODUCT. A market offering, such as a savings account, that can be immediately recognized as what is being sold. *See Also: account, market, offering, savings account*

FUNDAMENTAL VALUE. An asset's capital value, taken from its value as income plus interest, or from its use. *See Also: capital, interest, plus*

FUNDAMENTALIST. An investor who places more importance on a company's conditions and on the conditions of the economy in general than on the market's technical factors or the technical factors of a specific security. *See Also: security*

FUNDAMENTALS. A theory in which an investor can forecast stock market activity by looking at the relative data and statistics of a stock, the company's management and its earnings. *See Also: activity, earnings, market, stock, stock market*

FUNDED DEBT. Money raised when a long-term debt obligation, such as a bond, is issued. *See Also: bond, long-term debt, obligation*

FUNDED DEBT UNMATURED. A funded debt that matures in a year or more from the date it is issued. *See Also: funded debt*

FUNDED DEBTS TO NETWORKING CAPITAL. Divide the funded debt by net working capital to determine whether the long-term debts are in the proper proportion. The ratio should not be higher than 100 percent. *See Also: capital, funded debt, net, ratio, working capital*

FUNDED DEFICIT. A government issues bonds for the sole purpose of retiring a deficit. *See Also: deficit*

FUNDED RESERVE. A reserve invested in an interest-earning security. *See Also: reserve, security*

FUNDING. Refinancing a debt before the debt matures, or providing capital for a business or organizational venture. *See Also: capital*

FUNDS MANAGEMENTS. A bank's balance is continuously adjusted and rearranged to increase profits as long as the liquidity is kept intact and the investments are safe. *See Also: balance, liquidity*

FUNDS RATE. The interest rate a bank charges when loaning money to another bank or to a government securities dealer. *See Also: bank, dealer, interest, interest rate, securities*

FUNNEL SINKING FUNDS. A sinking fund in which the issuer has combined payments from several issues so the profits can be used to retire the most expensive of the issues. *See Also: fund, retire, sinking fund*

FURTHEST MONTH. The month that is the furthest away from settling an options or commodities contract, or the last month it can be settled. *See Also: contract*

FUTURE INCOME GROWTH SECURITIES. A bond issued by Paine Webber at discount which, after a specific number of years, pays a fixed interest rate based on a $1,000 par value. *See Also: bond, discount, fixed interest rate, interest, interest rate, par, par value*

FUTURE VALUE OF A DOLLAR. The rate at which a dollar will grow with a specific interest rate compounded over a designated length of time. *See Also: interest, interest rate, time*

FUTURE WORTH. The expected amount of an item in the future.

FUTURES. Commodities which are sold to be delivered at a future date.

FUTURES CALL. Commodities are sold at the request of an investor who holds an option to buy the commodities at a certain price as long as the option is exercised by a predetermined date. *See Also: option*

FUTURES COMMISSION MERCHANT. A business that handles buy and sell orders for commodities futures contracts or exchange-traded commodity options. *See Also: commodity, futures*

FUTURES CONTRACT. An agreement to sell or buy a specific amount of a commodity or security at a specific time, with the contract executed on one of the exchanges. *See Also: commodity, contract, exchanges, security, time*

FUTURES EXCHANGE. A securities or commodities exchange designed to handle the trading of futures contracts only. *See Also: exchange, futures, handle, securities*

FUTURES MARKET. A market where futures contracts on commodities and securities are traded. *See Also: futures, market, securities*

FUTURES SPREAD. Buying one commodities contract and selling another at the same time to take advantage of price differences. *See Also: contract, take, time*

401(K) PLAN. An employee can deposit up to 10 percent of his or her gross salary in a company fund, with the fund invested in stocks, bonds, or money markets. Income tax is deferred on the amount the employee puts into the fund. *See Also: fund, gross*

48-HOUR RULE. Final pool details of any TBA mortgage-backed security trade must be furnished by the seller by no later than 3 p.m. of the second business day before the settlement date. *See Also: business day, pool, security, settlement date, TBA*

529 PLAN. A reference to Section 529 of the Internal Revenue Code, a 529 plan is a state-operated investment plan designed to help families save for future college costs. The federal tax law provides special tax benefits to the family as long the plan satisfies a basic requirements are met. *See Also: internal revenue, investment*

G

G. In newspaper stock listings, this designates earnings in Canadian dollars. *See Also: earnings, stock*

GAIN. An investment's realized or unrealized profits.

GAIN ON DISPOSAL. Selling an asset, which wasn't expected to be sold or converted to cash for more than its book value. *See Also: asset, book, book value, cash*

GALLOPING INFLATION. A time when prices and wages are going up so quickly that the trend cannot be controlled by normal means. *See Also: time, trend*

GAMBLING. Buying and selling securities without checking into the wisdom of investing in those particular issues. *See Also: securities*

GAMMA. The amount that delta will change, given a price change in the underlying options contract. This measures the sensitivity of the delta to price changes. *See Also: change, contract, delta, options contract, price change*

GAP. A period when a stock's high and low prices do not overlap its high and low prices from the previous day during which no trade was made. This will occur when some extraordinarily positive or negative news is received on a stock or a commodity. *See Also: commodity, low, stock*

GARAGE. A nickname given to the New York Stock Exchange's annex floor, which is north of the exchange's primary trading floor. *See Also: floor, stock, trading floor*

GARN-ST. GERMAIN DEPOSITORY INSTITUTIONS ACT. The Depository Institutions Deregulation Committee must authorize the issuance of money market deposit accounts, and the accounts must be equal to money market mutual funds. The accounts cannot have a minimum maturity, and must have up to three automatic and three third-party transfers a month. *See Also: committee, depository, Depository Institutions Deregulation Committee, deregulation, market, maturity, money market*

GARNISHMENT. The withholding of wages by a court order. If a court has entered a judgment against a person for failure to pay a debt, the court also can order the person's employer to withhold all or part of that person's wages until the debt has been completely paid. *See Also: failure, order, pay, withholding*

GATEWAY. A computer system that facilitates electronic access by remote users across incompatible networks that use different protocols. *See Also: remote*

GATHER IN THE STOPS. Selling enough shares of a stock to force the price down to the level of stop orders. When the stop orders are activated, the price is driven down even farther, to the level of even more stop orders, thereby creating a snowballing effect. *See Also: level, snowballing, stock, stop*

GAZELLE COMPANY. A company whose earnings are growing at a very fast pace. *See Also: earnings*

GAZUMP. To raise the price of something, such as real estate, after agreeing on a lower price. *See Also: estate, on, real estate*

GAZUNDER. Occurs when a buyer reduces an already agreed upon bid for property, such as real estate, prior to exchanging contracts. *See Also: estate, real estate*

GEARING. As England's version of leverage, this is the difference between fixed-interest capital and equity capital. *See Also: capital, equity, equity capital, leverage*

GENERAL ACCOUNT. A customer's margin account in which a broker makes equity transactions for that customer. *See Also: account, broker, equity, margin, margin account*

GENERAL BONDED DEBT. A government's outstanding bond indebtedness excluding utility and special assessment bonds. *See Also: assessment, bond, outstanding, utility*

GENERAL LEDGER. A balance sheet that contains all of a company's financial statements, including the offsetting credit and debit accounts. *See Also: balance, balance sheet, credit, debit*

GENERAL LIEN. A claim against a person's personal property, excluding real estate, that carries the stipulation that the holder of the lien can take possession of the personal property to satisfy a debt. The property to be seized is not limited to the property which caused the debt. *See Also: estate, personal property, real estate, take*

GENERAL LOAN AND COLLATERAL AGREEMENT. A contract with which a broker-dealer can borrow money from a bank using listed securities as collateral so he or she can buy inventory, finance a new securities issue, or carry a customer's margin account. *See Also: account, bank, broker-dealer, carry, collateral, contract, inventory, issue, listed securities, margin, margin account, securities*

GENERAL LONG-TERM DEBT. A government unit's long-term debt that can be paid from general revenues. *See Also: long-term debt*

GENERAL MANAGEMENT INVESTMENT COMPANY. An investment firm that does not specialize in any particular type of investment, so it can diversify when market conditions make doing so wise. *See Also: firm, investment, market*

GENERAL MANAGEMENT TRUST. A trust fund that is not fully invested or limited to investing in one particular type of security. *See Also: fully invested, fund, security, trust*

GENERAL MORTGAGE. A blanket loan that covers all of a borrower's property and carries a lower priority in liquidation than mortgages that cover specific parcels. *See Also: liquidation, priority*

GENERAL MORTGAGE BOND. A bond that the issuing company secures with all or most of its property, even if the property is mortgaged. *See Also: bond*

GENERAL MOTORS BELLWETHER. A theory which says that when the common stock of General Motors reaches a new high, the general market will go up for four months; if it reaches a new low, the general market trend will follow suit for four months. If, within those four months, the General Motors stock does not set another high or low, the general market trend will reverse. *See Also: common stock, low, market, market trend, new high, new low, stock, trend*

GENERAL OBLIGATION BOND. A municipal bond with the issuer fully backing, in credit and in faith, the obligation. *See Also: bond, credit, municipal bond, obligation*

GENERAL PARTNERSHIP. An unincorporated business owned by at least two persons, with each being liable and each profiting in compliance with a predetermined plan.

GENERAL REVENUE SHARING. The federal government provides a certain amount of money to all centralized government entities, such as the 50 states, cities, villages, townships, Indian tribes, and counties, with each entity allowed to do whatever it wants with the funds.

GENERAL SERVICES ADMINISTRATION (GSA). A federal agency that buys, sells, manages, and maintains the government's property, as well as stockpiling strategic materials. The GSA sometimes issues government-backed participation certificates that are subject to federal taxes, but are exempt from local and state taxes. *See Also: GSA, local*

GENERALISTS. Securities that trade at more than $100 a share, so named after the General Electric Company, as its stock did trade above this price. *See Also: share, stock*

GENERALLY ACCEPTED ACCOUNTING PRINCIPLES. The procedures and rules that govern accepted accounting practices as defined and supervised by the Financial Accounting Standards Board, a self-regulatory organization. *See Also: Financial Accounting Standards Board, self-regulatory organization, standards*

GENERIC SECURITIES. Utilized to analyze the historic experience of a security, generic securities, or "generics," represent the most active security or contract over a given amount of time. For example, analyzing the performance of generic 30-year Treasury securities represents the yield levels of all the active 30-year Treasuries over the given amount of time. *See Also: contract, securities, security, time, treasuries, yield*

GENSAKI. A short-term Japanese money market. *See Also: market, money market*

GENSAKI RATE. A rate applied to repurchase agreements involving Japanese bonds that are traded in yen. *See Also: repurchase, yen*

GESTATION REPO. A reverse repurchase agreement between a mortgage firm and a securities dealer in which the firm sells agency-guaranteed, mortgage-backed securities, and simultaneously agrees to repurchase them at a predetermined price and date. *See Also: dealer, firm, mortgage, repurchase, repurchase agreement, reverse repurchase agreement, securities*

GHOSTING. The illegal act of two or more market makers colluding to influence or manipulate a stock's price. *See Also: market*

GIC. Good-Till-Canceled Order. *See Also: order*

GIFT TAX. A tax assessed against a person who gives money or an asset to another person without receiving fair compensation; there is an annual exclusion of $10,000 per recipient. For example, if Donna Schmidt gave Daniel Schwarz a $100,000 car, but charged him only $1 for it, Donna Schmidt would have to pay a tax based on $89,999 ($100,000 minus the $1 he paid equals $99,999, and $99,999 minus the $10,000 exclusion equals $89,999). The tax was designed to prevent people from transferring ownership to avoid taxes or to protect property from any pending legal action, such as bankruptcy. *See Also: asset, bankruptcy, exclusion, legal, minus, pay*

GIFTS TO MINORS ACT. Allows an adult to act as custodian of a minor's investment account without being appointed by a court. The purchases, dividends, and interest all are in the child's name. Because the stocks are considered gifts, they cannot be revoked. *See Also: account, and interest, custodian, interest, investment, name*

GIGA. A prefix that refers to billion or billions. For example, one billion bytes is expressed as 1 gigabyte, 1gb or just g. *See Also: G*

GILT. A British word used to connote a debt obligation from the United Kingdom. *See Also: obligation*

GILT-EDGED. Describes securities issued by a company that historically has achieved high profits and has proven its ability to make interest and dividend payments. *See Also: dividend, interest, securities*

GIM. Good-This-Month Order. *See Also: order*

GINNIE MAE. A commonly-used nickname for the Government National Mortgage Association. *See Also: mortgage*

GINNIE MAE CERTIFICATE UNIT TRUST. A government-backed mortgage with a maturity of 12 years or less which carries a reinvestment option. A broker will take all of the monthly interest and principal payments and put them into a market-rate money fund. *See Also: broker, fund, interest, maturity, mortgage, option, principal, put, reinvestment, take*

GINNIE MAE II. Serviced through Chemical Bank, this security is based on a number of different mortgage pools with varying rates and maturities from various parts of the United States. *See Also: bank, mortgage, security*

GINNIE MAE MORTGAGE-BACKED SECURITY. A pass-through security which pays interest plus principal. Congress has authorized this wholly-owned corporation of the U.S. government to provide guaranteed and timely payment of principal and interest on its securities. *See Also: and interest, corporation, interest, pass-through security, plus, principal, securities, security*

GINNIE MAE TRUSTS. A closed-end investment trust made up of Ginnie Maes with units available in lesser denominations than regular Ginnie Maes. *See Also: investment, investment trust, trust*

GINZY. An illegal futures contract arranged at a price that is not favorable to the executing broker. *See Also: broker, contract, futures, futures contract*

GISCARDS. A bond backed by the French government. *See Also: bond*

GIVE AN INDICATION. An investor enters a firm buy order for a specific number of a newly issued security, thereby expressing an interest in the issue. *See Also: buy order, firm, interest, issue, order, security*

GIVE AN ORDER. An investor tells his or her broker to buy or sell a specific number of a particular security, often with a predetermined price limit. *See Also: broker, limit, price limit, security*

GIVE ME A LOOK AT. A phrase brokers use when asking for a price and size quote on a particular security. *See Also: security, size*

GIVE UP. When one broker executes an order for another broker's client, the commission gets split, but the client does not have to pay anything extra. *See Also: broker, client, commission, order, pay, split*

GIVE-OUT ORDER. An investor tells his or her broker to have a specialist execute a particular order for securities or commodities. *See Also: broker, order, securities, specialist*

GIVE-UP ORDER. An underwriter refuses to directly sell a security. *See Also: security*

GLAMOUR STOCKS. Securities that are popular because investors believe the prices will go up faster than the general market. Glamour stocks normally have high price/earnings ratios, and usually sell at prices beyond their projected potentials. *See Also: market*

GLASS-STEAGALL ACT. Prevents commercial banks from underwriting corporate securities and from owning broker-dealer affiliates. *See Also: broker-dealer, securities, underwriting*

GLOBAL CERTIFICATE. The total debt of a foreign debt security offering. *See Also: debt security, offering, security*

GLOBAL MARKETS. A world-wide market, whether horizontal or vertical, that minimizes barriers to trade. *See Also: market*

GLOBALIZATION. An organization's expansion into areas outside its domestic region.

GLOCAL. Integrating a global presence into their local focus. This could include translations, currency converters, cultural elements, etc. *See Also: currency, local*

GLOW WORM. Nickname for the stock of Corning Glass, the stock symbol for which is GLW. *See Also: stock, symbol*

GLUT. To oversupply.

GNMA. Government National Mortgage Association. *See Also: mortgage*

GNMA IIS. Collateralized by multiple-issuer mortgage pools, or Custom Pools, registered holders of these securities receive aggregate principal and interest payments from a central paying agent on all of their GNMA II certificates. Principal and interest payments are expected to be paid on the 20th day of each month. *See Also: agent, and interest, custom pools, GNMA, interest, mortgage, paying agent, principal, securities*

GNMA IS. Collateralized by single-issuer mortgage pools, registered holders of these securities receive separate principal and interest payments on each of their certificates. Principal and interest payments are expected to be paid on the 15th day of each month. *See Also: and interest, interest, mortgage, principal, securities*

GNMA MIDGET. A term given to GNMA pass-through securities that are backed by fixed rate mortgages with 15-year terms. *See Also: fixed rate, GNMA, securities, term*

GNOMES. Freddie Mac "Gnomes" are securities backed by a pool of 15-year fixed-rate mortgages and issued under its cash program. *See Also: cash, pool, securities*

GNOMES OF ZURICH. A nickname the British gave to Swiss bankers involved in foreign exchange speculation during the 1964 sterling crisis. *See Also: exchange, foreign exchange, speculation*

GNP. Gross National Product. *See Also: gross*

GO AROUND. When the Federal Open Market Committee accepts bids from those banks and investment houses that are allowed to directly buy and sell. *See Also: committee, Federal Open Market Committee, investment, market, open, open market*

GO LONG. When an investor buys stock because he or she either needs to cover a short position or expects the price to go up. *See Also: position, short position, stock, to go*

GO PRIVATE. In accordance with Securities and Exchange Commission rules, a company buys back all of its outstanding shares of stock in an effort to change the company's status from publicly held to privately held. *See Also: change, commission, exchange, outstanding, privately held, publicly held, securities, stock*

GO PUBLIC. A privately owned company becomes a publicly held company by selling shares of ownership publicly after registering with the Securities and Exchange Commission and meeting the SEC's requirements. *See Also: commission, exchange, publicly held, securities*

GO SHORT. An investor who expects a particular stock's price to drop sells shares of that stock, even though he or she does not actually own the stock. *See Also: drop, stock*

GO-GO FUND. A mutual fund invested in highly speculative common stocks, with investors looking for high, short-term profits. *See Also: fund, mutual fund, speculative*

GOING AHEAD. Brokers unethically trading for their own accounts before settling deals for their customers.

GOING AWAY. One or more municipal bond serial maturities that an institutional account purchased in a block, or another deal bought to use as inventory for future sales. *See Also: account, bond, inventory, municipal bond*

GOING BUSINESS. A company that has been continuously fiscally responsible and profitable and is expected to continue in the same manner.

GOING-CONCERN VALUE. The value one company has to another company or to individuals. When this value is greater than the value of its assets, the difference is described as goodwill, an intangible asset. *See Also: asset, goodwill, intangible asset*

GOLD BOND. A bond issued by a gold-mining operation, with interest tacked on to the price of gold. *See Also: bond, interest, with interest*

GOLD BRICK. A security that originally looks like a sound investment, but later turns out to be worthless. *See Also: investment, security*

GOLD BUG. An analyst who is partial to gold investing, recommending to investors that gold is a safe place to put money because a depression or hyperinflation could push up its price. In reality, gold is a safe investment because it holds value, but it's not usually very profitable. For example, one ounce of gold 50 years ago would buy a high-quality wool suit. Today, that same ounce of gold will buy that same suit because the price of each has risen equally. *See Also: analyst, depression, hyperinflation, investment, put*

GOLD CERTIFICATE. Legal tender that can be converted to gold on demand because it is backed by gold. Few countries today still back their currency with gold. *See Also: currency, demand, tender*

GOLD CERTIFICATE ACCOUNT. Backed by government-owned gold and serving as legal reserve, these documents are what is on hand from the U.S. Treasury. *See Also: legal, reserve*

GOLD EXCHANGE STANDARD. A system in which only central banks and foreign governments are allowed to convert a particular currency into gold. *See Also: currency, governments*

GOLD FIX. When dealers in precious metals set the price of gold.

GOLD HOARDING. People convert their cash and other assets into large quantities of gold bullion in an effort to hedge inflation. The hoarders believe the value of the dollar will drop, so they invest in gold, which historically has held its value and has increased in value in tandem with inflation. *See Also: bullion, cash, drop, hedge, inflation*

GOLD MARKET. A foreign exchange market specializing in gold trading. *See Also: exchange, foreign exchange, market*

GOLD MUTUAL FUND. A mutual fund with investments divided among shares of gold mining companies. *See Also: fund, mutual fund*

GOLD POINTS. The difference between the foreign exchange rates of gold standard countries, with the points equal to the exchange's par rate plus or minus the cost of transportation. *See Also: exchange, foreign exchange, gold standard, minus, par, plus*

GOLD POOL. Representatives from the seven Central Banks try to keep the price of gold stable by trading gold within a specific price range. The seven representatives are from Belgium, Italy, the Netherlands, Switzerland, the United Kingdom, the United States, and Germany. *See Also: price range, range*

GOLD SHARES. Stock issued by a company that mines gold.

GOLD STANDARD. When a government agrees to convert any or all of its currency into a specific amount of gold on demand. In other words, the country's currency is backed by an amount of gold equal to the currency's face value. *See Also: currency, demand, face value*

GOLDEN HANDCUFFS. A contract in which a broker agrees to stay with the same firm and receive profitable commissions and bonuses; or upon leaving the firm, agrees to repay a lot of the money he or she earned while with the firm. Such agreements were designed to deter brokers from continuously changing firms and taking their prior clients with them. *See Also: broker, contract, firm, lot*

GOLDEN PARACHUTE. If a company is taken over, this provides the company's executives with profitable benefits (such as a large severance check and stock allowances) so that they will be financially secure in the event that they are let go. *See Also: check, stock*

GOLDILOCKS SCENARIO. An economic scenario in which both corporate earnings and the overall economy stay not too hot and not too cold. *See Also: earnings*

GOOD BUYING. When investors buy securities based on sound, reasonable information. *See Also: securities*

GOOD DELIVERY. A stock certificate that is in good condition, is properly endorsed, and is accompanied by any required legal documents when presented to transfer the stock's ownership from one investor to another. *See Also: certificate, legal, stock, stock certificate, transfer*

GOOD FAITH CHECK. Included with all bids on a bond sale. If the bonds are awarded to a syndicate that does not follow through on the agreement, this check is held to be used as liquidated damages. A losing bidder's good-faith check is returned to him or her. *See Also: bond, check, sale, syndicate*

GOOD FAITH DEPOSIT. When an investor establishes an account with a brokerage Finn, the firm usually requires a deposit of 25 percent of the purchase price; this is because the firm is unfamiliar with the investor's credit. *See Also: account, credit, firm*

GOOD MONEY. A nickname for federal funds, as the holder can use the money immediately instead of waiting for it to clear a bank. *See Also: bank, clear, federal funds*

GOOD NAME BROKER. When a mismatch exists between the buying and selling broker, the Securities Industry Automated Clearing will suggest the name of this contra broker so an easier and quicker settlement can be reached. *See Also: broker, contra broker, easier, industry, name, securities*

GOOD QUALITY. The stock of a company that has good financial status and historically has made prompt dividend and interest payments. *See Also: and interest, dividend, interest, stock*

GOOD THROUGH. An investor tells his or her broker to buy or sell a specific amount of securities, usually with a specific price limit, within a predetermined time frame. *See Also: broker, frame, limit, price limit, securities, time*

GOOD TICKET. Financially successful.

GOOD TO THE LAST DROP. If a clearing house member fails to transfer the debits and credits from a day's trading, the other clearing house members must make good on the transactions. *See Also: clearing house, fails, house, transfer*

GOOD-THIS-MONTH ORDER (GTM). An investor tells his or her broker to buy or sell a specific amount of securities within a specific price limit, with the order expiring at the end of the month. *See Also: broker, limit, order, price limit, securities*

GOOD-TILL-CANCELED ORDER (GIC). An investor makes an order to buy or sell a specific number of a particular security, with the order remaining effective until the order is filled or until the investor cancels the order. *See Also: order, security*

GOODWILL. An intangible asset calculated as the premium between the price at which a company is purchased and the book value of the company. Also, goodwill refers to how well a company treats its customers. *See Also: asset, book, book value, intangible asset*

GOOSE JOB. A trader who faces a limited supply of a stock illegally tries to push the price up to increase its demand. *See Also: demand, stock, supply, trader*

GOPHER. A protocol, now virtually vanquished by the Web, designed to allow users to search, retrieve and display documents over the Internet. *See Also: Internet, protocol, Web*

GORDON MODEL. A standard developed by professor Myron Gordon in which a stock's theoretical value can be determined by using equity investors' required rate of return to discount the stock's expected cash dividends. *See Also: cash, discount, equity, rate of return, required rate of return, return, theoretical value*

GOVERNING COMMITTEE. The governing unit of any securities or commodities exchange. *See Also: exchange, securities, unit*

GOVERNMENT AGENCY SECURITIES. Debt securities, such as Ginnie Maes, issued by branches of the U.S. government, but not guaranteed by the government. *See Also: securities*

GOVERNMENT BILLS. U.S. government-issued debt securities that mature in a year or less. *See Also: securities*

GOVERNMENT BOND. A 10 year or longer U.S. government-issued debt security that carries the highest rate available. *See Also: debt security, security*

GOVERNMENT NATIONAL MORTGAGE ASSOCIATION (GNMA). A government corporation that buys Veterans Administration and Federal Housing Administration mortgages, then issues bonds on pools of the mortgages. An investor in such a bond, commonly referred to as a Ginnie Mae, receives monthly dividends through the mortgagee's payments on principal and interest. *See Also: and interest, bond, corporation, Ginnie Mae, interest, principal*

GOVERNMENT NATIONAL MORTGAGE ASSOCIATION MORT-GAGE-BACKED SECURITIES DEALERS ASSOCIATION. An organization of Ginnie Mae dealers that pools its resources for training, lobbying, trading, and other industry-oriented topics for people interested in Ginnie Maes. *See Also: Ginnie Mae*

GOVERNMENT NATIONAL MORTGAGE ASSOCIATION STANDBY. A put option on a Ginnie Mae. *See Also: Ginnie Mae, option, put, put option*

GOVERNMENT NOTES. Conservative, U.S. government-issued debt securities that trade easily and mature in one to 10 years. *See Also: securities*

GOVERNMENTS. A nickname for U.S. Treasury securities. *See Also: securities*

GRACE PERIOD. The time between the date a loan payment is due and the date the loan will be called in or canceled, or when the borrower will be considered guilty of default. *See Also: time*

GRADING OF SECURITIES. Securities are rated according to the issuing company's financial strength, management ability, and stability so they can be compared against other securities. *See Also: securities*

GRADUATED PAYMENT ADJUSTABLE MORTGAGE LOAN. An adjustable-rate mortgage with low early payments that increase over time and level off after a few years. With the adjustable rate, both the borrower and the lender share the risk of changing interest rates. *See Also: interest, level, low, mortgage, risk, share, time*

GRADUATED PAYMENT MORTGAGE. A real estate mortgage that has a fixed interest rate, but monthly payments that rise during the first 10 years. The 10 years of payment increases reduces the principal, which ultimately reduces the life of the loan. *See Also: estate, fixed interest rate, interest, interest rate, mortgage, principal, real estate*

GRADUATED SECURITY. A security that has been moved from one exchange to a more prestigious exchange in order to widen its trading range. For example, a security that was moved from a regional to a national exchange would be a graduated security. *See Also: exchange, order, range, security, trading range*

GRAHAM-DODD METHOD. A theory in which investors should buy securities that had undervalued assets because the prices would eventually increase to their true value. They also said investors should buy stock in companies with assets that exceed liabilities and long-term debt, and with low price-earnings ratios. In addition, Graham and Dodd also said investors should market their shares when the shares reach a profit of 50 to 100 percent. *See Also: long-term debt, low, market, profit, securities, stock, undervalued*

GRAIN. A measure equal to 0.002 troy ounce or 0.0648 gram. *See Also: gram*

GRAIN PIT. The area of a commodities exchange where brokers transact business; different areas represent different contract periods. *See Also: contract, exchange*

GRAM. A metric measure equal to 0.03215 troy ounce or 15.432 grains.

GRAMM-RUDMAN ACT. Federal legislation that required the national deficit to be erased by 1991. *See Also: deficit*

GRANDFATHER CLAUSE. A stipulation included in most new rules, regulations, and laws that protects people who already are engaging in the practice outlined in the law from being restricted by the law. For example, if Joe Smith owned a store in a neighborhood that later was zoned for residential use only, he still could maintain his store because he was conducting business at the location before the new zoning law took effect. New businesses, however, could not be established in the area. In the securities industry, if a new examination is required of people wishing to be financial advisors, those who already serve as financial advisors don't have to take the test. *See Also: industry, securities, take, test*

GRANNY BOND. A government savings bond available in England to retired citizens and citizens receiving money from the government. *See Also: bond, savings bond*

GRANTOR. The person who establishes or puts money into a trust. *See Also: trust*

GRAPHICAL USER INTERFACE. Also referred to as GUI, graphical-based visual interface that uses icons, menus and a mouse to provide easy interaction between the user and the computer program. *See Also: GUI, mouse*

GRAPHICS. Pictures or images in digital format.

GRATUITY FUND. When a member of one of the stock exchanges dies, his or her next of kin receives a benefit from this fund, which ranges from $20,000 to $100,000. The fund is made up of contributions from exchange members. *See Also: exchange, exchanges, fund, stock*

GRAVELED. The London equivalent to bottoming out. This occurs when a stock's price starts to go up after it has hit a low, which then sparks interest in the security because of its low price. *See Also: hit, interest, low, security, to go*

GRAVEYARD MARKET. A bear market in which investors who sell theft shares lose money, and other potential investors stay away from the market altogether. The market is so named because the people who are inside can't get out, and the ones who are outside don't want to get in. *See Also: away from the market, bear, bear market, market*

GRAY CHIPS. Stocks of small- and medium-sized companies, as opposed to blue chips. *See Also: chips*

GRAY KNIGHT. The second bidder in a corporate takeover attempt, who hopes to take advantage of any hostilities that may exist between the first bidder and the corporation. A corporation doesn't solicit this second party. *See Also: corporation, take, takeover*

GRAY MARKET. A broker-dealer buys shares of an open-end mutual fund above the net asset value, in order to resell the shares to his or her clients. *See Also: asset, broker-dealer, fund, mutual fund, net, net asset value, order*

GRAY MARKETS. A product that is sold at different prices geographically.

GREAT DEPRESSION. When the U.S. stock market crashed on October 29, 1929, almost every nation in the world plunged into a depression, with supplies exceeding demands, businesses failing, and the job market squeezing closed. The Great Depression, seen by many as the worst financial crisis in America's history, continued until the mid-1930s. *See Also: depression, job, market, stock, stock market*

GREED INDEX. A system of grading portfolio managers. The lower the score, the more bearish, thus more preferable. A manager can receive up to 10 points in each of 10 categories which include: institutional activity, preference of stocks to bonds, money manager of personal investments, and invests for aggressive growth. *See Also: activity, aggressive growth, manager, portfolio, preference, score*

GREEN. Typically used in the mortgage-backed securities markets, green indicates mortgages that are not yet seasoned. A green mortgage is one that is typically less than 30 months old. *See Also: mortgage, securities*

GREEN SHOE. This underwriting agreement clause allows the syndicate to buy more shares at the original offering price so it can safely cover shares it sold short. *See Also: offering, offering price, syndicate, underwriting, underwriting agreement*

GREENMAIL. An investor buys a large block of stock with the intention of selling it to a corporate raider at a premium, or selling it back to the company at a higher premium to keep it out of the hands of the corporate raider. *See Also: at a premium, block of stock, premium, raider, stock*

GRESHAM'S LAW. Sir Thomas Gresham, an English economist, theorized that if a country has two forms of currency, citizens will hoard the currency with the higher intrinsic value, thus forcing the other currency out of circulation. *See Also: currency, intrinsic value*

GROSS. The total amount of cash or assets before taxes are paid. *See Also: cash*

GROSS ESTATE. The total value of a person's assets before any deductions for taxes, funeral expenses, attorney fees, or administration costs. After these items are deducted, the remainder is the person's net estate. *See Also: estate, net, net estate*

GROSS HIT. When a Web page is downloaded, it can be counted in two ways. A gross hit includes the number of components on a Web page that are accessed. (For example, six gross hits may include one text file and five graphic files.) A net hit is considered the entire page. *See Also: gross, hit, net, net hit, on, Web, Web page*

GROSS LEASE. Typically a short-term rental agreement, in which the owner agrees to pay all expenses such as utilities, insurance, and repairs. *See Also: insurance, pay*

GROSS NATIONAL PRODUCT (GNP). A measure based on the current market prices of the total of all goods and services produced in the United States, with the amount expressed in dollars. *See Also: current, market*

GROSS PROFIT. The amount of money an investor profits before paying taxes or commissions.

GROSS SALES. A company's total sales, with no deductions for customer returns, discounts, or adjustments.

GROSS SELECTION. Any choice made before the final choice.

GROSS SPREAD. The amount an underwriter charges the seller when he or she resells a block of securities. The fee includes management costs, underwriting fees, and selling concessions. *See Also: securities, underwriting*

GROSS UNDERWRITING SPREAD. The difference between the cost of a new security and the amount that goes to the issuer. *See Also: security*

GROSS YIELD. A discounted bond's yield to maturity before any taxes are paid. *See Also: maturity, yield, yield to maturity*

GROSS YIELD TO REDEMPTION. A British term used to describe a security's interest yield plus its annual capital gain if it is redeemed. *See Also: capital, capital gain, gain, interest, interest yield, plus, term, yield*

GROUP AVERAGES. An entire industry's average of market prices, price/earnings ratios, and earnings per share. *See Also: average, earnings, market, share*

GROUP NET. The manager of a municipal securities syndicate is given a buy order in which the buyer, who is not a member of the syndicate, agrees to pay the public offering price and promises to leave the entire spread in the syndicate's account for their benefit. *See Also: account, buy order, manager, offering, offering price, order, pay, public offering, public offering price, securities, spread, syndicate*

GROUP OF TEN. The 10 largest free industrialized nations, which work together to keep the world economic scene stable. The nations are: Belgium, Canada, France, Italy, Japan, the Netherlands, Sweden, the United Kingdom, the United States, and Germany.

GROUP SALE. The sale of a block of securities to an institutional investor, with the securities coming from the underwriting syndicate's pot. *See Also: institutional investor, pot, sale, securities, underwriting*

GROUP SALES. A syndicate manager sells offerings registered with the Securities and Exchange Commission to institutional investors, with the shares being pulled from the syndicate's pot. *See Also: commission, exchange, manager, pot, securities, syndicate, syndicate manager*

GROUPWARE. Software that supports the interaction of multiple users on a network. Shared communications may include data, such as email, meeting scheduling and file distribution applications. *See Also: on*

GROWING EQUITY MORTGAGE. A home real estate mortgage with the first principal and interest payments based on 25 years, then increasing four percent per year. The increase helps reduce the principal mount, so the equity is increased and the mortgage actually is amortized in 15 years. *See Also: and interest, equity, estate, home, interest, mortgage, principal, real estate*

GROWTH FUND. A mutual fund that invests in stocks with a long term capital appreciation objective. *See Also: appreciation, capital, capital appreciation, fund, mutual fund, term*

GROWTH IN EARNINGS PER SHARE. Primary earnings per share's annual percentage growth for a restated five-year period. *See Also: earnings*

GROWTH INDUSTRY. A business or an entire industry that is reaching higher profit and sales levels than the general market, with the trend expected to continue. *See Also: industry, market, profit, trend*

GROWTH PORTFOLIO. A securities portfolio comprised of stocks that are expected to increase quickly in price. *See Also: portfolio, securities*

GROWTH STOCK. A stock that financial experts predict will rise quickly in price because the issuing company is in an expanding industry or in the midst of some new and potentially popular technology. *See Also: industry, stock, technology*

GSA. General Services Administration.

GUARANTEE. To be liable for paying a debt if the person originally responsible for the debt defaults.

GUARANTEE LETTER. A commercial bank issues this document on behalf of a customer who has written a put option. The letter guarantees that the dollar amount involved will be paid if the option is exercised. *See Also: bank, commercial bank, option, put, put option*

GUARANTEE OF SIGNATURE. A bank or brokerage house issues a document certifying that a customer's signature is genuine. Such documents usually are required when a security's ownership is transferred from one person to another. *See Also: bank, brokerage house, house*

GUARANTEED ACCOUNT. One brokerage client guarantees another client's account, with the equity from the guarantor's account used in the account he or she is guaranteeing. *See Also: account, client, equity*

GUARANTEED BOND. A bond that is issued by one company but backed by another. *See Also: bond*

GUARANTEED CERTIFICATE OF DEPOSIT. A bank-issued certificate of deposit with flexible terms, guaranteed principal, and reinvestment rates. *See Also: certificate, principal, reinvestment*

GUARANTEED DEBT. A public company's debt that the federal government guarantees as a contingent liability. *See Also: liability*

GUARANTEED INCOME CONTRACT. An insurance company contract in which a corporation makes a large capital investment through its pension and profit-sharing plans, and the insurance company guarantees a specific rate of return on the invested capital over a period of three to 10 years. The insurance company takes on all interest, market, and credit risks involved with the security that serves as collateral for the obligation. *See Also: capital, collateral, contract, corporation, credit, insurance, interest, invested capital, investment, market, obligation, pension, rate of return, return, security*

GUARANTEED INSURANCE TRUST. Created for small- and medium-sized retirement funds, a broker will use a group of these trusts to form a unit trust, then he or she will sell participation units with face values as low as $1,000. *See Also: broker, low, trust, unit*

GUARANTEED INVESTMENT CONTRACT. A short-term, public bond with a fixed rate of return. *See Also: bond, fixed rate, rate of return, return*

GUARANTEED MORTGAGE CERTIFICATE. A security with income passed from the debtor, through an intermediary to the investor, with the owner of the security holding an undivided interest in a parcel of conventional mortgages bought by the Federal Home Loan Mortgage Corporation. *See Also: corporation, home, interest, intermediary, mortgage, mortgage corporation, security*

GUARANTEED SPREAD. A customer agrees to buy a new security at a price to be determined, and the broker-dealer, in turn, agrees to buy the securities the customer already is holding at a spread somewhere between the two prices. *See Also: broker-dealer, securities, security, spread, turn*

GUARANTEED STOCK. A preferred stock with dividend payments guaranteed by a company other than the issuer. *See Also: dividend, preferred stock, stock*

GUERRILLA. A syndicate that tries to outbid an independent bidder on a new municipal bond issue. *See Also: bond, issue, municipal bond, outbid, syndicate*

GUERRILLA GROUP. A municipal underwriting group with only a few members who assume large financial risks. *See Also: underwriting*

GUERRILLA MARKETING. A small business' approach to marketing that consists of creative, low-cost, often unconventional techniques that is going "all out" to achieve success.

GUI. Graphical User Interface.

GUN JUMPING. Illegally soliciting orders for a security before the Securities and Exchange Commission has approved the issue, or buying a security after receiving inside information that is not available to the public. *See Also: commission, exchange, inside information, issue, securities, security*

GUNSLINGER. An investor who puts money into speculative ventures. *See Also: speculative*

GUY TO THE HEAD. Used to draw attention away from plans to take over a company, often when the takeover would be a friendly one. *See Also: take, takeover*

H

***

HACKER. An enthusiast of computer programming, often with informal or no training. Hacker also, refers to a programmer with the malicious intent of gaining unauthorized access to computer systems.

HAIRCUT. A way of computing a broker-dealer's net capital by valuating securities, depending on the type of security and its market risk. *See Also: capital, market, market risk, net, net capital, risk, securities, security*

HAIRCUT FINANCE. A person who borrows money using securities as collateral. *See Also: collateral, securities*

HALF STOCK. Any stock that has a $50 par value. *See Also: par, par value, stock*

HALF-HEDGED OPTION. An option writer sells two option contracts for every 100 shares of the underlying stock he or she owns. *See Also: option, option writer, stock*

HAMMERING THE MARKET. The persistent selling of stocks to drive the prices down. *See Also: drive*

HAND SIGNALS. The manner in which brokers formerly signaled price quotes and executions on the American Stock Exchange. *See Also: exchange, stock, stock exchange*

HANDLE. The total percentage amount of a bid or asked price. In most cases the handle is omitted because industry professionals presumably already know the percentage amount involved. For example, if a bid is quoted as "8-14," the professional will know the price actually is 87 8/16 bid and 87 14/16 asked because he or she knows the security's current market price. *See Also: asked price, current, industry, market, market price, professional*

HANDLING CHARGE. A brokerage fee for handling small orders.

HANDWRITING RECOGNITION. A software application that recognizes the handwriting of its users.

HANG SENG INDEX. Similar to the Dow Jones Average but more reflective, this index charts the price movements of 33 stocks listed on the Hong Kong Stock Exchange. *See Also: average, Dow Jones Average, exchange, index, stock, stock exchange*

HARD CURRENCY. A national currency from an economically and politically stable nation, such as Switzerland, France, or the United States, with the currency holding worldwide confidence. *See Also: currency*

HARD DOLLAR. Payments made by a customer for services such as research and investigations.

HARD MONEY INVESTMENTS. Investments in gold, silver, or a foreign currency that has undergone little inflation. *See Also: currency, foreign currency, inflation*

HARD SPOT. Securities that remain strong in a weak market. *See Also: market*

HARD STOP. A strong economic environment that is slowing down, and headed toward a recession. *See Also: recession*

HART-SCOTT-RODINO ACT. A law requiring a corporation that is trying to buy into another company to notify the Federal Trade Commission and the Justice Department if the firm is planning to spend more than $15 million or buy 15 percent or more of that other company. *See Also: commission, corporation, Federal Trade Commission, firm*

HATCH. The reference to an incubator lending support to a startup company with such offerings as injecting cash, advising on strategy, providing office equipment, recruiting services, and legal and accounting assistance. *See Also: cash, incubator, legal, on, startup, support*

HATCHERY. An establishment, usually an office setting operated by an incubator, where start-up companies are incubated. *See Also: incubator, start-up*

HEAD AND SHOULDERS. When a security's central price peak is higher than the surrounding peaks. *See Also: peak*

HEART ATTACK MARKET. After President Dwight D. Eisenhower suffered a heart attack in 1955, the Dow Jones Industrial Average dropped 6.5 percent. *See Also: average, Dow Jones Industrial Average, industrial, president*

HEAVY. A lot of offers to sell a particular security, which will cause its price to drop. *See Also: drop, lot, security*

HEAVY INDUSTRY. An industry which manufactures basic products such as steel, oil, or mining. *See Also: industry*

HEAVY MARKET. When sell orders exceed buy orders, securities and commodities prices drop. *See Also: drop, securities*

HEDGE. A measure used to offset losses or potential losses. For example, gold and oil often are used as investments to hedge, or offset, inflation. *See Also: inflation, offset*

HEDGE CLAUSE. A disclaimer that absolves a writer, who has obtained information from a presumably sound source, from responsibility if information in letters or research documents is found to be inaccurate.

HEDGE FUND. An investing fund, typically used by wealthy individuals and institutions, which pursues aggressive strategies that are unavailable to mutual funds. These strategies may include selling short, extensive leveraging, program trading, swaps, arbitrage, and derivatives. The fund typically receives performance-based compensation, ranging up to 20% of the gains and 1% or 2% of the underlying principal. The term hedge fund is derived from a strategy, which is still actively used today, involving speculative investments in stocks and options, while selling short the stocks and options of other companies engaged in the same industry. Because hedge funds are private investment partnerships, they are limited under securities law to 99 sophisticated U.S. investors but unlimited for foreign investors. *See Also: fund, industry, investment, mutual fund, securities, selling short, speculative*

HEDGED TENDER. When a seller believes the buyer will accept less than the full amount of a stock tendered, he or she will sell a portion short for protection. *See Also: full, stock*

HEDGER. A person who, in order to avoid losing his or her cash position in the market, tries to offset potential losses. *See Also: cash, cash position, market, offset, order, position*

HEDGING. Selling foreign currency forward to local currency to protect the money against any changes in the exchange rate. *See Also: currency, exchange, exchange rate, foreign currency, forward, local*

HEL. Home Equity Loan Security. *See Also: equity, home, security*

HEMLINE THEORY. A theory that securities prices move in accordance with the hemlines on women's skirts. *See Also: securities*

HERFINDAHL INDEX. A statistical analysis for determining when an industry is so saturated that a merger would be anticompetitive. *See Also: industry, merger*

HICCUP. A temporary market drop. *See Also: drop, market*

HIDDEN ASSETS. A company's assets that are not readily apparent by studying the company's balance sheet. *See Also: balance, balance sheet*

HIDDEN INFLATION. The quality of goods and services drops, while prices may not rise. While hidden inflation affects the economy, it does not appear on any of the major indexes. *See Also: inflation*

HIGH CREDIT. The maximum one-time trade credit a company receives from a supplier. *See Also: credit, trade credit*

HIGH FLYERS. A speculative security that goes either up or down in price by several points on any given trading day. *See Also: security, speculative, trading day*

HIGH TECH. A company that manufactures or is connected with the sale or distribution of highly advanced computers, machines, or concepts. *See Also: sale*

HIGH WATER MARK. An investment account's peak value over a stated period of time.

HIGH-GRADE BONDS. A bond that has been classified as AAA or AA by the Standard & Poors rating service. Such rankings are given to bonds issued by strong, stable companies with high levels of proven management ability. *See Also: bond, service, Standard & Poors, Standard & Poors Rating*

HIGH-LOW INDEX. Predicts market pattern changes by defining the year's highs and lows on a moving average. *See Also: average, highs, market, moving average*

HIGH-PREMIUM CONVERTIBLE DEBENTURE. A bond that protects the holder against inflation by providing higher returns and a long-term equity kicker. *See Also: bond, equity, equity kicker, inflation, kicker*

HIGH-QUALITY STOCK. The stock of a company that historically has paid dividends in a timely manner, has shown good management, and has demonstrated fiscal responsibility. *See Also: stock*

HIGH-RATIO LOAN. A mortgage that is more than 80 percent of the sales price. *See Also: mortgage*

HIGH-RISK STOCK. An investment in a security with a volatile price, usually stock of a company with a high price-earnings ratio and a small capital structure. *See Also: capital, capital structure, investment, ratio, security, stock, volatile*

HIGH-SPECULATION SECURITY. A security from a company that has a high price-earnings ratio is considered a risky investment. *See Also: investment, ratio, security*

HIGHBALLING. A dealer illegally buys a customer's securities above the current market value so the dealer doesn't have to take a loss. When the customer exchanges his or her holdings for other holdings, which also are sold above the market value, the dealer takes the loss on the purchase, thereby giving the dealer a gain on the sale. *See Also: above the market, current, current market value, dealer, exchanges, gain, market, market value, sale, securities, take*

HIGHS. The total number of stocks that have made a new 52-week high in a daily session. *See Also: session*

HISTORICAL COST. All of the data on financial statements must be detailed with each entry's original cost to the company. *See Also: original cost*

HISTORICAL VOLATILITY. Volatility levels based on actual historical prices. *See Also: actual*

HIT. The act of accessing a Web page on a server. A net hit is considered the entire page, whereas a gross hit counts all the elements on the page. For example, six gross hits may include one text file and five graphic files. *See Also: gross, gross hit, hit, net, net hit, on, server, Web, Web page*

HOLD. A stock an investor buys and keeps because it is expected to have growth. *See Also: stock*

HOLDER IN DUE COURSE. A person or firm takes on an obligation that is complete and regular with the provision that he or she takes possession before the obligation is overdue and with the verification that it has not been dishonored. *See Also: dishonored, firm, obligation*

HOLDER OF RECORD. A person who holds a stock at the close of business on the stock's record date. That person will be entitled to receive the dividends. *See Also: at the close, close, record date, stock*

HOLDING COMPANY. One company owns enough shares of another company to hold voting control. *See Also: hold*

HOLDING COMPANY AFFILIATE. One company owns enough shares of a bank to hold voting control over the bank's board of directors. *See Also: bank, board of directors, hold*

HOLDING PAGE. A brokerage account that shows all of a client's transactions and holdings. *See Also: account, brokerage account*

HOLDING PERIOD. The length of time a person holds on to an investment or a company holds on to an asset. *See Also: asset, investment, time*

HOLDING PERIOD YIELD. Add the dividend yield to the percentage change in a stock's capital value during a specific time period to obtain this figure, which provides a measure of an investment's return. *See Also: capital, change, dividend, dividend yield, return, time, yield*

HOLDING THE MARKET. An investor buys enough shares of a security to increase interest and thereby cut down on a price decline. *See Also: interest, security*

HOME. A term a seller uses for a buyer when looking for a buyer in a tight market. For example, a seller would say, "I'm looking for a home for 15,000 shares of ABC stock." *See Also: market, stock, term, tight market*

HOME EQUITY LOAN (HEL). Security bonds that are backed by second mortgages or lines of credit. Home equity loan securities are collateralized by equity that exists in the market value of a home, the difference between the home's market value and the balance of any existing first mortgage. *See Also: balance, credit, equity, home, market, market value, mortgage, securities*

HOME IMPROVEMENT MORTGAGES. A type of mortgage that lets home owners finance home improvements. *See Also: home, mortgage*

HOME LOAN BANK BOARD. A panel that oversees the Federal Loan Bank System. *See Also: bank*

HOME NETWORKING. Two or more computers in a home interconnected to form a local area network (LAN). Users are able to share peripherals, such as printers and scanners, and simultaneously use a single Internet connection. *See Also: home, Internet, local, local area network, share*

HOME RUN. An investor makes a significant profit in a short time. *See Also: profit, time*

HOMEOWNER'S EQUITY ACCOUNT. A homeowner can borrow on the equity in his or her home through a line of credit. *See Also: credit, equity, home, line of credit*

HOMEPAGE. The first page or starting point of a Web site that typically includes general information about the site, as well as hyperlinks to key points on the site. Homepage is also used as a reference to a company's Web site. *See Also: on, point, Web, Web site*

HONEYCOMBED WITH STOPS. When the securities market contains a lot of stop orders. *See Also: lot, market, securities, stop*

HONEYPOT. An electronic-commerce Web site designed to lure, and catch, hackers who are looking to steal information, such as credit-card numbers. Honeypots are often used to divert the attention of attackers from legitimate systems. *See Also: Web, Web site*

HORIZON ANALYSIS. Measures an investment's discounted cash flow by studying changes from the time of the investment's maturity. The analysis provides a comparison with different types of investments so investors can fill their individual portfolio needs appropriately. *See Also: cash, cash flow, discounted cash flow, fill, maturity, portfolio, time*

HORIZONTAL E-MARKETPLACE. An online business-to-business marketplace that connects buyers and sellers, and serves a broad range of industries. A horizontal exchange may, for example, facilitate MRO (maintenance, repair and operations goods) or logistics services for many industries. *See Also: exchange, MRO, online, operations, range*

HORIZONTAL MARKET. A market that serves a broad range of industries. *See Also: market, range*

HORIZONTAL MERGER. When one company buys another company that is involved in the same type of business.

HORIZONTAL SPREAD. Buying and selling the same types of option contracts with the same underlying security and the same striking price, but with different expiration dates. *See Also: expiration, option, security, striking price, underlying security*

HOSPITAL REVENUE BOND. A city- or state-issued tax-exempt bond taken out to finance the construction of a new hospital or nursing home, which subsequently will be operated as a nonprofit organization. *See Also: bond, home, nonprofit organization, tax-exempt bond*

HOSTING. Internet based transaction services provided by an outside company. For example, a company may choose to outsource the maintenance of hardware, software and connections to the Internet of a company's Web site. *See Also: Internet, maintenance, transaction, Web, Web site*

HOT ISSUE. A newly issued stock that rises quickly in price. *See Also: issued stock, stock*

HOUSE. A broker-dealer company or a firm involved in investment banking. *See Also: broker-dealer, firm, investment*

HOUSE ACCOUNT. The account a brokerage firm uses for its own transactions. *See Also: account, firm*

HOUSE CALL. Occurs when a broker notifies a customer that the equity in the customer's account has dropped below the maintenance level. If the customer fails to bring the account to a higher level, the broker can liquidate the account. *See Also: account, broker, equity, fails, level, maintenance*

HOUSE MAINTENANCE REQUIREMENT. What a brokerage firm determines is the lowest level a customer's margin account can hit before further collateral is required. *See Also: account, collateral, firm, hit, level, margin, margin account*

HOUSE OF ISSUE. An investment bank that underwrites and distributes securities. *See Also: bank, investment, investment bank, securities*

HOUSE PAPER. A subsidiary or affiliate accepts a commercial bill of exchange drawn by the parent company. *See Also: affiliate, bill of exchange, exchange, subsidiary*

HOUSE RULES. A broker-dealer firm's rules regarding how customer accounts should be handled. *See Also: broker-dealer*

HOUSING AND URBAN DEVELOPMENT. A federal agency that guarantees loans and takes other measures to provide housing for low- and middle-income citizens.

HOUSING BOND. An uncallable bond issued by a housing authority and used to finance construction of low- and middle-income housing, factories, or pollution-control plants. *See Also: bond*

HOUSING STARTS. One of the 12 leading economic indicators, with changes that can drastically affect banking, construction, or hardware, among other industries. *See Also: economic indicators, indicators, leading economic indicators*

HTML. Hypertext Markup Language. *See Also: hypertext*

HTTP. Short for HyperText Transfer Protocol, HTTP is a set of instructions, or protocol, made by a computer program that enables HTML files to be transferred over the Internet. *See Also: HTML, hypertext, hypertext transfer protocol, Internet, protocol, transfer*

HTTPS. Short for HyperText Transfer Protocol Secure, HTTPS is a secured version of HTTP that utilizes certificates to encrypt all communications between the server and client. *See Also: client, HTTP, hypertext, hypertext transfer protocol, hypertext transfer protocol secure, protocol, server, transfer*

HULBERT RATING. Hulbert Financial Digest outlines how well different investment advisories fared in accuracy over the years, who followed their recommendations, and how much they profited or lost. *See Also: investment*

HUMAN ACTION THEORY. The foundation of the Austrian school of economics, which states that every human action is motivated by a person's desire for a higher level of mental well-being. *See Also: Austrian School of Economics, foundation, level*

HUMPTY DUMPTY FUND. A unit investment trust made up of shares of American Telephone and Telegraph and its regional companies. *See Also: investment, investment trust, trust, unit, unit investment trust*

HUNG UP. An investor's money is tied up in securities that have dropped below the original purchase price. If the investor sells the shares, he or she will suffer a great financial loss. However, if he or she holds on to the shares, they may drop even lower. *See Also: drop, purchase price, securities*

HURDLE RATE. The minimum rate of return on an investment. *See Also: investment, rate of return, return*

HYBRID ANNUITY. An insurance firm allows an investor to mix the benefits from fixed-rate and variable-rate annuities. *See Also: firm, insurance*

HYPERINFLATION. Out-of-control inflation that cannot be reined by ordinary means. *See Also: inflation*

HYPERLINK. Text or graphics on an electronic document that, when triggered by a command, such as a mouse click, links to another location in the same document or an entirely new document. *See Also: mouse, on*

HYPERTEXT. The reference to a Web-based system of associative links that enable information browsing and retrieval among related documents. Hypertext is enabled on Web pages via HTML programming. *See Also: HTML, on, Web*

HYPERTEXT MARKUP LANGUAGE. Also referred to as HTML, a computer language used for creating documents that can be seen on the Internet. *See Also: HTML, Internet, on*

HYPERTEXT TRANSFER PROTOCOL. *See Also: HTTP*

HYPERTEXT TRANSFER PROTOCOL SECURE. *See Also: HTTPS*

HYPOTHECATED ASSET. An asset that has been pledged, but physical possession and title have not been transferred. *See Also: asset*

HYPOTHECATED STOCK. A stock pledged as collateral on a loan. *See Also: collateral, stock*

HYPOTHECATION AGREEMENT. A client signs this document to open a margin account, pledging securities so that money can be borrowed against those securities. *See Also: account, client, margin, margin account, open, securities*

I

I. Appears in stock listing to indicate that a dividend already has been paid or has been omitted or deferred. *See Also: dividend, listing, stock*

I BUY. Used by over-the-counter brokers to acknowledge a transaction for a security in his or her own account. The expression stresses the broker's role as a dealer. *See Also: account, dealer, security, transaction*

ICANN. Short for the Internet Corporation for Assigned Names and Numbers, ICANN is responsible for issuing IP addresses and domain names. *See Also: corporation, Internet, Internet Corporation for Assigned Names and Numbers, IP*

ICQ. An instant messaging (IM) service that sounds like "I seek you." The program can be set to notify the user when others are online, such as friends, family and business associates. *See Also: Instant Messaging, online, service*

IDEAL PORTFOLIO. The perfect portfolio an investor would hold if all of his or her assets were available to be invested. *See Also: hold, portfolio*

IDENTIFIED SHARES. The portion of an investor's multiple holdings in the same security, purchased at different prices, that the investor wants to sell off. *See Also: security, sell off*

IDLE MONEY. Money in cash available for investing. *See Also: cash*

IF COME ORDER. A customer order to buy a bond issue if the broker-dealer can obtain the bond from its current holder. *See Also: bond, broker-dealer, current, issue, order*

IFX OPTION. International Option. *See Also: option*

IGNITION. The point at which a marketplace achieves a status of becoming more efficient than the traditional physical market or channel. *See Also: market, point*

IM. Instant Messaging.

IMMEDIATE ANNUITY. An annuity that begins making payments one period after a lump sum has been purchased. *See Also: annuity*

IMPLIED CALL. A home owner's right to prepay (or call) the mortgage at any time. *See Also: home, mortgage, right, time*

IMPLIED VOLATILITY. The market's prediction of expected volatility, calculated from current option prices and using option pricing models. *See Also: current, option, volatility*

IMPUTED VALUE. A reasonable or logical value a company does not record in its books, including those not yet available.

IN CONCERT. Two or more people join forces to reach a specific investment goal. *See Also: investment*

IN FOR A BID. An institutional investor asks a broker-dealer for a bid on a block of securities from the broker-dealer's proprietary account. The commitment becomes binding following negotiations as long as the broker-dealer can execute the deal on the exchange floor. *See Also: account, broker-dealer, exchange, exchange floor, floor, institutional investor, proprietary account, securities*

IN GEAR. The even and parallel rise in two or more economic indicators, such as two of the Dow Jones averages. *See Also: averages, economic indicators, indicators*

IN HAND. A firm order a broker must execute for a customer within a specific, limited time frame, usually during the same morning or afternoon. *See Also: broker, firm, firm order, frame, order, time*

IN SIGHT. The amount of commodities that are to be delivered to a specific place.

IN THE MONEY. An option contract that has a below-the-market strike price on the underlying stock for a call, and an above-the-market strike price for a put. *See Also: contract, option, option contract, put, stock*

IN TOUCH WITH. When a seller knows someone is interested in purchasing a security, even though that potential buyer has not entered an actual order. *See Also: actual, an actual, order, security*

IN-AND-OUT TRADE. An investor buys a security and then sells it immediately in the hopes of making a short-term profit. *See Also: profit, security*

IN-LINE TRANSACTION. Indicates a person buying or selling a block of securities is looking for a contra buyer or seller, and agrees to complete the deal at the prevailing market price. *See Also: market, market price, securities*

INACTIVE ACCOUNT. A brokerage account in which there has been no activity over a long period of time. *See Also: account, activity, brokerage account, time*

INACTIVE ASSET. An asset a company does not continuously use in its production processes, such as a backup generator. *See Also: asset*

INACTIVE BOND CROWD. Exchange-listed bonds that do not trade frequently.

INACTIVE MARKET. When the market's trading volume drops below its normal level. *See Also: level, trading volume, volume*

INCENTIVE FEE. A bonus paid to commodities trading advisors for providing outstanding services or for producing outstanding results. *See Also: outstanding*

INCENTIVE STOCK OPTION. Executive compensation in which the executive pays no tax when exercising a stock option. If the executive holds the stock for more than a year, the difference between the exercise price and the sale price is considered a long-term capital gain. *See Also: capital, capital gain, exercise, exercise price, gain, option, sale, stock, stock option*

INCHOATE. Not completed, or recently begun.

INCHOATE INTEREST. Indicates the person has a future interest in a piece of property. *See Also: interest*

INCOME ACCOUNT. Part of a portfolio that is devoted to holding onto money that is available for spending. *See Also: portfolio*

INCOME AVERAGING. Personal income tax is computed by averaging the current year's income with the income received during each of the three previous years. By using this method, a taxpayer is not hit with a large tax increase if his or her income rises by 140 percent or more in a year. *See Also: averaging, current, hit*

INCOME BASIS. The amount of interest or dividend dollars compared to the amount the investor paid for a security. *See Also: dividend, interest, security*

INCOME BONDS. A bond issued by a reorganized company, with interest paid out only when, and if, enough interest is accumulated. *See Also: bond, interest, with interest*

INCOME DIVIDENDS. The amount paid to mutual fund investors, with dividends, interest, and short-term capital gains earned and paid from the fund's portfolio securities after operating expenses are deducted. *See Also: capital, fund, interest, mutual fund, portfolio, securities*

INCOME FUND. A mutual fund that provides investors with short-term high income instead of long-term principal growth. *See Also: fund, mutual fund, principal*

INCOME INVESTMENT COMPANY. A management investment fund that tries to provide the highest income possible to its fund holders. *See Also: fund, investment*

INCOME LIMITED PARTNERSHIP. A limited partnership designed to achieve high income, which then uses tax shelters to protect its profits from taxes. *See Also: limited partnership, partnership*

INCOME PORTFOLIO. Securities designed to provide investors with short-term high income instead of long-term growth.

INCOME STATEMENT. A part of a company's annual report that tells how much money the company made or lost in the previous year after all expenses are deducted. *See Also: annual report*

INCOME STOCKS. Usually considered conservative securities with returns in the form of dividends rather than capital gains. *See Also: capital, securities*

INCONVERTIBILITY. When a security or other investment cannot be exchanged for another security or for cash. *See Also: cash, investment, security*

INCREMENTAL COST OF CAPITAL. The weighted average of additional costs raised in a specific time period associated with debt issues and equity classes composing the firm's capital structure. *See Also: average, capital, capital structure, equity, time*

INCUBATOR. An association of services, usually backed by an investing organization, designed to encourage and support early-stage businesses. Offering shared resources, incubators offer services that may include financing, office space, office support, office equipment, management support, advice on strategy, technical assistance, recruiting services, and legal and accounting assistance. *See Also: legal, offer, offering, on, support*

INCURRED LOSSES. The number of transactions in which a company or an individual has lost money, with the transaction occurring within a specific time period. *See Also: time, transaction*

INDENTURE. The part of a bond that specifies its terms and obligations. *See Also: bond*

INDEPENDENT AUDIT. An audit conducted by someone not within or associated with the firm undergoing the audit. *See Also: audit, firm*

INDEPENDENT BROKER. A member of the New York Stock Exchange who executes orders on behalf of overworked floor brokers. *See Also: exchange, floor, New York Stock Exchange, stock, stock exchange*

INDEPENDENT TRADING EXCHANGE. Also referred to as ITE, business-to-business e-marketplaces that are operated independently of industry-related companies, and are formed and owned by individuals with backgrounds in specific industries, technology companies, or others. *See Also: technology*

INDEX. A statistical composite that tracks changes in the economy or in the financial markets. *See Also: composite*

INDEX CALL. A bond issue stipulation in which the issuer can retire the bond at a price connected to the prevailing government bond rate instead of the more commonly used fixed-dollar price. *See Also: bond, government bond, issue, retire*

INDEX FUND. A fund made up of securities that parallel a major market index. The portfolio carries most of the same securities that are listed in the index and carries them in the same proportion. This type of investing is also known as an index program. *See Also: fund, index, index program, market, market index, portfolio, securities*

INDEX FUTURES. A promise to buy or sell a standard amount of stock index by a particular date through a broker licensed by the Commodity Futures Trading Commission. *See Also: broker, commission, commodity, commodity futures trading commission, futures, index, stock, stock index*

INDEX OF COINCIDENT ECONOMIC INDICATORS. Compiled from a collection of indicators issued by the U.S. Department of Commerce. This index uses such items as retail sales and personal income to come up with a value that many believe accurately reflects the current state of the economy. *See Also: commerce, current, index, indicators, to come*

INDEX OF INDUSTRIAL PRODUCTION. A federal index that measures the state of the economy by comparing changes in U.S. industrial, mining, and utility production. *See Also: index, industrial, utility*

INDEX OF LAGGING ECONOMIC INDICATORS. Compiled from a collection of indicators issued by the U.S. Department of Commerce. This index uses such items as outstanding business loans and trade inventories' book values to come up with a value that many believe accurately reflects the former state of the economy. *See Also: book, commerce, index, indicators, outstanding, to come*

INDEX OF LEADING ECONOMIC INDICATORS. An index compiled from a collection of indicators issued by the U.S. Department of Commerce. This index uses items, such as unemployment and factory orders, to come up with a value that is believed will accurately reflect the future state of the economy. *See Also: commerce, index, indicators, to come*

INDEX OPTION. An option that is based on a stock index instead of an underlying security, with the option paying in cash instead of shares when exercised. The Options Clearing Corporation issues these index options. *See Also: cash, corporation, index, option, security, stock, stock index, underlying security*

INDEX PROGRAM. *See Also: fund, index, index fund.*

INDEXING. The organizing and weighing of a person's investments in line with one of the major stock indexes. *See Also: stock*

INDICATED ORDER. An expressed interest in buying or selling a security. Following an indicated order, the broker can try to find a contra buyer or seller, but cannot execute the transaction without a binding order from the person who originally expressed the interest. *See Also: broker, interest, order, security, transaction*

INDICATED YIELD. The amount a stock is expected to yield during a specific time period. This yield is based on market projections for that specific security. *See Also: market, security, stock, time, yield*

INDICATION. The price range in which a security can be traded. *See Also: price range, range, security*

INDICATION OF INTEREST. A client's non-binding indication of a possible purchase of a new issue received before the effective date. *See Also: effective date, indication, issue, new issue*

INDICATIVE OFFER. In response to an RFQ, a non-binding offer a supplier sends to a buyer. This process helps to move toward an estimate of the final product and price. *See Also: offer, RFQ*

INDICATORS. Factors that accurately depict financial trends are also used to predict future economic movements.

INDIRECT EXPENSE. Any business expense that is not associated with a particular department or function, such as rent, utilities, insurance, and taxes.

Such costs usually are distributed evenly over a company's departments because all of the departments benefit equally from them. *See Also: expense, insurance*

INDIRECT GOODS. Products that support business operations but are not used directly in an end-product. Examples include office products used to support administrative functions and maintenance, repair, and operations products (MRO), such as office supplies, company travel or materials used to maintain equipment used for production. Indirect goods are products that support business operations. *See Also: maintenance, operations, support*

INDIRECT LABOR COSTS. The amount of money a company spends on employees who are not involved in the actual production of the finished products. Indirect labor costs could be associated with the salaries paid to maintenance workers, secretaries, or inspectors. *See Also: actual, maintenance*

INDIVIDUAL ACCOUNT. Any account that is held in only one person's name. *See Also: account, name*

INDIVIDUAL IDENTIFICATION. The method by which brokers segregate fully paid and excess-margin securities. Through this method, brokers register the securities in the customer's name or tag the securities with identification marks. *See Also: name, register, securities, segregate, tag*

INDIVIDUAL RETIREMENT ACCOUNT. Employed persons make deductible payments of up to $2,000 into this tax-sheltered fund, from which withdrawals will be made to the owner without a penalty between the ages of 59 1/2 and 70 1/2. *See Also: fund*

INDIVIDUAL RETIREMENT ACCOUNT ROLLOVER. A person who loses his or her job and receives a pension distribution in a lump sum can reinvest the amount in his or her IRA within 60 days. The amount, therefore, falls under the IRA's tax shelter. *See Also: IRA, job, pension*

INDORSEE. The person to whom a financial instrument is payable. *See Also: financial instrument, instrument*

INDORSOR. The person to whom a negotiable instrument is payable, but who signs that payment over to another person. *See Also: instrument, negotiable, negotiable instrument*

INDUSTRIAL. Companies that produce and distribute goods and services. Those that are followed closely by market analysts, such as Dow Jones, will be used to devise indexes to determine market trends. *See Also: market*

INDUSTRIAL BOND. A bond issued by a company that produces and distributes goods and services. The money raised from the debt will be used for expansion, working capital, or the retirement of other debts. *See Also: bond, capital, working capital*

INDUSTRIAL COLLATERAL. Brokers who borrow in the call money market present this stock exchange collateral, represented by the broker's traded stocks, to the lender. *See Also: call money, call money market, collateral, exchange, market, money market, stock, stock exchange*

INDUSTRIAL PRODUCTION. A Federal Reserve Board statistic that is reissued once a month and provides the total amount of U.S. output from mines and factories. *See Also: Federal Reserve Board, reserve*

INDUSTRIAL REVENUE BOND. A municipal bond issued to raise money for construction of a corporate building, factory, or other venture. Principal and interest on the bond are paid through the venture's proceeds. *See Also: and interest, bond, interest, municipal bond, principal, proceeds*

INDUSTRIAL STOCKS. An industrial corporation's common stock, excluding the common stock of banks, railroads, or utilities companies. *See Also: common stock, industrial, stock*

INDUSTRY. A specific segment of business, with all related businesses falling into the same segment. The businesses, while following their own financial paths, generally experience the same overall market trends that other businesses within the same industry experience. For example, while Shell and Exxon compete, they also both are hurt by low import prices, and helped by oil embargoes. *See Also: low, market*

INDUSTRY FUND. A mutual fund with most of its investments in preferred stocks and bonds derived from industrial companies with the objective of high income and preservation of capital. *See Also: capital, fund, industrial, mutual fund, preservation of capital*

INDUSTRY SPONSORED EXCHANGE. Also referred to as ISE, business-to-business online exchanges formed and owned by one or more companies in a particular industry that are competitors in the business world, but collaborate online for mutually beneficial purposes, such as aggregating purchases from the same suppliers or sharing technology costs. *See Also: exchanges, industry, ISE, online, technology*

INDUSTRY SPONSORED MARKETPLACE. Also referred to as ISM, business-to-business online exchanges formed and owned by one or more companies in a particular industry that are competitors in the business world, but collaborate online for mutually beneficial purposes, such as aggregating purchases from the same suppliers. *See Also: exchanges, industry, ISM, online*

INFANT INDUSTRY ARGUMENT. Some new industries say they need protection from imports or other international competition while they are trying to establish themselves. They seek help from their government by asking that import duties and tariffs be imposed.

INFLATION. The rise in the costs of goods and services, with the value of the currency going down. *See Also: currency*

INFLATION ACCOUNTING. A company's ledger reflects the effects inflation has had on its business. *See Also: inflation, ledger*

INFLATION HEDGE. An investment that is expected to go up in value enough to offset the declining value of the dollar during inflation. *See Also: inflation, investment, offset, to go*

INFLATION RATE. The rate of change at which prices rise. *See Also: change*

INFLATION-PROOFING. A person protects his or her savings and other fixed-income investments from the effects of inflation by tying the investments to a standard that reflects any changes in purchasing power, such as an index. *See Also: index, inflation, purchasing power*

INFLATIONARY GAP. The difference between the amount of private and public investment funds available and the total amount of savings. Many believe the inflationary gap sets the pace for inflation. *See Also: gap, inflation, investment*

INFLATIONARY RISK. The potential an investment has for losing purchasing power during its lifetime. The risk is that the investment will be worth less once it is liquidated. *See Also: investment, purchasing power, risk, worth*

INFOMEDIARY. An independent company that helps buyers make informed buying decisions by providing competitive data, research, advice and other information or services. Also, a third party that maintains consumer privacy and acts on the behalf of an individual's best interests. *See Also: on*

INFORMATION SERVICES. Also known as IS, an organization's department that is responsible for computers, networking and data management.

INFORMATION SUPERHIGHWAY. A term used by United States Vice President Al Gore in the early 1990s when referring to an emerging high-speed global communications network. Also referred to as the Infobahn. *See Also: president, term*

INFORMATION TECHNOLOGY. Also known as IT, an organization's management of information using computers.

INFRASTRUCTURE. An underlying foundation, such as equipment and support services, of an organization or system. The infrastructure for a network system may include phone lines and servers. *See Also: foundation, infrastructure, support*

INGOT. A bar of precious metal, such as gold or silver.

INHERITANCE TAX RETURN. A document the executor or administrator of an estate must file with the state government to determine the amount of tax due on an inheritance. *See Also: estate*

INITIAL EQUITY. The amount of money or securities a brokerage house requires a customer to have to open a margin account. *See Also: account, brokerage house, house, margin, margin account, open, securities*

INITIAL MARGIN. The amount a customer must have in his or her margin account to take a long or short position in the market. *See Also: account, margin, margin account, market, position, short position, take*

INITIAL PUBLIC OFFERING. Also known as an IPO, this is a company's initial offering of stock to the public. After the initial offering, the shares will trade in the secondary market. When deciding to offer stock for the first time, a corporation will hire an investment bank, or underwriter, which acts as the advisor and the distributor. *See Also: equity, IPO, issue, securities, time*

INJUNCTION. Prohibits a person or company from participating in specific activities following an accusation that the person or company is violating the regulations of the Securities and Exchange Commission. The prohibition usually remains in effect until an inquiry can be completed. *See Also: commission, exchange, securities*

INSCRIBED. A government bond with records held by a Federal Reserve Bank. *See Also: bank, bond, Federal Reserve Bank, government bond, reserve, reserve bank*

INSIDE DIRECTOR. A company director who holds a large block of the company's stock. *See Also: director, stock*

INSIDE INFORMATION. Information that is known by a company's directors and officers, but is not available to the public. Generally, this information consists of facts concerning conditions that could affect the price of a company's securities. Trading securities using the advantage of having inside information is illegal. *See Also: securities*

INSIDER BUYING AND SELLING. Officers or directors in a publicly traded corporation buy or sell securities from that corporation. *See Also: corporation, securities*

INSIDER TRADING SANCTIONS ACT. A federal law that allows the Securities and Exchange Commission to sue people who illegally trade securities. The law enables the SEC to seek up to three times the profit earned or three times the losses avoided by the person or company involved in the illegal activity. *See Also: activity, commission, exchange, profit, SEC, securities*

INSOLVENCY. This occurs when a debtor cannot meet financial obligations, and his or her assets are not sufficient to meet those obligations, even after liquidation. *See Also: liquidation*

INSTALLMENT SALE. An asset is sold with payments to be made regularly over a specified period of time, or money is lent with the principal and interest to be repaid regularly over a specified period of time. *See Also: and interest, asset, interest, principal, time*

INSTALLMENT SALES CONTRACT. An agreement in which a property buyer receives possession of the property, but not actual title until the entire loan is paid. *See Also: actual*

INSTANT MESSAGING. Also referred to as IM, a live Web-based chat service that can alert users when other pre-defined users are currently using the service. The service allows users to send messages or communicate in a private chat room. *See Also: ICQ, IM, service*

INSTITUTIONAL BROKER'S ESTIMATE SYSTEM. A compilation of estimates by analysts on how much public companies are expected to make in the future.

INSTITUTIONAL BROKERAGE FIRM. A brokerage house that specializes in handling investments of large organizations that invest their assets. *See Also: brokerage house, house*

INSTITUTIONAL BUY-SELL RATIO. Measures the enthusiasm of institutional investors by dividing institutional selling into institutional buying.

INSTITUTIONAL DELIVERY SYSTEM. A system that paves the way for trade notifications and settlements between the institutional investors of broker-dealers. Through the system, transfers, payments, and deliveries are made between the custodian banks and the broker-dealers. *See Also: custodian*

INSTITUTIONAL HOUSE. A brokerage firm that has financial institutions and profit-sharing plans, instead of individuals, as clients. *See Also: firm*

INSTITUTIONAL INVESTOR. A large organization that invests its assets and buys large blocks of securities. *See Also: securities*

INSTITUTIONAL LENDER. A financial institution that directly or indirectly invests in mortgages.

INSTITUTIONAL MARKET. Corporations and financial institutions use this market of short-term investments and commercial paper for investing large sums of money for short-term profits. *See Also: commercial paper, market, paper*

INSTITUTIONAL NETWORKS CORPORATION. A computer network subscribers use to complete transactions without using a broker. *See Also: broker*

INSTRUMENT. Any security. *See Also: security*

INSTRUMENTALITY. Any federal agency, such as the Federal Land Bank, with obligations that are backed by the government's full faith and credit. *See Also: bank, credit, Federal Land Bank, full, full faith and credit*

INSUBSTANTIAL QUANTITY. The limit that broker-dealers can allocate on hot issues, as prescribed by the National Association of Securities Dealers. *See Also: limit, securities*

INSURANCE. System where an individual or a company, concerned about potential hazards pays premiums to an insurance company. Pools of money are collected, categorized by the hazard, out of which losses sustained by the contributors are paid.

INSURED MUNICIPAL BOND. A municipal bond with principal and interest protected by insurance, which is paid for by the issuer. Such bonds carry higher ratings because of the protection involved. *See Also: and interest, bond, carry, insurance, interest, municipal bond, principal*

INTANGIBLE ASSET. An item that is considered valuable, but without physical substance. Examples of intangible assets include goodwill, reputation and patents. *See Also: asset*

INTANGIBLE COST. A business cost that is tax deductible, such as those incurred in oil drilling, geological surveys, or management fees.

INTANGIBLE PROPERTY. The title and deed to a piece of property.

INTANGIBLE TAX. A state tax on individual bank deposits, including stocks and bonds. *See Also: bank*

INTANGIBLE VALUE. The total value of any corporation's intangible assets.

INTEGRATED MARKETMAKING. A dealer who continuously bids on equity securities and on over-the-counter options on underlying securities. *See Also: dealer, equity, securities*

INTEGRATED SERVICES DIGITAL NETWORK. Also referred to as ISDN, a digital phone service that operates at high speeds. *See Also: digital, ISDN, service*

INTELLECTUAL PROPERTY. Also referred to as IP, knowledge assets that has commercial value, including copyrighted property, and patents. *See Also: IP*

INTENSITY. The degree to which the market, in a specific trading period, is filled with either overbuying or overselling. *See Also: market*

INTER ALIA. Appears in legal complaints to indicate the specific charges and inferred other charges made against broker-dealers and their firms. Translated, the Latin words mean "among other things." *See Also: legal*

INTER VIVOS TRUST. A trust established for transferring a piece of property from one person to another. *See Also: trust*

INTERACTIVE MARKETING. Software applications that personalize marketing messages by offering customers or prospects direct input in response to questions, cash-back offers or other marketing techniques. This interaction enables the software to learn more about their interests, preferences, and motivations. *See Also: offering*

INTERAMERICAN DEVELOPMENT BANK. Owned by several Western nations, this bank promotes and advances the development of the member countries in Latin America. *See Also: bank*

INTERBANK BID RATE. The rate at which a clearing member buys, or offers to sell, U.S. dollars for immediate delivery from another member in exchange for transaction currency. *See Also: clearing member, currency, delivery, exchange, transaction*

INTERBANK MARKET. A market wherein investors can spot and forward currency transactions. *See Also: currency, forward, market, spot*

INTERBANK RATES. The interest rates effective when one bank lends money or assets to another bank. *See Also: bank, interest*

INTERCHANGE AUTHORIZATION. The amount an authorizing member can approve transactions on behalf of the issuer. The member can approve the transaction alone if the amount is at the specified amount or less than the specified amount. If it is more than the amount specified, the issuer must approve the transaction. *See Also: transaction*

INTERCOMMODITY SPREAD. The price difference between the long and short positions of two different, but related commodities, such as gold and silver.

INTERCORPORATE STOCKHOLDING. A form of restraint-of-trade in which one company holds stock in another company and uses those share holdings to hinder its competition. Such activities are illegal. *See Also: share, stock*

INTERDELIVERY SPREAD. Buying one month of a commodity contract, and selling another month of the same contract. *See Also: commodity, contract*

INTEREST. The amount of money a lender charges for the use of a borrower's principal. *See Also: principal*

INTEREST ACCRUAL PERIOD. The period of time when interest is accumulated between interest payments. *See Also: interest, time*

INTEREST ACCRUED. The amount of interest that has been earned, but not yet paid. *See Also: interest*

INTEREST ASSUMPTION. That rate at which an investment in an investment plan's assets is expected to produce returns. *See Also: investment*

INTEREST BEARING. A debt instrument that pays interest instead of paying dividends. *See Also: debt instrument, instrument, interest*

INTEREST CHARGES. The cost of carrying a customer's margin account, including brokerage fees. *See Also: account, margin, margin account*

INTEREST DIFFERENTIAL. The difference between one interest rate and another. *See Also: interest, interest rate*

INTEREST EQUALIZATION TAX. A defunct 15 percent tax on interest that foreign borrowers of U.S. capital had to pay in the 1960s and early 1970s. The tax led to the development of the Eurobond. *See Also: capital, Eurobond, interest, pay*

INTEREST ON INTEREST. Compound interest, which is computed with each forthcoming interest payment, based on the principal plus the previous earned interest amount. With simple interest, payments are based only on the principal amount. *See Also: interest, plus, principal, principal amount, simple interest*

INTEREST RATE. The periodic compensation, expressed as a percentage of principal, that a borrower pays a lender for the use of money. The term Interest Rates typically refers to a general category of lending, such as Treasury rates, credit-card rates or mortgage rates. *See Also: interest, mortgage, principal, term*

INTEREST RATE FUTURES MARKET. A market for trading financial futures contracts on some government securities, commercial paper, and currencies. *See Also: commercial paper, financial futures, futures, market, paper, securities*

INTEREST RATE OPTION. An options contract on a financial instrument. *See Also: contract, financial instrument, instrument, options contract*

INTEREST RATE RISK. The risk that interest rates will rise and an investment in a fixed-income security will decrease in value. *See Also: interest, investment, risk, security*

INTEREST RATE SWAP. The periodic exchange of cash flows, as per a predetermined agreement, whereby two investors exchange fixed interest rates for floating interest rates. Interest for the floating and fixed portions is based on the same notional amount. The periodic exchange of these cash flows are for the life of the swap. *See Also: cash, exchange, interest, swap*

INTEREST SHORTFALL. An interest shortfall on loans underlying a CMO issue occurs when there is a deficiency in collections. The deficiency results when, on a class of securities, the amount of interest actually paid is less than the amount scheduled to be paid. This may occur upon the default of mortgage loans, foreclosures or other liquidations of defaulted mortgage loans that result in a prepayment, or when mortgagors fully or partially prepay principal. Interest on the amount prepaid is generally accrued only up to the date of prepayment. *See Also: class, CMO, default, interest, issue, mortgage, prepayment, principal, securities*

INTEREST WARRANT. A document in which a company asks an issuer to pay all interest due on the issuer's notes and other debts. *See Also: interest, pay*

INTEREST YIELD. The interest rate on a security, computed using the price at which the security was purchased to amortize premiums paid or to accrue discounts received. *See Also: interest, interest rate, security*

INTEREST-BEARING NOTE. A note in which the issuer has agreed to pay the face value plus interest. *See Also: face value, interest, note, pay, plus*

INTERIM BORROWING. Selling short-term paper while expecting a bond to be issued. *See Also: bond, paper*

INTERIM CLOSING. Closing a company's account books before the end of the company's fiscal year without computing profits and losses. *See Also: account, fiscal year*

INTERIM DIVIDEND. Generally a quarterly dividend, this is declared and paid before earnings have been announced. *See Also: dividend, earnings, quarterly*

INTERIM REPORT. A regular report, issued monthly or biannually, that updates stockholders on progress and developments within the company. Like the interim statement, the report acts as a supplement to the company's annual report. *See Also: annual report, interim statement, statement, UPDATES*

INTERIM STATEMENT. A company puts out a financial report that covers only part of its fiscal year to supplement its annual report. A quarterly statement, for example, would be an interim statement. *See Also: annual report, fiscal year, quarterly, statement*

INTERLOCKING DIRECTORATE. A person serving as a director on the boards of two or more companies. This is legal as long as the companies do not compete with each other. *See Also: director, legal*

INTERMARKET. Trading the same security on at least two different stock exchanges, or selling one type of bond while buying another type. *See Also: bond, exchanges, security, stock*

INTERMARKET SPREAD. Buying a commodity that is deliverable on one exchange while selling the same commodity on another exchange. *See Also: commodity, exchange*

INTERMARKET TRADING SYSTEM (ITS). A computer network that connects six stock exchanges so brokers and market makers can contact each other to execute orders. These six exchanges are the American, Boston, Midwest, New York, Pacific, and Philadelphia. *See Also: exchanges, market, stock*

INTERMEDIARY. An agent, broker or financial institution who can give advice and act as a middle person between a company and a client conducting investment business. Also, an aggregator and facilitator of transactions by bringing buyers and sellers together. *See Also: aggregator, client, investment*

INTERMEDIATE CREDIT BANK. One of 12 Federal Intermediate Banks that other financial institutions use for discounting intermediate-term agricultural paper. *See Also: paper*

INTERMEDIATE TERM. A time frame, usually between six and 12 months in regard to stocks, and one to 10 years for debt instruments. *See Also: frame, time*

INTERMEDIATE TREND. A security's price movement that falls within a larger, general trend. *See Also: movement, trend*

INTERMEDIATE-TERM CREDIT. Credit that has been extended for three to 10 years. *See Also: extended*

INTERMEDIATION. The process by which funds flow through a financial institution into investments or borrowers.

INTERMOUNTAIN POWER AGENCY. A political subdivision of Utah that issues municipal revenue bonds to finance its activities, which include owning, buying, building, and operating the electrical plants within the state.

INTERNAL AUDIT. A department of a company that conducts audits of that same company's financial records.

INTERNAL CONTROL. A company's system of maintaining an efficient, well-managed business with protected assets and well-regulated policies.

INTERNAL EXPANSION. The amount by which a company's assets grow through internally generated cash, accretion, or appreciation. *See Also: accretion, appreciation, cash*

INTERNAL FINANCING. A company uses retained earnings to expand its business. *See Also: earnings, retained earnings*

INTERNAL RATE OF RETURN. Because interest rates and depreciation cause shifts in property values, it is difficult to compute actual returns on a real estate investment. Therefore, this rate is computed by dividing net rents and the residual value, minus mortgage interest, into the actual dollar amount invested in the property. *See Also: actual, depreciation, estate, interest, investment, minus, mortgage, net, real estate, residual value*

INTERNAL REVENUE. All of the United States government's income from federal taxes except for money received through import or customs duties.

INTERNAL REVENUE SERVICE (IRS). The U.S. agency empowered to collect and administer the accumulation of all internal revenue taxes. *See Also: accumulation, internal revenue*

INTERNALIZATION. A broker buys or sells securities for a customer within his or her own brokerage firm without going to the exchange floor to execute a deal. *See Also: broker, exchange, exchange floor, firm, floor, securities*

INTERNATIONAL BANK FOR RECONSTRUCTION AND DEVELOPMENT. An agreement to help finance the reconstruction of Europe following World War II. The bank now helps developing countries to build an infrastructure. *See Also: bank, infrastructure*

INTERNATIONAL BANKING AND INVESTMENT SERVICES. A computer network based in Valley Forge, Pennsylvania, which traders can use to buy securities for their own accounts. The network provides traders with confirmations, currency positions, credit information, and settlements. *See Also: credit, currency, securities*

INTERNATIONAL COMMERCIAL EXCHANGE. A commercial market for trading currency futures. *See Also: currency, currency futures, futures, market*

INTERNATIONAL CORPORATION. A company that does business in more than one country.

INTERNATIONAL DEPOSITORY RECEIPT. A receipt given for a foreign corporation's share certificates. *See Also: share*

INTERNATIONAL FUNDS. Any funds that can be used to buy securities that are traded on foreign exchanges. *See Also: exchanges, securities*

INTERNATIONAL MONETARY FUND. A United Nations financial agency that establishes currency exchange rates and tries to maintain a world balance of trade. *See Also: balance, balance of trade, currency, exchange*

INTERNATIONAL MONETARY MARKET. The part of the Chicago Mercantile Exchange where futures contracts on precious metals, foreign currencies, and Treasury bills are traded. *See Also: Chicago Mercantile Exchange, exchange, futures*

INTERNATIONAL MONEY MANAGEMENT. A company that handles multinational investments uses this strategy to attain higher interest earnings and reduce risks by taking advantage of changes in exchange rates. *See Also: earnings, exchange, interest*

INTERNATIONAL MUTUAL FUND. A mutual fund with investments in international securities and foreign currencies. *See Also: fund, international securities, mutual fund, securities*

INTERNATIONAL OPTION. An equal and transferable foreign currency option cleared by the Options Clearing Corporation and traded on the London and Philadelphia stock exchanges. This instrument is also known as an IFX option. *See Also: cleared, corporation, currency, exchanges, foreign currency, foreign currency option, IFX option, instrument, option, stock*

INTERNATIONAL SECURITIES. Listed and unlisted securities that are traded on exchanges throughout the world. *See Also: exchanges, securities*

INTERNET. Short for internetwork, the Internet is a worldwide collection of interconnected computer networks. It is a three-level hierarchy that is composed of backbone networks, mid-level networks and backbone networks. To facilitate the exchange of information, all computers on the Internet use a common set of rules, or protocols. TCP/IP (Transmission Control Protocol/Internet Protocol). Until the advent of the World Wide Web (WWW), Internet users would use specific commands to access data. The Web is the multimedia portion of the Internet, and provides an attractive interface that consists of text, graphics, sound, animation, and hyperlinks that allow easy movement from one Web page to another. Individuals and businesses can access the Internet through Internet service providers (ISP). The Internet was originally developed as a project for the United States military during the cold war called ARPANet, it was then used for government, academic and commercial research and communications. *See Also: exchange, movement, multimedia, on, protocol, service, TCP/IP, Web, Web page, World Wide Web*

INTERNET ACCOUNT. An account with an ISP that provides Internet access. *See Also: account, Internet, ISP*

INTERNET COMMUNITY. A reference to people with a similar interest gathering on the Web to exchange ideas or information. *See Also: exchange, interest, Web*

INTERNET CORPORATION FOR ASSIGNED NAMES AND NUMBERS. *See Also: ICANN.*

INTERNET NETWORK INFORMATION CENTER. Also referred to as InterNIC, a group of organizations that provide primary directory and registration services for the American part of the Internet. *See Also: Internet, InterNIC, registration*

INTERNET PROTOCOL. Also known as IP, this protocol is responsible for moving data from node to node. IP forwards each packet based on a four-byte destination address, the IP number. *See Also: IP*

INTERNET RELAY CHAT. Also referred to as IRC, a program that facilitates real-time chat among Web users by typing messages back and forth across the Internet. IRC typically consists of channels, devoted to specific topics. Any Web user can create a channel; all messages typed in a given channel are viewed by anyone that enters the channel. *See Also: Internet, IRC, real-time chat, Web*

INTERNET SERVICE PROVIDER. Also referred to as ISP, a company that provides access (cable, telephone, ISDN, mobile, etc.) to the Internet. ISPs provide a network of servers, routers, and modems that make it easy for individuals or businesses to connect to the Internet backbone. Also referred to a business that provides Internet services such as web sites or web site development. *See Also: Internet, ISDN, ISP, sites, Web, Web site*

INTERNET TELEPHONY. The hardware and software that enables voice or fax via the Internet, rather than the traditional telephone company infrastructure. Internet telephony enables users to talk, for example, to another user anywhere in the world for the price of the Internet connection. *See Also: infrastructure, Internet*

INTERNET TIME. The implication that events occur at a faster rate, such as simply using a computer to quickly access information from anywhere around the world. Also, sociologically implies that the Internet is affecting the pace of the planet. *See Also: around, Internet*

INTERNET2. The next generation high-speed Internet. While there are many being developed, Internet2 typically refers to an initiative by the U.S. Government and over 100 universities. This is designed specifically for education and scientific research. Other Internet2 projects include the White House's Next-Generation Internet (NGI), which is a high-speed networking initiative, and The National Science Foundation's vBNS is a high-speed backbone. *See Also: Internet, U*

INTERNIC. Internet Network Information Center. *See Also: Internet*

INTEROPERABILITY. The ability of systems or products from multiple vendors to easily work together.

INTERPOLATION. A statistical analysis used to determine a bond's price or yield when the bond's maturity falls between listed maturity dates. To find the price or yield, determine how far away the bond falls from the listed maturity, and adjust the price accordingly. *See Also: bond, maturity, yield*

INTERPOSITIONING. This potentially unethical practice exists when one broker uses another broker to execute a deal between a client and the market. By doing this, the client ends up paying more and receiving less, because he or she is paying for two agency transactions instead of one. *See Also: broker, client, market*

INTERPRODUCT COMPETITION. A company that offers similar goods to the same market, such as two different kinds of soft drinks. *See Also: market*

INTERSTATE COMMERCE COMMISSION. A government agency that oversees interstate transportation companies and regulates equipment trust certificate offerings. *See Also: certificate, equipment trust certificate, trust*

INTERSYMPATHY BETWEEN STOCKS. The prices of similar securities usually follow the same trends. *See Also: securities*

INTERVALS. A schedule of exercise prices, expressed in points, upon which options are introduced. *See Also: exercise*

INTERVENTION. An agency that handles currency transactions can maneuver exchange rates between the currencies it handles. *See Also: currency, exchange*

INTERVENTION CURRENCY. The foreign currency a country uses to make sure the standard exchange rate margins are maintained. *See Also: currency, exchange, exchange rate, foreign currency, margins*

INTESTATE. When a person dies without leaving a last will and testament.

INTRANET. A company's or organization's private network using Web technology or proprietary technology, for internal use. For example, companies have Web servers that provide information that is available only to employees. The system is typically secured by use of a firewall. *See Also: firewall, technology, Web*

INTRAPRENEUR. A person who takes risk within a large corporation to develop new ideas into business ventures. *See Also: corporation, risk*

INTRASTATE SECURITIES OFFERING. A company in one state sells its securities only to citizens of another state. *See Also: securities*

INTREPRENEURIALISM. A large corporation invests in a new, small company to take advantage of any new technology that the new company may be developing. *See Also: corporation, take, technology*

INTRINSIC VALUE. In a call option, the amount the underlying security's current market value exceeds the option's strike price. In a put option, the amount the option's strike price exceeds the underlying security's current market value. *See Also: call option, current, current market value, market, market value, option, put, put option*

INTRODUCING BROKER. A futures commission broker and National Futures Association member who gives another member a customer execution and clearance. *See Also: broker, commission, commission broker, execution, futures, National Futures Association*

INVENTORY. A balance sheet entry that represents all materials involved in a company's manufacturing processes, including all goods produced as well as all raw materials. *See Also: balance, balance sheet*

INVENTORY FINANCING. A bank finances a dealer's inventory of consumer or capital goods. The dealer uses the inventory as collateral for the loan. *See Also: bank, capital, capital goods, collateral, dealer, inventory*

INVENTORY TURNOVER. A company divides the cost of its goods sold by its average inventory for the year. This ratio helps the company to determine how efficiently it is using its assets in its turnover of sellable goods. *See Also: average, inventory, ratio, turnover*

INVERSE DEMAND PATTERN. When prices and trading volumes change at the same rate and at the same time, and more securities are sold at higher prices than at lower ones. *See Also: change, securities, time*

INVERSE FLOATING RATE CMO. A CMO bond that acts as a complement to floating rate securities. Its coupon periodically adjusts inversely to the floating rate index. Considered a bullish investment, inverse floating rate securities earn higher interest payments as interest rates fall and the underlying mortgage collateral prepays faster. *See Also: bond, CMO, collateral, coupon, fall, floating rate securities, index, interest, inverse floating rate securities, investment, mortgage, securities, underlying mortgage*

INVERSE FLOATING RATE SECURITIES. A debt instrument whose coupon inversely adjusts periodically with changes in a specified index, such as LIBOR. Considered a bullish investment, floating rate securities earn higher interest payments as interest rates decrease. *See Also: coupon, debt instrument, floating rate securities, index, instrument, interest, investment, LIBOR, securities*

INVERTED MARKET. When distant-month commodity futures contracts sell at lower prices than near-month commodity futures contracts. *See Also: commodity, futures*

INVERTED SCALE. A serial bond offering with short-term yields that are higher than the long-term yields. *See Also: bond, offering*

INVERTED YIELD CURVE. A graph of yields from similar securities with short-term yields that are higher than their long-term yields. *See Also: securities*

INVESTED CAPITAL. An amount received in exchange for equity capital. *See Also: capital, equity, equity capital, exchange*

INVESTMENT. Cautiously using money to make more money, with the smallest amount of risk. Using money to make more money without regard to risk is considered gambling. *See Also: gambling, risk*

INVESTMENT ADVISORS ACT. Requires the registration of people and companies who provide investment advice and guidance for a fee. *See Also: investment, registration*

INVESTMENT ADVISORY SERVICE. A company that provides advice and guidance in securities investing. Many companies, the advisors of which must be registered with the Securities and Exchange Commission, specialize in guiding clients toward specific types of investments, such as growth stocks. *See Also: commission, exchange, securities*

INVESTMENT ASSETS. Cash, bonds, stocks, other assets or investments that will produce income for the investor or that will appreciate in value.

INVESTMENT BANK. A financial institution provides an assortment of services, including acting as an intermediary between an issuer of new securities and the investing public. Other services may include secondary stock offerings, underwriting counseling, facilitating mergers and acquisitions and other corporate reorganizations. The investment bank will also engage in the trading of their own account, and act as a principal or agent when selling securities to both individual and institutional clients. *See Also: account, agent, bank, intermediary, investment, principal, securities, stock, underwriting*

INVESTMENT BANKER. A person who acts as an intermediary between a company that needs money and a person who wants to invest in the company. To make the exchange, the banker aids in a number of functions, such as underwriting a securities issue. *See Also: exchange, intermediary, issue, securities, underwriting*

INVESTMENT BANKERS ASSOCIATION. A national organization established in 1912 and made up of bankers involved in investment activity. *See Also: activity, investment*

INVESTMENT BANKING HOUSE. A firm that buys large blocks of corporate and government securities and then sells the securities to investors to finance the corporation's capital needs. *See Also: capital, firm, securities*

INVESTMENT BILL. A discounted bill of exchange that an investor buys and holds until maturity. *See Also: bill of exchange, exchange, maturity*

INVESTMENT CERTIFICATE. A document verifying that a person has money invested in a savings and loan association. The document indicates the investment amount, but it does not provide the holder with any stockholder rights, such as voting rights. *See Also: investment, rights, savings and loan association, stockholder, voting rights*

INVESTMENT CLUB. A group of people who do not invest as a profession, but who pool their money together to invest. *See Also: pool*

INVESTMENT COMPANY. A firm that pools money from investors and puts the funds into securities. *See Also: firm, securities*

INVESTMENT COMPANY ACT. This act requires the registration of investment companies. *See Also: investment, registration*

INVESTMENT COMPANY AND VARIABLE CONTRACT PRODUCTS. A limited Securities and Exchange Commission registration that allows a person to sell or manage either shares of an investment company or annuity contracts. *See Also: annuity, commission, exchange, investment, investment company, registration, securities*

INVESTMENT CREDIT. A company that invests in specific asset categories can have a portion of its income tax liability reduced, as long as the credit is claimed in the same year the purchase is made. *See Also: asset, credit, liability*

INVESTMENT FEATURE. An investment's main characteristics and qualities, including income and growth potential, financial safety, and tax advantages. *See Also: safety*

INVESTMENT GRADE. The rating of a bond from AAA down to BBB according to Standard & Poors system is considered to be suitable for prudent investors. *See Also: bond, Standard & Poors*

INVESTMENT HISTORY NASD. term pertaining to sales of hot issues. The amount of shares purchased by an individual is governed by previous shares purchased in accordance with his or her investment history of a particular investment. *See Also: investment, term*

INVESTMENT IN DEFAULT. An investment in which interest or dividend payments are in default. *See Also: default, dividend, interest, investment*

INVESTMENT INCOME. Any money earned from an investment. *See Also: investment*

INVESTMENT LETTER. A private contract between a buyer and seller in which the buyer promises that the security is being purchased as an investment and not for resale, so he or she therefore will hold on to it for a specific length of time, usually two years. This occurs frequently in private placements. *See Also: contract, hold, investment, security, time*

INVESTMENT MANAGER. A person authorized to invest money for another person or for a corporation. *See Also: corporation*

INVESTMENT OBJECTIVE. The mount of money an investor expects to realize on an investment. Also, the goals of a portfolio. *See Also: investment, portfolio, realize*

INVESTMENT POLICY STATEMENT. A statement that tells how much risk the fiduciaries are willing to assume with pension fund assets and that spells out desired courses of action. *See Also: fund, pension, risk, statement*

INVESTMENT PORTFOLIO A collection of securities a person owns. *See Also: securities*

INVESTMENT PROPERTY. Real estate a person buys with the intent of making a profit, either through renting the property or through a quick sale. *See Also: estate, profit, sale*

INVESTMENT SECURITIES. All investments purchased for a portfolio instead of for a quick sale. *See Also: portfolio, sale*

INVESTMENT SKELETON. A worthless, speculative security, or a speculative security that fails to meet a person's investment objectives. *See Also: fails, investment, security, speculative*

INVESTMENT STRATEGY. A plan of investing among choices such as stocks, bonds, cash, commodities, and real estate. *See Also: cash, estate, real estate*

INVESTMENT TAX CREDIT. When a person buys certain tangible assets, he or she can receive a 10 percent tax credit during that same year. The credit is provided to stimulate the purchase of assets that will increase employment or public service opportunities. *See Also: credit, service, tax credit*

INVESTMENT TRUST. Any company or trust that invests its capital in another company or trust. *See Also: capital, trust*

INVESTMENT VALUE. The amount a bond would be worth if it did not have a conversion feature. The value is determined by adding the value of the coupons to the principal amount after the principal amount is discounted by the current interest rate for a similar bond. *See Also: bond, conversion, current, interest, interest rate, principal, principal amount, worth*

INVESTOR FALLOUT. A risk incurred by originators of mortgage collateral during the mortgage pipeline period when the originator of the loans commits loan terms to the borrowers and obtains commitments from investors at the time of application. *See Also: collateral, mortgage, mortgage pipeline, originator, pipeline, risk, time*

INVESTOR RELATIONS DEPARTMENT. An exchange-listed company will have a staff member responsible for acting as the intermediary between the company and an investor. While the duties of the person in charge vary from company to company, the job is similar to a public relations job. This person disseminates pertinent information to the public and usually is responsible for showing the company in a good light. *See Also: intermediary, job*

INVESTORS SERVICE BUREAU. A service offered by the New York Stock Exchange that answers questions regarding all types of securities investments. *See Also: exchange, New York Stock Exchange, securities, service, stock, stock exchange*

INVISIBLE WEB. Also referred to as the deep Web, Web-based information that isn't contained on static Web pages. This information is held in back-end systems that build Web pages for users upon their request. *See Also: deep Web, on, Web*

INVOLUNTARY INVESTOR. An investor who paid a high price for a security and because the price later dropped, he or she cannot sell the security without losing a lot of money. *See Also: lot, security*

INVOLUNTARY LIEN. A lien, such as property tax increases, placed on a person's property without that person's consent. IO An interest only bond. *See Also: bond, interest, stripped bond*

IOU. An informal agreement to repay a debt.

IP. Intellectual Property or Internet Protocol.

IP ADDRESS. The Internet protocol address is the numeric address that uniquely identifies a particular computer on the Internet. This number is assigned to every computer on the Internet, represented by four numbers separated by dots (e.g., 111.111.111.1). *See Also: address, Internet, Internet protocol, on, protocol*

IPO. an IPO is a company's initial offering of stock to the public. After the initial offering, the shares will trade in the secondary market. When deciding to offer stock for the first time, a corporation will hire an investment bank, or underwriter, which acts as the advisor and the distributor. *See Also: bank, corporation, distributor, initial public offering, investment, investment bank, market, offer, offering, secondary market, stock, time*

IRA. Individual Retirement Account. *See Also: account*

IRC. Internet Relay Chat. *See Also: Internet*

IRISH DIVIDEND. Nickname for when a stock split ends with fewer shares outstanding. *See Also: outstanding, shares outstanding, split, stock*

IRRATIONAL CALL OPTIONS. The name given to the implied call options that are embedded in mortgage-backed securities. These calls are considered irrational because interest rates may be well below the threshold to refinance, but mortgagors do not exercise the right to refinance. *See Also: exercise, implied call, interest, name, right, securities*

IRREVOCABLE LETTER OF CREDIT. A document in which an issuer agrees to accept drafts and to charge them against his or her own account during a specific time period. *See Also: account, time*

IRREVOCABLE TRUST. A trust that the creator cannot alter or end unless the beneficiary agrees. *See Also: trust*

IRS. Internal Revenue Service. *See Also: internal revenue, service*

IS. Information services.

ISDN. Integrated Services Digital Network. *See Also: digital*

ISE. Industry Sponsored Exchange. *See Also: exchange, industry*

ISLAND REVERSAL. A gap that marks a number of trades on both the up and down side when these fall in the middle of a market trend reversal. *See Also: fall, gap, market, market trend, reversal, trend*

ISM. Industry Sponsored Marketplace. *See Also: industry*

ISP. Internet Service Provider. *See Also: Internet, service*

ISSUE. A security issued by a company that is at least partially public-owned. *See Also: security*

ISSUE PRICE. The price at which a new security will be sold to the public. *See Also: security*

ISSUED AND OUTSTANDING. Stock that is owned by the public or by the company's directors.

ISSUED CAPITAL STOCK. A company's capital stock that has either been sold publicly or traded for goods and services. *See Also: capital, capital stock, stock*

ISSUED STOCK. The total number of a company's publicly held stocks plus the number of shares the company holds as treasury stock. *See Also: plus, publicly held, stock, treasury stock*

J

JACQUES COUSTEAU OPTION. An option that has lost value because the current market price has fallen below the original exercise price. *See also: current, exercise, exercise price, market, market price, option*

JAJO. Represents January, April, July, and October, which are the expiration months of successively offered option contracts. It also represents interest and dividend payments that are due quarterly. *See Also: dividend, expiration, interest, option, quarterly*

JAMES BOND. Nickname for a U.S. Treasury bond that matures in the year 2007, so named because the maturity date is James Bond's agent number in the popular series of movies. *See Also: agent, bond, maturity, Treasury bond*

JAPANESE AUCTION. A forward auction process in which bidding begins at a low price and increases in fixed amounts. As price levels rise, unwilling bidders withdraw until the last, winning bidder remains. *See Also: forward, forward auction, low*

JAPANESE DEPOSITORY RECEIPT. A receipt that represents ownership of a certain number of stock shares of a non-Japanese company. The JDR is the Japanese equivalent to the American Depository Receipt. *See Also: depository, JDR, stock*

JARGON. Terms and vocabulary that are particular to one general field or industry. *See Also: industry*

JAVA. A programming language, invented by Sun Microsystems, that is used to bring deliver applications over the Internet. It is designed to operate on many different types of computers. Java is an interpreted, object-orientated program language with a syntax and structure similar to the programming language C++. *See Also: Internet, on*

JAVASCRIPT. An adjunct to the programming language Java, JavaScript is a cross-platform WWW scripting language that creates interactive documents in HTML pages. The language is popular because of its functionality, and because it's easier to learn and use. *See Also: easier, HTML, Java, World Wide Web*

JDR. Japanese Depository Receipt. *See Also: depository*

JELLY ROLL SPREAD. A long and short position in the same index option with different classes-a put and a call-having different expiration dates. *See Also: expiration, index, index option, option, position, put, short position*

JEOPARDY CLAUSE. A stipulation in a Eurocurrency agreement that guarantees certain actions will be taken to protect the market if some events curtail the lender's activities or Euromarket operations. *See Also: Eurocurrency, market, operations*

JOB. A foreign bank that deals with other banks on its own behalf. *See Also: bank*

JOB LOT. A trading unit of commodities or securities that is less than a round lot, which usually is equal to 100 shares of stock, and varies in the futures market with each individual commodity. *See Also: commodity, futures, futures market, lot, market, round lot, securities, stock, trading unit, unit*

JOBBER. A London market maker similar to a U.S. exchange specialist. *See Also: exchange, maker, market, market maker, specialist*

JOBBER'S TURN. In England, the difference between a jobber's bid and ask prices, the equivalent to a spread on the American market. *See Also: ask, market, spread*

JOHN DOE. The legal name given to anyone whose name is unknown. *See Also: legal, name*

JOINT ACCOUNT. An account held by two or more people, with each person equally sharing all profits, privileges, and liabilities associated with the account. *See Also: account*

JOINT ACCOUNT AGREEMENT. All people who hold a joint account must sign this document, which authorizes each person to make transactions on the account. *See Also: account, hold, joint account*

JOINT AND SURVIVOR ANNUITY. An annuity that pays dividends to two or more people, usually a husband and wife. After one of the beneficiaries dies, the other continues to receive his or her share of the payments, but not those of the decedent's. *See Also: annuity, share*

JOINT BOND. A bond that is issued by one party, but guaranteed by another, or a bond that has more than one issuer. *See Also: bond*

JOINT CONTRACT. An agreement in which two or more people consent to be joint obligators to another party.

JOINT ENDORSEMENT. Two or more signatures are required on a financial instrument that has been made payable to those two or more people. The instrument is nonnegotiable without the signatures of everyone named as a payee. *See Also: financial instrument, instrument, nonnegotiable*

JOINT PHOTOGRAPHIC EXPERTS GROUP. *See Also: JPEG*

JOINT TENANCY. Two or more people jointly and equally own a piece of property. If one of the owners dies, his or her share is divided proportionately among the other owners. *See Also: share*

JOINT TENANCY WITH RIGHT OF SURVIVORSHIP (JTWROS). A joint account held with a brokerage firm or a bank with the agreement that if one should die, the ownership of the account assets would be transferred to the joint tenant(s). *See Also: account, bank, firm, joint account*

JOINT VENTURE. Two or more people unite to form a business.

JOINT VENTURE TENDER. Two or more companies combine their resources and capital to take over another company, after which the companies will share in the venture equally. *See Also: capital, share, take*

JPEG. Short for Joint Photographic Experts Group, JPEG is a compressed file format for graphics. *See Also: Joint Photographic Experts Group*

JTWROS. Joint Tenancy With Right of Survivorship. *See Also: joint tenancy, right, right of survivorship, tenancy*

JUDGMENT CURRENCY CLAUSE. A stipulation in a Eurocurrency credit agreement guaranteeing lenders that they will not lose any money if the loan is made in one currency and a court passes judgment in a different currency with an unfavorable exchange rate. *See Also: credit, credit agreement, currency, eurocurrency, exchange, exchange rate*

JUMBO CERTIFICATE OF DEPOSIT. A certificate of deposit with a denomination of at least $100,000, usually purchased by institutional investors. *See Also: certificate, denomination*

JUNIOR. An investor exchanges securities that mature in one to five years for securities that mature in five or more years. *See Also: exchanges, securities*

JUNIOR BOND. A debt instrument that falls subordinate to other bonds from the same issuer if that issuer defaults or becomes subject to financial claims. *See Also: debt instrument, instrument*

JUNIOR REFUNDING. Issuing securities that mature in five or more years to refinance a government debt that matures in one to five years. *See Also: securities*

JUNIOR SECURITIES. A stock or bond that falls subordinate to other claims on the issuer's cash or assets. For example, preferred stock is junior to a debenture, and common stock is junior to preferred stock. *See Also: bond, cash, common stock, debenture, junior, preferred stock, stock*

JUNIOR STOCK PLAN. A benefit plan that provides an executive with the right to exchange specially issued shares of stock for common stock after an executive has been with a company for a specified length of time. *See Also: common stock, exchange, right, stock, time*

JUNK BOND. A speculative bond with a rating of BB or lower from Moody's or Standard & Poors. *See Also: bond, speculative, Standard & Poors*

JUNK FINANCING. Using unsecured, high-interest securities with low credit ratings to raise capital. *See Also: capital, credit, low, securities*

JURY OF EXECUTIVE OPINION. A panel of experts combine knowledge to make individual forecasts, which later form a composite prediction. *See Also: composite*

K

K. Follows a number to indicate that the number should be multiplied by 1,000.

KAFFIR. Any gold mining company in South Africa, or South African gold mining shares.

KANSAS CITY BOARD OF TRADE. A Kansas City, Missouri commodities exchange with brokers specializing in futures contracts and agricultural commodities. *See Also: City, exchange, futures*

KARAT. A measure of gold content, with one karat equal to 1/24 pure gold. For example, 24-karat gold would be pure gold.

KEEP IN MIND. A customer tells a market maker at which quantities and prices he or she would be willing to buy or sell a security. *See Also: maker, market, market maker, security*

KEEP WELL AGREEMENT. A contract between one company and another in which the first company agrees to make sure its subsidiary maintains a minimum financial ratio and net worth to protect a future deal between the subsidiary and the second company. *See Also: contract, net, net worth, ratio, subsidiary, worth*

KEIRETSU. A Japanese term referring to a network, or coalition, of businesses with mutual interests. Oftentimes, the companies will own interests in each other or in a mutual common interest. An example of this would be a vertically linked group of manufacturers, each with ownership in their suppliers of raw materials. *See Also: coalition, interest, term, will*

KEOGH PLAN. A self-funded, tax-sheltered, invested pension plan available to self-employed people and to people who work for unincorporated businesses without company-sponsored plans. Nearly any investment, except for collectibles and precious metals, can be used in a Keogh. *See Also: investment, pension, pension plan*

KERB DEALING. Commodities market transactions that transpire after the exchange has closed for the day. *See Also: exchange, market*

KERNEL. A set of functions that make up the essential core of an operating system. The kernel controls such essentials as security, low-level hardware interfaces and resource allocation. *See Also: resource, security, up*

KEY INDICATOR OPERATIONAL REPORT. A weekly report from New York Stock Exchange members who carry and clear customer accounts to the exchange. The exchange can tell if any of the members are having business problems that could effect the net capital of members. *See Also: capital, carry, clear, exchange, net, net capital, New York Stock Exchange, stock, stock exchange*

KEY INDUSTRY. An industry that is vitally important to the country's economy, such as the defense and automobile industries. *See Also: industry*

KEYNESIAN ECONOMIC THEORY. John Maynard Keynes theorized that investment capital and the multiplier effect of such investments influence economic growth and income. *See Also: capital, investment, multiplier effect*

KICKBACK. A cash reward for dealers who discount installment purchase paper. Also, the illegal practice of secretly paying a seller for awarding a contract. *See Also: cash, contract, discount, paper*

KICKER. A security feature or stipulation providing added rights, benefits, or liabilities. *See Also: rights, security*

KILL. To cancel an order. *See Also: order*

KILLER BEES. A team of specialists a corporation will hold on retainer to protect the company from a hostile takeover by using such tactics as issuing tender offers or holding proxy contests. *See Also: corporation, hold, proxy, takeover, tender*

KILLING. Receiving outstanding profits from investments in the stock market. *See Also: market, outstanding, stock, stock market*

KILO. A prefix that refers to a thousand or thousands. For example, one thousand bytes is expressed as 1 kilobyte, 1kb or just k. *See Also: K*

KIND ARBITRAGE. Profitably buying and selling identical securities in the same market at about the same time, with the profit coming from the price differences in separate trading values. *See Also: market, profit, securities, time*

KINKED DEMAND. An industry that has only a few companies and no price leader often has a demand curve that becomes continuous at the market price. *See Also: demand, industry, market, market price*

KIOSK. A stand-alone booth that provides Internet-based information to users. Kiosks may exist in hotels, public places such as airports or companies may place kiosks inside their own stores as a way for consumers to obtain additional information about the organization that is sponsoring the kiosk. Organizations generally provide information about products or services, or to let consumers seek additional products or services that may not be positioned at that location.

KITCHEN SINK BONDS. Also called cash-flow bonds, kitchen-sink bonds are created by repackaging the cash flows of derivative bonds, such as CMOs, that may be illiquid or risky on a stand-alone basis-everything is included but the "kitchen sink." These securities are placed into a trust to create new bonds based on the cash flows of the entire trust. Insufficient information about the underlying securities and the characteristics of the structure of the trust make it extremely difficult for investors to analyze these securities. *See Also: cash, securities, trust*

KIWIS. Nickname for the United States Student Loan Marketing Association, also referred to as a Sallie Mae, which is a five-year floating rate note with the interest rate denominated in New Zealand dollars. *See Also: floating rate note, interest, interest rate, note, Sallie Mae*

KNIFE. Nickname for the New York Futures Exchange, derived from the exchange's initials NYFE. *See Also: exchange, futures, futures exchange, NYFE*

KNOCKED DOWN. A price that has been reduced.

KNOW YOUR CUSTOMER RULE. On the New York Stock Exchange, brokers are instructed to know all pertinent facts about a customer and their customer's accounts before they allow the customer to open a brokerage account. *See Also: account, brokerage account, exchange, New York Stock Exchange, open, stock, stock exchange*

KNOWLEDGE MANAGEMENT. The management of knowledge, via a network system, in an organization for the purposes such as reducing redundancy and sharing ideas.

KONDRATIEFF WAVE THEORY. Soviet economist Nikolai Kondratieff theorized in the 1920s that Western capitalistic societies would go through rising and declining supercycles that lasted 50 to 60 years each. Kondratieff said he predicted the 1929 stock market crash, which led to the Great Depression, because the American economy also crashed in 1870. *See Also: crash, depression, Great Depression, market, stock, stock market*

KRUGERRAND. A South African gold bullion coin with one troy ounce of gold. *See Also: bullion, bullion coin*

L

L. The symbol for a pound sterling, Great Britain's primary currency. *See Also: currency, pound, symbol*

L-COMMERCE. Location-based commerce.

LABOR INTENSE INDUSTRY. A company or an industry that requires a large number of employees, compared to its total capital investment. *See Also: capital, industry, investment*

LAFFER CURVE. Economics professor Arthur Laffer theorized that economic output would increase if marginal tax rates were reduced. The curve is used to describe supply-side economics. *See Also: supply-side economics*

LAGGING ECONOMIC INDICATORS. An economic measure used to confirm, after the fact, the financial condition and stability of a particular industry or the economy in general. *See Also: industry*

LAISSEZ-FAIRE CAPITALISM. French for "let do," this is a capitalistic theory that says the economy works best when market forces are allowed to operate freely and without intervention. *See Also: intervention, market*

LAN. Short for Local Area Network, a communications network that connects computer-related hardware within a single building, such as an office, or several nearby buildings, such as a university. One or more LANs that are connected are called a Wide Area Network, or WAN. *See Also: local, local area network, WAN, wide area network*

LAND DEVELOPMENT LOAN. A person or company uses a mortgage to obtain a financial advance to improve a piece of land so that the site will be ready for construction. *See Also: mortgage*

LANDOWNER ROYALTY. A person who owns land which oil or gas is drawn. He or she receives a fee for the drilling fund-usually 12.5 percent of the well's gross production-but doesn't own part of the oil or gas, because the owner has not contributed financially to the development of the well. *See Also: gross*

LAPPING. An individual solicits people to take part in an investment opportunity, fraudulently takes their money, then uses their money to repay people who were recruited into the scheme earlier. Known also as a Ponzi scheme, such a scheme could continue indefinitely. *See Also: investment, Ponzi scheme, take*

LAPSED OPTION. An expired options contract that was never exercised. *See Also: contract, options contract*

LAST IN, FIRST OUT (LIFO). A company lists the production costs of the items most recently added to its inventory first on its inventory balance sheet, as opposed to the first in, first out method. *See Also: balance, balance sheet, inventory*

LAST SALE. A security's most recent transaction, often used to describe the closing sale on the last trading day. *See Also: last trading day, sale, trading day, transaction*

LAST TRADING DAY. The last and final day a futures contract can be settled. *See Also: contract, futures, futures contract*

LATE TAPE. When an exchange's announcement of trades and prices falls behind trading activity. *See Also: activity*

LAUNDER MONEY. To transfer money through a number of different financial institutions and businesses to conceal its illegal source. *See Also: transfer*

LAY UP. The easy execution of a buy or sell order, so named for the seemingly effortless basketball move. *See Also: execution, order, sell order*

LBO. Leveraged Buy Out. *See Also: leveraged*

LEAD GENERATING. In return for providing information and other services, lead generating Web sites will collect personal information from consumers or businesses. These leads will then be sold to interested sellers. *See Also: return, sites, Web, will*

LEAD UNDERWRITER. The first insurance underwriter to accept a line on a risk. *See Also: insurance, risk*

LEADING ECONOMIC INDICATORS. A measure used to predict the financial condition and stability of a particular industry or the economy in general, represented by such indicators as the unemployment rate. *See Also: indicators, industry*

LEADS AND LAGS. The manner in which international payments are made. A lead occurs if experts predict a country's currency will drop in value. Upon such a prediction, importers with overseas currency obligations will rush to pay their debts so they will not increase after the currency devaluates. A lag occurs when the exporters, under the same circumstances, do not rush to convert export receipts in foreign currency because of the potential devaluation. *See Also: currency, devaluation, drop, foreign currency, pay*

LEAKAGE. The release of private, nonpublic information prior to an official public announcement. *See Also: nonpublic information*

LEASE UP. To fill a commercial building with paying tenants who sign lease agreements. *See Also: fill*

LEASE-PURCHASE AGREEMENT. A contract that applies a portion of the lease payments toward purchase of the same property. *See Also: contract*

LEASEHOLD IMPROVEMENT. The changing or modification of a leased piece of property, with modification costs added to the fixed assets.

LEDGER. The final bookkeeping entry record which accounts for every transaction and has an entry for every transaction within every account. *See Also: account, transaction*

LEDGER DEBT BALANCE. The amount of money a customer owes his or her broker for all fees, including commissions and interest. *See Also: and interest, broker, interest*

LEFT-HAND FINANCING. To borrow money using assets listed on the left side of the corporate balance sheet in double-entry bookkeeping. By using this method and these assets, asset-rich companies can get money at lower costs. *See Also: balance, balance sheet*

LEG. One side or the other of a straddle option position. *See Also: option, position, straddle*

LEG INTO A HEDGE. An investor tries to create an offsetting position in a security by executing one side of a straddle option position (leg) now, then executing the other side later when a better price prevails. *See Also: option, position, security, straddle*

LEGACY APPLICATION. *See Also: ;egacy system*

LEGACY BUSINESS. A traditional bricks and mortar business.

LEGACY SYSTEM. Application programs or computer systems that remain in use, such as mainframe computers, even though newer technologies have been installed. *See Also: mainframe*

LEGAL. A New York Stock Exchange computer network used for customer complaints, enforcement information, and the results of audits conducted on member firms. *See Also: exchange, New York Stock Exchange, stock, stock exchange*

LEGAL ASSET. Any asset a person or company can use to pay a debt. For example, securities would be considered a legal asset. *See Also: asset, legal, pay, securities*

LEGAL CAPITAL. The portion of a company's capital surplus that makes up its par value. The capital surplus is the difference between the common shares' aggregate par value and the price at which they were sold. *See Also: capital, capital surplus, par, par value*

LEGAL INVESTMENT. The investments, usually high grade, that are appropriate for a fiduciary to buy for portfolios that he or she manages. *See Also: fiduciary*

LEGAL LIST. A state-approved list of investment alternatives that are appropriate for fiduciaries and regulated companies, such as financial institutions, to invest in. *See Also: investment*

LEGAL MONOPOLY. A company, such as a utilities company, that has the exclusive legal right to provide a specific service within a geographical area as long as the company agrees to have its rates and policies regulated. *See Also: legal, right, service*

LEGAL TRANSFER. A security registered to such an extent that several documents are required before the security can be transferred. Most selling brokers must be responsible for putting the documents in order because most buying brokers won't accept a security that requires a legal transfer. *See Also: legal, order, security, transfer*

LEGEND. A story about a successful investment, whether true or mythical, that the investor prides. Also, an explanatory table of the symbols used on a chart, map, or illustration. *See Also: chart, investment, on, story*

LEHMAN INVESTMENT OPPORTUNITY NOTE (LION). This security, marketed by Lehman Brothers Kuhn Loeb, represents ownership interest in the future interest and future principal payments of U.S. government securities. The security is more commonly known as a LION and is similar to Treasury Investors Growth Receipts and Certificate of Accrual on Treasury Securities, commonly referred to as TIGRs and CATS, respectively. *See Also: CATS, certificate, interest, LION, principal, securities, security*

LENDER OF LAST RESORT. Federal Reserve banks can borrow against securities to fulfill reserve requirements with fewer restrictions than imposed by the Federal Reserve System; the system therefore becomes the lender of last resort. *See Also: reserve, securities*

LENDING AGREEMENT. An investor signs an agreement with his or her broker that allows the broker's firm to lend out securities held in the investor's margin account. *See Also: account, broker, firm, margin, margin account, securities*

LENDING FLAT. When a borrower doesn't pay a fee and a lender doesn't pay interest; typically done when a person borrows securities using cash as collateral. *See Also: cash, collateral, pay, securities*

LENDING SECURITIES. The securities a client borrows from his or her broker to make a short sale, with a cash amount equal to the value of the securities delivered to the buyer's broker. *See Also: broker, cash, client, sale, securities, short sale*

LESSEE. A person who pays to rent an asset or property from another person for a designated period of time. *See Also: asset, time*

LESSEE MEMBER. A person who pays an exchange member for use of the membership for a specific time period. *See Also: exchange, time*

LESSOR. A person who owns an asset or property and allows someone else to use that asset or property for a specified amount of money and a designated period of time. *See Also: asset, time*

LETTER BOND. A debt instrument that was sold privately, with the buyer allowed to transfer or resell the instrument under terms stipulated in an investment letter. *See Also: debt instrument, instrument, investment, investment letter, transfer*

LETTER OF ADMINISTRATION. A court will issue this document to authorize a court-appointed administrator to settle the estate of a person who died without leaving a will. *See Also: estate, issue, settle*

LETTER OF CREDIT. Through this document, a commercial bank authorizes a broker-dealer to borrow money, as needed, to meet its obligations. In turn, the broker-dealer pays the bank an annual fee based on a percentage of the amount. *See Also: bank, broker-dealer, commercial bank, turn*

LETTER OF FREE CREDIT. Through this document, a broker-dealer attests that a client has enough money to pay for the securities he or she has purchased. The buying broker-dealer delivers this document on behalf of his or her client to the selling broker-dealer. *See Also: broker-dealer, client, pay, securities*

LETTER OF INDEMNIFICATION. One party in a business contract agrees to pay the other party for any losses that the other party incurs in the proposed venture. *See Also: contract, pay*

LETTER OF INTENT. An investor buying into a mutual fund signs a document agreeing to buy enough shares of the fund during the next 13 months to qualify for a reduced sales charge. *See Also: fund, mutual fund, sales charge*

LETTER SECURITY. A stock or bond not registered with the Securities and Exchange Commission which, therefore, cannot be sold in a public exchange. A company privately issues a letter security to certain key people with the stipulation that the stock cannot be resold or transferred publicly. *See Also: bond, commission, exchange, public exchange, securities, security, stock*

LETTER STOCK. Stock issued to shareholders when a company creates new classes of shares for one or more of its businesses. For example, General Motors created letter-class shares for its Hughes Electronics and Electronics Data Systems units. *See Also: classes of shares*

LETTER TESTAMENTARY. A court issues this document authorizing the executor of an estate to settle the estate as quickly as possible under the terms of the will. *See Also: estate, settle*

LEVEL. The price at which a security can be bought or sold. *See Also: security*

LEVEL 1 SERVICE OF NASDAQ. A computer subscription service, available to brokerage firms, that provides the highest and lowest price offers of securities traded through the National Association of Securities Dealers Automated Quotation. *See Also: quotation, securities, service, subscription*

LEVEL 2 SERVICE OF NASDAQ. A computer subscription service, available to institutional investors and traders, that provides the names of market makers and their bids on securities traded through the National Association of Securities Dealers Automated Quotation. *See Also: market, quotation, securities, service, subscription*

LEVEL 3 SERVICE OF NASDAQ. A computer subscription service, available to registered market makers, that provides the names of market makers and their bids on securities traded through the National Association of Securities Dealers Automated Quotation. *See Also: market, quotation, securities, service, subscription*

LEVEL ACCRUAL. Earned income is recognized by dividing the number of months before maturity into the interest balance. *See Also: balance, interest, maturity*

LEVEL CHARGE PLAN. A program used for buying additional shares of a mutual fund over a specified length of time, with the sales charge assessed each time additional shares are purchased and with that sales charge based on the total dollar amount of each purchase. *See Also: fund, mutual fund, sales charge, time*

LEVERAGE. In investments, this is the control of a large amount of money by a smaller amount of money, such as buying on margin. In finance, this is the relationship of debt to equity on a company's balance sheet in the form of the debt-to-equity ratio. *See Also: balance, balance sheet, buying on margin, debt-to-equity ratio, equity, margin, on margin, ratio*

LEVERAGE FACTOR. The ratio of a leveraged security's price to its working assets. *See Also: leveraged, ratio*

LEVERAGE FUND. A mutual fund that borrows money to increase the number of securities it can buy so it can increase its returns. *See Also: fund, mutual fund, securities*

LEVERAGE TRANSACTION MERCHANT. A futures commission merchant who can deal in certain over-the-counter futures instruments as long as they were doing business before June 1, 1978, when off-exchange futures trading was made illegal. Aside from qualifying under the grandfather clause, such merchants also must be registered with the Commodities Futures Trading Commission. *See Also: commission, futures, futures commission merchant, grandfather clause, off-exchange*

LEVERAGED. A company that borrows money at a fixed-interest rate to obtain a higher rate of return on its total invested capital. *See Also: capital, invested capital, rate of return, return*

LEVERAGED BUY OUT (LBO). A person, company, group of company employees, or entity that borrows money to buy controlling interest in a company. This is usually done by using the company's assets as security for the loans taken out by the acquiring party and repaying the loans from the company's cash flow. *See Also: cash, cash flow, controlling interest, interest, security*

LEVERAGED COMPANY. A company that has both equity and debt accounting for its total capital. *See Also: capital, equity*

LEVERAGED EMPLOYEE STOCK OPTION PLAN. A plan into which a company deposits payments each year out of its revenue, deducting the full amount from taxable income. Shares of stock are distributed among the accounts of employees as the loan is paid off. This method helps to alleviate the threat of an unwanted corporate takeover. *See Also: full, stock, takeover, taxable income*

LEVERAGED HEDGE. An investment that can produce disproportionately high profits compared to its original purchase price. *See Also: investment, purchase price*

LEVERAGED INVESTMENT COMPANY. A dual-purpose fund that has income as well as capital shares, with dividends going to income shares and capital gains going to capital shares. The charter of the open-end investment company allows the borrowing of capital from a bank or another lender. *See Also: bank, capital, charter, fund, investment, investment company*

LEVERAGED LEASE. An equipment lease financed by a nonrecourse loan so that the lessee can use the equipment without putting out any money and the lessor can retain the residual depreciation value when the lease expires. *See Also: depreciation, lessee, lessor, nonrecourse loan*

LEVERAGED OPTION. To promote share ownership for each share of company stock held or invested, an employee receives a certain number of additional options. Under such an option plan, the number of shares exercised increases based on stock price movement or financial performance. *See Also: movement, option, share, stock*

LEVERAGED STOCK. A stock that can produce disproportionately high profits compared to its original purchase price. *See Also: purchase price, stock*

LIABILITY. Any debt, both current and potential. *See Also: current*

LIBOR. London Interbank Offering Rate. *See Also: offering*

LIFE CYCLES. A system used to study and analyze different companies and products as they progress through the developmental phases of pioneering, expansion, stabilization, and decline. *See Also: stabilization*

LIFE INSURANCE. The payment of a stipulated sum of money, upon the death of the insured, to the designated beneficiary.

LIFE OF CONTRACT. The time period extending from the first to the last day of a futures contract. *See Also: contract, futures, futures contract, time*

LIFE OF DELIVERY. The time between when a commodities trade is initiated and the last transaction's delivery date. *See Also: delivery, delivery date, time*

LIFETIME VALUE OF A CUSTOMER. Businesses, particularly online companies with high customer acquisition costs, analyze the return of that investment over time. The lifetime value of a customer reflects the total amount of revenue expected from a customer over time, less the cost of acquiring that customer. The resulting number is then discounted to a present value figure. *See Also: acquisition, investment, online, present value, return, time*

LIFO. Last in, first out.

LIFT. A market-average measure of a security's price increase. *See Also: average*

LIFT A LEG. Closing one side of a straddle option position while leaving the other side open. *See Also: open, option, position, straddle*

LIFT A SHORT. An investor closes a short position by buying a futures contract for the same commodity with the same delivery date. *See Also: commodity, contract, delivery, delivery date, futures, futures contract, position, short position*

LIGHT BID, LIGHT OFFER. An equity trader uses this to indicate his or her bid is not equal to or better than the best prevailing bid or offer. Market movements up or down will create institutional interest. *See Also: equity, interest, market, offer, or better, trader*

LIKE KIND ASSETS. Two or more assets that are so similar that the selling of one and the buying of the other cancel each other out. For tax purposes, no transaction at all has taken place. *See Also: transaction*

LIMIT. The highest price fluctuation that the commodities exchange will allow from an item's previous settlement price. Each exchange sets its own limits. *See Also: exchange, fluctuation, settlement price*

LIMIT ORDER. An investor tells his or her broker to buy securities or commodities at or below a specific maximum price, or to sell securities or commodities above or at a specific minimum price. *See Also: broker, securities*

LIMIT ORDER INFORMATION SYSTEM. An electronic system that gives the location, number, and prices of specialists' offers and bids on the different exchanges. *See Also: exchanges*

LIMIT PRICE. The maximum amount at which a broker can buy a security for a client, or the minimum amount at which a broker can sell a security for a client, with the client determining that amount. *See Also: broker, client, security*

LIMIT SYSTEM. A computer network through which subscribers can find out about securities traded on all participating exchanges, and including information such as the specialist, the number involved in the deal, and the bid and offer prices. *See Also: exchanges, offer, securities, specialist*

LIMIT UP, LIMIT DOWN. The most a commodity's price is allowed to move during one trading day. *See Also: trading day*

LIMIT-OR-MARKET-ON-CLOSE ORDER. An investor tells his or her broker to buy a specified number of shares of a certain security at a certain price. If the broker cannot execute the order as specified, he or she is to execute it as a market order as close to the specifications as possible and as close to the end of the trading day as possible. *See Also: broker, close, market, market order, order, security, trading day*

LIMITED ACCESS TO BOOKS AND RECORDS. A person who holds stock in a company is allowed to inspect some of the company's records. *See Also: stock*

LIMITED AUDIT. Selected items are examined to determine the effectiveness of a company's internal controls, mathematical accuracy, legality, and the completeness of all transactions, with the results of the selected items' analysis generalized to cover all items, even those not examined.

LIMITED COMPANY. The British equivalent to a U.S. company that has been incorporated.

LIMITED DISCRETION. A customer authorizes his or her registered representative to make certain trades without any authorization. *See Also: registered representative*

LIMITED DIVIDEND CORPORATION. A company with a ceiling on the amount of dividends it can pay on its capital stock. *See Also: capital, capital stock, pay, stock*

LIMITED EXERCISE OPTION. An options contract that cannot be exercised until the fifth business day before the contract expires. *See Also: business day, contract, options contract*

LIMITED LIABILITY. A stockholder or partner in a partnership or corporation who holds liability for only as much as his or her investment. *See Also: corporation, investment, liability, partnership, stockholder*

LIMITED PARTNERSHIP. A partnership with at least one of the partners holding only a limited liability. *See Also: liability, limited liability, partnership*

LIMITED TAX BOND. A municipal bond based on the taxation value of the municipality's real estate. *See Also: bond, estate, municipal bond, real estate*

LIMITED TRADING AUTHORIZATION. *See Also: Limited Discretion.*

LINE CHART. A graph that charts a security's or the general market's price changes during a specific time period, with one line connecting the prices. *See Also: time*

LINE OF CREDIT. An arrangement between a person and a financial institution that allows the person to borrow up to a certain amount of money for a predetermined time period without providing any additional credit information. *See Also: credit, time*

LINUX. The name is derived from its creator's name, Linus Torvalds and the open source operating system from which it is derived. Linux is an implementation of the Unix kernel originally written from scratch with no proprietary code. *See Also: kernel, name, open, UNIX*

LION. Lehman Investment Opportunity Note. *See Also: investment, note*

LIPPER MUTUAL FUND INDUSTRY AVERAGE. The average performance of all mutual funds, as reported quarterly and annually by Lipper Analytical Services. *See Also: average, quarterly*

LIQUID. Having enough assets that easily can be converted to cash to retire all short-term debts. *See Also: cash, retire*

LIQUID ASSETS. Assets that easily can be converted into cash, such as money market fund shares, Treasury bills, and bank deposits. *See Also: bank, cash, fund, market, money market, money market fund*

LIQUID MARKET. A market in which securities or commodities are easily bought and sold because of the willingness of interested buyers and sellers to trade large quantities at reasonable prices. *See Also: market, securities*

LIQUID SAVING. Savings of a person, a company, or a trust that is in cash, or assets that can easily be converted into cash. *See Also: cash, trust*

LIQUID SECURITIES. Stocks and bonds that are easily converted to cash. *See Also: cash*

LIQUID YIELD OPTION NOTE. Also known as a LYON, this callable, zero-coupon security combines the capital needs of an investment banking customer with the investment needs of a retail customer. Put and call options on the note become operative in the third year after it is issued. The put and call prices reflect fixed interest rates, and therefore, increase over time. *See Also: capital, interest, investment, LYON, note, put, security, time*

LIQUIDATING DIVIDEND. The distribution of assets from a company that is going out of business.

LIQUIDATING MARKET. A market in which securities are aggressively sold at relatively low prices. *See Also: low, market, securities*

LIQUIDATING VALUE. The amount of money an asset is expected to cost when the company that owns it goes out of business. *See Also: asset*

LIQUIDATION. Selling an asset, or closing a company and mining all of the company's assets into cash. *See Also: asset, cash*

LIQUIDITY. There are three types of liquidity. Market liquidity refers to the number of buyers and sellers that participate in an exchange. Liquidity of assets refers to the degree to which assets of a company or an investment can easily be sold or converted into cash. Product Liquidity refers to the number of transactions executed to sell a product. The larger the critical mass, and the more active the buyers and sellers, the greater the liquidity. *See Also: critical mass, liquidity, market, market liquidity*

LIQUIDITY DIVERSIFICATION. A portfolio manager invests in bonds which all have different maturities. *See Also: manager, portfolio, portfolio manager*

LIQUIDITY EVENT. See Exit Strategy. *See Also: exit*

LIQUIDITY FUND. A California company will pay a limited partner 25 to 30 percent below the appraised value for interest in a real estate limited partnership. *See Also: estate, interest, limited partnership, partnership, pay, real estate, real estate limited partnership*

LIQUIDITY RATIO. Comparison of a company's cash and marketable securities to its current liabilities. *See Also: cash, current, current liabilities, marketable securities, securities*

LISTED OPTION. A put or call option that a particular securities exchange has approved for trading. *See Also: call option, exchange, option, put, securities*

LISTED OPTION CONTRACT. A stock option contract that is traded in an organized auction market on a member-exchange's floor, and has a preset strike price and expiration date. *See Also: auction, auction market, contract, expiration, expiration date, floor, market, option, option contract, stock, stock option*

LISTED SECURITIES. Any security that a particular registered exchange has accepted for trading. *See Also: exchange, registered exchange, security*

LISTING. Achieved through meeting all of an exchange's trading requirements and through receiving that exchange's approval for trading.

LISTING AGREEMENT. A contract that a company and a stock exchange sign when the company wants its shares listed for trading on that exchange. *See Also: contract, exchange, stock, stock exchange*

LISTING REQUIREMENTS. Rules and regulations a security must meet before it can be traded on a particular exchange. *See Also: exchange, security*

LITIGATION. Involvement in a civil lawsuit.

LITTLE BOARD. Nickname for the American Stock Exchange, which has the second-largest trading volume of all exchanges. The Big Board is the New York Stock Exchange, which has the largest trading volume. *See Also: big board, exchange, exchanges, New York Stock Exchange, stock, stock exchange, trading volume, volume*

LOAD. The commission fee charged (up to 8.5 percent) for buying shares of an open-end mutual fund to cover expenses. *See Also: commission, fund, mutual fund*

LOAD FUNDS. A mutual fund that a brokerage firm sells for a sales charge. *See Also: firm, fund, mutual fund, sales charge*

LOAD SPREAD OPTION. A contractual plan for paying the sales charge on mutual funds. *See Also: actual, contractual plan, sales charge*

LOAD UP. An investor speculatively buys a security or commodity and pays up to his or her financial limit. *See Also: commodity, limit, security*

LOADING. Funds are added to the prorated market price of the underlying securities to cover fees and overhead costs. *See Also: market, market price, overhead, securities*

LOADING CHARGE. A fee, up to 8.5 percent, that is charged on open-end investment funds when new securities are sold. The fee is used to cover all selling costs. *See Also: investment, securities*

LOAN CONSENT AGREEMENT. A contract required by the Securities and Exchange Commission, authorizing a securities broker to lend securities carried in a customer's account. *See Also: account, broker, commission, contract, exchange, securities*

LOAN CROWD. Members of a stock exchange who either lend or borrow securities to cover their brokerage customers' short sales. *See Also: exchange, securities, stock, stock exchange*

LOAN SHARK. A lender that charges excessive rates of interest, usually above legal rates. *See Also: interest, legal*

LOAN VALUE. The maximum amount a brokerage firm can lend to a client for buying securities on margin. *See Also: client, firm, margin, on margin, securities*

LOAN-CLOSING PAYMENTS. The expenses involved in selling and finalizing a mortgage loan. *See Also: mortgage*

LOAN-TO-VALUE RATIO. The ratio of a property's appraised value to the amount of the mortgage. *See Also: mortgage, ratio*

LOANED FLAT. A loan without interest. *See Also: interest, without interest*

LOANED STOCK. A brokerage firm lends stock to an investor who is selling short in order to cover delivery of the shares to the buyer. *See Also: delivery, firm, order, selling short, stock*

LOBSTER TRAP. Used by companies with outstanding convertible securities to stop unfriendly takeovers. A lobster trap prevents a person who holds 10 percent or more of the company's voting shares from converting their holdings into common shares of stock. The system is so named after the real lobster traps, which net large lobsters while allowing smaller fish to escape through the net. *See Also: fish, net, outstanding, securities, stock, stop*

LOCAL. A commodities exchange trader who works in the pit and sells for his or her own account. *See Also: account, exchange, pit, trader*

LOCAL AREA NETWORK. *See Also: LAN*

LOCAL BILL. A document that verifies an investor's transactions.

LOCAL SERVICE PROVIDER. Also referred to as LSP, companies that help Web site operators globalize their operations. These services may include translations, currency converters, overcoming international trading barriers, and other cultural elements. The goal is to adapt a site for local markets so users feel the product or service has been designed specifically for them. *See Also: currency, local, LSP, operations, service*

LOCATION-BASED COMMERCE. Transaction of business via wireless devices such as cellular telephones and personal digital assistants that is based on positioning technologies. For example, a nearby restaurant may transmit an electronic coupon to a user's wireless device, which in turn may signal the user with an audio signal. *See Also: current, Internet, on, sale*

LOCK AWAY. A long-term security in England. *See Also: security*

LOCKED MARKET. When bid and offer prices are the same in a highly competitive market. *See Also: market, offer*

LOCKED OUT. Current market conditions are preventing an investor from taking advantage of buying potentially profitable securities. *See Also: market, securities*

LOCKED-IN. A position an investor is in when he or she has not held onto a security for a long enough period and therefore cannot sell it to his or her advantage. Examples of being locked-in include benefiting from a capital gains treatment, owning a low-interest bond during a period of rising interest rates, investing in a commodities position when the exchange has established an up or down limit per day and the investor cannot get out, and so forth. *See Also: bond, capital, exchange, interest, limit, position, security*

LOCKOUT BONDS. The lockout bond in a CMO tranche typically receives principal payments similar to a sequential pay bond, until the first PAC bond begins paying its scheduled principal payments. Once the PAC bond's principal payments commence, the companion bond receives principal payments that exceed the PAC bond's scheduled principal payments, as determined by the PAC bond's PAC band. *See Also: bond, CMO, PAC band, pay, principal, sequential pay bond, tranche*

LOCKOUT PERIOD. A time measure that indicates the return of principal is being delayed. The Lockout Period begins at a bond's settlement date and ends at its first scheduled principal payment. *See Also: principal, return, settlement date, time*

LOCKOUT TAC BONDS. A type of targeted amortization class bond that partially or wholly pays down principal payments prior to the commencement of principal payments to the first PAC class. Once the PAC class starts to make principal payments, the lockout TAC bond has second priority. *See Also: amortization, bond, class, principal, priority*

LOCKUP. A security that has been pulled out of circulation as a long-term investment and placed in a safe deposit box. *See Also: investment, long-term investment, security*

LOCO. A term used to identify the place a commodity is being traded. *See Also: commodity, term*

LOGIN. The process of identifying oneself to a database to access a network or remote system. Also, the act of entering an identification and password in which to gain access to a network or remote system. *See Also: gain, remote*

LOGOFF. The process of disconnecting from a Web site, network or remote system. *See Also: remote, Web, Web site*

LOGON. The process of identifying oneself to a database to connect to a network or remote system. *See Also: remote*

LOGOUT. The process of taking an action, whether typing a logout command or clicking a logout button on the Web, in order to disconnect from a network or remote system. *See Also: on, order, remote, Web*

LOLLIPOP TACTIC. A method a company uses to stop an unfriendly takeover bid. With this method, some stockholders can tender shares at a premium price if the unwanted bidder buys a predetermined number of the outstanding shares. The deal, therefore, becomes profitable to everyone except the person attempting the takeover. *See Also: at a premium, outstanding, premium, stop, takeover, tender*

LOMBARD RATE. The interest rate Germany's central bank charges to other commercial banks when the banks borrow money using German securities as collateral. The Lombard rate is Germany's equivalent to the U.S. Federal Reserve System's discount rate. *See Also: bank, central bank, collateral, discount, discount rate, interest, interest rate, reserve, securities*

LOMBARD STREET. England's financial district.

LONDON INTERBANK BID RATE. In England's Eurodollar market, this is the interest rate at which American dollar deposits can be traded again within the British banking community. *See Also: interest, interest rate, market*

LONDON INTERBANK OFFERING RATE (LIBOR). In England's Eurodollar market, this is the interest rate banks charge each other on short-term money. *See Also: interest, interest rate, market*

LONDON INTERNATIONAL FINANCIAL FUTURES EXCHANGE. A British futures exchange where arbitrageurs, hedgers, and speculators can trade selected financial instruments that are subject to interest rate changes. *See Also: exchange, futures, futures exchange, interest, interest rate*

LONDON METAL EXCHANGE. An exchange where members trade in metals such as lead and copper. *See Also: exchange*

LONDON OPTIONS. English options contracts for commodities, such as cocoa.

LONDON STOCK EXCHANGE. A major European stock exchange. *See Also: exchange, stock, stock exchange*

LONG BOND. A bond that doesn't mature for at least 10 years. *See Also: bond*

LONG CALL. Ownership of a call option contract on an opening purchase. *See Also: call option, contract, opening purchase, option, option contract*

LONG COUPON. A newly issued bond with the first coupon not redeemable for at least six months. *See Also: bond, coupon, first coupon*

LONG HEDGE. An investor locks in a future yield on a fixed-income security by buying a futures contract, whereby he or she could lose money if interest rates increase, or by purchasing a call option, whereby he or she could lose money if interest rates do not drop. *See Also: call option, contract, drop, futures, futures contract, interest, option, security, yield*

LONG INTEREST. Collectively holding on to a specific security or a group of securities as an investment. *See Also: investment, securities, security*

LONG LEG. The position of an investor who holds an offsetting position. *See Also: position*

LONG MARKET VALUE. The daily market value in an investor's margin account, as determined by the value of its long-position securities. *See Also: account, margin, margin account, market, market value, securities*

LONG OF EXCHANGE. A trader trades foreign bills in an amount that exceeds his or her outstanding bills. *See Also: outstanding, trader*

LONG ON THE BASIS. An investor buys currency or spot goods and hedges them by selling futures. *See Also: currency, futures, spot*

LONG POSITION. An investor achieves a long position through buying a security (ownership) before selling because of an expected price increase. *See Also: position, security*

LONG PUT. An investor buys a put option contract on an opening purchase transaction. *See Also: contract, opening purchase, option, option contract, put, put option, transaction*

LONG SALE. Any time an investor sells securities that he or she owns. *See Also: securities, time*

LONG SIDE. A long interest. *See Also: interest*

LONG SQUEEZE. Occurs when prices drop and people holding long positions are forced to liquidate their positions. *See Also: drop*

LONG STOCK. Securities an investor buys because he or she believes the prices will go up.

LONG-TERM CAPITAL GAINS. The amount of money an investor earns by holding on to an investment for more than a year. *See Also: investment*

LONG-TERM CAPITAL LOSSES. The amount of money an investor loses by holding on to an investment for more than a year. *See Also: investment*

LONG-TERM CORPORATE DEBT. An obligation that will not be due for more than a year after the contract is signed. *See Also: contract, obligation*

LONG-TERM DEBT. A debt obligation that takes 10 years at the least to mature. *See Also: obligation*

LONG-TERM FINANCING. An obligation that will not be due for at least a year. *See Also: obligation*

LONG-TERM INSTITUTIONAL EQUITY. An institution can create a longer term stake by financing with additional preferred stocks and convertible debts. *See Also: term*

LONG-TERM INVESTMENT. An investor buys a security and holds on to it for more than a year because its growth potential is much greater than its short-term profits through a sale would be. *See Also: sale, security*

LONG-TERM LIABILITY. A debt that falls due in more than a year, but usually indicating an obligation that will last 10 or more years. *See Also: obligation*

LONG-TERM MORTGAGE. A home mortgage with a life of 40 years or more. *See Also: home, mortgage*

LONG-TERM RECEIVABLES AND INVESTMENTS. Long-term debts owed to a company plus the company's investments. *See Also: plus*

LONG-TERM TREND. The direction prices are expected to move during a specific future time period. *See Also: time*

LOOK BACK. A company's past records are audited in a search for mistakes that already have become obvious to a bank's auditing department.

LOOK-BACK OPTION. A commodities put or call option that allows the holder to buy or sell at the best available price during the option's life. *See Also: call option, option, put*

LOOPHOLE. The process of circumventing the law without violating its letter. A tax-sheltered investment exploits a loophole in the tax law. *See Also: investment*

LOOPHOLE CERTIFICATE OF DEPOSIT. A federally insured bank can pay the market interest rate, as pegged to the weekly Treasury bill auction, on deposits of $10,000 or more. The bank lends a customer the difference between his or her deposit amount and $10,000. The loan is a paper transaction, so the customer never actually receives the money which the bank deposits in his or her account and then withdraws six months later. *See Also: account, auction, bank, interest, interest rate, market, paper, pay, transaction, Treasury bill, Treasury bill auction*

LOSS RESERVE. An account established to provide for defaulted loans or other account receivables. *See Also: account, receivables*

LOST OPPORTUNITY. An investment that does not earn as much as the current interest rate. *See Also: current, interest, interest rate, investment*

LOT. A trading unit. *See Also: odd lot, round lot, trading unit, unit*

LOT SIZE. The quantity or size of an item that is ordered. *See Also: size*

LOW. The lowest price a security, or the market in general, reached during a specific time period. *See Also: market, security, time*

LOW DOWN PAYMENT MORTGAGES. A mortgage type that requires down payments that are lower than traditional mortgages. These mortgages are attractive to homebuyers with limited income and savings. *See Also: mortgage*

LOW GRADE. A securities rating that indicates a particular security is not worth investing in because the issuer probably will not be able to meet financial obligations and has a poor reputation in the industry. *See Also: industry, securities, security, worth*

LOW WATER MARK. An investment account's peak value over a stated period of time. *See Also: investment, peak, time*

LSP. Local Service Provider. *See Also: local, service*

LUXURY TAX. The taxes assessed against all nonessential items, such as hot tubs or built-in swimming pools.

LYON. Liquid Yield Option Note. *See Also: liquid, note, option, yield*

M

M. The abbreviation for one thousand. When following a number, it indicates the number is to be multiplied by 1,000 (For example, 3M would equal 3,000).

M-COMMERCE. Transaction of business via wireless devices such as cellular telephones and personal digital assistants. *See Also: digital*

M1. A money supply category consisting of currency in public circulation, credit union share account balances, negotiable order of withdrawal account balances, automatic transfer account balances, demand deposits, and travelers checks. *See Also: account, credit, currency, demand, money supply, negotiable, order, share, supply, transfer*

M2. A money supply category consisting of all money in the M1 category plus Eurodollar deposits, savings and other small deposits, and private holdings in money market mutual funds. *See Also: M1, market, money market, money supply, plus, supply*

M2M. Manufacturer to Manufacturer or Mobile to Mobile.

M3. A money supply category deposits and institutional shares in money market mutual funds. *See Also: market, money market, money supply, supply*

M4. A money supply category consisting of all money in the M1, M2, and M3 categories, plus banker's acceptance, commercial paper, and U.S. savings bonds. *See Also: acceptance, banker's acceptance, commercial paper, M1, M2, M3, money supply, paper, plus, supply*

MACARONI DEFENSE. A strategy used by a company seeking to avoid a hostile takeover. The target company will issue a large number of bonds that must be redeemed at a higher price if the company is taken over. *See Also: takeover, target, will*

MACINTOSH. Introduced by Apple Computer in 1984, a family or 32-bit computers that was widely sold due to its graphical user interface, mouse, and windows.

MACROECONOMICS. A nation's inflation rate, price levels, unemployment figures, and industrial production, among other data used to study the country's economy as a whole. *See Also: industrial, industrial production, inflation, inflation rate*

MACROHEDGE. An investment hedge that reduces an organization's net portfolio risk. *See Also: hedge, investment, net, portfolio, risk*

MAE WEST SPREAD. A strategy that brings the investor profits when the market is stagnating, and involves a combination of a short straddle and a long strangle. *See Also: combination, market, straddle, strangle*

MAGIC MORTGAGE. Promoted by the Mortgage Guarantee Insurance Corporation, this is a method that allows a person to buy a house with a low down payment as long as the buyer pays a yearly interest fee to the loan's insurer. *See Also: corporation, guarantee, house, insurance, interest, low, mortgage*

MAGIC SIXES. A group of undervalued stocks, with each trading at less than 60 percent of its book value, having a price-earnings ratio of six or lower, and having an annual yield higher than six percent. *See Also: annual yield, book, book value, ratio, undervalued, yield*

MAIL BOMB. The flooding of an e-mail address with e-mail messages, oftentimes with intent to crash or spam the recipient's system. Mail bombing is considered an act of harassment. *See Also: address, crash, e-mail, e-mail address, spam*

MAIN STREET. A description for the investing public. Wall Street is used to describe the professional investment community. *See Also: investment, professional, Street, Wall Street*

MAINFRAME. A centralized computer that is capable of supporting hundreds, or even thousands, of users simultaneously for one-way computing processes. *See Also: supporting*

MAINTENANCE. The amount of cash and securities an investor has deposited in his or her account to fulfill his or her margin requirements. *See Also: account, cash, margin, securities*

MAINTENANCE BOND. A financial obligation with materials and workmanship that are guaranteed after a contract has been fulfilled, with the guarantee lasting a predetermined time. *See Also: contract, guarantee, obligation, time*

MAINTENANCE CALL. A broker's request for cash or securities when the equity in his or her client's margin account falls below the brokerage firm's maintenance requirements. Unless the client deposits enough cash or securities to bring the account up to the required level, the broker can sell some of the client's securities to make up for the deficit. *See Also: account, broker, cash, client, deficit, equity, level, maintenance, margin, margin account, securities*

MAINTENANCE EXCESS. The amount a client's equity exceeds the minimum maintenance requirements in his or her margin account. *See Also: account, equity, maintenance, margin, margin account, minimum maintenance*

MAINTENANCE FEE. The cost a brokerage firm charges yearly to maintain some accounts. *See Also: firm*

MAINTENANCE MARGIN. A margin sale must occur below this margin or level, which is set by the lender. *See Also: level, margin, margin sale, sale*

MAINTENANCE OF INVESTMENT ORGANIZATION. The income charges and administration expenses of the firm which carries investments in leased property or securities. *See Also: firm, securities*

MAINTENANCE, REPAIR, AND OPERATIONS. Also referred to as MRO, a procurement term used to describe routine purchases, but not purchases essential to a business's output. MRO includes items such as office supplies, computers, and equipment maintenance. *See Also: maintenance, MRO, procurement, term*

MAJOR BOTTOM. When market prices have dropped to the lowest expected value. *See Also: market*

MAJOR TREND. The general direction that stock prices are moving, disregarding any minor, temporary shifts. *See Also: stock*

MAJOR-BRACKET UNDERWRITER. An investment banking group that continuously subscribes to the largest portion of a new securities issue. *See Also: investment, issue, securities*

MAJORITY SHAREHOLDER. The person who holds the most voting shares of a company's stock. If a person owns 51 percent of the stock, he or she automatically is the majority shareholder. However, if ownership of the shares is widely scattered among many different stockholders, the majority shareholder may own a lot less than 50 percent, as long as he or she owns more shares than anyone else. *See Also: lot, shareholder, stock*

MAJORITY-OWNED SUBSIDIARY. A subsidiary with more than 51 percent of its outstanding stock owned by the parent company. *See Also: outstanding, outstanding stock, stock, subsidiary*

MAKE A LINE. When a security's price movement remains in a narrow range for a long time. *See Also: movement, range, time*

MAKE A MARKET. The maintaining of firm bid and offer prices on a specific security by always being ready to buy and sell round lots of the security at publicly quoted prices. The dealer on the over-the-counter market is called the market maker and the specialist on the exchanges. *See Also: dealer, exchanges, firm, firm bid, maker, market, market maker, offer, security, specialist*

MAKER. The person or company who signs a check or other obligation. *See Also: check, obligation*

MAKING UP PRICE. A delivered security's price.

MALFEASANCE. An illegal action.

MALONEY ACT. A law that regulates over-the-counter securities and holds the registered securities' associations responsible for supervising and making sure the regulations are obeyed. *See Also: securities*

MANAGED ACCOUNT. An investment account held by one or more people with a bank trust department or an investment firm entrusted with deciding what investments to make and when to make them. The investors pay management fees in any profits or losses, with each person responsible for an amount that is in proportion to the amount he or she invested. *See Also: account, bank, bank trust department, firm, investment, pay, trust*

MANAGEMENT AUDIT. The overall analysis of a management's performance and effectiveness.

MANAGEMENT COMPANY. A farm that handles other people's investments and supervises their portfolios.

MANAGEMENT FEE. An investment manager charges investors this cost for handling their portfolios or mutual funds, or for taking care of shareholder relations and administration. The charge is based on a percentage of the particular fund's asset value. *See Also: asset, investment, investment manager, manager, shareholder*

MANAGEMENT STOCK. Those shares of stock owned by a company's management. *See Also: stock*

MANAGER. The bank that manages a Eurocredit or a security issue. *See Also: bank, issue, security*

MANAGER'S FEE. The underwriter in a public offering imposes this charge on the issuer in return for handling the new series. *See Also: offering, public offering, return*

MANAGING UNDERWRITER. The investment banking firm for an underwriting group, which was formed to buy and distribute a new securities issue. An agreement among underwriters gives this agent authority to buy, carry, and distribute the issue, to ensure compliance with federal and state laws, to determine how many shares each group member receives, to sell at discount to the selling group, and to initiate the public market offering. *See Also: agent, agreement among underwriters, carry, discount, firm, investment, issue, market, offering, public market, securities, selling group, underwriting*

MANIPULATION. The illegal buying or selling of a security to create the false impression that active trading exists in an effort to convince other people to buy more shares or sell the ones they own. Manipulation is done to influence prices so the person doing the manipulating can achieve a more advantageous market. *See Also: market, security*

MANUFACTURED HOUSING (MHS) LOANS. Securities backed by loans on manufactured homes, or prefabricated homes, built to the specifications of the Housing and Urban Development (HUD) Act. *See Also: Housing and Urban Development*

MANUFACTURER TO MANUFACTURER. Also referred to as M2M and MtoM, a form of business-to-business commerce that connects manufacturers to other manufacturers. *See Also: commerce, M2M*

MAPLE LEAF SERIES. A Euro-Canadian warrant to buy a particular amount of a Canadian government bond issue. Created by the Merrill Lynch Capital Markets Inc., this product is not available to investors in the United States. *See Also: bond, capital, capital markets, government bond, issue, warrant*

MARGE A TERME. A forward margin in France. *See Also: forward, forward margin, margin*

MARGIN. The amount of money a client deposits with his or her broker, against which the client can borrow when he or she wants to buy securities. *See Also: broker, client, securities*

MARGIN ACCOUNT. The brokerage account established for a client who wants to buy securities. The client borrows against the account. *See Also: account, brokerage account, client, securities*

MARGIN AGREEMENT. The document that provides the rules and regulations concerning margin accounts, including the amount of money and securities the client must maintain in the account. *See Also: account, client, margin, securities*

MARGIN BUYING. An investor uses a broker's credit to buy securities. *See Also: credit, securities*

MARGIN CALL. A broker's request for a customer to deposit enough money in the customer's margin account to bring the balance back up to the initial margin requirement. If the customer fails to do so, the broker is allowed to liquidate the account. *See Also: account, back up, balance, broker, fails, initial margin, margin, margin account, margin requirement*

MARGIN DEPARTMENT. A brokerage firm department responsible for making sure customers comply with the firm's margin rules and regulations, and for monitoring margin debits, credits, short sales, and purchases. *See Also: firm, margin*

MARGIN LOAN. A call loan with an investment as collateral. *See Also: call loan, collateral, investment*

MARGIN MINIMUM REQUIREMENT. Set by the Federal Reserve Board, this is the minimum amount of money or marginable securities an investor must have deposited in his or her margin account to buy more securities on margin. The minimum is a percentage of the total value of the securities the investor wants to buy. *See Also: account, Federal Reserve Board, margin, margin account, marginable, on margin, reserve, securities*

MARGIN OF PROFIT. The ratio of a company's net sales to its gross profits. To obtain the margin of profit, a company would divide its net sales into its gross profits. The margin provides an indication of the company's operating efficiency and pricing policies. *See Also: gross, indication, margin, net, net sales, profit, ratio*

MARGIN OF SAFETY. The difference between a bond issue's price and the value of its underlying property. *See Also: bond*

MARGIN REQUIREMENT. The minimum amount a brokerage firm requires a customer to have deposited in his or her margin account. *See Also: account, firm, margin, margin account*

MARGIN SALE. When assets are sold to fill a margin call requirement. *See Also: fill, margin, margin call*

MARGIN SECURITY. A security a customer can buy or sell in his or her brokerage margin account. *See Also: account, margin, margin account, security*

MARGINABLE. Securities that can be used for buying on margin. *See Also: buying on margin, margin, on margin*

MARGINAL ACTIVITY. A company with revenues that barely meet its obligations.

MARGINAL ANALYSIS. The amount a value increases when one variable is increased by one unit of another variable. *See Also: unit*

MARGINAL BORROWER. A person who will borrow money as long as the interest charge is not increased. *See Also: interest*

MARGINAL BUYER. A person who will buy an item as long as the price is not increased.

MARGINAL COST. The potential increase or decrease in a company's total costs if it had one more or one less unit of output. In most companies, these costs drop as volume increases because of bulk discounts and the more efficient use of equipment. For other companies, the cost may go up because increased production requires additional employees. Even those companies whose costs drop reach a point where the cost will begin to rise because additional personnel are needed and more intense supervision is required. *See Also: drop, point, unit, volume*

MARGINAL EFFICIENCY OF CAPITAL. The annual percentage yield a company's last additional unit of capital earns, which represents the market interest rate at which undertaking a capital investment becomes profitable. If the market rate is 12 percent, it would not be profitable to undertake any project that has less than a 12 percent rate of return. *See Also: capital, interest, interest rate, investment, market, rate of return, return, unit, yield*

MARGINAL LENDER. A person who will lend money as long as the interest charge is not lowered. *See Also: interest*

MARGINAL PAIR. The marginal seller and marginal buyer, along with the first seller whose offer is above the current market price and the first buyer whose bid is below the current market price. *See Also: current, marginal buyer, marginal seller, market, market price, offer*

MARGINAL REVENUE. The degree to which a company's total revenue would change by adding one unit of output. The marginal revenue is determined by the difference between the total revenue produced before the unit was added and the total revenue produced after the unit was added. If the price of the unit does not change, the marginal revenue will equal the unit's price. *See Also: change, unit*

MARGINAL SELLER. A person who will sell a security as long as the price is not reduced. *See Also: security*

MARGINAL TAX RATE. The amount of additional tax imposed on a company with each additional dollar of income because of the U.S. progressive income tax system.

MARGINAL TRADING. A person borrows part of the money necessary to buy a security or commodity. *See Also: commodity, security*

MARGINED SECURITIES. Securities an investor buys on credit and holds as collateral in his or her margin account. *See Also: collateral, credit, margin*

MARGINS. The par value's range within which the spot exchange rate of a member nation's currency is permitted to move. *See Also: currency, exchange, exchange rate, par, range, spot, spot exchange rate*

MARK DOWN. The amount that a security's selling price is reduced to cover commissions to a market maker in the over-the-counter market. A reduction in the price of an underwriter's municipal bond offering to entice buyers when there is a lack of interest at the original price. *See Also: bond, interest, maker, market, market maker, municipal bond, offering*

MARK TIME. When the prices of a number of transactions in the commodities and securities markets fail to indicate any trend. *See Also: securities, trend*

MARK TO MARKET. A daily accounting procedure whereby the investor adjusts a security to the current market price. *See Also: current, market, market price, security*

MARK UP. The amount a dealer adds to a security's actual price to arrive at the purchase price to cover commissions to the market maker in the over-the-counter market. *See Also: actual, dealer, maker, market, market maker, purchase price*

MARKET. A place where products, services, and securities are sold to the public. Market also indicates the general supply and demand for a particular security. *See Also: demand, securities, security, supply*

MARKET ANALYSIS. A study followed by a prediction of the movement expected from a particular security or commodity, or from the market in general, with emphasis placed on supply and demand. *See Also: commodity, demand, market, movement, security, supply*

MARKET AREA. The area where a commodity purchase or sale directly affects the prevailing price of that commodity. *See Also: commodity, sale*

MARKET AUCTION PREFERRED STOCK. A variable rate issue that a Dutch auction resets every 49 days. The security is immediately callable. *See Also: auction, dutch auction, issue, security*

MARKET AVERAGE. The measure of a group of securities to gauge the market movement as a whole. The term often refers to the Dow Jones Industrial Average. *See Also: average, Dow Jones Industrial Average, industrial, market, movement, securities, term*

MARKET BOTTOM. The lowest point a market indicator reaches during a specific time period. *See Also: market, point, time*

MARKET BREADTH. The number of shares of a particular security that are traded during a particular time period. Generally, this term refers to the overall strength and trading volume of the market by such measures as advance/

decline figures and volume momentum. *See Also: market, momentum, security, term, time, trading volume, volume*

MARKET CANNIBALIZATION. A company's sales of an existing product adversely affected by selling a new product.

MARKET CAPITALIZATION. A company's worth as indicated by the price of its outstanding shares of stock. *See Also: outstanding, stock, worth*

MARKET CYCLE. When an increase in prices follows a period of lower prices, or when a drop in prices follows a period of higher prices. *See Also: drop*

MARKET DATA SYSTEM. A communications system that displays a summary of trading volumes on the New York Stock Exchange. *See Also: exchange, New York Stock Exchange, stock, stock exchange*

MARKET EQUILIBRIUM. Occurs after buyers and sellers refuse to trade at the prevailing prices.

MARKET EXCESS RETURN. The percentage that a predicted return exceeds the risk-free rate of return. *See Also: rate of return, return, risk-free rate of return*

MARKET IF TOUCHED ORDER (MIT). An investor's order to buy or sell a security or commodity as soon as it can be bought or sold at a predetermined market price. *See Also: commodity, market, market price, order, security*

MARKET INDEX. A group of numbers (with arbitrary values assigned to proportionately represent real values) that provide a gauge to track specific securities, industries, and markets. *See Also: securities*

MARKET INSTINCT. The ability to understand, interpret, and use market signals, such as volume trading and price shifts. *See Also: market, volume*

MARKET IS OFF. Indicates that the prices of securities dropped after a previous closing. *See Also: securities*

MARKET LEADERS. When the stock of a major influential company is considered a reflection of the market in general. *See Also: market, stock*

MARKET LETTER. A newsletter sent to brokerage clients. The newsletter examines market trends, interest rates, the economy, as well as investment recommendations. *See Also: interest, investment, market*

MARKET LIQUIDITY. Occurs when an investor can buy or sell a security near the price at which the security last sold. *See Also: security*

MARKET MAKER. 1) In a stock exchange, market makers help to provide liquidity by accepting the risk of holding a particular number of shares of a security, allowing people to buy and sell those shares from them. 2) On the Internet, market makers in vertical or horizontal markets help match buyers and sellers. In this instance, the market maker may or may not take possession of the goods or services. *See Also: exchange, Internet, liquidity, maker, market, market maker, on, risk, security, stock, stock exchange, take*

MARKET MAKER IDENTIFIER. A four-letter acronym or code the National Association of Securities Dealers uses to represent broker-dealers who actively use the NASD's Automated Quotations. *See Also: securities*

MARKET MAVEN. Used to denote an expert or connoisseur of the markets.

MARKET MULTIPLE. A price-earnings ratio. The market multiple helps an investor determine whether a stock is overpriced or underpriced. *See Also: market, ratio, stock, underpriced*

MARKET NEUTRAL. An investing strategy in which both long and short positions are taken. Theoretically, the opposing positions will result in neither a gain or a loss, regardless of the movement of the underlying securities. *See Also: gain, movement, securities, will*

MARKET OPENING. The first transaction of the day on an exchange. *See Also: exchange, transaction*

MARKET ORDER. An investor's order to buy or sell a security or commodity at the best price. *See Also: commodity, order, security*

MARKET ORDER SYSTEM OF TRADING. A computer system that connects the Toronto Stock Exchange with the American Stock Exchange and through which orders for dual-listed stocks can be automatically executed at the best price. *See Also: exchange, stock, stock exchange, Toronto Stock Exchange*

MARKET OUT CLAUSE. A stipulation in some underwriting agreements that releases underwriters from the purchase commitment if some development negatively affects the overall securities market. *See Also: market, securities, underwriting*

MARKET OVERSIGHT SURVEILLANCE SYSTEM. A computer surveillance system that monitors market activity for the Securities and Exchange Commission. *See Also: activity, commission, exchange, market, securities*

MARKET POTENTIAL. The amount of a commodity or security that is expected to sell during a specific time period. *See Also: commodity, security, time*

MARKET PRICE. The last price at which a security or commodity publicly sold. *See Also: commodity, security*

MARKET REPORT. A verbal or written statement from the exchange floor that a transaction has been executed at a specific price. *See Also: exchange, exchange floor, floor, statement, transaction*

MARKET RESEARCH. A study and analysis of a prospective company's or product's size, characteristics, and market potential. In the securities market, market research refers to the study and analysis of volume, price changes, and market potential; all of these indicators show potential price movements. *See Also: indicators, market, market potential, securities, size, volume*

MARKET RISK. The risk an investor takes when owning securities because the prices could go up or down, with all movements beyond the investor's control. *See Also: risk, securities*

MARKET SECURITIES. Stock or bonds that are publicly traded.

MARKET SENTIMENT. Positive or negative public attitudes that affect trends in the securities or commodities markets. *See Also: securities*

MARKET SHARE. The percentage of an industry's total sales that belong to a specific product or a particular company.

MARKET STABILIZATION. An organization tries to hinder the market to affect prices. The Securities and Exchange Commission normally prohibits this practice. *See Also: commission, exchange, market, securities*

MARKET SWING. A cyclical shift in a security's price.

MARKET TIMING. This occurs when economic factors indicate the economy is strong and interest rates are favorable for buying or selling securities. *See Also: and interest, interest, securities*

MARKET TONE. When traders are willing to deal actively, with minimal price differences between bid and ask prices. *See Also: ask*

MARKET TOP. The highest point a market indicator reaches during a specific time period. *See Also: market, point, time*

MARKET TREND. The general market movement, either up or down. *See Also: market, movement*

MARKET UNCERTAINTY. An investor's opinions and attitudes change in such a way that the investment's market price changes. *See Also: change, market, market price*

MARKET VALUE. The last price for which a security or commodity was bought or sold. *See Also: commodity, security*

MARKET VALUE-WEIGHTED INDEX. An index with components that are stressed according to the total market value of their outstanding shares. *See Also: index, market, market value, outstanding*

MARKET VERSUS QUOTE. A security's market price at the last price it was executed versus the current bid and ask. *See Also: ask, current, market, market price*

MARKET VOLUME. The number of shares traded in one day on a particular exchange. *See Also: exchange*

MARKET-INDEXED CD. The market-indexed certificate of deposit protects an investor's principal while offering the potential to share in stock price gains. These hybrid securities are typically linked to a stock market index, such as the S&P 500, where the investor will receive a stated portion of the upside appreciation, while the principal is protected by the safety of the CD. These securities typically appeal to conservative investors wanting to participate in a particular market, such as stocks, while protecting their assets. *See Also: appreciation, cd, certificate, index, market, market index, offering, principal, safety, securities, share, stock, stock market, upside*

MARKET-ON-THE-CLOSE ORDER. An investor's order to his or her broker to buy or sell a security at the close of the trading day, or as near to the close as possible. *See Also: at the close, broker, close, order, security, trading day*

MARKET-ON-THE-OPENING ORDER. An investor's order to his or her broker to buy or sell a security at the opening of the trading day, or as near to the opening as possible. *See Also: at the opening, broker, order, security, trading day*

MARKETABILITY. The speed and case with which a specific security can be bought and sold. *See Also: security*

MARKETABLE LIMIT ORDER. An investor tells his or her broker to buy at or below a maximum price, or sell at or above a minimum price, with the specified prices better than the current market. These orders can be executed immediately. *See Also: broker, current, market*

MARKETABLE SECURITIES. Stocks or bonds that can be bought and sold easily and quickly.

MARKETPLACE SERVICE PROVIDER. Also referred to as MSP, a company that provides services to e-marketplaces, such as building, designing, operating, and hosting. *See Also: hosting, MSP*

MARKING. At the close, an investor executes an option contract that does not reflect the contract's fair value, with the execution bringing the investor's account into a better equity position. *See Also: account, at the close, close, contract, equity, execution, fair value, option, option contract, position*

MARRIED PUT. An investor buys a put option to sell a specific number of a security at a specific price by a specific time. The option is purchased from the same underlying company at the same time the investor buys the securities, so the investor can hedge the price paid for the securities. *See Also: hedge, option, put, put option, securities, security, time*

MASSACHUSETTS RULE. A rule that governs trust fund investing. Included in this rule are limitations on those securities in which a fund can be invested. *See Also: fund, securities, trust*

MASSACHUSETTS TRUST. A business organized as a trust where shareholders have a limited liability. *See Also: liability, limited liability, trust*

MASTER LIMITED PARTNERSHIP. An investment that offers some tax shelter advantages as well as publicly traded securities. *See Also: investment, securities*

MASTER NOTES. Paper that a large company with good credit can issue to a bank, but not to another company. *See Also: bank, credit, issue*

MASTER TRUST. A pool of trusts or assets involved in a trust agreement. *See Also: pool, trust*

MATCH FUNDS. A person who borrows money has the same repayment date as a loan which that person makes out to someone else. For example, a person borrows money that is to be repaid by January 16, then lends someone else money, with that loan to be repaid by January 16.

MATCHED AND LOST. When two securities brokers are competing against each other to execute a trade, with both representing the same price, a coin is flipped. The "matched and lost" is the report of that coin toss for the broker who lost. The losing broker tells his or her client the security was not available in sufficient quantity to execute the deal at the price the client stipulated. *See Also: broker, client, securities, security*

MATCHED BOOK. A securities dealer's account when his or her borrowing costs equal the interest he or she earned for loaning money to customers and other brokers. *See Also: account, interest, securities*

MATCHED MATURITIES. A financial institution coordinates the maturities of a customer's loans and certificates of deposits to ease the problems that result when interest rates rise or fall sharply. *See Also: fall, interest*

MATCHED ORDERS. In a practice that the Securities and Exchange Commission prohibits, an investor offsets buy and sell orders in a particular security to create the false impression that the security is being actively traded, which causes its price to go up. *See Also: commission, exchange, securities, security, to go*

MATCHED SALE PURCHASE TRANSACTION. The Federal Reserve Bank of New York sells government securities to a securities dealer against the payment of federal funds, after which the dealer must agree to sell the securities back by a predetermined date. In turn, the Federal Reserve Bank pays the dealer an interest rate equal to the discount rate. *See Also: bank, dealer, discount, discount rate, Federal Funds, Federal Reserve Bank, interest, interest rate, reserve, reserve bank, securities, turn*

MATCHING. Assets that are denominated in a specific currency to lower the risks involved in foreign exchange rates. *See Also: currency, exchange, foreign exchange*

MATRIX TRADING. Two brokers trade bonds in different classes, or in the same class but with different ratings, in an effort to take advantage of differences in the yield spreads. *See Also: class, take, yield*

MATURE ECONOMY. The economy of a country with a stabilized or declining population along with stabilized economic growth. While consumer spending increases, government spending on roads and factories drops. Many Western European economies have reached maturity. *See Also: maturity*

MATURED. A contract or other obligation that has been completely paid and whose terms have been completely fulfilled. *See Also: contract, obligation*

MATURITY. The date the principal amount of a bond or other debt instrument becomes due, or the date an installment loan must be completely paid. *See Also: bond, debt instrument, instrument, principal, principal amount*

MATURITY BASIS. A ratio that compares the interest, in dollars, due on a bond to the bond's maturity value. In calculating the maturity basis, no consideration is given to any discounts or premiums that were in effect when the bond was purchased. *See Also: basis, bond, consideration, interest, maturity, ratio*

MATURITY DISTRIBUTION OF LOANS AND SECURITIES. Provides the amounts of loans, acceptance holdings, and government securities due within a specific time period. *See Also: acceptance, securities, time*

MAXIMUM CAPITAL GAINS MUTUAL FUND. A mutual fund directed at achieving the highest returns for its investors, with a policy of investing in smaller, fast-growing companies with volatile stock. While the fund may earn large, quick profits for the investors, it also is subject to quick, dramatic losses. *See Also: fund, mutual fund, stock, volatile*

MAY DAY. Fixed minimum brokerage commissions became prohibited in the U.S. on May 1, 1975, after which brokers could charge whatever fee they wanted. The change created an opening for both discount brokers and a diversified and specialized brokerage industry. *See Also: change, discount, diversified, industry*

MBSCC. Mortgage-Backed Securities Clearing Corporation. *See Also: corporation, securities*

MCFADDEN ACT. A federal law that allows each state to regulate commercial banks within that state.

MCIC INDEMNITY CORPORATION. An MGIC Investment Corporation subsidiary that insures some municipal bonds. *See Also: corporation, investment, MGIC Investment Corporation, subsidiary*

MEAN RETURN. The expected returns of all of the investments in a portfolio, an analysis of which determines the relationship between risks and returns. *See Also: portfolio*

MEASURING GAP. A price gap that copies the most recent movement. *See Also: gap, movement, price gap*

MECHANIC'S LIEN. A claim the state can hold against a building until contractors, laborers, and suppliers involved in the construction are paid in full. If the company that contracted for the building liquidates before these people are paid, the state can give them priority over any other creditors. *See Also: full, hold, priority*

MEDIUM OF EXCHANGE. Any negotiable instrument that is commonly accepted as payment for goods or services or for settling a debt. The instrument is accepted without any consideration given to the person's credit-worthiness. For example, U.S. dollars are a medium of exchange. *See Also: consideration, exchange, instrument, negotiable, negotiable instrument*

MEDIUM OTHER THAN CASH. Any negotiable instrument other than cash that is commonly accepted as payment for goods or services or for settling a debt. For example, checks, notes, and credit are considered media other than cash. *See Also: cash, credit, instrument, negotiable, negotiable instrument*

MEDIUM-TERM BOND. A debt instrument with a maturity of two to 10 years. *See Also: debt instrument, instrument, maturity*

MEDIUM-TERM NOTE. An unsecured obligation that matures in nine months to 15 years. *See Also: obligation*

MEETING BOND INTEREST AND PRINCIPAL. Principal and interest payments are being made when they fall due. *See Also: and interest, fall, interest*

MEGAGOTH. A company that has the ability to offer more services than any similar firm that has capital totaling at least $25 billion. *See Also: capital, firm, offer*

MEGAGRANT. A large grant of options or shares that is usually only given out one time to key executives. This grant may be several times the size of a normal grant. *See Also: size, time*

MEMBER BANK. A bank that is a member of the Federal Reserve System. *See Also: bank, Federal Reserve System, reserve*

MEMBER CORPORATION. A company registered as a broker or as a dealer that has at least one employee as a member on one of the securities exchanges. *See Also: broker, dealer, exchanges, securities*

MEMBER FIRM. A brokerage firm or a company that is a member of an organized stock exchange. *See Also: exchange, firm, stock, stock exchange*

MEMBER TAKEDOWN. When an underwriting syndicate member agrees to buy bonds at a discount from the member's account and sell them to the customer at the public offering price. *See Also: account, at a discount, discount, offering, offering price, public offering, public offering price, syndicate, underwriting, underwriting syndicate*

MEMBER'S RATE. The commission an exchange member must pay when the member is not also a member of the clearing association. *See Also: commission, exchange, pay*

MEMBERS' SHORT-SALE RATIO. Achieved by dividing all short sales into all shares that members sold short for their own accounts during a specific time period. *See Also: time*

MEMBERSHIP CORPORATION. A company that members can join by paying a fee, but that does not issue any stocks. *See Also: issue*

MEMBERSHIP DUES. The annual fees that exchange members pay to remain members of the exchange. *See Also: exchange, pay*

MERCANTILE AGENCY. An agency that provides one company with the credit ratings of another company that they expect to do business with. A mercantile agency also collects overdue accounts. *See Also: credit*

MERCHANT BANK. A British commercial bank. A merchant bank is different from an American commercial bank, because a merchant bank is allowed to underwrite new issues of corporate securities, where an American commercial bank is not. *See Also: bank, commercial bank, securities*

MERGER. When two or more companies voluntarily combine to form one company, with only one of the companies maintaining its identity.

MERGER CONVERSION. When the depositors of a mutual institution can vote on a merger, even though the acquiring company does not give them any money or stock shares. The depositors will be offered the stock first in an offer that equals the mutual's market value. *See Also: market, market value, merger, offer, stock*

MESSAGE SWITCHING. A computer network that connects the different trading areas of an exchange to member firms. *See Also: exchange*

METAMARKETS. An e-marketplace that connects customers with the providers of goods and services they need to fill their needs. These goods and services may be offered by the marketplace or by third-party providers. *See Also: e-marketplace, fill*

METAMEDIARY. Providers of the resources necessary to fulfill the needs of a buyer or seller, by either directly or indirectly offering goods and services. For example, a metamediary may facilitate a transaction between a buyer and seller of office equipment, and provide additional services such as credit, fulfillment, and inspection. *See Also: credit, fulfillment, offering, transaction*

METCALF'S LAW. Robert M. Metcalfe, inventor of Ethernet, expressed the power of a connected network as increasing exponentially by the number of computers that are connected. Mathematically, this is represented as the number of members squared. *See Also: ethernet, M*

MEZZANINE BRACKET. An underwriter who, next to the major underwriters, subscribes to the next largest portion of the issue. *See Also: issue*

MEZZANINE FINANCING. A takeover is financed through preferred stock or convertible subordinated debentures to expand the company's equity capital and to satisfy creditors that the new owners are making a substantial financial commitment to the company. *See Also: capital, equity, equity capital, preferred stock, stock, subordinated, takeover*

MEZZANINE LEVEL. The time before a company goes public when venture capitalists enter with a lower risk than if they had entered earlier. Investors who enter at this time can expect early capital appreciation because market values can increase at the initial public offering. *See Also: appreciation, capital, capital appreciation, initial public offering, market, offering, public offering, risk, time*

MGIC INVESTMENT CORPORATION. A company that provides insurance on some municipal bonds, mortgages, and commercial leases. *See Also: insurance*

MICROECONOMICS. A study of an economy's individual parts, such as an individual industry. *See Also: industry*

MICROHEDGE. A hedge that reduces the risk involved in owning a security or an asset. *See Also: asset, hedge, risk, security*

MICROMARKETPLACE. A vertical business-to-business portal that enables buyers within a geographic region or particular industry, or other grouping to make informed purchasing decisions. The marketplace aggregates content, vendors' offerings, and other value-added services. *See Also: industry, portal*

MICROPAYMENT. Small financial transactions, typically up to $1. Digital cash is one technology that enables these transactions. *See Also: cash, digital, digital cash, technology, up*

MID-AMERICA COMMODITY EXCHANGE. A commodities exchange in Chicago. *See Also: exchange*

MIDDLE-OF-THE-ROAD STAND. To avoid predicting or voicing an opinion on how securities prices probably will change. Such a stand is neither bullish nor bearish. *See Also: change, securities*

MIDDLEWARE. A mediator that manages the interaction between an application program and a database. A Web server is considered middleware because it sits between Web browser software and a database. *See Also: server, Web, Web browser*

MIDGET. A Government National Mortgage Association mortgage pool with a 15-year maturity. Other than the maturity, the midget is the same as a regular Ginnie Mae-the average Ginnie Mae has a 30-year maturity. *See Also: average, Ginnie Mae, maturity, mortgage, mortgage pool, pool*

MIDWEST STOCK EXCHANGE (MSE). A securities exchange that handles transactions of its own listed securities as well as some of those traded on the New York Stock Exchange. The MSE is in Chicago. *See Also: exchange, listed securities, MSE, New York Stock Exchange, securities, stock, stock exchange*

MIDWEST STOCK EXCHANGE AUTOMATED EXECUTION SYSTEM. An electronic system that connects the Midwest Stock Exchange with the Intermarket Trading System and through which dual-listed stocks can be immediately executed at the best price. *See Also: exchange, intermarket, stock, stock exchange*

MILL. Equal to 0.1 percent.

MINI MANIPULATION. A manipulative deal on a stock option contract that is small enough to be difficult to detect, but large enough to change the option position. When the manipulator holds a large position in an underlying option, the movement can be multiplied many times. *See Also: change, contract, movement, option, option contract, position, stock, stock option*

MINI-WAREHOUSE LIMITED PARTNERSHIP. Two or more people form a partnership to invest in small warehouses and then rent space in the warehouses for people to store furniture or other belongings. While most of the profits come from rents, the partners also receive tax benefits from depreciation and capital gains after the warehouse is sold. *See Also: capital, depreciation, partnership*

MINIMUM LENDING RATE. The interest rate the Bank of New England charges British banks to borrow. *See Also: bank, interest, interest rate*

MINIMUM MAINTENANCE. The least amount of equity a brokerage firm requires a customer to maintain in his or her margin account. *See Also: account, equity, firm, margin, margin account*

MINIMUM PRICE CHANGES OMITTED. An announcement that appears on a stock exchange's tape if the reporting of trades are 10 or more minutes late. After the announcement, only prices that have gone up or down more than 1/8 of a point from the previous transaction are printed. *See Also: point, stock, tape, transaction*

MINIMUM VARIATION. One-eighth of a point in securities transactions, and 1/32 of a point in transactions of bonds and government notes. *See Also: government notes, point, securities*

MINIMUM YIELD. The lesser of the yield to call or the yield to maturity. *See Also: maturity, yield, yield to call, yield to maturity*

MINNEAPOLIS GRAIN EXCHANGE. A commodity exchange located in Minneapolis. *See Also: commodity, exchange*

MINOR TREND. Small daily price changes in the securities or commodities markets. *See Also: securities*

MINORITY INTEREST. Ownership of stock shares with no voting control, or with less than controlling interest. *See Also: controlling interest, interest, stock*

MINORITY INVESTMENT. A person's holdings in a company when those holdings total less than 50 percent of the company's voting shares.

MINORITY STOCKHOLDER. An investor who owns less than 50 percent of a company's voting shares.

MINT PAR OF EXCHANGE. Divide the weight of one country's monetary unit, such as gold or silver, by the weight of the similar metal of another country's monetary unit. *See Also: unit*

MINT PRICE OF GOLD. The price a government will pay for gold when that gold is delivered to the mint. *See Also: pay*

MINT RATIO. The difference between the weight of one metal to another, along with each metal's national currency unit equivalent. *See Also: currency, unit*

MINUS. The discount at which a closed-end mutual fund sells below the fund's net asset value. *See Also: asset, discount, fund, mutual fund, net, net asset value*

MINUS YIELD. A convertible bond selling at a premium that is higher than the bond's interest yield. *See Also: at a premium, bond, interest, interest yield, premium, yield*

MINUSTICK. A transaction executed at a price lower than the previous transaction. *See Also: transaction*

MINUTE BOOK. A company's official record of its stockholder and board of directors meetings. *See Also: board of directors, stockholder*

MIPS. Short for million instructions per second, a measure of the power of processing power. Because MIPS is often a misleading measure, due to differing measuring techniques and because different computers behave differently with instructions, adversaries of this measuring technique redefine it as Meaningless Indicator of Processor Speed. *See Also: processing*

MIRROR SITE. A server that contains a duplicate of a Web site or FTP site that exists on another server. By using mirror sites, or mirroring, heavy traffic from users can be directed from the primary server to the exact copy on a mirrored site. *See Also: FTP, heavy, on, server, sites, Web, Web site*

MISCELLANEOUS LIABILITIES. A bookkeeping entry that represents liabilities for which payments, for tax or legal reasons, have not been determined yet. *See Also: legal*

MISCELLANEOUS STOCK. The securities of a company that is not part of any particular industry. *See Also: industry, securities*

MISSING THE MARKET. An investor's limit order that a broker could not fill because the security's market price jumped too far from the investor's limit price. *See Also: broker, fill, limit, limit order, limit price, market, market price, order*

MIT. Market If Touched Order. *See Also: market, order*

MIXED. A market that follows no trend and that has many price shifts, with some prices going up and others going down. *See Also: market, trend*

MIXED ACCOUNT. A margin account that holds both long and short positions in the securities market. *See Also: account, margin, margin account, market, securities*

MIXED COLLATERAL. In securing a loan, a borrower uses a variety of different types of securities as collateral. *See Also: collateral, securities*

MIXED CURRENCY. A currency that contains both notes and precious metals. *See Also: currency*

MIXING RATES. A variety of foreign exchange rates that are used in specific categories of items traded overseas. *See Also: exchange, foreign exchange*

MM. The abbreviation for one million; when following a number, it indicates the number is to be multiplied by 1,000,000. For example, 3MM would equal 3,000,000.

MOBILE COMMERCE. *M-commerce*

MOBILE HOME CERTIFICATE. A governmental National Mortgage Association security that represents a mortgage on a mobile home. The securities carry shorter maturities, but the same guarantees as the normal Ginnie Maes. *See Also: carry, home, mortgage, securities, security*

MOBILE TO MOBILE. Communications between users via wireless devices such as cellular telephones and personal digital assistants. An example of this includes sending text messages or files, such as images or video. *See Also: digital*

MODELING. An economic system model is designed and manipulated so that any possible changes and the impact of those changes can be analyzed.

MODEM. Short for Modulator/DEModulator, this is an electronic device that allows one computer to communicate with another over a telephone line by translating digital data into analog signals. The modem modulates the digital data into analog signals. The signals are sent over the telephone lines, where a modem demodulates the signals into digital signals that can be read by the receiving computer. *See Also: digital*

MODERN PORTFOLIO. An investment theory in which investment managers classify, estimate, and control investment risks and returns. *See Also: investment*

MODIFIED DURATION. Modified duration is the duration of a bond, but modified to express the percentage price change as the result of a small change in the bond's yield. *See Also: bond, change, duration, price change, yield*

MODIFIED LEGAL LIST. Allows fiduciaries in some states to put most of the money in funds on the legal list and the rest of the money in securities that are not on the list. *See Also: legal, legal list, put, securities*

MOMENTUM. The pace and the strength of a specific security's, industry's, or market indicator's price movements. In the stock market, technical analysts measure momentum by charting the trends of prices and volume. *See Also: market, stock, stock market, volume*

MOMENTUM INDICATOR. A gauge that uses prices and trading volumes to determine the market's strength and its general health, and to find possible market turning points. *See Also: market*

MOMO. Slang for momentum in the movement of an index's or security's price. *See Also: momentum, movement*

MONETARISM. An economic system where changes in the money supply prompt economic and price fluctuations. *See Also: in the money, money supply, supply*

MONETARY AGGREGATES. Money supply. *See Also: supply*

MONETARY INDICATOR. A gauge used to determine what effect the Treasury Department and Federal Reserve will have on equity and on the bond market. *See Also: bond, equity, market, reserve*

MONETARY INFLATION. When the money supply increases. *See Also: money supply, supply*

MONETARY POLICY. The way the money supply is managed. In the United States, for example, the Federal Reserve Board establishes the monetary policy. *See Also: Federal Reserve Board, money supply, reserve, supply*

MONETIZE. To establish as a currency or legal tender. Also refers to the conversion of a business idea into currency. *See Also: conversion, currency, legal, tender*

MONEY BROKER. A financial institution that acts as an intermediary between borrowers and lenders. *See Also: intermediary*

MONEY CENTER BANK. A bank in one of the world's major financial centers, such as London, Tokyo, or Chicago, that has large lenders, money market buyers, and securities purchasers. A money center bank also lends money to governments and international corporations. *See Also: bank, governments, market, money market, securities*

MONEY FUNDS. A mutual fund in which an investor owns shares, usually at one dollar each, in an account that is similar to a bank account. *See Also: account, bank, fund, mutual fund*

MONEY MARKET. An international market for dealers who trade short-term government and corporate financial instruments such as a banker's acceptance, commercial paper, negotiable certificates of deposit, or Treasury bills. *See Also: acceptance, banker's acceptance, commercial paper, market, negotiable, paper*

MONEY MARKET ACCOUNT. A savings account with a higher interest rate for a time savings account with a minimum required balance. *See Also: account, balance, interest, interest rate, savings account, time*

MONEY MARKET BROKER. A financial institution that buys, sells, and transfers short-term credits and instruments.

MONEY MARKET CENTER BANK. A large, metropolitan bank that actively issues and trades short-term financial instruments such as commercial paper, bankers' acceptance, and certificates of deposit. *See Also: acceptance, bank, commercial paper, paper*

MONEY MARKET CERTIFICATE. A savings instrument with a minimum face value of $10,000 and a 26-week maturity, and with the interest rate tied to a six-month Treasury bill. *See Also: face value, instrument, interest, interest rate, maturity, Treasury bill*

MONEY MARKET DEPOSIT ACCOUNT. A bank account that requires a minimum deposit of $1,000, allows the drawing of only three checks a month, while permitting unlimited transfers through automatic teller machines. It has an interest rate comparable to that found on money market mutual funds. *See Also: account, bank, interest, interest rate, market, money market*

MONEY MARKET FUND. A mutual fund with investments directed in short-term money market instruments only, which normally can be withdrawn with 24-hour's notice without penalty. *See Also: fund, market, money market, mutual fund*

MONEY MARKET INSTRUMENT. A short-term bill or note that is easily marketable and carries little risk of default. *See Also: default, note, risk*

MONEY MARKET PREFERRED STOCK. An equity security with a dividend paid every 49 days, at which time the rate is changed to reflect the current market rate. *See Also: current, dividend, equity, equity security, market, security, time*

MONEY MARKET RATES. The current interest rates on a variety of different money market instruments. Typically, the rate is based on the fund's security, liquidity, size, and maturity. *See Also: current, interest, liquidity, market, maturity, money market, security, size*

MONEY MARKET SECURITIES. High-quality securities with market prices that are tied more closely to the prevailing interest rates than to the underlying company's general economic health. *See Also: interest, market, securities*

MONEY MULTIPLIER SECURITY. A zero-coupon offering that offers the investor a choice of maturities. Because long-term securities cost less than short-term securities, investors can profit greatly because all can be redeemed at par at maturity. *See Also: at par, maturity, offering, par, profit, securities*

MONEY PRICE. The amount it costs to buy one unit of a commodity. *See Also: commodity, unit*

MONEY RATE. The interest rate a lender charges a borrower. *See Also: interest, interest rate*

MONEY RATE OF RETURN. Divide the value of assets into the annual dollars received through those assets.

MONEY SPREAD. A vertical spread, occurring when a client buys a long option, while simultaneously selling another option in the same class and with the same expiration dates, with different strike prices. *See Also: class, client, expiration, option, spread, vertical spread*

MONEY SUPPLY. Bank deposits that can be withdrawn on command, and any currency held outside of a commercial bank. *See Also: bank, commercial bank, currency*

MONEY SUPPLY INDICATOR. The percentage of change in the money supply when it is adjusted for the percentage change in the Consumer Price Index. The indicator is useful when the money supply steadily increases and inflation remains low; at this time, the prices of securities normally increase. *See Also: change, in the money, index, inflation, money supply, price index, securities, supply, time*

MONOPOLY. A company or group of connected companies that controls all of the production and distribution of a product or service without any competition. Because of the lack of competition, prices generally are high and little concern is given to the needs of consumers. Most monopolies are illegal. *See Also: service*

MONTHLY INVESTMENT PLAN. Offered by the New York Stock Exchange, this method allows smaller investors to buy stocks by paying a specified minimum amount each month. *See Also: exchange, New York Stock Exchange, stock, stock exchange*

MONTHLY STATEMENT. A report a brokerage firm sends each client monthly, outlining such information as the dates, amounts, credits, debits, and balances involved in each individual transaction. *See Also: client, firm, transaction*

MONTREAL EXCHANGE REGISTERED REPRESENTATIVE ORDER ROUTING AND EXECUTION SYSTEM. A computer network that connects the Montreal Stock Exchange with the Boston Stock Exchange, through which traders can execute orders in U.S. dollars on whichever exchange offers the best price. *See Also: Boston Stock Exchange, exchange, Montreal Stock Exchange, stock, stock exchange*

MONTREAL STOCK EXCHANGE. A securities exchange in Montreal. *See Also: exchange, securities*

MOOCH. A person who wants to make big money fast, so he or she invests in securities without first investigating the market. *See Also: market, securities*

MOODY'S INVESTORS SERVICE. A company that analyzes and rates securities, and provides a variety of other investment information to investors. MIG 1 is the highest rating, and MIG 4 is the lowest, but even MIG 4 represents an adequate rating of bank quality and investment grade. *See Also: bank, bank quality, investment, investment grade, securities*

MOORE'S LAW. In 1965, Intel co-founder Gordon Moore remarked that going forward processing power would double every 18 months. His well-known law has proven extraordinarily precise. *See Also: forward, processing*

MORAL HAZARD. The risk that the behavior of one or more parties will change after entering into a contract. *See Also: change, contract, risk, will*

MORAL OBLIGATION BONDS. A revenue-backed, state-issued municipal bond upon which the state will pay principal and interest in the event of default. *See Also: and interest, bond, default, interest, municipal bond, pay, principal*

MORAL SUASION. The moral, but not legal, ability of the Federal Reserve System to ensure compliance with its policies through well-placed influence. *See Also: Federal Reserve System, legal, reserve*

MORATORIUM. When a debtor legally can delay paying an obligation. *See Also: delay, obligation*

MORNING LOAN. The unsecured loan a bank makes to a stockbroker so the stockbroker can deliver stocks to a customer until the customer can pay the broker. *See Also: bank, broker, pay, stockbroker*

MORTGAGE. A loan, usually to buy property, with other property used as collateral. *See Also: collateral*

MORTGAGE BANKER. The intermediary between the institution that originates the mortgage and the investor who buys the mortgage. *See Also: intermediary, mortgage*

MORTGAGE BANKERS ASSOCIATION OF AMERICA. A professional organization that promotes better investor services. *See Also: professional*

MORTGAGE BANKING. The combining of property-backed mortgage loans to form a pool, with shares sold to investors. For a fee, the seller services the investment for the life of the loan. *See Also: investment, mortgage, pool*

MORTGAGE BANKING COMPANY. An expert or specialist in the buying and selling of government-backed mortgages. *See Also: specialist*

MORTGAGE BOND. A corporate bond backed by the mortgage on a particular piece of property, with a first mortgage bond backed by the first mortgage, a second mortgage bond backed by the second mortgage, and a general mortgage backed by either the third or some other mortgage on the same property. *See Also: bond, corporate bond, first mortgage bond, general mortgage, mortgage, second mortgage bond*

MORTGAGE BOND SECURITIES CLEARING CORPORATION. An organization that helps investors in mortgage-backed securities transfer ownership and allows trade comparisons by book entry debits and credits. *See Also: book, securities, transfer*

MORTGAGE BROKER. An agent who arranges property loans but does not service the loans after the financing is set. *See Also: agent, service*

MORTGAGE CERTIFICATE. A document that verifies and provides the details of an interest in a mortgage or in part of a mortgage. The mortgage certificate is not a negotiable instrument or an obligation to pay. *See Also: certificate, instrument, interest, mortgage, negotiable, negotiable instrument, obligation, pay*

MORTGAGE CHATTEL. A personal property mortgage. *See Also: mortgage, personal property*

MORTGAGE COMPANY. A mortgage or a mortgage agent for large mortgagees. The company collects payments and retains all records. *See Also: agent, mortgage*

MORTGAGE CORPORATION. A government-sponsored corporation that buys some conventional residential mortgages from corporation members, then packages the mortgages and sells them publicly. *See Also: corporation*

MORTGAGE CORRESPONDENT. A lender's agent who processes the actual loans. *See Also: actual, agent*

MORTGAGE CREDIT CERTIFICATES. An annual credit offered by cities and states that provides a mortgage subscriber with a federal tax credit. Through this program, cities and states can promote housing projects and subsidize mortgage payments at the federal government's expense. *See Also: credit, expense, mortgage, subscriber, tax credit*

MORTGAGE DEPARTMENT. The area of a lending institution where counselors, loan officers, and recording employees handle mortgage work. *See Also: handle, mortgage*

MORTGAGE DURATION. A modified form of duration for mortgage-backed securities to account for the impact of changes in prepayment speeds resulting from changes in interest rates. *See Also: account, duration, interest, prepayment, securities*

MORTGAGE IN POSSESSION. A creditor who takes over a mortgaged property's income if the debtor defaults on the mortgage loan. *See Also: creditor, mortgage*

MORTGAGE INVESTMENT TRUST. A real estate investment trust that puts money in long-term, usually guaranteed mortgages, and makes short-term construction loans. *See Also: estate, investment, investment trust, real estate, trust*

MORTGAGE LIEN. A mortgage that is used as collateral for a debt. *See Also: collateral, mortgage*

MORTGAGE LOAN LEDGER RECORD. A record of all principal, interest, and charges involved in a mortgage transaction. *See Also: interest, mortgage, principal, transaction*

MORTGAGE NOTE. Proof of indebtedness that outlines how the mortgage is to be repaid. *See Also: mortgage*

MORTGAGE PARTICIPATION CERTIFICATE. A mortgage purchased by the Federal Home Loan Mortgage Association and resold as a pass-through security. The security represents an undivided interest in a mortgage pool. *See Also: home, interest, mortgage, mortgage pool, pass-through security, pool, security*

MORTGAGE PASS-THROUGH SECURITIES. A pool of residential mortgage loans, with the interest and principal distributed to the investor each month. *See Also: interest, mortgage, pool, principal*

MORTGAGE PATTERN. The way mortgage payments are arranged. *See Also: mortgage*

MORTGAGE PAY-THROUGH BONDS. A pay-through bond is a debt obligation of the issuer, secured by mortgage collateral that is owned by the issuer. Because the cash flow is based on the cash flow from the mortgage collateral, the principal and interest cash flow must be sufficient to cover principal and interest payments on the bonds. *See Also: and interest, bond, cash, cash flow, collateral, interest, mortgage, obligation, principal*

MORTGAGE PIPELINE. The time period during which applications are accepted from prospective mortgage borrowers to the date at which the loans are marketed. *See Also: mortgage, time*

MORTGAGE POOL. A group of mortgages on the same class of property with the same interest rates and maturities. *See Also: class, interest*

MORTGAGE POOL ORIGINATOR. A mortgage banker who groups together similar classes of mortgages and then issues securities to reflect fractional interests in the pool. The originator also distributes interest and principal payments to certificate holders. *See Also: certificate, interest, mortgage, mortgage banker, originator, pool, principal, securities*

MORTGAGE PORTFOLIO. All of the mortgage loans a bank holds and claims as assets. *See Also: bank, mortgage*

MORTGAGE PREMIUM. When the legal interest rate is lower than the prevailing market rate on mortgages and when mortgage money is in short supply, a bank or other lender will charge this fee for providing a mortgage. *See Also: bank, interest, interest rate, legal, market, mortgage, supply*

MORTGAGE REAL ESTATE INVESTMENT TRUST. Uses an investor's funds as a leveraged investment, with the trust lending money it borrowed from a commercial bank. Investors in the trust hope to profit from the difference between the bank's and the borrower's interest. *See Also: bank, commercial bank, interest, investment, leveraged, profit, trust*

MORTGAGE ROLL. Selling mortgage bonds for settlement in one month, while simultaneously buying them back for settlement in a later month. Investors hope to buy them at a cheaper level. *See Also: level, mortgage*

MORTGAGE SERVICING. The supervision and administration of a mortgage loan. The person or institution who services a mortgage collects payments, monitors principal and interest payments, handles all escrow duties, and forecloses when necessary. *See Also: and interest, escrow, interest, mortgage, principal*

MORTGAGE-BACKED CERTIFICATES. A bank-issued certificate in a large denomination that covers a mortgage pool insured by a private mortgage insurance company. *See Also: certificate, denomination, insurance, mortgage, mortgage pool, pool*

MORTGAGE-BACKED SECURITIES CLEARING CORPORATION (MBSCC). A clearing division for the comparison, netting, and margining of GNMA, Fannie Mae, and Freddie Mac forward transactions. The MBSCC is a wholly owned subsidiary of the Midwest Stock Exchange Incorporated. *See Also: exchange, Fannie Mae, forward, Freddie Mac, GNMA, MBCC, stock, stock exchange, subsidiary*

MORTGAGE-BACKED SECURITY (MBS). A debt instrument with a pool of real estate loans as the underlying collateral. These financial instruments are designed to channel funds from the capital markets to the mortgage borrowers. *See Also: capital, capital markets, channel, collateral, debt instrument, estate, instrument, mortgage, pool, real estate*

MORTGAGE-BACKED SECURITY (MBS). *See Also: Pass-Through Security, security*

MORTGAGEE CLAUSE. An insurance contract stipulation in which the proceeds will be payable to the mortgagee. *See Also: contract, insurance, proceeds*

MOST ACTIVE LIST. A list of the securities that traded the heaviest volume in one day. *See Also: securities, volume*

MOTHER GOOSE. A short, simple summary that explains a company's prospectus. *See Also: prospectus*

MOTHERBOARD. The primary circuit board in a computer. The motherboard houses the central processing unit's chip, the controller circuitry, the bus, memory sockets, expansion slots, and other components. Daughter boards, which are additional boards, can be added to the motherboard. *See Also: processing*

MOUSE. A part of the GUI, or graphical user interface, of computers, the mouse is a device used to move a cursor around a computer screen. *See Also: around, graphical user interface, GUI, screen*

MOVABLE EXCHANGE. An instrument that is quoted in the currency of the nation being owed a payment instead of the nation paying the debt. *See Also: currency, instrument*

MOVEMENT. Any upward or downward shift, no matter how large or how slight, in a security's price.

MOVING AVERAGE. A price average that is continuously adjusted, with each new added price changing the overall average, during a particular time period and therefore accurately reflects values. *See Also: average, time*

MP3. A format used for the compression of audio signals that lets users quickly download sound files, such as music, with minimal hard drive storage required. Although MP3 files save disk space and download time, it does not sacrifice quality. *See Also: download, drive, time*

MPEG. Short for Moving Picture Experts Group, a format used for the compression of audio and video signals that is used on the Web. *See Also: on, picture, Web*

MRO. Maintenance, Repair, and Operations. *See Also: maintenance, operations*

MS-DOS. Short for Microsoft Disk Operating System, the forerunner to the graphical user interface used in Windows, MS-DOS created in six weeks by Tim Paterson at Seattle Computer Products, who is said to have regretted it ever since. Microsoft licensed the technology in order to have an on-time demonstration for IBM. *See Also: demonstration, graphical user interface, order, technology, Windows*

MSE. Midwest Stock Exchange. *See Also: exchange, stock, stock exchange*

MSP. Marketplace Service Provider. *See Also: service*

MULTI VERTICAL. A business that is involved in a broad array of industries, typically with an expertise in each industry. This differs from horizontal exchanges, which simply provide one service that spans across industries. *See Also: exchanges, industry, service*

MULTI-UNIT AUCTION. An auction in which multiple, identical units, such as ten-year Treasury securities, are available to be bid on by one or more bidders. *See Also: on*

MULTICURRENCY CLAUSE. A Eurocurrency loan stipulation that allows the borrower to repay the loan in a different currency as long as he or she takes out another Eurodollar loan immediately. *See Also: currency, Eurocurrency*

MULTIMANAGEMENT SYSTEM. A plan sponsor uses at least two investment managers to provide diversification. *See Also: diversification, investment, sponsor*

MULTIMEDIA. The delivery of any combination of text, sound, video, and animated graphics. *See Also: combination, delivery*

MULTINATIONAL CORPORATION. A company that conducts business globally that has fixed assets in at least one foreign country.

MULTIPLE CAPITAL STRUCTURE COMPANY. A corporation with several different classes of securities outstanding. *See Also: corporation, outstanding, securities*

MULTIPLE COMMODITY RESERVE DOLLAR. To set a reserve of some items, an investor will try to keep a constant dollar ratio between gold and other commodities. The investor redeems dollars for gold or for the reserved items, and the gold and the items are always converted into dollars. *See Also: ratio, reserve*

MULTIPLE CURRENCY PRACTICE. When at least two exchange rates are effective at the same time, with one at least one percent higher or lower than the par value. *See Also: exchange, par, par value, time*

MULTIPLE CURRENCY SECURITIES. Stocks or bonds for which the owner can choose the currency of the payments. *See Also: currency*

MULTIPLE CURRENCY SYSTEM. When foreign exchange is controlled to such an extent that foreign currency can be exchanged only through the government or through a controlled bank. *See Also: bank, currency, exchange, foreign currency, foreign exchange*

MULTIPLE EXCHANGE. Occurs when three or more people or companies are involved with several different pieces of property.

MULTIPLE OPTION PUT SECURITY. A municipal bond with a 30-year maturity and with two-, three-, and five-year put options. Because of the put options, the bond will trade as close to par as if it were a short-term bond. *See Also: bond, close, maturity, municipal bond, par, put*

MULTIPLIER EFFECT. A theory that even a minor event can cause great changes in another area because everything economic is connected, so even a small change will cause a domino effect. *See Also: change*

MUNICIPAL ASSISTANCE CORPORATION FOR THE CITY OF NEW YORK. A government agency that provides financial assistance to New York City by issuing bonds to keep the city from going through bankruptcy. The corporation can redeem city obligations, incur debt, and oversee the city's financial situation. *See Also: bankruptcy, City, corporation, redeem*

MUNICIPAL BOND. A city- or state-issued debt instrument. Interest on such instruments is exempt from federal income tax. If the bond was issued in the bondholder's state of residence, state and local taxes will be exempt. *See Also: bond, debt instrument, instrument, interest, local*

MUNICIPAL BOND COMPARISON SYSTEM. A system that takes the Municipal Securities Rulemaking Board's trade information and clears the transactions by getting a contra party to accept trade terms and by offering book entry debits and credits to promote a settlement. *See Also: book, offering, securities*

MUNICIPAL BOND FUND. A mutual fund that concentrates investments in tax-exempt municipal obligations. *See Also: fund, mutual fund*

MUNICIPAL BOND INSURANCE ASSOCIATION. A group of insurance companies that insure interest and principal on some municipal bonds. *See Also: insurance, interest, principal*

MUNICIPAL IMPROVEMENT CERTIFICATE. A local government issues this tax-exempt certificate in lieu of bonds in order to finance such improvements, such as widening sidewalks or street repairs. The obligation is paid from special assessments made against people who benefit from the improvements. *See Also: certificate, local, obligation, order, Street*

MUNICIPAL INSURED NATIONAL TRUST. A tax-free bond fund, offered by Moseley, Hallgarten, Estabrook, and Weeden, that offers monthly payments from a portfolio containing municipal securities. *See Also: bond, bond fund, fund, portfolio, securities*

MUNICIPAL INVESTMENT TRUST. A unit trust of diversified portfolio investments concentrated in municipal securities. Such trusts provide investors with tax-exempt monthly income. *See Also: diversified, portfolio, securities, trust, unit*

MUNICIPAL NOTE. A municipal-issued, short-term debt instrument. *See Also: debt instrument, instrument, short-term debt*

MUNICIPAL OPTION. One dealer offers to sell bonds to another dealer at a specific price, with the offer good only for a specific time period. *See Also: dealer, offer, time*

MUNICIPAL REVENUE BOND. A government bond issued to pay for projects, such as bridges or sewers. After the project is completed, revenues from the project, such as tolls or other user fees, are used to pay off the bond. *See Also: bond, government bond, pay*

MUNICIPAL SECURITIES RULEMAKING BOARD. A panel that issues the rules and regulations of registering municipal bonds.

MUNIFACTS. A service that provides available data on newly issued municipal bonds. *See Also: service*

MUTILATED SECURITY. A security with a certificate that has the name of the issue or the issuer obscured, or with a portion of the certificate missing so the security cannot be identified. With such a security, the transfer agent must guarantee all ownership rights for the buyer. *See Also: agent, certificate, guarantee, issue, name, rights, security, transfer, transfer agent*

MUTUAL ASSOCIATION. A savings and loan that is owned by its depositors, with deposits representing ownership shares. Such associations do not issue stocks. *See Also: issue*

MUTUAL COMPANY. A company with ownership and profits distributed among members. Each member receives an amount directly related to the amount of business each member does with the company.

MUTUAL FUND. An investment company that puts an investor's money in a variety of areas, usually securities, and that must redeem the shares at net asset value upon demand. *See Also: asset, demand, investment, investment company, net, net asset value, redeem, securities*

MUTUAL FUND CASH RATIO. A percentage comparison of a mutual fund's cash to the fund's total assets. A high ratio of cash to assets is favorable because it means the investor has more funds available for investing. *See Also: cash, ratio*

MUTUAL FUND CORPORATION. A trust company or commercial bank that holds onto a mutual fund's securities, makes transfers, and pays and collects stockholders' investments. *See Also: bank, commercial bank, securities, trust, trust company*

MUTUAL FUND CUSTODIAN. A commercial bank or other institution that holds a mutual fund's assets for safekeeping. *See Also: bank, commercial bank, safekeeping*

MUTUAL SAVINGS BANK. A savings bank organized for the benefit of depositors. Income distributed to the depositors after expenses are deducted. *See Also: bank, savings bank*

MUTUAL WILLS. An arrangement in which a husband and wife agree to leave everything to each other.

N

NAKED OPTIONS. The person selling a put or call option does not own the underlying security. *See Also: call option, option, put, security, underlying security*

NAKED POSITION. A long or short position the holder has not hedged as prices fluctuate. The write of a call option, for example, is naked if the investor doesn't own the underlying security, and is partially hedged if he or she does own the underlying security because the potential risk is much greater if the price rises. *See Also: call option, option, position, risk, security, short position, underlying security, write*

NAME. A participant in a foreign exchange market transaction. *See Also: exchange, foreign exchange, market, participant, transaction*

NARROW MARKET. Occurs when securities are traded with little difference between the bid and asked prices. *See Also: bid and asked, securities*

NARROWING THE SPREAD. Occurs when a broker-dealer bids higher than the last bid price, or offers a lower price than the last offer price. By doing this, the broker-dealer narrows the price spread between bids and offers. *See Also: bid price, broker-dealer, offer, price spread, spread*

NASD. National Association of Securities Dealers. *See Also: securities*

NASDAQ. National Association of Securities Dealers Automated Quotations. *See Also: securities*

NATIONAL ASSOCIATION OF INVESTMENT CLUBS. An organization that helps to establish investment clubs, through which investors pool their money and make common investments. *See Also: investment, pool*

NATIONAL ASSOCIATION OF SECURITIES DEALERS (NASD). An organization of brokers and dealers who trade securities in the United States. Supervised by the Securities and Exchange Commission, the NASD regulates all over-the-counter brokers and dealers. *See Also: commission, exchange, NASD, securities*

NATIONAL ASSOCIATION OF SECURITIES DEALERS AND INVESTMENT MANAGERS. A self-regulating organization of licensed securities dealers who do not have to apply for a license every year before they can deal in securities. *See Also: securities*

NATIONAL ASSOCIATION OF SECURITIES DEALERS AUTO-MATED QUOTATION INDEXES. Seven indexes that act as gauges and which average the trading prices of more than 3,000 American over-the-counter companies. The seven indexes cover banks, industrials, insurance companies, other financial institutions, transportations, utilities, and a composite. *See Also: average, composite, insurance*

NATIONAL ASSOCIATION OF SECURITIES DEALERS AUTO-MATED QUOTATION OPTIONS AUTOMATED EXECUTION SYS-TEM. A computer network over which NASD members can trade and execute over-the-counter put and call options. The members can use the computer to trade up to three contracts on an option series. *See Also: NASD, option, option series, put*

NATIONAL ASSOCIATION OF SECURITIES DEALERS AUTOMATED QUOTATIONS (NASDAQ). A national computer network through which securities dealers execute and post transactions as well as record prices. The NASDAQ is the major method of over-the-counter trading. *See Also: NASDAQ, post, securities*

NATIONAL ASSOCIATION OF SECURITIES DEALERS FIVE PER-CENT POLICY. A nonbinding NASD recommendation that brokerage commissions, markups, and markdowns should be near five percent on most transactions. NASD members do not need to adhere to this policy when executing small transactions, transactions that are difficult to complete, or mutual fund transactions. *See Also: fund, mutual fund, nasd*

NATIONAL ASSOCIATION OF SECURITIES DEALERS FORM FR-1. A document that foreign broker-dealers who are not syndicate members sign when they want to subscribe to a hot issue. Upon signing the certificate, the broker-dealer agrees that he or she understands and will adhere to the NASD's rules on hot issues. *See Also: broker-dealer, certificate, hot issue, issue, syndicate*

NATIONAL ASSOCIATION OF SECURITIES DEALERS RULES OF FAIR PRACTICE. NASD regulations that cover the ethics of brokers and dealers to make sure that they all deal fairly with their customers.

NATIONAL BANK. A commercial bank that is chartered with the U.S. Comptroller of the Currency instead of the state in which it does business. Such banks must be members of the Federal Reserve System. *See Also: bank, commercial bank, comptroller of the currency, currency, Federal Reserve System, reserve*

NATIONAL CRIME INFORMATION CENTER. A Securities and Exchange Commission computer network that registers lost or stolen securities. A broker-dealer can use the network to verify the ownership of a security for sale. *See Also: broker-dealer, commission, exchange, sale, securities, security*

NATIONAL DEBT. The total amount of money the U.S. government owes, including all Treasury bills, Treasury bonds, and other debt obligations.

NATIONAL FARM LOAN ASSOCIATION. An agricultural cooperative that can secure financing for farm mortgages when subscribing to a local Federal Land Bank. *See Also: bank, cooperative, Federal Land Bank, local*

NATIONAL FUTURES ASSOCIATION. An organization that regulates the commodities industry and that requires membership of commodity pool operators, commodity trading advisors, and futures exchange members. *See Also: commodity, exchange, futures, futures exchange, industry, pool*

NATIONAL HOUSING ACT. A law that established the Federal Housing Administration, which insures home mortgages, provides home improvement loans, and finances low-income housing projects. The law also established the Federal Savings and Loan Insurance Corporation, which insures member association accounts for up to $5,000. *See Also: corporation, home, insurance*

NATIONAL INCOME. All of the income a nation earns through its goods and services.

NATIONAL MARKET ADVISORY BOARD. A 15-member panel appointed by the Securities and Exchange Commission, that makes recommendations to the SEC on establishing, operating, and regulating the securities market. Members serve between two and five years. A majority of members come from within the securities industry. *See Also: commission, exchange, industry, market, SEC, securities*

NATIONAL MARKET SYSTEM. A nationwide computer network that links all markets for a particular security so that everyone can have access to all bid and ask prices and can execute transactions based on the best prices available. *See Also: ask, security*

NATIONAL QUOTATION BUREAU. A commerce clearing house subsidiary that provides subscribers with daily over-the-counter quotes. *See Also: clearing house, commerce, house, subsidiary*

NATIONAL QUOTATION SERVICE (NQS). A National Quotation Bureau system that lists corporate bonds, over-the-counter securities, their market makers, and bid and ask prices. The NQS reports on those OTC stocks that are not quoted by the National Association of Securities Dealers Automated Quotation system. *See Also: ask, market, National Quotation Bureau, NQS, quotation, securities*

NATIONAL SECURITIES CLEARING CORPORATION. An independent clearing organization that member firms use to execute transactions with other member firms.

NATIONAL SECURITIES EXCHANGE. Any securities exchange that has been registered with the Securities and Exchange Commission. *See Also: commission, exchange, securities*

NATIONAL SECURITIES TRADE ASSOCIATION. An organization of over-the-counter brokers and dealers. Among other activities, the association provides lobbying services on behalf of brokers and dealers.

NATIONAL STOCK EXCHANGE (NSE). A third New York City Stock Exchange. The NSE was established in 1960. *See Also: City, exchange, NSE, stock, stock exchange*

NATIONALIZATION. Occurs when a government takes over a company's assets and operations. *See Also: operations*

NATURAL FINANCING. A transaction in which financing is not necessary because the seller pays the buyer in cash. *See Also: cash, transaction*

NATURAL INTEREST RATE. The interest rate at which the demand for loans equals the savings supply. *See Also: demand, interest, interest rate, supply*

NATURAL MONOPOLY. A company that holds a monopoly when no other company is able to compete because of variables beyond either company's control. For example, an agricultural business that holds a monopoly on a particular produce item because no one else can farm that item holds a natural monopoly. Other companies may not be able to farm the item because of climate or because of a lack of available labor. *See Also: monopoly*

NATURAL SELLER. An investor who is selling a security he or she has in his or her portfolio. *See Also: portfolio, security*

NEAR MONEY. A debt instrument such as a bond that is near its redemption or maturity date. *See Also: bond, debt instrument, instrument, maturity, redemption*

NEAR OPTION. The side of a spread option position that expires first. *See Also: option, position, spread, spread option*

NEAR TERM. A market performance evaluation that indicates a period from one to five weeks. *See Also: evaluation, market*

NEARBY DELIVERY. The closest active month a commodities futures agreement can be delivered. *See Also: futures*

NEAREST MONTH. In a group of commodity futures or options contracts, this represents the contract that expires first. *See Also: commodity, contract, futures*

NEGATIVE AMORTIZER. A home mortgage that is lower than the average current rate, with the difference added to the principal. Such mortgage payments increase in amount as time goes on. *See Also: average, current, home, mortgage, principal, time*

NEGATIVE CARRY. When a security's percentage of return is less than the interest rate charged on the loan the investor used to buy the security. For example, if the investor is buying a bond that has a 10 percent rate of return using funds from a loan that charges an 11.5 percent interest rate, the bond would have a negative carry. *See Also: bond, carry, interest, interest rate, rate of return, return, security*

NEGATIVE CASH FLOW. Occurs when a company is spending more money than it is taking in.

NEGATIVE CONVEXITY. Most commonly seen in mortgage-backed securities because of mortgagors' tendencies to prepay mortgage loans when interest rates drop. Negative convexity represents prices that tend to move with the direction of interest rates. *See Also: convexity, drop, interest, mortgage, securities*

NEGATIVE INCOME TAX. A subsidy that low-income residents receive to bring them up to the subsistence level when their yearly income is below that level. To receive the subsidy, the residents first must file a tax return that verifies their poverty-level income. *See Also: level, return*

NEGATIVE INTEREST. Money that has been deducted from the interest amount. *See Also: interest*

NEGATIVE INTEREST TAX. The Swiss government imposes this tax occasionally on new bank accounts held by foreigners when the account balances exceed a particular level. That level usually is about 100,000 francs. *See Also: account, bank, level*

NEGATIVE PLEDGE CLAUSE. An indenture agreement stipulation in which the company guarantees that it will not pledge any of its assets if such a pledge would decrease a debt-holder's security. *See Also: indenture, pledge, security*

NEGATIVE WORKING CAPITAL. When a company's current liabilities exceed its current assets. *See Also: current, current assets, current liabilities*

NEGATIVE YIELD. Occurs when savings returns are less than the inflation rate plus taxes. *See Also: inflation, inflation rate, plus*

NEGATIVE YIELD CURVE. The graph that occurs when charting the following situation: the interest rate on a short-term fixed-income security is higher than the interest rate on a long-term fixed-income security with the same class and rating. *See Also: class, interest, interest rate, security*

NEGOTIABLE. Any instrument that can be sold or transferred easily. *See Also: instrument*

NEGOTIABLE CERTIFICATE OF DEPOSIT. A negotiable money market instrument that trades on the open market with high returns and low risks. *See Also: instrument, low, market, money market, money market instrument, negotiable, open, open market*

NEGOTIABLE INSTRUMENT. An ownership certificate that can be transferred without registering that transfer with the original issuer. *See Also: certificate, transfer*

NEGOTIABLE ORDER OF WITHDRAWAL ACCOUNT (NOW ACCOUNT). An interest-bearing account on which the holder can draw checks. Such an account is a combination savings-checking account. *See Also: account, combination*

NEGOTIABLE PAPER. A negotiable instrument used to take out short-term business loans. *See Also: instrument, negotiable, negotiable instrument, take*

NEGOTIABLE SECURITY. A security with an easily-transferable title. *See Also: security*

NEGOTIATED BID. As opposed to a competitive bid, this occurs when a security's issuer and the underwriting syndicate mutually agree on a price after holding meetings and discussions on the subject. *See Also: competitive bid, syndicate, underwriting, underwriting syndicate*

NEGOTIATED SALE. When two or more parties agree to a securities transaction price without going through any competitive bidding. *See Also: securities, transaction*

NEGOTIATED UNDERWRITING. The underwriting of a new securities issue. The issuing company and the underwriting manager negotiate the spread between the price paid to the issuer and the offering price, instead of having that spread determined through competitive bidding. Corporate stocks and bonds normally are issued through a negotiated underwriting, and utilities issues are issued through competitive bidding. *See Also: issue, manager, offering, offering price, securities, spread, underwriting*

NELLIE MAES. New England Education Loan Marketing Corporation. *See Also: corporation*

NEST EGG. The assets and money a person conservatively invests or sets aside for his or her retirement.

NET. The difference between the value of a sale, whether positive or negative, and the cost of completing that sale. *See Also: sale*

NET ASSET VALUE. Determined by subtracting the liabilities from the portfolio value of a fund's securities and dividing that figure by the number of outstanding shares. *See Also: outstanding, portfolio, securities*

NET ASSETS. The difference between a company's assets and its liabilities.

NET AVAILS. The money a borrower receives on a discounted note, with the amount equal to the note's face value, less the amount of the discount. *See Also: discount, face value, note*

NET BALANCE. The amount that falls due after any refunds have been subtracted.

NET BONDED DEBT. The gross bonded debt, which is a government's direct debt in outstanding bonds, minus cash and assets. *See Also: cash, gross, minus, outstanding*

NET BORROWED RESERVES. The amount of money borrowed minus any excess reserves. *See Also: excess reserves, minus*

NET CAPITAL. A company's net worth minus assets that cannot be sold at their full value. *See Also: full, minus, net, net worth, worth*

NET CAPITAL REQUIREMENT. A Securities and Exchange Commission regulation that outlines the net capital ratio, which is the aggregate, customer-related indebtedness along with cash and other assets that can be converted easily into cash. *See Also: capital, cash, commission, exchange, net, net capital, ratio, securities*

NET CHANGE. The difference between a security's current price and the price at which it closed after the last trading session. *See Also: current, session*

NET CURRENT ASSETS. The amount by which a company's current assets exceed its current liabilities. *See Also: current, current assets, current liabilities*

NET DOWN. Occurs when a taxpayer offsets short-term gains with short-term losses, and long-term gains with long-term losses to reach a final figure in both columns. If the investor ends up with a net loss in one column and a net gain in the other, he or she must offset the gains and losses again. *See Also: gain, net, offset*

NET EARNINGS. The amount by which gross operating income exceeds gross operating expenses, subtracted by the applicable taxes. *See Also: gross, operating income*

NET ESTATE. The amount an estate is worth after all management expenses have been subtracted. *See Also: estate, worth*

NET FOR COMMON STOCK. A preferred stock's net income after dividends have been subtracted during a period of accrual. *See Also: net, net income*

NET FOREIGN INVESTMENT. The amount a country's foreign assets and liabilities change through trade, investment income, and cash gifts. *See Also: cash, change, investment, investment income*

NET HIT. When a Web page is downloaded, it can be counted in two ways. A net hit is considered the entire page. A gross hit includes the number of components on a Web page that are accessed. A net hit is considered the entire page. *See Also: gross, gross hit, hit, net, on, Web, Web page*

NET INCOME. The profit after all expenses have been deducted. *See Also: profit*

NET INCOME MULTIPLIER. An estimated property value achieved by dividing the monthly net rent into the selling price. *See Also: net*

NET INCOME PER SHARE OF COMMON STOCK. The dollar amount of earnings from one common stock share after all costs, including taxes and depreciation, have been subtracted. *See Also: common stock, depreciation, earnings, share, stock*

NET INTEREST COST. A debt security issuer's interest expense for the security's life. *See Also: debt security, expense, interest, security*

NET INVESTMENT INCOME. The profit from an investment minus commissions and other expenses. *See Also: investment, minus, profit*

NET INVESTMENT INCOME PER SHARE. The average dollar amount of dividend and interest earnings an investment company receives from each individual security share after all costs, including taxes and depreciation, have been subtracted. *See Also: and interest, average, depreciation, dividend, earnings, interest, investment, investment company, security, share*

NET LEASE. A lease in which the tenant pays all maintenance costs, taxes, insurance, etc. *See Also: insurance, maintenance, tenant*

NET LIQUID ASSETS. The difference between a company's cash and marketable securities and its current liabilities. *See Also: cash, current, current liabilities, marketable securities, securities*

NET LISTING. The commission amount a broker receives beyond the security's selling price. *See Also: broker, commission*

NET LONG-TERM DEBT. The total long-term debt, minus sinking fund investment assets and other reserve funds held for redeeming the debt. *See Also: fund, investment, investment assets, long-term debt, minus, reserve, sinking fund*

NET MARKET. An online exchange or a central hub that facilitates transactions among buyers and sellers. *See Also: exchange, online*

NET MARKET MAKER. An online company that facilitates buying and selling among participants. The net market maker may act as an agent or principal. *See Also: agent, maker, market, market maker, net, net market, online, principal*

NET NATIONAL PRODUCT (NNP). Gross national product minus the capital consumption allowances (depreciation). *See Also: capital, capital consumption, consumption, minus*

NET OPERATING INCOME. A company's net operating income after minority interest and taxes are subtracted and before investment profits, losses, and preferred dividend payments are added or subtracted. *See Also: dividend, interest, investment, minority interest, net, operating income*

NET OPTION. A contract that gives a buyer the right to buy a piece of property at a specific price. *See Also: contract, right*

NET OUT. A brokerage client's market position is established by determining how much margin he or she must post at the exchange. *See Also: exchange, margin, market, position, post*

NET POSITION. The difference between open contracts held long and open contracts held short in the same commodity. *See Also: commodity, open*

NET PRESENT VALUE (NPV). An investment evaluation method in which the net present value of all cash outflows and inflows is calculated with a discount rate or a required rate of return. The net present value of a good investment is positive. *See Also: cash, discount, discount rate, evaluation, investment, net, present value, rate of return, required rate of return, return*

NET PROCEEDS. The amount of money an investor receives from selling a security, with the cost of completing the sale subtracted. *See Also: sale, security*

NET PROFIT. Total earnings after all debts, expenses, and taxes have been deducted. *See Also: earnings*

NET PROFIT ON NET SALES. To measure a company's profitability, divide its net sales into its net earnings. *See Also: earnings, net, net earnings, net sales, profitability*

NET PROFITS ON NET WORKING CAPITAL. Subtract a company's total current debt from its total current assets, which provides the owner's equity in the current assets. The difference represents the financial cushion with which the company can carry inventories and receivables and can pay for the day-to-day operations of the business. *See Also: carry, current, current assets, equity, operations, pay, receivables*

NET PROFITS ON TANGIBLE NET WORTH. To determine a company's profitability, divide its net profits after taxes by its tangible net worth, which is obtained by subtracting liabilities from assets, then subtracting the intangible assets. *See Also: net, net worth, profitability, tangible net worth, worth*

NET QUICK ASSETS. After removing a company's inventory from its current assets, subtract the company's current liabilities from the remaining assets to compute its net quick assets. *See Also: current, current assets, current liabilities, inventory, net*

NET RADIO. Radio programming over the Internet, using streaming technology to Webcast the audio programming. *See Also: Internet, streaming, technology*

NET REALIZED CAPITAL GAINS PER SHARE. An investment company's long-term capital gains from selling a security added to the net of its long-term capital losses, with the sum divided by the number of outstanding shares. The gains are distributed among stockholders each year, with the amount each stockholder receives in direct proportion to the percentage of the investment company portfolio he or she owns. *See Also: capital, investment, investment company, long-term capital gains, long-term capital losses, net, outstanding, portfolio, security, stockholder*

NET REVENUE AVAILABLE FOR DEBT SERVICE. To determine revenue bond issue coverage, subtract an organization's operating and maintenance expenses, not including bond interest or depreciation, from its gross operating revenue. *See Also: bond, depreciation, gross, interest, issue, maintenance, revenue bond*

NET ROADSHOW. A pre-offering roadshow that is delivered over the Internet. The presentation is hosted by the issuing company's management for mostly institutional investors. Audiences are usually selected by the underwriter. *See Also: Internet*

NET SALES. A balance sheet item that indicates sales receipts minus the cost of the sales. *See Also: balance, balance sheet, minus*

NET SALES TO INVENTORY. To determine a company's stocks-to-sales ratio, divide its inventory into its annual net sales. The figure is compared with the ratios of other companies. *See Also: inventory, net, net sales, ratio*

NET SALES TO NETWORKING CAPITAL. Divide a company's net working capital into its net sales. This is a gauge to determine the extent to which a company is implementing its working capital and its margin of operating funds. *See Also: capital, margin, net, net sales, working capital*

NET SALES TO TANGIBLE NET WORTH. The measurement of a company's relative capital turnover, by dividing a company's tangible net worth into its net sales. *See Also: capital, capital turnover, net, net sales, net worth, tangible net worth, turnover, worth*

NET SHARES MARKET. In Europe, most U.S. equity securities are traded in dealer markets with banks and brokers as principals; they are the net of commissions. *See Also: dealer, equity, net, securities*

NET SURPLUS. A company's total earnings after operating expenses, taxes, insurance, dividend payments, and other costs have been deducted. *See Also: dividend, earnings, insurance*

NET TANGIBLE ASSETS PER SHARE. Subtract a company's intangible assets from its total assets to find its total tangible assets. Subtract all liabilities and the preferred stock's par value from the total tangible assets. Then, divide the remainder by the total number of outstanding common shares to obtain the net tangible assets per share. *See Also: net, outstanding, par, par value, share*

NET TRANSACTION. When the buyer and the seller of a security are charged no additional fee in the transaction. *See Also: security, transaction*

NET UNREALIZED APPRECIATION. The appreciation between a person's investment costs and the current market value of his or her holdings. *See Also: appreciation, current, current market value, investment, market, market value*

NET UNREALIZED DEPRECIATION. The depreciation between a person's investment costs and the current market value of his or her holdings. *See Also: current, current market value, depreciation, investment, market, market value*

NET VOLUME. The difference between the uptick and downtick volumes. *See Also: downtick, uptick*

NET WORTH. The difference between a company's or individual's assets and liabilities.

NET YIELD. A security's rate of return minus all related out-of-pocket costs, such as commissions. *See Also: minus, rate of return, return*

NET YIELD TO REDEMPTION. A company's gross yield to redemption, which is a security's interest yield plus the yearly capital gains it would earn if it were held to redemption, minus taxes. *See Also: capital, gross, gross yield, gross yield to redemption, interest, interest yield, minus, plus, redemption, yield*

NETIQUETTE. The Internet rules of etiquette which apply to communication or an online service. This may include e-mail, chat rooms, or privacy issues. For example, it is considered improper netiquette to only use capital letters when writing correspondence because it is considered an act of yelling. *See Also: capital, e-mail, Internet, online, service*

NETIZEN. An Internet citizen. *See Also: Internet*

NETWORK A. A Consolidated Tape Association subscription service that reports on successive New York Stock Exchange-listed round-lot transactions, even if the transaction was not executed on the NYSE. *See Also: consolidated tape, NYSE, service, stock, subscription, tape, transaction*

NETWORK B. A Consolidated Tape Association subscription service that reports on successive American Stock Exchange-listed round-lot transactions, even if the transaction was not executed on the ASE. *See Also: consolidated tape, service, stock, subscription, tape, transaction*

NETWORK COMPUTER. A desktop computer that is designed to connect to a network. Applications are typically accessed not from the user's computer, but from a server on the network. The saving of data, upgrades, and maintenance are performed on the server, not the computer. *See Also: maintenance, on, server*

NETWORK EFFECT. The theory that as more participants are added to a network, those additional participants will attract even more participants. This term is often used when describing the benefits of the Internet as it relates to B2B exchanges or viral marketing. *See Also: exchanges, Internet, term, viral, will*

NETWORK INTERFACE CARD. *See Also: NIC.*

NETWORK PC. Also called an appliance denotes a low-cost PC or related device designed for Internet access and other specialized business uses, but without the full capabilities of today's personal computer and software. *See Also: full, Internet, personal computer*

NEUTRAL. An investing belief or portfolio structure that is neither bullish nor bearish. *See Also: portfolio*

NEUTRAL HUB. A business-to-business e-marketplace that is independent of any particular party, and does not favor any participant in a transaction. *See Also: e-marketplace, participant, transaction*

NEUTRAL MONEY. When a dollar could be converted into a commodity at a specific price to stabilize the price level. *See Also: commodity, level*

NEUTRAL SPREAD. In a market with a narrow spread, this is a long call at a lower price and two short calls at a higher price. *See Also: long call, market, spread*

NEUTRAL TREND. When a security's price remains even, with the prevailing price trend moving laterally. *See Also: trend*

NEW ACCOUNT REPORT. A document that broker-dealers must prepare and update on customers' investment objectives, financial situation, and investment background. *See Also: investment, update*

NEW ECONOMY. Describes knowledge-driven industries that are on the cutting edge of technology, such as information technology. *See Also: information technology, on, technology*

NEW ENGLAND EDUCATION LOAN MARKETING CORPORATION. A private Massachusetts company that buys student loan notes issued through the U.S. Higher Education Act. The firm then publicly issues tax-exempt bonds, with the proceeds used to buy education loans from eligible lenders. These securities are commonly referred to as Nellie Maes. *See Also: firm, Nellie Maes, proceeds, securities*

NEW ENGLAND NEGOTIABLE ORDER OF WITHDRAWAL AC-COUNT. A NOW account, which is a combination checking-savings account, with a federally chartered association in Connecticut, Maine, Rhode Island, or Vermont. The NOW account authority was expanded in 1979 to include these areas. *See Also: account, combination*

NEW HIGH. The highest price of a security during a specific time period. *See Also: security, time*

NEW HIGHS. A group of securities has reached its highest price in a year. *See Also: securities*

NEW ISSUE. A security publicly offered for sale for the first time. *See Also: sale, security, time*

NEW ISSUE MARKET. The market in which new securities issues are publicly sold. *See Also: market, securities*

NEW LOW. A security has reached its lowest price during a given time period. *See Also: security, time*

NEW LOWS. A group of securities has reached its lowest price in a year. *See Also: securities*

NEW MONEY. A new bond that has a greater par value than a bond that was retired after a call option was exercised or after it matured. *See Also: bond, call option, matured, option, par, par value*

NEW MONEY APPROACH TO INVESTMENT INCOME. An investment method in which investment income from a group annuity contract is allocated according to the rate of return earned on new investments that were made in the same year each block of contributions was received. *See Also: annuity, contract, investment, investment income, rate of return, return*

NEW MONEY PREFERRED. Preferred stock that was issued after October 1, 1942, with the shares providing the holder with an 85 percent tax exclusion on cash dividends. *See Also: cash, exclusion, stock*

NEW YORK CALL MONEY. Money a brokerage firm borrows to meet financial obligations after extending credit to a client's margin account. *See Also: account, credit, firm, margin, margin account*

NEW YORK CASH EXCHANGE (NYCE). A regional organization of commercial banks that uses a central computer network to provide customers with automated teller services.

NEW YORK COFFEE AND SUGAR EXCHANGE. The primary U.S. market for trading coffee and sugar futures contracts. *See Also: futures, market*

NEW YORK CURB EXCHANGE. The original name of the American Stock Exchange. *See Also: exchange, name, stock, stock exchange*

NEW YORK FUTURES EXCHANGE (NYFE). A New York Stock Exchange subsidiary that deals in the trading of financial futures contracts. *See Also: exchange, financial futures, futures, New York Stock Exchange, stock, stock exchange, subsidiary*

NEW YORK INSURANCE EXCHANGE. The chief market insurance brokers carry out large transactions with numerous different underwriters. *See Also: carry, insurance, market*

NEW YORK INTERBANK OFFERED RATE. The interest rate that deposits in U.S. financial center banks trade in the United States. *See Also: interest, interest rate*

NEW YORK MERCANTILE EXCHANGE. A New York commodities exchange that deals in futures contracts on agricultural products, currency, petroleum, and precious metals. *See Also: currency, exchange, futures*

NEW YORK PLAN. A plan in which equipment ownership is transferred through equipment trust certificates. *See Also: trust*

NEW YORK STOCK EXCHANGE. The largest stock exchange in the United States with over 1,500 security listings. *See Also: exchange, security, stock, stock exchange*

NEW YORK STOCK EXCHANGE AVERAGES. A composite market indicator that profiles the general market condition through the prices of 25 industrial and railroad stocks. *See Also: composite, industrial, market*

NEW YORK STOCK EXCHANGE COMMON STOCK INDEX. A composite indicator that profiles the common stock market through the prices of all common stocks listed with the NYSE. A new index is calculated continuously and printed every 30 minutes. *See Also: common stock, composite, index, market, nyse, stock, stock market*

NEW YORK STOCK EXCHANGE COMPOSITE INDEX. A gauge which averages the trading prices of all of the common shares of companies listed on the New York Stock Exchange. The four subgroup indexes are the financials, industrials, transportations, and utilities. *See Also: averages, exchange, New York Stock Exchange, stock, stock exchange*

NEW YORK STOCK EXCHANGE VOLUME. All shares traded on the New York Stock Exchange in one day. *See Also: exchange, New York Stock Exchange, stock, stock exchange*

NEWBY A term that describes anyone that is new, or a "baby," to anything Internet related. This could be a reference to an Internet user that is new to the Internet or an online community. *See Also: Internet, online, term*

NEWS TICKER. A brokerage house machine that provides business news that could have an effect on securities prices. *See Also: brokerage house, house, securities*

NEWSGROUP. A specific topic on an Internet message board. Participants post initial comments, then replies from other participants are posted. Thereafter, more replies are posted to replies, and so on. *See Also: Internet, on, post, topic*

NEWSREADER. An application that enables a user to read, download, and reply to newsgroup messages. *See Also: download, newsgroup*

NEXT DAY CONTRACT. A securities transaction in which the payment and delivery must be made the next day. *See Also: delivery, securities, transaction*

NEXT GENERATION INTERNET. Also referred to as NGI, a multi-agency Federal research and development program that began October 1, 1997, to develop advanced networking technologies and revolutionary applications that require advanced networking. These capabilities are intended to run 100 to 1,000 times faster end-to-end than the speed of the Internet at the time the mission commenced. *See Also: Internet, NGI, research and development, run, time*

NGI. Next Generation Internet. *See Also: Internet*

NIC. A network interface card is an adapter card that is placed inside a computer to provide a connection to a network. *See Also: network interface card*

NICKEL. A move in the bond market of five basis points either up or down. *See Also: basis, bond, market*

NIFTY FIFTY. The 50 favorite stocks of institutional investors.

NINE-BOND RULE. A New York Stock Exchange regulation that if a member firm receives an order for nine or fewer listed bonds, the order must be sent to the exchange floor. If the order cannot be filled on the floor within one hour, the firm can fill the order in the over-the-counter market. *See Also: exchange, exchange floor, fill, firm, floor, market, member firm, New York Stock Exchange, order, stock, stock exchange*

NINETY-DAY SAVINGS ACCOUNT. A passbook savings account that pays interest based on 90-day deposits, with substantial interest penalties assessed if the money is withdrawn before the end of 90 days. *See Also: account, interest, passbook savings, savings account*

NNP. Net National Product. *See Also: net*

NO LIEN AFFIDAVIT. A document in which a property-owner verifies that work on a piece of property has been completed, and that the property is not encumbered by any liens or mortgages. *See Also: encumbered*

NO LOAD. Without any sales charge. *See Also: sales charge*

NO NEAR BID-OFFER. When the bid or offer price for a security is significantly above or below the last bid or offer price. *See Also: offer, security*

NO PAR VALUE. A security that has no face value. *See Also: face value, security*

NO PAR VALUE STOCK. A company's issued stock that holds no par value but has a value assigned in the company's ledgers. *See Also: issued stock, no par value, par, par value, stock*

NO PASSBOOK SAVINGS. A savings account in which no passbook is used. Instead, the teller issues receipts for deposits or withdrawals. A monthly transaction statement is mailed to the depositor for his or her records (also called a Statement Savings Account). *See Also: account, savings account, statement, transaction*

NO REVIEW OFFERING. An accelerated public securities offering that can be used by large issuers who already have outstanding publicly held securities. After registering with the Securities and Exchange Commission, the issuer can make the offering in two to three days. *See Also: commission, exchange, offering, outstanding, publicly held, securities*

NO-ACTION LETTER. A letter sent to the Securities and Exchange Commission when the writer is considering taking civil or criminal recourse against another party, but is not sure that the other party's actions were really illegal or improper. The SEC provides an opinion on the situation, but takes no civil or criminal action against anyone involved. *See Also: commission, exchange, recourse, SEC, securities*

NO-LIMIT ORDER. An investor's request to have his or her broker buy a security with no price restrictions. *See Also: broker, security*

NO-LITIGATION CERTIFICATE. A document that a bond attorney verifies that no lawsuits are pending in connection with the validity of a bond issue. *See Also: bond, issue*

NO-LOAD MUTUAL FUND. A mutual fund that carries no sales charge. *See Also: fund, mutual fund, sales charge*

NODE. An addressable point, or processing location, on a computer network. *See Also: on, point, processing*

NOMINAL. A security's face value. *See Also: face value*

NOMINAL ACCOUNT. An account used for analyzing surplus account changes, including income accounts that are closed into surplus at the end of the fiscal year. *See Also: account, fiscal year*

NOMINAL ASSET. An asset with little or no worth, or with a worth that is difficult to determine. Judgments and many intangible assets are considered nominal assets. *See Also: asset, nominal, worth*

NOMINAL CAPITAL. The face value or par value of a company's issued securities. *See Also: face value, par, par value, securities*

NOMINAL EXERCISE PRICE. To determine a Government National Mortgage Association option contract's dollar value, multiply its strike price by a Ginnie Mae certificate's unpaid principal balance, with an eight percent interest rate. *See Also: balance, Ginnie Mae, interest, interest rate, mortgage, option, principal, principal balance*

NOMINAL INTEREST RATE. The coupon rate of a bond, which represents the amount of interest due to the bond holder. *See Also: bond, bond holder, coupon, coupon rate, interest*

NOMINAL QUOTATION. A broker's bid and offer price that estimates a security's value when a broker refuses to execute the deal at the prices given. *See Also: broker, offer*

NOMINAL YIELD. Divide a fixed-income security's par value into its annual payout to reach this yield, which is stated as a percentage. *See Also: par, par value, payout, yield*

NOMINALLY ISSUED. Certified securities that have been properly prepared for delivery. *See Also: delivery, securities*

NOMINALLY OUTSTANDING. Securities that the issuing company buys back, but keeps alive instead of retiring.

NOMINEE. The name that appears on a security's certificate when that name is different from the beneficial owner. *See Also: beneficial owner, certificate, name*

NONASSENTED SECURITIES. Securities in which the owner refuses to agree to the term changes of a defaulted security. *See Also: security, term*

NONASSESSABLE STOCK. A security for which the owner cannot be penalized or held accountable if the issuer becomes insolvent. Most stocks are nonassessable stocks. *See Also: security*

NONBORROWED RESERVES. Reported weekly via the Federal Reserve System, this provides the total of member bank reserves less a member bank's discount window borrowings. *See Also: bank, discount, discount window, Federal Reserve System, member bank, reserve, window*

NONCALLABLE. A security that cannot be redeemed before it matures. *See Also: security*

NONCARRY. A market that handles transactions involving perishable commodities. *See Also: market*

NONCASH. Any financial instrument that is not currency. *See Also: currency, financial instrument, instrument*

NONCLEARING HOUSE STOCK. Any securities that have not been cleared through the New York Stock Exchange Clearing Corporation. Over-the-counter securities are considered nonclearing house securities. *See Also: cleared, corporation, exchange, house, New York Stock Exchange, securities, stock, stock exchange*

NONCLEARING MEMBER. A member of the National Association of Securities Dealers or a member of a securities exchange who does not maintain his or her own operations. Such a person pays another member a fee to use his or her operations to execute settlements. *See Also: exchange, operations, securities*

NONCOMPETITIVE BID. An individual applies for a new government securities issue; the cost is established at the average price paid by brokers submitting competitive bids. *See Also: average, securities*

NONCONTINGENT PREFERENCE STOCK. A synonym for a share of cumulative preferred stock. *See Also: cumulative preferred stock, preferred stock, share, stock*

NONCONTRIBUTORY. A group insurance policy in which the policy holder, instead of his or her employer, pays the entire premium. *See Also: insurance, policy holder, premium*

NONCUMULATIVE DIVIDENDS. If a company fails to pay a dividend when it is due, it does not accrue and the shareholder loses it forever. *See Also: dividend, fails, pay, shareholder*

NONCUMULATIVE PREFERRED STOCK. Preferred stock with omitted dividends that are not cumulative. *See Also: stock*

NONCURRENT ASSET. Any asset that will not be sold, converted to cash, or transferred within a company's normal cycle, which usually lasts one year. Fixed assets, intangible assets, and leasehold improvements are all considered noncurrent assets. *See Also: asset, cash, cycle*

NONCURRENT LIABILITIES. A claim that will not fall due for one year or more. *See Also: fall*

NONDIVERSIFIED MANAGEMENT COMPANY. A management investment firm that is not subject to asset allocation limits. However, it is not eligible for specific tax exemptions. Such firms must register their intentions with the Securities and Exchange Commission. *See Also: allocation, asset, commission, exchange, firm, investment, register, securities*

NONEXEMPT. A bond that cannot be redeemed for a specific time period. *See Also: bond, time*

NONFORFEITURE OPTION. One of four possible life insurance contract privileges, including a stipulation that allows the policy holder to cash the policy, and one that permits the policy holder to take out a loan for an amount up to the policy's cash value. *See Also: cash, contract, insurance, life insurance, policy holder, take*

NONINSURED FUND. Any mutual fund or pension fund that is invested, but not with an insurance company. *See Also: fund, insurance, mutual fund, pension*

NONINTEREST-BEARING BOND. A discounted bond or note that earns no interest, but is redeemable at its face value at maturity. *See Also: bond, face value, interest, maturity, note*

NONINVESTMENT PROPERTY. Any property that is not purchased to create income for the buyer.

NONLEDGER ASSET. Any asset that a company does not list in its general ledger. Accrued dividends, for example, are considered nonledger assets. *See Also: asset, general ledger, ledger*

NONLEGAL INVESTMENT. Any investment that cannot legally be used for trust fund investing. *See Also: fund, investment, trust*

NONMARKET RISK. The volatility of portfolio securities, when that volatility is not reflective of any general market trend. *See Also: market, market trend, portfolio, securities, trend, volatility*

NONMARKETABLE LIABILITIES OF THE U.S. GOVERNMENT. A foreign, medium-term, nonmarketable government security that cannot be paid before maturity except under special conditions. For example, an export-import bank certificate of participation falls into this category. *See Also: bank, certificate, certificate of participation, maturity, security*

NONMARKETABLE SECURITIES. Securities that are difficult to sell for some specific reason, e.g., their lack of a secondary trading market. *See Also: E, market, trading market*

NONMEMBER BANK. A bank that is not a Federal Reserve System member. *See Also: bank, Federal Reserve System, reserve*

NONMEMBER FIRM. A brokerage firm that is not a member of a specific securities exchange. For example, a company that is a member of the New York Stock Exchange would be a nonmember at the American Stock Exchange. *See Also: exchange, firm, New York Stock Exchange, securities, stock, stock exchange*

NONNEGOTIABLE. An instrument or document that does not meet the requirements of negotiability. Such a document cannot be transferred without assignment. *See Also: assignment, instrument*

NONNEGOTIABLE CERTIFICATE OF DEPOSIT. A nonnegotiable instrument that brings high returns with low risk, but cannot be withdrawn early without incurring heavy penalties. *See Also: heavy, instrument, low, nonnegotiable, nonnegotiable instrument, risk*

NONNEGOTIABLE INSTRUMENT. An instrument that cannot easily be sold or transferred. *See Also: instrument*

NONPARTICIPATING GROUP ANNUITY CONTRACT. An insurance company contract in which the company provides the policy holder with income. *See Also: contract, insurance, policy holder*

NONPRODUCTIVE LOAN. A commercial bank loan that subsequently increases the economic spending power in the economy, but does not increase output. A loan to pay for a leveraged buyout would be considered a nonproductive loan. *See Also: bank, buyout, commercial bank, leveraged, pay*

NONPROFIT ORGANIZATION. A chartered, tax-exempt business in which an officer or stockholder cannot legally receive any profits. *See Also: officer, stockholder*

NONPUBLIC INFORMATION. Any information about a company that could cause the company's stock to go up or down in price if it were released publicly. Corporate officers who are privy to nonpublic information cannot legally trade shares using the information because doing so would give them an unfair advantage over other investors. *See Also: stock, to go*

NONPURPOSE LOAN. A loan that will not be used to trade securities subject to the Federal Reserve System's credit regulations, but that has securities used as collateral. *See Also: collateral, credit, reserve, securities*

NONQUALIFIED. A document, instrument, or investment that does not meet the requirements for tax preference. *See Also: instrument, investment, preference*

NONQUALIFYING ANNUITY. An annuity that is not bought in an Internal Revenue Service-approved pension plan, and is purchased with after-tax dollars. However, the annuity's original investment dollars can still fall under an appropriate tax shelter. *See Also: annuity, fall, internal revenue, investment, pension, pension plan*

NONQUALIFYING STOCK OPTION. An issuing company grants such an option, usually to an executive, to buy a specific number of shares of a security at a specific price by a specific date. The difference between the option price and the fair market value is considered earned income in the year the option is exercised, and the difference is taxable. *See Also: earned income, fair market value, market, market value, option, security*

NONRECOURSE LOAN. When a limited partner borrows money to finance his or her part in the partnership using his or her partial ownership as collateral for the loan. If the borrower defaults on the loan, the lender can take the partial ownership, but no other assets. In a recourse loan, the lender also can take the assets. *See Also: collateral, partnership, recourse, recourse loan, take*

NONRECURRING CHARGE. A one-time income or a one-time expense listed on a corporation's ledger. *See Also: expense, ledger*

NONREFUNDABLE. A bond with the stipulation that the issuer cannot retire the issue with funds from a second bond issue. *See Also: bond, issue, retire*

NONRESIDENT AFFIDAVIT. A document that says a brokerage account holder is not a resident of the State of New York. Such a document, which no longer is used, would make the owner exempt from stock transfer taxes. Today, the tax is subject to a 100 percent rebate, making the affidavit no longer necessary. *See Also: account, affidavit, brokerage account, rebate, stock, transfer*

NONRESIDENT-OWNED INVESTMENT CORPORATION. An open-ended company, most often Canadian, with stock shares and funded indebtedness owned exclusively by people who do not live in the country, and thereby promoting foreign investments in the country. *See Also: stock*

NONREVENUE RECEIPTS. A collection that does not represent revenue and in which the liability is recorded in the same fund that the proceeds and account receipts are placed. *See Also: account, fund, liability, proceeds*

NONSTICKY JUMP BONDS. CMO bonds whose principal paydown is altered by the incident of a triggering event. Each time a trigger event occurs, the bond's payment priority changes to a new priority, then reverts to its prior priority each time the triggering event is not met. *See Also: paydown, principal, priority, time*

NONSTOCK CORPORATION. A nonprofit company in which members do not own stock shares. A charitable corporation, for example, would be considered a nonstock corporation. *See Also: corporation, stock*

NONSTOCK MONEY CORPORATION. A financial institution or insurance company that does not issue stock. A credit union, for example, would be considered a nonstock money corporation. *See Also: corporation, credit, insurance, issue, stock*

NONTAXABLE DIVIDEND. Money paid out to stockholders as returns or as capital. The dividend is not taxable when it is distributed, but the security's cost basis must be reduced by the dividend amount. *See Also: basis, capital, cost basis, dividend*

NONTAXABLE SECURITY. A security that is exempt from some taxes. Some municipal securities, for example, are at least partially exempt from income taxes. *See Also: securities, security*

NONVOTING STOCK. A company's stock that contains no voting rights. *See Also: rights, stock, voting rights*

NORMAL BETA. The desired portfolio risk. *See Also: portfolio, risk*

NORMAL EXERCISE OFFERING. An option that can be exercised any time before its expiration date. *See Also: expiration, expiration date, option, time*

NORMAL INVESTMENT PRACTICE. A practice in which hot issues can be ethically allocated to a decision maker's personal institutional account. For example, if a bank officer has made 15 purchases at $2,000 each from an underwriter in the past two years, the underwriter could ethically allocate $2,000 in a hot issue to the officer's account. *See Also: account, bank, hot issue, issue, officer*

NORMAL RETURN. A specific investment's standard return. *See Also: return*

NORMAL SALE. A usual real estate transaction in which all parties are satisfied and in which no unusual problems occur. *See Also: estate, real estate, transaction*

NORMAL TRADING UNIT. The minimum number of security shares that can be bought or sold. When fewer are involved in a transaction they are considered odd lots. *See Also: security, transaction*

NORTH AMERICAN SECURITIES ADMINISTRATOR ASSOCIA-TION. An association of securities administrators from the U.S., Mexico, and Canada organized to provide cooperation and to coordinate national and international securities regulations. *See Also: international securities, securities*

NOT A DELIVERY. When a document or instrument is invalid because it does not meet the necessary requirements to complete the transaction. *See Also: instrument, transaction*

NOT HELD ORDER. A market order or limit order that gives the floor broker the right to use his or her own discretion in the price and time of filling the order. *See Also: broker, floor, floor broker, limit, limit order, market, market order, order, right, time*

NOT RATED. Indicates that a recognized rating service has not rated a particular security. *See Also: security, service*

NOT SUBJECT TO CALL. A bond or note that cannot be redeemed before maturity. *See Also: bond, maturity, note*

NOTARIAL ACKNOWLEDGMENT. A notary public's acknowledgment that a legal instrument was properly executed in his or her presence. *See Also: instrument, legal*

NOTARIAL CERTIFICATE. The document a notary public issues and signs to acknowledge that a legal instrument was properly executed in his or her presence. *See Also: instrument, legal*

NOTARIZED DRAFT. A withdrawal order that a notary public signs and confirms that the person who signed the draft personally signed it in the notary's presence, and that the person was, indeed, the indicated person. *See Also: draft, order*

NOTCOM. In contrast to a pure dotcom, which only has a Web presence, a notcom has no Web presence, but only exists in the form of bricks and mortar. *See Also: contract, Web*

NOTE. A legal document that is evidence of a debt and that requires payment within a specific time period. *See Also: legal, time*

NOTE ISSUANCE FACILITY. An underwriting organization that deals in transactions involving offshore Eurodollar notes and Eurodollar certificates of deposit. *See Also: offshore, underwriting*

NOTICE ACCOUNT. A savings account in which the owner promises to tell the financial institution in advance before making a withdrawal. Such accounts earn higher interest rates than most other savings accounts. *See Also: account, interest, savings account*

NOTICE DAY. The day of or after a notice of intent is issued to a futures contract holder. *See Also: contract, futures, futures contract*

NOTICE OF SALE. A municipal issuer's advertisement announcing its intention to sell a new issue and to invite municipal underwriters to enter bids for the issue. *See Also: issue, new issue*

NOTING A BILL. After a notary public presents a bill of exchange and protests nonpayment, he or she adds this notation to the bill. Among other information, the notation includes the reason for nonpayment. *See Also: bill of exchange, exchange*

NOVATION. An investor substitutes one debt for another debt by paying the dollar difference between the two.

NPV. Net Present Value. *See Also: net, present value*

NQS. National Quotation Bureau. *See Also: quotation*

NSE. National Stock Exchange. *See Also: exchange, stock, stock exchange*

NUCLEAR WAR. When at least two companies compete with each other to take over a third company. The action is so named because it is usually destructive to all involved. *See Also: take*

NUMERAIRE. A French standard of measuring values that is similar to international monetary system exchange rates. *See Also: exchange*

NUMISMATIC. A coin that carries a premium over its metal content because of its rarity. *See Also: premium*

NYFE. New York Futures Exchange. *See Also: exchange, futures, futures exchange*

NYSE. New York Stock Exchange. *See Also: exchange, stock, stock exchange*

O

OAS. Option Adjusted Spread. *See Also: option, spread*

OBLIGATION. Any legal debt. *See Also: legal*

OBLIGATION BOND. A mortgage bond with a face value that is higher than the underlying property's value. *See Also: bond, face value, mortgage, mortgage bond*

OBLIGATORY MATURITY. A compulsory maturity on a debt obligation that is not optional or does not carry the rights of early redemption. *See Also: carry, maturity, obligation, redemption, rights*

OCC. Options Clearing Corporation. *See Also: corporation*

OCR. Short for Optical Character Recognition, a computer's ability to recognize characters optically. For example, a hard copy version of text can be scanned into a computer. An OCR software program creates a text file on the computer, which can be edited and formatted just like any other text file. *See Also: on, optical character recognition*

ODD LOT. A quantity of stock traded that amounts to less than a normal trading amount. For example, for actively traded stocks, odd lots may involve 1-99 shares, with round lots trading in multiples of 100 shares. Odd lots for inactively traded stocks may involve 1-9 shares, with round lots trading in multiples of 10. *See Also: stock, transaction*

ODD LOT BUY/SELL RATIO. To determine odd-lot investors' attitudes toward the market, divide the odd-lot selling into the odd-lot buying. *See Also: market*

ODD LOT DEALER. An exchange member who buys odd lots from and sells odd lots to other exchange members. *See Also: exchange*

ODD LOT DIFFERENTIAL. A fee a broker charges to a customer for executing an odd-lot transaction. *See Also: broker, transaction*

ODD LOT HOUSE. A brokerage firm that deals in odd-lot transactions, which are deals for fewer than 100 shares. *See Also: firm*

ODD LOT INDEX. This composite average indicator, which measures odd-lot purchases, is used to determine odd-lot investors' attitudes toward the market. *See Also: average, composite, market*

ODD LOT ORDERS. Any stock transaction that involves fewer than 100 shares of stock. *See Also: stock, transaction*

ODD LOT SHORT SALE RATIO. To determine whether the odd-lot market is positive or negative, divide odd-lot sales into odd-lot short sales. If the figure is at least three percent, the market is considered to be positive. *See Also: market*

ODD LOT SHORT SALES. This composite average indicator, which measures odd-lot sales, is used to determine odd-lot investors' attitudes toward the market. *See Also: average, composite, market*

ODD LOT THEORY. A theory which contends that record highs in odd-lot transactions will precede a drop in the general market because small investors are usually wrong. *See Also: drop, highs, market*

ODD LOT TRADER. A broker or dealer who handles transactions that involve fewer than 100 shares of stock. *See Also: broker, dealer, stock*

ODD LOT TREND. A market indicator that compares the volume of odd-lot buying to the volume of odd-lot selling. Some analysts believe that high odd-lot selling indicates that the market is on the rise, while high odd-lot buying indicates that the market will drop. *See Also: drop, market, volume*

OFF THE BOARD. A securities transaction that is not completed on a particular exchange. An odd-lot transaction, for example, would be considered an off-the-board deal. *See Also: exchange, securities, transaction*

OFF THE CURVE. Describes a corporate debt security when the Treasury yield curve is used as a benchmark in the corporate debt security's pricing. *See Also: benchmark, debt security, security, yield, yield curve*

OFF-BALANCE-SHEET FINANCING. A system of financing that is not clearly defined, described, or displayed on a company's balance sheet. *See Also: balance, balance sheet*

OFF-BUDGET AGENCY. A government-sponsored and government-guaranteed agency that does not appear in the federal budget, such as the Federal Home Loan Mortgage Association. *See Also: budget, home, mortgage*

OFF-EXCHANGE. A commodities firm that is registered with the Commodity Futures Trading Commission, but that is not a member of one of the 10 regulated futures exchanges, which oversee members' daily activities. *See Also: commission, commodity, Commodity Futures Trading Commission, exchanges, firm, futures*

OFF-FLOOR ORDER. An order made off of the New York Stock Exchange floor, usually taking precedence over orders made on the floor. *See Also: exchange, exchange floor, floor, New York Stock Exchange, order, precedence, stock, stock exchange*

OFF-THE-RUN ISSUE. An equity security that is inactively traded and that attracts little interest. *See Also: equity, equity security, interest, security*

OFFER. To present for sale. *See Also: sale*

OFFER WANTED. A term used by a dealer who wants another dealer to make an offer on a particular security. *See Also: dealer, offer, security, term*

OFFERED DOWN. Securities sold at prices that are lower than the last price quote or the last transaction involving the same securities. *See Also: securities, transaction*

OFFERING. A security that is being presented for sale. *See Also: sale, security*

OFFERING CIRCULAR. The prospectus to which potential investors are entitled. A company offering a new securities issue for sale must provide this detailed financial statement to anyone interested in buying shares. *See Also: issue, offering, prospectus, sale, securities, statement*

OFFERING DATE. The first day a security is publicly offered for sale. *See Also: sale, security*

OFFERING LIST. The document a security's seller provides with the quantity and price of the security to be sold *See Also: security*

OFFERING PRICE. The price for which a new securities issue will be sold publicly. *See Also: issue, securities*

OFFERING SALE. The prices or yields to maturity at which an underwriter offers the different maturities of a serial bond issue. *See Also: bond, issue, maturity*

OFFERING SCALE. The price at which an underwriter will sell each of a bond issue's serial maturities. The price is stated in points, fractions, or as a yield to maturity. *See Also: bond, maturity, yield, yield to maturity*

OFFICE OF MANAGEMENT AND BUDGET (OMB). A federal agency that prepares the President of the United States's budget and submits it to Congress, helps prepare Congressional appropriations, and reviews the performance of other government agencies. *See Also: budget, president*

OFFICE OF SUPERVISORY JURISDICTION. A department or office that oversees National Association of Securities Dealers members to make sure that the members follow NASD procedures. Every NASD member must have at least one office of supervisory jurisdiction at its firm. *See Also: firm, NASD, securities*

OFFICER. A person who has some limited legal and management rights and responsibilities to act on behalf of a company. Officers normally include the president, vice president, secretary, and treasurer. *See Also: legal, president, rights, treasurer*

OFFICIAL EXCHANGE RATE. The monetary authority of one country applies this ratio to determine how much its currency is worth compared to the currency of another country. *See Also: currency, ratio, worth*

OFFICIAL NOTICE OF SALE. Made by a municipal securities issuer who is soliciting competitive bids for an upcoming issue. The notice details such information as the security's par value and condition, and the name of the municipal official who can provide further information on the issue. *See Also: issue, name, par, par value, securities*

OFFICIAL STATEMENT. A prospectus for a new municipal bond offering. *See Also: bond, municipal bond, offering, prospectus*

OFFLINE. The reference to a real-world event or situation, as opposed to being online. *See Also: online*

OFFSET. To liquidate or close a futures position. *See Also: close, futures, position*

OFFSETS TO LONG-TERM DEBT. Reserve fund assets that are held for redeeming the long-term debt, and credit-fund assets that are pledged to redeem the debt incurred while financing the funds' loan activities. *See Also: fund, long-term debt, redeem*

OFFSHORE. Describes a financial institution, organization, or fund outside of the United States that is not restricted by U.S. securities laws unless its securities are sold in the United States. *See Also: fund, securities*

OFFSHORE FUND. A mutual fund that has its headquarters in a foreign country. *See Also: fund, mutual fund*

OFFSHORE TRUST. A personal, foreign trust, usually in a country that does not significantly tax the trusts. *See Also: trust*

OFX. Open Financial Exchange. *See Also: exchange, open*

OLIGOPOLY. A system in which a small number of companies control the total market supply of a specific good or service. These companies can control the market price. In a perfect oligopoly, all companies produce the exact same item. In an imperfect oligopoly, the companies produce items that are similar, but not identical. In an oligopoly, price competition is essentially nonexistent, so prices tend to be higher than they would have been in a competitive market. The tobacco industry, for example, is an oligopoly, as are the airlines that serve the same routes. *See Also: industry, market, market price, service, supply*

OLIGOPSONY. A system in which a small number of large and powerful buyers control the purchasing power for a specific good or service. The companies, therefore, can control the purchase price, so oligopsony prices usually are lower than would be expected in a competitive market. For example, because tobacco companies buy all of the small tobacco growers' output, the companies can control the prices they pay the growers for that tobacco. *See Also: market, pay, purchase price, purchasing power, service*

OMB. Office of Management and Budget. *See Also: budget*

OMITTED DIVIDEND. A dividend a company was supposed to declare, but didn't. For example, if a company is having financial troubles, its board of directors may decide that saving money is more important than paying the stockholders. Omitted dividends usually cause the company's stock to drop in price. *See Also: board of directors, declare, dividend, drop, stock*

OMS. Opportunity Management System.

ON. The number of points that represent how much higher a cash commodity is than a particular futures month. *See Also: cash, cash commodity, commodity, futures*

ON A SCALE. Occurs when a customer buys or sells equal amounts of a specific stock at prices that are spaced by a constant interval as the market price goes up or down. *See Also: market, market price, stock*

ON ACCOUNT. An open account in which a seller expects payment after the security or commodity is delivered, with a note documenting the debt obligation. *See Also: account, commodity, note, obligation, open, security*

ON BALANCE. The difference between the quantity of securities involved in offsetting sales and purchases. For example, if a person sold 3,000 shares of a security, then bought 4,000 shares of the same security, he or she bought 1,000 shares on balance. *See Also: balance, securities, security*

ON BALANCE VOLUME. The net of volumes of transactions executed at price increases and transactions executed at price decreases. When the former is higher, the net is considered positive. *See Also: net*

ON BID. Occurs when a broker completes an odd-lot transaction by selling at the bid price or buying at the offer price instead of waiting for the next round-lot purchase in the security to determine the price. *See Also: bid price, broker, offer, security, transaction*

ON LEND. In England, the lending of borrowed funds to another person or company.

ON MARGIN. Securities an investor buys when he or she has borrowed at least part of the purchase price from his or her broker. *See Also: broker, purchase price*

ON THE FLY. A user's request for information that requires an immediate customized response, usually from back-end systems. If the request is generated on the Web, once the requested information has been found, the Web pages are then instantly customized for the user. *See Also: on, request for information, Web*

ON THE MONEY. When the strike price in a put or call option equals the price of the underlying security. *See Also: call option, option, put, security, underlying security*

ON-FLOOR ORDER. An order that originates on an exchange floor. *See Also: exchange, exchange floor, floor, order*

ONE CANCELS THE OTHER. An alternative order in which a client wants one of two orders executed. When one order is executed, the other automatically is canceled. *See Also: alternative order, client, order*

ONE NIGHT STAND. A reference to entering into an investment with the objective of holding the security for the long term, only to sell it the next trading day. *See Also: investment, security, term, trading day*

ONE PERCENT BROKER. A broker who charges a fee to arrange the borrowing and lending of securities between dealers and institutional investors. The fee is one percent of the interest rate the lender pays to use the cash collateral. *See Also: broker, cash, collateral, interest, interest rate, securities*

ONE-CLICK SHOPPING. Web site functionality that enables customers to easily place an order by clicking on a single button for each item they would like to buy, instead of filling out an order form for each item. *See Also: on, order*

ONE-MAN PICTURE. A price quote from only one market maker. *See Also: maker, market, market maker*

ONE-SIDE MARKET. Describes a broker who will buy or sell securities, but will not do both. *See Also: broker, securities*

ONGOING BUYER. A buyer who wants to accumulate many shares of a specific security makes continuous purchases in that security. When done with limit or scale orders, the buyer usually will achieve a better average price than he or she would have by buying a large block at one time. *See Also: average, limit, scale, security, time*

ONGOING SELLER. A seller who wants to distribute a lot of shares of a specific security makes continuous sales in that security. When done with limit or scale orders, the seller usually will achieve a better average price than he or she would have by selling a large block at one time. *See Also: average, limit, lot, scale, security, time*

ONLINE. The reference to a user that is connected to a network, such as the Internet. *See Also: Internet*

ONLINE BANKING. Banking that is performed over the Internet or other network connection. Benefits to consumers include around-the-clock access, money transfers, access to historical data and, oftentimes, lower fees. *See Also: Internet*

ONLINE BILL PAYING. Customers' ability to receive and pay bills electronically. *See Also: pay*

ONLINE BROKERS. Internet-based intermediaries that facilitate transactions between buyers and sellers. Typically, a commission is charged for their services. Also a reference to online investing companies. *See Also: commission, online*

ONTOLOGY. A standardized hierarchy of relationships in a particular domain of knowledge or practices.

OPD. A stock symbol used to indicate a security's opening transaction when that transaction is at a price that went up or down substantially from the previous closing price. OPD also can indicate the first transaction of the day following a delayed opening. *See Also: closing price, delayed opening, opening transaction, stock, symbol, transaction*

OPEC. Organization of Petroleum Exporting Countries.

OPEN. A security's first trade of the day.

OPEN ARCHITECTURE. The reference to a technology infrastructure that has specifications that are public, not proprietary. An open architecture enables other developers to add additional functionality and flexibility to the technology. *See Also: infrastructure, open, technology*

OPEN CONTRACT. A contract that was bought or sold even though the transaction involved in the contract was not completed by a subsequent sale, repurchase, or commodity delivery. *See Also: commodity, contract, delivery, repurchase, sale, transaction*

OPEN CREDIT. Credit that is given to a customer even though the customer hasn't yet proven that he or she is creditworthy.

OPEN END CLAUSE. A mortgage clause in which the property is pledged against future additional cash advances or loans, with the lender agreeing to pay such advances. *See Also: cash, mortgage, pay*

OPEN END FUNDS. Mutual funds that are offered by an investment company. Shares in open end funds are redeemed at its net asset value. The number of shares are not fixed. This contrasts to closed-end mutual funds, which have a fixed number of shares, usually trade on a secondary market, and can sell at a premium or discount to its net asset value. *See Also: asset, at a premium, discount, investment, investment company, market, net, net asset value, open, premium, secondary market*

OPEN END INDENTURE. A limited secured bond indenture that permits the repledging of collateral for additional bonds. *See Also: bond, collateral, indenture, secured bond*

OPEN END INVESTMENT. COMPANY An investment firm that continually issues new securities to the public. The proceeds are then put into other investments. The company must buy back the shares on demand. *See Also: demand, firm, investment, proceeds, put, securities*

OPEN END INVESTMENT TRUST. An investment trust in which the trustee can invest in securities that were not originally included in the trust. *See Also: investment, investment trust, securities, trust, trustee*

OPEN END MORTGAGE. A bond collateralized by property, carrying the stipulation that further bonds can be issued with the same property used as collateral again. *See Also: bond, collateral*

OPEN FINANCIAL EXCHANGE. Also known as OFX, an open protocol for the online transfer of financial data. OFX was originally comprised, and built, using technologies from several companies previously competing for the leading technology. The OFX technology can directly connect financial institutions with their customers, for the purposes of facilitating transactions. This includes transferring funds, making payments, downloading statements, etc. *See Also: OFX, online, open, protocol, technology, transfer*

OPEN INTEREST. The total number of option and futures contracts that have not been closed, liquidated, or delivered. *See Also: futures, option*

OPEN MARKET. A public market that is open and available to all prospective buyers and sellers. *See Also: market, open, public market*

OPEN MARKET CREDIT. The short-term financing through which a commercial paper house can buy notes and then resell them publicly. *See Also: commercial paper, commercial paper house, house, paper*

OPEN MARKET OPERATION. The market through which the Federal Reserve System publicly buys and sells government securities to expand or contract the credit supply. *See Also: contract, credit, Federal Reserve System, market, reserve, securities, supply*

OPEN MARKET PAPER. A note or a bill of exchange that is sold to financial institutions, which a person with good credit can draw upon and make payable to himself or herself. *See Also: bill of exchange, credit, exchange, note*

OPEN MARKET RATES. When supply and demand directly affects the interest rates of debt instruments that trade on the open market. Rates established through a Federal Reserve System discount or through a bank's commercial loan rates, for example, would not represent open market rates. *See Also: commercial loan, demand, discount, Federal Reserve System, interest, market, open, open market, reserve, supply*

OPEN MORTGAGE. A mortgage that can be paid off at any time before maturity. *See Also: maturity, mortgage, time*

OPEN ORDER. Any unexecuted order to buy or sell securities that has not been canceled; a good-till-canceled order. *See Also: order, securities*

OPEN OUTCRY. Occurs on a commodities exchange when traders shout their buy and sell orders. When one trader shouts a buy order and another trader responds to that buy order, or unknowingly shouts a sell order for the same commodity, the contact is recorded. *See Also: buy order, commodity, exchange, order, sell order, trader*

OPEN PROSPECTUS. A document used to seek financial backing without saying exactly how the money will be invested.

OPEN REPO. A repo with no definite term and an agreement made on a day-to-day basis. Either party may terminate the agreement at will. *See Also: basis, term*

OPEN SOURCE CODE. Software in which the program source code is openly available to developers and users. This openness enables developers to customize the application. New innovations are, in turn, shared within the programming community. The Linux operating system is an example of open source software. *See Also: Linux, open, source code, turn*

OPEN TRADE. A deal that has not been closed or canceled.

OPENING AUTOMATED REPORT SERVICE. A computer network that market specialists from the New York and American stock exchanges use to open and reopen the market for a specific security. *See Also: exchanges, market, open, security, stock*

OPENING BLOCK. A security's first transaction during a particular trading session. *See Also: session, transaction*

OPENING PRICE. The price of a security at its first transaction during a particular trading session. *See Also: security, session, transaction*

OPENING PURCHASE. The transaction that creates or increases an investor's long position in an option trade. *See Also: long position, option, position, transaction*

OPENING RANGE. The difference between the highest and the lowest opening prices of a particular commodity. Often a commodity will have several opening and closing prices during one trading session. Orders can be filled within this range at any time during that trading session. *See Also: commodity, range, session, time*

OPENING ROTATION. The trading rotation in which the price and volume of buy and sell orders are in balance. *See Also: balance, trading rotation, volume*

OPENING SALE. The transaction that creates an investor's short position in an option trade. *See Also: option, position, short position, transaction*

OPENING TRANSACTION. Indicates the first time a particular futures or option contract has been bought or sold. *See Also: contract, futures, option, option contract, time*

OPERATING ASSET. Any asset involved in a company's operations that directly and regularly creates income for a company. Stocks and real estate, while creating some income, are not considered operating assets because they do not produce income regularly, and they are not directly related to the company's production or operations. *See Also: asset, estate, operations, real estate*

OPERATING BUDGET. Any budget that covers all expenses except capital expenses. *See Also: budget, capital*

OPERATING CAPITAL. The money a company uses to pay for its daily operations. *See Also: operations, pay*

OPERATING COSTS. The amount of money a company needs to pay for equipment, utilities, and other necessities in maintaining its operations. *See Also: operations, pay*

OPERATING INCOME. The total amount of money a company makes through its earning assets and services. *See Also: earning assets*

OPERATING INTEREST. In property development and operations, this is the royalty interest subtracted from the mineral interest. *See Also: interest, operations, royalty*

OPERATING LOSSES. Any loss that a company incurs during its normal operations. *See Also: operations*

OPERATING MARGIN. To determine this expense margin, divide a company's net sales into its operating costs. *See Also: expense, margin, net, net sales, operating costs*

OPERATING PROFIT. Any profit a company makes through its normal operations. *See Also: operations, profit*

OPERATING RATIO. To determine this margin of profit gauge, divide a company's cost of goods sold into its operating income. *See Also: cost of goods sold, margin, margin of profit, operating income, profit*

OPERATING RESERVES. A company's balance sheet accounts that represent the net accumulated balances for amortization, damages, injuries, pensions, and insurance. *See Also: amortization, balance, balance sheet, insurance, net*

OPERATING STATEMENT. A financial statement that includes the company's net costs, expenses, profits, and sales during a specific time period. *See Also: net, statement, time*

OPERATING SURPLUS. A company's profits after it subtracts its operating costs. *See Also: operating costs*

OPERATIONS. A broker-dealer's functions in clearing, executing, settling, and recording his or her customer's transactions.

OPINION SHOPPING. A company hires an auditor who will provide a positive auditing report, even if the audit results would not normally be positive. *See Also: audit*

OPPORTUNITY COST. The maximum profit an alternative plan of action would provide. *See Also: profit*

OPPORTUNITY MANAGEMENT SYSTEM. Also referred to as OMS, a software system that maintains sales opportunity data and related information, with each sales lead tracked. Information stored in the data base may include names, company data, status of sale, potential for sales, etc. *See Also: base, OMS, sale*

OPRA. The Option Price Reporting Authority is operated by the American Stock Exchange, Chicago Board Options Exchange, Pacific Exchange and Philadelphia Stock Exchange. Its purpose is to provide a uniform quote system covering these exchanges. *See Also: exchange, exchanges, option, Philadelphia Stock Exchange, stock, stock exchange*

OPT-IN MAILING LIST. A mailing list, typically an e-mail list, that allows members to join only upon request. *See Also: e-mail*

OPT-OUT MAILING LIST. A mailing list, typically an e-mail list, that allows members to discontinue their membership upon request. *See Also: e-mail*

OPTICAL CHARACTER RECOGNITION. *See Also: OCR*

OPTICAL FIBER. A hair-width thin plastic or glass fiber capable of transmitting beams of light.

OPTIMUM CAPACITY. The level of a company's production that leads to the lowest price per unit. For example, if a company produces 10,000 staplers at four dollars each, but can manufacture the staplers at three dollars each if it mass produces 15,000, the latter figure is its optimum capacity. *See Also: level, unit*

OPTION. A contract that provides the right, but not the obligation, to buy or sell a specific amount of a specific security within a predetermined time period. One call option contract gives the buyer the right to purchase, or a put buyer to sell, 100 shares of the underlying stock in exchange for a premium based on the time value. The seller of the contracts is called the writer. *See Also: call option, contract, exchange, obligation, option contract, premium, put, right, security, stock, time, time value*

OPTION ACCOUNT. A charge account through which a customer can pay either a percentage of the balance, with an additional service charge, or the entire balance amount after 30 days. Also, an account which has been approved to trade options. *See Also: account, balance, pay, service*

OPTION ACCOUNT AGREEMENT FORM. A document that all options contract customers must sign to verify that they will abide by the Options Clearing Corporation regulations. The form also contains a customer's financial position and his or her investment background. *See Also: contract, corporation, investment, options contract, position*

OPTION ADJUSTED SPREAD (OAS). A method of evaluating option components, such as call options and put options, of fixed-income securities. OAS methodology defines the value of the options as additional basis yield spread, or the options cost. *See Also: basis, OAS, option, put, securities, spread, yield, yield spread*

OPTION CONTRACT. The document giving the buyer the right to buy or sell a specific quantity of a security by a specific date at a specific price. *See Also: right, security*

OPTION DAY. The date an options contract expires. *See Also: contract, options contract*

OPTION MUTUAL FUND. A mutual fund that buys or sells options to increase its share's value. Because of the leverage options created, such investments can multiply the fund's earnings several times over if the options are exercised properly and invested wisely. *See Also: earnings, fund, leverage, mutual fund*

OPTION ORDER. A detailed and specific order to establish or cancel an options contract, with all of the pertinent information outlined. *See Also: contract, options contract, order*

OPTION PREMIUM. The dollar price per share that an option holder pays the option writer for the option privileges. *See Also: dollar price, option, option writer, share*

OPTION SERIES. A listed option class with a specific price and a specific expiration date. *See Also: class, expiration, expiration date, listed option, option*

OPTION SPREAD. Occurs when an investor simultaneously holds a long and short position in the same option class. *See Also: class, option, position, short position*

OPTION TENDER BOND. A variable-rate, tax-exempt bond with a put option in its indenture and an interest rate that is adjusted twice a year. If the bondholder does not like the new interest rate, he or she can tender the bond at the end of the year for its full principal amount plus any accrued interest. *See Also: accrued interest, bond, full, indenture, interest, interest rate, option, plus, principal, principal amount, put, put option, tax-exempt bond, tender*

OPTION TRADING RIGHT HOLDER. A person who is licensed by the New York Stock Exchange to trade NYSE-listed index options, but who is not a member of the exchange. *See Also: exchange, index, New York Stock Exchange, stock, stock exchange*

OPTION WRITER. An option seller who gives the buyer the right to buy a security if it is a call option, or sell a security if it is a put option. *See Also: call option, option, put, put option, right, security*

OPTIONAL DATE. The date a corporation or a government can redeem its note or other obligation if certain designated requirements are met. *See Also: corporation, note, obligation, redeem*

OPTIONAL DIVIDEND. A dividend that the recipient can take in cash or have reinvested at his or her discretion. *See Also: cash, dividend, take*

OPTIONAL PAYMENT BOND. A bond in which the holder can choose to have either principal and interest payments or both made in foreign or domestic currencies. *See Also: and interest, bond, interest, principal*

OPTIONS CLEARING CORPORATION (OCC). A company that processes options transactions.

OPTIONS CLEARING CORPORATION PROSPECTUS. The Securities and Exchange Commission requires that all options customers must be given this disclosure statement before the options contracts can be approved for trading. *See Also: commission, disclosure, exchange, securities, statement*

OPTIONS CONTRACT. The agreement between the writer and the holder of a put or call option. *See Also: call option, option, put*

OPTIONS MARKET. The market in which financial futures contracts are bought and sold. *See Also: financial futures, futures, market*

OPTIONS PRICE REPORTING AUTHORITY. A subscription service that reports option prices and transactions. *See Also: option, service, subscription*

OPTIONS PRINCIPAL MEMBER. An investor who bought the right to buy and sell listed options. The investor can buy such rights from an exchange or from an exchange member, but can buy and sell the options only on that particular exchange. *See Also: exchange, right, rights*

OPTIONS TO PURCHASE OR SELL SPECIFIED MORTGAGE SECURITIES. A customized group of put and call options on mortgage-backed securities that are combined according to coupon, exercise price, expiration date, and issue. Created by Merrill Lynch Mortgage Capital Corporation, these securities normally are referred to as Oppsoms. *See Also: capital, corporation, coupon, exercise, exercise price, expiration, expiration date, issue, mortgage, put, securities*

OR BETTER. An investor's limit order to buy or sell at the price indicated or at a better price, if possible. *See Also: limit, limit order, order*

ORDER. A customer's instructions to his or her broker for buying or selling a security. Such an order may specify price, time limits, or quantity. *See Also: broker, security, time*

ORDER BOOK OFFICIAL. A Pacific or Philadelphia stock exchange official who takes options orders that cannot be immediately executed. The official then trades later and notifies the person who submitted the order that the transaction is finally made. *See Also: exchange, order, Philadelphia Stock Exchange, stock, stock exchange, transaction*

ORDER CONFIRMATION TRANSACTION. Permits members of the National Association of Securities Dealers to negotiate over-the-counter option transactions for more than three contracts while using the National Association of Securities Dealers Automated Quotations Options Automated Execution System, which normally limits the number of permitted contracts to three. *See Also: execution, option, over-the-counter option, securities*

ORDER DEPARTMENT. The broker-dealer's office that routes buy and sell instructions to the trading floors of different exchanges, and executes over-the-counter transactions. *See Also: exchanges*

ORDER GOOD UNTIL A SPECIFIED TIME. A market order or a limit order that a broker will hold in the trading crowd or will execute until a specific time, after which any unexecuted portion will be canceled. *See Also: broker, crowd, hold, limit, limit order, market, market order, order, time, trading crowd*

ORDER SUPPORT SYSTEM. A Chicago Board Options Exchange system for disseminating information about securities orders. *See Also: exchange, securities*

ORDER TICKET. A document that provides a customer's directions to the registered representative concerning each specific securities transaction. *See Also: registered representative, securities, transaction*

ORDINARY ASSET. An asset a company regularly buys and sells as part of its business. For example, real estate would represent an ordinary asset to a real estate broker. *See Also: asset, broker, estate, real estate*

ORDINARY DISCOUNT. The difference between an item's current value, with an assumed interest rate that will accumulate to the value at maturity, and the item's value at maturity. *See Also: current, interest, interest rate, maturity*

ORDINARY GAIN. The amount of money a company will make by selling an asset that is not a capital asset. *See Also: asset, capital, capital asset*

ORDINARY INCOME. Any and all income except that earned from capital gains. *See Also: capital*

ORDINARY INTEREST. Simple interest based on a 360-day year. The difference between ordinary interest and exact interest, which is based on a 365-day year, can be substantial when a large sum of money is involved. *See Also: exact interest, interest*

ORDINARY SHARES. British common stock. *See Also: common stock, stock*

ORDINARY STOCK. Common stock or equity stock. *See Also: equity, stock*

ORDINARY VOTING. Occurs in board of directors elections when each stockholder gets one vote for each share he or she owns. *See Also: board of directors, share, stockholder*

ORGANIZATION CHART. A chart of the relationship between authority and responsibility within a company. An organization chart, for example, maps out who has the most responsibility, and to whom each employee is answerable. *See Also: chart*

ORGANIZATION OF ARAB PETROLEUM EXPORTING COUNTRIES. An association of Arabian oil exporters that sets international oil prices and settles disputes among Arab nations. OPEC includes the members of the Organization of Petroleum Exporting Countries plus Bahrain, Egypt, and Syria, and excluding Ecuador, Gabon, Indonesia, Iran, Nigeria, and Venezuela. *See Also: OPEC, plus*

ORGANIZATION OF PETROLEUM EXPORTING COUNTRIES (OPEC). An association of 13 Middle East, South American, Eastern, and African oil exporting countries that sets international oil prices.

ORGANIZED EXCHANGE. The place where securities or commodities are bought and sold according to a prescribed set of rules and regulations. *See Also: securities*

ORGANIZED MARKET. An organization of traders that operates under a specific set of rules and regulations and, using those guidelines, trades in commodities or securities. *See Also: securities*

ORIGINAL COST. All costs that were incurred when buying an asset. *See Also: asset*

ORIGINAL FACE. For mortgage-backed securities, original face is the total amount of all individual mortgagees at the time the mortgages are pooled. *See Also: securities, time*

ORIGINAL ISSUE. The first stock a company issues when it is first trying to raise capital for establishing business. *See Also: capital, stock*

ORIGINAL ISSUE DISCOUNT. A bond with its par value discounted at the time it is issued. The difference between the purchase price and the adjusted price is considered income in addition to any interest that may be paid. If held to maturity, no capital gains tax will be paid since the gain is considered interest. *See Also: bond, capital, capital gains tax, gain, interest, maturity, par, par value, purchase price, time*

ORIGINAL MARGIN. The amount of money a brokerage customer is supposed to have when beginning a transaction. *See Also: transaction*

ORIGINAL MATURITY. The time between a bond's issue date and the maturity date at the time it is issued. *See Also: issue, maturity, time*

ORIGINATION FEE. A tax-deductible service charge assessed against the person or company that originates the mortgage loan processing. *See Also: mortgage, processing, service*

ORIGINATOR. A financial institution that is the first to mortgage a pool of loans, with the descriptive term used only after the pool is resold. *See Also: mortgage, pool, term*

OTHER INCOME. Appears on a profit and loss statement to indicate income received by unconventional income sources. Other income can indicate a one-time profit, or income received infrequently. *See Also: profit, profit and loss statement, statement*

OTHER LOANS FOR PURCHASING OR CARRYING SECURITIES. A loan one broker will make to another broker to buy or carry securities. *See Also: broker, carry, securities*

OTHER LONG-TERM DEBT. A long-term debt that is neither a mortgage bond nor a debenture. For example, serial notes would be classified as other long-term debts. *See Also: bond, debenture, long-term debt, mortgage, mortgage bond*

OUT OF ORDER EXECUTIONS. A technique that compensates for delays when the microprocessor is forced to wait for slower components by handling instructions in a different order than specified by the programs. *See Also: order*

OUT OF THE MONEY. Occurs when the strike price of a call option is higher than the price of the underlying investment, or when the strike price of a put option is lower than the price of the underlying security. *See Also: call option, investment, option, put, put option, security, underlying security*

OUT THE WINDOW. Describes a new securities issue when it is marketed aggressively, quickly, and successfully to investors. Such issues tend to be hot issues after distribution. *See Also: issue, securities*

OUT TRADING. A trading-floor mistake in which an order is mistakenly lost while a trader assumes the transaction has been completed. *See Also: order, trader, transaction*

OUTBID. To offer a securities seller a higher price than any other bidder. *See Also: offer, securities*

OUTRIGHT TRANSACTION. A forward exchange or a purchase sale that does not have a corresponding transaction spot. *See Also: exchange, forward, sale, spot, transaction*

OUTSIDE BROKER. A trader who deals in unlisted stocks and who is not a stock exchange member. *See Also: exchange, stock, stock exchange, trader*

OUTSIDE DIRECTOR. A member of a corporation's board of directors who is not a company employee. Such directors can bring fresh and unbiased opinions to the board. *See Also: board of directors*

OUTSIDE FINANCING. When a company issues securities to finance expansion instead of using its own retained earnings. *See Also: earnings, retained earnings, securities*

OUTSIDE SECURITY. A security that is not listed on one of the major exchanges in the issuing company's region. *See Also: exchanges, security*

OUTSIDER. Any investor who is a member of the general public, as opposed to a corporate officer who owns stock in his or her company. *See Also: officer, stock*

OUTSTANDING. Any instrument that has not been redeemed, paid, or canceled, or any stock issued to shareholders. *See Also: instrument, stock*

OUTSTANDING OPTION. An options contract issued by the Options Clearing Corporation that remains open-it has not expired, been exercised, or canceled. *See Also: contract, corporation, options contract*

OUTSTANDING STOCK. All of a company's ownership shares of stock that have been publicly purchased or that are owned by the company's officers. Shares that the company has repurchased are not considered outstanding stock. *See Also: outstanding, stock*

OVER THE COUNTER. The market for securities that are not listed on one of the major exchanges. The National Association for Securities Dealers Automated Quotations provides prices for over-the-counter securities. *See Also: exchanges, market, securities*

OVER-THE-COUNTER INDEX OPTION. An index of the 100 most highly capitalized, unlisted securities which will provide profit for investors who correctly gauge short-term, over-the-counter price movements. It also provides investors with a hedge against other over-the-counter securities in their portfolio. *See Also: hedge, index, portfolio, profit, securities*

OVER-THE-COUNTER MARGIN STOCK. A stock that is sold only in the over-the-counter market, with the issuer meeting certain requirements so broker-dealers can extend credit on the short purchase or short sale. *See Also: credit, market, sale, short purchase, short sale, stock*

OVER-THE-COUNTER OPTION. An option with negotiated premium, striking price, and expiration date. *See Also: expiration, expiration date, option, premium, striking price*

OVER-THE-COUNTER STOCK INDEX FUTURE. An over-the-counter contract in which a customer agrees to a delivery date that is based on a stock price index's quoted value. *See Also: contract, delivery, delivery date, stock*

OVERALL MARKET PRICE COVERAGE. A figure that provides the extent to which the market value of a security class is covered if the issuing company were liquidated. To obtain the coverage, divide a company's tangible assets by the sum of the security issue's market value and the book value of the company's liabilities, along with any security issues that have a prior claim. *See Also: book, book value, class, market, market value, security*

OVERALLOTTING. Offering a security for sale publicly when more shares are confirmed than are available because the issuer mistakenly believed that some investors would not confirm their orders. *See Also: sale, security*

OVERBANKED. An underwriting in which the initial allotment to syndicate members is greater than the total number of shares to be offered. *See Also: syndicate, underwriting*

OVERBOUGHT. Occurs when speculative buying pushes a security's bid price unreasonably high. *See Also: bid price, speculative*

OVERCAPITALIZED. Occurs when a company's capital stock has a higher value than its corporate assets. *See Also: capital, capital stock, stock*

OVERHANG. A large block of securities or commodities contracts that would push prices down if released into the market. *See Also: market, securities*

OVERHEAD. A company's expenses that are not directly related to production, such as rent and utilities.

OVERHEATING. An economy that is growing and expanding so quickly that inflation may result. In such an economy, demand far exceeds supply, which pushes prices up. *See Also: demand, inflation, supply*

OVERINVESTMENT THEORY. A theory that proposes that business managers will invest too much in the economy when they see increasing demands during an upswing, and then make major investment cuts during the ensuing downswing when they realize that they expanded too much. *See Also: investment, realize*

OVERISSUE. Occurs when a company issues more stock shares than it was authorized to issue. The company's registrar must work to cancel the orders for enough shares to bring the number back to the allowable limit. *See Also: issue, registrar, stock*

OVERLAPPING DEBT. Municipal securities with either two or more issuers or with two or more municipalities responsible for the issue. *See Also: issue, securities*

OVERNIGHT POSITION. A broker-dealer's description of his or her securities inventory at the end of a trading day. The securities in inventory represent the broker-dealer's overnight long position with those securities. *See Also: inventory, long position, position, securities, trading day*

OVERSOLD. Occurs when, during heavy selling, a security's price is higher than the established downside trend. Because the price is extended, an upward movement probably will occur. *See Also: downside trend, extended, heavy, movement, trend*

OVERSOLD MARKET. This situation occurs when speculative long interest drops sharply and the speculative short interest subsequently increases. Usually, the market increases again quickly following an oversold market. *See Also: interest, long interest, market, oversold, short interest, speculative*

OVERSPECULATION. Occurs when speculators cause the market activity to be unusually heavy. *See Also: activity, heavy, market*

OVERSTAY THE MARKET. Describes a person who has held on to a long position for too long and subsequently will suffer a financial loss. *See Also: long position, position*

OVERSUBSCRIBED. Occurs when investors want to buy more shares of a new security than will be available. When this happens, the price of the security immediately goes up. *See Also: security*

OVERTRADING. A dealer, who also is an underwriter, offers to pay more for a security than it is worth, if the customer agrees to buy a portion of a new issue. *See Also: dealer, issue, new issue, pay, security, worth*

OVERVALUED. Describes a security with a current market price that is too high (considering the company's earnings, history, and price-earnings ratio). A security that is overvalued will probably drop in price. *See Also: current, drop, earnings, market, market price, security*

OVERWRITING. Describes a call option with an underlying security that is overpriced and is therefore expected to drop in value. Because of the expected drop, the call writer does not expect the option to be exercised. *See Also: call option, drop, option, security, underlying security*

OWNER FINANCING. A home loan made by the property seller instead of by a financial institution. At times, the seller offers lower interest rates, or will finance a home when the buyer cannot qualify for a loan from a financial institution. *See Also: home, interest*

OWNER OF RECORD. The person whose name appears on a company's books as the owner of a specific quantity of the company's securities, and who is eligible for any benefits from those shares. *See Also: name, securities*

P

P. Appears in newspaper stock listings to designate a put option. *See Also: option, put, put option, stock*

P/E. The relationship between the price of a stock and its earnings per share. This figure is determined by dividing the stock's market price by the company's earnings per share figure. The higher the P/E, the more earnings growth investors are expecting. A growth stock will typically have a higher price/earnings ratio than a stock that is expected to grow at a slower rate. Stocks with a higher P/E, usually over 20, are considered riskier than stocks with a lower P/E, which have proven earning potential. *See Also: earnings, growth stock, market, market price, ratio, share, stock*

P2P. Peer to Peer.

PAC BAND. A PAC bond's sinking fund schedule, established by identifying collateral principal payments at two different prepayment rates; a lower range and an upper range. Prepayments within the PAC band ensure that the sinking fund schedule for the PAC bond will be met. *See Also: bond, collateral, fund, prepayment, principal, range, sinking fund*

PAC II BOND. A type of planned amortization class bond, but with less extension risk and call protection than a typical PAC bond. If collateral payments in a CMO structure slow down, principal payments will be paid to PAC bonds first, then to PAC II bonds. Companion bonds typically will be next to receive principal payments. Conversely, if collateral payments in a CMO structure decrease dramatically, principal payments will be paid to companion bonds first, then to PAC II bonds, leaving PAC bonds last to receive principal payments. *See Also: amortization, bond, class, CMO, collateral, companion bonds, principal, risk*

PAC IO BOND. Priced at a very high premium-to-par value, this type of PAC bond makes only interest payments. PAC IOs adhere to a specific schedule of interest payments, which are met if prepayment rates on the underlying collateral occur at the designated PAC band. *See Also: bond, collateral, interest, PAC band, prepayment*

PAC MAN DEFENSE. To avoid a hostile takeover or merger, the target company tries to buy control of the raider. *See Also: merger, raider, takeover, target*

PAC PRINCIPAL-ONLY (PO) BOND. Offered at a deep discount to par value, this type of PAC bond makes only principal payments. PAC POs adhere to a specific schedule of principal payments, which are met if prepayment rates on the underlying collateral occur at the designated PAC band. *See Also: bond, collateral, discount, PAC band, par, par value, prepayment, principal*

PACIFIC STOCK EXCHANGE. A California stock exchange with two centers (one in Los Angeles and the other in San Francisco) that are electronically connected. *See Also: exchange, stock, stock exchange*

PACKET. 1) A British block of securities. *See Also: securities* 2) A message contained within a document that is being electronically transmitted that holds the destination address. *See Also: address*

PACKET SWITCHING. Protocols in which electronically transmitted messages are divided into packets before they are sent, so that even though the packet may not travel together, all are recompiled into the original data upon arrival at the destination. *See Also: packet*

PAGE VIEWS. The number of times a single Web page is accessed by all users, regardless of whether or not they are repeat users. *See Also: Web, Web page*

PAID-IN CAPITAL. The amount above par value that a company received for selling its stock. *See Also: above par, par, par value, stock*

PAID-IN SURPLUS. A company's balance sheet entry of the difference between the dollar value actually received from issued shares along with their par value. *See Also: balance, balance sheet, par, par value*

PAID-UP CAPITAL. The total of the par value of a company's stock and the given value of its no-par securities for which the company receives full consideration. *See Also: consideration, full, par, par value, securities, stock*

PAID-UP STOCK. Capital stock the buyer has paid for in cash, goods, or services in an amount that equals or is greater than the stock's par value. *See Also: cash, par, par value, stock*

PAINTING THE TAPE. A form of manipulation in which a broker illegally enters matched orders to create the false impression of an active market and heavy trading in a particular security. *See Also: broker, heavy, manipulation, market, matched orders, security*

PAIR TRADE. A stock-investing strategy in which one stock is purchased, while selling short an equal dollar amount of a similar or related stock, typically of a competitor with similar products or end markets that are closely correlated. This strategy is generally used when buying a stock that is considered undervalued, while shorting another stock that is considered overvalued. *See Also: overvalued, selling short, stock, undervalued*

PAIRED SHARES. The common stock of two companies with the same management, with shares of the two companies sold as a unit. *See Also: common stock, stock, unit*

PANIC. Occurs when the public suddenly loses confidence in the economy, resulting in massive bank withdrawals, stock sales, etc. A panic can lead to a depression. *See Also: bank, depression, stock*

PAPER. Short-term notes such as corporate commercial paper. *See Also: commercial paper*

PAPER INVESTMENT. A paper claim or a promise-backed investment. *See Also: investment, paper*

PAPER LOSS. The loss an investor would incur if he or she sold a security or closed his or her position, but that is unrealized because he or she holds on to the security. *See Also: position, security*

PAPER MONEY. Bank notes or deposits that serve as money.

PAPER PROFIT. The profit an investor would make if he or she sold a security or closed his or her position, but that is unrealized because he or she holds on to the security. *See Also: position, profit, security*

PAPER TITLE. Although not a proper title, a paper title is written verification that proves ownership of a security. *See Also: paper, security*

PAPERLESS. Proof that a person owns a security electronically, even though the owner does not physically hold a certificate. *See Also: certificate, hold, security*

PAPILSKY RULES. A National Association of Securities Dealers regulations modification concerning the allocation of new securities issues to related people, selling concessions made in exchange for research services, and securities that an underwriter takes in a trade. The modifications were made after an investor named Papilsky sued an investment adviser. *See Also: adviser, allocation, exchange, investment, securities*

PAR. Any security whose market value is equivalent to its face value at the time of redemption. A bond with a face value of $1000 is at par when it is selling for $1000. *See Also: at par, bond, face value, market, market value, redemption, security, time*

PAR BOND. A bond with a current market value that is equal to its redemption value. *See Also: bond, current, current market value, market, market value, redemption, redemption value*

PAR CAP. The seller of a Government National Mortgage Association security cannot deliver a substitute Ginnie Mae with an interest rate that requires the contract's dollar price to be adjusted above the security's par value. *See Also: dollar price, Ginnie Mae, interest, interest rate, mortgage, par, par value, security*

PAR EXCHANGE RATE. The amount one country's money is worth in another country's money. *See Also: worth*

PAR ITEM. Any instrument that can be redeemed for its par or face value on demand. *See Also: demand, face value, instrument, par*

PAR VALUE. The face value or nominal value of a stock, bond or other financial instrument. This value, unrelated to market value, is established by the issuer at the time of issuance. The par value for stock would be the stock certificate's face value. For debt securities, if a bond's market price is above the par value, it would be selling at a premium; if its value is below par value, it would be selling at a discount. *See Also: at a discount, bond, discount, face value, par, share, stock*

PAR VALUE OF CURRENCY. The currency values, or exchange rates, are determined through supply and demand according to the buying and selling of other countries that use the same currency. The par value of currency determines the ratio of one country's currency unit to the currency unit of another country. *See Also: currency, demand, exchange, par, par value, ratio, supply, unit*

PARALLEL COMPUTING. A computer processing architecture in which a single computer has more than one processor, each with its own memory, working simultaneously. *See Also: processing*

PARALLEL PORT. A socket on a computer, linked directly to the bus, that transmits data in parallel, usually one byte at a time. *See Also: on, time*

PARAMOUNT TITLE. A title that supersedes all other titles, such as an original title.

PARENT CORPORATION. One company that owns another company or that owns part of another company.

PARENT GUARANTEED. Describes debt securities issued by a subsidiary, but with principal and interest guaranteed by the subsidiary's parent corporation. *See Also: and interest, corporation, interest, parent corporation, principal, securities, subsidiary*

PARETO'S LAW. Hypothesized by Italian-Swiss economist Vilfredo Pareto, this proposes that the pattern of income distribution remains the same, despite a nation's policies on taxation and public assistance. According to the theory, 80 percent of a country's income benefits only 20 percent of the population, and 20 percent of the customers account for 80 percent of a business's sales volume. Pareto postulated that the only way to improve the economic status of the poor is to increase the country's overall output and income levels. *See Also: account, volume*

PARIS BOURSE. France's national stock exchange. *See Also: exchange, stock, stock exchange*

PARITY. Price or value equality. For example, if a bond is convertible into 100 shares of common stock, with the stock's market price at five dollars per share, the bond, to be selling at parity, would have a value of $500. *See Also: bond, common stock, market, market price, share, stock*

PARITY CLAUSE. A mortgage clause in which no note obtained through the mortgage has priority over any other note obtained through it. *See Also: mortgage, note, priority*

PARITY PRICE. The price for one commodity that is pegged to either another price or a composite average of prices. *See Also: average, commodity, composite*

PARKING. An investor will put money into a safe investment to protect it while looking into other investments. *See Also: investment, put*

PARTIAL COVERED WRITING. An options position with both covered and uncovered calls written on the same underlying security. *See Also: position, security, uncovered, underlying security*

PARTIAL DELIVERY. A delivery against a contract sale with the delivery amount less than the contract's total amount. *See Also: contract, delivery, sale*

PARTIAL EXECUTION. Occurs when only part of a round-lot order is executed with the investor's permission. *See Also: order*

PARTIAL WRITE. An investment strategy in which the investor writes a call option against some of the stock that he or she owns so that if the price stays low, he or she will keep the premium and increase his or her cash flow; if the price goes up, he or she can buy back the option and, while the premium is lost, hold on to the stock that now is worth more. *See Also: call option, cash, hold, investment, investment strategy, low, option, premium, stock, worth*

PARTIALLY AMORTIZED MORTGAGE. A mortgage paid in part by amortization and in part at maturity. *See Also: amortization, maturity, mortgage*

PARTIALLY PAID BONDS. The initial public offering of a dollar-denominated bond sold to a foreign investor when that investor pays 20 to 30 percent of the purchase price immediately and the balance at a specified future date. *See Also: balance, bond, initial public offering, offering, public offering, purchase price*

PARTICIPANT. A member of an underwriting syndicate. *See Also: syndicate, underwriting, underwriting syndicate*

PARTICIPATE BUT DO NOT INITIATE. An investor's trading instructions in which his or her large order cannot initiate market activity, but can be filled in normal market trading. Large institutional investors often will use these instructions to avoid having the order negatively affect market prices. *See Also: activity, market, order, trading instructions*

PARTICIPATING BOND. An industrial bond that provides the owner with both debt and equity participation. *See Also: bond, equity, industrial, industrial bond*

PARTICIPATING BROKER-DEALERS. Broker-dealers who are not members of the underwriting syndicate, but who do assist the syndicate in selling the new issue. *See Also: issue, new issue, syndicate, underwriting, underwriting syndicate*

PARTICIPATING CERTIFICATE. A document that verifies partial ownership in a stock. *See Also: stock*

PARTICIPATING EXCHANGE. A national securities exchange that the Securities and Exchange Commission has approved to trade options issued by the Options Clearing Corporation. *See Also: commission, corporation, exchange, national securities exchange, securities*

PARTICIPATING GROUP ANNUITY CONTRACT. An insurance contract in which income is distributed to 10 or more participants and in which the company and participants share, in varying degrees, the mortality risk and the investment experience. *See Also: contract, insurance, investment, risk, share*

PARTICIPATING INCENTIVE PREFERRED STOCK. The convertible, participating, and nontransferable voting stock that a potential takeover target will issue to its business constituents to stop the raider from buying 100 percent of the equity. Issuing the securities thus protects a constituent's financial interests. *See Also: equity, issue, raider, securities, stock, stop, takeover, target, voting stock*

PARTICIPATING MORTGAGE. A mortgage that offers an interest in future income from mortgaged property or another form of participation. *See Also: interest, mortgage*

PARTICIPATING PREFERRED STOCK. A preferred stock that pays additional dividends after all common stock dividends have been paid. *See Also: common stock, preferred stock, stock*

PARTICIPATING TRUST. A unit investment trust with shares that reflect interest in an underlying mutual fund investment. *See Also: fund, interest, investment, investment trust, mutual fund, trust, unit, unit investment trust*

PARTICIPATION CERTIFICATE. A certificate representing interest in a separate class of shares. Participation certificates typically carry similar economic rights to ordinary shares, but no voting rights. *See Also: interest, mortgage, mortgage pool, pool, security*

PARTICIPATION DIVIDENDS. Profits that a member of a cooperative receives, with the amount proportionate to the amount of business he or she has provided the cooperative. *See Also: cooperative*

PARTICIPATION LOAN. Two or more lenders make a loan, with one of the lenders administering the loan. Participation loans make it possible for a large borrower to obtain the needed capital, even if the loan amount exceeds each lender's legal lending limit. For example, a bank cannot lend an amount that exceeds 10 percent of its capital. *See Also: bank, capital, legal, limit*

PARTLY PAID. Stocks held in an investor's margin account. *See Also: account, margin, margin account*

PARTNERSHIP. A company owned by at least two people, with each owner sharing in direction, responsibility, management, and debt liability. *See Also: liability*

PARTNERSHIP CERTIFICATE. A written document filed with a bank that verifies members of a partnership, including limited and silent partners, and that indicates how much of the business each partner owns. *See Also: bank, partnership*

PASS. A planned, open market purchase of securities by the Federal Reserve to inject reserves into the banking system. *See Also: market, open, open market, reserve, securities*

PASS-THROUGH RATE. The net interest rate passed through to the investor in a MBS after service fees, management fees, and guarantee fees have been deducted from the gross mortgage coupon. *See Also: coupon, gross, guarantee, interest, interest rate, MBS, mortgage, net, service*

PASS-THROUGH SECURITY. A debt instrument in which security holders own an undivided portion of the cash flows from the pool of mortgages backing the security. Because these securities are interest-rate sensitive, prepayments can be irregular and dispersed over time; the securities remain outstanding as long as any mortgages in the pool are outstanding. *See Also: cash, debt instrument, instrument, outstanding, pool, securities, security*

PASSBOOK SAVINGS. A customer savings account with a bank, savings and loan, or other federally insured financial institution that allows the customer to withdraw money easily. A record of the transactions is kept in a small booklet, which the customer presents to the bank teller when making a deposit or withdrawal. The government allows the financial institutions to charge whatever interest rate they want. *See Also: account, bank, interest, interest rate, savings account*

PASSED DIVIDEND. Occurs when a company does not pay a regularly scheduled dividend because it wants to keep the earnings within the company as a result of financial problems, or because it needs the money to expand operations. *See Also: dividend, earnings, operations, pay*

PASSIVE BOND. A debt security that pays no interest, such as those issued by a charitable corporation. *See Also: corporation, debt security, interest, security*

PASSIVE INCOME. Income that is generated by limited partnerships and rental activities.

PASSIVE MANAGEMENT. An investment strategy that seeks an average performance, adjusted for risk. *See Also: average, investment, investment strategy, risk*

PATENT. A government-issued license that gives the holder a monopoly on the use of a new design, invention, or process. *See Also: monopoly*

PAY. A bond's currency denomination. *See Also: currency, denomination*

PAY TO ORDER. A stipulation in a negotiable instrument that names the person to whom the instrument is payable. *See Also: instrument, negotiable, negotiable instrument*

PAY UP. An investor pays an above-the-market price for a security that he or she believes is a wise investment. *See Also: investment, security*

PAY-THRO A UGH BONDS. debt instrument with the issuer guaranteeing the bond through a mortgage pool it owns. The bond's monthly interest and principal payments have features similar to that of a pass-through security. *See Also: bond, debt instrument, instrument, interest, mortgage, mortgage pool, pass-through security, pool, principal, security*

PAYABLE DATE. The date in which principal and interest distribution payments are made. *See Also: and interest, interest, principal*

PAYABLE IN EXCHANGE. A negotiable instrument must be paid with its issuer's funds. *See Also: instrument, negotiable, negotiable instrument*

PAYABLES. All of a company's accounts or redeemable notes.

PAYBACK PERIOD. The length of time it takes to realize a profit from an investment. *See Also: investment, profit, realize, time*

PAYDOWN. Part, but not all, of the repaid principal. *See Also: principal*

PAYING AGENT. The financial institution or company treasurer who is named in a bond indenture as the person or organization responsible for repaying principal, periodically paying the interest on behalf of the bond's issuer. *See Also: bond, indenture, interest, principal, treasurer*

PAYMENT DATE. The day that dividends or stock is scheduled to be paid to stockholders. *See Also: stock*

PAYMENT DELAY. The number of days between the first day of the month after the issuance month and the day the servicer remits the principal and interest of the pass-through security to the investor. *See Also: and interest, interest, pass-through security, principal, security, servicer*

PAYMENT FOR ORDER FLOW. Money that trading firms give to brokerage firms in exchange for their customer's orders. *See Also: exchange*

PAYOUT. The amount of a company's holdings that are distributed as dividends to stockholders.

PAYOUT RATIO. The percentage of a company's earnings that holders of common stock receive in cash dividends. *See Also: cash, common stock, earnings, stock*

PAYROLL DEDUCTION PLAN. A plan that allows an employee to accumulate mutual fund shares or shares in some other investment by having his or her employer withhold regular payments directly from his or her paycheck. *See Also: fund, investment, mutual fund*

PAYROLL-BASED STOCK OWNERSHIP PLAN. A fund that allows a company that contributed 0.5 percent of its payroll to take that same amount in a tax credit. *See Also: credit, fund, take, tax credit*

PCS. (Short for Personal Communications Service) A U.S. Federal Communications Commission (FCC) term that describes U.S.-deployed digital cellular technologies. PCS systems are digital, carried over cellular links, and can bundle such services as voice communications, voice mail, text messaging. *See Also: commission, digital, personal communications service, service, term*

PDA. (Short for Personal Digital Assistant, a handheld computer, either pen or keyboard based, that is designed to perform functions such as applications that are run on a standard computer, like games, word processing applications, photo albums, scheduling and calendaring, calculator and wireless features such as Internet access, e-mail and mobile telephony. *See Also: digital, e-mail, Internet, on, personal digital assistant, processing, run*

PDF. A method for distributing formatted documents over the Internet. Adobe, the company that originated the technology, produces special reader software, called Acrobat, that is required in order to view the PDF document. *See Also: Internet, order, technology*

PE RATIO. The relationship between the price of a stock and its earnings per share. This figure is determined by dividing the stock's market price by the company's earnings per share figure. The higher the P/E, the more earnings growth investors are expecting. A growth stock will typically have a higher price/earnings ratio than a stock that is expected to grow at a slower rate. Stocks with a higher P/E, usually over 20, are considered riskier than stocks with a lower P/E, which have proven earning potential. *See Also: earnings, growth stock, market, market price, P/E, ratio, share, stock*

PEAK. The highest point a security or a market indicator reaches during a specific time period. Prices will begin to drop after reaching a peak. *See Also: drop, market, point, security, time*

PEER TO PEER. Also referred to as P2P and PtoP, A type of Internet-based network that enables a group of users, using the same P2P networking program, to connect with each other to directly access files from one another or through a mediating server. *See Also: P2P, server*

PEGGED PRICE. The fixed price of a commodity. *See Also: commodity, fixed price*

PEGGING. A security's offer price is maintained by a bid that is slightly below that price. *See Also: offer*

PEGGING THE MARKET. An illegal form of manipulation in which an underwriting syndicate sets up a fund to stabilize the stock's price by fixing a bid at the offering price during the offering's initial stages. *See Also: fund, manipulation, offering, offering price, syndicate, underwriting, underwriting syndicate*

PENALTY BID. Permissible under SEC Rule 10b-7, a syndicate's effort to stabilize the price of a newly issued security. *See Also: SEC, security*

PENALTY CLAUSE. A contractual stipulation that imposes financial penalties if the contract terms are not obeyed or if a loan payment is late. *See Also: actual, contract*

PENALTY PLAN. A critical name for a mutual fund, named because of the penalties incurred if the investor does not complete the involved contract. *See Also: contract, fund, mutual fund, name*

PENALTY SYNDICATE BID. A syndicate manager's stabilizing bid which carries the provision that selling concessions will be withheld from, and a penalty will be assessed against, any syndicate members whose customers offer to sell the securities back to the syndicate. *See Also: offer, securities, stabilizing bid, syndicate*

PENETRATION PRICING. A company issues shares at a low initial price in an effort to quickly gain a large portion of the market. *See Also: gain, low, market*

PENNANT. A security's chart pattern that forms a triangle, or pennant. Usually, this indicates that the security's price either will rise or fall as the apex is reached. *See Also: chart, fall, triangle*

PENNY STOCK. A low-priced share of stock that is usually traded for less than $1 a share. These stocks are normally issued by speculative companies with a short or erratic revenue and earnings history. *See Also: earnings, share, speculative, stock*

PENSION. A French money market borrowing against securities that the lender holds in pension until repaid. *See Also: market, money market, securities*

PENSION BENEFIT GUARANTY CORPORATION. A federal corporation that guarantees pension benefits in plans that clearly define benefits for more than 25 employees. The corporation administers terminated plans and places liens on the company's assets for any pension benefits that were promised but not delivered. *See Also: corporation, pension*

PENSION PLAN. A company- or government-sponsored plan that provides regular income to retired or disabled employees. In most cases, the recipients of pension funds have to pay taxes on the money only as they receive it. *See Also: on the money, pay, pension*

PENSION RESERVE. An accounting of the amount of money a company must pay in the future to its pension or retirement account. *See Also: account, pay, pension*

PENSION TRUST. A pension fund that a company establishes to provide retired and disabled employees with an income, even if the employees have not made any contributions to the fund. *See Also: fund, pension*

PENTAPHILIA THEORY. A theory that the stock market will go up in calendar years that are divisible by five, such as 1990, 1995, and 2000. *See Also: calendar, market, stock, stock market*

PER CAPITA DEBT. A general obligation bond's total bonded debt divided by the issuing municipality's population. *See Also: obligation*

PER CAPITA TAX. A tax determined by dividing the amount of money needed by the number of people who will pay the tax. As such, each person pays the same amount, despite the person's income or use of the resulting services. *See Also: pay*

PER SHARE NET. The number of outstanding shares divided into the company's earnings after it has paid taxes. *See Also: earnings, outstanding*

PERCENT RETURN ON INVESTMENT. The amount of money a company receives compared to the amount of money invested in the company.

PERCENTAGE LEASE. A lease stipulating that a company will pay rent in an amount equal to a percentage of its gross sales or profits. *See Also: gross, gross sales, pay*

PERCENTAGE ORDER. A customer's order to his or her broker to buy or sell a specific number of shares after a particular number of the same shares have been traded in one trading day. *See Also: broker, order, trading day*

PERFECT COMPETITION. Occurs in the market when buyers and sellers have no power to influence a good's or a service's market price, because everyone has an equal knowledge of the market and discrimination is nonexistent. Perfect competition is a goal, but not a truly realistic one. *See Also: market, market price*

PERFECT LIEN. A legal, documented security interest in an asset, with the creditor's claim protected. *See Also: asset, interest, legal, security*

PERFECT TITLE. A complete, legal, and total title. *See Also: legal*

PERFORMANCE APPOINTMENT MARKET MAKER. An exchange member who has to maintain two-sided markets in specific classes of options traded on the Chicago Board Options Exchange. In return for providing market depth and for supplementing the activities of competitive market makers, the CBOE provides performance appointment market makers with a number of economic advantages. *See Also: CBOE, depth, exchange, market, return*

PERFORMANCE BOND. A surety debt security that protects the buyer in case the seller does not fulfill the contract terms. For example, if a person added a garage onto his or her house, he or she could request a performance bond from the contractor so that if the construction work was not satisfactory, he or she would be reimbursed or financially compensated. *See Also: bond, contract, debt security, garage, house, security, surety*

PERFORMANCE FEE. An incentive fee that a customer pays his or her mutual fund manager when the manager's investment strategies help the fund outperform the general market averages during a specific time period. *See Also: averages, fund, incentive fee, investment, manager, market, mutual fund, time*

PERFORMANCE FUND. A mutual fund with investments concentrated in speculative common stock for short-term profits. *See Also: common stock, fund, mutual fund, speculative, stock*

PERFORMANCE INDEX. An index of an investment's performance, including dividends and other distributions. *See Also: index*

PERFORMANCE OPTION. An option where the grant, exercise price, or vesting is contingent upon the company's performance. *See Also: exercise, exercise price, option, vesting*

PERFORMANCE STOCK. A growth stock, which is a security that is expected to increase in price either in a short time or over a long period. *See Also: growth stock, security, stock, time*

PERFORMANCE UNIT PLANS. An incentive plan providing executives with cash bonuses or stock shares when a company reaches its profit goals. *See Also: cash, profit, stock*

PERIOD OF DIGESTION. The time period after a new security issue is released in which the security's market price is established and during which the price could go through considerable volatility. *See Also: issue, market, market price, security, time, volatility*

PERIOD OF REDEMPTION. The time during which a mortgagor can call in the title and property by paying off the debt. *See Also: time*

PERIODIC PAYMENT PLAN. A mutual fund in which the investor makes payments at regular intervals in exchange for fund benefits. *See Also: exchange, fund, intervals, mutual fund*

PERIODIC PURCHASE DEFERRED CONTRACT. A fixed or variable annuity contract in which the investor makes regular, fixed payments, and payouts are deferred until the investor determines which payout method he or she wants. *See Also: annuity, contract, payout, variable annuity*

PERIODICALLY ADJUSTABLE RATE TRUST SECURITIES. A pass-through mortgage trust made up of municipal loans, so interest is exempt from federal taxes. *See Also: interest, mortgage, trust*

PERIODICITY. The market condition as it is affected by different cycle shifts. *See Also: cycle, market*

PERL. Practical Extraction and Reporting Language is a script language similar in syntax to the C programming language. PERL includes many UNIX facilities. PERL is the preferred programming choice for CGI programs. *See Also: UNIX*

PERMANENT ASSET. A fixed asset. *See Also: asset, fixed asset*

PERMANENT CAPITAL. Any stock or retained earnings that do not have to be repaid. *See Also: earnings, retained earnings, stock*

PERMANENT FINANCING. Any long-term debt or equity financing. *See Also: equity, equity financing, long-term debt*

PERMANENT INCOME. The average amount of income expected over a specific time period. *See Also: average, time*

PERMANENT MORTGAGE REAL ESTATE INVESTMENT TRUST. A trust that makes long-term loans for developing commercial and residential construction projects. *See Also: trust*

PERMANENT PORTFOLIO. A group of securities remaining unchanged from year to year. *See Also: securities*

PERMISSION-BASED MARKETING. A sales method in which individuals consent to receive marketing information about specific products or services.

PERPENDICULAR SPREAD. An investment strategy that includes using options with the same expiration dates with different strike prices. This spread can be bullish or bearish. *See Also: expiration, investment, investment strategy, spread*

PERPETUAL BOND. A bond with either no maturity date or a maturity date that is so far in the future that the bond will pay interest indefinitely. *See Also: bond, interest, maturity, pay*

PERPETUAL INVENTORY. A company's accounting system in which the on-hand inventory continuously is reflected in the book inventory through a daily record of physical inventory and the dollar amounts, each of which is periodically reconciled. *See Also: book, inventory*

PERPETUAL WARRANT. A warrant to buy a specific amount of a company's common shares at a particular price, with the warrant carrying no expiration date. *See Also: expiration, expiration date, warrant*

PERPETUITY. An annuity or bond with payments lasting indefinitely. *See Also: annuity, bond*

PERSONAL AREA NETWORK. Also referred to as PAN, an individual's network of devices, such as personal digital assistants, computers and peripherals, digital camera, mobile phone, headsets and other wearable devices. *See Also: digital*

PERSONAL COMMUNICATIONS SERVICE. *See Also: PCS.*

PERSONAL COMPUTER. Also referred to as PC, a general-purpose microprocessor designed for use by only one person at a time. *See Also: time*

PERSONAL DIGITAL ASSISTANT. *See Also: PDA.*

PERSONAL FINANCE COMPANY. A company that loans people small amounts of money at high interest rates to fill personal needs. *See Also: fill, interest*

PERSONAL FINANCIAL STATEMENT. An individual's account of obligations and income sources. *See Also: account*

PERSONAL HOLDING COMPANY. A company with no more than five people owning more than 50 percent of the stock which receives at least 60 percent of its income through investments instead of through business activities. *See Also: stock*

PERSONAL PROPERTY. A person's rights and ownership in chattels, which is all property other than real estate. *See Also: estate, real estate, rights*

PERSONAL SAVINGS. The difference between a person's disposable personal income and his or her expenses.

PERSONAL SECURITY. An unsecured loan backed by the borrower's net worth and business stature instead of by collateral. *See Also: collateral, net, net worth, worth*

PERSONAL SERVICE INCOME. A company's or an individual's earned income. *See Also: earned income*

PERSONAL SURETY. Surety that is provided by an individual instead of an insurance company. *See Also: insurance*

PERSONALIZATION. Tailoring information for individuals, based on preferences that have been learned about them. This information is usually obtained from interaction with the individual, whether by asking questions or simply observing the user's preferences as he or she looks around the Web site. Applications, such as collaborative filtering software, are often used in determining users' preferences. *See Also: around, collaborative filtering, on, Web, Web site*

PERSONALTY. Describes an individual's personal property. *See Also: personal property*

PESO. The primary monetary unit of Spain and other countries colonized by Spain, such as Argentina, Mexico, and the Philippines. *See Also: unit*

PETITION IN BANKRUPTCY. A document used to voluntarily declare bankruptcy. *See Also: bankruptcy, declare*

PETROBOND. A Mexican financial instrument backed by a number of Mexican barrels of oil. *See Also: financial instrument, instrument*

PETRODOLLARS. The large dollar balances that oil-producing countries, earned through oil sales, have deposited in financial institutions worldwide.

PETTY CASH. Money set aside, in cash or a bank deposit, to be used as change for small transactions. *See Also: bank, cash, change*

PHANTOM STOCK PLAN. A corporate incentive plan in which corporate officers will receive bonuses if the company's common stock increases in value. *See Also: common stock, stock*

PHILADELPHIA EXCHANGE. An exchange that has a futures contract on its own over-the-counter index. The Philadelphia Exchange is affiliated with the Philadelphia Stock Exchange. *See Also: contract, exchange, futures, futures contract, index, Philadelphia Stock Exchange, stock, stock exchange*

PHILADELPHIA PLAN. A method of transferring equipment ownership through equipment trust certificates, with a trustee holding the equipment title until the entire debt is paid. *See Also: trust, trustee*

PHILADELPHIA STOCK EXCHANGE. A Pennsylvania stock exchange that serves as an alternate exchange for many others, including the exchanges in New York, by actively trading the other exchange's listed securities. *See Also: exchange, exchanges, listed securities, securities, stock, stock exchange*

PHONY DIVIDENDS. An illegal act in which a company pays dividends from the money it receives from people buying shares, instead of from stock earnings. *See Also: earnings, stock*

PHYSICAL ACCESS MEMBER. A person who pays an annual fee for the right to use the New York Stock Exchange trading floor for buying and selling securities. A physical access member cannot vote on any exchange matters and is not entitled to any compensation if the exchange liquidates. *See Also: exchange, floor, New York Stock Exchange, right, securities, stock, stock exchange, trading floor*

PHYSICAL COMMODITY. The tangible commodity, such as corn or soybeans, that a seller delivers to the buyer of a commodities contract. *See Also: commodity, contract*

PHYSICAL VERIFICATION. Occurs when an auditor physically inspects a company's inventory to verify its existence and value. *See Also: inventory*

PICKUP. Bonds with similar coupon rates and maturities are swapped at a basis price that is beneficial to the swapper. *See Also: basis, basis price, coupon*

PICKUP BOND A bond with a high coupon and a short callable date. If interest rates drop, the issuer probably will call the bonds. The investor will get higher-than-expected returns because of the premium the issuer pays. *See Also: bond, coupon, drop, interest, premium*

PICTURE. The prices at which a dealer will trade. *See Also: dealer*

PIECE-OF-THE-ACTION FINANCING. A loan agreement where the lender receives interest plus a percentage of an income property's gross profits or the borrowing company's net profits. *See Also: gross, interest, net, plus*

PIGGYBACK EXCEPTION. A Securities and Exchange Commission rule that a company can substitute frequent and regular stock quotes in an actively traded market for other factual information the company must submit. The SEC allows the substitution because the market will not trade if the company hesitates at all in providing positive and negative information. *See Also: actual, commission, exchange, market, SEC, securities, stock, substitution*

PIGGYBACK REGISTRATION. Occurs when an issuer making a primary distribution allows those who privately bought stock earlier to include their shares in the offering. Such primary-secondary distributions are so described in the issue's prospectus. *See Also: offering, primary distribution, prospectus, stock*

PIL. (Short for Profits, Interest rates and Liquidity) PIL is a methodology used to formulate a predicted value for a stock index. *See Also: index, interest, liquidity, stock, stock index*

PINCH. A quick rise in prices.

PING. A short message that is sent from one computer to another, which elicits an immediate response.

PINK SHEETS. A quotation service that provides bid and ask prices and the market maker's name for over-the-counter stocks that are not listed by the National Association of Securities Dealers Automated Quotations. The quotes, printed on pink paper, are distributed to brokerage firms daily, but do not include stocks listed in newspapers. *See Also: ask, market, name, paper, quotation, securities, service*

PIP. A foreign exchange figure equaling 0.00001 of a unit. *See Also: exchange, foreign exchange, unit*

PIPELINE. The underwriting procedures that precede the public offering. *See Also: offering, public offering, underwriting*

PIT. The trading area in a futures exchange. *See Also: exchange, futures, futures exchange*

PITBOSS. A Chicago Board Options Exchange member who assists floor officials in several areas of concern, such as settling disputes over rule violations and overseeing quotation accuracy. *See Also: exchange, floor, quotation*

PITI. The abbreviation for principal, interest, taxes, and insurance. *See Also: insurance, interest, principal*

PIVOTAL STOCK. A stock that does or can influence the market activity of other stocks. *See Also: activity, market, stock*

PLACEMENT. Securities distribution, either public or private.

PLACEMENT MEMORANDUM. A document that a syndicate manager prepares in the Eurocredit market to provide pertinent information to other potential syndicate managers that will help them decide whether to join in the credit. *See Also: credit, manager, market, syndicate, syndicate manager*

PLACEMENT RATIO. The percentage of new municipal issues involving at least $1 million that has been syndicated and sold in the last week.

PLACING POWER. The success of a broker in selling securities. *See Also: broker, securities*

PLAIN ENGLISH. In an effort to make companies' registration statements for their initial public offerings of stock apply more clear, concise and understandable, the Securities and Exchange Commission mandates that "plain English" be applied. Prospectuses, typically densely written documents laden with legalistic language and technological lingo, were often enigmatic to the average investor. The companies are ordered to write prospectuses using an active voice, short sentences, and common language. Additionally, risk factors must be written more clearly and confusing language, such as double negatives, be omitted. *See Also: average, clear, commission, exchange, registration, risk, securities, stock, write*

PLAIN VANILLA. A traditional, routine security offering with no special features. *See Also: offering, security*

PLAINTIFF. The person or company that initiates a court action against a defendant.

PLAN COMPANY. A company registered with the Securities and Exchange Commission that sells contractual funds on behalf of the fund's underwriter. The company is certified as a participating unit investment trust. *See Also: actual, commission, exchange, investment, investment trust, securities, trust, unit, unit investment trust*

PLAN COMPLETION INSURANCE. A group term life insurance policy for investors in a mutual fund contract plan. If the investor dies before the contract is completed, the difference between his or her contributions and the total plan amount is paid to the custodian financial institution, which completes the plan with the insurance money and holds the shares for the investor's estate. *See Also: contract, custodian, estate, fund, insurance, life insurance, mutual fund, term*

PLAN HOLDER. A person who owns shares in a pension plan. *See Also: pension, pension plan*

PLANNED AMORTIZATION CLASS (PAC). A CMO tranche that pays principal based on a predetermined paydown schedule. The schedule is derived from the amortization of collateral at two different prepayment speeds. The paydown schedule will be met if prepayments occur inside the PAC band, between the two defined prepayment speeds. *See Also: amortization, CMO, collateral, PAC band, paydown, prepayment, principal, tranche*

PLANT. A company's fixed assets, including real estate and equipment. *See Also: estate, real estate*

PLATEAU. A horizontal price movement after a period of increasing prices. Plateaus often indicate uncertainty, and usually are followed by a price drop. *See Also: drop, movement*

PLATFORM. The type of operating system on which applications execute. Common platforms include Microsoft Windows, Apple, Linux and Unix. *See Also: Linux, on, UNIX, Windows*

PLATO. A computer teaching and testing system, designed by the Control Data Corporation, for investment industry examinations, such as those involved in blue sky qualifying. *See Also: corporation, industry, investment, testing*

PLAY. A speculative investment. *See Also: investment, speculative*

PLC. *See Also: Project Loan Certificates.*

PLEDGE. To transfer property to a lender as security for a loan or other obligation. *See Also: obligation, security, transfer*

PLEDGED ASSETS. Bank-owned securities used as collateral for government deposits. *See Also: collateral, securities*

PLEDGED LOAN. A mortgage that is used to secure a loan. *See Also: mortgage*

PLEDGED SECURITIES. Securities used as collateral for a long- or short-term debt. *See Also: collateral, short-term debt*

PLEDGED-ACCOUNT MORTGAGE. A mortgage in which part of the borrower's down payment pays for a pledged savings account, which helps pay the first year's monthly mortgage payments. *See Also: account, mortgage, pay, savings account*

PLOW BACK. Instead of distributing dividends to stockholders, a company holds on to its earnings so the money can be reinvested in the business. *See Also: earnings*

PLUM. Additional or unexpected profits or dividends.

PLUNGE. A quick, sudden drop in the market or a security's price. *See Also: drop, market*

PLUNGER. A person who invests in speculative securities. *See Also: securities, speculative*

PLUNK DOWN. To pay for in cash. *See Also: cash, pay*

PLUS. Follows a security's price quote to indicate a point fraction in 64ths. *See Also: fraction, point*

PLUS-TICK RULE. A Securities and Exchange Commission regulation that round-lot short sales of listed securities must be at a price that reflects an increase over the last different transaction price, unless the last price already reflects an increase. *See Also: commission, exchange, listed securities, securities, transaction*

PLUSTICK. A transaction completed at a higher price than the previous transaction. *See Also: transaction*

PO. A principal only bond. *See Also: bond, principal, stripped bond*

POINT. Used to quote securities prices. One point for a stock equals one dollar; for a bond, one point equals $10, assuming a $1,000 par value. *See Also: bond, par, par value, securities, stock*

POINT AND FIGURE CHART. A measure of price changes and the direction of the changes without any consideration for volume or time. *See Also: consideration, time, volume*

POINT OF PRESENCE. Also referred to as POP, the closest site at which a user may connect to an Internet server or other remote site. This is usually the location of an ISP or telephone company. This is also the point at which a long distance carrier connects to a local site. *See Also: Internet, ISP, local, point, POP, remote, server*

POINT OF SALE. The point at which a product is paid and delivered, whether at a physical location or at an online location. *See Also: online, point*

POISON PEN. A corporate warrant transferring a stockholder's right to consider tender offers for his or her shares to the board of directors. *See Also: board of directors, right, tender, warrant*

POISON PILL. A method used by a board of directors to discourage a takeover bid by making the company less attractive to the potential raider. A poison pill normally indicates a company has distributed convertible preferred stock shares as dividends to the existing stockholders, with the stock convertible to a number at least equal to the number of outstanding shares. The stockholders have no desire to convert the stock because of the dividend adjustments, unless the company is to be taken over. The raider's takeover, in turn, would increase the price of the stock many times over again, so the price the raider would have to pay for the company also would increase many times over. *See Also: board of directors, dividend, outstanding, pay, preferred stock, raider, stock, takeover, turn*

POLICY HOLDER. A person covered by insurance. *See Also: insurance*

POLICY LOAN. A low-interest insurance company loan with the policy's surrender value used as collateral. *See Also: collateral, insurance*

POLICY VALUE. The amount of money an insurance policy is worth at maturity. *See Also: insurance, maturity, worth*

POLYOPSONY. Occurs when the market has so few buyers that their actions materially affect stock prices, but the number is great enough that the buyers cannot significantly judge the effect of their actions on the other buyers. *See Also: market, stock*

POLYPOLY. Occurs when the market has so few sellers that their actions materially affect stock prices. However, the number is great enough that the sellers cannot significantly judge the effect of their actions on the other sellers. *See Also: market, stock*

PONZI SCHEME. Named after Charles Ponzi, who cost investors millions of dollars in the 1920s. In this scheme, people are promised high returns on an investment, with the money taken from new investors used to pay off earlier investors. Such a scheme theoretically could go on indefinitely, except that the amount owed to investors will continue to balloon. *See Also: balloon, investment, pay*

POOL. A group of debt instruments, with another security representing an undivided interest. *See Also: interest, security*

POOL DAY. The second business day before the settlement date of a TBA mortgage-backed security. *See Also: business day, security, settlement date, TBA*

POOL FINANCING. When a municipal financing sponsor floats an issue with several municipalities underwriting the expenses and, in turn, receives lower interest rates. *See Also: interest, issue, sponsor, turn, underwriting*

POOL ISSUE DATE. The date at which the pass-through security was issued, not the origination date of the underlying mortgages. *See Also: pass-through security, security*

POOL MATURITY DATE. The date at which the latest maturing mortgage in the pool matures. *See Also: mortgage, pool*

POOLED INCOME FUND. A fund to which contributors transfer property and retain income interest, then transfer the rest to a charity. *See Also: fund, interest, transfer*

POOLING OF INTEREST. When one company merges with another company, all assets and liabilities also are merged, and the difference between the acquired company's purchase price and its net tangible value is entered on the balance sheet as goodwill. *See Also: balance, balance sheet, goodwill, net, purchase price, tangible value*

POOLING OPERATION. A company that solicits and accepts money from other funds for the purpose of trading commodity futures contract deliveries. *See Also: commodity, contract, futures, futures contract*

POOP. A reference to an individual who claims to have inside information, and releases the information publicly. An individual with "poop" may or may not have accurate information. *See Also: inside information*

POOP AND SCOOP. The unethical method of spreading fabricated information with the intention of later buying the stock at more favorable prices. If the false information is negative, the security will be purchased at lower prices; using false information that is positive, the security will be shorted at higher prices. Once the truth is revealed investors will profit from a rebound in the price of the stock. *See Also: profit, security, spreading, stock, will*

POPULARIZING. An exchange specialist's advertisements, marketing activities, or sales literature that promotes his or her activities. *See Also: exchange, sales literature*

PORK BELLY. A speculative commodity involving frozen pork. *See Also: commodity, speculative*

PORTAL. A Web site that acts as a gateway, or entrance, to the Web. Portals offer such services as a search engine, directory, e-mail, news and other services. *See Also: e-mail, gateway, offer, search engine, Web, Web site*

PORTFOLIO. Either a combination of assets, or the entirety of a person's investments. *See Also: combination*

PORTFOLIO BETA SCORE. A portfolio's volatility, determined by the beta coefficients of its securities, with a beta one reflecting the same volatility as the general market. A higher beta would reflect securities that are more volatile, and a beta of less than one would be less volatile than the general market. *See Also: beta, market, securities, volatile, volatility*

PORTFOLIO MANAGER. Any broker, dealer, or other person who makes daily investment decisions on behalf of another person. *See Also: broker, dealer, investment*

PORTFOLIO OPTIMIZATION. After considering all of the securities available, an investor selects those securities that will minimize risk and maximize returns. *See Also: risk, securities*

PORTFOLIO PUMPING. End-of-quarter trading by portfolio managers designed to boost a fund's quarterly performance results. Using this tactic, portfolio managers will buy additional shares of small stocks that are already owned by the fund. This buying can improve the share price, which enhances the end-of-quarter value of the stock and the portfolio as a whole. *See Also: fund, portfolio, quarterly, share, stock, will*

PORTFOLIO THEORY. An investment strategy in which an investor controls the amount of risks and returns by determining the relationship among the securities in a portfolio instead of their individual characteristics. *See Also: investment, investment strategy, portfolio, securities*

POSITION. The nature of investment account holdings. For example, an investor who owns securities has a long position in those securities, and an investor who sells short, which is selling securities he or she doesn't own in anticipation of buying them back at a lower price, holds a short position. *See Also: account, anticipation, investment, long position, securities, short position*

POSITION BID. A broker's bid when that broker wants to buy a large block of securities for his or her own account to accommodate an institutional client. *See Also: account, broker, client, securities*

POSITION BUILDING. The establishment of net long or net short positions for a portfolio, which cuts down on the number of securities the account executive must follow while increasing the risks. *See Also: account, account executive, net, portfolio, securities*

POSITION LIMITS. An options exchange regulation that prohibits investors from holding 2,000 or more put or call contracts against the same underlying security on the same side of the market. *See Also: exchange, market, put, security, underlying security*

POSITION OFFER. A broker's offer when that broker wants to sell a large block of securities for his or her own account to accommodate an institutional client. *See Also: account, broker, client, offer, securities*

POSITION TRADER. A commodities broker who tries to achieve long-term profits by taking only calculated risks and by dealing in contracts that have durations of six months or longer. *See Also: broker*

POSITIVE CARRY. Occurs when money is borrowed to buy interest-bearing securities and the income received from the securities exceeds the loan's interest rate. For example, if an investor borrows money at 11 percent interest to buy a security that will produce 12.5 percent interest, the investor will have a positive carry. *See Also: carry, interest, interest rate, securities, security*

POSITIVE YIELD CURVE. A graph that displays the relationship between the maturities and yields of securities with the same issuer or with similar credit ratings. When the graph has a positive yield curve, the longer-term securities have higher yields than the shorter-term securities. *See Also: credit, securities, yield, yield curve*

POST. The area of an exchange floor where specific securities are traded and where the exchange specialist accepts bids and offers and provides price quotes. *See Also: exchange, exchange floor, floor, securities, specialist*

POST 30. A special New York Stock Exchange trading post for transactions involving inactive stocks and round lots of fewer than 100 shares. *See Also: exchange, New York Stock Exchange, post, stock, stock exchange, trading post*

POST EXECUTION REPORTING. A computer network for routing market, limit, and odd-lot orders, and executing those orders for members of the American Stock Exchange. See *Also: exchange, limit, market, stock, stock exchange*

POST-MARKET TRADING. Trading after the close of the regular trading session. Post-market trading can refer to intercompany trading, via an ECN, or an international exchange. *See After-Hours Trading.*

POST OFFICE PROTOCOL. Also referred to as POP, the protocol used by mail clients, such as browser software, to retrieve messages from a mail server. *See Also: POP, protocol, server*

POSTAL SERVICE. A federal agency that issues debt securities to pay for capital improvements, using its own assets as collateral. *See Also: capital, collateral, pay, securities*

POSTDATED. Any instrument or document that carries a date that is later than the date it was signed. *See Also: instrument*

POT. Shares of a newly issued security that are held to fill institutional orders. *See Also: fill, security*

POT IS CLEAN. An underwriting syndicate manager's announcement to account members that all shares reserved for institutional sales have, indeed, been sold. *See Also: account, syndicate, underwriting, underwriting syndicate*

POT LIABILITY. An underwriter's financial liability for those securities in the pot that remain unsold after the manager removes price restrictions. *See Also: liability, manager, pot, securities*

POT PROTECTION. An issuer's promise to an institution that the institution definitely will receive a specific number of securities from a pot. *See Also: pot, securities*

POTENTIAL STOCK. The difference between the amount of capital stock a company has authorized to be issued and the total amount of stock that actually has been issued. For example, if a company has authorized the issuing of 30,000 shares of stock and 20,000 actually have been issued, the potential stock would total 10,000. *See Also: capital, capital stock, stock*

POUND. The primary monetary unit of Great Britain. *See Also: unit*

POWER OF ATTORNEY. One person's authorization for another person to sign the first person's name on a legal document, or for that other person to vote on behalf of the first person. *See Also: legal, name*

PRACTICAL EXTRACTION AND REPORTING. *See Also: PERL*

PRAECIPIUM. A borrower must pay a Euromarket credit manager a fee, of which the manager will deduct and keep a portion, and the rest of which is divided among the other management group members. The praecipium is the portion that the manager keeps. *See Also: credit, manager, pay*

PRE-MARKET INDICATOR. Also referred to as PMI, an indicator that reflects pre-market trading in NASDAQ 100 stocks. The PMI was invented to help investors better determine the opening level of the NASDAQ stock market. *See Also: level, market, NASDAQ, pre-market trading, stock, stock market*

PRECAUTIONARY LIQUIDITY BALANCE. The cash, securities, or other assets that an investor holds onto and uses in case of an emergency. *See Also: cash, securities*

PRECEDENCE. A broker's right to buy a security before other brokers, even though the other brokers could complete the transaction. A broker is given precedence based on the time of his bid and the size of that bid. *See Also: broker, right, security, size, time, transaction*

PRECEDENCE OF ORDER. One security's priority over another security when buy or sell orders are received. *See Also: priority, security*

PRECOMPUTE. When the interest on an installment loan is determined by deducting the amount of annual interest from the loan's face value as the loan's proceeds are disbursed, or by adding the amount of annual interest to the total amount that will be repaid in equal installments. *See Also: face value, interest, proceeds*

PREEMPTIVE RIGHT. A shareholder's privilege to maintain his or her proportionate share of company ownership when the company offers additional stock shares for sale publicly. The company usually lets the existing stockholders have the first crack at the new shares before offering the stock to the general public. *See Also: offering, sale, share, stock*

PREFERENCE. The broker who receives priority after reaching an impasse with another broker who has offered the same amount for the same number of shares. Because neither broker holds precedence, the broker who entered the crowd first receives preference. *See Also: broker, crowd, precedence, priority*

PREFERENCE AS TO ASSETS. After a company liquidates and before declared dividends are distributed, the holders of preferred stock can make a claim for payments before the holders of common stock are entitled to their claims. *See Also: common stock, preferred stock, stock*

PREFERENCE INCOME. Income a person does not list in his or her adjusted taxable income. If the amount exceeds a specific limit, the person must compute an alternative minimum tax. *See Also: alternative minimum tax, limit, taxable income*

PREFERENCE SETTING. The selection of parameters on software tools according to likes and dislikes. When used on Web browsers, for example, users can change such settings as colors, size and type of fonts, and security settings. *See Also: change, on, security, size, Web*

PREFERENCE STOCK. Preferred stock that has priority over ensuing preferred and common stock issues when dividends are paid, and when proceeds are distributed following liquidation. *See Also: common stock, liquidation, priority, proceeds, stock*

PREFERRED DIVIDEND COVERAGE. The ratio of the annual preferred stock dividends to the company's after tax income. *See Also: after tax, preferred stock, ratio, stock*

PREFERRED DIVIDENDS PAYABLE. A record of how much in dividends a company owes to preferred stockholders.

PREFERRED PREFERRED. A preferred stock that has priority over other preferred stock of the same company in dividends and claims. *See Also: preferred stock, priority, stock*

PREFERRED STOCK. A type of capital stock that represents a portion of ownership in a company, with the shares usually carrying fixed dividends, and typically no voting rights. Preferred stock holders receive dividend payments before common stock holders. *See Also: capital, capital stock, common stock, dividend, rights, stock, voting rights*

PREFERRED STOCK FUND. A mutual fund with investments concentrated in preferred stocks to preserve capital and achieve higher income. *See Also: capital, fund, mutual fund*

PREFERRED STOCK RATIO. A company's total capitalization divided into the par value of its outstanding preferred stock. *See Also: capitalization, outstanding, par, par value, preferred stock, stock, total capitalization*

PREGNANCY NOTES. A debt instrument that postpones payments for 10 months. *See Also: debt instrument, instrument*

PRELIMINARY AGREEMENT. A contract between a company and an underwriter of a company's securities, which serves as a temporary commitment until the final registration statement is issued. The registration statement replaces the preliminary agreement after the underwriter and company agree on the offering's potential for success, and the securities' terms and conditions. *See Also: contract, registration, registration statement, securities, statement*

PRELIMINARY OFFICIAL STATEMENT. A detailed, preliminary report, similar to a prospectus, that covers a new municipal securities offering. *See Also: offering, prospectus, securities*

PRELIMINARY PROSPECTUS. An early, detailed registration report that covers a new securities issue. The preliminary prospectus does not offer the security for sale and does not list the security's expected price. *See Also: issue, offer, prospectus, registration, sale, securities, security*

PRELIMINARY TITLE REPORT. A company's title statement after conducting a title search and before it issues an insurance commitment binder. *See Also: binder, insurance, statement*

PREMIUM. The amount for which a security is selling above its par value. *See Also: par, par value, security*

PREMIUM BOND. A bond that sells at a price that is higher than its face value. The premium is the amount the price exceeds a bond's face value. *See Also: bond, face value, premium*

PREMIUM FOR RISK. An investment's yield after subtracting its basic, prevailing yield at the time. *See Also: time, yield*

PREMIUM INCOME. An investor's income from selling either a put or a call option. *See Also: call option, option, put*

PREMIUM ON BOND. The percentage over a bond's face value for which it can be bought, sold, or redeemed. *See Also: face value*

PREMIUM ON CAPITAL STOCK. The amount over a stock's cash value for which it can be bought or sold. See *Also: cash*

PREMIUM ON FUNDED DEBT. The amount over a funded debt security's cash value for which it can be issued or assumed. *See Also: cash, funded debt*

PREMIUM ON SECURITIES. The amount over a security's value for which it can be bought or sold.

PREMIUM OVER BOND VALUE. The difference between a convertible bond's market value and the general market price of a regular bond from the same issuer. *See Also: bond, market, market price, market value*

PREMIUM OVER CONVERSION VALUE. The difference between the market price of a convertible stock or bond and the price at which it can be convened. *See Also: bond, market, market price, stock*

PREMIUM RAID. Occurs in Great Britain when an investor quickly buys a sizable percentage of a company's securities at a price higher than the current market price. The purchases are made so quickly that few of the company's stockholders can take advantage of the chance to sell their stock at the premium price. *See Also: current, market, market price, premium, securities, stock, take*

PREMIUM RECAPTURE. The length of time needed for a convertible security's yield advantage to recoup its conversion value premium. *See Also: conversion, conversion value, premium, time, yield, yield advantage*

PREMIUM STOCK. A stock that generates profits at a greater rate than that displayed by the general market. *See Also: market, stock*

PRE-MARKET HIGH. The highest price paid for a security during the pre-market trading session. *See Also: pre-market trading, security, session*

PRE-MARKET LAST SALE. The last price in which a security traded during the current day's pre-market trading session. *See Also: current, pre-market trading, security, session*

PRE-MARKET LOW. The lowest price paid for a security during the post-market, or after-market, trading session. *See Also: after-market, security, session*

PRE-MARKET PERCENT CHANGE. The percent increase or decrease between the last sale of the regular-day's trading session and the last sale of the current day's pre-market trading session. *See Also: current, last sale, pre-market trading, sale, session*

PRE-MARKET TRADING. Trading prior to the open of the regular trading session. Pre-market trading can refer to inter-company trading, trading via an ECN, or on an international exchange. *See Also: ECN, exchange, on, open, session*

PRE-MARKET VOLUME. The total number of shares in which a security traded during the current day's pre-market trading session. *See Also: current, pre-market trading, security, session*

PRE-SYNDICATE BID. A bid entered to stabilize the price of a security prior to the effective date of a secondary offering. *See Also: effective date, offering, security*

PREPAID CHARGE PLAN. A contractual mutual fund with a sales charge that is paid in the fund's early years. *See Also: actual, fund, mutual fund, sales charge*

PREPAID EXPENSES. A balance sheet entry that includes items that normally must be paid in advance. *See Also: balance, balance sheet*

PREPAYMENT. When a brokerage firm pays a selling client for a security before the transaction's predetermined settlement date. A principal payment on a mortgage loan that is greater than the amount actually due. *See Also: client, firm, mortgage, principal, security, settlement date*

PREPAYMENT PENALTY. A bank charge that a borrower must pay for a loan without a prepayment clause when the borrower repays the loan before it reaches maturity. *See Also: bank, maturity, pay, prepayment*

PREPAYMENT PRIVILEGE. A mortgage clause that gives the mortgagor the right to pay off the debt before it matures. *See Also: mortgage, pay, right*

PREREFUNDING. When a bond issuer uses a second bond issue to pay for the future refunding of an outstanding bond which is not yet callable. *See Also: bond, issue, outstanding, pay, refunding*

PREROGATIVES. One person's rights or privileges that no one else can possess. *See Also: rights*

PRESALE ESTIMATES. The price range within which an auction house believes an item will sell. *See Also: auction, house, price range, range*

PRESALE ORDER. A buy order that a municipal syndicate manager has accepted for part of the issue, even though all of the offering's details have not been released. *See Also: buy order, issue, manager, order, syndicate, syndicate manager*

PRESCRIBED RIGHT TO INCOME AND MAXIMUM EQUITY (PRIME). One of two component parts of a unit trust, sponsored by the Americus Shareowner Service Corporation, which separates the income portion of a stock from its potential appreciation. The prime is the income producing portion and the score (special claim on residual equity) is the potential appreciation. This unit trust, which trades on the NYSE, allows investors who want to enhance their income or appreciation a conservative, leveraged approach. *See Also: appreciation, corporation, leveraged, NYSE, prime, score, service, stock, trust, unit*

PRESENT VALUE. The discounted value of an amount that will be payable at a specific future date. *See Also: discounted value*

PRESENT VALUE OF EXPECTED CASH FLOW. The amount of money a company expects to make from holding an asset with the interest rate discount subtracted. *See Also: asset, discount, interest, interest rate*

PRESERVATION OF CAPITAL. An investment with the goal of securing the value of the principle by avoiding speculative situations. *See Also: investment, speculative*

PRESIDENT. A company's second-highest officer, falling in rank just below the company's board chairperson. The president is elected to the position by the company's board of directors and reports directly to the board. *See Also: board of directors, officer, position*

PRESIDENTIAL ELECTION CYCLE THEORY. A theory that stocks will drop in price immediately after a new president is elected, after which the president will raise taxes or take other unpopular steps to correct the economic problems. After two years, the stocks will go up because the president, as an incumbent, is looking for a strong economy at election time. After the election, the cycle starts over again. *See Also: cycle, drop, president, take, time*

PRESOLD ISSUE. An issue of government or municipal securities that has been sold even before the coupon rate or price has been announced. *See Also: coupon, coupon rate, issue, securities*

PRESUMPTIVE UNDERWRITER. An investor who buys 10 percent of a company's stock in a public offering and resells the stock for a profit within two years. *See Also: offering, profit, public offering, stock*

PRETAX EARNINGS. A company's net income before federal taxes have been subtracted. *See Also: net, net income*

PRETAX RATE OF RETURN. A security's yield before taxes have been subtracted. *See Also: yield*

PREVIOUS CLOSE. The closing price of a security for the previous trading session. *See Also: closing price, security, session*

PRICE ALERT. Occurs when a security's price pushes above or below a previous resistance level and exceeds its previous high or low point during a specific time period. A strength or weakness in the market can be measured by totaling all the stocks that have upside or downside breakouts. *See Also: level, low, market, point, resistance level, time, upside*

PRICE AVERAGING. Buying several equal amounts of a security at different prices to achieve a better overall price per share. For example, if an investor bought 100 shares of a stock at $10 a share, then bought 100 shares at $16 a share, and then bought 100 shares at $20 a share, the overall price per share would be $15.33, while the stock's price continued to climb. *See Also: security, share, stock*

PRICE CHANGE. The net rise or drop in a security's market price. *See Also: drop, market, market price, net*

PRICE GAP. Occurs when a security's price range in one day does not overlap its price range from the day before. *See Also: price range, range*

PRICE INDEX. A gauge that measures price changes for different goods and services compared to an earlier period.

PRICE INFLATION. Occurs when general price levels increase.

PRICE LIMIT. The highest amount a futures contract is allowed to fluctuate from the previous record's settlement price. *See Also: contract, futures, futures contract, settlement price*

PRICE LOCO. An item's purchase price. *See Also: purchase price*

PRICE POTENTIAL. A technical, analytical estimate of a security's future market value. *See Also: market, market value*

PRICE RANGE. The highest and lowest prices in which a security traded during a specific time period. *See Also: security, time*

PRICE SPREAD. The difference between a security's bid and ask prices. *See Also: ask*

PRICE SUPPORT. A government-set minimum price for farm products designed to protect farmers against low prices for their goods. If prices drop below the minimum level, the government pays the difference. *See Also: drop, level, low*

PRICE TAKER. An investor whose securities transactions are so small that they have no impact on the market. *See Also: market, securities*

PRICE TALK. An underwriter's preliminary discussion of a negotiated issue's offering price or a competitive issue's bid price. *See Also: bid price, offering, offering price*

PRICE TRANSPARENCY. Pricing that is known to both buyer and seller. Price transparency typically results in lower prices and even reduced or eliminated transaction costs. *See Also: transaction*

PRICE-EARNINGS RATIO (P/E). The relationship between the price of a stock and its earnings per share. This figure is determined by dividing the stock's market price by the company's earnings per share figure. The higher the P/E, the more earnings growth investors are expecting. A growth stock will typically have a higher price/earnings ratio than a stock that is expected to grow at a slower rate. Stocks with a higher P/E, usually over 20, are considered riskier than stocks with a lower P/E, which have proven earning potential. *See Also: earnings, growth stock, market, market price, P/E, ratio, share, stock*

PRICE-LEVEL-ADJUSTED ADJUSTING MORTGAGE. A mortgage plan with the outstanding loan balance indexed and with the interest rate net of any inflation premium. Because the payments are based on the interest rate, the outstanding balance at the end of the year is adjusted for inflation. The initial payments are lower than most other types of mortgages. *See Also: balance, inflation, interest, interest rate, mortgage, net, outstanding, premium*

PRICE-VOLUME ALERT. A price breakout combined with a volume breakout. A breakout occurs when a security's price pushes above or below a previous resistance level. *See Also: breakout, level, resistance level, volume*

PRICE-WEIGHTED INDEX. An index in which component stocks are weighted by their individual prices with lower-priced stocks having a smaller impact than those with higher prices. *See Also: index*

PRICE/DIVIDEND RATIO. A company divides its stock's annual dividend per share into the current market value per share. *See Also: current, current market value, dividend, market, market value, share*

PRICE/EARNINGS RATIO (P/E). The relationship between the price of a stock and its earnings per share. This figure is determined by dividing the stock's market price by the company's earnings per share figure. The higher the P/E, the more earnings growth investors are expecting. A growth stock will have a higher price/earnings ratio than a stock that is expected to grow at a slower rate. Stocks with a higher P/E, usually over 20, are considered riskier than stocks with a lower P/E, which have proven earning potential. *See Also: earnings, growth stock, market, market price, p/e, ratio, share, stock*

PRICED OUT OF THE MARKET. Occurs when an item is priced so high that no one will buy it, which ultimately leads to a drop in sales. *See Also: drop*

PRICEY. An underpriced bid or an overpriced offer. *See Also: offer, underpriced*

PRIMARY DEALER. A group of dealers and banks that can buy and sell government securities while working directly with the Federal Reserve Bank of New York. *See Also: bank, Federal Reserve Bank, reserve, reserve bank, securities*

PRIMARY DISTRIBUTION. The first time a new securities issue is offered publicly for sale. The primary distribution usually involves an investment banker selling the issue as an over-the-counter security. *See Also: investment, investment banker, issue, sale, securities, security, time*

PRIMARY EARNINGS. A company's net income after taxes and preferred dividends, divided by the number of outstanding common shares. *See Also: net, net income, outstanding*

PRIMARY MARKET. The market in which investment bankers first sell newly issued securities to investors. *See Also: investment, market, securities*

PRIMARY OFFERING. The first time a company publicly sells its stock. *See Also: stock, time*

PRIMARY POINTS. The main agricultural commodities exchanges. *See Also: exchanges*

PRIMARY TREND. A market trend or price movement that lasts for a long period of time, sometimes as long as several years. *See Also: market, market trend, movement, time, trend*

PRIME. Prescribed Right to Income and Maximum Equity. *See Also: equity, right*

PRIME INVESTMENT. A high-quality, low-risk investment expected to bring in high profits. *See Also: investment*

PRIME PAPER. Commercial paper that Moody's Investors Services has given a rating of P, with the rating broken into three categories: P-3 is high quality, P-2 is higher quality, and P-1 is the highest quality. *See Also: paper*

PRIME RATE. The interest rate on loans that commercial banks quote as an indication of the rate being charged on loans to its best commercial customers. Interest rates on other loans often are based on the prime rate, which is frequently more, but can be less, based on past and potential future trends. *See Also: indication, interest, interest rate, prime*

PRINCIPAL. 1) For debt instruments, the face value or par value of a bond, not including the interest. Also, the remaining balance of an obligation. 2) The amount of money that a client invests, or the client's capital. 3) An individual with supervisory responsibilities at a securities firm. *See Also: balance, bond, capital, client, face value, firm, interest, obligation, par, par value, securities*

PRINCIPAL AMOUNT. A debt security's par value, or a loan's face amount. *See Also: face amount, par, par value*

PRINCIPAL BALANCE. Outstanding and unpaid balances, less interest, on any debt or obligation. *See Also: interest, obligation*

PRINCIPAL ORDERS. A broker/dealer buying or selling for its own account. *See Also: account*

PRINCIPAL STOCKHOLDER. Any shareholder who owns 10 percent or more of a company's voting stock. *See Also: shareholder, stock, voting stock*

PRINCIPAL SUM. The same as "principal," or the total amount of a financial obligation, such as a loan, less interest. *See Also: interest, obligation*

PRINCIPAL TRANSACTION. When one or both parties in a securities transaction act as a principal when dealing for their own account. *See Also: account, principal, securities, transaction*

PRINCIPAL WINDOW. The amount of time between the first and last payment of principal. *See Also: principal, time*

PRINCIPALS. A company's stockholders.

PRINT. The exchange-tape record of securities transactions. *See Also: securities*

PRIOR DEDUCTIONS METHOD. An improper interest or dividend calculation in which senior obligations are subtracted from the earnings first, then the junior issues are subtracted from the balance. *See Also: balance, dividend, earnings, interest, junior*

PRIOR LIEN. A mortgage that has priority over other mortgages. *See Also: mortgage, priority*

PRIOR LIEN BOND. A debt instrument that has priority over the issuing company's other issues. *See Also: debt instrument, instrument, priority*

PRIOR PREFERRED STOCK. Preference stock that has priority over ensuing preferred and common stock issues when dividends are paid, and when proceeds are distributed following liquidation. *See Also: common stock, liquidation, priority, proceeds, stock*

PRIOR REDEMPTION. A debt paid before maturity. *See Also: maturity*

PRIOR REDEMPTION PRIVILEGE. Occurs when the holder of a called bond is allowed to redeem the bond before maturity, or before the bond's call dates. *See Also: bond, maturity, redeem*

PRIOR SALE. When demand for an item exceeds supply, and an investor offers it for sale at a specific price based on that short supply, the investor will sell the item to the first bidder. Potential bidders will be told beforehand that the supply is limited, and the first bidder will receive the item. Subsequent bidders will be out of luck because of the prior sale. *See Also: demand, sale, supply*

PRIOR STOCK. *See Also: Preferred Stock*

PRIORITY. The first broker to make the highest bid or the lowest offer. Because the broker has priority, he or she always receives at least partial execution of the order. *See Also: broker, execution, offer, order, partial execution*

PRIVATE AUCTION. An auction in which the identity of the buyer or seller is concealed.

PRIVATE DISTRIBUTION. A company distributing its securities to a small, select group of investors. *See Also: securities*

PRIVATE EXCHANGE. A single seller or buyer exchange that is open to its buyers or sellers. For example, a manufacturer will create a private exchange to offer its products to buyers. *See Also: exchange, offer, open, will*

PRIVATE EXPORT FUNDING CORPORATION. A private company that loans money to foreign importers of American goods and services, with the Export-Import Bank guaranteeing the loan's principal and interest. This is also guaranteed by the United States government's full faith and credit. *See Also: and interest, bank, credit, full, full faith and credit, interest, principal*

PRIVATE LIMITED PARTNERSHIP. With memberships sold through an investment advisor, this type of partnership has no more than 35 limited partners and is not registered with the Securities and Exchange Commission. It is designed to create tax benefits, income, or capital gains for its members. Such partnerships often will invest in research, real estate, or oil and gas drilling. *See Also: capital, commission, estate, exchange, investment, partnership, real estate, securities*

PRIVATE OFFERING. A company offering a new stock issue to a small, select group of no more than 25 investors. *See Also: issue, offering, stock*

PRIVATE PLACEMENT. A large block of securities offered for sale to an institutional investor or a financial institution through private negotiations. Also, the sale of securities to a small group of investors (generally 35 or less) which is exempt from SEC registration requirements. The investors execute an investment letter stating that the securities being purchased are for investment without a view towards distribution. *See Also: institutional investor, sale, securities*

PRIVATE SECTOR. The section of the economy controlled by corporations and individuals, as opposed to the public sector, which is controlled by the government. *See Also: public sector, sector*

PRIVATE SECTOR PASS-THROUGH. A bank-issued, nongovernment, mortgage-backed security that is sometimes privately guaranteed. *See Also: security*

PRIVATE TRUST. As opposed to a charitable trust fund, this is a trust fund with limited designated beneficiaries, such as family members. *See Also: charitable trust, fund, trust*

PRIVATE WIRE FIRM. A large brokerage house that uses telegraphs to communicate between branches. *See Also: brokerage house, house*

PRIVATELY HELD. Either a company owned by a few people, or the shares of a company that have never been offered publicly for sale. *See Also: sale*

PRIVATELY OWNED CORPORATION. A company owned by only a few people, with those people chiefly responsible for the company's operations and holding the majority of stock. *See Also: operations, stock*

PRIVILEGE DEALER. A trader who sells options contracts. *See Also: trader*

PRIVILEGE ISSUE. A convertible or participating security, or a stock that carries a purchase warrant. *See Also: security, stock, warrant*

PRO. A person with a high degree of skill or knowledge, held in high regards by others for his or her accomplishments and know-how. An investor with an impressive trading record, for example, is considered a pro.

PRO FORMA. A financial statement reflecting the company's financial condition using hypothetical data to determine the effects of an idea that has been proposed, but not yet consummated. *See Also: statement*

PRO RATA. A method of equally and proportionately allocating money, profits or liabilities by percentage. For example, if a gas company is found to have overcharged consumers and is subsequently forced to pay rebates, each consumer would get an amount proportionate to the amount he or she over-paid in the first place. *See Also: pay*

PRO RATE CANCELLATION. When a bond or other contract is canceled and the premium is charged according to the actual length of ownership. *See Also: actual, bond, contract, premium*

PROCEEDS. The profit a seller receives for selling assets. The amount of the proceeds is calculated by subtracting all fees and commissions from the total sale price. *See Also: profit, sale*

PROCEEDS SALE. Securities sold in the secondary market, with proceeds from the sale used to buy securities in the secondary market. *See Also: market, proceeds, sale, secondary market, securities*

PROCESS EFFECTS. An increase in consumer spending and private investments that follows a public works project.

PROCESSING. A lender's preparation and consideration of a mortgage application. *See Also: consideration, mortgage*

PROCUREMENT. The activities involved in the process of generating an order for a buyer. *See Also: order*

PROCUREMENT HUB. An e-marketplace which specializes in MRO or routine purchases such as office supplies, tickets, or other products that are essential to running a business. *See Also: e-marketplace, MRO*

PRODUCE EXCHANGE. An agricultural commodities exchange for trading futures contracts. *See Also: exchange, futures*

PRODUCER. A broker who brings in a large amount of profits and commissions for his or her firm. *See Also: broker, firm*

PRODUCERS' PRICE INDEX. Used to gauge inflation trends, this is a market index that measures price changes for goods sold to their final users. *See Also: index, inflation, market, market index*

PRODUCTION RATE. The coupon rate for issuing Government National Mortgage Association pass-through securities, with the interest rate set at 0.5 percent below the Federal Housing Administration mortgage rate. *See Also: coupon, coupon rate, interest, interest rate, mortgage, securities*

PROFESSIONAL. A person who buys and sells securities for a living. *See Also: securities*

PROFESSIONAL CORPORATION. A company that specializes in providing professional services, such as medical care, legal services, or psychiatric counseling. *See Also: legal, professional*

PROFILE A control mechanism in a software program or Web-based application that is intended to be modified by the user in order to customize the program's behavior. *See Also: order*

PROFILING. A summary or analysis of data, noting certain characteristics, behavioral patterns or other data. Profiling is commonly used among advertising companies to more efficiently target advertisements. *See Also: target*

PROFIT. The amount an investment earns or the amount a company earns through its business activities. *See Also: investment*

PROFIT AND LOSS ACCOUNT. An account transferred from the accounts receivable to a different account and subtracted from the accounts receivable balance because it is considered uncollectible. *See Also: account, accounts receivable, balance*

PROFIT AND LOSS RESERVE. An amount of money a company sets aside to take care of uncollectible accounts. *See Also: take*

PROFIT AND LOSS STATEMENT. A company's accounting statement that shows net profits, losses, income sources, and expenses. *See Also: net, statement*

PROFIT AND LOSS SUMMARY ACCOUNT. A company's account of all income and expenses, transferred to this summary ledger at the end of the company's fiscal year. *See Also: account, fiscal year, ledger*

PROFIT CENTER. A company's department, branch, or subsidiary that is directly responsible for generating its own profits. For example, a newspaper's advertising and circulation departments would be considered the newspaper's profit centers, while the news department would not be. *See Also: profit, subsidiary*

PROFIT MARGIN. A company divides its net sales into its net income to measure, through a percentage figure, its profitability. *See Also: net, net income, net sales, profitability*

PROFIT ON FIXED ASSETS. The profit from a fixed asset sold for a price above its book value. *See Also: asset, book, book value, fixed asset, profit*

PROFIT ON NET WORTH RATIO. By dividing a company's net worth into its net profit after taxes, the resultant number can determine how well the company is investing its funds. *See Also: net, net profit, net worth, profit, worth*

PROFIT-SHARING PLAN. A fund that a company sets up and through which employees can share in the company's success, often through the distribution of stock shares. *See Also: fund, share, stock*

PROFIT-SHARING SECURITIES. Stocks or bonds purchased for employees through a profit-sharing plan. *See Also: profit-sharing plan*

PROFIT-TAKING. Describes when stock is being sold for capital gains. *See Also: capital, stock*

PROFITABILITY. The ability of a company to generate profits.

PROFITABILITY INDEX. A company's predicted future cash flow divided by its initial investment. *See Also: cash, cash flow, investment*

PROFITABILITY RATIO. The degree and ratio through which a company can determine its profitability.

PROGRAM BUYING. The initial stock purchase determined by a large spread, or premium, between the stock's price and the futures' contract prices. *See Also: contract, premium, spread, stock*

PROGRAM EXECUTION PROCESSING. A system in which orders for multiple issues can be issued easily and simultaneously through an institutional investor's portfolio. *See Also: portfolio*

PROGRAM SELLING. A stock sale determined by a small spread or premium. *See Also: premium, sale, spread, stock*

PROGRAM TRADING. Institutional buying and selling of huge amounts of stocks based on the spread, or premium between an index future and the market prices of the stocks involved. *See Also: index, market, premium, spread*

PROGRESSIVE PAYMENTS. Money that a contractor or supplier periodically receives while properly and satisfactorily completing his or her work. The regular payments reduce the initial total amount of working capital the contractor or supplier actually needs to complete the job. *See Also: capital, job, working capital*

PROGRESSIVE TAX. An income tax system in which people who have higher incomes pay a higher rate of income tax than those with lower incomes so that the people who make lesser amounts do not end up paying a disproportionate share. People who have higher incomes, for example, have more tax breaks and shelters available to them than the poorer segment of society, so they end up paying a lower percentage of taxes on a straight percentage tax system. *See Also: pay, share*

PROJECT LINK. A Nobel Prize-winning economic model that connects all of the world's economies and predicts the effects that changes in one country's economy will have on another country's economy.

PROJECT LOAN CERTIFICATES (PLC). A Ginnie Mae program, which securitizes project loans. *See Also: Ginnie Mae, project loans*

PROJECT LOAN SECURITIES. Securities backed by project loans.

PROJECT LOANS. Mortgages on multiple-family housing complexes, including nursing homes and hospitals; they are typically HUD-guaranteed and FHA-insured.

PROJECT NOTE. A government-issued, guaranteed, short-term debt security that finances public housing construction. *See Also: debt security, security, short-term debt*

PROJECTED MATURITY. Given a particular prepayment assumption, the date on which a tranche is expected to completely retire. *See Also: prepayment, retire, tranche*

PROJECTION. The forecast of expected future price movements based on historical performances.

PROMISSORY NOTE. A written commitment to pay another party a specific amount of money by a specific date. For example, a note is a promissory note. *See Also: note, pay*

PROMOTER. The intermediary between those proposing a business venture and the people with money to invest in business ventures. *See Also: intermediary*

PROMPT DATE. The date a metal must be delivered to fill purchase contract terms on the London Metal Exchange. *See Also: contract, exchange, fill, London Metal Exchange*

PROPERTY ASSESSMENT. A determination of a property's value, with taxes based on that assessed value.

PROPERTY CAPITAL. Ownership of debts or securities. *See Also: securities*

PROPERTY DIVIDENDS. Dividends that a company pays in the stock shares of another company. The company may have received the stock shares through selling property. *See Also: stock*

PROPORTIONAL REPRESENTATION. An equalizing method of electing a company's board of directors in which each stockholder gets as many votes as he or she has shares of stock, multiplied by the number of board vacancies. Such methods give smaller shareholders the ability to obtain representation on the board. *See Also: board of directors, stock, stockholder*

PROPORTIONAL TAX. A tax based on a percentage rate that remains the same as the tax base increases. *See Also: base, tax base*

PROPORTIONATE SHARE OF ASSETS. After a company liquidates or dissolves, and after its debts have been satisfied and the holders of preferred stock have been paid, the holders of the company's common stock divide the remaining assets among themselves. *See Also: common stock, preferred stock, stock*

PROPRIETARY ACCOUNT. An account that reflects the company's financial condition. It provides an exact inventory count, the dollar amount of earnings, and the dollar amount of the company's reserves, among other statistics. *See Also: account, earnings, inventory*

PROPRIETOR. A person who has an exclusive interest in a company or other business venture and who is personally responsible for all liabilities. *See Also: interest*

PROPRIETORSHIP. A company that is owned by only one person, with that person holding all financial liabilities and receiving all profits.

PROSPECT. Any potential business customer or potential investor.

PROSPECTUS. A document the Securities and Exchange Commission requires a company to provide to prospective investors upon issuing new securities. The prospectus includes information such as financial background of the company or the company's officers, and the company's investment potential. *See Also: commission, exchange, investment, securities*

PROTECTIVE COMMITTEE. A panel organized to protect and represent stockholders in negotiating defaulted securities. *See Also: securities*

PROTECTIVE COVENANT. A municipality's agreement to protect the buyers of its municipal issues, as well as promising to service, insure, and cover interest on the issue. *See Also: interest, issue, service*

PROTOCOL. Specifications or set of rules that describes how computers will communicate with one another on a network. These standards assure that different networks or programs can work together, while minimizing potential errors. The success of the Internet in many ways relies on the agreement of the software and hardware protocol standards of TCP/IP. *See Also: Internet, on, standards, TCP/IP, will*

PROVISIONAL ALLOTMENT LETTER. As the British equivalent to an American rights offering, the provisional allotment letter gives a company's current stockholders the right to buy additional shares from the company before the stock is offered publicly. *See Also: current, offering, right, rights, rights offering, stock*

PROXIMO. Next month.

PROXY. One person grants another person the right to vote on behalf of the first person in corporate matters. *See Also: right*

PROXY CONTEST. A person or group of people try to gather a sufficient number of proxies from stockholders to swing a corporate vote. *See Also: swing*

PROXY DEPARTMENT. The area of a brokerage firm that distributes financial statements, voting information, and other corporate publications to beneficial owners. The department acts as an intermediary between the issuing company and the beneficial owners, and votes on behalf of those owners. *See Also: firm, intermediary*

PROXY SERVER. A system designed to cache items from other Web servers to fulfill requests, thereby quickening users' access. A proxy server will receive the request from a client application, such as a Web browser, and attempt to fulfill the request locally on its server. If the requested data is not present, it will obtain the data from the remote server where the data resides. *See Also: client, on, proxy, remote, server, Web, Web browser, will*

PROXY STATEMENT. A report a company submits to stockholders that explains issues on which they will be asked to vote at an upcoming meeting.

PRUDENT INVESTMENT-COST STANDARD. A company's value is determined by subtracting the costs incurred through bad investments from the original cost of the company's assets. *See Also: original cost*

PRUDENT MAN RULE. An investment system in which the investor will invest conservatively to receive a stable income with little risk. *See Also: investment, risk*

PSA. Public Securities Association Model. *See Also: model, securities*

PUBLIC CORPORATION. A company that has publicly issued and sold ownership shares of stock. *See Also: stock*

PUBLIC CREDIT. A government's ability to obtain money, through bonds or notes, by promising to repay.

PUBLIC DEBT. Any government debt.

PUBLIC EXCHANGE. An independent or consortium-backed e-marketplace that is open to all qualified buyers and sellers. *See Also: e-marketplace, open*

PUBLIC FINANCING. Any funding received from a government or a government agency. *See Also: funding*

PUBLIC HOUSING AUTHORITY BOND. A long-term municipal debt security that finances low- and middle-income housing projects. *See Also: debt security, security*

PUBLIC KEY ENCRYPTION. A public key system using cryptography that uses two keys, a public key available to all and a secret key that is only available to the recipient. The public key can be used to encrypt data, and the private key is used to decrypt the data, making the data available in the original format or verifying the source of data.

PUBLIC LIMITED PARTNERSHIP. A partnership with shares sold publicly through a broker and registered with the Securities and Exchange Commission. *See Also: broker, commission, exchange, partnership, securities*

PUBLIC MARKET. A securities market with relevant information publicly available. *See Also: market, securities*

PUBLIC OFFERING. A company offers a large number of its shares to the general public for sale. *See Also: sale*

PUBLIC OFFERING PRICE. A company's asking price for its securities during their first public sale. *See Also: sale, securities*

PUBLIC ORDER EXPOSURE SYSTEM. A system through which customers are ensured that their orders are not crossed in-house before they have a chance to hit a better price in the public market. *See Also: hit, market, public market*

PUBLIC OWNERSHIP. The publicly owned portion of a company's stock that is actively traded. *See Also: stock*

PUBLIC SECTOR. The section of the economy that is controlled by the government, as opposed to the private sector which is controlled by corporations and individuals. *See Also: private sector, sector*

PUBLIC SECURITIES ASSOCIATION (PSA) MODEL. The most widely used prepayment model for mortgage-backed securities that describes mortgage prepayment behavior by combining the initial linear increase found in the Constant Prepayment Rate model with its subsequent leveling off at a constant rate. The PSA benchmark assumes the CPR increases linearly from zero over the first 30 months, then levels off at a constant CPR. *See Also: benchmark, CPR, mortgage, prepayment, PSA, securities*

PUBLIC UTILITIES. A publicly or privately owned company that sells electricity, natural gas, telephone service, water, or other utilities. Most utilities operate as monopolies in their respective geographical areas. *See Also: service*

PUBLIC UTILITY BOND. A high-quality, utility-issued debt instrument backed by building or equipment mortgages. *See Also: debt instrument, instrument*

PUBLIC UTILITY HOLDING COMPANY ACT. A law that requires publicly held trading companies involved in either the electrical or the natural gas business to register with the Securities and Exchange Commission. *See Also: commission, exchange, publicly held, register, securities*

PUBLIC UTILITY STOCK. A stable, high-yield, utility-issued equity stock. *See Also: equity, stock*

PUBLICLY HELD. A company with stock shares owned by a large number of people. *See Also: stock*

PUBLICLY TRADED INVESTMENT FUND. Any closed-end investment firm. *See Also: firm, investment*

PUKE. The point at which a short-term trade becomes so unprofitable that the investor is willing to close a trade at any price just to end the misery. The price at which the puking begins is called the puke point. *See Also: close, point, puke point*

PUKE POINT. The actual price at which an investor will puke, or close a trade regardless of price, just to end the misery. *See Also: actual, close, puke, will*

PULL. To cancel a securities order, to increase the offering price, or to lower the bid price. *See Also: bid price, offering, offering price, order, securities*

PULL. A user's request of data from another program or computer. In contrast to push technologies, pull technologies relies on a browser request before the requested information is delivered. *See Also: on, pull*

PULL THE PLUG ON THE MARKET. To cancel supporting bids that were entered just below a leading security's prevailing market price. *See Also: market, market price, supporting*

PUNT. A stock that probably will not bring the holder any profit. *See Also: profit, stock*

PUP. An inactive, low-priced security. *See Also: security*

PURCHASE ACQUISITION. One company pays cash for another company or pays in Treasury stock, with the cost higher than the acquired company's net tangible assets. *See Also: cash, net, stock, Treasury stock*

PURCHASE FUND. A clause in a preferred stock or bond contract that requires the issuer to buy a specific number of shares or bonds each year at a par value price or below. While the issuer is not actually required to make the purchases, the issuer is required to exert the best possible effort to do so. *See Also: bond, contract, par, par value, preferred stock, stock*

PURCHASE GROUP. An underwriting syndicate consisting of an organization of investment bankers that buys new securities issues from the issuer and resells the issues publicly. *See Also: investment, securities, syndicate, underwriting, underwriting syndicate*

PURCHASE OPTION. A rent-to-buy option that gives the renter the option to buy the property or equipment when the lease expires, with some of the rent or lease money going toward the purchase price. *See Also: option, purchase price*

PURCHASE ORDER. A buyer's written permission to a seller to deliver goods or services at a predetermined price.

PURCHASE OUTRIGHT. Paying the purchase price for an item in cash. *See Also: cash, purchase price*

PURCHASE PRICE. The price paid for a particular security. *See Also: security*

PURCHASE-MONEY MORTGAGE. A mortgage that a buyer provides a property seller instead of paying cash for a piece of property. A buyer may provide such a mortgage when he or she is unable to obtain mortgage money and another buyer cannot be found. *See Also: cash, mortgage*

PURCHASING POWER. The amount of goods or services that one unit of money or one unit of an asset can buy. *See Also: asset, unit*

PURCHASING POWER OF THE DOLLAR. The amount of goods or services available for one dollar during a specific time period compared to the amount of goods and services available for one dollar during another time period, with an inflation or deflation factor taken into consideration for each period. *See Also: consideration, deflation, factor, inflation, time*

PURCHASING POWER PARITY. The exchange rate at which one nation's price level equals another nation's price level. *See Also: exchange, exchange rate, level*

PURE PLAY. A company involved in only one line of business or medium, such as a restaurant chain or the Internet, as opposed to a conglomerate, which may be involved in a number of different businesses. *See Also: conglomerate*

PURE PREMIUM. A premium that equals a company's losses divided by exposure and that contains no commissions, taxes, or other fees. *See Also: exposure, premium*

PURPOSE LOAN. Money borrowed to buy, carry, or trade securities that uses other securities as collateral. *See Also: carry, collateral, securities*

PURPOSE STATEMENT. A document a borrower must provide the lender when margin securities are used as collateral for a loan. The document describes the purpose of the loan. *See Also: collateral, margin, securities*

PUSH TECHNOLOGY. In contrast to the traditional Web model of "pull" Web delivery, push technology is an application that automates the delivery of information via computer, pager, cellular telephone or PDA to users. Push technology is often used for time-sensitive information, like stock market updates. *See Also: delivery, market, PDA, stock, stock market, technology, UPDATES, Web*

PUT. Put option. *See Also: option*

PUT A LINE THROUGH IT. A British transaction wherein the buyer and seller mutually agree to cancel, so named because years ago transactions were written on a piece of paper, and putting a line through the deal would cancel it out. *See Also: paper, transaction*

PUT AND CALL BROKER. A broker who trades options contracts and who is not permitted on the stock exchange floor. *See Also: broker, exchange, exchange floor, floor, stock, stock exchange*

PUT BOND. A bond stipulation that allows the holder to redeem the bond at face value at a specific, predetermined time so that if interest rates go up, the holder can avoid losing money as long as the stipulation is operative. *See Also: bond, face value, interest, redeem, time*

PUT INTO PLAY. Rumors are spread and blocks of less than five percent of stock are purchased from a company that potentially could be a takeover target, but is not yet such a target. By doing so, the instigator or purchaser can woo others into buying blocks of the company's stock. *See Also: spread, stock, takeover, target*

PUT OPTION. An agreement that gives the buyer the right to sell a specific quantity of a particular security by a specific date. The option is not obligatory and is traded during its life. The holder hopes the stock will drop in price. *See Also: drop, option, right, security, stock*

PUT OUT A LINE. Occurs when an investor sells a large quantity of stock short over an extended period of time because he or she believes that prices will fall. *See Also: extended, fall, stock, time*

PUT SPREAD. When an investor writes a put option contract and buys a put option on the same underlying security, but with different expiration dates or different exercise prices. *See Also: contract, exercise, expiration, option, option contract, put, put option, security, underlying security*

PUT TO. A put option buyer's right to sell a round-lot share of a specific stock at a particular price to the option writer who sold an option on the stock. *See Also: option, option writer, put, put option, right, share, stock*

PYRAMIDING. An investor increases his or her holdings by using the highest level of available buying power in his or her margin account with both paper and real profits. *See Also: account, buying power, level, margin, margin account, paper*

Q

QQQ. Also referred to as the Q's, an exchange traded fund that comprises the 100 largest NASDAQ non-financial stocks. The Q's is viewed by some as a proxy for big technology stocks. *See Also: exchange, fund, NASDAQ, proxy, technology*

Q-RATIO. Economist James Tobin developed this theory to explain how stock prices affect capital spending and the general economy. The ratio is determined by comparing the market value of a company's physical assets to the amount of money it would take to replace those assets. If the ratio is greater than one, the stock market believes that one dollar of the company's assets is actually worth more than one dollar. *See Also: capital, market, market value, ratio, stock, stock market, take, worth*

Q-TIP TRUST. Represents a Qualified Terminable Interest Property Trust in which one spouse transfers specific asset income to the other spouse until that spouse's death after which the first spouse designates a third person to receive the assets and asset income. *See Also: asset, interest, trust*

Q'S. *See Also: QQQ*

QUALIFIED ACCEPTANCE. A counteroffer.

QUALIFIED EMPLOYEE STOCK OPTIONS. A company program in which its employees can buy stock shares from their company at a specific price within a predetermined time period, after which the offer expires. *See Also: offer, stock, time*

QUALIFIED ENDORSEMENT. A signature that limits an endorser's liability. For example, if Sam cashes Joe's check at the bank with a qualified endorsement and Joe's check bounces, Sam's account will not be debited. *See Also: account, bank, check, liability*

QUALIFIED OPINION. An auditor's opinion that is given with restrictions and limitations because of information that was not available during the audit. For example, if the company has a lawsuit pending against it, the results of that suit could dramatically change the auditing opinion. *See Also: audit, change*

QUALIFIED RETIREMENT PLAN. A private, tax-sheltered retirement plan approved by the Internal Revenue Service. *See Also: Internal Revenue Service*

QUALIFIED TRUST. A tax-deferred plan through which employees can build up a retirement or termination savings chest.

QUALIFYING ANNUITY. A tax-sheltered annuity that can be included in a profit-sharing plan or a retirement plan approved by the Internal Revenue Service. *See Also: annuity, Internal Revenue Service, profit-sharing plan, service*

QUALIFYING COUPON RATE. A Government National Mortgage Association coupon rate that is below the current production rate and therefore is deliverable against the contract. *See Also: contract, coupon, coupon rate, current, current production rate, mortgage, production rate*

QUALIFYING DIVIDEND. A dividend in which $100 can be deducted from an investor's income. *See Also: dividend*

QUALIFYING SHARE. A common stock share that gives a holder the right to be one of the issuing company's directors. *See Also: common stock, right, share, stock*

QUALIFYING UTILITY. A utility with stockholders who can defer taxes by reinvesting a maximum of $750 in dividends back into stock shares. The investors have to pay taxes on the deferred amount only after selling the stock. *See Also: pay, stock, utility*

QUALITATIVE ANALYSIS. A subjective analysis of a security, with the judgment not based on financial information, such as that found on a balance sheet or on an account statement. Instead, the judgment may be based on such issues as labor relations. *See Also: account, account statement, balance, balance sheet, security, statement*

QUALITY CONTROL. An inspection method of making sure a good or service lives up to high quality standards. *See Also: service, standards*

QUALITY OF EARNINGS. A company's additional earnings that come from higher sales instead of from inflation or some other source. During periods of inflation, most companies have low-quality earnings because sales actually drop while the company's asset values increase. *See Also: asset, drop, earnings, inflation*

QUALITY RATING. An evaluation, such as the Standard & Poors and Moody's rating, given to a security, with the grading based on such factors as the issuing company's financial condition, strength, and proven management ability. *See Also: evaluation, security, Standard & Poors*

QUALITY STOCK. A highly graded stock. *See Also: stock*

QUANTITATIVE ANALYSIS. An analysis of a security, with the judgment based on financial information such as that found on a balance sheet or on an income statement. *See Also: balance, balance sheet, income statement, security, statement*

QUARTER STOCK. Any stock with a $25-per-share par value. *See Also: par, par value, stock*

QUARTERLY. A three-month period that acts as a basis for the reporting of earnings or the paying of dividends. *See Also: basis, earnings*

QUARTERLY REPORT. Also referred to as Form 10Q, or 10Q, an unaudited document that is required to be filed quarterly SEC for all U.S. public companies. The report provides financial information and other selected material, such as significant changes or events that have occurred during the quarter.

QUARTILE. Statistics, such as performance gauges or ratios, that are grouped into four equal parts.

QUASI-CORPORATION. Any organization's political subdivision, such as an unincorporated village.

QUASI-MONEY. A bank note, deposit, or other asset that has the properties and characteristics of money. *See Also: asset, bank, note*

QUASI-PUBLIC CORPORATION. A privately owned company such as a non-public utility that provides the public with goods or services with a high degree of public responsibility; it is therefore government-regulated. *See Also: utility*

QUASI-RENT. The total returns from an investment in capital goods if they have no alternative use, or the returns over the alternative use if such a use exists. *See Also: capital, capital goods, investment*

QUASI-REORGANIZATION. A restructuring or reorganization that is undertaken to eliminate a deficit or to avoid bankruptcy, but that does not result in the formation of a new company. *See Also: bankruptcy, deficit, reorganization*

QUICK ASSET. A current asset that can be readily converted into cash. *See Also: asset, cash, current*

QUICK ASSET RATIO. *See Also: Quick Ratio.*

QUICK BUCK. Money made on a short-term investment or from a highly speculative venture. *See Also: investment, speculative*

QUICK RATIO. Also called the "acid ratio," this figure gauges a company's short-term liquidity by dividing its current liabilities into its cash, cash equivalents, and account receivables. *See Also: account, cash, cash equivalents, current, current liabilities, liquidity, ratio, receivables*

QUICK TURN. Occurs when a security is sold immediately after it is purchased, with the investor seeking short-term profits. *See Also: security*

QUID PRO QUO. Occurs when one item of value is traded for another item of the same value, even if that item is intangible, such as research information concerning a specific security. *See Also: security*

QUIET PERIOD. Companies in the midst of a securities offering are required by this SEC rule to avoid self-promotion. Exceptions to this rule include statements in carefully worded government filings, including IPO prospectuses. *See Also: IPO, offering, SEC, securities*

QUIET PERIOD. The 90 days, as required by the Securities and Exchange Commission, between an issuer's first public offering and the first time underwriters distribute research information about the issuing company. The purpose of the quiet period is to make sure that traders do not try to influence investors because the trader has a beneficial interest in the offering's secondary market. *See Also: beneficial interest, commission, exchange, interest, market, offering, public offering, quiet period, secondary market, securities, time, trader*

QUIET TITLE SUIT. A lawsuit or legal maneuver designed to remove a questionable claim filed against a property's title. *See Also: legal*

QUO WARRANTO. A lawsuit designed to determine who is in power or in charge of a corporation, or to test the authority of that person. *See Also: corporation, test*

QUOTATION. A figure that reflects a security's current transaction, bid, or ask price. *See Also: ask, current, transaction*

QUOTATION BOARD. A security's exchange board that displays a security's daily market prices, ticker symbol, transaction price, and the number of shares traded. *See Also: exchange, market, symbol, transaction*

QUOTATION TICKER. An exchange's ticker tape that displays transaction prices. *See Also: tape, ticker tape, transaction*

QUOTE MACHINE. An electronic system that provides transaction prices for securities. *See Also: securities, transaction*

QUOTE WIRE. An electronic connection between a brokerage house and the New York Stock Exchange that carries a listed security's highest bid and lowest offer prices. *See Also: brokerage house, exchange, house, New York Stock Exchange, offer, stock, stock exchange*

QUOTED PRICE. The last transaction price of any stock, bond, or commodity. *See Also: bond, commodity, stock, transaction*

R

R-SQUARED. The way in which a percentage of a portfolio's total returns represents the portfolio's beta measure. *See Also: beta*

RACKETEER INFLUENCED AND CORRUPT ORGANIZATION ACT (RICO). A federal law outlawing participation in organized crime, racketeering activities, and securities fraud. *See Also: securities*

RADAR ALERT. When a specific security is closely monitored to see if large chunks are being accumulated in a takeover attempt. If it is, company officials are notified immediately so they can take defensive steps. *See Also: security, take, takeover*

RAG STOCK. A security with a low price. *See Also: low, security*

RAID. A manipulative move to drive stock prices down. *See Also: drive, stock*

RAIDER. A person or company that is trying to buy a controlling interest in another company in an effort to take that company over. *See Also: controlling interest, interest, take*

RALLY. A sharp rise in the general level of the market, commodity futures, or a security's price after a period of a downward or sideways movement. *See Also: commodity, futures, level, market, movement*

RANDOM WALK. The path of stock prices, in that past prices cannot always be used to determine future prices because of the many and varied influences that can affect the prices. *See Also: stock*

RANGE. All of the prices that fall between a highest and lowest price during a specific time period. *See Also: fall, time*

RANGE FORWARD CONTRACTS. A forward exchange agreement designed to limit the downside currency risk and protect the upside profit potential. It allows the customer to choose either end of a currency range as well as the contract's expiration date, with the issuer choosing the other end of the currency range. *See Also: currency, exchange, expiration, expiration date, forward, limit, profit, range, risk, upside*

RANKING. Rating a security's performance during a specific time period, comparing it to the performance of other securities rated during the same time. *See Also: securities, time*

RAPID AMORTIZATION. A method for the owner of an asset to write off its cost for short-term tax savings. *See Also: asset, write*

RATABLE DISTRIBUTION. Occurs when the assets of an estate are distributed proportionally to all heirs. *See Also: estate*

RATE BASE. The base value that a regulatory panel establishes for a utility to determine the utility's allowed rate of return. The panel bases the value on the utility's operating costs. *See Also: base, operating costs, rate of return, return, utility*

RATE COVENANT. A municipal revenue bond with the provision that rates will be adjusted for the facility's use, so that revenues can provide maintenance, repairs, and bond debt service. *See Also: bond, debt service, maintenance, municipal revenue bond, revenue bond, service*

RATE OF RETURN. The rate of return is determined by dividing stockholders' equity into net income. This produces a security's yearly after tax profit, expressed as a percentage of the original capital investment, and serves as a measure of a company's profitability. *See Also: after tax, capital, equity, investment, net, net income, profit, profitability, return*

RATE REOPENER. Long-term financing with an interest rate that is adjusted every three to five years. In addition, the issuer is allowed to terminate the loan for a premium each time. *See Also: interest, interest rate, premium, time*

RATING OF SECURITIES. The determination of an issuing company's financial strength and stability, based on the company's management ability, debts, and payment history.

RATIO. The comparison of different financial variables and their relationship to one another.

RATIO ANALYSIS. Studying, interpreting, and comparing different financial ratios. *See Also: financial ratios*

RATIO BULL SPREAD. A call option spread with one long call option and two short call options all on the same underlying stock and with the same expiration date, but with the long call having a lower striking price. *See Also: call option, expiration, expiration date, long call, option, option spread, short call, spread, stock, striking price*

RATIO OF ACCOUNTS PAYABLE TO PURCHASES. Determines whether obligations are paid on time during one period compared to another period. *See Also: time*

RATIO OF CAPITAL TO FIXED ASSETS. Determines how long it probably will take to convert an owner's investments into fixed assets. *See Also: take*

RATIO OF COLLATERAL TO DEBT. Determines how effectively a stock margin can be achieved. *See Also: margin, stock*

RATIO OF FINISHED GOODS INVENTORY TO THE COST OF GOODS SOLD. Determines sales stability to gauge inventory turnover. This is measured by dividing the cost of goods sold by the average finished goods' inventory. *See Also: average, cost of goods sold, inventory, inventory turnover, turnover*

RATIO SCALE. A graph with the percentage difference between two prices that cover the same vertical distance.

RATIO SPREADING. Simultaneously buying one number of option contracts and selling a different number of option contracts on the same underlying security. *See Also: option, security, underlying security*

RATIO WRITER. When an owner of an underlying security writes more call option contracts than he or she actually could cover if they all were called. *See Also: call option, option, security, underlying security*

RE-INTERMEDIATION. While many e-marketplaces seek to disintermediate traditional channels, others are reintermediating, or bringing the traditional channels into the buying and selling process.

REACH BACK. An improper benefit through which a tax shelter, such as a limited partnership, can offer year-end deductions that cover the entire year-to-date, thus reaching back over the year. For example, an investor who entered a partnership in November could claim the partnership expense deductions for the entire year. *See Also: expense, limited partnership, offer, partnership*

REACH THROUGH. A broker carelessly enters a price quotation into the Intermarket Trading System (ITS) that falls below the best quote for that security. The ITS will reject the broker's quote. *See Also: broker, intermarket, intermarket trading system (ITS), quotation, security*

REACQUIRED STOCK. Stock shares that a company has issued to stockholders and then bought back.

REACTION. Occurs when a security's price changes directions, then stabilizes, usually following a lengthy and strong up or down price movement. *See Also: movement*

READING THE TAPE. An investor can determine a stock's price performance by reading the prices on a stock exchange's ticker tape. The investor can then judge whether the stock's price will go up or down. *See Also: stock, tape, ticker tape*

READY TRANSFERABILITY. The holder of a publicly traded security can sell or give away the security without the issuer's permission. *See Also: security*

REAL ACCOUNTS. Accounts with balances that are carried over to the next fiscal period instead of being canceled. Liabilities, for example, would be included in a real account. *See Also: account*

REAL CAPITAL. Equipment or machinery that is used in a company's production.

REAL EARNINGS. Income that has been adjusted to eliminate any effects from price changes.

REAL ESTATE. Any piece of land and all buildings and physical characteristics that are attached to it.

REAL ESTATE APPRECIATION NOTE. The loan a company takes out using real estate as collateral, with the loan carrying a fixed interest rate as well as the underlying property's accrued appreciation. *See Also: appreciation, collateral, estate, fixed interest rate, interest, interest rate, real estate*

REAL ESTATE INVESTMENT TRUST (REIT). A closed-end investment firm that deals in real estate investing. *See Also: estate, firm, investment, real estate*

REAL ESTATE LIMITED PARTNERSHIP. A public investment program that must be registered with the Securities and Exchange Commission. *See Also: commission, exchange, investment, securities*

REAL ESTATE LOAN. A loan with real estate used as collateral. *See Also: collateral, estate, real estate*

REAL ESTATE MORTGAGE INVESTMENT CONDUIT (REMIC). A vehicle which may be structured as corporations, partnerships, trusts, or a segregated pool of assets. This vehicle, created under the Tax Reform Act of 1986, not subject to taxation at the issuer level if it is in compliance with the requirements of the Act. This entity can hold the mortgages of any type of real property and issue multiple classes of ownership interests in the form of pass-through certificates, bonds, or other legal forms. *See Also: hold, issue, legal, level, pool*

REAL ESTATE OWNED. All bank-owned property except that taken in consideration of a defaulted loan. *See Also: consideration*

REAL ESTATE SETTLEMENT PROCEDURES ACT. A federal law that covers the costs involved with loan closings as well as property settlement activities. For example, the law requires lenders to disclose the actual closing costs and the land's previous selling price. *See Also: actual, closing costs*

REAL ESTATE SETTLEMENT PROCEDURES ACT AMENDMENTS. A federal amendment that slightly altered the previous procedures act. For example, the amendment says a lender can give a borrower a good faith estimate of the closing costs instead of the actual charges, and the lender does not have to disclose the land's previous selling price. *See Also: actual, closing costs*

REAL ESTATE SOLD ON CONTRACT. Occurs when the property buyer does not have enough of a down payment to take title to the property. The contract stipulates that, when the loan balance is reduced to a certain level, the buyer can refinance the property and take title to it. *See Also: balance, contract, level, take*

REAL INCOME. One person's purchasing power, or his or her income as adjusted for the rate of inflation. *See Also: inflation, purchasing power*

REAL INTEREST RATE. An interest rate from which the inflation rate has been subtracted. *See Also: inflation, inflation rate, interest, interest rate*

REAL INVESTMENT. An expense that creates a new capital asset. *See Also: asset, capital, capital asset, expense*

REAL MONEY. Coins that contain intrinsic value, as opposed to paper currency. *See Also: currency, intrinsic value, paper*

REAL PROPERTY TRANSACTION. When credit is extended because an interest in a piece of property will be used as collateral. *See Also: collateral, credit, extended, interest*

REAL RETURN. A return that has been adjusted for inflation. *See Also: inflation, return*

REAL STOCK. A long stock position versus a short position. *See Also: long stock, position, short position, stock*

REAL TERMS. A measure of the degree to which inflation has affected purchasing power. *See Also: inflation, purchasing power*

REAL TIME. Tasks that are time critical, and the response is immediate. For example, real-time quotes contain the most current listing of prices for stocks. *See Also: current, listing, time*

REAL-TIME CHAT. A live conversation between two or more individuals by writing messages online. Internet Relay Chat (IRC) is one program that facilitates real time chat. *See Also: online, real time, time*

REAL-TIME TRADE REPORTING. A requirement by NASDAQ imposed on market makers and other parties that maintain markets in NASDAQ-traded securities to report each trade immediately after execution. *See Also: execution, market, NASDAQ, on, securities*

REALIZATION ACCOUNT. A consolidated account summarizing all of the accounts of a company that is going out of business. The account reflects assets that are reduced to cash or applied to reduce the company's liabilities. *See Also: account, cash*

REALIZE. An investor's actual cash profit or loss, as opposed to a paper profit or loss. *See Also: actual, cash, paper, paper profit, profit*

REALIZED YIELD. The bond's return based on its original purchase price. *See Also: purchase price, return*

REALIZING. The repurchasing of a short sale, or any profiting from a liquidation sale. *See Also: liquidation, sale, short sale*

REALLOWANCE. Occurs when an underwriting syndicate allows members of the National Association of Securities Dealers to receive a sales commission for shares sold to the members' clients. *See Also: commission, securities, syndicate, underwriting, underwriting syndicate*

REALTOR. A real estate broker who belongs to a National Association of Realtors board. *See Also: broker, estate, real estate*

REAPPRAISAL. The second appraisal of a piece of property. *See Also: appraisal*

REASSESSMENT. The changing of a property's base value, usually as the result of a reappraisal. *See Also: appraisal, base, reappraisal*

REBATE. The return of a portion of money that has been paid. For example, a return of unearned interest to a borrower if the loan is paid off before maturity. *See Also: interest, maturity, return, unearned interest*

RECAPITALIZATION. When a company changes its financial structure (an exchange of bonds for stock, or bonds for another type of bond, for example). Companies often perform a recapitalization in the event of a bankruptcy or when a healthy company is seeking to improve its tax situation. *See Also: bankruptcy, bond, exchange, financial structure, stock*

RECAPITALIZATION SURPLUS. Occurs when a stock's par value is reduced and bonds are exchanged for securities that have a lower value. *See Also: par, par value, securities*

RECAPTURE. A contract stipulation that permits one person to at least partially retrieve asset ownership. For example, a contractor may be able to take a percentage of a development's profits. *See Also: asset, contract, take*

RECASTING A MORTGAGE. Changing a mortgage by altering its principal amount, interest rate, or maturity. *See Also: interest, interest rate, maturity, mortgage, principal, principal amount*

RECEDING MARKET. A period when the market's prices are dropping.

RECEIVABLES. Accounts receivable.

RECEIVABLES TURNOVER. A company can gauge the quality of its account receivables by comparing its net sales to the receivables' current value, which provides a ratio that helps the company determine the length of time that the receivables may remain outstanding. *See Also: account, current, net, net sales, outstanding, ratio, receivables, time*

RECEIVE VERSUS PAYMENT. A buyer pays the seller in cash for a security when that security is delivered. *See Also: cash, security*

RECEIVER. A court-appointed person who oversees a company that is going through bankruptcy. *See Also: bankruptcy*

RECEIVER'S CERTIFICATE. A document that represents the securities of a company that has gone through a receivership, which is similar to bankruptcy. Holders can publicly trade their receiver's certificates on the open market. *See Also: bankruptcy, market, open, open market, receivership, securities*

RECEIVERS' AND TRUSTEES' SECURITIES. The debt securities a court-appointed trustee issues. *See Also: securities, trustee*

RECEIVERSHIP. A form of bankruptcy in which a company can avoid liquidation. The company reorganizes with the help of a court-appointed trustee who helps to resolve the company's financial troubles. *See Also: bankruptcy, liquidation, trustee*

RECESSION. Occurs when a nation's living standards drop and prices increase. This downturn in economic activity is widely defined as a decline in a country's gross national product for at least two quarters. *See Also: activity, downturn, drop, gross, standards*

RECIPROCAL BUSINESS. One investor wants to buy or sell securities in a deal with a person who later will enter another deal with the investor. *See Also: securities*

RECLAIM. A security certificate is recovered after a flaw was found and corrected. *See Also: certificate, security*

RECLAMATION. In a securities transaction, the right to return a security or recover losses as a result of bad delivery or other irregularities in the settlement process. *See Also: bad delivery, delivery, return, right, securities, security, transaction*

RECLASSIFICATION OF STOCK. Occurs when a company changes its capital structure. *See Also: capital, capital structure*

RECOGNIZANCE. The recording of a former debt.

RECONVEYANCE. Occurs when a property title is transferred back to its original owner.

RECORD DATE. The date an investor must be registered with the issuing company as a security's owner of record to receive dividends or other ownership privileges. *See Also: owner of record*

RECORDATION. A written acknowledgment that a lien exists against a piece of property.

RECORDS OF ORIGINAL ENTRY. A record of all cash receipts and expenses, with entries recorded before they are made in the general ledger. *See Also: cash, general ledger, ledger*

RECOURSE. The right of a person who owns a negotiable instrument to insist that the former endorser make good on the instrument if the acceptor has refused to honor it. For example, if one person wrote a check to another person and the bank refused to honor the check, the first person, through recourse, can force the second person to honor the check. *See Also: bank, check, instrument, negotiable, negotiable instrument, right*

RECOURSE LOAN. A loan taken out by a partnership or other concern carrying the provision that if the borrower defaults, the lender can not only take the collateral, but also some of the partners' personal assets. *See Also: collateral, partnership, take*

RECOVERY. A period in which securities prices are climbing steadily after a period in which they dropped or were inactive. *See Also: securities*

RECOVERY RATE. The market price of bonds following a company's default on the bonds. This is expressed as a percentage of par or, similarly, cents on the dollar. *See Also: default, market, market price, on, par*

RECURRING CHARGES. Fees that continue regularly.

RED HERRING. A preliminary prospectus which explains that the prospectus is incomplete. Its name comes from the red print on the front page of some copies. *See Also: name, preliminary prospectus, print, prospectus*

REDEEM. The issuing company repurchases a bond at maturity by paying the holder its face value. *See Also: bond, face value, maturity*

REDEEMABLE BOND. A bond that the issuing company can buy back before maturity, usually by paying the holder a premium. *See Also: bond, maturity, premium*

REDEEMABLE STOCK. Any preferred stock that the issuing company can call in for redemption. *See Also: preferred stock, redemption, stock*

REDEMPTION. When a security's issuer repurchases the security. *See Also: security*

REDEMPTION FUND. A fund used to retire a debt. *See Also: fund, retire*

REDEMPTION NOTICE. A document that tells stockholders whose securities are being called in with the time and terms through which their securities will be redeemed. *See Also: securities, time*

REDEMPTION PERIOD. The time period that a debtor can buy back a piece of property by paying the total amount due on a foreclosed mortgage. *See Also: mortgage, time*

REDEMPTION PRICE. The price at which a bond can be redeemed before maturity or the price at which the shares from a mutual fund can be redeemed. *See Also: bond, fund, maturity, mutual fund*

REDEMPTION RIGHT. The right of a person who has defaulted on a mortgage to buy his or her property back after the court judgment. *See Also: mortgage, right*

REDEMPTION VALUE. The total amount that a security can be redeemed for. *See Also: security*

REDISCOUNT. When a bank that is a member of the Federal Reserve System uses a customer's pledged collateral as collateral for a loan the bank takes out from the Federal Reserve. *See Also: bank, collateral, Federal Reserve System, reserve*

REDLINING. The improper practice of some financial institutions to refuse to make home improvement loans or mortgages in a financially depressed area. The practice is called redlining because the institution may use a red marker to outline the area on a map. *See Also: home*

REDUCIBLE RATE BOND. A bond on which the issuer can reduce the interest rate and call premium. *See Also: bond, interest, interest rate, premium*

REFERENCE CURRENCY. Any cash that is used to pay bondholders. *See Also: cash, pay*

REFINANCING. An issuer sells new bonds at lower interest rates to raise money to pay off an older debt that had a higher interest rate. *See Also: interest, interest rate, pay*

REFLEX RALLY. A price correction from an oversold condition. The security's price moves up, but does not change the price's established trend. *See Also: change, correction, oversold, trend*

REFLEX REACTION. A price correction from an overbought condition. The security's price drops, but does not change the price's established trend. *See Also: change, correction, overbought, trend*

REFUNDING. When the proceeds of a security's sale are used to pay off the issuing company's existing debt securities. *See Also: pay, proceeds, sale, securities*

REFUNDING MORTGAGE. A mortgage loan that is refinanced with another loan. *See Also: mortgage*

REG FD. A Securities and Exchange Commission rule that seeks to provide all investors with equal access to material financial information. For example, if a company releases potentially market-moving information, the company cannot selectively disclose the information to certain analysts or big investors before releasing it to the public. Reg FD is short for Regulation Fair Disclosure. *See Also: commission, disclosure, exchange, securities*

REGIONAL BANK. A bank that operates in a specific area of the country, as opposed to a money center bank which operates at least nationally. *See Also: bank, money center bank*

REGIONAL FUND. A mutual fund with investments concentrated in companies located in a specific area of the country, such as Texas oil or Idaho potato products. *See Also: fund, mutual fund*

REGIONAL STOCK EXCHANGE. A national stock exchange located outside of New York City, such as the Philadelphia Stock Exchange, that lists securities that often are not listed elsewhere. *See Also: City, exchange, Philadelphia Stock Exchange, securities, stock, stock exchange*

REGISTER. To formally record.

REGISTERED AS TO INTEREST ONLY. Bonds with interest that are sent directly to the registered holder, with the face value payable only to the bearer. *See Also: bearer, face value, interest, registered holder, with interest*

REGISTERED AS TO PRINCIPAL ONLY. A coupon bond with its face value payable only to the registered holder at maturity. *See Also: bond, coupon, coupon bond, face value, maturity, registered holder*

REGISTERED BOND. A bond registered in the owner's name and payable only to that owner, as opposed to a bearer bond. *See Also: bearer, bearer bond, bond, name*

REGISTERED CHECK. A check that a bank issues on behalf of a customer who sets aside special funds for the check. For example, a bank-issued cashier's check or a money order would be considered a registered check. *See Also: bank, check, order*

REGISTERED COMPANY. A company registered with and regulated by the Securities and Exchange Commission. *See Also: commission, exchange, securities*

REGISTERED COMPETITIVE MARKET MAKER. A New York Stock Exchange floor broker who can make transactions with his or her own firm as well as for other brokerage firms, and who, upon request, must make a bid or offer on a security to maintain a fair market. *See Also: broker, exchange, exchange floor, firm, floor, floor broker, market, New York Stock Exchange, offer, security, stock, stock exchange*

REGISTERED COMPETITIVE TRADER. A New York Stock Exchange member who can trade for his or her own account, but 75 percent of his or her transactions must be stabilizing, which means they cannot be higher or lower than the last transaction's price. *See Also: account, exchange, New York Stock Exchange, stock, stock exchange*

REGISTERED COUPON BOND. A bond registered in the owner's name, but with interest coupons paid only by delivering the coupon to a disbursing agent. *See Also: agent, bond, coupon, disbursing agent, interest, name, with interest*

REGISTERED EQUITY MARKET MAKER. A competitive market maker on the American Stock Exchange. *See Also: exchange, maker, market, market maker, stock, stock exchange*

REGISTERED EXCHANGE. A securities exchange governed by the Securities and Exchange Commission, or a commodities exchange governed by the Commodities Exchange Commission. *See Also: commission, exchange, securities*

REGISTERED FORM. A document issued in the owner's name and payable only to that owner. *See Also: name*

REGISTERED HOLDER. The name that is recorded on the books of the issuer or on the books of the paying agent. Regardless of beneficial ownership on the record date, principal and interest payments are advanced to the registered holder. *See Also: agent, and interest, interest, name, paying agent, principal, record date*

REGISTERED HOME OWNERSHIP SAVINGS PLAN. A Canadian savings account in which a person can deposit up to $1,000 a year, to a total of $10,000, in tax-deductible income as long as the money eventually is used to buy a home. *See Also: account, home, savings account*

REGISTERED INVESTMENT COMPANY. An investment company that is certified by the Securities and Exchange Commission. *See Also: commission, exchange, investment, investment company, securities*

REGISTERED OPTIONS PRINCIPAL. An employee of an exchange-member firm who handles the options transactions of the member firm's customers. *See Also: firm*

REGISTERED OPTIONS TRADER. An American Stock Exchange specialist who deals in several of the exchange's options contracts and who must maintain a fair market in those options. *See Also: exchange, market, specialist, stock, stock exchange*

REGISTERED OVER-THE-COUNTER STOCK. An unlisted security that can be traded in a margin account. *See Also: account, margin, margin account, security*

REGISTERED REPRESENTATIVE. An employee of a stock exchange broker-dealer who advises and trades customers' accounts while generating commissions. *See Also: broker-dealer, exchange, stock, stock exchange*

REGISTERED REPRESENTATIVE RAPID RESPONSE PROGRAM. A New York Stock Exchange Communications computer through which member firms can quote execution prices to their customers without having to wait for the exchange floor to confirm the trade. *See Also: exchange, exchange floor, execution, floor, New York Stock Exchange, stock, stock exchange*

REGISTERED RETIREMENT SAVINGS PLAN. A Canadian retirement plan in which a person can deduct either $5,500 or 20 percent of his or her annual taxable income each year and deposit the amount in a bank account or mutual fund. *See Also: account, bank, fund, mutual fund, taxable income*

REGISTERED SECONDARY. A security sold by its owner, who is registered with the Securities and Exchange Commission, with a prospectus issued. The sale may perhaps be part of a primary secondary offering. *See Also: commission, exchange, offering, prospectus, sale, securities, security*

REGISTERED SECURITY. A security that was recorded with its issuer. *See Also: security*

REGISTERED TRADER. An exchange member who can trade on the exchange floor for his or her own account and whose transactions must meet certain requirements. *See Also: account, exchange, exchange floor, floor*

REGISTRAR. A person who keeps a bank's or a company's financial books and who oversees stock certificates. *See Also: stock*

REGISTRATION. A procedure through which the Securities and Exchange Commission must review and approve publicly traded securities before they can be publicly sold. *See Also: commission, exchange, securities*

REGISTRATION FEE. A Securities and Exchange Commission fee charged on a public securities offering. *See Also: commission, exchange, offering, securities, Securities and Exchange Commission Fee*

REGISTRATION STATEMENT. A document that spells out a company's public securities sales. The document must be filed with the Securities and Exchange Commission. *See Also: commission, exchange, securities*

REGRESSION ANALYSIS. A method of comparing two investment variables to determine an independent variable's impact on a dependent variable, with the end result providing a prediction on future performance. For example, a computer manufacturer may determine what effect a population burst will have on the manufacturer's business. *See Also: investment*

REGRESSIVE TAX. A tax system in which a community's taxes will drop as the community's tax base increases. *See Also: base, drop, tax base*

REGULAR DIVIDEND. The dividend rate that the issuing company's board of directors sets. *See Also: board of directors, dividend*

REGULAR LOT. A normal security or commodity trading unit. *See Also: commodity, security, trading unit, unit*

REGULAR SPECIALIST. A stock exchange member who must maintain a fair and orderly market in a group of specific stocks by accepting orders from other members by buying and selling for his or her own account *See Also: exchange, market, stock, stock exchange*

REGULAR-WAY DELIVERY (SETTLEMENT). A securities transaction in which the selling broker delivers the security to the buying broker, who in turn pays the selling broker within five business days after the transaction transpires. Other securities such as governments, options, and money market funds settle on the next business day. *See Also: broker, business day, governments, market, money market, securities, security, settle, transaction, turn*

REGULAR-WAY SALE. Any sale that is not a short sale. *See Also: sale, short sale*

REGULARITY OF DIVIDENDS. A company's pattern of paying dividends may be used as a gauge for investors to determine a wise investment. *See Also: investment*

REGULATED COMMODITIES. Commodities that the Commodities Futures Trading Commission governs and regulates. *See Also: commission, Commodities Futures Trading Commission (CFTC), futures*

REGULATED INVESTMENT COMPANY. A company that invests money for other people. The company issues and publicly sells stock shares, then invests the proceeds. *See Also: proceeds, stock*

REGULATION. A Securities offerings between $50,000 and $300,000 must file a prospectus, though a less-detailed one than is required from an offering of more than $300,000. *See Also: offering, prospectus*

REGULATION D. A private placement issue that is sold by the issuer directly to investors. The underwriter is not used for this type of transaction. Although the size of the issue is not limited, the sale is restricted to a maximum of 35 nonaccredited investors. *See Also: issue, placement, private placement, sale, size, transaction*

REGULATION G. Regulates the amount of credit that can be extended for buying securities in some situations that otherwise are unregulated. *See Also: credit, extended, securities*

REGULATION Q. A Federal Reserve System ceiling on the interest rates that banks pay. *See Also: Federal Reserve System, interest, pay, reserve*

REGULATION T. Regulates the amount of credit that brokers or dealers can extend to customers who want to buy securities. *See Also: credit, securities*

REGULATION T CALL. A brokerage firm's margin call. *See Also: margin, margin call*

REGULATION T EXCESS. The amount of credit a broker-dealer can extend to a margin account customer above the amount of credit the customer already is using. *See Also: account, broker-dealer, credit, margin, margin account*

REGULATION U. Regulates the amount of credit a bank can extend to customers who want to buy securities. *See Also: bank, credit, securities*

REGULATION W. Regulates commercial credit concerning loan maturities and down payments for consumer products, such as cars and expensive appliances. *See Also: commercial credit, credit*

REGULATION X. Regulates the type and amount of credit extended to people for buying, carrying, or trading securities. *See Also: credit, extended, securities*

REGULATION Z. Regulates, oversees, and enforces the Truth in Lending Act, which covers disclosure requirements. *See Also: disclosure, Truth in Lending Act*

REHYPOTHECATION. When a stockbroker uses the securities from a client's margin account as collateral for a bank loan to finance the debit balance in the client's account. *See Also: account, balance, bank, collateral, debit, margin, margin account, securities, stockbroker*

REINVESTMENT. When dividends and capital gains are put back into buying more shares. *See Also: capital, put*

REINVESTMENT PRIVILEGE. The right of mutual fund investors to have their dividend payments automatically put back into additional mutual fund shares. *See Also: dividend, fund, mutual fund, put, right*

REINVESTMENT RATE. The rate of return achieved through reinvesting the proceeds from the sale of a fixed-income investment. *See Also: fixed-income investment, investment, proceeds, rate of return, return, sale*

REINVESTMENT RISK. Because a bond's yield to maturity is based on the reinvestment of interest, reinvestment risk is the risk that an investor will not reinvest coupon payments below the calculated yield to maturity. *See Also: coupon, interest, maturity, reinvestment, risk, yield, yield to maturity*

REIT. Real Estate Investment Trust. *See Also: estate, investment, investment trust, real estate, trust*

REJECTION. A buyer's refusal to accept delivery of a security. *See Also: delivery, security*

RELATIONSHIP TRADING. Basis trading in which an investor hedges by taking advantage of unusual price movements. The investor will buy or sell securities while simultaneously taking the opposite position with options contracts. *See Also: position, securities*

RELATIVE PRIORITY. Occurs in a reorganization when creditors take losses in inverse proportion to their seniority. *See Also: reorganization, take*

RELATIVE STRENGTH. A security's market performance compared to other securities in its industry. *See Also: industry, market, securities*

RELATIVE VALUE. The value comparison of one security or commodity to another. *See Also: commodity, security*

RELEASE CLAUSE. A stipulation in a mortgage contract that frees a portion of the covered property after a percentage of the mortgage is paid. *See Also: contract, mortgage*

RELEASE LETTER. A document that a syndicate manager sends to other syndicate members with details of the offering. *See Also: manager, offering, syndicate, syndicate manager*

RELEASE OF PREMIUMS ON FUNDED DEBTS. Occurs when a portion of the sale premium is credited to income each fiscal period, based on a comparison of the fiscal period to a security's maturities. *See Also: premium, sale*

RELIEF SPECIALIST. An exchange member who can take over for a regular specialist if such a need should arise. *See Also: exchange, regular specialist, specialist, take*

RELOAD OPTION. An option to buy company stock, granted with the provision that, upon exercise, if the exercise price is paid in previously owned shares, a new option is automatically granted for the number of shares used in the exercise. *See Also: exercise, exercise price, option, stock*

RELOADER. A person who can sell additional securities to an investor who wanted to buy only a smaller, more limited number. *See Also: securities*

REMAINDER BENEFICIARY. A trust beneficiary who can immediately receive the principal after the earlier beneficiary has ended his or her interest. *See Also: interest, principal, trust*

REMAINDER ESTATE. Occurs when one grant simultaneously creates two or more estates. The interest on each estate depends on and remains after the other estates have ended. *See Also: estate, interest*

REMAINDER MEN. The final trust or estate beneficiaries. *See Also: estate, trust*

REMARGINING. When an investor puts up additional securities or money because the equity in his or her margin account has fallen below accepted levels. *See Also: account, equity, margin, margin account, securities*

REMARKETED PREFERRED STOCK. A preferred stock with a dividend rate that is reset to a new level by a remarketing agent, or redistributor, at the end of each dividend period. The new rate is subject to certain restraints, usually relative to commercial paper rates. The dividend payments and periods in an issue also may change in order to meet issuer and investor needs. *See Also: agent, change, commercial paper, dividend, issue, level, order, paper, preferred stock, stock*

REMIC. Real Estate Mortgage Investment Conduit. *See Also: estate, investment, mortgage, real estate*

REMIT. To pay for goods or services. *See Also: pay*

REMOTE. Resources or devices that a user accesses via a network, directly connected to the users computer.

REMOTE ACCESS. The ability to access a network from a location other than a user's local access point. *See Also: local, point*

RENEGOTIABLE RATE MORTGAGE. A 20- to 30-year real estate loan with interest rates fixed for three to five years, after which the interest rate is changed according to the average national mortgage rate. *See Also: average, estate, interest, interest rate, mortgage, real estate, real estate loan, with interest*

RENTES. Austrian, Italian, or French bonds and the annual interest payment on those bonds. *See Also: interest*

RENTIER. A person who lives on fixed-investment income.

REOPEN AN ISSUE. Occurs when the Treasury sells more outstanding shares of an old government security at prevailing prices with the same conditions. *See Also: outstanding, security*

REORGANIZATION. A form of involuntary bankruptcy in which the company can avoid liquidation. The company's financial structure changes and its management is replaced by a court-appointed trustee, who tries to solve the company's financial troubles. *See Also: bankruptcy, financial structure, liquidation, trustee*

REORGANIZATION BOND. A bond that a company issues to raise much needed capital while it is going through the process of bankruptcy reorganization. *See Also: bankruptcy, bond, capital, reorganization*

REORGANIZATION DEPARTMENT. The cashiering area where one security can be exchanged for another. Rights can be executed and tender offers can be transacted. *See Also: rights, security, tender*

REPATRIATION. Occurs when a person's or a company's assets are returned from a foreign country to that person's or company's home country. *See Also: home*

REPEAT PRICES OMITTED. A consolidated tape designation that appears when the tape is late and therefore only a security's first transaction price is printed instead of all of the security's transaction prices. *See Also: consolidated tape, tape, tape is late, transaction*

REPLACEMENT COST ACCOUNTING. An accounting method in which the difference between an asset's original cost and the current replacement cost can be further depreciated. *See Also: current, original cost*

REPORTING LIMIT. The number of futures contracts in which an investor can hold a position before he or she must report that position to the commodities exchange. *See Also: exchange, futures, hold, position*

REPRESENTATIONS AND WARRANTIES. Legal opinions and performance guarantees in a contract, with the signing attorney responsible for backing the contract. *See Also: contract*

REPRESENTATIVE BID AND ASK PRICES. An old system used by the National Association of Securities Dealers Automated Quotation in which the median bid and median offer prices were quoted. *See Also: offer, quotation, securities*

REPRESENTATIVE MONEY. Money that is fully backed by a commodity or by a monetary metal, such as gold or silver. *See Also: commodity*

REPURCHASE. A security's issuer buys back shares.

REPURCHASE AGREEMENT. An agreement in which an investor sells an investment to another investor with the provision that the first investor can buy it back for a specific price by a specific date. *See Also: investment*

REQUEST FOR A REPORT. An investor's inquiry to a brokerage house on the status of a securities order. *See Also: brokerage house, house, order, securities*

REQUEST FOR INFORMATION. Also referred to as RFI, a preliminary step to a request for proposal (RFP) in which a company solicits potential vendors for information about their products and services

REQUEST FOR PROPOSALS. Also referred to as RFP, an invitation by a company to suppliers to bid on products or services. *See Also: on*

REQUEST FOR QUOTATION. Also referred to as RFQ, an invitation by a company to suppliers to bid on supplying easily described products or services. *See Also: on*

REQUIRED RATE OF RETURN. The rate of return an investor must reach on an investment to keep the systematic risk from pushing the investment's value down. *See Also: investment, rate of return, return, risk, systematic risk*

REQUIRED RETURN. The lowest return an investment needs to become profitable. *See Also: investment, return*

REQUISITIONIST. A person or group of people who want to take over a company's management. *See Also: take*

RESCIND. To cancel an offer or a contract. *See Also: contract, offer*

RESEARCH AND DEVELOPMENT. A company's department or branch that seeks new, more efficient ways to conduct its business or improve its goods or services. Normally, the more money a company invests in research and development, the faster the company grows.

RESEARCH AND DEVELOPMENT LIMITED PARTNERSHIP. An investment through which investors can finance a research and development venture and, in turn, receive a percentage of any new development's profits. *See Also: investment, research and development, turn*

RESEARCH DEPARTMENT. The department in a financial institution or brokerage house that analyzes securities and commodities and makes predictions on future movements. *See Also: brokerage house, house, securities*

RESERVE. Capital that is set aside to take care of future losses or demands. *See Also: take*

RESERVE BANK. A bank that is a member of the Federal Reserve System. *See Also: bank, Federal Reserve System, reserve*

RESERVE CITY BANK. A Federal Reserve member bank in a city that has a Federal Reserve District bank or branch. *See Also: bank, City, member bank, reserve*

RESERVE FOR RETIREMENT OF SINKING FUND BONDS. A fund set aside so the issuer will have enough money by a certain date to redeem outstanding bonds. *See Also: fund, outstanding, redeem*

RESERVE FUND. A cash or a liquid asset created to meet an upcoming expense. *See Also: asset, cash, expense, liquid*

RESERVE PRICE. The minimal price at which a seller will sell an item. Reserve prices are commonly used at auctions. *See Also: reserve, will*

RESERVE REQUIREMENT. The percentage amount of a bank's deposits that a bank must keep in its vault or in a noninterest-bearing reserve bank account. *See Also: account, bank, reserve, reserve bank*

RESERVE SPLIT. Occurs when the number of capital shares are reduced, but the total dollar amount stays the same because each share's par value increases. A company can achieve a reverse split by substituting one new share for a number of outstanding shares, thus increasing the par value of each while decreasing the actual number of outstanding shares. *See Also: actual, capital, outstanding, par, par value, reverse split, share, split*

RESIDENTIAL ENERGY CREDIT. A tax credit homeowners can claim on their federal income tax forms when they improve the energy efficiency of their homes through insulation, storm window installation, or other home additions and improvements. *See Also: credit, home, tax credit, window*

RESIDUAL BOND CMO. bonds that represent the residual interest of the cash flows of a CMO transaction. *See Also: cash, CMO, interest, residual interest, transaction*

RESIDUAL INTEREST. The remainder of all cash flows of a bond issue after all service and administrative expenses have been met. *See Also: bond, cash, issue, service*

RESIDUAL SECURITY. A convertible security, or a security with rights or warrants, that possesses traits which could result in a reduced amount of earnings per share. Such dilution would increase the number of common shares that compete for the same earnings, reducing the earnings per share. *See Also: convertible security, dilution, earnings, rights, security, share*

RESIDUAL VALUE. *See Also: salvage value.*

RESIDUARY CLAUSE. The contract or the will clause that distributes all of a decedent's property after all taxes and debts have been satisfied. *See Also: contract*

RESIDUARY ESTATE. All of the assets and property left in an estate after all taxes and debts have been satisfied. *See Also: estate*

RESIDUARY LEGATEE. The person who receives all of the assets and property left in an estate after all taxes and debts have been satisfied. *See Also: estate*

RESIDUARY TRUST. A trust into which all of an estate's assets and property are deposited after all taxes and debts have been satisfied. *See Also: trust*

RESISTANCE LEVEL. A security's price level at which persistent selling occurs at a certain price to stop a price increase. Technicians believe that a breakout above a resistance level will lead to new highs. *See Also: breakout, highs, level, new highs, stop*

RESOLUTION. An individual's intention, or a security's clause that expresses an intention.

RESOURCE. Anything of value or that can be used in exchange for something else. *See Also: exchange*

RESPONDEAT SUPERIOR. When a complaint is made against a company's employee, either because of the employee's error or oversight, the complaint is made against that employee's superior, as the superior is responsible for supervising the employee.

RESTING ORDER. Any securities order that remains in effect until the order cannot be filled because of high market prices if it is a buy order or because of low market prices if it is a sell order. *See Also: buy order, low, market, order, securities, sell order*

RESTORATION PREMIUM. The extra charge a person must pay to restore an instrument that has dropped in value to its original value. *See Also: instrument, pay*

RESTRICTED ACCOUNT. A margin account that has fallen below margin requirements. *See Also: account, margin, margin account*

RESTRICTED ASSET. Any resource that has a limited legal use, such as an asset from a revenue bond indenture. *See Also: asset, bond, indenture, legal, resource, revenue bond*

RESTRICTED LIST. A list of securities issuers and specific issues that cannot be traded, but can be sold only for a customer who does not solicit the sale. A broker-dealer usually gives the restricted list to the firm's selling employees. *See Also: broker-dealer, sale, securities*

RESTRICTED SHARES. A common stock that will not pay dividends until a specific event has occurred, such as the company achieving a certain earnings level. *See Also: common stock, earnings, level, pay, stock*

RESTRICTED STOCK. Stock that is not registered under the Securities Exchange Act of 1933. Unregistered stock may include stock obtained through a private placement or a company's stock option plan. Holders of restricted stock are not permitted to sell until a certain time period has been met, typically two years. SEC Rule 144 governs the sale of restricted stock. *See Also: option, placement, private placement, securities, Securities Act of 1933, stock, stock option, unregistered stock*

RESTRICTED STOCK OPTION. An employee's privilege to buy a specific amount of his or her company's capital stock during a specific time period for the current market price. *See Also: capital, capital stock, current, market, market price, stock, time*

RESTRICTED SURPLUS. The part of a company's retained earnings that it cannot use to pay dividends. *See Also: earnings, pay, retained earnings*

RESTRICTIVE COVENANTS. A bond indenture that limits the debtor from taking certain actions to protect the creditor. *See Also: bond, creditor, indenture*

RESTRICTIVE ENDORSEMENT. The endorsement on a securities certificate that names one person or one company name. *See Also: certificate, name, securities*

RESTRIKE. A coin that was stamped at the U.S. Mint after the date marked on the coin.

RESYNDICATION LIMITED PARTNERSHIP. A partnership that buys property which previously was owned by another partnership, thus enabling the new partners to take new tax credits and depreciation after the previous partners exhausted their credits and depreciation benefits. *See Also: depreciation, partnership, take*

RETAIL AUTOMATIC EXECUTION SYSTEM. A computer system for the quick execution of five or fewer option orders on the Chicago Board Options Exchange. *See Also: exchange, execution, option*

RETAIL HOUSE. A brokerage firm with retail investors, not institutional investors, as customers. *See Also: firm*

RETAIL INVESTOR. An individual investor as opposed to an institutional investor. *See Also: institutional investor*

RETAIL REPO. A collateralized loan with the bank borrowing from the lender. Basically, the depositor buys the collateral, then sells it back to the bank, which pays the initial price plus interest for a flexible amount of time, usually less than 90 days. This money is not insured since it is considered an investment, not a deposit. *See Also: bank, collateral, interest, investment, plus, time*

RETAINED EARNINGS. The portion of a company's earnings that it does not pay out to stockholders. *See Also: earnings, pay*

RETAINED EARNINGS STATEMENT. A detailed financial record of annual and past dividend payments, which accompanies the company's annual report. *See Also: annual report, dividend*

RETENTION. That part of an underwriting member's takedown that can be sold after enough shares are held back to ease institutional and selling group sales. For example, if the member has a takedown of 20,000 shares and holds on to 5,000 shares for institutional and selling group sales, the member's retention is 15,000. *See Also: group sales, selling group, takedown, underwriting*

RETENTION RATE. As the opposite of a dividend payout ratio, this is a percentage of a company's profits after taxes have been paid that can be credited to its retained earnings. *See Also: dividend, dividend payout ratio, earnings, payout, payout ratio, ratio, retained earnings*

RETENTION REQUIREMENT. A broker must retain 50 percent of the customer's margin account proceeds to lower the customer's debt. The customer can withdraw the other 50 percent. *See Also: account, broker, margin, margin account, proceeds*

RETIRE. To cancel or redeem a securities issue. *See Also: issue, redeem, securities*

RETIRED SECURITIES. A company's outstanding shares that the company calls back in or cancels and thus can no longer be sold. *See Also: outstanding*

RETIREMENT OF DEBT. When principal is paid off. *See Also: principal*

RETRACTABLE LOAN. A debt security on which the issuer can regularly change the interest rate. The investor can redeem the security for its par value if the new interest rate is not profitable. *See Also: change, debt security, interest, interest rate, par, par value, redeem, security*

RETREAT. Describes a drop in prices. *See Also: drop*

RETROACTIVE RESTORATION. A bond stipulation which states that its original coverage will be restored after a loss is paid to take care of potential future losses. *See Also: bond, take*

RETURN. An investment's profits, whether through interest or dividends. *See Also: interest*

RETURN OF CAPITAL. Nontaxable cash payments to shareholders that represent a return of invested capital instead of a dividend distribution. The investor decreases the investment's cost by the payment amount. *See Also: capital, cash, dividend, invested capital, return*

RETURN ON ASSETS. One can determine a company's profitability by dividing its total assets into its net income. *See Also: net, net income, profitability*

RETURN ON EQUITY. A stockholder's equity divided into net income. *See Also: equity, net, net income, stockholder's equity*

RETURN ON INVESTED CAPITAL. A company's total capitalization divided into its net income and interest expense. *See Also: and interest, capitalization, expense, interest, net, net income, total capitalization*

RETURN ON INVESTMENT. Divide an investment into the pretax income to obtain a figure that represents the relationship of investment and profit. *See Also: investment, profit*

RETURN ON NET WORTH. A stockholder can determine his or her rate of return by comparing the issuing company's after tax net profit to its net worth. *See Also: after tax, net, net profit, net worth, profit, rate of return, return, stockholder, worth*

RETURN ON SALES. To determine a company's operating efficiency, one can compare the percentage of its net sales that represent before-tax profits to that same figure from prior time periods. The percentage that represents that the company is operating efficiently will vary from industry to industry. *See Also: industry, net, net sales, time*

REVALUATION. The changing of the value of a country's currency not by market fluctuations but on decisions made by authorities. *See Also: currency, market*

REVENUE ANTICIPATION NOTE. A short-term municipal note that the government has backed with expected revenues. *See Also: municipal note, note*

REVENUE APPLICATION NOTES. A short-term note that a company or bank distributes to raise money because it is expecting to receive an amount of revenue with which it can pay off the notes. *See Also: bank, note, pay*

REVENUE BOND. A revenue bond that is backed by a tax placed on a special project, such as the construction of a toll road. *See Also: bond*

REVENUE INDEXED MORTGAGE BOND. A real estate-backed security with interest payments supplemented by a predetermined percentage of the issuer's earnings. *See Also: earnings, interest, security, with interest*

REVENUE SHARING. When the federal government or any larger governmental entity returns some tax money to a local government or any other smaller governmental entity. *See Also: local*

REVERSAL. Occurs when a security's price movement changes, with the new direction continuing at least for several days. A down reversal occurs when the price drops; an up reversal occurs when the price starts going up. *See Also: down reversal, movement, up reversal*

REVERSE A SWAP. A second transaction in bonds that reestablishes a client's original portfolio position, thereby eliminating any effects from the market changes that have transpired. For example, if a yield spread expanded, making it profitable to sell one bond and buy another, then returned to its original condition, the investor would make a reverse swap by selling the bond that was purchased and buying back the bond that was sold. *See Also: bond, market, portfolio, position, spread, swap, transaction, yield, yield spread*

REVERSE ANNUITY MORTGAGE. This mortgage enables an elderly property owner to receive an income for life in return for gradually relinquishing ownership in the property. *See Also: collateral, mortgage*

REVERSE AUCTIONS. An auction process in which sellers compete for the lowest price to sell goods or services. Unlike a forward auction, prices only move down. Since buyer power is key to reverse auctions, they work either for large enterprises or when practiced by aggregators, which aggregate demand of many buyers, small or large. *See Also: demand, forward, forward auction*

REVERSE CONVERSION. A technique, usually implemented by brokerage firms, that involves simultaneously selling an underlying security short, buying a call and selling a put, all with the same striking price. The options will hedge against a sharp rise, while the brokerage firm collects the interest received by investing money in short-term money market installments. *See Also: firm, hedge, interest, market, money market, put, security, striking price, underlying security*

REVERSE DOLLAR ROLL. An investor who owns a high-coupon Government National Mortgage Association bond sells it after interest rates drop, but agrees to buy it back in a month, thus obtaining higher returns in a short time. *See Also: bond, drop, interest, mortgage, time*

REVERSE HEDGE. The owner of common stock sells a convertible security short because he or she believes the premium over conversion parity will drop so he or she can close the position at a profit. *See Also: close, common stock, conversion, conversion parity, convertible security, drop, parity, position, premium, profit, security, stock*

REVERSE MORTGAGE. This mortgage enables an elderly property owner to receive an annual income, using the value of the home as collateral. At the end of the term, or at the death of the borrower, the loan is repaid plus interest when the property is sold. *See Also: collateral, home, interest, mortgage, plus, term*

REVERSE REPURCHASE AGREEMENT. A customer sells a group of securities to a broker-dealer under the provision that the customer will buy them back by a predetermined date for a specific price. The difference between the amount the customer received for the securities and the amount he or she will pay the broker-dealer when buying them back represents the interest. *See Also: broker-dealer, interest, pay, securities*

REVERSE SPLIT. Used to reduce the number of outstanding shares. For example, an investor with two shares will have only one share after a one for two reverse split. *See Also: outstanding, share, split*

REVERSE TARGETED AMORTIZATION CLASS (TAC) BONDS. TAC bonds adhere to a specified principal paydown schedule that will be met as long as the collateral prepayment speed decreases below the original pricing speed, as compared to regular TAC bonds which pay principal when prepayment speeds increase above the original pricing speed. *See Also: collateral, pay, paydown, prepayment, principal*

REVERSE YIELD GAP. Occurs when a fixed-interest security earns more than an industrial security. *See Also: industrial, security*

REVOCABLE TRUST. A contract that deeds a piece of income-producing property to a person's beneficiaries, with the holder able to change the contract or cancel it any time he or she wants. Because the property automatically goes to the owner's beneficiaries according to the contract's terms, it does not go through probate. *See Also: change, contract, time*

REVOLVING LINE OF CREDIT. A line of credit a bank extends to a customer, with the amount available to the customer whenever he or she needs it. *See Also: bank, credit, line of credit*

REVOLVING UNDERWRITING FACILITIES. A long-term debt contract between a group of investment bankers and the issuer of Eurodollar securities in which the underwriter offers three- to six-month obligations at more profitable short-term rates, then continues to offer the notes as previously issued ones mature. *See Also: contract, investment, long-term debt, offer, securities*

RFF. Request For Firm Offers. *See Also: firm*

RFI. Request for Information.

RFP. Request for Proposal.

RFQ. Request for Quotation. *See Also: quotation*

RIALTO. Any commodities or securities exchange. *See Also: exchange, securities*

RICH. A price that is too high.

RIDING THE YIELD CURVE. During times in which a positively shaped yield curve exists, bond investors will enjoy the coupon payments of longer-term bonds even as the security approaches maturity; in other words, an investor in a five-year bond will earn the interest payment of that bond even though, four years later, it will be a one-year bond. This can be a profitable strategy for traders when interest rates for maturities are less than the bond decrease. *See Also: bond, coupon, interest, security, yield, yield curve*

RIGGED MARKET. A market with securities prices that have been manipulated to attract unsuspecting buyers. *See Also: market, securities*

RIGGING. Any illegal stock price manipulation. *See Also: manipulation, stock*

RIGHT. A stipulation in a securities contract that allows the holder to subscribe to other securities at a specific ratio. *See Also: contract, ratio, securities*

RIGHT OF ACCUMULATION. The right of a mutual fund investor to reinvest if the value of the fund's holdings exceeds a certain price level. *See Also: fund, level, mutual fund, right*

RIGHT OF REDEMPTION. The fight to take back a piece of property by paying off the mortgage. *See Also: mortgage, take, take back*

RIGHT OF RESCISSION. The right to cancel a contract within three business days with full refund and no penalty. This right, granted by the Federal Consumer Credit Protection Act of 1968, protects consumers from high pressure sales and other sales tactics. *See Also: Consumer Credit Protection Act of 1968, contract, credit, full, right*

RIGHT OF SURVIVORSHIP. When two people own a piece of property and one dies, the deed is automatically transferred to the other person.

RIGHT OF WAY. The right of the public to allow utilities or transportation companies to use land that will benefit the general public. *See Also: right*

RIGHTS. The option a company gives to shareholders in which the shareholders can buy a pro rata share of a new common stock issue at a specific price. Because the rights carry a market value, they can be actively traded. *See Also: carry, common stock, issue, market, market value, option, pro, pro rata, share, stock*

RIGHTS OF SHAREHOLDERS. The rights of stockholders to vote on company matters, such as board election, charter changes, reorganization, and merger proposals. *See Also: charter, merger, reorganization, rights*

RIGHTS OFFERING. A company gives the holders of common stock the right to buy a proportionate number of new issue shares at a lower price before the new issue is offered publicly. *See Also: common stock, issue, new issue, right, stock*

RIGHTS ON. A security that carries the right for the investor to buy a pro rata amount of any new offerings. *See Also: pro, pro rata, right, security*

RING. A commodity exchange's trading area, or the area in the New York Stock Exchange where commodities are traded. *See Also: commodity, exchange, New York Stock Exchange, stock, stock exchange*

RINGING UP. Occurs when two commodities brokers settle a deal before the contracts mature and before the contracts are deliverable. Such practices enable the brokers to take care of their commitments before the last minute so they will have time to take care of other deals that may become more pressing. *See Also: settle, take, time*

RISING BOTTOMS. The chart pattern that occurs when a security's or a commodity's low prices are moving up, which indicates that the basic price support levels also are moving up. *See Also: chart, low, price support, support*

RISK. The probability that an investment will earn the amount of profit that it is supposed to earn. The chance an investment will drop in value. *See Also: drop, investment, profit*

RISK ARBITRAGE. Occurs when an arbitraguer buys stock shares of a target company and then sells the shares to the raider. *See Also: raider, stock, target*

RISK AVERSE. A wise investor given two investment alternatives with equal returns and different risks will take the investment with the lesser risk. *See Also: investment, risk, take*

RISK CAPITAL. Investment capital.

RISK OF CAPITAL. The possibility that part of an investment will be lost. *See Also: investment*

RISK OF INFLATION. The possibility that an investment will have a lower buying power after awhile because of the effects of inflation. *See Also: buying power, inflation, investment*

RISK OF SELECTION. The possibility that an investor, given several investment alternatives, will choose the wrong or least profitable one. *See Also: investment*

RISK OF TIMING. The possibility that an investor will put money into a security at an unwise time, such as right before the price is about to drop. *See Also: drop, put, right, security, time*

RISK PREMIUM. The amount above the risk-free rate that investors seek before they will put money into a risky asset. *See Also: asset, put*

RISK REWARD. The most an investment can lose compared to the most the investment can gain. *See Also: gain, investment*

RISK-ADJUSTED DISCOUNT RATE. The risk-free rate plus a risk premium investment advisors use to determine the present value of a speculative income source. This figure is based on an investment's characteristics. *See Also: investment, plus, premium, present value, risk, risk premium, speculative*

RISK-FREE ASSET. A noncallable bond such as a government security with inflation as the only risk. *See Also: bond, inflation, noncallable, risk, security*

RISK-FREE RATE OF RETURN. The return on a default-free Treasury security. *See Also: return, security*

RISKLESS TRANSACTION. Occurs when a broker-dealer takes a position in a security only after receiving a firm buy order, thereby eliminating any risk involved in taking a position. *See Also: broker-dealer, buy order, firm, order, position, risk, security*

RISKRATING. A method of determining the relative, estimated risk of a mortgage investment. *See Also: investment, mortgage, risk*

ROAD SHOW. Pre-offering meetings, also hosted online and over the telephone, by the issuing company's management for mostly institutional investors. Audiences are usually selected by the underwriter. *See Also: online*

ROBINSON-PATMAN ACT. A 1936 law prohibiting price discrimination, false brokerage deals, and excessive quantity discounts.

ROLL DOWN. An options position is closed and a new position with a lower exercise price is established immediately. *See Also: exercise, exercise price, position*

ROLL FORWARD. An options position is closed and a new position with a later expiration date is established. *See Also: expiration, expiration date, position*

ROLL UP. An options position is closed and a new position with a higher exercise price is established immediately. *See Also: exercise, exercise price, position*

ROLL-UP. The process by which a company grows by acquiring other companies. Roll-ups are also known as consolidators.

ROLL-UP FUND. An investment fund that pays no dividends, with money concentrated in world currencies. Returns are considered capital gains and not income. *See Also: capital, fund, investment*

ROLLING OVER. Exchanging a near option for a far option on the same underlying security, with both options carrying the same striking price. *See Also: far option, near option, option, security, striking price, underlying security*

ROLLING STOCK. A transportation company's movable equipment, including cars, trucks, and trains.

ROLLOVER. An investor takes money from a maturing security, such as a futures or options contract, and invests it in longer-term securities. *See Also: contract, futures, options contract, securities, security*

ROLLOVER CERTIFICATE OF DEPOSIT. Also called a "roly-poly certificate of deposit," this is a package of 12 six-month CDs, each of which matures in three years. *See Also: certificate*

ROLLOVER MORTGAGE. A short-term mortgage in which the unpaid balance is refinanced every two or three years and thus the interest rate is adjusted each time it is refinanced. *See Also: balance, interest, interest rate, mortgage, time*

ROLY POLY CERTIFICATE OF DEPOSIT. A group of six-month certificates of deposit with expiration dates stretching over at least two years. As one matures, the investor is required to buy another for the same price to replace it. *See Also: expiration*

ROOK. To cheat.

ROTH IRA. The result of the Taxpayer Relief Act of 1997, this type of IRA is also known as a "back-loaded" IRA because contributions to the plan are not deductible, but withdrawals, subject to certain rules, can be completely tax-free in retirement. Earnings withdrawals are subject to penalties until age 59 1/2, and withdrawals are not mandatory at age 70 1/2; the account's unused balance can be passed tax-free to heirs. *See Also: balance, earnings, IRA*

ROUND DOWN. Buying a specific amount of securities through the fixed dollar amount system of investing while leaving a surplus in the account. The investor buys as much as he or she can with the amount in the account. *See Also: account, securities*

ROUND LETTER. A person who wades in packages of 100 shares of actively traded securities or 10 shares of inactive securities. *See Also: securities*

ROUND LOT. The smallest transaction that will not involve a service fee for being small, usually 100 shares. *See Also: service, service fee, transaction*

ROUND LOT CASH BUY-SELL RATIO. The cash account selling of round lots divided into the cash account buying of round lots. *See Also: account, cash, cash account*

ROUND LOT MARGIN BUY-SELL RATIO. Margin account selling divided into margin account buying. *See Also: account, margin, margin account*

ROUND LOT SHORT-COVER RATIO. The total round lot shares covered divided into the round lot shares shorted. *See Also: lot, round lot*

ROUND TRIP. As the basis upon which a commodities commission is charged, this refers to the opening and closing prices of a futures position. *See Also: basis, commission, futures, position*

ROUND TRIP TRADE. A security or commodity bought and sold within a short time period. *See Also: commodity, security, time*

ROUND UP. Buying a specific amount of securities through the fixed dollar amount system of investing while leaving a debit in the account. The investor pays the additional amount. *See Also: account, debit, securities*

ROUTER. Hardware or software that finds the best path for a data packet from one computer to another. Routers look at the destination address, and determine all possible paths to the destination address. Once the most expedient route is determined, based on factors such as Internet traffic and the most direct route, the router then directs the data to that address. *See Also: address, Internet, on, packet*

ROYALTY. Payment to the owner of a patent or copyrighted materials such as books, movies, properties, or products. *See Also: patent*

ROYALTY TRUST. An oil or gas company spins off property to its shareholders, which means it will not be taxed at the corporate level and will offer high returns to stockholders. *See Also: level, offer*

RSA. Short for its creators's names, Ron Rivest, Adi Shamir, and Leonard Adleman, RSA is public key algorithms that are based on calculations involving large integers, with the larger the key increasing the size of the integers. *See Also: on, size*

RULE 144. A Securities and Exchange Commission regulation that covers the selling of restricted securities. *See Also: commission, exchange, securities*

RULE 15C3-1. Minimum net capital requirements for broker/dealers that are established by the SEC. *See Also: capital, capital requirements, net, net capital, SEC*

RULE 15C3-3. This "Customer Protection Rule" requires broker/dealers to establish special reserve accounts for its customers' protection and to maintain custody or control of certain customer securities. *See Also: reserve, securities*

RULE 405. A New York Stock Exchange regulation that members must know specific information about their customers, their customers' accounts, and their customers' transactions. This "know-your-customer-rule" deals with the suitability of certain investments for individuals with different conditions. *See Also: exchange, know your customer rule, New York Stock Exchange, stock, stock exchange, suitability*

RULE OF 20. A theory that says the annual inflation rate added to the price-earnings ratio of the Dow Jones Industrial stocks should add up to 20, because as inflation rises, the P/E ratios drop. *See Also: drop, industrial, industrial stocks, inflation, inflation rate, P/E, ratio*

RULE OF 72. To determine how long it would take for an investor to double his or her money, divide the fixed rate of compound interest into 72. *See Also: compound interest, fixed rate, interest, take*

RULE OF 78. A system of calculating interest refunds when a debt is paid off early. The sum of the numbers one through 12 equals 78, thus, assuming equal monthly payments, the interest for the last month would be 12/78, the second would be 11/78, and so on. *See Also: interest*

RULES OF FAIR PRACTICE. Regulations of the National Association of Securities Dealers that govern ethical practices, such as fair pricing and proper disclosure. *See Also: disclosure, securities*

RUMORTRAGE. Trading or arbitraging a security, based on a rumor. *See Also: on, security*

RUN. A market maker's list of offerings, including bid and offer prices and par values. Also, when a security's price rapidly increases. *See Also: market, offer, par*

RUN ON A BANK. Occurs when a large number of a bank's depositors want to withdraw their money at the same time. Because a bank does not keep all of the money on hand, it could be in danger of closing its doors. *See Also: bank, time*

RUN RATE. A company's revenues over the next 12 months if the current revenue growth rate remains unchanged. *See Also: current*

RUNAWAY INFLATION. A swift rise in prices that special controls will not be able to reign. *See Also: swift*

RUNDOWN. The dollar amounts available in a municipal bond issue series. *See Also: bond, issue, municipal bond*

RUNDOWN ORDER. An order to buy stock at descending price ranges, such as $20 to $19. *See Also: order, stock*

RUNNING AHEAD. Illegal practice occurring when a registered representative enters a personal order to buy or sell a security before entering a similar order for a client. *See Also: client, order, registered representative, security*

RUNNING BOOK. The activities of a person who specializes in trading a specific stock on the exchange floor. *See Also: exchange, exchange floor, floor, stock*

RUNNING IN THE SHORTS. An investor buys a number of varied securities that are sold short in an effort to push the price up because doing so encourages the sellers to buy the securities back, which will push the prices up even further. *See Also: securities*

RUNNING THROUGH THE POT. Occurs when a syndicate manager calls back some shares that the syndicate has taken down and puts them into the pot for institutional investors. *See Also: manager, pot, syndicate, syndicate manager*

RUNOFF. The ticker tape that shows an exchange's closing prices. *See Also: tape, ticker tape*

RUNUP ORDER. An order to buy stock at ascending price ranges, such as $22 to $23. *See Also: order, stock*

S

S. Indicates a stock split or a stock dividend when it appears in newspaper stock listings. *See Also: dividend, split, stock, stock dividend*

S & P INDEXES. Standard and Poors Indexes. *See Also: Standard & Poors*

SADDLED. A situation in which an investor pays more than the market price for a security, then is forced to hold onto it because its value has failed to increase to the price paid. *See Also: hold, market, market price, security*

SAFE HARBOR. An action to avoid legal and tax consequences. *See Also: legal*

SAFEKEEPING. A brokerage action to store and protect an investor's securities by segregating and identifying the securities. *See Also: securities*

SAFETY. A minimal risk that creates the investor belief that an investment will not lose money. *See Also: investment, risk*

SAFETY OF INCOME. The probability that a company will continue making timely interest and dividend payments. *See Also: dividend, interest*

SAFETY OF PRINCIPAL. The probability that money invested with a particular company will remain stable.

SAFETY STOCK. A group of securities held to prevent stockouts. *See Also: securities*

SAG. Occurs when a security's price drops slightly after demand for the security has been depleted. *See Also: demand, security*

SAIF. Savings Association Insurance Fund. *See Also: fund, insurance*

SALARY REDUCTION PLAN. A program in which an employee can have a percentage of his or her gross salary withheld and invested in his or her choice of securities or money markets. The employer, in turn, matches the contributions up to a predetermined limit. The employee does not have to pay taxes on the amount contributed or on any profits until he or she leaves the company. *See Also: gross, limit, pay, securities, turn*

SALE. Occurs when a buyer and a seller agree on a price in a securities transaction. *See Also: securities, transaction*

SALE AND LEASE BACK. An agreement in which a company sells an item to another company or to an investor, then agrees to lease the item back for a specific length of time. Such agreements can be profitable because of the tax advantages they provide. *See Also: time*

SALE AND SERVICING AGREEMENT. A secondary market transaction in which the seller-servicer supplies, and the buyer purchases loans every so often, as prescribed in the agreement. *See Also: market, secondary market, transaction*

SALE ON APPROVAL. A contract with the seller retaining the risk and the buyer not taking title until he or she indicates approval. *See Also: contract, risk*

SALE OR RETURN. A contract with the buyer taking immediate title unless he or she returns the goods to the seller. *See Also: contract*

SALES AGREEMENT. A contract in which a seller agrees to transfer goods or services to the buyer for a predetermined price. *See Also: contract, transfer*

SALES CHARGE. A fee that an open-end investment company charges for buying fund shares. *See Also: fund, investment, investment company*

SALES LITERATURE. Any written material that promotes a specific investment by detailing its advantages. The material is distributed to potential investors. *See Also: investment*

SALES LOAD. Sales charge.

SALES TAX. A state or city tax placed on a purchase based on the dollar amount of that purchase. *See Also: City*

SALLIE MAE. Nickname for the United States Student Loan Marketing Association.

SALT-DOWN STOCK. Occurs when an investor buys securities and keeps them for a long time, even if the securities show large paper profits. *See Also: paper, securities, time*

SALVAGE VALUE. The realized value of an asset at the end of its useful life. Also called residual value and scrap value.

SAM. Shared Appreciation Mortgage. *See Also: appreciation*

SAME-DAY SUBSTITUTION. This occurs when an investor sells one security and buys another of equal value in the same day. *See Also: security*

SAME STORE SALES. A comparison measure for the retail industry that analyzes new sales from existing stores that have been open for a year or more. *See Also: industry, open*

SAMMIE BEE. Nickname for a small business administration loan. *See Also: small business administration loan*

SAMURAI BOND. A debt instrument denominated in Japanese yen, but not issued by a Japanese agency or company. *See Also: debt instrument, instrument, yen*

SANDBAG. A strategy used by management of a company to delay action by a potential acquirer. Management might employ this strategy in the hope that a better deal might surface. *See Also: delay*

SANDWICH BONDS. This CMO bond is structured so that principal cash flows are first directed to reduce the bond's principal amount for the given payment date to the maximum balance. Interest on the accrual bond will be allocated to the Sandwich bond if available cash flows to the bond fall short of the maximum balance amount. *See Also: balance, bond, cash, CMO, fall, interest, payment date, principal, principal amount*

SANTA CLAUS RALLY. A rise in stock prices that sometimes occurs during the week between Christmas and New Year's day. *See Also: stock*

SAR. Stock Appreciation Right. *See Also: appreciation, stock, stock appreciation right*

SATISFACTION OF MORTGAGE. The document issued by the lender verifying that a mortgage has been paid in full. *See Also: full, mortgage*

SATISFACTION PIECE. A document verifying that a debt has been paid.

SATURATION. Occurs when supply exceeds demand to such a degree that the prices must drop to absorb any further supply. *See Also: demand, drop, supply*

SATURATION POINT. The point where supply starts to exceed demand. *See Also: demand, point, supply*

SATURDAY NIGHT SPECIAL. One company's sudden attempt to takeover another company by tendering a public offer, so named because of a series of such attempts in the 1960s, most of which were announced during the weekends. *See Also: offer, takeover*

SAUCER PATTERN. A price chart that displays little activity after a steady price decline followed by a slight upturn. *See Also: activity, chart, steady*

SAVER'S SURPLUS. The difference between the interest a saver received and the higher amount of interest at which he or she would have agreed to loan money, if a demand for loans had existed. For example, if a person earned eight percent interest on his or her savings, but would have earned 8.5 percent interest if he or she had loaned the money instead of saving it, 0.5 percent would be the saver's surplus. *See Also: demand, interest*

SAVINGS ACCOUNT. Money deposited in a bank, with the account paying interest and the funds payable on demand of the depositor. Such accounts normally carry no penalties for early withdrawal. *See Also: account, bank, carry, demand, interest*

SAVINGS AND INVESTMENT THEORY. A theory that business cycles occur when people save more or less than the amount invested in new capital. *See Also: capital*

SAVINGS AND LOAN ASSOCIATION. A government-chartered financial institution that carries customer deposits and makes real estate mortgage loans. *See Also: estate, mortgage, real estate*

SAVINGS ASSOCIATION INSURANCE FUND (SAIF). Formerly the Federal Savings and Loan Insurance Corporation, this fund insures deposits of up to $100,000 per account. *See Also: account, corporation, fund, insurance*

SAVINGS BANK. A government-chartered bank that invests a customer's deposits in real estate, mortgages, government bonds, and other permissible securities. *See Also: bank, estate, real estate, securities*

SAVINGS BANK LIFE INSURANCE. An over-the-counter method of buying limited amounts of life insurance coverage from a bank without using an agent. *See Also: agent, bank, insurance, life insurance*

SAVINGS BOND. A U.S. Treasury bond that cannot be traded on the public market. *See Also: bond, market, public market, Treasury bond*

SAVINGS DEPOSIT. A bank account deposit that bears interest which can be withdrawn upon demand without prior notice. *See Also: account, bank, demand, interest*

SBA. Small Business Administration.

SBO. Settlement Balance Order. *See Also: balance, order*

SCALABILITY. The ability to accommodate expanding computing demands, in terms of the number of users on the systems or the demands of new or additional applications. *See Also: on*

SCALE. Represents the number of bonds, their maturity dates, interest rates, and offering prices in the initial offering of a serial bond issue. *See Also: bond, interest, issue, maturity, offering*

SCALE. The ability ramp up, or climb rapidly, in a business or technological sense as little effort is required to quickly expand. *See Also: up*

SCALING. Occurs when an investor places a series of buy and sell orders at different prices or at different times instead of placing only one order for all of the securities. *See Also: order, securities*

SCALPER. A market maker who excessively marks up or marks down securities that carry little risk to the market maker. *See Also: carry, maker, market, market maker, risk, securities*

SCALPING. An unethical and sometimes illegal practice where a trader will buy securities for his or her firm's account. Then, the trader will improperly try to influence investors to buy the securities in an effort to drive the price up. *See Also: account, drive, securities, trader*

SCHEDULE 13-D. A form the Securities and Exchange Commission requires the buyer of five percent of a registered equity security to file within 10 days of the purchase. *See Also: commission, equity, equity security, exchange, securities, security*

SCHEDULE 13-G. A short form the Securities and Exchange Commission requires the owner of five percent of a registered equity security to file at the end of the year. *See Also: commission, equity, equity security, exchange, securities, security*

SCHEDULE C. A regulation from the National Association of Securities Dealers requiring the registration of principals, financial principals, and representatives. *See Also: principals, registration, securities*

SCHEDULED CASH FLOWS. The contractual payments, not including possible prepayments, of principal and interest for the loans backing a mortgage-backed security. *See Also: actual, and interest, interest, principal, security*

SCHULDSCHEIN. Collateralized ownership in a German loan, with the lending bank participating in an underwriting syndicate. After the first 90 days, ownership of the security cannot be transferred more than three times before it matures. *See Also: bank, security, syndicate, underwriting, underwriting syndicate*

SCIENTER. To knowingly transact a fraudulent securities deal. *See Also: securities*

SCM. Supply Chain Management. *See Also: supply, supply chain*

SCORCHED EARTH TACTIC. A takeover target tries to discourage the takeover either by selling its most valuable and attractive assets or by entering a long-term contract. *See Also: contract, takeover, target*

SCORE. Special Claim on Residential Equity. *See Also: equity*

SCOREX SYSTEM. See Securities Communication, Order Routing, and Execution. *See Also: execution, order, securities, securities communication, order routing, and execution*

SCOTTISH DIVIDEND. A reverse split in which, for example, a company trades two shares for one. *See Also: reverse split, split*

SCRAP VALUE. Salvage value.

SCREEN. To search for securities that meet certain investment goals and criteria, such as a certain price/earnings ratio. *See Also: investment, ratio, securities*

SCRIP. A document that a company issues to indicate ownership of a share fraction, usually following a stock split. Some companies pay dividends in scrip instead of in cash when they are short of money. *See Also: cash, fraction, pay, share, split, stock*

SCRIPOPHILY. The hobby of collecting old securities certificates. *See Also: securities*

SCRIPT KIDDIES. Hackers that use ready-made software, often available for educational purposes, to attack vulnerable computer systems. Script Kiddies are typically technological neophytes.

SEALED BID AUCTION. Auction type in which each bidder makes a discreet single and the highest bidder wins.

SEALING. Concealed bids, usually enclosed in sealed envelopes, that all are opened at the same time, with the best bid accepted immediately. *See Also: time*

SEARCH ENGINE. Software that users access on the Internet to search through massive databases of Web pages. Users are presented with a list of results that best match their key words. Internet-based results are offered with links, which enable users to easily access that Web page. *See Also: Internet, on, Web, Web page*

SEASONAL STOCK. A company whose sales vary due to seasonal effects, such as weather and holidays. For example, a toy manufacturer typically has greater sales during the Christmas season.

SEASONAL TREND. A consistent, short-lived rise or drop in business or economic activity that regularly occurs as a result of changes in climate, holidays, vacations, and so on. *See Also: activity, drop*

SEASONED SECURITY. A publicly held security, so any future transaction would involve a deal between two investors and not between the issuer and an investor. *See Also: publicly held, security, transaction*

SEAT. A securities or commodities exchange membership. *See Also: exchange, securities*

SEC. Securities and Exchange Commission. *See Also: commission, exchange, securities*

SECOND MARKET. The over-the-counter securities market with the exchanges being the first. *See Also: exchanges, market, securities*

SECOND MORTGAGE BOND. A bond backed by a mortgage, with the first mortgage bonds taking priority over the second. *See Also: bond, mortgage, priority*

SECOND MORTGAGE LENDING. A mortgage secured by a piece of property that already has been pledged on another mortgage. The first mortgage always has priority over the second. *See Also: mortgage, priority*

SECOND PARTNER. Also called a secret partner, this is an active partner whose association with the company is not public knowledge.

SECOND PREFERRED STOCK. One preferred stock issue that ranks below another preferred stock issue in priority in dividend payments and on assets in the case of a liquidation. *See Also: dividend, issue, liquidation, preferred stock, priority, stock*

SECOND ROUND. The venture capital stage between startup and the mezzanine level when a company has matured to a point where it can either accept a management's leveraged buyout or an initial public offering. *See Also: buyout, capital, initial public offering, level, leveraged, matured, mezzanine level, offering, point, public offering, startup, venture capital, venture capital*

SECONDARIES. Small, speculative companies that investors are attracted to because of their potential for major advances. *See Also: speculative*

SECONDARY BANK RESERVE. High-grade securities that easily can be converted into cash. *See Also: cash, securities*

SECONDARY DISTRIBUTION. When an issuing company publicly offers a large block of stock for sale after the stock's primary distribution. *See Also: block of stock, primary distribution, sale, stock*

SECONDARY FINANCING. A second loan using the same collateral as the first loan, with the first loan having priority over the second. *See Also: collateral, priority*

SECONDARY MARKET. A securities transaction that takes place after the initial distribution. *See Also: securities, transaction*

SECONDARY MORTGAGE MARKET. The trading of existing mortgage loans and mortgage-backed securities. *See Also: mortgage, securities*

SECONDARY MOVEMENT. A sharp price rally in a bear market, or a sharp drop in a bull market. *See Also: bear, bear market, bull, bull market, drop, market, rally*

SECONDARY REACTION. A price change that moves against the general market trend. *See Also: change, market, market trend, price change, trend*

SECTION 403 PLAN. A section of the Internal Revenue Code that allows the employees of some charitable groups or of some public schools to create tax-sheltered retirement plans, with the programs normally invested in mutual funds or annuities. *See Also: internal revenue*

SECTOR. Bonds in the same class with similar ratings, close maturity dates, and similar coupons that are expected to have parallel movements. *See Also: class, close, maturity*

SECULAR TREND. An up or down long-term market trend, with no regard to seasonal variations, in the price or levels of commodities, inflation, the stock market, and so on. *See Also: inflation, market, market trend, stock, stock market, trend*

SECURED ACCOUNT. Any collateralized account. *See Also: account*

SECURED BOND. A bond for which the issuer has set aside assets as collateral to ensure timely interest and principal payments. *See Also: bond, collateral, interest, principal*

SECURED DEBT. Any collateralized debt.

SECURED LOAN. A loan with collateral pledged in exchange for funds. *See Also: collateral, exchange*

SECURITIES. Usually describes stocks and bonds, but can be expanded to describe any financial instrument. *See Also: financial instrument, instrument*

SECURITIES ACT OF 1933. A law that regulates securities markets by requiring, among other things, registration before any sale and by requiring disclosure of all pertinent information about the issuing company. *See Also: disclosure, registration, sale, securities*

SECURITIES ACT OF 1934. A law that created the Securities and Exchange Commission to govern securities markets, which outlawed price manipulation, the misrepresentation of facts, and other possible abuses. *See Also: commission, exchange, manipulation, securities*

SECURITIES ACTS AMENDMENTS OF 1975. A law that calls for a national market system and a national process through which securities transactions can be cleared and executed. *See Also: cleared, market, national market system, securities*

SECURITIES ANALYST. A brokerage employee who reviews and judges securities investments, as well as the financial condition of publicly-held companies. *See Also: securities*

SECURITIES AND COMMODITIES EXCHANGES. National exchanges which trade securities, options, and futures contracts by members for their customers and personal accounts. *See Also: exchanges, futures, securities*

SECURITIES AND EXCHANGE COMMISSION (SEC). The governmental agency that regulates and supervises the securities industry. The commission administers federal laws, formulates and enforces rules to protect against malpractice, and provides investors with the fullest disclosure possible. *See Also: commission, disclosure, industry, securities*

SECURITIES AND EXCHANGE COMMISSION FEE. The SEC imposes a one-cent charge on every $300 involved in a securities transaction. The seller normally pays the fee, which applies only to exchange-registered equity securities. *See Also: equity, SEC, securities, transaction*

SECURITIES AND EXCHANGE COMMISSION ORGANIZATION MEMBER. A broker-dealer who is registered with the SEC and is not a member of the National Association of Securities Dealers or of a national exchange. *See Also: broker-dealer, exchange, SEC, securities*

SECURITIES COMMUNICATION, ORDER ROUTING, AND EXECUTION. Commonly referred to as the SCOREX System, this is a Pacific Stock Exchange computer network through which members can automatically send and execute market orders of less than 600 shares at the best available Intermarket Trading System price. *See Also: exchange, intermarket, market, Pacific Stock Exchange, SCOREX system, stock, stock exchange*

SECURITIES DEPOSITORY. The place where a security's certificate is physically filed before a bookkeeping transfer. *See Also: certificate, transfer*

SECURITIES INDUSTRY ASSOCIATION. An organization of broker-dealers that is aimed at training members' employees and lobbying for members' interests.

SECURITIES INDUSTRY AUTOMATION CORPORATION. A company that handles a trading communications system for the American and New York stock exchanges. *See Also: exchanges, stock*

SECURITIES INVESTOR PROTECTION CORPORATION (SIPC). A private, government-sponsored company that insures brokerage accounts for up to $500,000 in securities with $100,000 for cash in case the brokerage firm goes bankrupt. *See Also: cash, firm, securities*

SECURITIES LOAN. When one broker-dealer loans securities to another broker-dealer to complete a short sale. *See Also: broker-dealer, sale, securities, short sale*

SECURITIZATION. Pooling loans into packages of securities in Great Britain. *See Also: securities*

SECURITY. Any investment, such as stocks, rights, warrants, bonds or notes that represents ownership, rights to ownership, or a creditor relationship with a corporation or governmental unit. Security can also represent any type of collateral offered by a debtor to a lender to secure a loan. *See Also: collateral, corporation, creditor, investment, rights, unit*

SECURITY ELEMENT. Any type of collateral. *See Also: collateral*

SECURITY INSTRUMENT. Either the mortgage or the deed to property that has been pledged as collateral. *See Also: collateral, mortgage*

SECURITY MARKET LINE. The ratio of an asset's expected rate of return and its systemic risk. *See Also: rate of return, ratio, return, risk*

SECURITY PURCHASE CONTRACT. A debt instrument that converts to an equity security of the same issuer after a specific date. *See Also: debt instrument, equity, equity security, instrument, security*

SECURITY RATINGS. Evaluations of the credit and investment risk of securities which are rated by independent agencies. *See Also: credit, investment, risk, securities*

SECURITY VALUATION MODEL. A theory that says a common stock's value can be reached by adding the discounted present value to the total expected dividends. *See Also: present value*

SEED MONEY. The first money put into a business venture, usually a loan, that allows those opening the business to move closer to a startup. *See Also: put, startup*

SEEK A MARKET. To try to find orders for the appropriate security to complete a transaction. *See Also: security, transaction*

SEGREGATE. To separate a client's securities from the broker's securities. *See Also: securities*

SEGREGATED SECURITIES. A client's securities kept separate from a broker-dealer's securities; that a broker-dealer cannot use to transact the firm's business. *See Also: broker-dealer, securities*

SELECTED DEALER AGREEMENT. An underwriting syndicate's contract for distributing new securities, with the agreement stipulating the syndicate members' rights and responsibilities, such as the obligation to sell the securities at the agreed upon price. *See Also: contract, obligation, rights, securities, syndicate, underwriting*

SELF TENDER. Often used to fend off a takeover attempt, a company will buy back a specific number of its outstanding stock shares. *See Also: outstanding, outstanding stock, stock, takeover*

SELF-DEALING. A transaction between company officers, family members, or business associates with no concern for interest payments. *See Also: interest, transaction*

SELF-DIRECTED INDIVIDUAL RETIREMENT ACCOUNT. An IRA in which a holder governs an account and an account's investment direction. *See Also: account, investment, IRA*

SELF-LIQUIDATING. An asset that easily can be converted to cash, or with a value that ultimately can be recovered in full. *See Also: asset, cash, full*

SELF-LIQUIDATING ASSET PURCHASE (SLAP). This is a method in which a newly issued debt is used to buy a company that has a high level of cash flow. The large cash flow is used to pay off the debt issue. *See Also: cash, cash flow, issue, level, pay*

SELF-REGULATORY ORGANIZATION. A stock exchange, securities, or commodities organization that is registered with the Securities and Exchange Commission and that is responsible for making sure members obey rules and regulations. *See Also: commission, exchange, securities, stock, stock exchange*

SELF-SUPPORTING. Occurs when project revenue will amount to enough alone, without help, to pay off the bonds that funded the project. For example, if the taxes assessed against people who get a new sewer line will be sufficient to pay off the bond issued. *See Also: bond, pay*

SELL AT BEST. This is said when an over-the-counter broker-dealer asks another broker-dealer to help sell part of a market order at the best available price. *See Also: broker-dealer, market, market order, order*

SELL OFF. When prices are dropping because of heavy-selling pressure.

SELL ORDER. An investor's directions to his or her broker to liquidate a specific number of shares. *See Also: broker*

SELL OUT. Occurs when a buyer refuses to accept delivery or pay the agreed upon price. A sell out also occurs when a broker liquidates a margin account because the investor has failed to bring the account up to the minimum level following a margin call. *See Also: account, broker, delivery, level, margin, margin account, margin call, pay*

SELL PLUS. A market order to sell a security at a price higher than that security's last transaction price. *See Also: market, market order, order, security, transaction*

SELL SIGNAL. A market gauge that indicates a security could soon drop in price. *See Also: drop, market, security*

SELL THE BOOK. A seller's request to sell as many shares as possible at the best bid price. *See Also: bid price*

SELL-DOWN. The security shares an underwriting syndicate offers to those who are not syndicate members. *See Also: security, syndicate, underwriting, underwriting syndicate*

SELL-OUT NOTICE. A notice from a broker to a client telling the client he or she must pay an amount due immediately or the broker will begin selling the client's securities to satisfy the debt. *See Also: broker, client, pay, securities*

SELL-OUT PROCEDURE. When a buying broker fails to honor a contract by refusing to pay for securities he or she agreed to buy, the selling broker can turn around and sell the securities to someone else without notifying the defaulting buyer, or the seller can hold the buyer liable for any losses incurred because of the default. *See Also: around, broker, contract, default, fails, hold, pay, securities, turn*

SELL-SIDE APPLICATIONS. E-commerce software applications that address a company's online sales strategy. These solutions include transaction and payment processors, and catalogs. *See Also: address, online, transaction*

SELLER DRIVEN AUCTION. A forward auction model in which suppliers offer items for sale and multiple buyers bid on the items, driving prices up. *See Also: forward, forward auction, offer, on, sale, up*

SELLER FINANCING. Occurs when a buyer cannot get a loan to buy an asset or a piece of property, so the seller instead of a bank provides a secondary trust or a mortgage through which the buyer pays the money back in monthly installments. *See Also: asset, bank, mortgage, trust*

SELLER'S 30. A contract that gives the seller the option of delivering the security certificate within 30 days. *See Also: certificate, contract, option, security*

SELLER'S CALL. Buying a commodity that is the same quality as described in a contract establishing its future price. *See Also: commodity, contract*

SELLER'S MARKET. Occurs when demand exceeds supply, which benefits anyone trying to sell a security or other asset. *See Also: asset, demand, security, supply*

SELLER'S OPTION TRADE. A transaction in which the seller can, after notifying the buyer in writing, deliver the security's certificate on or before the day the option expires in 60 days, instead of settling the transaction in a regular-way delivery. *See Also: certificate, delivery, option, transaction*

SELLER'S SEVEN SALE. Occurs when the seller agrees not to deliver the security certificate to the buyer for at least seven days. *See Also: certificate, security*

SELLING AWAY. Occurs when a broker sells a security that his or her firm has not authorized the broker to sell. *See Also: broker, firm, security*

SELLING BELOW THE MARKET. Occurs when one security is selling for less than other similar securities. *See Also: securities, security*

SELLING CLIMAX. Describes a downward price trend that suddenly creates a volume increase, which plunges the price dramatically. *See Also: trend, volume*

SELLING CONCESSION. Brokers who receive a commission to help distribute a securities offering. *See Also: commission, offering, securities*

SELLING DIVIDENDS. An improper activity in which a trader influences his or her client to buy investment company securities only so he or she can receive an approaching dividend. In essence, the customer is actually paying for the dividend with his or her own money because the dividend already is included in the fund's net asset value. *See Also: activity, asset, client, dividend, investment, investment company, net, net asset value, securities, trader*

SELLING FLAT. Occurs when an invest or buying a bond does not have to pay any additional amount, such as accrued interest, other than the bond's actual purchase price. *See Also: accrued interest, actual, bond, interest, pay, purchase price*

SELLING GROUP. A group of dealers that helps an underwriting syndicate distribute a new or secondary issue by distributing the securities to the public. The group, in turn, receives a commission from the sales. *See Also: commission, issue, securities, syndicate, turn, underwriting, underwriting syndicate*

SELLING ON BALANCE. Occurs when supply exceeds demand and thus prices are falling and securities are being sold in high volume. *See Also: demand, securities, supply, volume*

SELLING ON THE GOOD NEWS. Occurs when an investor sells his or her holdings in a security after the release of positive information about that security. They believe the stock has reached its top price and that profit taking will occur. *See Also: profit, security, stock, top*

SELLING SHORT. *See Also: sale, short sale*

SELLING THE CROWN JEWELS. Often used to fend off a takeover attempt, a company will sell some of its more valuable assets to make the company less attractive to the raider. *See Also: raider, takeover*

SELLING THE INTERMARKET SPREAD. Occurs when an investor simultaneously sells short a Treasury bill future and buys a certificate of deposit futures contract. *See Also: certificate, contract, futures, futures contract, Treasury bill*

SELLING, GENERAL, AND ADMINISTRATIVE EXPENSES (SG&A). An expense section of a company's profit and loss statement that includes items such as advertising, salaries, commissions, travel, entertainment, and promotion. *See Also: expense, profit, profit and loss statement, statement*

SENIOR BOND. A bond that has priority over other bonds in claiming assets and dividends. *See Also: bond, priority*

SENIOR DEBT. Any debt security that takes priority over other debts from the same issuer. *See Also: debt security, priority, security*

SENIOR REFUNDING. Occurs when securities that mature in five to 12 years are replaced with securities that have original maturities of 15 years or longer. Senior refunding often is done to reduce interest costs, to extend a maturity date, or to consolidate several different issues. *See Also: interest, maturity, refunding, securities*

SENIOR REGISTERED OPTION PRINCIPAL. A company's officer responsible for customer accounts and for customer options transactions. *See Also: officer*

SENIOR SECURITIES. Debt and equity securities that have priority over other securities when claiming assets and dividends. *See Also: equity, priority, securities*

SENSITIVE MARKET. Also describes an insecure market in which the release of either positive or negative information will cause major price shifts. *See Also: market*

SENTIMENT INDICATOR. A market gauge that indicates changes in investors' moods, psychology, and strategies. *See Also: market*

SEP. Simplified Employee Pension Plan. *See Also: pension, pension plan*

SEPARATE ACCOUNT. Describes a variable annuity in which the issuer cannot commingle the investor's funds with the issuer's funds because the investor holds all of the risk. The investment, therefore, is kept in a separate account. *See Also: account, annuity, investment, risk, variable annuity*

SEPARATE CUSTOMER. Describes the highest level of customer protection that the Securities Investor Protection Corporation provides. The SIPC keeps one investor's cash, margin, and special bond accounts separate from another customer's by listing a security's ownership under the investor's name. *See Also: bond, cash, corporation, level, listing, margin, name, securities, SIPC*

SEPARATE PROPERTY. Property that is not jointly owned.

SEPARATE TRADING OF REGISTERED INTEREST AND PRIN-CIPAL OF SECURITIES (STRIPS). A U.S. Treasury method of selling interest and principal payments separately on certain qualified government-issued securities. *See Also: bond, interest, principal, securities, stripped bond*

SEQUENTIAL PAY BOND. A bond that begins principal payments after classes with an earlier principal priority have paid to zero. Sequential pay bonds receive principal payments until their balances are paid to completely paid. *See Also: bond, pay, principal, priority*

SEQUENTIAL TRANSACTIONS. When a security is heavily traded on an exchange, the exchange's ticker tape lists the transactions in consecutive order by volume and by price, but without constantly repeating the identifying stock symbol. *See Also: exchange, order, security, stock, symbol, tape, ticker tape, volume*

SERIAL BONDS. A group of bonds from the same issue that have different maturity dates. *See Also: issue, maturity*

SERIAL BONDS PAYABLE. A liability account of the face values of outstanding serial bonds. *See Also: account, liability, outstanding, serial bonds*

SERIES 7 EXAM. A test of the basic understanding of the securities industry required and administered by the NASD of all registered representative candidates. The multiple choice test is developed by the New York Stock Exchange. *See Also: exchange, industry, nasd, New York Stock Exchange, registered representative, securities, stock, stock exchange, test*

SERIES BOND. One bond that is offered publicly on a number of different dates instead of on one particular issue date. *See Also: bond, issue*

SERIES E BOND. A former government savings bond series, issued from World War II to 1979, that will pay the owner interest for up to 40 years of ownership. The Series E Bond was replaced by the Series EE Bond, for which it can be exchanged. *See Also: bond, E, interest, pay, savings bond, Series EE bond*

SERIES EE BOND. A discounted, nontransferable U.S. government savings bond. These bonds are sold in denominations of at least $25 and mature in seven to 10 years. *See Also: bond, savings bond*

SERIES HH BOND. A nontransferable U.S. government current income bond that sells at face value. These bonds are sold in denominations of at least $500 and mature in 10 years. *See Also: bond, current, face value*

SERIES OF OPTIONS. A group of call or put option contracts, with each based on the same underlying security, having the same striking price, and expiring on the same date. *See Also: option, put, put option, security, striking price, underlying security*

SERVER. A host computer on a network that holds information, such as Web sites, responds to requests for information. Requests can include links to other Web pages, access to specific information on a data base, video, etc. *See Also: base, on, sites, Web*

SERVICE. To make regular interest and sinking fund payments on a long-term obligation. *See Also: fund, interest, obligation, sinking fund*

SERVICE FEE. The difference between interest borrowers pay as part of their payments and the interest investors receive. This amount is retained by the mortgage servicer. *See Also: interest, mortgage, pay, servicer*

SERVICER. The party that collects periodic payments from borrowers and passes the remaining balance of principal and interest to the lender or investor. The servicer may retain a portion of the interest, generally 50 to 75 basis points per year. *See Also: and interest, balance, basis, interest, principal*

SERVICING A MORTGAGE. The financial preparation, bookkeeping, analysis, and follow-up care of a mortgage pool. These services carry a fee, which is subtracted from the borrower's mortgage payments. *See Also: carry, mortgage, mortgage pool, pool*

SESSION. One trading day. *See Also: trading day*

SETTLE. To finalize a securities transaction, usually with the physical delivery of the security and the payment of the purchase price. *See Also: delivery, purchase price, securities, security, transaction*

SETTLEMENT BALANCE ORDER (SBO). After a firm has netted its transactions with other participants in the Clearing Division of the Mortgage-Backed Securities Clearing Corporation, the SBO is the net position of the firm. The resultant position is the actual receive/delivery obligations of each participant for each coupon, or class. *See Also: actual, class, corporation, coupon, firm, net, net position, participant, position, SBO, securities*

SETTLEMENT DATE. The day that securities must be delivered and paid to complete a transaction. *See Also: securities, transaction*

SETTLEMENT PRICE. A commodity's closing price. *See Also: closing price*

SETTLOR. A person who created a trust between two living people, as opposed to a person who creates a trust through a will. *See Also: trust*

SEVERALLY AND JOINTLY. An Eastern account, with the underwriting syndicate agreeing to buy a municipal issue in which the syndicate members, both individually and as a group, will be responsible for any unsold securities. *See Also: account, eastern account, issue, securities, syndicate, underwriting, underwriting syndicate*

SEVERALLY BUT NOT JOINTLY. A Western account, with the underwriting syndicate agreeing to buy part of a corporate issue in which the syndicate members individually, but not as a group, will be responsible for any unsold securities. For example, if one member sells all of his or her shares, but another member does not, the first will not be liable for the securities that the second member did not sell. *See Also: account, issue, securities, syndicate, underwriting, underwriting syndicate, western account*

SG&A. Selling, General, and Administrative Expenses. *See Also: selling*

SHADOW CALENDAR. An issue that, because of a Securities and Exchange Commission backlog, or because of a volatile market, has no effective registration date yet available. *See Also: commission, exchange, issue, market, registration, securities, volatile*

SHADOW MARKET. Occurs when options and futures are manipulated because of their high level of leverage. *See Also: futures, level, leverage*

SHADOW PRICE. The price at which a security would sell under equilibrium conditions. *See Also: security*

SHADOW WARRANT. Occurs when additional loan interest payments are tied to a common stock's market performance. *See Also: interest, market*

SHAKEOUT. Occurs when market conditions change and create an atmosphere in which marginally financed participants in an industry are eliminated. *See Also: change, industry, market*

SHARE. A stock unit that represents a portion of company ownership. *See Also: stock, unit*

SHARE BROKER. A discount broker who bases his or her commissions on the number of shares that are involved in the deal. The more shares involved, the lower the commission per share. *See Also: broker, commission, discount, discount broker, share*

SHARE CAPITAL. Capital that stockholders provide.

SHARE OF BENEFICIAL INTEREST. A security that represents an undivided interest in a debt security pool. *See Also: debt security, interest, pool, security*

SHARE REGISTER. A company's record of who owns the publicly held shares. *See Also: publicly held*

SHARE REPURCHASE PLAN. A plan that allows a company to buy back its outstanding shares, usually because the shares are undervalued. The plan helps the company increase its stock's market value because the reduction of outstanding shares pushes up the earnings per share. *See Also: earnings, market, market value, outstanding, share, undervalued*

SHAREBUILDER INVESTMENT PLAN. A plan in which a bank depositor's account is regularly debited for an amount that will be invested in the securities market the next day. *See Also: account, bank, market, securities*

SHARED APPRECIATION MORTGAGE. A Shared Appreciation Mortgage (SAM) is a mortgage in which a borrower pays a lower interest rate to the lender in exchange for some portion of the underlying properties' appreciation. SAMs are more attractive to borrowers who live in housing markets with little or no appreciation. *See Also: appreciation, exchange, interest, interest rate, mortgage*

SHARED APPRECIATION NOTE. A fixed-rate mortgage with the borrower and lender sharing in the value appreciation's equity interest during the mortgage's life. *See Also: equity, interest, mortgage*

SHARED EQUITY MORTGAGE. Occurs when an investor makes the down payment for a home buyer, then pays a portion of the monthly mortgage payments, in exchange for a percentage of the home's appreciation. *See Also: appreciation, exchange, home, mortgage*

SHAREHOLDER. Any person who owns units of a company's stock. *See Also: stock*

SHARES AUTHORIZED. The maximum number of stock shares a company can sell as prescribed in its articles of incorporation. The company can sell more shares only if the board passes a charter amendment increasing the maximum number of shares authorized. *See Also: articles of incorporation, charter, stock*

SHARES OUTSTANDING. Amount of stock, or shares, held by shareholders. *See Also: stock*

SHARING AGREEMENT. An agreement outlining how costs will be accounted for and how revenues distributed among the partners in a limited partnership. *See Also: limited partnership, partnership*

SHARK. A company that tries to take over another company when it is vulnerable to such an act. *See Also: take*

SHARK REPELLENT. Used to describe a company's actions when it changes its charter to make the company less attractive to a corporate raider. *See Also: charter, raider*

SHARK WATCHER. A company that watches for early indications of a takeover attempt, identifies the raider, then solicits proxies of any client company that probably will become a target. *See Also: client, raider, takeover, target*

SHAVE. An extra charge added to a security purchase when the buyer wants to extend the delivery time. *See Also: delivery, security, time*

SHEARED. An unsuccessful broker or dealer. *See Also: broker, dealer*

SHELF DISTRIBUTION. A company officer's right to sell shares from his or her portfolio within nine months after their effective date. *See Also: effective date, portfolio, right*

SHELF REGISTRATION. A Securities and Exchange Commission registration that carries the right for a security to be sold at some unspecified future date. *See Also: commission, exchange, registration, right, securities, security*

SHELL COMPANY. An issuing company that has no assets and no operations. While the company is not necessarily a cover for fraud, its securities are high risk. *See Also: operations, risk, securities*

SHERMAN ANTI-TRUST ACT. Passed in 1890, this law was designed to curtail monopolies and cartels and their growing influence on the nation's economy by limiting and restricting businesses that dominate a specific industry. Such domination allows the companies to manipulate prices. *See Also: industry*

SHIBOSAI. A private, Japanese placement market. *See Also: market, placement*

SHINGLE THEORY. A broker's responsibility to treat clients fairly and equally when he or she advertises, or "hangs out a shingle," to do business publicly.

SHOGUN SECURITY. A U.S. corporation-issued, dollar-denominated security distributed in Japan. *See Also: security*

SHOP. A broker-dealer's office, or the production area of a company.

SHOPPING BOTS. Automated programs designed to collect products or prices for comparison purposes.

SHOPPING CART. A feature on many e-commerce sites that allows buyers to place more than one item on hold, while the buyer continues to browse the site. The buyer can later proceed to a checkout page, in which all the items will appear. *See Also: e-commerce, hold, on, sites, will*

SHORT AGAINST THE BOX. Occurs when an investor sells the same number of securities short that he or she owns. *See Also: securities*

SHORT BOND. Either a bond that once had a long maturity but that now is nearing that maturity date, or any bond that has been sold short. *See Also: bond, maturity*

SHORT CALL. A call option sold on an opening sale transaction. *See Also: call option, opening sale, option, sale, transaction*

SHORT COUPON. A newly issued bond with a first coupon due in less than six months. *See Also: bond, coupon, first coupon*

SHORT COVERING. Occurs when an investor buys securities or commodities to close a short position or to return a security that previously was borrowed. *See Also: close, position, return, securities, security, short position*

SHORT DATES. Any date falling within the next month.

SHORT EXEMPT. A short-sale order that does not require the sale to be made on an uptick, such as one that is part of an arbitrage transaction. *See Also: arbitrage, order, sale, transaction, uptick*

SHORT FUNDED. Occurs when an investor buys short-term money at a high interest rate because he or she believes interest rates will soon fall, making it cheaper to obtain lendable funds. *See Also: fall, interest, interest rate*

SHORT HEDGE. A method of reducing the risk of a security's falling value without requiring ownership of that security, such as buying a put option or selling short against the box. *See Also: against the box, option, put, put option, risk, security, selling short, short against the box*

SHORT INTEREST. The total number of shares investors have sold short but have not yet bought back.

SHORT INTEREST RATIO. The average daily trading volume during a specific time period, divided into the total number of shares that an investor has sold short. *See Also: average, time, trading volume, volume*

SHORT INTEREST THEORY. Predicts an upward price movement when short interest is 1.5 to two times higher than the security's average daily volume. *See Also: average, interest, movement, short interest, volume*

SHORT LEG. A short option that is part of a spread position. *See Also: option, position, spread, spread position*

SHORT MARKET VALUE. The current market value of securities sold short. *See Also: current, current market value, market, market value, securities*

SHORT OF THE MARKET. Occurs when an investor holds a short position in a security because he or she believes the security's price will drop. *See Also: drop, position, security, short position*

SHORT POSITION. An investor's situation after shorting a security, option, or futures contract. *See Also: contract, futures, futures contract, option, security*

SHORT PURCHASE. Occurs when an investor buys stock to cover a previous short sale in the same security. *See Also: sale, security, short sale, stock*

SHORT PUT. A put option sold on an opening sale transaction. *See Also: opening sale, option, put, put option, sale, transaction*

SHORT SALE. The sale of a security that the seller does not own, based on the belief that the seller will be able to buy it back at a lower price, thus profiting from the difference. Short sales can be executed only through a brokerage margin account, with the brokerage firm loaning the seller the security so he or she can deliver it to the buyer. *See Also: account, firm, margin, margin account, sale, security*

SHORT SALE RULE. A Securities and Exchange Commission regulation that all short sales must be on a zero-plus tick or on an uptick. *See Also: commission, exchange, securities, tick, uptick*

SHORT SQUEEZE. A situation in which the price of a security or futures contract moves up sharply, forcing traders with short positions to buy back the position in order to cover and prevent losses. *See Also: contract, futures, futures contract, order, position, security*

SHORT SWING. Occurs when a company's directors, officers, stockholders, or others with access to inside information, transact a profitable deal by buying and then selling back the company's securities within six months (or selling the securities and then buying them back within six months). Such transactions normally are prohibited, and the company often can recover any profits, because U.S. securities laws assume the directors, officers, or stockholders acted on inside information, which is illegal. *See Also: inside information, securities*

SHORT TENDER. An illegal practice in which a person accepts a tender offer by delivering borrowed securities. According to the Securities and Exchange Commission, only long securities can be included in a tender offer. *See Also: commission, exchange, offer, securities, tender, tender offer*

SHORT TERM. For purposes of capital gains tax, an investment of one year or less. *See Also: capital, capital gains tax, investment*

SHORT-TERM AUCTION RATE (STAR). This is a money market, cumulative preferred stock with a dividend rate that a Dutch auction adjusts every 49 days. If a holder is unhappy with the new dividend, he or she can redeem the stock at any of the seven yearly auctions. *See Also: auction, cumulative preferred stock, dividend, Dutch auction, market, money market, preferred stock, redeem, stock*

SHORT-TERM CAPITAL GAIN. The profit from an investment held for one year or less. *See Also: investment, profit*

SHORT-TERM CAPITAL LOSS. The loss from an investment held for one year or less. *See Also: investment*

SHORT-TERM DEBT. A bond or other debt instrument that will mature within the next five years. *See Also: bond, debt instrument, instrument*

SHORT-TERM INDEXED LIABILITY TRANSACTIONS (STILTS). A debt that the issuer can convert into commercial paper at a specific interest spread for a series of short-term rollover periods. *See Also: commercial paper, interest, paper, rollover, spread*

SHORT-TERM INVESTMENT FUND (STIF). This is a pool of money invested in money markets that matures in less than 90 days. *See Also: pool*

SHORT-TERM NOTE ISSUANCE FACILITY. Since it was replaced by the revolving underwriting facilities, this once represented the placing of one-to five-year Eurodebt securities. *See Also: revolving underwriting facilities, securities, underwriting*

SHORT-TERM SAVINGS ACCOUNT. An account the depositor closes within two years of the date he or she opened it. *See Also: account*

SHORT-TERM SECURITY. A security that is payable on demand and that matures in a year or less. *See Also: demand, security*

SHORT-TERM TRADING. Holding an investment for a brief period of time with the hopes of making a quick profit. *See Also: investment, profit, time*

SHORTCUT FORECLOSURE. A mortgage clause that allows the lender to sell the property if the borrower defaults. *See Also: mortgage*

SHORTS. A British, gilt-edged security that matures in less than five years. *See Also: gilt-edged, security*

SHOW STOPPER. A legal maneuver a company takes to fend off a takeover attempt. A company will convince government officials to pass certain laws that would make a takeover impossible. *See Also: legal, pass, takeover*

SHRINKS. Common stock purchases. *See Also: stock*

SHUT-OFF RATE. A high mortgage rate established to discourage potential home buyers. *See Also: home, mortgage*

SICK MARKET. A weak market. *See Also: market*

SIDE COLLATERAL. Collateral that is too small to cover the total loan amount.

SIDE-BY-SIDE TRADING. Occurs when an investor simultaneously trades a security and an option on that security on the same exchange. *See Also: exchange, option, security*

SIDELINER. An investor who closes out his or her positions, then waits for a better time to get in the market. *See Also: market, time*

SIDEWAYS MARKET. Occurs when market prices remain relatively stable, not moving up or down to any great degree. *See Also: market*

SIGHT DRAFT. A negotiable instrument similar to a check used to immediately transfer money from a buyer to a seller. Aside from the buyer's signature, the draft includes the paying agent's name. *See Also: check, draft, instrument, name, negotiable, negotiable instrument, transfer*

SIGNAL. A gauge that indicates when a price is expected to rise or fall, thus giving an investor a way of knowing when to buy or sell a particular security. *See Also: fall, security*

SIGNATURE AUTHORITY. Occurs when one person gives another person permission to trade for the first person's account. *See Also: account*

SILENT PARTNER. A limited partner who does not vote on management aspects.

SILENT SALES. An illegal procedure through which a homeowner secretly sells his or her home without notifying the local government or the original mortgagor of the ownership transfer. This type of sale sometimes occurs because the buyer refuses to pay a new mortgage rate or is unable to obtain a mortgage. *See Also: home, local, mortgage, pay, sale, transfer*

SILICON VALLEY. A geographic region southeast of San Francisco noted for its abundance of high-technology design and manufacturing companies. Also refers to a start-up company that is involved in high-technology, and located in Northern California. *See Also: start-up*

SILVER THURSDAY. Occurred on March 27, 1980, when the Hunt brothers failed to meet a margin call for $100 million in silver futures contracts, which had disastrous effects on the commodities and financial markets. Their brokerage firm later covered the call, but the damage had already been done. *See Also: firm, futures, margin, margin call*

SIMPLE ARBITRAGE. Arbitrage that an investor can achieve by using three markets. *See Also: arbitrage*

SIMPLE INTEREST. Interest that is based on the original principal amount instead of compounding. *See Also: compounding, principal*

SIMPLE MAIL TRANSFER PROTOCOL. *See Also: SMTP*

SIMPLE MAJORITY. This occurs when the owners of at least 50 percent of a company's outstanding shares agree to vote together on a corporate matter. *See Also: outstanding*

SIMPLIFIED EMPLOYEE PENSION PLAN (SEP). A plan in which a company contributes vested, tax-sheltered funds on behalf of employees who are at least 25 years or older and who have worked for the company for at least three years. The amounts usually are based on company profits, so the plan becomes a pension-profit-sharing plan combination. *See Also: combination*

SINGLE CAPITAL STRUCTURE COMPANY. A company that has issued only one class of securities. *See Also: class, securities*

SINGLE DEBT. An accounting method in which the lender records installment payments as a lump sum.

SINGLE LIABILITY. When a person is responsible for a company's liabilities, but only for the percentage he or she originally invested.

SINGLE MONTHLY MORTALITY (SMM). A prepayment measure that expresses the rate at which a specified percentage of the remaining mortgages in a pool will prepay per month. It is expressed as a percentage of the mortgage balance outstanding at the beginning of a period. SMM includes only prepayments, not contractual principal payments. *See Also: actual, balance, mortgage, outstanding, pool, prepayment, principal*

SINGLE OPTION. Used to differentiate between a put and a call option, or between a spread and a swaddle. *See Also: call option, option, put, spread*

SINGLE PREMIUM DEFERRED ANNUITY (SPDA). A tax-deferred investment in which a person makes a lump-sum payment to an insurance company or to a mutual fund selling the annuity, with the annuity depreciating over the years. Such annuities have no ceiling on the amount a person can contribute. *See Also: annuity, fund, insurance, investment, mutual fund*

SINGLE-PURCHASE CONTRACT. An annuity in which the investor can make lump-sum purchases and can receive immediate or future payments. *See Also: annuity*

SINGLE-STATE MUNICIPAL BOND FUND. A mutual fund with investments concentrated in obligations from governments within one state. *See Also: fund, governments, mutual fund*

SINKER. A bond that carries a sinking fund stipulation. *See Also: bond, fund, sinking fund*

SINKING FUND. A fund that a company sets aside each year to retire outstanding bonds or preferred stock. *See Also: fund, outstanding, preferred stock, retire, stock*

SINKING FUND BOND. A bond issued with the stipulation that the issuer has, indeed, set up a fund through which the bond can be redeemed. *See Also: bond, fund*

SINKING FUND REQUIREMENTS. The amount that a sinking fund must regularly increase so the fund will have enough money to redeem the bonds at maturity. *See Also: fund, maturity, redeem, sinking fund*

SIPC. Securities Investor Protection Corporation. *See Also: corporation, securities*

SITES. A British purchase in which the item is in a sealed container, so that the buyer will not know what he or she is getting until after buying the item.

SIZE. The number of shares available at the bid and ask prices. *See Also: ask*

SIZE OF THE MARKET. The number of round lots that are being bid at the specialist's highest book price, and the number that simultaneously is being offered at the specialist's lowest book price. *See Also: book*

SIZED OUT. Occurs when a broker cannot cross stock at a block trader's price because another broker is offering a larger number of shares at the trader's price, making the other broker's offer more attractive. *See Also: broker, offer, offering, stock*

SKIMMING PRICES. A high initial price followed by several price drops. Skimming allows the seller to attract as many buyers as possible at the highest price before dropping the price some more, which attracts more buyers at that next level. *See Also: level*

SKIP-DAY SETTLEMENT. Occurs when a security is to be paid for and delivered on the second day after the transaction date. *See Also: security, transaction*

SKIP-PAYMENT PRIVILEGE. An installment mortgage stipulation in which a borrower can skip a payment if previous payments have been made ahead of schedule. *See Also: mortgage*

SKIRT LENGTH THEORY. The theory that the rise and fall of hemlines is a predictor for the direction of the stock market. *See Also: fall, market, stock, stock market*

SLAP. Self-Liquidating Asset Purchase. *See Also: asset, self-liquidating*

SLATED VALUE. As opposed to a market value or par value, this is a per-share value a security carries only for accounting purposes. *See Also: market, market value, par, par value, security*

SLD LAST SALE. Appears on an exchange's consolidated tape to indicate "sold last sale" when a great change has occurred between transactions in a securities issue, with the change usually consisting of one or two points, depending on the issue's price. *See Also: change, consolidated tape, issue, securities, tape*

SLEEPER. An underpriced stock that unexpectedly rises sharply in price. *See Also: stock, underpriced*

SLEEPING BEAUTY. A takeover target company that a raider has not yet approached. *See Also: raider, takeover, target*

SLIDE. Occurs when a bookkeeper mistakenly moves the decimal point on a figure when recording the figure on the company's books. *See Also: point*

SLMA. Student Loan Marketing Association.

SLOW MARKET. A market with little trading activity. *See Also: activity, market*

SLUGS. Nonmarketable U.S. Treasury securities sold to states and municipalities, which deposit the securities into escrow accounts until they need to pay off their own bonds upon maturity. *See Also: escrow, maturity, pay, securities*

SLUMP. A temporary, but steady, decline in market prices. *See Also: market, steady*

SMA. Special Miscellaneous Account.

SMALL BUSINESS ADMINISTRATION (SBA). A government agency that provides management advice and government-guaranteed loans to small businesses. SBA securities are exempt from state and local taxes, but not from federal taxes. *See Also: local, securities*

SMALL BUSINESS ADMINISTRATION LOAN. Commonly referred to as a Sammie Bee, this is an SBA loan with a unit trust certificate as collateral. A commercial bank will combine these loans into $1 million to $25 million, SBA-backed pools, and then will sell the pools to institutional investors. *See Also: bank, certificate, collateral, commercial bank, Sammie Bee, SBA, trust, unit*

SMALL BUSINESS INVESTMENT COMPANY. A federal agency that, under the auspices of the Small Business Administration, loans money to small businesses.

SMALL CAP. A company with a small amount of capitalization. *See Also: capitalization*

SMALL INVESTOR. As opposed to an institutional investor, this individual usually buys stock shares in small, odd-lot quantities. *See Also: institutional investor, stock*

SMALL ORDER EXECUTION SYSTEM. A National Association of Securities Dealers program through which over-the-counter deals involving not more than 1,000 shares of a qualified issue can be matched immediately to the best available price. *See Also: issue, securities*

SMALL SAVER CERTIFICATE. A savings account in which the money must remain deposited for at least 30 months, but deposits need not be any larger than $100, with interest rates tied to U.S. Treasury security yields. *See Also: account, interest, savings account, security, with interest*

SMALL TO MEDIUM SIZED ENTERPRISES. Also referred to as SME, a term that segments businesses and other organizations somewhere in between SOHOs (small office home office) and larger enterprises. The European Union defines SMEs as legally independent companies with up to 500 employees. *See Also: home, SME, term, up*

SMART CARDS. Similar to credit cards, smart cards are plastic cards that contain, depending on the type, a microprocessor and a memory chip, or just a memory chip. The chip is a memory device for storing information, such as telephone numbers, addresses, medical information and cash. The microprocessor component enables additional functionality such as adding, deleting, and manipulating data.

SMART MONEY. A wise investor who has more knowledge and experience in the market than the average investor. *See Also: average, market*

SMASH. A dramatic drop in market prices. *See Also: drop, market*

SMBS. Stripped Mortgage-Backed Security. *See Also: security*

SME. Small to Medium Sized Enterprises.

SMM. Single Monthly Mortality.

SMTP. Short for Simple Mail Transfer Protocol, a standard Internet protocol used for delivery of e-mail. *See Also: protocol, transfer*

SNAKE. A European agreement to let a nation's currencies flow freely in the open market, with a charting of the configuration resembling a snake, unless certain conditions or measures are exceeded. *See Also: market, open, open market*

SNOWBALLING. Occurs when a stop order is executed and causes the market to drop or increase even more, depending on whether the market had been going up or down. When the market reacts, more stop orders are executed. *See Also: drop, market, order, stop, stop order*

SOCIAL CONSCIOUSNESS MUTUAL FUND. A mutual fund with investments directed to bring capital appreciation and with the investments made in companies that meet certain social criteria. For example, such a fund would not have investments in tobacco companies or known polluters. *See Also: appreciation, capital, capital appreciation, fund, mutual fund*

SOCIALISM. A system of government in which the government controls all production, utilities, manufacturing, etc., and in turn pays for its citizens' medical care and equally provides income to workers. *See Also: turn*

SOCIALLY RESPONSIBLE INVESTMENT. An investment that carries a lower rate of return, but that provides society with many benefits. For example, a socially responsible investment would describe an investment made in a company that provided many jobs for the area. *See Also: investment, rate of return, return*

SOCIETY FOR WORLDWIDE INTERBANK FINANCIAL TELE-COMMUNICATIONS (SWIFT). A computer network for transferring financial data and foreign currencies.

SOFT ARBITRAGE. An arbitrage achieved between the public sector and private paper. *See Also: arbitrage, paper, public sector, sector*

SOFT CURRENCY. A nation's currency that cannot be exchanged for another country's hard currencies because the first is fixed at an unrealistic exchange rate and is not backed by gold. The former Soviet Union's ruble, for example, was soft currency. *See Also: currency, exchange, exchange rate*

SOFT DOLLARS. Research and brokerage services, instead of hard dollars, are used to pay for underwriting credits and portfolio transaction commissions. *See Also: pay, portfolio, transaction, underwriting*

SOFT LANDING. Occurs when inflation ends without causing a depression. *See Also: depression, inflation*

SOFT MARKET. A relatively inactive market with little demand and in which a small amount of selling pressure will drive prices down. *See Also: demand, drive, inactive market, market*

SOFT SPOT. Securities that are weak when the rest of the market is strong and on the upswing. *See Also: market*

SOFTWARE PIRACY. The unauthorized copying, distribution, or use of software.

SOHO. Short for Small Office/Home Office, a segment of the business market comprised of professionals who work at home or in small offices. *See Also: home, market*

SOLD TO YOU. One trader's confirmation to another that an offer was accepted. *See Also: confirmation, offer*

SOLD-OUT MARKET. A commodity futures contract that is not available because offerings are limited or because of contract liquidations. *See Also: commodity, contract, futures, futures contract*

SOLE PROPRIETORSHIP. A business owned by one person who carries all liabilities and receives all profits.

SOLVENCY. A company's ability to meet its financial obligations.

SOLVENT DEBTOR SECTION. A federal law that requires a company to buy back its own bonds at a discount to pay income tax on the difference between the bond's original sale price or its face value and the discount repurchase price. *See Also: at a discount, discount, face value, pay, repurchase, sale*

SOPHISTICATED INVESTOR. A wealthy investor who studies market trends and, based on experience and knowledge, invests large sums of money. *See Also: market*

SOURCE AND APPLICATIONS OF FUNDS STATEMENT. The comparison of a company's financial situations in two or more different accounting periods.

SOURCE CODE. When a programmer creates a software application, it is in the form of source code. To execute the application, the programmer then translates the source code into a language, often using a utilities called a compiler or an assembler.

SOURCING. The identification and procurement of goods and services. On the Internet, sourcing ranges from simple commodities to fully automated solutions that capture and simplify the inherent complexity involved. *See Also: Internet, on, procurement*

SOVEREIGN RISK. A person's risk involved in foreign investments because of currency value changes or because of government instability. *See Also: currency, risk*

SPACE ARBITRAGE. Simultaneously selling and buying the same security on two different exchanges to take advantage of price differences. *See Also: exchanges, security, take*

SPAM. Stupid Person's AdvertiseMent is unsolicited junk email. Also refers to the sending of messages, usually advertisements, to discussion groups, bulletin boards, newsgroups, etc.

SPDA. Single Premium Deferred Annuity. *See Also: annuity, deferred annuity, premium*

SPECIAL ARBITRAGE ACCOUNT. A margin account in which a customer receives advantageous credit terms when he or she simultaneously buys a security and sells it in a different market, or simultaneously buys one security and sells an equal one in the same market to profit from any price differences. *See Also: account, credit, margin, margin account, market, profit, security*

SPECIAL ASSESSMENT BOND. A municipal bond issued to pay for a civic project, such as a sewer or a road improvement, with those who benefit from the project assessed a special tax. *See Also: bond, municipal bond, pay*

SPECIAL BID. A fixed bid for a block of stock in which the buyer pays for all transaction costs. *See Also: block of stock, stock, transaction*

SPECIAL BOND ACCOUNT. A brokerage account used to show the firm's purchasing power from bonds that were bought on margin. *See Also: account, brokerage account, margin, on margin, purchasing power*

SPECIAL CASH ACCOUNT. A margin account in which a customer can buy or sell any security long, with all securities delivered within seven days. *See Also: account, margin, margin account, securities, security*

SPECIAL CLAIM ON RESIDUAL EQUITY (SCORE). One of two component parts of an Americus Trust for which holders receive no dividends, but do receive the trust's asset value up to an agreed upon per-share dollar value. The other component is the Prescribed Right To Income and Maximum Equity, better known as PRIME. *See Also: Americus Trust, asset, equity, PRIME, right, trust*

SPECIAL COMMODITY ACCOUNT. A brokerage account through which a customer can buy and sell commodities and commodity futures contracts. *See Also: account, brokerage account, commodity, futures*

SPECIAL CONVERTIBLE DEBT SECURITY ACCOUNT. A margin account in which a customer can finance a short sale of a bond that is easily convertible into margin stock, or that carries a subscription warrant to margin stock. *See Also: account, bond, margin, margin account, sale, short sale, stock, subscription, subscription warrant, warrant*

SPECIAL DEAL. Occurs when the underwriter of investment company securities pays another dealer's employee in connection with the sale. The National Association of Securities Dealers prohibits this practice. *See Also: investment, investment company, sale, securities*

SPECIAL DEPOSITORY. Any bank that the U.S. Treasury allows to receive deposits from the sale of government bonds. *See Also: bank, sale*

SPECIAL DEVISE. A gift of property.

SPECIAL DRAWING RIGHTS. An International Monetary Fund credit against which specific nations can draw to pay off their payment deficits. *See Also: credit, fund, International Monetary Fund, pay*

SPECIAL FINANCING MORTGAGES. Mortgages that are offered to specific groups of people, including native Americans, people with disabilities, and people living in rural areas.

SPECIAL INSURANCE PREMIUM FUNDING ACCOUNT. A brokerage account through which the customer can buy a life insurance policy, with the equity placed in shares of a registered investment company or trust bought along with the policy. *See Also: account, brokerage account, equity, insurance, investment, investment company, life insurance, registered investment company, trust*

SPECIAL ISSUES. U.S. Treasury securities for investing in government trust fund reserves. *See Also: fund, securities, trust*

SPECIAL LOAN. A loan with unusual collateral and normally carrying a higher interest rate. *See Also: collateral, interest, interest rate*

SPECIAL MISCELLANEOUS ACCOUNT (SMA). A special brokerage account that shows how much unpledged money a customer has available in his or her margin account. *See Also: account, brokerage account, margin, margin account*

SPECIAL OFFERING. An issuing company's secondary distribution that has been registered in detail with the Securities and Exchange Commission. *See Also: commission, exchange, secondary distribution, securities*

SPECIAL OMNIBUS ACCOUNT. A broker-dealer account in which a second broker-dealer who is registered with the Securities and Exchange Commission can transact for the customers without giving out their names. *See Also: account, broker-dealer, commission, exchange, securities*

SPECIAL OPTION. An over-the-counter option that still is effective and that a broker-dealer or a customer in the secondary market offers to resell. *See Also: broker-dealer, market, option, over-the-counter option, secondary market*

SPECIAL PARTNER. A business partner who does not actively participate in the company's management, and who is responsible for the company's liabilities up to the percentage of investment that he or she originally made. *See Also: investment*

SPECIAL SECURITY. A Federal National Mortgage Association security that a bank purchases with deposits from a tax-exempt savings certificate. *See Also: bank, certificate, mortgage, security*

SPECIAL SITUATION. Occurs when a security will earn higher-than-average profits because of a unique and unexpected event involving the security itself or the issuing company. *See Also: average, security*

SPECIAL SUBSCRIPTION ACCOUNT. A margin account through which a client can receive credits to buy a margin security by exercising a right or warrant. *See Also: account, client, margin, margin account, margin security, right, security, warrant*

SPECIAL TAX BOND. A municipal revenue bond with a luxury tax, such as one on liquor, which pays for the debt service. *See Also: bond, debt service, luxury tax, municipal revenue bond, revenue bond, service*

SPECIALIST. An exchange member whose job is to maintain an orderly market in a specific group of securities by buying and selling for his or her own account and for clients. *See Also: account, exchange, job, market, securities*

SPECIALIST BLOCK PURCHASE. Occurs when a specialist buys a large block of stock for his or her own account. *See Also: account, block of stock, specialist, stock*

SPECIALIST BLOCK SALE. Occurs when a specialist sells a large block of stock for his or her own account. *See Also: account, block of stock, specialist, stock*

SPECIALIST MANAGER. An investment manager who researches and handles only one class of investments. *See Also: class, investment, investment manager, manager*

SPECIALIST MARKET. A market where investment information can be obtained only through a dealer. *See Also: dealer, investment, market*

SPECIALIST PERFORMANCE EVALUATION QUESTIONNAIRE. A series of questions the New York Stock Exchange has floor brokers answer concerning specialists and their performances. The questionnaire is used to screen specialists. *See Also: exchange, floor, New York Stock Exchange, screen, stock, stock exchange*

SPECIALIST UNIT. A group of at least three specialists responsible for maintaining an orderly market in specific stocks. *See Also: market*

SPECIALIST'S ACCOUNT. A brokerage account through which exchange specialists and market makers who deal in listed options can take advantage of credit to pay for their dealer inventories. *See Also: account, brokerage account, credit, dealer, exchange, market, pay, take*

SPECIALIST'S BOOK. The book a specialist uses to keep track of all limit, stop, and market orders for which he or she is responsible. *See Also: book, limit, market, specialist, stop*

SPECIALIST'S SHORT-SALE RATIO. A comparison of the amount of stock a New York Stock Exchange specialist sold short, to the total number of short sales. The ratio provides a gauge of how the specialists perceive the market and whether they believe the market will be moving up or down. *See Also: exchange, market, New York Stock Exchange, ratio, specialist, stock, stock exchange*

SPECIALIZED MUTUAL FUND. A mutual fund with investments concentrated in a specific industry. *See Also: fund, industry, mutual fund*

SPECIFIC RISK. A risk that involves the issuing company only-not other securities from other issuers and not securities from other companies in the same industry. *See Also: industry, risk, securities*

SPECTAIL DEALER. A broker-dealer who spends more time taking speculative positions in his or her own account than he or she does on retail customers. *See Also: account, broker-dealer, speculative, time*

SPECULATION. The risk that an investment will, indeed, bring higher profits. *See Also: investment, risk*

SPECULATION INDICATOR. A gauge used to determine how much of a risk investors are willing to take by putting money into a speculative security. *See Also: risk, security, speculative, take*

SPECULATIVE. An unproven, high-risk investment. *See Also: investment*

SPECULATIVE POSITION. An open, unhedged position. *See Also: open, position*

SPECULATOR. A person who will invest in high-risk securities because he or she believes they will bring higher returns. *See Also: securities*

SPEECH RECOGNITION. Software that enables a computer to hear sounds by digitizing sounds sound patterns. These sound patterns are then associated with sound patterns in a data base. When the associations are found, the computer can utilize those digital words as if they had been typed into the computer. Speech recognition is the basis behind voice activated programs that can enable users to operate a computer using commands and for dictation purposes. *See Also: base, basis, digital*

SPIDER. A program that automatically searches the World Wide Web by finding documents and all linked documents. Search engines utilize spiders to index key words and pages for future retrieval. *See Also: index, Web, World Wide Web*

SPIKE. A quick, dramatic price increase.

SPIN OFF. A dividend made up of assets, such as another company's stock, that is distributed to stockholders. Also, a company divestiture resulting in the transfer of assets or an entire subsidiary. *See Also: dividend, stock, subsidiary, transfer*

SPINOUT. A strategy in which a new business venture is derived from non-core assets or technologies from another business. The new business will then be a spin-off to new investors. *See Also: will*

SPLIT. Occurs when stock shares are divided into a larger or smaller number of stock shares. For example, the issuing company will issue two stocks for every one turned in, which would cut the stock's par value in half. *See Also: issue, par, par value, stock*

SPLIT CLOSE. Occurs when one closing index average is higher, while another closing index average is lower on the same day. *See Also: average, index*

SPLIT COMMISSION. A transaction commission that is divided between the executing broker and the person who brought the deal to the broker's attention. *See Also: broker, commission, transaction*

SPLIT DOWN. A company charter amendment that diminishes the number of issued shares while proportionately pushing up the issue's par value. *See Also: charter, par, par value*

SPLIT FUNDS. A British mutual fund with two classes of security shares: capital shares and income shares. *See Also: capital, fund, mutual fund, security*

SPLIT INVESTMENT COMPANY. A closed-end investment company that issues two different capital stock issues, one paying investment dividends and the other paying dividends from investment appreciation. *See Also: appreciation, capital, capital stock, investment, investment company, stock*

SPLIT OFF. Occurs when a stockholder trades in shares of a controlling company for shares of a subsidiary. *See Also: stockholder, subsidiary*

SPLIT OFFERING. Occurs when a bond issue consists of both serial maturities and term maturities. *See Also: bond, issue, term*

SPLIT OPENING. Occurs when a security opens at two different prices, usually because traders simultaneously entered their first quotes on the same security. *See Also: security*

SPLIT ORDER. A large securities transaction that is broken into several smaller transactions to avoid causing market fluctuations in the security's price. *See Also: market, securities, transaction*

SPLIT RATING. Occurs when two bond rating services give the same issue two different ratings. *See Also: bond, bond rating, issue*

SPLIT UP. *See Also: split*

SPLIT-SCHEDULE LOAN. A mortgage with an interest rate that lasts only a few years, after which it is amortized according to a schedule. *See Also: interest, interest rate, mortgage*

SPONSOR. A person who acts as an officer or a board director of an unincorporated company. *See Also: director, officer*

SPONSORSHIP. Occurs when several professional investors, such as broker-dealers, actively support a particular security. *See Also: professional, security, support*

SPOOFING. The action of misleading a computer system into believing a user is another identity, by circumventing network security. This is accomplished by impersonating a valid TCP/IP address that exists inside of the network. *See Also: address, security, TCP/IP*

SPOT. Available for immediate delivery. *See Also: delivery*

SPOT COMMODITY. A commodity that will be delivered upon settlement, as opposed to the delivery of a futures contract. *See Also: commodity, contract, delivery, futures, futures contract*

SPOT DELIVERY MONTH. The nearest month from purchase in which a commodity can be delivered. *See Also: commodity, nearest month*

SPOT EXCHANGE RATE. The amount of one country's currency needed to buy a unit of another country's currency, with the purchase requiring immediate delivery. *See Also: currency, delivery, unit*

SPOT LENDING. Mortgages originated by processing applications taken directly from prospective borrowers. *See Also: processing*

SPOT LOAN. As opposed to a housing development mortgage, this is a single mortgage made on a single-family home. *See Also: home, mortgage*

SPOT MARKET. Also known as a cash or physical market, this market represents the immediate delivery of an underlying instrument by which a futures or options contract is based. *See Also: commodity, contract, futures, futures contract, transaction*

SPOT MONTH. The month in which a formerly traded commodity is to be delivered. *See Also: commodity*

SPOT NEWS. A news report that could temporarily affect market prices. *See Also: market*

SPOT PRICE. The price quoted for a cash commodity. *See Also: cash, cash commodity, commodity*

SPOT SALE. The purchase of an item to be delivered immediately.

SPOT SECONDARY. A secondary offering made without a registration statement. *See Also: offering, registration, registration statement, statement*

SPOTTED MARKET. A market with small up and down price movements, but showing no major trends. *See Also: market*

SPOUSAL INDIVIDUAL RETIREMENT ACCOUNT. An IRA opened in the name of a spouse who is not employed outside of the home, with the employed spouse making the contributions. The maximum annual amount that can be contributed for both spouses is $2,250. If both spouses worked, $2,000 could be contributed for each for a total of $4,000. *See Also: home, IRA, name*

SPOUSAL REMAINDER TRUST. A method in which income-earning assets are transferred to a person who is taxed at a lower rate, such as a child. Income from the trust is distributed to the beneficiary for costs such as paying for his or her college education. *See Also: trust*

SPREAD. The difference between the bid price and the ask price. *See Also: ask, bid price*

SPREAD BANKER. A commercial banker who matches the maturities of the loans he or she has taken out to the maturities of loans he or she has extended in an effort to profit from the interest rate differences. *See Also: extended, interest, interest rate, profit*

SPREAD LOAD. A mutual fund in which the sales charge principal is paid during the contract's first four years, with the rest paid in equal payments throughout the contract's life. *See Also: fund, mutual fund, principal, sales charge*

SPREAD LOAN. A mutual fund with the principal part of the sales charge paid in the first four years, with the rest paid in equal installments for the life of the contract. *See Also: contract, fund, mutual fund, principal, sales charge*

SPREAD OPTION. Occurs when an investor buys and sells option contracts of the same class on the same underlying security with one or more of the terms in each being different. *See Also: class, option, security, underlying security*

SPREAD ORDER. An order for a listed option that the investor plans to use in a spread strategy. *See Also: listed option, option, order, spread*

SPREAD POSITION. A client account with long and short options on the same underlying security and of the same class. *See Also: account, class, client, security, underlying security*

SPREAD SHEET. The ledger sheet of a company's financial statement, with all income and expenses laid out in columns and rows. *See Also: ledger, statement*

SPREAD SWAP. An illegal practice in which an underwriter agrees to buy an investor's securities in exchange for the investor buying the new issue, with the price set before the registration statement is effective. *See Also: exchange, issue, new issue, registration, registration statement, securities, statement*

SPREADING. Buying and selling option contracts of the same class on the same underlying security to profit from price differences. *See Also: class, option, profit, security, underlying security*

SQUATTING. Registering a trademarked, branded or otherwise generally recognized Internet domain name for the purpose of reselling it at a profit. *See Also: domain name, Internet, name, profit*

SQUAWK BOX. A telephone system broker-dealers use to communicate with the firm's different branches, departments, and offices.

SQUEEZE. Occurs when securities or commodities futures begin increasing in price and investors who sold them short must cover their short positions to avoid major losses, thus driving up the prices even more. *See Also: futures, securities*

SSL. Short for Secured Sockets Layer, a protocol designed to provide the secure transmission of communications via the Internet. Web pages that utilize SSL start with HTTPS. *See Also: HTTPS, Internet, protocol, Web*

STABILIZATION. A lateral price movement usually preceding a change in price direction. *See Also: change, movement*

STABILIZING BID. The bid price that an underwriter will offer immediately after a new security is issued to maintain the security's market level. *See Also: bid price, level, market, offer, security*

STAGFLATION. A period of stagnation and inflation. *See Also: inflation, stagnation*

STAGGERED BOARD. A company's board of directors with terms that are offset so stockholders do not vote for all board members at the same time. For example, if terms run three years and the board has 12 members, four new members are elected each year. A staggered board often will discourage a corporate raider because the raider cannot take over the entire board all at once. *See Also: board of directors, offset, raider, run, take, time*

STAGGERING MATURITIES. A method that bond investors use to reduce risk through buying short-, medium- and long-term bonds. If interest rates go up, the short-term bonds will hold their value better, and if interest rates drop, the long-term bonds will increase faster in value. *See Also: bond, drop, hold, interest, risk*

STAGNATION. Occurs when a country's economy slows substantially.

STAGS. Sterling Transferable Accruing Government Securities. *See Also: securities*

STAKE-OUT INVESTMENT. Occurs when one holding company buys another holding company's nonvoting, convertible preferred stock, with the hope that banking laws will change to allow some interstate banking. After such a change, the first company will have a claim on the second company. *See Also: change, holding company, preferred stock, stock*

STAMPED SECURITY. A security certificate that has been stamped to indicate it has been altered since it was originally issued. *See Also: certificate, security*

STANDARD & POORS. An investment service that rates securities. *See Also: investment, securities, service*

STANDARD & POORS INDEX. As a market performance gauge, this index checks the movement of 500 of the most commonly held stocks, and generalizes the findings to predict the potential movements of other securities and market volatility. *See Also: index, market, movement, securities, volatility*

STANDARD & POORS INDEXES. An average of securities traded on the New York Stock Exchange as determined by multiplying the price of each issue by the number of outstanding shares. *See Also: average, exchange, issue, New York Stock Exchange, outstanding, securities, stock, stock exchange*

STANDARD & POORS RATING. A rating of stocks and bonds of risk with AAA, AA, A, and BBB considered investment grade, indicating minimal risk. *See Also: investment, investment grade, risk*

STANDARD COST. Normal production costs that include no unforeseen conditions. A company can determine its cost efficiency by calculating the difference between standard costs and actual costs. *See Also: actual*

STANDARD DEDUCTION. The amount of money a taxpayer can deduct from his or her annual income on their tax forms without itemizing.

STANDARD DEVIATION. A measure of the degree to which an individual probability value varies from the distribution mean. The higher the number, the greater the risk. *See Also: risk*

STANDARD INDUSTRIAL CLASSIFICATION SYSTEM. A numbering system used to identify companies and to provide information about that company. The numbers indicate the business's industry and are used by analysts and researchers. *See Also: industry*

STANDARD STOCKS. Stock from established, well-run companies.

STANDARDIZED EXPIRATION DATES. The Options Clearing Corporation has three fixed expiration dates for its options; each period runs for three months. *See Also: corporation, expiration*

STANDARDS. Protocols that are established to facilitate the interoperability of products or services, particularly in the software industry. *See Also: industry, interoperability*

STANDBY COMMITMENT. A contract between a company and a banking group in which the banking group agrees to buy a portion of a securities issue offered in a rights offering after the current shareholders fail to buy all that was offered during the prescribed period. *See Also: contract, current, issue, offering, rights, rights offering, securities*

STANDBY FEE. The commission an underwriter receives when he or she agrees to buy any stock shares left after current stockholders have exercised their rights offering. *See Also: commission, current, offering, rights, rights offering, stock*

STANDBY UNDERWRITING. Occurs when a company that issues rights hires an investment banker preparing to buy the remaining shares and to take over the rights that investors do not exercise. *See Also: exercise, investment, investment banker, rights, take*

STANDSTILL. A contract between a securities issuer and the owner of a large block of the securities in which the holder agrees not to buy any more shares or sell the shares he or she owns without the issuer's permission. *See Also: contract, securities*

STAR. Short-Term Auction Rate

START-UP. A new business venture that has recently begun operations, typically in need of capital. *See Also: capital, operations*

STARTUP. The point of a new business venture when an investor will provide the beginning company with venture capital. *See Also: capital, point, venture capital*

STATE BANK. A bank that falls under a state's regulations, as opposed to a national bank, which fails under the auspices of the federal government. *See Also: bank, fails, national bank*

STATED CAPITAL. The amount of money that stockholders contribute to the company.

STATED PERCENTAGE ORDER. An order to buy a block of stock large enough to represent a specific percentage of the security's market volume. *See Also: block of stock, market, market volume, order, stock, volume*

STATEMENT. A summary of charges, expenses, and purchases, as well as a description of financial condition.

STATEMENT ANALYSIS. An analyst studies a company's accounting statements and analyzes such ratios as turnover and current, then determines the company's future financial potential. *See Also: analyst, current, turnover*

STATEMENT OF CHANGES IN FINANCIAL POSITION. The part in a company's annual report that shows changes in the company's working capital. *See Also: annual report, capital, working capital*

STATEMENT OF CONDITION. A summary of the status of a company's assets, liabilities, and equity. *See Also: equity*

STATEMENT OF POLICY. Securities and Exchange Commission standards governing investment companies and covering such issues as disclosure, commissions, and management approaches. *See Also: commission, disclosure, exchange, investment, standards*

STATEMENT SAVINGS ACCOUNT. A savings account in which the depositor keeps his or her own records, tracking deposits and withdrawals. The financial institution, in turn, sends the depositor regular statements summarizing the account, against which the depositor can check his or her own records. This is also called a No Passbook Account. *See Also: account, check, savings account, turn*

STATION. The area in a stock exchange where a specialist completes transactions. *See Also: exchange, specialist, stock, stock exchange*

STATUTE OF LIMITATIONS. U.S. securities laws prohibit civil actions on most securities matters after three years. *See Also: securities*

STATUTORY INVESTMENT. A state-approved investment through which a trustee can administer a trust. *See Also: investment, trust, trustee*

STATUTORY MERGER. Occurs when two companies merge into one, with one of the companies maintaining its identity.

STATUTORY UNDERWRITER. A person who inadvertently performs underwriting functions, and therefore subjects himself or herself to Securities and Exchange Commission regulations regarding the sale of unregistered securities. *See Also: commission, exchange, sale, securities, underwriting*

STATUTORY VOTING. Occurs when each stockholder gets one vote for each share he or she owns for each board director to be elected. *See Also: director, share, stockholder*

STAYING POWER. An investor's financial ability to hold on to an investment that has dropped in value. *See Also: hold, investment*

STEADY. A market that is not moving up or down much. *See Also: market*

STEENTH. Designates a bid that is quoted in 16ths.

STEPPED COSTS. Costs that incrementally climb as volume increases. *See Also: volume*

STEPPED COUPON SECURITIES. A bond series with all issues paying the same interest rate each year, but with that rate increasing periodically. *See Also: bond, interest, interest rate*

STERILE INVESTMENT. An investment in a precious metal that does not pay any dividends. *See Also: investment, pay*

STERLING SECURITY. Either a bond denominated in British sterling pounds, or a corporate bond issued in Great Britain. *See Also: bond, corporate bond*

STERLING TRANSFERABLE ACCRUING GOVERNMENT SECURITIES (STAGS). A British, zero-coupon bond based on British Treasury bonds. *See Also: bond*

STICKY. Also known as stickiness, the ability to retain participants on a Web site. *See Also: on, Web, Web site*

STICKY DEAL. An underwriting issue that will most probably be hard to market. *See Also: issue, market, underwriting*

STICKY JUMP BONDS. CMO bonds whose principal paydown is altered by the incident of a triggering event. If an initial trigger event is met, the bond's payment priority changes to a new priority, and remains in its new priority for the life of the bond. *See Also: bond, paydown, principal, priority*

STICKY PRICES. Prices that are not subject to major price fluctuations either up or down.

STIF. Short-Term Investment Fund. *See Also: fund, investment*

STILTS. Short-Term Indexed Liability Transactions. *See Also: liability*

STOCK. A unit of company ownership, which is represented by shares, that acts as a claim on the underlying corporation's earnings and assets. *See Also: earnings, unit*

STOCK AHEAD. Occurs when one investor's orders were put in before another investor's orders on the exchange floor, so the price could change before the later investor's order comes up for execution. *See Also: change, exchange, exchange floor, execution, floor, order, put*

STOCK ALLOTMENT. The number of shares an underwriting manager sets aside for each syndicate member to distribute. *See Also: manager, syndicate, underwriting*

STOCK APPRECIATION RIGHT. A Stock Appreciation Right (SAR) is a contractual right, often granted in tandem with an option, that allows the option holder to receive cash (or stock) amounting to the gain on the stock between the grant date and the date the SAR is exercised. *See Also: appreciation, cash, gain, on, option, right, SAR, stock, stock appreciation right*

STOCK ASSESSMENT. The amount of money a stockholder must pay to make up for negative developments in the issuing company's activities. *See Also: pay, stockholder*

STOCK ASSOCIATION. A capital stock corporation in which investors sink operating capital by buying ownership interest in stock. *See Also: capital, capital stock, corporation, interest, operating capital, stock*

STOCK BUSINESS. Describes a dealer who buys a portion of a new municipal bond issue for his or her own account in hopes of making a quick profit by reselling the bonds. *See Also: account, bond, dealer, issue, municipal bond, profit*

STOCK CERTIFICATE. A document that verifies stock ownership and details such information as the security's par value, the number of shares involved, the issuing company's name, and the owner's name. *See Also: name, par, par value, stock*

STOCK CLEARING CORPORATION. A company that handles the delivery of securities and payments between exchange members. *See Also: delivery, exchange, securities*

STOCK COMPANY. A company with stockholders providing all of the operating capital, paying all losses, and sharing all profits. *See Also: capital, operating capital*

STOCK DISCOUNT. The amount a stock's par value exceeds its paid-in capital. *See Also: capital, paid-in capital, par, par value*

STOCK DIVIDEND. A portion of a company's retained earnings that are distributed to stockholders, with the amount dependent on the number of shares the stockholder owns. *See Also: earnings, retained earnings, stockholder*

STOCK EXCHANGE. An institution wherein members can trade stocks, bonds, and other financial instruments.

STOCK EXCHANGE AUTOMATED QUOTATIONS. Similar to the National Association of Securities Dealers Automated Quotations, this British system allows market makers to quote prices on 3,500 actively and inactively traded British and international securities. *See Also: international securities, market, securities*

STOCK INDEX. A measure in value changes among a group of similar securities, with the gauge used to predict possible future movements. A group of similar securities are measured to determine differences and trends. *See Also: securities*

STOCK INDEX FUTURE. A futures contract using a stock index as its base. *See Also: base, contract, futures, futures contract, index, stock, stock index*

STOCK INDEX OPTION. A put or call option with any profit or loss settled in cash. *See Also: call option, cash, option, profit, put*

STOCK JOBBER. A British commission broker. *See Also: broker, commission, commission broker*

STOCK JOBBING. Price manipulation. *See Also: manipulation*

STOCK LIST. A registered exchange's investigation into a company that wants to list its securities on that exchange, or wants its securities approved for unlisted trading. *See Also: exchange, securities, unlisted trading*

STOCK LOAN BUSINESS. A brokerage firm branch designated for earning profits from lending securities. *See Also: firm, lending securities, securities*

STOCK MARKET. The organized trading of securities on one of the many exchanges. *See Also: exchanges, securities*

STOCK OPTION. A contract that provides the right, but not the obligation, to buy or sell a specific amount of a specific security within a predetermined time period. One call option contract gives the buyer the right to purchase, or a put buyer to sell, 100 shares of the underlying stock in exchange for a premium based on the time value and volatility. The seller of the contracts is called the writer. Stock options are also used as a form of employee compensation, generally through an employee stock ownership plan (ESOP). *See Also: below the market, market, market value, time*

STOCK POWER. A document that gives one party permission to transfer stock ownership into another person's name. *See Also: name, stock, transfer*

STOCK PURCHASE PLAN. Also known as ESOP, or employee stock ownership plan, a company plan that allows employees to buy shares of the company's stock through a contribution system. This plan gives employees of the company the right to buy shares in the company, usually at or below the market price. These stock options are usually restricted as to when they can be exercised and sold. These plans are intended to motivate employees, often providing tax benefits to the company. *See Also: commission, stock*

STOCK PURCHASE TRUST. A program through which the surviving stockholder of a closed company can buy a deceased stockholder's shares. *See Also: stockholder*

STOCK RATINGS. A judgment of the issuing company's financial strength and management ability, with high ratings given to stocks that probably will increase in value.

STOCK RECORD. A brokerage firm department responsible for handling and following all of the firm's securities, identifying their owners, and keeping track of the securities' locations daily. *See Also: firm, securities*

STOCK REGISTRAR. A fiduciary who certifies that a company has not issued more shares than are allowed in the company's charter. *See Also: charter, fiduciary*

STOCK RIGHTS. A stockholder's right to buy shares of the company's new issue at a predetermined price. The number of shares the stockholder can buy is set according to his or her current holdings. *See Also: current, issue, new issue, right, stockholder*

STOCK TABLES. A newspaper listing of market information, such as stock opening and closing prices, trading volumes, and price/earnings ratios. *See Also: listing, market, stock*

STOCK TICKER. An old device that printed trading information on a narrow ticker tape. *See Also: tape, ticker tape*

STOCK WATCHER. A New York Stock Exchange computer network used to follow the movements and transactions of NYSE-listed securities. *See Also: exchange, New York Stock Exchange, securities, stock, stock exchange*

STOCK YIELD. A security's rate of return, as determined by its market value and dividend payments. *See Also: dividend, market, market value, rate of return, return*

STOCK-BONUS TRUST. A program through which a company gives employees stock shares to reward them for high productivity. *See Also: stock*

STOCKBROKER. A person registered to trade securities for customers. *See Also: securities*

STOCKHOLDER. A person who has ownership units in a publicly held company. *See Also: publicly held*

STOCKHOLDER OF RECORD. The stockholder whose name is registered with the issuing company or with the transfer agent and who is entitled to dividend payments. *See Also: agent, dividend, name, stockholder, transfer, transfer agent*

STOCKHOLDER'S EQUITY. A company's net worth, which is its liabilities subtracted from the value of its assets. *See Also: net, net worth, worth*

STOP. The lowest rate the central bank will charge dealers who trade their government securities in for cash. *See Also: bank, cash, central bank, securities*

STOP ORDER. A request to buy or sell a security as soon as the security's price hits a specific level. *See Also: level, security*

STOP PAYMENT. Occurs when a check issuer asks the bank to refuse to honor the check. The issuer is usually charged a fee for this request. *See Also: bank, check*

STOP-LIMIT ORDER. A request to buy or sell a security, directing the broker to make the order a limit order as soon as the security's price hits a predetermined stop level. *See Also: broker, level, limit, limit order, order, security, stop*

STOP-LOSS ORDER. An investor's order to his or her broker to sell a security if its price drops to a specified level. *See Also: broker, level, order, security*

STOP-OUT PRICE. The lowest price that will be accepted at a Treasury auction. *See Also: auction*

STOP-OUT RATE. The lowest interest rate the Federal Reserve will allow a nonbank dealer to pay on a repurchase agreement. *See Also: dealer, interest, interest rate, pay, repurchase, repurchase agreement, reserve*

STOPPED OUT. Occurs if an order is executed at the specialist's guaranteed price. *See Also: order*

STOPPED STOCK. An order with a price that a specialist has guaranteed to the exchange member. The member then can seek a better price-if one is unavailable, he or she still can lake advantage of the guaranteed price. *See Also: exchange, order, specialist*

STORY. A scenario for buying a specific stock as described by an analyst. For example, the analyst may tell the potential investor about positive factors that are influencing the issuing company's management. *See Also: analyst, stock*

STRADDLE. Occurs when an investor buys a put option and a call option on an underlying security with the same expiration price and maturity date. *See Also: call option, expiration, maturity, option, put, put option, security, underlying security*

STRAIGHT BOND. A bond that cannot be converted. *See Also: bond*

STRAIGHT INVESTMENT. An investment made because of its current value and income and not because of any expected increase. *See Also: current, investment*

STRAIGHT MORTGAGE. A mortgage on which the borrower must pay interest, with the full mortgage amount falling due at the end of the mortgage period. *See Also: full, interest, mortgage, pay*

STRAIGHT-LINE DEPRECIATION. A method in which the company's cost of a qualified asset can be apportioned in equal amounts over the length of the asset's life. To obtain the amount that can be depreciated, subtract the asset's salvage value at the end of its useful life from the asset's original cost. *See Also: asset, original cost, salvage value*

STRAIGHT-LINE INTEREST. Annually computed interest payments based on a percentage of the unpaid balance. *See Also: balance, interest*

STRANGLE. Selling an out of the money call and a put option with the same expiration date on the same underlying security. To profit, the investor would have to see minor volatility in the security's market. *See Also: expiration, expiration date, market, option, out of the money, profit, put, put option, security, underlying security, volatility*

STRAP OPTIONS. Occurs when an investor buys one put and two calls with the same series on the same underlying security. *See Also: put, security, underlying security*

STRATEGIC ALLIANCE. Two or more companies that agree to collaborate toward a similar goal.

STRATEGICS. A precious metal investment. *See Also: investment*

STREAMING. A system in which sound or video files can be delivered to a computing device over the Internet. The system allows the user to begin playing the file before the downloading has been completed. *See Also: Internet*

STREET. A nickname for Wall Street or any other city's or country's major financial center. *See Also: Wall Street*

STREET BROKER. Any over-the-counter broker who is not an exchange member. *See Also: broker, exchange*

STREET CERTIFICATE. A securities certificate with a blank endorsement by an owner with a guaranteed signature. This allows the security to be transferred without it having to be recorded on the company's books. *See Also: blank endorsement, certificate, securities, security*

STREET NAME. Describes securities that are being held in the name of a broker for a customer. *See Also: broker, name, securities*

STREET PRICE. The price of a security that is involved in a transaction not connected to one of the exchanges. *See Also: exchanges, security, transaction*

STREET SIDE. The brokerage side of a broker-customer relationship.

STRETCHING THE PAYABLES. Occurs when accounts payable are deferred past the due date.

STRIKE FROM THE LIST. An exchange order to stop all transactions in a specific security. *See Also: exchange, order, security, stop*

STRIKESUIT. A minority stockholder's lawsuit designed to convince management to buy out his or her shares.

STRIKING PRICE. The exercise price, or the price at which an option holder can buy an asset. *See Also: asset, exercise, exercise price, option*

STRINGENCY. Occurs when interest rates are rising and finding credit is difficult. *See Also: credit, interest*

STRIP. An option strategy in which the investor buys one call and two puts on the same underlying security, all with the same exercise price and expiration date. *See Also: exercise, exercise price, expiration, expiration date, option, security, underlying security*

STRIPPED BOND. A bond which can be bought in either a principal only (PO) or interest only (IO) package. *See Also: bond, interest, principal*

STRIPPED MORTGAGE-BACKED SECURITY. A security that is created by redistributing the cash flows from the underlying mortgage-backed security collateral into the principal and interest components. Stripped Mortgage-Backed Securities are used to meet the special needs of investors. *See Also: and interest, cash, collateral, interest, principal, securities, security*

STRIPPED TREASURY OBLIGATIONS. Zero-coupon Treasury bonds that mature in three months to 29 years, and are backed by the full faith and credit of the U.S. Government. *See Also: credit, full, full faith and credit*

STRONG HANDS. A person who holds on to an investment for a long period of time, as opposed to a person who buys and sells quickly to make a fast profit. *See Also: investment, profit, time*

STRONG MARKET. Occurs when demand exceeds supply. *See Also: demand, supply*

STUDENT LOAN MARKETING ASSOCIATION (SLMA). A "Sallie Mae" security based on a pool of student loans, which financial institutions make to college students; guaranteed by the U.S. government's full faith and credit. *See Also: credit, full, full faith and credit, pool, security*

SUBCHAPTER M. An Internal Revenue Service regulation that gives investment companies special tax allowances when they distribute at least 90 percent of their income to stockholders. *See Also: Internal Revenue, investment, service*

SUBCHAPTERS CORPORATION. A small company taxed as a partnership and which, as such, has some taxable income and liabilities falling on the shoulders of the individual officers' tax reports. *See Also: partnership, taxable income*

SUBJECT MARKET. A trader's quote that has yet to be confirmed and authorized by the trader's customer.

SUBJECT PRICE. A negotiated, estimated price, subject to confirmation. *See Also: confirmation*

SUBJECT TO OPINION. An auditor's statement in an audit report stipulating that the results fairly represent the publicly owned company's financial status subject to some specific adjustments. *See Also: audit, statement*

SUBJECT TO PRIOR SALE. When the market is strong, the supply of a security is limited, and buy orders exceed the security's supply, bid orders often will be filed early so the investor will be able to obtain whatever amount of the limited security is available. Those investors filing their bids later will not be able to buy the security, because none will be left. *See Also: market, security, supply*

SUBJECT TO REDEMPTION. Stocks that a company can call in without notifying the shareholders ahead of time. *See Also: time*

SUBMISSION. A mortgage banker's offer to sell mortgage shares to an investor. *See Also: mortgage, offer*

SUBMITTAL NOTICE. The notice a broker sends to a property owner when that property has been offered for sale. It includes the property's offering price and the potential buyer's name and address. *See Also: address, broker, name, offering, offering price, sale*

SUBMORTGAGE. Occurs when a mortgage lender pledges that mortgage as collateral for his or her own loan. *See Also: collateral, mortgage*

SUBORDINATED. A security with a lower priority than other securities when dividends and assets are distributed in liquidations or bankruptcies. *See Also: priority, securities, security*

SUBORDINATED DEBENTURE. A high-risk debenture, the holder of which may receive lower payments than other creditors of the same issuer. *See Also: debenture*

SUBORDINATED DEBT INSTRUMENT. A bond over which another bond has priority in case of liquidation or asset distribution. *See Also: asset, bond, liquidation, priority*

SUBORDINATED EXCHANGEABLE VARIABLE-RATE NOTE. A note that allows a company to borrow at low, short-term interest rates and that guarantees the company access to capital for a longer time. The interest rate floats for five years, then is fixed for another five years, after which the company can exchange the notes for others with fixed interest rates. *See Also: capital, exchange, interest, interest rate, low, note, time*

SUBORDINATED INTEREST. A financial property interest that is inferior in claims to another financial interest in that same property. *See Also: interest*

SUBSCRIBER. An investor who promises to buy a specific number of shares of a newly issued security. *See Also: security*

SUBSCRIPTION. An agreement to buy a certain number of shares of a newly issued security. *See Also: security*

SUBSCRIPTION CAPITAL. The money an issuer receives from the public in a new securities offering. *See Also: offering, securities*

SUBSCRIPTION CASH RECORD. A cash record of all a capital stock subscriber's payments, including the down payment. *See Also: capital, capital stock, cash, stock*

SUBSCRIPTION LIST. A document a subscriber signs verifying the number of shares he or she has agreed to buy. *See Also: subscriber*

SUBSCRIPTION PRICE. The set, established price at which a new security is offered publicly for sale. *See Also: sale, security*

SUBSCRIPTION PRIVILEGE. The right that a stockholder has to buy a portion of the company's new offering in proportion to the number of shares he or she already holds. *See Also: offering, right, stockholder*

SUBSCRIPTION RATIO. The number of subscription rights a stockholder needs to subscribe to one share or to a convertible bond. *See Also: bond, rights, share, stockholder, subscription*

SUBSCRIPTION RIGHT. A security that provides the number of rights a stockholder has when subscribing to either new shares or new convertibles. For example, a stockholder would receive one right for each share he or she owned. *See Also: right, rights, security, share, stockholder*

SUBSCRIPTION WARRANT. A subscription right that is valid longer and carries the probability it will be more profitable when exercised. *See Also: right, subscription, subscription right*

SUBSCRIPTIONS RECEIVABLE. A company's account that indicates how much each capital-stock subscriber owes to the company for his or her shares. *See Also: account, subscriber*

SUBSIDIARY. A company owned by and controlled by another company.

SUBSIDIARY COIN. A coin denominated in an amount less than a dollar, such as a U.S. quarter or dime. *See Also: dime*

SUBSTANTIVE. Describes the situation in which corporate activities will affect stockholders directly.

SUBSTITUTION. One security is sold and another purchased to replace it in order to take advantage of price differences while maintaining the same volume of ownership. *See Also: order, security, take, volume*

SUBSTITUTION OF COLLATERAL. Occurs when a borrower substitutes one collateral, such as property, for another collateral, such as securities. *See Also: collateral, securities*

SUITABILITY. Guidelines that brokers in speculative securities must follow to make sure the investors actually can afford to assume such risks. *See Also: securities, speculative*

SUM-OF-THE-YEARS' DIGITS METHOD. An accelerated depreciation method that creates higher depreciation charges and higher tax savings in a fixed asset's earlier years. The method is based on an inverted scale for the total number of years in the asset's useful life. *See Also: accelerated depreciation, depreciation, inverted scale, scale*

SUMMARY COMPLAINT PROCEEDINGS. A National Association of Securities Dealers code, stating that a person charged with NASD code violations may, in some cases, plead guilty to a minor infraction as long as the person pays a fee and promises not to appeal. *See Also: NASD, securities*

SUNDRY ASSET. An asset that the company does not use in day-to-day production, but that it plans to hold on to for a long period of time. Undeveloped land, for example, would be considered a sundry asset. *See Also: asset, hold, time*

SUNRISE INDUSTRIES. Growth industries that will be vital to the future economy, such as the electronics industry. *See Also: industry*

SUNSET PROVISION. A legal provision that indicates the law or provision will expire on a certain future date. *See Also: legal*

SUNSHINE LAW. A law that opens government meetings, including those of the Securities and Exchange Commission and the Commodities Futures Trading Commission, to the public. *See Also: commission, exchange, futures, securities*

SUPER BOWL THEORY. An investment strategy theory that predicts that when a member of the National Football League wins the Super Bowl the stock market will go up, and when a member of the American Football League wins, the stock market will drop. *See Also: drop, investment, investment strategy, market, stock, stock market*

SUPER DOT. An automated order processing and trade reporting system through which New York Stock Exchange members can quickly execute price orders. *See Also: exchange, New York Stock Exchange, order, processing, stock, stock exchange*

SUPER MAJORITY. When at least 80 percent of a company's outstanding shares are voted for or against a company issue or a board member. *See Also: issue, outstanding*

SUPER NOW ACCOUNT. A Negotiable Order of Withdrawal Account that pays money market rates and through which depositors who have at least a $2,500 balance are given unlimited checking account privileges. *See Also: account, balance, market, money market, money market rates, negotiable, order*

SUPER PRINCIPAL-ONLY (PO) BONDS. Structured as highly leveraged Companion bonds, Super POs make only principal payments and are sold at a deep discount to par value. *See Also: companion bonds, discount, leveraged, par, par value, principal*

SUPER RESTRICTED ACCOUNT. A defunct description of a brokerage account margined at less than 30 percent of the account securities' market value. *See Also: account, brokerage account, market, market value*

SUPER SINKER BOND. A bond with a long-term coupon and a short-term maturity. *See Also: bond, coupon, maturity*

SUPER STOCK. A security that will multiply several times in value. *See Also: security*

SUPER TRUST. A fund created to refunnel union employees' benefit money to finance construction projects. *See Also: fund*

SUPERPRIME INSTRUMENT. A nonrenewable, 10-day note that costs only slightly more than the amount a bank pays itself for funds. *See Also: bank, note*

SUPERSEDED SURETY RIDER. A continuing coverage clause in a new fidelity bond that takes the place of another bond. The holder is protected against any losses from the preceding bond as long as the chain of riders remains unbroken. *See Also: bond, fidelity bond*

SUPERVISORY ANALYST. An exchange member employee who, after passing a written examination, can authorize publicly distributed research reports. *See Also: exchange*

SUPPLEMENTAL AGREEMENT. A contract that supersedes a previous contract, with the newer contract including additional provisions and elaborating clauses. *See Also: contract*

SUPPLY. The number of shares available publicly for sale. *See Also: sale*

SUPPLY AND DEMAND INDICATORS. A gauge that measures how much money is coming in and out of the market. *See Also: market*

SUPPLY AREA. An area on a price chart indicating a price's resistance level. *See Also: chart, level, resistance level*

SUPPLY CHAIN. The entire network of processes that transforms raw materials into intermediate and finished goods, and the distribution of those finished products to buyers.

SUPPLY CHAIN MANAGEMENT. Also referred to as SCM, The coordination of processes, including producing, shipping and distribution.

SUPPLY-SIDE ECONOMICS. An economic theory that says tax cuts will stimulate large private investments from wealthy business people, which, in turn, will benefit the economy as a whole. *See Also: turn*

SUPPORT. The price level that buyer demand is expected to keep a security's price from dropping below. *See Also: demand, level*

SUPPORT LEVEL. The price at which buyers have tended to purchase a security, thus overcoming the downward pressure from sellers. *See Also: security*

SUPPORTING. Occurs when an investor buys securities at prices that will keep their values from dropping in an effort to discourage people from exercising their put options. *See Also: put, securities*

SUPPORTING ORDERS. Buy orders entered in order to support a security's price. *See Also: order, support*

SUPPORTING SCHEDULES. A supplementary report of information added either to a company's balance sheet or to its profit and loss statement. *See Also: balance, balance sheet, profit, profit and loss statement, statement*

SUPPORTING THE MARKET. Occurs when a bid falls at or slightly below a security's prevailing market price, The bid is usually designed to balance the price and to encourage it to go up. *See Also: balance, market, market price, to go*

SURCHARGE. One charge that is added on top of another charge. *See Also: top*

SURETY. A security that protects the holder in case a party owing money to the issuer defaults or, for example, if a company officer embezzles money from the company. *See Also: officer, security*

SURF. The nonlinear act of clicking from one Web site to another. *See Also: Web, Web site*

SURPLUS EQUITY. The amount by which a margin account security's market value exceeds the amount needed to satisfy a margin requirement. *See Also: account, margin, margin account, margin requirement, market, market value*

SURPLUS RESERVES. A company's financial reserve that is not available for paying dividends. *See Also: reserve*

SURPRISE. A company's earnings report that differs positively or negatively from the consensus forecast. *See Also: earnings, earnings surprise*

SURROGATE COURT CERTIFICATE. A probate court document that lists a trustee who is authorized to settle an estate. *See Also: estate, settle, trustee*

SURTAX. The tax a company or individual must pay after attaining a certain income level. *See Also: level, pay*

SURVEILLANCE DEPARTMENT OF EXCHANGES. An exchange department that watches for unusual securities transactions that could indicate illegal activity is under way. *See Also: activity, exchange, securities*

SUSHI BOND. A Japanese bond denominated in Eurodollars. *See Also: bond, Eurodollars*

SUSPENSE ACCOUNT. A broker-dealer's account of security balance discrepancies. *See Also: account, balance, security*

SUSPENSION. Occurs when a brokerage employee is either permanently or temporarily stopped from working because he or she has violated securities regulations. *See Also: securities*

SUSPENSION OF TRADING. Occurs when an exchange temporarily halts trading in a particular security to stabilize the market. *See Also: exchange, market, security*

SWAP. Occurs when a government agrees to borrow a foreign currency from the issuing country to pay for an intervention in the foreign exchange market. Also, the sale of one security to purchase another security with similar features. *See Also: currency, exchange, foreign currency, foreign exchange, intervention, market, pay, sale, security*

SWAP FUND. A pooled investment portfolio fund with several investors, each sharing in a proportionate percentage of the earnings. The fund was designed to diversify the investors' holdings without their having to pay capital gains tax on stock sales. *See Also: capital, capital gains tax, earnings, fund, investment, investment portfolio, pay, portfolio, stock*

SWAP RATE. The difference between the spot price of one nation's currency and the current futures trading prices. *See Also: currency, current, futures, spot, spot price*

SWAPTION. An interest rate swap agreement in which the purchaser pays an initial fee for the option to enter into an interest rate swap at a later date at a specified price. *See Also: interest, interest rate, interest rate swap, option, swap*

SWEAT EQUITY. Work performed in exchange for a share of ownership. *See Also: exchange, share*

SWEEP ACCOUNT. A central assets account that allows an investor to transfer cash into an interest-bearing account such as a money-market mutual fund. *See Also: account, cash, central assets account, fund, mutual fund, transfer*

SWEETENER. An additional value included with a proposal to make the deal more attractive.

SWEETHEART DEAL. A very attractive deal that one party gives to another.

SWEETENING A LOAN. Occurs when an investor deposits additional securities to margin a loan after the existing securities have dropped in value. Sweetening a loan is done either to maintain the margin level or to improve its condition. *See Also: level, margin, securities*

SWIFT. Society for Worldwide Interbank Financial Telecommunications.

SWIMMING MARKET. A strong, active securities market. *See Also: market, securities*

SWING. A price movement, usually in the opposite direction of the previous movement. *See Also: movement*

SWING LINE. A bank line of credit through which a customer can borrow a predetermined amount of money each day. *See Also: bank, bank line, credit, line of credit*

SWING TRADING. A short-term trading style that seeks to profit from either general fluctuations or momentum in a security or index. *See Also: index, momentum, profit, security, short-term trading*

SWINGER. A financial manager who handles a heavy volume of business. *See Also: heavy, manager, volume*

SWISS FRANC. Switzerland's primary monetary unit. *See Also: unit*

SWISS FRANC NOTE. A Eurodebt denominated in Swiss francs with a maturity of five to 10 years. *See Also: maturity*

SWITCH ORDER. An investor's request to simultaneously buy one stock and sell another because of beneficial price differences. *See Also: stock*

SWITCHING. Selling some securities from a portfolio and replacing them with different securities. *See Also: portfolio, securities*

SWITCHING COSTS. The costs incurred for consumers or companies to alter a practice or buying pattern.

SYMBOL. An acronym used to identify securities that are traded on a ticker tape or exchange, or are listed in newspapers. *See Also: exchange, securities, tape, ticker tape*

SYNCHROVEST. An investment in which the investor buys varying amounts of a stock or a mutual fund, depending on how the investment performs. For example, if the price of the shares drops, the investor puts more money into the investment, and if the price goes up, he or she buys fewer shares. *See Also: fund, investment, mutual fund, stock*

SYNDICATE. A group of investment bankers that underwrites and distributes a new securities issue. *See Also: investment, issue, securities*

SYNDICATE ACCOUNT. An underwriting syndicate's financial condition. *See Also: underwriting*

SYNDICATE AGREEMENT. A contract, creating an underwriting group. *See Also: contract, underwriting*

SYNDICATE LETTER. An invitation to investment bankers to participate in an underwriting group. The letter typically details the rules of such an agreement. *See Also: investment, underwriting*

SYNDICATE MANAGER. The lead underwriter who, among other things, is in charge of organizing the syndicate, distributing member participation shares, and making stabilizing transactions. *See Also: lead underwriter, syndicate*

SYNDICATE RESTRICTIONS. The binding requirements to which an underwriting syndicate must adhere. The restrictions govern such things as distribution and price limits. *See Also: syndicate, underwriting, underwriting syndicate*

SYNDICATE TERMINATION. After a security has been issued and distributed, the underwriting syndicate is released from its restrictions. *See Also: security, syndicate, underwriting, underwriting syndicate*

SYNERGY. Occurs when, after two companies merge, the new company has higher earnings than the two previous companies combined. *See Also: earnings*

SYNTHETIC PUT. An unregistered over-the-counter put option that a broker-dealer issues to accommodate a client's request for a put option. The investor shorts stock and simultaneously buys a call option. *See Also: broker-dealer, call option, option, put, put option, shorts, stock*

SYSTEMATIC RISK. A risk that all assets possess, or that all securities of the same class have in common. *See Also: class, risk, securities*

SYSTEMS INTEGRATORS. An individual or company that builds complete computer systems by assimilating components from more than one vendor, and does not typically create original code. *See Also: vendor*

SYSTEMS SOFTWARE. Also known as the operating system, systems software manages computer resources. Software is generalized as being either systems software or applications software.

T

T. Appears in newspaper stock listings to indicate the security's main trading place is the Toronto Stock Exchange. *See Also: exchange, stock, stock exchange, Toronto Stock Exchange*

T1 LINE. A communications link connected directly to a network that offers very high transmission speeds.

TAC II BOND. A type of TAC bond which possesses increased prepayment protection at higher prepayment speeds than originally used at pricing. *See Also: bond, prepayment*

TAC INTEREST-ONLY (IO) BOND. Priced at a very high premium-to-par value, this type of TAC bond makes only interest payments. TAC IOs adhere to a specific schedule of interest payments, which is met if prepayment rates on the underlying collateral occur at the initial pricing speed. *See Also: bond, collateral, interest, prepayment*

TAC PRINCIPAL-ONLY (PO) BOND. Offered at a deep discount-to-par value, this type of TAC bond makes only principal payments. TAC POs adhere to a specific schedule of principal payments, which are met if prepayment rates on the underlying collateral occur at the initial pricing speed. *See Also: bond, collateral, prepayment, principal*

TACKING. Occurs when a third mortgage holder tacks the first mortgage onto the third so he or she will have a superior claim over the second mortgage. *See Also: mortgage, third mortgage*

TAFT-HARTLEY ACT. A 1947 federal law that restricts unions from refusing to bargain in good faith, coercing employees to join, and participating in sympathy strikes, among other things. *See Also: bargain*

TAG. The codes used to format HTML documents. These codes can either be single, or compound, in which initial and closing tags are required. *See Also: HTML*

TAG ALONG RIGHTS. A right that can be given to minority shareholders to ensure they receive the same terms as a majority shareholder. *See Also: majority shareholder, right, shareholder*

TAG ENDS. Indicates that only a small number of debt securities are available from the underwriting syndicate because the rest have been sold. *See Also: securities, syndicate, underwriting, underwriting syndicate*

TAIL. The difference between the lowest bid accepted and the average bid in a U.S. Treasury auction. *See Also: auction, average*

TAILGATING. Occurs when a registered representative buys a security for a customer, then buys more shares of the same security for his or her own account. *See Also: account, registered representative, security*

TAKE. Indicates that buyers are accepting another broker's offering price to complete a transaction. *See Also: offering, offering price, transaction*

TAKE A FLIER. When an investor knowingly makes a risky investment. *See Also: investment*

TAKE A POSITION. When an investor creates a long or short position. *See Also: position, short position*

TAKE BACK. Occurs when a syndicate regains those securities it had allotted for the selling group. *See Also: securities, selling group, syndicate*

TAKE IT. A broker's indication that he or she will buy a specific security at a specific price. *See Also: indication, security*

TAKE ON A LINE. Occurs when an investor buys a large block of stock over a period of time because he or she expects the stock's price to climb. *See Also: block of stock, stock, time*

TAKE PROFITS. Occurs when an investor earns money from selling a security. *See Also: security*

TAKE UP. Occurs when an investor pays all that is due on a margined security so he or she can take full ownership of that security. *See Also: full, security, take*

TAKE-OR-PAY CONTRACT. A contract binding a buyer to pay the seller a minimum mount of money, even if the seller does not provide the buyer with the promised goods or services. These contracts protect bondholders. *See Also: contract, pay*

TAKEDOWN. The number of securities for which an underwriting syndicate member is financially responsible. *See Also: securities, syndicate, underwriting, underwriting syndicate*

TAKEOUT. The amount of money an investor withdraws to sell one security and buy another at a lower price. *See Also: security*

TAKEOVER. The attempt of one company to buy another company, either in a hostile or friendly manner.

TAKEOVER ARBITRAGE. Occurs when an investor buys and/or sells securities issued by a company targeted for a takeover, or the acquiring company, because the investor believes such a transaction will bring him or her a profit. *See Also: profit, securities, takeover, transaction*

TAKEOVER CANDIDATE. Any company that is vulnerable to a takeover, or is looking to be taken over by another company. *See Also: takeover*

TAKER. A person who borrows money or securities. *See Also: securities*

TAKING A BATH. Occurs when an investor is losing a lot of money on an investment. *See Also: investment, lot*

TAKING A VIEW. Indicates a British prediction of interest rates, security prices, and yields. *See Also: interest, security*

TAKING DELIVERY. Accepting the delivery of securities to complete a transaction. *See Also: delivery, securities, transaction*

TALON. Any special coupon that carries extra income or rights. *See Also: coupon, rights*

TANDEM OPTION. A stock option that carries qualified as well as nonqualified plans. *See Also: nonqualified, option, stock, stock option*

TANDEM PLAN. A plan in which the Government National Mortgage Association pays above-the-market value for some mortgages and simultaneously sells them through the Federal National Mortgage Association in the secondary market. By doing this, the GNMA pays for housing projects without having to put out much money. *See Also: GNMA, market, mortgage, put, secondary market*

TANDEM SPREAD. A strategy in which an investor buys one security and sells another short to take advantage of price differences between the two. *See Also: security, take*

TANGIBLE ASSET. An asset with physical substance, such as a machine. An intangible asset would be an asset without physical substance, such as goodwill, reputation and patents. *See Also: asset, intangible asset*

TANGIBLE COST. The amount of money it costs to buy oil and gas drilling equipment that can be used over a period of time. *See Also: time*

TANGIBLE NET WORTH. Achieved by subtracting a company's intangible assets from its tangible assets.

TANGIBLE VALUE. The difference between a stock option contract's exercise price and the underlying security's market price. *See Also: exercise, exercise price, market, market price, option, stock, stock option*

TAP CERTIFICATE OF DEPOSIT. A one-month, as-required certificate of deposit in denominations of at least $25,000. *See Also: certificate*

TAP ISSUE. A securities offering with the same terms and conditions as a previous issue, even though the prices may be different. The tap issue is so named because the issuer is tapping the same market. *See Also: issue, market, offering, securities*

TAPE. Short for a ticker tape, which is an exchange's system for physically recording and reporting securities transactions and volume information. *See Also: securities, ticker tape, volume*

TAPE DANCING. Occurs when a trader pays an institutional investor 1/8 to 1/4 over the last transaction price for a block of equity securities, then imposes a heavier commission in an effort to cushion trading losses and to make it appear on the ticker tape as if buyers are anxious to buy the stock, a notion that attracts speculators. *See Also: commission, equity, institutional investor, securities, stock, tape, ticker tape, trader, transaction*

TAPE IS LATE. A condition in which heavy trading causes a delay for the real-time quotes. *See Also: delay, heavy*

TAPE PRICE. The last price shown on ticker tape for a specific security. *See Also: security, tape, ticker tape*

TAPE RACING. Occurs when a broker improperly buys or sells a security using the knowledge that a client plans to execute a large order in the same security shortly thereafter. *See Also: broker, client, order, security*

TAPE READING. A method of analyzing and predicting price movements by studying only the information appearing on an exchange's ticker tape, such as the price and trading volume. *See Also: tape, ticker tape, trading volume, volume*

TARGET. A company that another company wants to buy out.

TARGET PRICE. The price to which an investor expects his or her newly purchased securities to rise. *See Also: securities*

TARGET STOCK. Stock issued to shareholders when a company creates a new class of shares for one of its businesses. As opposed to a spin-off, shareholders don't actually own the assets of the unit when holders receive separate common stock in the unit. The target stock's performance is still tied to the unit's earnings and the parent company retains the power to seize assets or divert earnings without shareholder approval. *See Also: class, common stock, earnings, shareholder, stock, target, unit*

TARGETED AMORTIZATION CLASS (TAC) BONDS. A CMO tranche that has a specified principal paydown schedule that will be met as long as the collateral prepayment speed does not decline below the pricing speed. At higher prepayment rates, excess principal payments may be allocated to non-TAC classes. If a shortfall of prepayments occurs, arrears will be paid to the TAC, causing its average life to lengthen. *See Also: arrears, average, average life, CMO, collateral, paydown, prepayment, principal, tranche*

TARIFF. An import and export tax imposed usually to balance competition. *See Also: balance*

TAW. The amount of money necessary to completely finance a new business venture.

TAX ABATEMENT. A cut or refund in taxes because the amount paid was too high or was improperly imposed.

TAX ADJUSTMENT ACT. A 1966 federal law that, among other things, reinstated the excise taxes on transportation equipment and on telephone service rates. *See Also: service*

TAX AND LOAN ACCOUNT. A government-owned demand deposit account in a commercial bank, with companies and people who owe Social

Security payments, or employee withholding taxes as depositors. *See Also: account, bank, commercial bank, demand, demand deposit, deposit account, security, withholding*

TAX ANTICIPATION BILL. A Treasury-issued, short-term debt instrument issued to meet short-term financial needs. *See Also: debt instrument, instrument, short-term debt*

TAX ANTICIPATION NOTE. A short-term, municipal note issued to meet short-term financial needs, and which is repaid upon maturity with tax receipts. *See Also: maturity, municipal note, note*

TAX ANTICIPATION OBLIGATION. A government-issued debt instrument that will be repaid with tax receipts. *See Also: debt instrument, instrument*

TAX AVOIDANCE. Legal methods a taxpayer can use to reduce his or her tax liabilities.

TAX BASE. The taxable portion of any asset or property. *See Also: asset*

TAX BASIS. The total price an investor paid for a security, including the brokerage commission. *See Also: commission, security*

TAX BRACKET. The tax schedule level in which a taxpayer's income falls, with each level carrying a different percentage level of tax liability. For example, a person earning more money would fall in a higher tax bracket and therefore would be responsible for paying a higher percentage of tax. *See Also: bracket, fall, level, liability*

TAX CAPITALIZATION. To capitalize a tax at an assumed interest rate, divide the interest rate into the tax change, then subtract that amount from the asset's value before the tax change. *See Also: capitalize, change, interest, interest rate*

TAX CERTIFICATE. A government-issued document that verifies the title transfer of a tax-delinquent property. If the owner does not pay the delinquent amount, the certificate holder can foreclose. *See Also: certificate, pay, transfer*

TAX COST. The base figure representing the difference between the amount of money paid for a property and the amount of money for which the property is sold. This difference determines a taxable gain or loss. *See Also: base, gain*

TAX COURT OF THE UNITED STATES. A federal court that has jurisdiction over Internal Revenue Service tax disputes. *See Also: Internal Revenue Service*

TAX CREDIT. A reduction in tax liabilities, expressed as a percentage of the individual's tax bracket. *See Also: bracket, tax bracket*

TAX DEDUCTION ACT. A 1975 law that provided, among other things, increased standard deductions, low-income credits, and increased investment tax credits. *See Also: investment*

TAX DEED. The deed that is given to a person who buys property that was sold because of tax delinquency. *See Also: delinquency*

TAX DEFERRED. An investment that allows a person to put off paying income taxes on money deposited into the investment until he or she actually takes possession of the money. For example, many retirement accounts are tax deferred. *See Also: investment, put*

TAX EQUITY AND FISCAL RESPONSIBILITY ACT. A federal law that imposed levies and improved taxpayer compliance to increase revenues.

TAX EQUIVALENT. The payment a government-owned utility makes to other government units instead of paying taxes. *See Also: utility*

TAX EVASION. Occurs when a taxpayer illegally falsifies his or her financial records in an effort to avoid paying taxes.

TAX EXEMPTION. A right attached to some assets and activities that frees them from paying taxes. *See Also: right*

TAX LEASE. A long-term lease on a tax-delinquent property that is given when the law prevents the property from actually being sold.

TAX LIEN. A government lien on property that has been imposed because the property-owner is delinquent in paying taxes.

TAX LIENS RECEIVABLE. An account of delinquent taxes and all legal claims against those delinquent properties. *See Also: account, legal*

TAX LIMIT. A law that limits all government-imposed tax ceilings.

TAX LOOPHOLE. Any tax exemption. *See Also: exemption, tax exemption*

TAX MANAGED UTILITY MUTUAL FUND. A reinvesting mutual fund that concentrates investments in utility securities. Because interest and dividends are reinvested in the fund, investors profit only by selling shares. *See Also: fund, interest, mutual fund, profit, securities, utility*

TAX OFFSET. Occurs when one tax is eliminated because another tax has been paid.

TAX ON NET INVESTMENT INCOME. A four percent excise tax imposed on a tax-exempt, private foundation's net investment income. *See Also: excise tax, investment, investment income, net, net investment income*

TAX PREFERENCE ITEM. An asset the Internal Revenue Service requires a taxpayer to count when adding together the alternative minimum tax liability. A tax-shelter deduction, for example, would be a tax preference item. *See Also: alternative minimum tax, asset, deduction, Internal Revenue, liability, preference, service*

TAX REDUCTION ACT STOCK OWNERSHIP PLAN. A program, running from 1975 to 1981, that allowed a company to take a one percent tax credit on its capital investments if the company contributed one percent to its employee stock ownership plan. *See Also: capital, credit, employee stock ownership plan, stock, take, tax credit*

TAX REDUCTION AND SIMPLIFICATION ACT. A 1977 law that cut taxes by $34 billion and simplified tax forms.

TAX REFORM ACT OF 1969. A federal law limiting corporate tax benefits, such as accumulated earnings credits and multiple surtax exemptions. *See Also: earnings, surtax*

TAX REFORM ACT OF 1976. A federal law that restricted tax benefits. Among other things, the law set a capital gains tax on home sales, extended the holding period for long-term capital gains, and limited home-office use deductions. *See Also: capital, capital gains tax, extended, holding period, home, long-term capital gains*

TAX REFORM ACT OF 1984. A federal law aimed at reducing the national deficit. Among other things, the law raised the liquor tax, extended a telephone excise tax, and tightened tax-shelter partnership rules. *See Also: deficit, excise tax, extended, partnership*

TAX SEARCH. A records search conducted to find out if a piece of property has any history of tax delinquency. *See Also: delinquency*

TAX SELLING. Occurs when an investor sells a security in an effort to achieve a capital loss, which provides tax breaks. *See Also: capital, security*

TAX SHIELD. The tax-exempt depreciation charged against a person's income. *See Also: depreciation*

TAX SHIFTING. Occurs when a manufacturer or service-provider passes its tax liabilities on to the consumer. For example, a service station must pay gasoline tax, so the station owner adds that tax onto the price of gasoline. *See Also: pay, service, station*

TAX STRADDLE. Occurs when an investor takes off-setting positions in the commodities market to achieve short-term capital gains. By taking a short-term loss in the same year he or she received the capital gains, the net position is not taxed and the investor receives long-term gains the next year on the remaining position. *See Also: capital, market, net, net position, position*

TAX SWAPPING. Occurs when an investor sells a security for a loss at the end of the tax year to take advantage of tax breaks on capital losses. Then, he or she invests the tax savings in another security believing that security offers a better chance for profit. *See Also: capital, profit, security, take*

TAX TITLE. A property title issued on property that was sold because of tax delinquency. *See Also: delinquency*

TAX UMBRELLA. A company's current and past losses that it can carry over to a subsequent year to shield future earnings. *See Also: carry, current, earnings*

TAX WAIVER. A document that accompanies a will and states either that estate taxes have been paid, or do not need to be paid immediately. *See Also: estate*

TAX-ADVANTAGED INVESTMENT. A tax-free investment or an investment that lowers the holder's tax liabilities. *See Also: investment*

TAX-BASED INCOME POLICY. An extra corporate income tax imposed if the company raises employees salaries above a certain level. If the company keeps salaries below the government-set limit, it receives a corporate income tax break. *See Also: break, level, limit*

TAX-EXEMPT BOND. A municipal debt security that pays the holder interest that is free from federal, state, and local taxes if the investor resides in the state offering the bond. *See Also: bond, debt security, interest, local, offering, security*

TAX-EXEMPT DEFERRED INTEREST SECURITY. A tax-exempt security issued at a discount. The security pays no interest for a specific number of years, after which it becomes a bond with a fixed par value, and pays interest twice a year. *See Also: at a discount, bond, discount, interest, par, par value, security, tax-exempt security*

TAX-EXEMPT SECURITY. Any municipal security, so named because the interest usually is at least partially tax-exempt. *See Also: interest, security*

TAX-FREE INSTRUMENT. A government-issued debt security that pays the holder tax-free interest or dividends, or interest or dividends with reduced tax liabilities. *See Also: debt security, interest, security*

TAX-FREE ROLLOVER. A person who receives a lump-sum pension distribution can avoid paying taxes on the amount by depositing it into an Individual Retirement Account or into some other tax-deferred program. *See Also: account, individual retirement account, pension*

TAX-LOSS CARRY FORWARD. The dollar amount of a net capital loss that taxpayers can carry over to subsequent years on their tax forms to reduce tax liability. *See Also: capital, carry, liability, net, net capital*

TAX-LOSS SELLING. To avoid capital-gains taxes, investors will sell stocks that show losses, which can be balanced against the gains. *See Also: will*

TAX-MANAGED FUND. A fund in which investment earnings constantly are reinvested. Because the fund doesn't bring the investor profit without selling all shares, the investor does not have to pay taxes on the fund's increased value. *See Also: earnings, fund, investment, pay, profit*

TAXABLE DISTRIBUTION. An amount of money distributed on which the receiver must pay taxes. *See Also: pay, receiver*

TAXABLE EQUIVALENT YIELD. A bond that yields taxable income compared to a tax-exempt bond's yield. *See Also: bond, taxable income, yield*

TAXABLE ESTATE. The total amount of a deceased person's estate after all administrative, funeral, transfer, and other costs have been subtracted. *See Also: estate, transfer*

TAXABLE EVENT. An occasion that can be taxed. For example, the issuing of dividend payments would be considered a taxable event. *See Also: dividend*

TAXABLE GIFT. An asset transferred to another person, with the asset worth more than the government-allowed exemption. *See Also: asset, exemption, worth*

TAXABLE INCOME. The amount of a company's or an individual's yearly income that is subject to tax after all legal and appropriate credits, adjustments, and deductions have been applied. *See Also: legal*

TAXABLE VALUE. An assessed value of assets, income, or property, with the government using the value to determine the amount of tax due on the assets, income, or property.

TAXONOMY. A system for organizing items based on similar qualities. *See Also: on*

TAXPAYER IDENTIFICATION NUMBER. A nine-digit number, usually an individual's social security number, used to identify every taxpayer in the United States. *See Also: security*

TBA. To Be Announced.

TCP. Short for Transmission Control Protocol, TCP is responsible for breaking up messages into datagrams, then reassembles them at the final stop, or client. TCP verifies the data, and resends any data from the server that is lost along the way, and places the information back in the correct order. *See Also: client, order, protocol, server, stop, up*

TCP/IP. Short for Transmission Control Protocol and the Internet Protocol, it is result of a Department of Defense (DOD) research project to connect a number different networks designed by different vendors into a network of networks, or the Internet. These protocols let different types of computers communicate with each other. *See Also: Internet, Internet protocol*

TDMA. Time Division Multiple Access is a digital cellular telephone technology that increases data transmission by dividing each cellular channel into three time slots. *See Also: digital, technology, time*

TEAR SHEET. Standard & Poors's individual stock comments, which the firm lists in a loose-leaf binder from which it tears out the appropriate individual sheets to send to interested customers. *See Also: binder, firm, stock*

TECHIE. Used in reference to computer-related technology, an individual with expert knowledge of or is very enthusiastic about technology. *See Also: technology*

TECHNICAL ADJUSTMENT. A short-term reversal of the current market trend, usually the reaction to investors overbuying or overselling. *See Also: current, market, market trend, reaction, reversal, trend*

TECHNICAL ANALYSIS. Studying and interpreting the supply of, and demand for, securities or markets, with the end result a prediction of future trends. The technician utilizes charts and computer programs to identify and project price trends. The technician's analysis includes studying such measures as price movements and trading volumes to determine certain patterns, such as resistance and supply levels, head and shoulders formations, and moving averages. *See Also: demand, securities, supply*

TECHNICAL CORRECTION. A short-term, temporary reversal of the current market trend. *See Also: current, market, market trend, reversal, trend*

TECHNICAL DIVERGENCE. Occurs when one market average does not conform to the pattern or movement of another market average. *See Also: average, market, market average, movement*

TECHNICAL DROP. The drop in a security's or commodity's price caused by market conditions and not by any changes in supply and demand. *See Also: demand, drop, market, supply*

TECHNICAL INDICATORS. Charts, ratios, graphs, or other methods of evaluating market trends and deeming possible future trends. *See Also: market*

TECHNICAL MARKET ACTION. The market activity caused by volume, odd-lot transactions, and other technical factors. *See Also: activity, market, volume*

TECHNICAL MOVE. A fluctuation in a stock's price interpreted as a self-adjusted movement. *See Also: fluctuation, movement*

TECHNICAL POSITION. The position of the market when it is affected by internal conditions, such as short-term interest or steady price declines. *See Also: interest, market, position, steady*

TECHNICAL RALLY. A short-term price increase in a declining market, indicating a surge of bargain buying but not a permanent change in the overall market condition. *See Also: bargain, change, market*

TECHNICAL SIGN. A security's price movement that represents the onset of a short-term price trend. *See Also: movement, trend*

TECHNICALLY STRONG MARKET. A market with high trading volume and increasing prices. *See Also: market, trading volume, volume*

TECHNICALLY WEAK MARKET. A market with high trading volume and decreasing prices. *See Also: market, trading volume, volume*

TECHNICIAN. An analyst (also called a chartist) that uses indicators such as ratios and graphs to predict future market trends instead of studying an issuing company's management and fundamentals. *See Also: analyst, fundamentals, indicators, market*

TECHNILIST. A newsletter a financial institution sends to subscribers with recommendations on what securities to buy or sell and at what prices. *See Also: securities*

TECHNOLOGY. The practical application of science and knowledge created to assist in achieving a particular goal, particularly commerce or industry. Technology is also jargon for hardware, software, protocols, particularly in regards to an object or sequence of operations. *See Also: commerce, industry, jargon, operations*

TED SPREAD. The spread, or value, between Treasury bill contracts and Eurodollar contracts. The behavior of this spread is viewed as a gauge of bank profitability and financial stability. A narrowing TED spread is a bullish indicator in that the difference in both the cost of Treasury debt and bank debt declines. *See Also: bank, profitability, spread, Treasury bill*

TELECOMMUTING. Working for an organization remotely, usually at home, by using a computer and telephone to communicate with the organization.

TELEGRAPHIC TRANSFER. The electronic transfer of money wherein the receiving firm actually remits the funds, and the sender then owes the receiving firm the money. *See Also: firm, transfer*

TELEPHONE BOOTHS. A communications booth on an exchange floor that members use to obtain buy and sell orders and to provide transaction information. *See Also: exchange, exchange floor, floor, transaction*

TELEPHONE SWITCHING. Occurs when a telephone is used to shift assets from one mutual fund to another. *See Also: fund, mutual fund*

TEMPORARY AGENT TRANSFER PROGRAM. Using the National Association of Securities Dealers' Central Registration Depository, the North American Securities Administrators Association designed a program through which salespeople can obtain temporary registration before they file their permanent registration forms. *See Also: Central Registration Depository, depository, registration, securities*

TEMPORARY RECEIPT. A document acknowledging security ownership until the engraved certificate is ready. *See Also: certificate, security*

TEMPORARY SPECIALIST. An exchange member who temporarily takes over for a specialist in all capacities if that specialist cannot, for some reason, perform his or her duties. *See Also: exchange, specialist*

TEN BAGGER. A stock that rises tenfold. *See Also: stock*

TEN PERCENT GUIDELINE. A city's bonded debt never should exceed 10 percent of the city-owned real estate's market value. *See Also: market, market value*

TEN-FORTY. A government bond that can be redeemed in 10 years and is due after 40 years. *See Also: bond, government bond*

TEN-K REPORT. The annual report that any company issuing listed securities must file with the Securities and Exchange Commission. *See Also: annual report, commission, exchange, listed securities, securities*

TENANCY. Any property ownership.

TENANCY AT SUFFERANCE. A person who takes title to a property and then retains that property even after the title or interest has ended. *See Also: interest*

TENANCY AT WILL. An estate that a lessor or lessee can end at any time. *See Also: estate, lessee, lessor, time*

TENANCY FOR YEARS. A tenancy that lasts a predetermined number of years, and in which no party has any right to terminate the tenancy before the end of that period. *See Also: right, tenancy*

TENANCY IN COMMON ACCOUNT. A savings account owned by at least two people. *See Also: account, savings account*

TENANT. A person who is part owner of a security or a joint account. *See Also: account, joint account, security*

TENANTS BY THE ENTIRETY. When a husband and wife jointly own an asset piece of property or margin account. *See Also: account, asset, margin, margin account*

TENANTS IN COMMON. A form of joint ownership by two or more people whereby the portion owned by one who dies is passed to his or her heirs rather than to another party in the agreement.

TENDENCY. The probability or likelihood of a security's price to shift up, down, or sideways.

TENDER. To formally bid on a security. *See Also: security*

TENDER OFFER. One company's public announcement that it plans to buy as many shares of another company's securities as possible, usually in an effort to take that company over. *See Also: securities, take*

TENDER OPTION PUT SECURITY. A long-term municipal security with a short-term put option that gives the owner the right to redeem the security at par, which, in essence, makes the long-term security a short-term trading instrument. *See Also: at par, instrument, option, par, put, put option, redeem, right, security, short-term trading*

TENDERABLE. A commodity that meets the commodity exchange's quality standards and delivery requirements. *See Also: commodity, delivery, standards*

TENNESSEE VALLEY AUTHORITY (TVA). A government agency established in 1933 to develop the Tennessee River area using money raised through the issuing of debt securities. *See Also: securities*

TENOR. A bond's maturity. *See Also: maturity*

TERA. A prefix that refers to trillion or trillions. For example, one trillion bytes is expressed as 1 terabyte. *See Also: terabyte*

TERABYTE. One trillion bytes.

TERM. The time between the issuing date and the date of maturity. *See Also: date of maturity, maturity, time*

TERM BOND. An issue with all of the bonds in the series maturing on the same date. *See Also: issue*

TERM BONDS PAYABLE. A liability record of outstanding bonds and their face value. *See Also: face value, liability, outstanding*

TERM CERTIFICATE. A certificate of deposit that matures in two to five years and pays interest twice a year. *See Also: certificate, interest*

TERM FEDERAL FUNDS. A commercial bank's excess reserves that it loans at negotiated interest rates for longer-than-normal periods of time. *See Also: excess reserves, interest, time*

TERM ISSUE. A bond issue with each bond in the issue maturing in the same future year. *See Also: bond, issue*

TERM LOAN. A loan that lasts a specific time period. *See Also: time*

TERM MORTGAGE. A mortgage with all interest to be paid within a predetermined time, after which the principal is due. *See Also: interest, mortgage, principal, time*

TERM REPURCHASE AGREEMENT. A repurchase agreement that lasts a longer-than-normal period of time. *See Also: repurchase, repurchase agreement, time*

TERMINAL. A device that contains a display screen and keyboard, which communicates with another computer, such as a network server or mainframe. A terminal can be a dumb terminal, a smart terminal, or an intelligent terminal. *See Also: dumb terminal, mainframe, screen, server*

TERMINAL MARKET. A futures market. *See Also: futures, futures market, market*

TERMINATION CLAIM. The predetermined, allowable level of the appreciation in a stockholder's shares. *See Also: appreciation, level*

TERTIARY MOVEMENT. Small, unimportant, daily price shifts.

TEST. Occurs when a price is challenging a resistance level. If the price does not break through the level, the resistance level is said to have passed the test. *See Also: break, level, resistance level*

TESTAMENTARY ACCOUNT. A savings account with funds invested in some sort of trust, with a beneficiary to receive all of the money upon the account holder's death. *See Also: account, savings account, trust*

TESTAMENTARY DISTRIBUTION. The distribution of a person's estate after the person's death. *See Also: estate*

TESTAMENTARY GUARDIAN. A person named in a will to take over the guardianship of a child. *See Also: take*

TESTAMENTARY TRUST. A contract that allows one person to administer another person's assets after the second person's death. *See Also: contract*

TESTATE. Describes a person who died without leaving a will.

TESTING. A market price that challenges the resistance level, but will not break through that level. *See Also: break, level, market, market price, resistance level*

THE BOND BUYER. A newspaper published daily that lists indexes and statistics from fixed-income markets.

THEORETICAL VALUE. Any evaluation that considers only mathematical variables, but no other market situations. *See Also: evaluation, market*

THEORY OF CONTRARY OPINION. A theory that says that when no great difference of opinion exists, the majority will be wrong.

THIN CORPORATION. A company with debts that greatly outweigh its equity. *See Also: equity*

THIN MARKET. A market with little interest in buying or selling a particular security, which prompts large price fluctuations in the few shares that are traded. *See Also: interest, market, security*

THINLY-HELD STOCK. Shares owned by a small group of people, resulting in wide price fluctuations even when the trading volume is low. *See Also: low, trading volume, volume*

THIRD MARKET. Occurs when a trader who is not a member of an exchange trades exchange-listed securities either over the counter or off the board. *See Also: exchange, off the board, over the counter, securities, trader*

THIRD MORTGAGE. A mortgage that falls beneath the first and second mortgage in claims priority. *See Also: mortgage, priority*

THIRD-PARTY ACCOUNT. An illegal brokerage account that one person carries in his or her name, even though another person actually owns the account. *See Also: account, brokerage account, name*

THIRD-PARTY BROKER. A broker who routinely executes institutional trades, then returns a portion of his or her fee to a fund such as a pension program. *See Also: broker, fund, pension*

THIRD-PARTY CHECK. A check that is payable to someone other than the bearer. *See Also: bearer, check*

THIRD-PARTY REPURCHASE AGREEMENT. A broker's deal with a bank customer in which the bank guarantees the loan and the broker uses government securities as collateral. *See Also: bank, broker, collateral, securities*

THIRTY-DAY VISIBLE SUPPLY. A list of securities that will be offered publicly within 30 days. *See Also: securities*

THIRTY-DAY WASH RULE. With this regulation, the Internal Revenue Service prohibits an investor who suffered a loss on a stock sale from using that loss for tax benefits if the investor bought the stock back 30 days after the sale date, or owned the stock for only 30 days before the sale. *See Also: internal revenue, sale, service, stock*

THREAD NEEDLE STREET. London's financial district.

THREE-AGAINST-ONE RATIO WRITING. Occurs when an investor sells three call options for every 100 shares of the underlying security he or she owns. *See Also: security, underlying security*

THREE-HANDED DEAL. A securities issue that puts together serial maturity bonds with two-term maturity bonds. *See Also: issue, maturity, securities*

THRESHOLD COMPANY. A company run by entrepreneurs and not by seasoned professionals, but that still is on the brink of becoming a mature company. *See Also: run*

THRIFT INSTITUTION. A savings and loan, credit union, or savings bank. *See Also: bank, credit, savings bank*

THROUGH THE MARKET. Occurs when a new bond offering has a lower yield-to-maturity than comparable outstanding bonds. *See Also: bond, offering, outstanding*

THROW AWAY OFFER. An approximate bid or offer price that is not binding and is not a definite transaction quote. *See Also: offer, transaction*

TICK. A security's successive transaction prices. *See Also: transaction*

TICK INDEX. Subtract an exchange's downtick volume from its uptick volume to determine the net tick volume. *See Also: downtick, net, tick, tick volume, uptick, volume*

TICK VOLUME. The downtick volume compared to the uptick volume of a certain security in one trading day. *See Also: downtick, security, trading day, uptick, volume*

TICKER TAPE. An exchange's system for physically recording and reporting securities transactions and volume information. The ticker tape also is referred to as a ticker or a tape. *See Also: securities, tape, volume*

TICKLER. A financial institution's list of bonds and their maturity dates, with such an index reminding the institution of which bonds will fall due and when. *See Also: fall, index, maturity*

TIDAL WAVE PURCHASE. A cash-rich corporate raider quickly and openly buys up all of the target company's outstanding stock, catching the target off guard. *See Also: outstanding, outstanding stock, raider, stock, target*

TIE GAUGE THEORY. A lighthearted market indicator that says when men's ties are wider, stock prices decline, and when men's ties are narrower, stock prices rise. *See Also: market, stock*

TIER. Differentiates one class of securities from another. *See Also: class, securities*

TIFFANY LIST. The nickname for a group of companies that issue high-grade commercial paper. *See Also: commercial paper, issue, paper*

TIGHT MARKET. An active, competitive market with little difference between bid and offer prices. *See Also: market, offer*

TIGHT MONEY. Occurs when there is not enough money to lend, often because of the government's attempts to ebb inflation by manipulating the money reserves. *See Also: inflation*

TIGR. Treasury Investment Growth Receipt. *See Also: investment*

TIME. The time at which a security traded. *See Also: security, trusts for investments in mortgages (TIME)*

TIME BARGAIN. An agreement between a buyer and seller to trade a specific security at a particular price at a specific future date. *See Also: security*

TIME BILL. A bill of exchange with a fixed payment date. *See Also: bill of exchange, exchange, payment date*

TIME CERTIFICATE OF DEPOSIT. A financial instrument with a specific amount and maturity date. *See Also: financial instrument, instrument, maturity*

TIME DEPOSIT. A deposit in an interest-paying account that requires the money to remain on account for a specific length of time. If the depositor withdraws the money before the end of that period, he or she must pay a heavy interest penalty. *See Also: account, heavy, interest, on account, pay, time*

TIME DRAFT. A post-dated financial instrument that transfers money from one person to another. *See Also: financial instrument, instrument*

TIME ORDER. A market order that becomes a limit order on a specific date or at a specific time. *See Also: limit, limit order, market, market order, order, time*

TIME SHARING. A computer environment that enables many users to use a computer, and work independently, simultaneously.

TIME SPREAD. An option strategy in which the investor buys and sells option contracts with the same exercise prices but different expiration dates. *See Also: exercise, expiration, option*

TIME VALUE. A part of a stock option contract's premium that shows how much time is left before the contract expires, thereby indicating how much the premium exceeds the contract's intrinsic value. *See Also: contract, intrinsic value, option, premium, stock, stock option, time*

TIME WARRANT. A negotiable, government obligation with a term that is shorter than bonds. Time warrants often are used to pay people and companies for goods provided or for services rendered. *See Also: negotiable, obligation, pay, term, time*

TIME WEIGHTED RATE OF RETURN. The investment performance of assets held for a specific time period. *See Also: investment, time*

TIME-SHARE. A type of ownership interest that allows use of the property for a fixed or variable time period. Time-sharing exists for many types of properties, including real estate, boats, airplanes, etc. *See Also: estate, interest, real estate, time*

TIMES FIXED CHARGES. The bond interest and preferred stock dividend coverage that a company's income provides. *See Also: bond, dividend, interest, preferred stock, stock, stock dividend*

TIMES INTEREST AND PREFERRED DIVIDEND EARNED. A preferred stock's earnings protection, achieved by dividing the interest and preferred dividend requirements into the net earnings per year. *See Also: dividend, earnings, interest, net, net earnings*

TIMES INTEREST EARNED. A bond's earnings protection, achieved by dividing its interest requirements for the year into its net earnings per year. *See Also: earnings, interest, net, net earnings*

TIMING. The proper time to buy or sell securities, according to impending trends. *See Also: securities, time*

TIN PARACHUTE. A plan that offers benefits to all employees who lose their jobs following a corporate takeover. This employee protection plan attempts to guarantee employees' health and life insurance benefits, severance pay, and out placement assistance. *See Also: guarantee, insurance, life insurance, pay, placement, takeover*

TIP. An inducement to buy or sell securities, with the tip carrying the assumption that it is based on inside information. *See Also: inside information, securities*

TIPPEE. A person who accepts inside information. *See Also: inside information*

TIPSTER. A person who claims he or she has inside information on an investment. *See Also: inside information, investment*

TIPSTER SHEET. A list of recommended securities. *See Also: securities*

TITLE DEED. A document verifying property ownership.

TITLE DEFECT. A situation that challenges property ownership.

TITLE GUARANTY COMPANY. A company paid by a property buyer to research real estate files in order to determine the property's legal status, delinquencies, or defects. *See Also: estate, legal, order, real estate*

TO BE ANNOUNCED (TBA). Securities sold into the forward delivery market are sold with details provided on a TBA basis. *See Also: basis, contract, delayed delivery, delayed delivery contract, delivery, forward, market, TBA*

TO COME. The number of shares that will be sold, but that have not yet been transferred.

TO GO. The number of shares that will be purchased, but that have not yet been transferred.

TO THE BUCK. An offer when the bid and offer amounts are close, and the offer is a round point. *See Also: close, offer, point*

TOEHOLD PURCHASE. Buying less than five percent of a company's outstanding stock before the company notifies the Securities and Exchange Commission about the purchase. *See Also: commission, exchange, outstanding, outstanding stock, securities, stock*

TOLL REVENUE BOND. A municipal bond that will be repaid from toll revenue generated by the project the bond was issued to finance. *See Also: bond, municipal bond*

TOM-NEXT. Tomorrow's business day to the next business day. A next business day settlement. *See Also: business day*

TOMBSTONE. A public announcement that a new security will be offered for sale. A tombstone is not, however, an advertisement to buy the security, but merely an announcement that it will be available. *See Also: sale, security*

TON. Nickname for $100 million.

TOP. A security's highest price during a particular time period. *See Also: time*

TOP HEAVY. Occurs when a security, commodity, or the general market is priced so that it is expected to fall. *See Also: commodity, fall, market, security*

TOP MANAGEMENT. A company's highest ranking officers. *See Also: ranking*

TOP-DOWN APPROACH TO INVESTING. An investment strategy that involves initially studying broad trends, such as the economy, then picks an industry, followed by a company within that industry that will probably benefit the most from the trends. *See Also: industry, investment, investment strategy*

TOPIC. A British information system that provides timely transaction information to subscribing investors. *See Also: transaction*

TOPPING A BID. Occurs when an investor bids a higher amount than the prevailing market price. *See Also: market, market price*

TOPPING OUT. Occurs when a security's steadily increasing price stabilizes and then begins to decline.

TOPPY. Occurs when the general market or an individual security hits its resistance level and subsequently drops. *See Also: level, market, resistance level, security*

TORONTO STOCK EXCHANGE. A major Canadian securities exchange governed by the Ontario Securities Corn mission. The TSE lists both Canadian and American securities. *See Also: exchange, securities, TSE*

TORRENS CERTIFICATE. A document that shows the name of the person who owns a title. *See Also: name*

TOTAL ASSET TURNOVER. Obtained by dividing a company's total operating assets into its sales.

TOTAL CAPITALIZATION. A company's complete capital structure. *See Also: capital, capital structure*

TOTAL COST. The amount of money it costs to buy a security, including the purchase price, fees, and commissions. *See Also: purchase price, security*

TOTAL DEBT TO TANGIBLE NET WORTH. In order to determine whether a company's creditors own more equity in the company than a company's owners, divide the company's tangible net worth into its total current and long-term debts. If the figure is higher than 100 percent, the creditors own more of the company. *See Also: current, equity, net, net worth, order, tangible net worth, worth*

TOTAL OF PAYMENTS. All of the amount financed plus all finance charges involved with the loan. *See Also: plus*

TOTAL RETURN. An investment's current cash flow combined with its ultimate gains or losses. *See Also: cash, cash flow, current*

TOTAL RETURN INVESTMENT. A low-risk investment which provides income with growth. *See Also: investment*

TOTAL VOLUME. The number of shares or contracts traded on all exchanges and in all marketplaces. *See Also: exchanges*

TOTTEN TRUST. A trust in which the initiator deposits money in his or her name, but which is designed to benefit another person. The initiator can cancel the trust at any time, but after his or her death, the fund is transferred to the beneficiary. *See Also: fund, name, time, trust*

TOUCH OFF THE STOPS. Occurs when stop orders become market orders because the price indicated in the order was hit. *See Also: hit, market, order, stop*

TOUT. A subjective endorsement of an investment. *See Also: investment*

TRACKING STOCK. Companies offer tracking shares to fully value the performance of a specific piece of their business. Unlike common stocks, tracking shares don't represent ownership interest in the underlying company, nor are the holders of the shares privy to many of the voting rights and protections given to shareholders that hold shares in a parent company. *See Also: hold, interest, offer, rights, voting rights*

TRADE ACCEPTANCE AND RECONCILIATION SERVICE. Sponsored by the National Association of Securities Dealers, this is a computer network through which over-the-counter contracts can be compared and problems can be resolved. *See Also: securities*

TRADE CREDIT. An account that a supplier keeps for the company buying its goods or services. The account outlines all of the purchases as well as the buying company's payment record. The supplier's trade liabilities are included in its accounts payable. *See Also: account*

TRADE DATE. The day a securities transaction is negotiated and executed. *See Also: securities, transaction*

TRADE DEFICIT. The amount by which a country's imports exceed its exports, creating a negative balance of trade. *See Also: balance, balance of trade*

TRADE HOUSE. A brokerage firm that buys and sells futures and actuals for its own account and for the accounts of customers. *See Also: account, firm, futures*

TRADE PROCESSING AND OPERATIONS DEPARTMENT. A broker-dealer's area responsible for processing all securities transactions. *See Also: processing, securities*

TRADE SUPPORT SYSTEM. Used at the Chicago Board Options Exchange to transmit price information. *See Also: exchange*

TRADE SURPLUS. The amount by which a country's exports exceeds its imports, creating a positive balance of trade. *See Also: balance, balance of trade*

TRADE THROUGH. A normally unethical practice in which an exchange member transacts a deal on the exchange floor even though a better price is available through the Intermarket Trading System. *See Also: exchange, exchange floor, floor, intermarket*

TRADEMARK. A slogan, emblem, or identifying mark registered to one company, to which it has exclusive rights. The company can obtain an exclusive trademark by registering its request with the government. *See Also: rights*

TRADER. A person who buys and sells securities for short-term profits. *See Also: securities*

TRADER'S MARKET. Occurs when market conditions are positive for profiting from short-term investments. *See Also: market*

TRADES ON TOP OF. The relationship between two debt instruments with little or no yield differentials. *See Also: yield*

TRADING. Buying and selling securities or commodities, typically on a short-term basis for quick profits.

TRADING AUTHORIZATION. An agreement in which an account owner allows another person to buy and sell securities for the owner's account. *See Also: account, securities*

TRADING COMMUNITIES. Centralized hubs or marketplaces that bring together buyers and sellers.

TRADING CROWD. A group of exchange members who gather to trade securities. *See Also: exchange, securities*

TRADING CURB. Trading that is restricted temporarily.

TRADING DAY. Any day a securities exchange is open, normally Monday through Friday except for holidays. *See Also: exchange, open, securities*

TRADING DIFFERENCE. The point-fraction difference between the price in an odd-lot transaction and the price of those securities if they had been purchased in a round lot. *See Also: lot, round lot, securities, transaction*

TRADING DIVIDENDS. Occurs when a company buys and sells securities to increase the number of annual dividends subject to a tax exclusion. *See Also: exclusion, securities*

TRADING DOWN. Occurs when an investor buys and sells high-risk or low-rated securities in an attempt to increase his or her capital gains. *See Also: capital, securities*

TRADING FLOOR. The area in an exchange where securities are bought and sold. *See Also: exchange, securities*

TRADING HALT. The temporary trading suspension of an exchange-traded security while material news from the issuer is being disseminated or for an imbalance of orders. Trading may also be halted for regulatory purposes by the exchange or the SEC. *See Also: exchange, SEC, security, suspension*

TRADING HOURS. The times a securities exchange is open, normally 9:30 a.m. to 4 p.m. *See Also: exchange, open, securities*

TRADING INDEX. Also known as TRIN, a technical analysis indicator to determine a stock exchange's intraday market movements. Calculated by dividing the advance-decline volume ratio into the advance-decline ratio. The New York and American stock exchanges calculate the TRIN once every minute. The TRIN measuring less than 1.0 is bullish while a higher number is bearish. *See Also: advance-decline, exchanges, market, ratio, short-term trading, stock, TRIN, volume*

TRADING INSTRUCTIONS. An investor's orders to his or her broker that limits a transaction through a stop order or other restriction. *See Also: broker, order, stop, stop order, transaction*

TRADING LIMIT. The price range within which a commodity can be bought or sold within a given day, with high and low limits marking the edges of that range. A commodity cannot be sold below the low limit or above the high limit. *See Also: commodity, limit, low, marking, price range, range*

TRADING MARKET. A low-volume market with few price fluctuations, in which professional traders, not the general public, make up most of the trading business for the day. *See Also: market, professional*

TRADING ON THE EQUITY. A high-risk practice in which a company issues a funded debt so it can leverage its investments. *See Also: funded debt, leverage*

TRADING ON THE PERIMETER. Occurs when the trading at an exchange's trading post is so active that many transactions are executed on the edge of the trading crowd. Because they are on the edge, the specialist is not always immediately aware of the deals. *See Also: crowd, post, specialist, trading crowd, trading post*

TRADING PAPER. A negotiable, short-term certificate of deposit. *See Also: certificate, negotiable*

TRADING PATTERN. The long-term direction of a security's price movements.

TRADING POST. The area of an exchange where one particular security is traded. *See Also: exchange, security*

TRADING RANGE. The price difference between a security's highest and lowest transaction price in a specific time period. *See Also: time, transaction*

TRADING RING. The New York Stock Exchange area where listed bonds are traded. *See Also: exchange, New York Stock Exchange, stock, stock exchange*

TRADING ROTATION. One method of opening the trading of option series, securities, and commodities futures contracts after which individual trading can continue. *See Also: futures, option, option series, securities*

TRADING THROUGH THE FUND'S RATE. A debt security with a yield to maturity that is lower than the federal fund's rate, which is vulnerable to interest rate changes. When this occurs often, the Federal Reserve probably is preparing to change its monetary policies. *See Also: change, debt security, interest, interest rate, maturity, reserve, security, yield, yield to maturity*

TRADING UNIT. A round lot.

TRADING UP. Occurs when an investor trades securities from his or her portfolio for securities with higher ratings, which thereby reduces the investor's portfolio risks. *See Also: portfolio, securities*

TRADING VARIATION. The fractions to which a security's price is rounded. For example, stocks are rounded up and down and traded in eighths.

TRADING VOLUME. The number of shares a security has traded on a particular exchange during a specific time period. *See Also: exchange, security, time*

TRADITIONAL VALUE FUNDS. A type of mutual fund that seeks out-of-favor stocks that sell at a discount to the overall market. Typically, this is measured by the ratio of their price to earnings, dividend yield or book value. *See Also: at a discount, book, book value, discount, dividend, dividend yield, earnings, fund, market, mutual fund, ratio, yield*

TRANCHE. French for "slice," this represents classes of bonds or securities designed to meet the needs of the issuer and the objectives of investors. *See Also: securities*

TRANS-CANADA OPTION. A Canadian put or call option with the underlying security issued by a Canadian company. *See Also: call option, option, put, security, underlying security*

TRANS-CANADA OPTIONS INC. A Canadian company that issues options with the underlying securities issued by Canadian companies. The options are traded in both the U.S. and Canada. *See Also: securities*

TRANSACTION. The execution of a securities deal. *See Also: execution, securities*

TRANSFER. To change ownership from one party to another. *See Also: change*

TRANSFER AGENT. A person who physically records the transfer of a securities ownership. *See Also: securities, transfer*

TRANSFER AND SHIP. A security owner's order to his or her broker to have the security registered in his or her name and shipped to the address on the account. *See Also: account, address, broker, name, order, security*

TRANSFER INITIATION REQUEST. A contract issued by the National Securities Clearing Corporation that approves the transfer of securities from one member's account to another. *See Also: account, contract, corporation, National Securities Clearing Corporation, securities, transfer*

TRANSFER JOURNAL. A company's book that shows all securities issued, transferred, and canceled. *See Also: book, securities*

TRANSFER PRICE. The price that one entity of a corporation charges another entity of the same corporation for completing a transaction. *See Also: corporation, transaction*

TRANSFER TAX. A modest tax on securities transactions, normally paid by the seller. *See Also: securities*

TRANSFERABLE NOTICE. A document a seller issues to announce his or her plans to deliver a commodity in order to fill a futures contract. The recipient is allowed to transfer the document to another party who will then receive the commodity. *See Also: commodity, contract, fill, futures, futures contract, order, transfer*

TRANSMITTAL LETTER. The letter a seller attaches to the document or securities he or she is sending to the buyer describing the shipment's purpose and contents. *See Also: securities*

TRAPPER. Nickname for a registered representative, so named because the business used to be so slow that representatives would have to try to "trap" their customers. *See Also: registered representative*

TREASURER. A company's officer who receives, manages, and invests the company's funds. If the company is publicly held, the treasurer also must maintain the market. *See Also: market, officer, publicly held*

TREASURIES. Nickname for any Treasury security. *See Also: security*

TREASURY BILL. A short-term discounted, government debt instrument of one year or less, issued in $10,000 denominations, that pays its face value at maturity. The government issues Treasury bills weekly. *See Also: debt instrument, face value, instrument, maturity*

TREASURY BILL AUCTION. A weekly Treasury Department auction in which short-term government obligations are sold. *See Also: auction*

TREASURY BOND. A long-term, Treasury-issued debt instrument issued at par and maturing in at least 10 years in minimum denominations of $1,000. Treasury bonds pay interest, which is exempt from state and local taxes, twice a year. *See Also: at par, debt instrument, instrument, interest, local, par, pay*

TREASURY CERTIFICATE. A short-term government security with a maturity of six months to a year that has been issued to ease Federal Reserve transfers to banks. *See Also: maturity, reserve, security*

TREASURY INVESTMENT GROWTH RECEIPT (TIGR). A Treasury bond that has been stripped of its coupons, with ownership of individual coupons, or of bond principal sold at a discount as a zero coupon. All interest is paid at maturity. *See Also: at a discount, bond, coupon, discount, interest, maturity, principal, treasury bond*

TREASURY NOTE. A medium-term, government debt instrument that is issued at par in $5,000 to $10,000 denominations, and matures in one to 10 years. Treasury notes pay interest that is exempt from state and local taxes biannually. *See Also: at par, debt instrument, instrument, interest, local, par, pay*

TREASURY RECEIPTS. Stripped Treasury bonds.

TREASURY STOCK. Stock a company issues then buys back, at which time it is placed in the company's treasury where it earns no dividends and carries no voting privileges. *See Also: time*

TREND. A prevailing price movement. *See Also: movement*

TRENDLESS. A price movement that fluctuates up and down to the extent that no specific trend can be identified. *See Also: movement, trend*

TRENDLINE. A chart slope representing price movements, connecting the highest and lowest prices of a security. Technical analysts use this line to indicate an uptrend or downtrend. *See Also: chart, security*

TRIANGLE. A charted price pattern that forms a triangle because the security's price has gone down, then up, then back down again.

TRIANGULAR ARBITRAGE. Arbitrage achieved through the exchange rates of three foreign currencies. *See Also: arbitrage, exchange*

TRICK. A long-term, municipal bond issue's special low coupon with a high yield, which allows a bidder to lower the issuer's net interest cost in an attempt to win the bid. *See Also: bond, coupon, interest, low, municipal bond, net, net interest cost, yield*

TRICKLE-DOWN THEORY. An economic theory stating that giving money to businesses is more important than giving money to consumers because if businesses are promoted and expanded, the individual ultimately will benefit.

TRIN. Trading Index. *See Also: arms index, index*

TRIPLE BOTTOM. A chart that shows a security's price has hit three bottom prices within a short time, but will not drop below the most recent low price. *See Also: bottom, chart, drop, hit, low, time*

TRIPLE EXEMPTION. A municipal bond that provides tax-exempt interest income to the holder. The triple exemption is so named because it is exempt from local, state, and federal taxes. *See Also: bond, exemption, interest, local, municipal bond*

TRIPLE NET LEASE. A rental contract in which the renter pays the property owner a fixed amount, then is responsible for maintenance and all other costs involved. *See Also: contract, maintenance*

TRIPLE OPTION PREFERRED STOCK. A preferred stock that gives the owner the right to sell the stock back to the issuing company quarterly for an equal amount of common stock or a debt security, or cash. *See Also: cash, common stock, debt security, preferred stock, quarterly, right, security, stock*

TRIPLE TAX EXEMPT. Municipal bonds that are exempt from federal, state, and local taxes on the interest paid to bondholders. Municipal bonds issued by possessions and territories of the United States (such as Puerto Rico) are triple tax exempt. Residents of the local states and localities that issue municipal bonds also enjoy the triple tax exemption. *See Also: exemption, interest, issue, local, tax exemption*

TRIPLE TOP. A chart that shows a security's price has hit three top prices within a short time, but will not rise above the most recent high price. *See Also: chart, hit, time, top*

TRIPLE WITCHING HOUR. The final hour of trading before equity, index options, and index futures contracts expire. Because of contract schedules, a triple witching hour will occur four times a year, each of which typically marks heavy trading. *See Also: contract, equity, futures, heavy, index, index futures*

TROUGH. An activity's economic bottom. *See Also: bottom*

TRUNCATION. The elimination, reduction, or consolidation of paper work to reduce operating expenses. Feeding information from paper documents into a computer system and then throwing the paper documents away would be an example of truncation. *See Also: consolidation, paper*

TRUST. A contract in which a person deposits and holds money, securities, or other assets for the ultimate benefit of another person. *See Also: contract, securities*

TRUST COMPANY. A financial institution that handles trust funds. *See Also: trust*

TRUST INDENTURE ACT. A federal law that requires issuing companies to fully disclose information about their securities as well as pertinent information concerning their own management. The law covers securities that were not included in the Securities Act of 1933. *See Also: securities, Securities Act of 1933*

TRUST INSTITUTION. Any company with at least one department handling trust business, even if the company's general business is in another field. *See Also: trust*

TRUST INSTRUMENT COMMITTEE. A trust institution panel of officers that oversees and decides how to invest the institution's trust funds. *See Also: trust, trust institution*

TRUSTEE. One person who is legally responsible for another person's investments, property, or other assets.

TRUSTEED FUND. Any accumulation of money held for a future use such as a retirement or an education. *See Also: accumulation*

TRUSTEED PENSION PLAN. A pension plan in which the company puts its contributions into a trust fund for investing. *See Also: fund, pension, pension plan, trust*

TRUSTEES SHARES. The certificates of beneficial interest in an investment company. *See Also: beneficial interest, interest, investment, investment company*

TRUSTS FOR INVESTMENTS IN MORTGAGES (TIME). This gives mortgage-backed securities bond characteristics, such as twice-a-year payments and repayment protection. *See Also: bond, securities*

TRUTH IN LENDING ACT. A federal law that requires lenders to provide the true cost of loans and all terms involved to the borrower.

TRUTH IN SECURITIES ACT. A law that requires full disclosure of information concerning publicly issued securities. *See Also: disclosure, full, full disclosure, securities*

TSE. Toronto Stock Exchange. *See Also: exchange, stock, stock exchange, Toronto Stock Exchange*

TUNNELING. Using the Internet to create a private and secure network between two computers. *See Also: Internet*

TURBO CASH COLLATERAL. An overcollateralization of securities, usually multitranche Automobile Loan securities or other transactions that contain excess spread, with the extra cash and principal from the underlying loans generated in the issue building to overcollateralize the securities. *See Also: automobile loan securities, cash, issue, principal, securities, spread*

TURKEY. A security that has lost money for its investors. *See Also: security*

TURN. Occurs when a price movement or trend changes directions. *See Also: movement, trend*

TURNAROUND. A security with a price that has rebounded. *See Also: security*

TURNAROUND SITUATION. Occurs when an unprofitable company becomes profitable by changing its internal management, marketing, or other corporate structure situation.

TURNKEY. A product manufactured to completion, then turned over to the user, who needs no expert knowledge to make the product work. A computer that needs no installation other than plugging it in would be an example of a turnkey.

TURNOVER. The number of securities in an investor's portfolio that were bought and sold within a specific time period. *See Also: portfolio, securities, time*

TURTLE BLOOD. A stable security with low volatility and a price that is not expected to increase quickly. *See Also: low, security, volatility*

TVA. Tennessee Valley Authority.

TWENTY PERCENT CUSHION RULE. A project funded by a municipal bond should produce revenue that exceeds 20 percent of the cost of maintaining and servicing the bond. *See Also: bond, municipal bond*

TWENTY-DAY PERIOD. Also called the cooling-off period, this is the time between the day a company files its registration statement with the Securities and Exchange Commission and the day the security can be publicly sold. *See Also: commission, exchange, registration, registration statement, securities, security, statement, time*

TWENTY-FIVE PERCENT RULE. A city's bonded debt never should exceed 25 percent of its yearly budget. *See Also: budget*

TWISTING. An unethical practice of persuading a person to switch from one mutual fund to another because the other carries an additional sales charge. *See Also: fund, mutual fund, sales charge*

TWO HUNDRED-DAY MOVING AVERAGE. A daily chart that looks at price averages over the past 200 days, which often provides a better indicator of trends. The averages include the reporting day's averages and the averages of the past 199 days. *See Also: averages, chart*

TWO-AGAINST-ONE RATIO WRITING. When an investor sells two call options for every 100 shares of the underlying security he or she owns. *See Also: security, underlying security*

TWO-DOLLAR BROKER. An exchange member who executes transactions for other brokers who are too busy to handle their own high-volume businesses. Two-dollar brokers are so named because they used to charge $2 for every 100-share deal. *See Also: exchange, handle*

TWO-HANDED DEAL. Occurs when two broker-dealers comanage a new securities distribution. *See Also: securities*

TWO-SIDED MARKET. A market in which firm bids and offered prices are offered. For example, the NASD mandates that NASDAQ market makers make both firm bids and offers for each security in which they make a market. *See Also: firm, make a market, market, NASD, NASDAQ, security*

TWO-TIER PRICING. Occurs in a takeover attempt when the raider pays the person who owns the controlling stock a higher price than the other stockholders. *See Also: raider, stock, takeover*

TWO-WAY TRADE. Occurs when an investor simultaneously buys one security and sells another. *See Also: security*

TWOFER. A long call at a lower striking price and two short calls at higher striking prices, with all expiring on the same date. *See Also: long call, striking price*

TYPE OF OPTIONS. Indicates either a call option or a put option. *See Also: call option, option, put, put option*

1099. An Internal Revenue Service form on which a taxpayer lists interest, dividend, and fee payments. *See Also: dividend, interest, internal revenue, service*

10Q. *See Also: quarterly, quarterly report.*

12B-1 FEE. Termed after an SEC rule, a fee that is charged by mutual funds to pay for advertising and marketing related expenses. *See Also: pay, SEC*

12B-1 MUTUAL FUND. A no-load mutual fund, typically a Class C share, which is registered with the Securities and Exchange Commission, in which investors pay a 12B-1 fee of one percent or less toward promotion expenses. Such promotion is necessary because no brokers are involved in the sale of such funds, so the fund manager must pay for advertising. *See Also: 12B-1 fee, commission, exchange, fund, manager, mutual fund, no-load mutual fund, pay, sale, securities*

U

U-4. An application used to register agents and representatives with an exchange and with the National Association of Securities Dealers. The registration provides the personal, legal, and business background of an applicant. *See Also: agents, exchange, legal, register, registration, securities*

U-5. A document used to notify an exchange and the National Association of Securities Dealers that an agent's registration has been terminated. *See Also: exchange, registration, securities*

U.S. RULE. A method in which a trust mortgage's payments are applied first to the interest due, and then to reducing the principal due. *See Also: interest, principal, trust*

U.S. TERMS. The number of American dollars needed to buy one unit of a foreign country's currency. *See Also: currency, unit*

UDDI. Universal Description Discovery and Integration.

ULTIMATE BENEFICIARY. A principal beneficiary that will receive the trust's principal amount in the final distribution. *See Also: principal, principal amount*

ULTIMO. The previous month.

ULTRA VIRES. An action a company takes when a prior event exceeds the boundaries of what is allowed according to the company's charter. Ultra vires often lead to shareholder or third-party suits. *See Also: charter, shareholder*

UNACCRUED. Income from payments made before their due date.

UNAMORTIZED BOND DISCOUNT. The difference between a bond's face value and the amount of money the issuing company received from selling the bond, minus any amortized portion. *See Also: bond, face value, minus*

UNAMORTIZED DISCOUNTS ON INVESTMENTS. The difference between a security's face value and the amount the issuing company received for selling the security, minus any amortized portion. *See Also: face value, minus, security*

UNAMORTIZED PREMIUMS ON INVESTMENTS. The unexpensed part of a security's purchase price that exceeded its par or market value. *See Also: market, market value, par, purchase price*

UNAPPROPRIATED PROFITS. The portion of a company's profits that the company has not paid out in dividends or used to retire existing debts. *See Also: retire*

UNASSENTED SECURITIES. Securities that the issuing company wants to change, but which have yet to receive stockholder approval. *See Also: change, stockholder*

UNAUTHORIZED GROWTH. A capital investment with different growth rates in different economic areas. *See Also: capital, investment*

UNAUTHORIZED INVESTMENT. A trust investment that the trust instrument has not approved. *See Also: instrument, investment, trust*

UNCALLED CAPITAL. The part of a company's issued share capital that the company has not called. *See Also: capital, share, share capital*

UNCERTIFIED SHARES. Fund shares an investor owns in his or her account, even though no stock certificates have been issued for the shares. *See Also: account, stock*

UNCOLLECTED FUNDS. Describes a check the bank returns to a customer when that customer wrote a check without having sufficient funds in his or her account to cover the check. *See Also: account, bank, check*

UNCOVER THE STOPS. Depressing a security's price to the extent that investors begin creating stop orders. *See Also: stop*

UNCOVERED. A short option position for which the seller does not own the underlying security and is therefore not in a hedged position. *See Also: option, position, security, underlying security*

UNCOVERED WRITER. A person who sells an option contract without owning any shares of the underlying security. *See Also: contract, option, option contract, security, underlying security*

UNDER REVIEW (UR). Indicates a bond a rating service has yet to rank. *See Also: bond, service*

UNDER THE RULE. When exchange officers buy or sell securities to complete a transaction that a delinquent exchange member entered but failed to settle. The delinquent member is charged with any price discrepancies. *See Also: exchange, securities, settle, transaction*

UNDERBANKED. A proposed underwriting in which the syndicate manager is having trouble recruiting other syndicate members to share in the underwriting risk. *See Also: manager, risk, share, syndicate, syndicate manager, underwriting*

UNDERBOOKED. A proposed underwriting in which the investing public's interest is extremely limited, so the supply of the security may outweigh the demand. *See Also: demand, interest, security, supply, underwriting*

UNDERCAPITALIZED. A company that does not have enough money to conduct its day-to-day business.

UNDERCUTTING AN OFFER. An attempt to sell securities below the prevailing offer price. *See Also: offer, securities*

UNDERLYING DEBT. A lower municipality's debt for which residents of a higher municipality have some responsibilities. A county, for example, would have an underlying debt if its residents had a partial liability for the debts of a city within that county. *See Also: City, liability*

UNDERLYING FUTURES CONTRACT. A futures contract upon which a futures option is written. *See Also: contract, futures, futures contract, option*

UNDERLYING MORTGAGE. A mortgage that takes priority over another mortgage, even though the senior mortgage is for a smaller amount. *See Also: mortgage, priority*

UNDERLYING SECURITY. The security on which an options contract is written. Underlying security is also the common stock which can be issued by a corporation to an investor who exercises a stock option, right offering, warrant, or convertible security. *See Also: common stock, contract, convertible security, corporation, offering, option, options contract, right, security, stock, stock option, warrant*

UNDERLYING SYNDICATE. The original syndicate members who underwrote a new securities issue. *See Also: issue, securities, syndicate*

UNDERMARGINED ACCOUNT. A margin account that has dropped below the margin requirement. *See Also: account, margin, margin account, margin requirement*

UNDERPRICED. Used to describe a stock price that is low compared to its potential future value. *See Also: low, stock*

UNDERTONE. The market's strong or weak base. *See Also: base*

UNDERVALUED. Occurs when a security's price is lower than its liquidation price or the market value placed on it by analysts. An undervalued stock justifies a higher market price and price/earnings ratio. *See Also: liquidation, market, market price, market value, ratio, stock*

UNDERWATER OPTION. *See Also: Jacques Cousteau option.*

UNDERWRITING. The business of investment bankers to assume the risk of buying new issues of securities from a corporation or government entity and distributing them to the public. The underwriters will profit from the difference in the purchase and selling price. *See Also: corporation, investment, profit, risk, securities*

UNDERWRITING AGREEMENT. The contract between an underwriting syndicate and the security's issuer, with the agreement spelling out the terms, price, and account settlement details. *See Also: account, contract, syndicate, underwriting, underwriting syndicate*

UNDERWRITING FEE. A spread that accrues to syndicate members in proportion to the number of shares for which each member was responsible. *See Also: spread, syndicate*

UNDERWRITING RECAPTURE. A syndicate member who also is a broker-dealer sells part of the underwriting to an institutional portfolio. *See Also: broker-dealer, portfolio, syndicate, underwriting*

UNDERWRITING SPREAD. The difference between the amount of money an issuer receives per security in a public offering, and the actual public offering price. *See Also: actual, offering, offering price, public offering, public offering price, security*

UNDERWRITING SYNDICATE. A group of people who contract with the securities issuer and, upon agreement, guarantee a new securities issue by buying the entire issue, then reselling it publicly. *See Also: contract, guarantee, issue, securities*

UNDIGESTED SECURITIES. A securities issue in which more shares are issued than the market can absorb. *See Also: issue, market, securities*

UNDILUTED STOCK. A security with an earnings per share that has not been reduced for any reason. *See Also: earnings, security, share*

UNDISTRIBUTED PROFIT. A company's earnings before those earnings have been divided among the company's owners or stockholders. *See Also: earnings*

UNDISTRIBUTED PROFITS TAX. A tax placed on a company's undistributed profits that is designed to discourage a company from holding on to the profits without having a sound business reason for doing so. Without the tax, a company could hold on to the profits, so stockholders could avoid paying income taxes on the distribution amounts. *See Also: hold*

UNDIVIDED ACCOUNT. A municipal securities underwriting with each syndicate member holding an undivided selling liability (also known as an Eastern Account). *See Also: liability, securities, syndicate, underwriting*

UNDIVIDED PROFITS. A bank account showing profits that have not been paid out as dividends or transferred to the surplus account. *See Also: account, bank*

UNDIVIDED RIGHT. The portion of ownership that cannot be separated from other ownership parts, such as those found in joint tenancy. *See Also: joint tenancy, tenancy*

UNEARNED DISCOUNT. A lending institution's account of interest that will be taken as income earned over the life of the loan. *See Also: account, interest*

UNEARNED INCOME. Income such as dividends, interest payments, or other income that is not earned through salaries or wages. *See Also: interest, other income*

UNEARNED INCREMENT. A property value increase caused by changing conditions that are beyond the property owner's control, as opposed to increases because of home improvements or other conditions over which the property owner has influence. *See Also: home*

UNEARNED INTEREST. Interest that a lending institution has not yet collected, but that is part of its earnings. *See Also: earnings*

UNENCUMBERED. An asset that has no liens and that is not pledged as collateral against a loan. *See Also: asset, collateral*

UNEVEN MARKET. A market with fluctuating prices. *See Also: market*

UNFUNDED DEBT. Any short-term debt, or a debt that is not protected by a bond. *See Also: bond, short-term debt*

UNIFIED CREDIT. A credit that can be applied only once in a person's life against that person's gift or estate taxes. *See Also: credit, estate*

UNIFORM COMMERCIAL CODE. A statute that standardizes commercial customs and practices, with many local modifications. *See Also: local*

UNIFORM GIFTS TO MINORS ACT. A state law which designates the distribution and administration of assets in the name of a child by a custodian who is of legal age. *See Also: custodian, legal, name*

UNIFORM PRACTICE CODE. A National Association of Securities Dealers regulation governing the execution, settling, and clearing of over-the-counter transactions. *See Also: execution, securities*

UNIFORM RESOURCE LOCATOR. Also referred to as URL, refers to the protocol of a Web document on the Internet. *See Also: Internet, on, protocol, Web*

UNIFORM SECURITIES AGENT STATE LAW EXAMINATION. A state test, administered by the National Association of Securities Dealers, given to people who want to become registered representatives. *See Also: securities, test*

UNISSUED COMMON STOCK. Common stock shares that a company has authorized to be issued publicly, but that have not yet been issued. Unissued common stock shares do not include those shares the company has reacquired. *See Also: common stock, stock*

UNIT. The group of exchange specialists who maintain an orderly market in a particular group of securities. *See Also: exchange, market, securities*

UNIT INVESTMENT TRUST. A portfolio made up of a variety of different income securities that are pooled together and sold to investors as units. Each unit represents a fractional, undivided interest in the portfolio's principal and income. *See Also: interest, portfolio, principal, securities, unit*

UNIT PRICE DEMAND ADJUSTABLE TAX-EXEMPT SECURITIES (UPDATES). This is a variable-rate municipal security with a put feature attached. The variable rate is reset each day, and interest is paid monthly. The investor can redeem the security once a month or once a week (depending on the security type) for its face value. *See Also: and interest, face value, interest, put, redeem, security*

UNIT STOCK INVESTMENT TRUST. An Americus Trust involving the Prescribed Right to Income and Maximum Equity (PRIME), in which investors receive dividend distributions and a partial asset value when the trust is dissolved, and the Special Claim On Residual Equity (SCORE), in which investors do not receive dividends, but do receive a partial asset value when the trust is dissolved. *See Also: Americus Trust, asset, dividend, equity, Prescribed Right to Income and Maximum Equity (PRIME), right, Special Claim on Residual Equity (SCORE), trust*

UNITARY INVESTMENT FUND. A mutual fund with no directors and no stockholder voting rights. *See Also: fund, mutual fund, rights, stockholder, voting rights*

UNITARY TAX. A state calculation in which a company's tax liabilities within that state are figured as a percentage of its total worldwide profits, not only on the profits of the company's subsidiary or branch within that state. *See Also: subsidiary*

UNITED STATES GOVERNMENT SECURITIES. Any debt issued by the U.S. Government, such as Treasuries or Series EE and HH savings bonds. *See Also: treasuries*

UNIVERSAL DESCRIPTIN DISCOVERY AND INTEGRATION. Also referred to as UDDI, a set of specifications that allows businesses to describe their e-business processes. The goal is to help improve collaboration between potential business partners. *See Also: e-business, UDDI*

UNIX. An operating system originally developed at the Bell Telephone Laboratories that is used on many Internet servers. It quickly gained in popularity because it can be run on many different computer platforms. *See Also: Bell, Internet, on, run*

UNLEVERAGED PROGRAM. A limited partnership that invests in real estate or other property or equipment and that borrows less than 50 percent of a property's purchase price to buy the property. *See Also: estate, limited partnership, partnership, purchase price, real estate*

UNLIMITED MORTGAGE. An open-ended mortgage. *See Also: mortgage*

UNLIMITED TAX BOND. A municipal securities issue to be repaid with general, unrestricted tax collections. *See Also: issue, securities*

UNLISTED OPTION. An option contract that is traded directly from the buyer to the seller and not traded on an organized exchange. An unlisted option is not issued by the Options Clearing Corporation. *See Also: contract, corporation, exchange, option, option contract, organized exchange*

UNLISTED STOCK. A security such as an over-the-counter stock that is not listed with a registered exchange. *See Also: exchange, registered exchange, security, stock*

UNLISTED TRADING. An exchange transaction involving an unlisted security. Such a transaction is allowed only with the special permission of the Securities and Exchange Commission. *See Also: commission, exchange, securities, security, transaction*

UNLOADING. When an investor sells securities or commodities that have dropped in price to prevent any further losses. *See Also: securities*

UNMARGINABLE. A security that cannot be used as margin for buying stock shares. *See Also: margin, security, stock*

UNPAID DIVIDEND. A dividend a company has declared, but not yet paid to stockholders. *See Also: dividend*

UNPARTED BULLION. A bullion that carries other metals besides the primary precious metal. *See Also: bullion*

UNREALIZED APPRECIATION. Occurs when a security's market value increases above its purchase price, but the owner does not sell it. The appreciation will remain unrealized, or a paper profit, until the investor sells the security. *See Also: appreciation, market, market value, paper, paper profit, profit, purchase price, security*

UNREALIZED LOSS. Occurs when a security's market value drops below its purchase price, but the owner does not sell it. The loss will remain unrealized, or a paper loss, until the investor sells the security. *See Also: market, market value, paper, paper loss, purchase price, security*

UNRECOVERED COST. The part of an investment that has not been amortized. *See Also: investment*

UNREGISTERED STOCK. Limited-issue stock that is not registered with the Securities and Exchange Commission. The issues are either confined to certain buyers or issued by a small company to raise money for a limited, specific purpose. *See Also: commission, exchange, securities, stock*

UNSEASONED SECURITY. A newly issued security with no prior exposure to the effects of supply and demand. *See Also: demand, exposure, security, supply*

UNSECURED DEBT. A debt obligation with no collateral and backed only by the debtor's creditworthiness. *See Also: collateral, obligation*

UNSTEADY MARKET. A market in which securities prices fluctuate to the point that specialists cannot identify any trends. *See Also: market, point, securities*

UNSUBSCRIBED SHARES. Shares in a securities offering that the underwriting syndicate has not yet sold to the public. *See Also: offering, securities, syndicate, underwriting, underwriting syndicate*

UNSYSTEMATIC RISK. A risk that is limited or unique to one asset or investment. A company can eliminate its unsystematic risk by diversifying its holdings. *See Also: asset, investment, risk*

UNVALUED STOCK. Stock for which the issuing company has recorded on its books as having no par or stated value. *See Also: par*

UNWIND A TRADE. A transaction that voids a previous transaction. For example, if an investor wanted to unwind the purchase of a security, he or she would sell it. *See Also: security, transaction*

UP. Follows a number to indicate the dollar amount that a security's price has increased.

UP REVERSAL. A sudden, short-term price increase in a security that has been dropping in value. *See Also: security*

UP ROUND. A venture capital round of financing that is priced at a higher valuation than the previous round. *See Also: capital, valuation, venture capital*

UP TREND. Occurs when a security's price continues to climb steadily over a period of time. *See Also: time*

UP-AND-OUT OPTION. An over-the-counter put option that will be canceled if the price goes up. *See Also: option, put, put option*

UPDATE. An upward trend in a security's price. *See Also: trend*

UPDATES. Unit Price Demand Adjustable Tax-Exempt Securities. *See Also: demand, securities, unit*

UPGRADE. Occurs when an investor sells the low-quality securities from his or her portfolio and replaces them by buying higher quality securities. *See Also: portfolio, securities*

UPLOAD. To send or transmit a file from one computer to another over the Internet. *See Also: Internet*

UPSET PRICE. The lowest price a seller will consider before selling an item, security, or property. *See Also: security*

UPSIDE. A security's price increase.

UPSIDE BREAK-EVEN. The most a security's price will have to rise before the investor starts to make a profit. *See Also: profit*

UPSIDE GAP. A gap that appears on a chart when a security's highest price on one day is lower than its lowest price on the next day. *See Also: chart, gap*

UPSIDE POTENTIAL. The price to which an investor expects a security to rise based on all fundamental and technical predictions. The upside potential of a stock may also be a buy-out price. *See Also: security, stock, upside*

UPSIDE TREND. A period of at least several months during which prices steadily climb, even if it is a market with a few temporary down reversals. *See Also: market*

UPSIDE-DOWNSIDE VOLUME RATIO. The total number of traded shares that dropped in value divided into the total number of traded shares that rose in value during a specific time period. *See Also: time*

UPSTAIRS MARKET. A brokerage firm area where a transaction involving a listed security is completed without sending that transaction to the exchange floor. The deal, for example, would be negotiated between one broker-dealer and another broker-dealer. *See Also: broker-dealer, exchange, exchange floor, firm, floor, security, transaction*

UPTICK. A security transaction made at a higher price than the previous transaction in the security. *See Also: security, transaction*

UPTICK-DOWNTICK BLOCK RATIO. The number of security blocks traded on downticks divided into the number waded on upticks. A ratio below 0.4 indicates the market is oversold, and a ratio above 1.0 indicates the market is overbought. *See Also: market, overbought, oversold, ratio, security*

UPVALUATION. Revaluation or restoring an inflated currency's purchasing power. *See Also: purchasing power*

UR. Under Review.

URL. Uniform Resource Locator. *See Also: resource*

USABLE BOND. A debenture with a detachable warrant, which allows the investor to use the bond's face value to subscribe to common stock. *See Also: common stock, debenture, face value, stock, warrant*

USENET. A giant public Internet-based collection of newsgroups for electronic news and mail, covering every imaginable topic. *See Also: topic*

USER FRIENDLY. The reference to an interface design, such as a Web page, that is easy for a user to learn and use. *See Also: Web, Web page*

USERNAME. The identification assigned to users of a computer network or remote server. Typing the username on the computer screen, oftentimes followed by a password, is a part of the login procedure. *See Also: login, on, remote, screen, server*

USURY. The loaning of money with interest. *See Also: interest, with interest*

UTILITY. Small helper software programs that handle isolated functions, such as compressing programs, converting files from one format to another, and font managers. *See Also: handle*

UTILITY REVENUE BOND. A municipal bond issued to pay for a utility service project such as a generating plant or sewer system. The bond is repaid through the revenues produced from the project. *See Also: bond, municipal bond, pay, plant, service, utility*

V

V FORMATION. On a vertical line chart, a V-shaped pattern indicates a bottoming out, thus a bullish movement, followed by a current uptrend. An inverted-V pattern indicates a bearish movement. *See Also: chart, current, line chart, movement*

VA LOANS. Veteran's Administration Loans.

VALEUR. A French security. *See Also: security*

VALUATION. An appraisal. *See Also: appraisal*

VALUATION RESERVE. To provide for any changes in a company's asset value, the company creates a reserve through a charge to expenses. *See Also: asset, reserve*

VALUE ASSET. To determine the value asset for each share of common stock, divide the number of common shares outstanding into the issuing company's net resources. To determine the value asset for each share of preferred stock, divide the number of preferred shares outstanding into the issuing company's net resources. *See Also: asset, common stock, net, outstanding, preferred stock, share, shares outstanding, stock*

VALUE BROKER. A discount broker who bases his or her rates on a percentage of each transaction's dollar value. Smaller orders, therefore, are less expensive when settled through a value broker. *See Also: broker, discount, discount broker*

VALUE CHANGE. The net change of all individual securities weighted to represent the number of shares outstanding. *See Also: change, net, net change, outstanding, securities, shares outstanding*

VALUE COMPENSATED. Buying or selling a foreign currency, with the transaction executed by cable, after which the buyer pays back the seller for the earlier value. *See Also: cable, currency, foreign currency, transaction*

VALUE DATE. A foreign currency settlement date. *See Also: currency, foreign currency, settlement date*

VALUE FUND. A mutual fund with investments concentrated in securities issued by companies with low price/earnings ratios. *See Also: fund, low, mutual fund, securities*

VALUE LINE INVESTMENT SURVEY. A service that rates securities for risk potential and timely investing using a computer model based on the issuing company's earnings momentum. The highest ranking is one, and the lowest is five. *See Also: earnings, momentum, ranking, risk, securities, service*

VALUE-ADDED TAX. A value-based excise tax added to a product at each production stage. *See Also: excise tax*

VANILLA TRANSACTION. Occurs when a company sells shares of its own stock or takes out long-term loans, lasting up to 30 years, at a fixed interest rate. *See Also: fixed interest rate, interest, interest rate, stock*

VARIABILITY. Rate of return fluctuations. *See Also: return*

VARIABLE ANNUITY. An annuity contract investing in a certain portfolio with lifetime retirement payments varying according to the results of the investments. *See Also: annuity, contract, portfolio*

VARIABLE COST. A cost that will change as production costs change (such as labor and equipment). *See Also: change*

VARIABLE INCOME SECURITY. A security with its dividend payments dependent on the company's ability to make a profit. *See Also: dividend, profit, security*

VARIABLE INTEREST PLUS. A defunct certificate of deposit with the interest rate tied to the Treasury rate, and against which the investor could borrow at an interest rate of one percent above the weekly rate that the CD was earning. *See Also: CD, certificate, interest, interest rate*

VARIABLE LIFE INSURANCE. A life insurance policy giving policy holders benefits based on the performance of the securities in the portfolio. *See Also: insurance, life insurance, portfolio, securities*

VARIABLE PORTFOLIO. A group of investments that changes with the securities's market value. *See Also: market, market value*

VARIABLE RATE CERTIFICATE. A savings certificate with the government-set interest rate varying according to the length of time for which the money was pledged. *See Also: certificate, interest, interest rate, time*

VARIABLE RATE CERTIFICATE OF DEPOSIT. A 360-day certificate of deposit with an interest rate tied to the issuing bank's rate on 90-day CDs and changed every 90 days accordingly. *See Also: certificate, interest, interest rate*

VARIABLE RATE DEMAND NOTE. A note that is payable on demand and bears interest rates tied to money market rates. *See Also: demand, interest, market, money market, money market rates, note*

VARIABLE RATE MORTGAGE. An amortized real estate loan with an interest rate that is adjusted twice a year. Payments vary according to the different interest rates on the loan, which usually will run 20 to 30 years. *See Also: estate, interest, interest rate, real estate, real estate loan, run*

VARIABLE RATIO PLAN. A formula investing plan in which part of the investment capital is in common stock and part is in bonds or preferred stock. *See Also: capital, common stock, investment, preferred stock, stock*

VARIABLE SPREAD. A strategy in which an investor simultaneously buys and sells options, with the number of options sold different from the number bought. Both are based on the same underlying security and have the same expiration dates, but varying exercise prices. *See Also: exercise, expiration, security, underlying security*

VARIANCE. A statistical difference in a distribution dispersion, calculated by adding together the squares of the mean deviations.

VARIANCE RULE. As defined by the Public Securities Association's standards for the uniform practice for good delivery and settlement of TBA agency-guaranteed mortgage backed securities, the variance rule describes the maximum allowable variance of mortgages originated from a round amount. For example, a $1 million pool isn't likely to be issued for exactly $1 million, but may be delivered for plus or minus the allowable variance. *See Also: delivery, good delivery, minus, mortgage, plus, pool, securities, standards, TBA, variance*

VAULT CASH. Cash that a bank keeps on reserve in its vault to take care of demand deposits and drafts. *See Also: bank, demand, reserve, take*

VC. Venture Capitalist or Venture Capital.

VEGA. Given a one percent change in implied volatility, vega is the amount that the option price should change. *See Also: change, implied volatility, option, volatility*

VELOCITY. The number of times a dollar is spent within a given time period; the turnover of money. *See Also: time, turnover*

VELOCITY OF MONEY. The turnover of money used to buy goods or services. To obtain the velocity of money, divide the country's money supply into its gross national product. *See Also: gross, money supply, supply, turnover, velocity*

VELOCITY SHOP. A mortgage lender who creates secondary lending markets to make money so it can increase the number of mortgages it sells, which allows it to make even more mortgages. *See Also: mortgage*

VENDOR. A person or company that supplies goods or services.

VENDOR FINANCING. A company will offer easier-than-market financing terms to its business customers. Companies with high-quality credit will use its high-grade balance sheet to finance products to customers with weaker credit profiles. The buyer in effect gets the product at much lower interest rates than it would otherwise have been able to get from a creditor, while the financing company assumes credit risk. Lower-credit quality companies, particularly start-ups, may offer easy or more-creative terms in order to win business and generate sales and hype in its products. *See Also: balance, balance sheet, credit, credit risk, creditor, interest, offer, order, risk, will*

VENTURE CAPITAL. Money that is invested in innovative enterprises or research in return for ownership in the enterprise. *See Also: investment, return*

VENTURE CAPITAL FUND. A mutual fund invested in securities of new companies and in the securities of companies that are not registered with the Securities and Exchange Commission. *See Also: commission, exchange, fund, mutual fund, securities*

VENTURE CAPITAL LIMITED PARTNERSHIP. An investment aimed at providing startup costs for beginning businesses, with investors receiving private stock shares. *See Also: investment, startup, stock*

VENTURE CAPITALIST. Also referred to as VC, a deal maker that will provide funds and advice to an innovative enterprise in return for ownership in the enterprise. *See Also: maker, return, VC, will*

VERTICAL E-MARKETPLACE. An online business-to-business marketplace that connects buyers and sellers, and specifically serves one industry. *See Also: industry, online*

VERTICAL LINE CHARTING. A chart that uses a vertical line to represent a security's high and low prices, and a horizontal line to represent the security's closing prices. *See Also: chart, low*

VERTICAL MARKET. A market that specifically serves one industry. *See Also: industry, market*

VERTICAL MERGER. Occurs when two companies, who control different ends of producing the same item, combine. For example, if a petroleum producer merges with a painting company, it would be considered a vertical merger. *See Also: merger, producer*

VERTICAL SPREAD. An investment strategy in which an investor holds long and short options of the same class that have the same expiration month, but different exercise prices. *See Also: class, exercise, expiration, expiration month, investment, investment strategy*

VESTED ESTATE. A property interest carrying current as well as future rights, but which has transferable current interest rights. *See Also: current, interest, rights*

VESTED INTEREST. A person's personal or financial right to an asset. *See Also: asset, right*

VESTED REMAINDER. A fixed property interest that doesn't allow the owner to take possession of the property until the previous estate is terminated. *See Also: estate, interest, take*

VESTING. Rights an employee receives for working at the same company a specified length of time. The rights normally include such things as pension payments, participation in a stock plan, and profit-sharing benefits. *See Also: pension, rights, stock, time*

VETERAN'S ADMINISTRATION LOANS. A program enacted by the government during the post-World War II era to provide veterans with the means for financing homes.

VETERANS ADMINISTRATION MORTGAGE. A Veterans Administration-guaranteed mortgage loaned to veterans or to their surviving spouses.

The loan requires a smaller down payment and carries a lower interest rate. *See Also: interest, interest rate, mortgage*

VI. Appears in newspaper stock listings to indicate a company that is going through a bankruptcy reorganization. *See Also: bankruptcy, reorganization, stock*

VICKREY AUCTION. Similar to an English auction, the highest bidder wins, except the winner pays the price offered by the second highest bidder. *See Also: English auction*

VIRAL. A self-propagating pattern of Internet use that grows exponentially among people. This practice is best used with a product or service that is easily adaptable and a very low sales cycle. *See Also: cycle, Internet, low, service*

VIRTUAL. The cyberspace reference to objects, activities, destination, etc. *See Also: cyberspace*

VIRTUAL CEO. An executive that joins an early stage enterprise, typically from concept to implementation, in return for compensation that may include ownership in the new enterprise, cash or both. The virtual CEO may not be involved on a daily basis, but participates more as a consultant. A virtual CEO may be involved in multiple enterprises simultaneously. *See Also: basis, cash, on, return, virtual*

VIRTUAL COMMUNITY. An Internet-based aggregation of users with common interests. Typical activities in a virtual community may include chatting, message posting, and personal directories. *See Also: aggregation, virtual*

VIRTUAL PRIVATE MARKETPLACE. A private Internet or extranet based e-marketplace that connects a buyer and a seller or one company with a number of buyers or sellers. This is in contrast to a business to business e-marketplace with many buyers and sellers. *See Also: e-marketplace, extranet, Internet*

VIRTUAL PRIVATE NETWORK. Also referred to as VPN, a data network that enables users to privately and securely access information, usually on a corporate network, extranet or intranet. Access can be provided via the Internet using a tunneling protocol and security procedures. *See Also: extranet, Internet, intranet, on, protocol, security, tunneling*

VIRTUAL REALITY. Computer simulations using 3D graphics, and oftentimes data gloves, that allow users to interact with the simulation.

VOICE OVER IP. Using the Internet to transmit voice data using the Internet protocol, or IP, instead of the standard public switched telephone network. *See Also: Internet, Internet protocol, IP, protocol*

VOID. Either a document that has been canceled or that has no legal standing or worth. *See Also: legal, worth*

VOIDABLE. A transaction that can be voided because it originally was not properly or legally executed. *See Also: transaction*

VOLATILE. The condition of fluctuating prices in a security without any marked trends. *See Also: security*

VOLATILITY. The extent to which a security's price fluctuates back and forth within a short time. *See Also: time*

VOLATILITY RATIO. To reach a company's volatility percentage for the year, subtract a security's lowest price for the year from its highest price, then divide the lowest price for the year into the remainder. For example, a stock's year high and low is 80 and 40, respectively. Divide the difference, 40 by 40, to get a volatility ratio of 100 percent. *See Also: low, ratio, volatility*

VOLUME. The total number of shares traded for a market or for a particular stock, bond, option, or futures contract. *See Also: bond, contract, futures, futures contract, market, option, stock*

VOLUME ALERT. Occurs when a security's volume surpasses its moving average during a specific time period. *See Also: average, moving average, time, volume*

VOLUME DELETED. Usually appears on an exchange's consolidated tape when the tape is running at least two minutes late. This announcement indicates that only stock symbols and transaction prices will be reported on the tape unless a transaction involves more than 5,000 shares. *See Also: consolidated tape, stock, tape, transaction*

VOLUME DISCOUNT. A discount often given to institutional investors when an order exceeds a certain level. *See Also: discount, level, order*

VOLUME OF TRADING. The sum of successive futures contract sales or successive futures contract purchases. *See Also: contract, futures, futures contract*

VOLUNTARY ACCUMULATION PLAN. A mutual fund in which the investor accumulates shares regularly over a prescribed time period, with the stockholder determining the spending intervals and the amount to be invested each time. *See Also: fund, intervals, mutual fund, stockholder, time*

VOLUNTARY ASSOCIATION. An unincorporated membership organization, with each member carrying an unlimited amount of financial responsibility.

VOLUNTARY BANKRUPTCY. Occurs when the debtor, not the creditor, petitions the U.S. District Court to reorganize and payoff any debts because of insolvency. *See Also: creditor, insolvency*

VOLUNTARY CONVEYANCE. The transfer of a title from one person to another without the transfer being imposed by the court. *See Also: transfer*

VOLUNTARY PLAN. A mutual fund program in which an investor can buy an unlimited additional number of shares whenever he or she wants. *See Also: fund, mutual fund*

VOLUNTARY TRUST. A voluntary deed transfer made to benefit a specific person or trustee for a specific purpose. *See Also: transfer, trustee*

VOLUNTARY UNDERWRITER. The opposite of a statutory underwriter in that this person intentionally and voluntarily buys a securities issue from the issuer and resells the issue publicly. *See Also: issue, securities, statutory underwriter*

VOODOO ACCOUNTING. Non-traditional accounting methods. This practice can be highly scrutinized, as it can lead to improper recognition of revenue.

VORTAL. Short for vertical portal, or vertical e-marketplace. *See Also: e-marketplace, portal, vertical e-marketplace*

VOTING RIGHTS. The rights of stockholders to elect the issuing company's board of directors and to vote on other corporate matters because the stockholders are, in essence, the company's owners. *See Also: board of directors, elect, rights*

VOTING STOCK. A security that gives the owner the right to vote on corporate matters. *See Also: right, security*

VOTING TRUST. When a stockholder temporarily turns over his or her voting rights to a trustee, whose decisions during that time are binding. *See Also: rights, stockholder, time, trustee, voting rights*

VPN. Virtual Private Network. *See Also: virtual*

VULTURE FUND. Nickname for a pool of money aimed at buying commercial property at distressed prices. *See Also: pool*

W

WAC. Weighted Average Coupon. *See Also: average, coupon*

WAITER. A British floor broker who assists brokers in obtaining market information and execution reports. *See Also: broker, execution, floor, floor broker, market*

WAITING PERIOD. The 20 days between a company's filing of its registration statement and the date the Securities and Exchange Commission has approved for the company's securities to be publicly sold. *See Also: commission, exchange, registration, registration statement, securities, statement*

WALK-AWAY MORTGAGE. A mortgage in which the lender cannot force the defaulting borrower to pay the difference between the loan balance and the price at which the property is sold at foreclosure. *See Also: balance, foreclosure, mortgage, pay*

WALL STREET. A street in Manhattan that is the primary financial district in the United States. Also used to describe the professional investment community. *See Also: Street*

WALL STREET JOURNAL. A highly respected newspaper that focuses on financial and corporate news.

WALLFLOWER. A stock that no longer is popular with investors. *See Also: stock*

WALLPAPER. A worthless securities certificate. *See Also: certificate, securities*

WAM. Weighted Average Maturity.

WAN. Wide Area Network.

WANTED FOR CASH. Indicates on an exchange's tape that a buyer will pay cash the same day for a block of securities. *See Also: cash, pay, securities, tape*

WAP. Wireless Application Protocol. *See Also: protocol,*

WAR BABIES. Securities issued from companies involved in the defense industry. *See Also: industry*

WAR CHEST. Cash that is set aside in anticipation of a future event, such as an acquisition or defense against a hostile takeover. *See Also: acquisition, anticipation, takeover*

WAREHOUSE RECEIPT. A document that lists the commodities an investor is homing in a warehouse for safekeeping. The investor can use the document to transfer ownership of the commodities without worrying about physically transferring the actual commodities. *See Also: actual, safekeeping, transfer*

WARRANT. A company-issued certificate that represents an option to buy a certain number of stock shares at a specific price before a predetermined date. Because it has a value of its own, it can be traded on the open market. *See Also: certificate, market, open, open market, option, stock*

WARRANT VALUE. An investor can determine a warrant's theoretical value by subtracting the common stock's exercise price from its market price, then multiplying the sum by the number of shares the warrant can buy. *See Also: exercise, exercise price, market, market price, theoretical value, warrant*

WARRANTS INTO NEGOTIABLE GOVERNMENT SECURITIES (WINGS). Options to buy a specific number of Treasury notes at a predetermined price to be delivered at a stated future date.

WARRANTS TO BUY TREASURY SECURITIES (WARTS). These represent rights to buy a specific amount of government issues at specific prices within six months to one year. *See Also: rights*

WASH SALE. A transaction in which an investor simultaneously buys and sells a security through two different brokers. Such a transaction is considered a manipulation, and is illegal if it artificially increases the security's trading volume or changes the price. *See Also: manipulation, security, trading volume, transaction, volume*

WASHINGTON METROPOLITAN AREA TRANSIT AUTHORITY. A municipal agency that issues federally guaranteed bonds to pay for the mass transit system in the Washington D.C. metropolitan area. *See Also: pay*

WASTING ASSET. An investment with a value that continually drops or delays, as it gets closer to its expiration date. *See Also: expiration, expiration date, investment*

WASTING TRUST. A trust fund with assets that are gradually dropping in value or are being consumed. *See Also: fund, trust*

WATCH FILING. A procedure by which an investor who incurs a loss from a low-risk investment brings that loss to the underwriter's attention. *See Also: investment*

WATCH LIST. A list of securities the exchange is monitoring for potential illegal practices. An exchange will, for example, watch a security that a broker-dealer is about to underwrite, or a security that is heavily traded by the issuing company's officers. *See Also: broker-dealer, exchange, securities, security*

WATCH MY NUMBER. Each broker is assigned an identification number, which is flashed on an annunciator board if the broker is being summoned to his or her firm's booth. When a broker leaves the exchange floor for a few minutes, he or she asks another broker to "watch my number" so the broker knows if he or she was summoned while away. *See Also: broker, exchange, exchange floor, floor*

WATERED STOCK. A security issue that adds no extra value to the issuing company's position. *See Also: issue, position, security*

WE OFFER RETAIL (WOR). This indicates the seller will assume all transaction costs. *See Also: transaction*

WEAK HOLDINGS. Securities a speculator will keep on margin only long enough to sell them. *See Also: margin, on margin, speculator*

WEALTH EFFECT. The tendency for individuals to spend more money as their assets rise. *See Also: tendency*

WEAL MARKET. A short-term drop in general market prices. *See Also: drop, market*

WEARABLE COMPUTER. A computer device that can be worn, whether strapped to the body or embedded into clothing. Commands can be input using a portable keyboard or a microphone using voice activated commands.

WEB. World Wide Web.

WEB BROWSER. A client-side software program that a computer user runs to view Web pages. *See Also: Web*

WEB PAGE. A document created with HTML, and accessed through the World Wide Web. A group of Web pages collectively form a Web Site. *See Also: HTML, Web, Web site, World Wide Web*

WEB SITE. An arrangement of interconnected Web pages contained within one domain name. The Web site usually includes a homepage, and is prepared and maintained as a group by a person or organization. *See Also: domain name, homepage, name, Web*

WEBCASTING. Broadcasting digital media over the Internet. *See Also: digital, Internet*

WEBMASTER. The individual responsible for administering and maintaining a Web site. This may include designing, developing, marketing, or maintaining the Web site. *See Also: Web, Web site*

WEEK ORDER. A buy or sell order that expires automatically if it cannot be executed on the exchange floor within a week. *See Also: exchange, exchange floor, floor, order, sell order*

WEIGHTED AVERAGE COST OF CAPITAL. The required rate of return a company must pay to raise long-term capital. *See Also: capital, pay, rate of return, required rate of return, return*

WEIGHTED AVERAGE COUPON (WAC). The average of the coupons in a pool of mortgage collateral, weighted by the sizes of the pools. *See Also: average, collateral, mortgage, pool*

WEIGHTED AVERAGE MATURITY (WAM). An average of the maturities of pools in the mortgage collateral weighted by the sizes of the pools. *See Also: average, collateral, mortgage*

WEIGHTING. Comparing the importance of one investment to another. *See Also: investment*

WELLHEAD PRICE. The price paid for gas drawn from leased property.

WELLS SUBMISSION. A procedure through which a person that the Securities and Exchange Commission is investigating can respond to the allegations in an attempt to get the SEC to drop its investigation. *See Also: commission, drop, exchange, SEC, securities*

WENT TO THE WALL. Either a person or company who has gone through bankruptcy. *See Also: bankruptcy*

WESTERN ACCOUNT. A plan in which each underwriting syndicate member is responsible for distributing only his or her agreed upon shares, and not the shares of any other syndicate member (also known as a Divided Account). *See Also: divided account, syndicate, underwriting, underwriting syndicate*

WHAT'S NEW. A section on a Web site devoted to the latest announcements, such as updates and changes to the site, new content additions, news and press releases. *See Also: on, UPDATES, Web, Web site*

WHEN DISTRIBUTED. A security traded before the final certificate has been printed. The investor will receive the certificate when it is completed. *See Also: certificate, security*

WHEN ISSUED. A security traded before it receives final authorization. The investor receives the certificate only after the final approval is granted. The transaction would be canceled automatically if the security failed to receive the approval. *See Also: certificate, security, transaction*

WHIPSAWED. Describes an investor who lost money on both sides of a price swing, such as an investor who bought a security just before the price dropped, then sold it right before the price rose again. *See Also: right, security, swing*

WHITE ELEPHANT. An asset or property that costs more to maintain than it is worth, or an asset or investment that will definitely lose money. *See Also: asset, investment, worth*

WHITE KNIGHT. A party a company chooses to merge with in order to fend off an unwanted corporate raider. *See Also: order, raider*

WHITE SHEET. A list the National Quotation Bureau publishes daily for market makers, which provides prices for over-the-counter securities traded in Chicago, Los Angeles, and San Francisco. *See Also: market, National Quotation Bureau, quotation, securities*

WHITE SQUIRE. A risky management anti-takeover maneuver in which the company places a large block of its shares into the hands of a friendly party whose financial interests are similar to the target company. *See Also: target*

WHITEHATS. Highly skilled hackers who break into computer systems without malicious intention. A whitehat will typically expose the weakness to the site operators, often leaving contact information. Some whitehats will offer their services for a fee. Unlike a whitehat, a blackhat will break into a system to destroy files or steal data. *See Also: blackhats, break, hacker, offer, will*

WHITE'S RATING. White's Tax Exempt Bond Rating Service ranks municipal bonds according to the municipal trading markets instead of the issuer's credit rating. The ranking gives investors an indication of a bond's expected yield. *See Also: bond, bond rating, credit, credit rating, expected yield, indication, ranking, service, yield*

WHOLE LIFE INSURANCE. An insurance policy which offers protection in the event the policy holder dies. The holder will pay a set annual premium during his or her lifetime while building up a cash value. Earnings on the cash are tax-deferred and can be used as collateral. *See Also: cash, collateral, earnings, insurance, pay, policy holder, premium*

WHOLE LOAN. A mortgage that is not part of any investment pool. *See Also: investment, mortgage, pool*

WHOLESALE PRICE INDEX. A Bureau of Labor Statistics gauge that measures price changes in goods sold wholesale.

WHOLESALER. A mutual fund underwriter. *See Also: fund, mutual fund*

WHOOPS BOND. Nickname for a bond issued by the Washington Public Power Supply System to pay for a nuclear power plant. *See Also: bond, pay, plant, supply*

WIDE AREA NETWORK. Also referred to as WAN, a network of computers that extends over a broad geographical area. A WAN typically consists of two or more Local Area Networks (LANs). The largest WAN in existence is the Internet. *See Also: Internet, local, WAN*

WIDE MARKET. A market with many investors. *See Also: market*

WIDE OPEN. An underwriting with additional securities available for sale because the syndicate members did not subscribe to all that was available, either because some members withdrew from the syndicate or because the syndicate had too few members to begin with. *See Also: sale, securities, syndicate, underwriting*

WIDE OPENING. A large price difference between the opening bid and ask prices. *See Also: ask*

WIDGET. A plastic tube that carries exchange information through an exchange's pneumatic tube system. Also, a hypothetical product used to illustrate an economical concept. *See Also: exchange*

WIDOW-AND-ORPHAN STOCK. A low-risk security paying high dividends that is issued by a noncyclical business or a business that is not seasonal. *See Also: security*

WILD CARD. An investment that carries either the highest interest rate allowed by law or an unlimited yield. *See Also: interest, interest rate, investment, yield*

WILDCAT DRILLING. A speculative oil or gas drilling venture in an area where no oil or gas previously has been found. *See Also: speculative*

WILDCAT SCHEME. A speculative investment that is not expected to succeed. *See Also: investment, speculative*

WILL. A document in which a person assigns the distribution of all of his or her assets after his or her death.

WILLIAMS ACT. A 1968 federal law requiring those planning to tender offers, to file their intentions with the target company, as well as with the Securities and Exchange Commission. The filing must include such information as cash sources and plans for the company once it has been taken over. *See Also: cash, commission, exchange, securities, target, tender*

WILSHIRE INDEX. A gauge of 5,000 securities, including a number of securities from smaller companies as well as some over-the-counter securities. Some say the gauge is more accurate than other indexes because of the wide cross section of securities used. *See Also: securities*

WINDFALL. An unexpected unspent profit or investment appreciation. *See Also: appreciation, investment, profit*

WINDFALL PROFITS TAX. Tax on the profits a particular company or industry must pay after receiving some sort of windfall. *See Also: industry, pay, windfall*

WINDING UP. Liquidating a company.

WINDOW. The limited time a person has to take advantage of a price situation or other favorable condition. *See Also: take, time*

WINDOW DRESSING. Temporary or superficial means of making a portfolio or security look more profitable. *See Also: portfolio, security*

WINDOW SETTLEMENT. The physical place where the selling broker delivers securities to the buying broker. Most deals, however, are settled through a depository instead of a window. *See Also: broker, depository, securities, window*

WINDOWS. The reference to the operating system developed by Microsoft that presents its information in a GUI, or graphical user interface, rather than via text-based commands. *See Also: graphical user interface, GUI*

WINGS. Warrants Into Negotiable Government Securities. *See Also: negotiable, securities*

WINNING A BID. The bid that is attractive and profitable enough to a seller to lead to a completed transaction. *See Also: transaction*

WINTEL. A computer environment that is composed of an operating system running Windows and an Intel microprocessor. *See Also: Windows*

WIPED OUT. An investor who lost all of his or her money in the market. *See Also: market*

WIRE HOUSE. An exchange-member firm connected to other offices by a communications system. *See Also: firm*

WIRE ROOM. A brokerage firm area that changes customer orders into floor tickets so the orders can be executed in the market with the best available prices. *See Also: firm, floor, market*

WIRELESS APPLICATION PROTOCOL. A protocol by which Web-based data is adapted for use in mobile devices, such as a PDA, cell phone or pager. *See Also: PDA, protocol*

WIRELESS MARKUP LANGUAGE. Also referred to as WML, the markup language that provides a light, less-intensive, version of a Web site so that is can easily be viewed on a handheld device that is WAP enabled. *See Also: on, site, WAP, Web, Web site*

WIRELESS PERSONAL AREA NETWORK. Also referred to as WPAN, a wireless network, typically for an individual. A WPAN will network devices such as personal digital assistants, computers and peripherals, digital camera, mobile phone, headsets and other wearable devices. *See Also: digital, will, WPAN*

WITH INTEREST. Used to indicate that a bond buyer must pay the bond seller all interest that accrued on the bond between the bond's last payment date and the transaction's settlement date. *See Also: bond, interest, pay, payment date, settlement date*

WITH OR WITHOUT. Instructions an investor gives his or her broker to sell an odd-lot limit order either for the stock quote or in the round-lot market, whichever comes first. *See Also: broker, limit, limit order, market, order, stock*

WITH PREJUDICE. Accompanies the dismissal of a legal action to indicate that the case cannot be reopened. If a case is closed without prejudice, it can be reopened. *See Also: legal*

WITH RIGHT OF SURVIVORSHIP (WROS, JTWROS). This is a joint account with the ownership of all assets automatically passing to the surviving tenant if the other tenant dies. *See Also: account, joint account, tenant*

WITHDRAWAL PLAN. A mutual fund program in which the investor receives monthly or quarterly fund distributions. *See Also: fund, mutual fund, quarterly*

WITHHOLDING. Occurs when a broker-dealer keeps part of the securities from an offering and sells the remaining portion to employees. *See Also: broker-dealer, offering, securities*

WITHHOLDING TAX AT THE SOURCE. A domestic issuer's obligation to withhold part of a foreign corporation's dividends and interest, usually 30 percent, to pay for the U.S. tax on those distributions. *See Also: and interest, interest, obligation, pay*

WITHOUT AN OFFER. A one-sided quote in which a dealer is willing to bid a certain price for a security, but is unwilling to sell it at that price, either because the dealer does not want to sell the security short or because the dealer does not actually have possession of the security. *See Also: dealer, security*

WITHOUT INTEREST. When a security that is in default is sold without interest, and the buyer does not make any additional accrued interest payments to the seller. *See Also: accrued interest, default, interest, security*

WOLF. An experienced speculator. *See Also: speculator*

WOLF PACK. Describes a situation where one investor buys a block of a company's stock, then signals a group of others to do the same on the premise that the issuing company is vulnerable to a takeover. *See Also: stock, takeover*

WOODEN TICKET. Occurs when a broker-dealer indicates he or she is executing an order to a customer when, in fact, the broker has not confirmed the order. A broker-dealer will improperly try this maneuver on the belief that market conditions will change before the actual execution. In this way, the broker-dealer hopes to earn larger profits. *See Also: actual, broker, broker-dealer, change, execution, market, order*

WOODY. Jargon for an upwardly moving stock or market in general. A trader may say "This market is getting a woody," or "This stock is going to get a woody after the company reports earnings." *See Also: earnings, market, stock, trader*

WOR. We Offer Retail.

WORDFLOW MARKETPLACE. An e-marketplace that provides its participants tools and services to manage and track projects, including various collaboration services. *See Also: e-marketplace*

WORKED OFF. A slight drop in a security's or commodity's price. *See Also: drop*

WORKFLOW. The automated distribution or organization of jobs, such as documents. The job is passed from one individual or one department to another in an efficient manner. *See Also: job*

WORKING ASSET. An asset, invested in securities, with a price that fluctuates along with common stock prices. *See Also: asset, common stock, securities, stock*

WORKING CAPITAL. A company's current liabilities subtracted from its current assets, which gives the company the amount of money it probably will need to maintain operations for a year. *See Also: current, current assets, current liabilities, operations*

WORKING CONTROL. The ability of those who own less than 50 percent of a corporation's stock to dictate corporate policy because of the wide dispersion of shares. *See Also: stock*

WORKING INTEREST. An investor's financial interest in an oil or gas drilling partnership, often with that interest representing borrowed capital and not equity. *See Also: capital, equity, interest, partnership*

WORKING ORDER. An investor's order to his or her broker to buy or sell a large block of stock gradually so that the transaction does not affect the stock's market price. *See Also: block of stock, broker, market, market price, order, stock, transaction*

WORKOUT MARKET. An estimated price quoted for a security. *See Also: security*

WORKSTATION. A computer designed for one user. The term describes either a terminal in a network, a personal computer, or a powerful computer designed for scientific computing, graphics and other tasks requiring high performance and memory. *See Also: personal computer, term, terminal*

WORLD BANK. The International Bank for Reconstruction and Development, established to provide loans for promoting the economic redevelopment of member countries. *See Also: bank, international bank for reconstruction and development*

WORLD RESERVE. In an antiques auction, a consignor sets this minimum price for the sale of an entire collection, which gives the auctioneer a range within to sell individual items from the collection. *See Also: auction, range, sale*

WORLD WIDE WEB. Also referred to as WWW, the multi-media portion of the Internet, used for accessing Internet resources. Using the hypertext transfer protocol (HTTP), users can access a massive network of computers, with an interface consisting of text, graphics, sound and animation. *See Also: hypertext, hypertext transfer protocol, Internet, protocol, transfer*

WORTH. An asset's or investment's total value.

WPAN. Wireless Personal Area Network.

WRAP-AROUND ANNUITY. An annuity that shelters dividends, interest, and capital appreciation from taxes, with the investor choosing the securities in which the annuity should be invested. The insurance company does not assume principal risk until the contract earns an annuity. *See Also: annuity, appreciation, capital, capital appreciation, contract, insurance, interest, principal, risk, securities*

WRAP-AROUND MORTGAGE. A low-interest mortgage made up of both an assumable mortgage from the previous seller and a new loan from the carrying bank. *See Also: assumable mortgage, bank, mortgage*

WRINKLE. A security feature that could potentially be profitable to the investor. *See Also: security*

WRITE. To sell a put or call option in an opening transaction. *See Also: call option, opening transaction, option, put, transaction*

WRITE OUT. Occurs when a specialist trades an order that is on his or her order books by having the broker who entered the order write the order, after which the specialist becomes the contrabroker. The broker who wrote the order receives all fees and commissions. *See Also: broker, order, specialist, write*

WRITE UP. An asset's book value increase that is not due to added costs or asset account adjustments reflected from an updated appraisal. *See Also: account, appraisal, asset, book, book value*

WRITEOFF. Charging an asset amount to a loss, which subtracts the asset's value from the company's profits and therefore lessens the company's tax liabilities. *See Also: asset*

WRITING CASH-SECURED PUTS. A put option seller who does not want to use a margin account can instead deposit cash equal to the option's exercise price with the broker. By doing this, the seller is not responsible for any further margin requirements, even if the underlying security's price changes. *See Also: account, broker, cash, exercise, exercise price, margin, margin account, option, put, put option*

WRITING PUTS TO ACQUIRE STOCK. An option seller who believes a stock's price will drop will write a put that can be exercised at that expected price. If the stock does go up, the option will not be exercised, and the seller still has earned a premium. If the price does, indeed, drop, the seller has obtained the security at a low price and, in addition, has earned a premium. *See Also: drop, low, option, premium, put, security, stock, write*

WRITTEN-DOWN VALUE. An asset's net book value after depreciation or amortization. *See Also: amortization, book, book value, depreciation, net*

WROS. With Right Of Survivorship.

X

X-DIS. Used to indicate that a securities buyer is not entitled to a dividend distribution. *See Also: dividend, securities*

XCH. Used to indicate that a securities transaction will be completed outside of the normal clearing procedures. *See Also: securities, transaction*

XD. Appears in newspaper stock listings to indicate a security is trading ex-dividends. *See Also: security, stock*

XENOCURRENCY. A currency that is traded in money markets outside of its own country. *See Also: currency*

XLS. Extensible Stylesheet Language.

XML. Short for eXtensible Markup Language, XML is a standard for describing information within a document, considered an innovation above EDI. XML describes information contained on a page or form. *See Also: on, XML*

XML ENABLED SOLUTION. A process that facilitates the transfer and sharing of XML based information across applications, firewalls, and corporations using the Web. *See Also: transfer, Web, XML*

XR. Appears in newspaper stock listings to indicate a security is trading ex-rights. *See Also: ex-rights, security, stock*

XW. Appears in newspaper stock listings to indicate a security is trading ex-warrants. *See Also: ex-warrants, security, stock*

XX. Used to indicate without securities or warrants. *See Also: securities*

Y

YANKEE AUCTION. A variation of the Dutch auction in which successful bidders pay what they bid as opposed to every successful bidder paying the price that is determined by the lowest qualified bidder. *See Also: Dutch auction, pay*

YANKEE BOND. A foreign bond denominated in U.S. dollars and registered with the Securities and Exchange Commission for sale in the United States. *See Also: bond, commission, exchange, sale, securities*

YANKEES. American securities traded in Great Britain. *See Also: securities*

YEAR-END DIVIDEND. An additional dividend that a board of directors approves for distribution to stockholders at the end of a company's fiscal year. *See Also: board of directors, dividend, fiscal year*

YELLOW BOOK. A listing of requirements for British market quotations. *See Also: listing, market*

YELLOW COLOR THEORY. A market theory that says that when yellow clothes, yellow furnishings, and yellow packaging are popular, the market will rise. *See Also: market*

YELLOW KNIGHT. One company that tries to take over another company, after which the two companies discuss a merger. *See Also: merger, take*

YELLOW SHEETS. A daily list the National Quotation Bureau publishes for market makers which provides over-the-counter corporate bond prices. *See Also: bond, corporate bond, market, national quotation bureau, quotation*

YEN. Japan's primary currency unit. *See Also: currency, unit*

YEN BOND. A bond denominated in Japanese yen. While not registered for sale in the United States, it can be traded in America after it has been traded for a reasonable length of time outside of the U.S. *See Also: bond, sale, time, yen*

YIELD. The dividends or interest a security will earn, with the yield expressed as a percentage of the amount paid for the security or of the security's par value. *See Also: interest, par, par value, security*

YIELD ADVANTAGE. The difference between a convertible security's current yield and its underlying common stock's current yield. *See Also: current, current yield, yield*

YIELD CURVE. A chart consisting of the yields of bonds of the same quality but different maturities. This can be used as a gauge to evaluate the future of the interest rates. An upward trend with short-term rates lower than long-term rates is called a positive yield curve while a downtrend is a negative or inverted yield curve. *See Also: chart, interest, inverted yield curve, positive yield curve, trend, yield*

YIELD EQUIVALENCE. A measurement used to compare the yield on a taxable investment versus a nontaxable investment. *See Also: investment, yield*

YIELD MAINTENANCE CONTRACT. Provides a price adjustment on mortgage securities (such as a Government National Mortgage Association security) upon delivery to give the buyer the same yield as that which was originally agreed upon. *See Also: delivery, mortgage, securities, yield*

YIELD SPREAD. A comparison between the yields of different quality issues.

YIELD TEST. The relationship of the yield of individual bonds in an insurance company's portfolio to the yield of taxable government bonds with the same maturity. *See Also: insurance, maturity, portfolio, yield*

YIELD TO ADJUSTED MINIMUM MATURITY. Provides the yield for a bond's shortest possible life. *See Also: yield*

YIELD TO AVERAGE LIFE. The yield achieved by substituting a bond's average maturity for the issue's fiscal maturity date. *See Also: average, maturity, yield*

YIELD TO CALL. The amount of money an investor would receive from a bond investment which is expressed as an average annual return from the purchase date to the call date. *See Also: average, bond, call date, investment, return*

YIELD TO LESSOR. A lease transaction's internal rate of return. *See Also: internal rate of return, rate of return, return*

YIELD TO MATURITY. A debt security's average return based on its interest income, capital gains, or capital losses incurred until the security matures. *See Also: average, capital, interest, return, security*

YIELD TO PUT. A bond's return if it is held until a specific date and is then sold back to the issuer for a particular price. *See Also: return*

YO-YO OPTION. An executive option program in which a company officer's option price is lowered by a dollar every time the company's stock price goes up by a dollar. *See Also: option, stock, time*

YO-YO STOCK. A volatile stock with a price that continually rises and falls quickly. *See Also: stock, volatile*

Z

Z. Appears in newspaper stock listings preceding a number to indicate that the number represents a total volume, so it should not be multiplied by 100. *See Also: stock, total volume, volume*

Z CERTIFICATE. A Bank of England certificate issued to discount houses instead of stock certificates so the houses can deal in gilt-edged securities with short maturities. *See Also: bank, certificate, discount, gilt-edged, securities, stock*

Z-BOND. *See Also: Accrual Bond.*

ZERIAL BOND. A stripped Treasury bond or other zero-coupon debt instrument issued in serial form. *See Also: bond, debt instrument, instrument, treasury bond*

ZERO BASIS. Occurs when a convertible bond is selling at such a high premium that the interest is equal to or less than the premium. *See Also: bond, interest, premium*

ZERO COUPON BOND. A bond sold at a deep discount that pays no interest until maturity, at which time the holder receives the bond's face value plus all accrued interest. While holders receive no interest on the bond until maturity, they are responsible for paying taxes each year on the unpaid interest. *See Also: accrued interest, bond, discount, face value, interest, maturity, plus, time*

ZERO DOWNTICK. Zero Minus Tick. *See Also: minus, tick, zero minus tick*

ZERO MINUS TICK. Also called a "zero downtick," this is a security transaction that occurs at the same price as the previous similar transaction in that same security, but less than the last different transaction in that security. *See Also: downtick, security, transaction*

ZERO PLUS TICK. Also called a "zero uptick," this is a security transaction that occurs at the same price as the previous similar transaction in that same security, but higher than the last different transaction in that security. *See Also: security, transaction, uptick*

ZERO RATE MORTGAGE. A mortgage that requires a hefty down payment with a one-time finance charge, after which the mortgage is repaid in monthly installments. Because the term of the loan is so short, it appears to be nearly interest free. *See Also: interest, mortgage, term*

ZERO UPTICK. *See Also: plus, tick, zero plus tick*

ZERO VOLATILITY SPREAD. A method used to evaluate the price of a bond. Zero Volatility Spread discounts cash flows along the Treasury curve rather than at a single point on the curve. This approach adjusts for the variance of interest rates. *See Also: bond, cash, interest, point, spread, variance, volatility*

ZERO-BASE BUDGETING. A budgeting method in which all spending must be justified, instead of only those expenses that exceeded the previous year's allocations. Budget lines, therefore, begin with a zero base with no consideration given to the previous year's levels. *See Also: base, budget, consideration*

ZERO-BRACKET AMOUNT. The portion of a person's income that is not subject to federal income tax. This standard deduction is already figured into Internal Revenue Service tax tables, so the taxpayer does not have to subtract the amount from his or her income before calculating tax liabilities. *See Also: deduction, internal revenue, service, standard deduction*

ZERO-COUPON EUROBONDS. A deep-discount American corporate issue that pays no interest. *See Also: interest, issue*

ZEROES. Nickname for zero coupon bonds. *See Also: coupon*

About the Author

R. J. Shook, is a recognized authority in his fields. As author of six business books and a decade of Wall Street experience, Shook spends his time consulting Wall Street firms and Internet ventures. Other books Shook has written include the popular *The Winner's Circle* series. Shook is a graduate of Babson College, and lives in Columbus, Ohio. More information about the author can be found by visiting *www.shookbook.com*.

DATE DUE

DEMCO 13829810